3 2 11/12

SOMETIMES THERE IS A VOID

SOMETIMES THERE IS A VOID

Memoirs of an Outsider

ZAKES MDA

Farrar, Straus and Giroux   New York

Farrar, Straus and Giroux
18 West 18th Street, New York 10011

Library of Congress Cataloging-in-Publication Data
Mda, Zakes.
    Sometimes there is a void : memoirs of an outsider / Zakes Mda. — 1st
American ed.
        p.   cm.
    Includes index.
    ISBN 978-0-374-28094-9 (hardcover : alk. paper)
    1. Mda, Zakes—Childhood and youth.   2. Mda, Zakes—Homes and
haunts—South Africa.   3. Mda, Zakes—Homes and haunts—Lesotho.
4. Authors, South African—20th century—Biography.   I. Title.

PR9369.3.M4 Z46 2012
828'.914—dc22
[B]

                                                        2011020817

                            www.fsgbooks.com

                    1   3   5   7   9   10   8   6   4   2

Paradoxically, academic writers are often inhibited when it comes to speaking directly, possibly because they were all little goody-goodies in junior high school, and they're being massed together in university departments, and when you put all the smartest in the class together, there's a tremendous anxiety about whether one can live up to the seriousness of the enterprise.

– Terry Castle

SOMETIMES THERE IS A VOID

CHAPTER ONE

THE SMELL OF LIFE is back on the pink mountain. Human life, that is, for other forms have always thrived here even after we had left. Before our return shrubs and bushes flourished, but their fused aromas highlighted an absence. The air was too crisp. Too clean and fresh. In spring aloes bloomed – hence the pinkness – and wild bees busied themselves with the task of collecting pollen for some hive that would invariably be located in a cleft of a dangerous-looking sandstone cliff. Now we have tamed the bees, and are keeping them in supers that dot the landscape. Bees have brought us back to the mountain.

Decades ago my grandfather's estate sprawled out on this mountainside. He, Charles Gxumekelana Zenzile Mda, was the headman of Qoboshane Village in the Lower Telle area, named for the Telle River that separated Lesotho from the Herschel District of the Cape Province in the Union of South Africa. A headman was the chief of a small village, and my grandfather was given that position by his brother-in-law, Edwin Mei, the original headman who pursued a better career as an interpreter at the magistrate's court in Sterkspruit. Edwin also gave Charles a huge chunk of Dyarhom Mountain where he planted vast orchards and built houses for his wife, Mildred Millicent Mda, who never forgot to remind everyone of her true royal breeding by repeating at the slightest provocation: *Undijonge kakuhle, ndiyintombi kaMei mna.* Don't mess with me, I am Mei's daughter.

Soon other families built their homesteads on the mountain, and my grandfather named the settlement Goodwell.

The elite of Qoboshane lived in Goodwell. Across the gravel road, just below my grandfather's estate, lived Mr Nyangintsimbi who, as the principal of Qoboshane Bantu Community School, taught me and my father before me. As a spindly boy of twelve I used to play with his son Christopher, though I was in awe of him because his father was the school principal. My own grandmother used to teach at that school. Her mantra, as she twisted your ear for not performing your tasks properly, was: 'One thing at a time, things done by halves never done right'. She said these words in English. Grandma always spoke in English when she was mad at us, whereas on all other occasions she spoke in her native isiXhosa. We came to regard English as a language of anger.

There were other homesteads on that mountain, but because the houses and kraals blended with the rocky terrain in perfect camouflage you knew of their presence only by the smoke that spiralled from each of them every morning and evening.

That was in 1960.

Today I am walking with Gugu on the ruins. I call them ruins, though nothing is left of the buildings. The stones long since became part of the landscape. Yet I remember where each house used to be. I show Gugu where the main house, *ixande*, stood. It was built of stone and roofed with corrugated iron. It was pure joy to sleep in that house when it rained because the sound of the raindrops created ear-shattering music on the roof. But when it thundered it got really scary; the rafters shook and we imagined all sorts of fire-breathing ogres dancing in the rain, creating all the mayhem.

As we walk the length of what used to be our yard surrounded by gigantic aloes, I point out to her where each house used to be: the grass-thatched rondavels, one used as a kitchen, another one as a pantry, the big four-walled thatched house with decorative patterns on the red mud walls. You had to climb many stone steps before you got to the mud stoep and the door. This house also served as our living room, except when there were important visitors: they would be welcomed on the sofas in the *ixande*.

We all slept in the thatched four-walled house. There weren't enough beds to go round; some of us slept on mats on the floor. In seasons of scarcity sleeping on the floor became a source of hilarity, like when we woke up one morning and discovered that Cousin Ethel's toes had been nibbled by rats and were caked in red. She had slept through it all.

The kitchen rondavel was the centre of our social life in the evenings. Not only did grandmother cook our food in a three-legged cast-iron pot in the hearth that was in the middle of the hut as fifteen or so grandchildren huddled together around the fire in a cold winter, we also told folk tales in this room. I remember that when my siblings and I were newly arrived from Johannesburg sitting here was an ordeal; we would cry streams from the pungent smoke that filled the hut. But after a few months our eyes, like those of the rest of the cousins, were inured to the smoke.

We each took turns telling stories that had been passed on to us by older relatives, who had in turn learnt them from those who came before them, from one generation to the next, beginning when time began.

We noted whenever Cousin Nobantu came to visit from Johannesburg that her stories would not be quite the same as ours. By that time I had already spent a year or so in this village and thought of myself as one of the villagers as Johannesburg became a receding memory, whereas

Cousin Nobantu only came to visit during school holidays. Although her stories would have the familiar characters that we had grown to love so much and the plots were no different from the plots we knew so well, her characters acquired Johannesburg slickness. Also, they spoke in isiZulu and in a lot of township slang, whereas our characters spoke in isiXhosa as spoken by the village people. Her characters were therefore more endearing than ours. isiZulu gave them the sophistication that villagers envied in Johannesburgers.

And then there was Cousin Nondyebo whose manner of narration transformed even those characters we knew as kind and gentle into bullies, quite reminiscent of her own bullying tendencies. She was older than the rest of us, and had even been to Lady Grey, a town that lay beyond our district headquarters of Sterkspruit. She was therefore the fountain of all wisdom.

But the stories that left us in stitches were Cousin Ethel's. Whereas we all told stories as they were passed down to us, Cousin Ethel invented new events and characters in the tried and tested folk tales. She even incorporated the rats that ate her toes in a story about Mamlambo, the water goddess who lives in the Mzintlava River but travels in lightning to visit other rivers, including the river that runs in a narrow valley between our own Dyarhom Mountain and the eSiqikini Mountain. The true Mamlambo is a beautiful goddess with the torso of a horse, the neck of a snake and the lower body of a fish. But Cousin Ethel added other features to this wonderful water creature, such as hair that was flaming red and spellbinding eyes that hypnotised toe-chomping culprits until she swallowed them. Oh, yes, Cousin Ethel's rats got their comeuppance from Mamlambo!

Stories continued even as we ate *umgqusho* – samp cooked with beans – and *umfino* – wild spinach – from a single basin. As our hands raced to the food and as we stuffed it in our mouths and swallowed without chewing properly so as to fill our stomachs before the basin was empty, storytellers continued unabated. Occasionally grandmother snapped at them, 'Don't talk with your mouth full' or 'If you don't chew your food you will be constipated and I'll have to unblock you with castor oil or an enema'.

Outside the kitchen rondavel was the smooth granite stone that was used for grinding maize, wheat and sorghum into flour, and another granite rock with a hole and a pestle for stamping maize into samp. On the clearing below the *ixande* was the space where the bus that travelled between Qoboshane and Sterkspruit, Dumakude Bus Service, was parked every night. My grandparents rented out the parking space, and a rondavel up the mountain where the driver slept, to the coloured family who owned the bus. The fact that Dumakude slept at our home was a source of pride to the hordes of grandchildren who lived at the estate.

And then there were the orchards; my grandfather's own source of pride. People wondered how he had turned the rocky mountain into a Garden of Eden. There were rows and rows of peach, apricot, quince, pear, apple, orange and pomegranate trees. There were also vines that bore both green and purple grapes, and cacti that bore red and green prickly pears. Figs had great prominence in the orchard, and my grandmother said it was in honour of our grandfather's father whose name was Feyiya, which means fig. In summer yellow cling peaches became our bane because we had to eat them as relish for hard porridge during hard times. Sometimes my grandfather's relatives from Lesotho would wade across the Telle River and bring us wild honey, which also helped in our battle with hard porridge.

It is hard to believe that I lived here for only two years – from 1960 to 1962 – when at the age of twelve I was banished from Johannesburg by my own parents for engaging in gang activities. My father had moved to Engcobo in the Transkei to serve articles under George Matanzima in order to be admitted as an attorney, while my mother remained in Johannesburg working as a registered nurse and midwife at the Dobsonville Clinic.

While she was at work at the clinic, which was just across the street from our four-roomed home, or cycling in the township delivering babies, I was playing truant from school and hanging out on shop verandas where I played the pennywhistle with other delinquent youths. Or I would be fighting in street gangs where I had become famous among my peers as a ducking champion, though my throwing of the stones that we used as weapons of war was reputed to be weak. On the occasions when I did go to school I spent most of the time in class drawing pictures. My talent was recognised when the teacher asked us to illustrate the poetry we were studying with appropriate pictures and I drew the Zulu warrior uPhoshozwayo as an illustration for a poem in his praise. With crayons, I brought his traditional dress of leopard skins and a shield and a spear to life. Then I signed the picture at the bottom right: 'by Zakes the Artist'.

That was the beginning of the name Zakes. I was given the name by a friend, Percy Bafana Mahlukwana, an artist in his own right, who later died in one of those gang wars. At the time there was a famous jazz saxophonist by the name of Zakes Nkosi in Alexandra Township. With my initials ZK, it seemed the logical thing to name me after this great man.

Sometimes I played truant from gang warfare and spent my time praying. I imagined that one day I would be a Catholic priest and go to heaven. I built an altar behind the house and on Saturdays and Sundays I lit candles and conducted a holy mass for myself. Sometimes the girl next door joined me and marvelled at my Latin chants: *Gloria Patri et Filio et Spiritu Sancto . . . Dominus vobiscum . . . et cum spiritu tuo . . . oremus.*

Because I thought she was my girlfriend, one day I asked her for *isinjonjo* – township slang for sex. She burst out in anger, threatening never to visit my altar again if I asked her to do 'silly things'. That was a relief! I wouldn't have known what to do if she had said yes. I immediately apologised and vowed on my life never to ask for *isinjonjo* ever again.

The last straw for my mother was when I was frogmarched home by a man who claimed I had robbed his daughter. That afternoon I had been loitering on the shop veranda as usual when a man and his weeping daughter, who was slightly younger than me, arrived. The daughter pointed at me as the boy who had robbed her of the money with which she had been sent to the store to buy a loaf of bread. I swear I had nothing to do with it, but when he searched me and found a big knife in my pocket the crime fitted me very well.

Not only had I disgraced my mother by engaging in criminal activities, I had also stolen a knife from her special set of *braai* knives and forks with carved ivory handles. My protestations that I had only carried the knife to impress my friends did not convince her. She had had enough of me, and she wrote to my father to fetch me and take me to his own parents at Qoboshane.

Under normal circumstances I loved visiting my grandparents in the village, particularly because I enjoyed travelling by train. It was always exciting to board at Park Station and then change trains in Bloemfontein after spending the whole night being lulled to sleep by the grinding rhythm of the wheels on iron, or to stand in the corridor looking out at the telephone poles passing very fast. If we were lucky we – my mother, my twin brothers Sonwabo and Monwabisi, my sister Thami, and my baby brother Zwelakhe – would have our own compartment with four berths, like bunk-beds. The greatest joy came from eating *umphako* – provisions for the road – of chicken and steamed bread carried in a cane and wicker basket. Sometimes we shared the compartment with another family, in which case we would share our respective *umphako*. Invariably they would also be carrying chicken and steamed bread in a similar basket. From Bloemfontein the train took us to Zastron, where we would catch a bus to Sterkspruit, and then take our trusty Dumakude Bus Service right to the doorstep of my grandparents' *ixande*.

But on this occasion of banishment the two-day train journey was a very unhappy one. I was leaving my friends in Johannesburg, and I wondered how I would cope in a village. My father didn't make things any better when he snapped at me in a café in Sterkspruit. He was at the counter buying fish and chips for our lunch and I was standing next to him. A mad woman in dirty tattered clothes approached me, smiling. She really scared me, so I moved to the other side of my father. But he thought I was afraid of a white boy, about my age, who had also approached the counter at the same time. He reprimanded me right there in public for giving way to the boy just because he was white and lectured me on how I was just as good as the boy and had no business to be afraid of white people. I just stood there feeling small; I dared not defend myself by saying that I was escaping the mad black woman and not the white boy.

When I came to live here grandfather had already lost some of his marbles, after an assassination attempt by a man called Gazi who stabbed him in the head with a knife. Apparently Gazi had been unhappy about one thing or another in grandfather's administration. After the stabbing Charles was no longer the grandfather I remembered on earlier visits, years before. The grandfather who sat in the shade of a gigantic boulder across the gravel road surrounded by his councillors, settling community disputes; who rode his horse Gobongwana, while singing its praises; who sat at his iron sewing machine making leather shoes while still singing praises to Gobongwana (we were proud that he was not just a cobbler who fixed soles like the old man on the veranda of Cretchley's store; he created shoes right from scratch); who stood in front of *ixande* in his brown riding breeches and gave sweets to a queue of grandchildren whenever he came from meetings in Sterkspruit; who never forgot to give a brief caress to his twenty-year-old dog Ngqawa, as it slept at the door; and who regaled us with stories of our revered ancestor Mhlontlo.

According to him, our clan, the amaMpondomise people, originally came from Qumbu in the eastern part of the Cape Province – the region that was named Transkei by subsequent colonial governments. Then one day Mhlontlo, who was a paramount chief in that area, killed the British resident magistrate. It happened in 1880, the very year my grandfather was born. First, Mhlontlo invited the magistrate to a ceremony at Sulenkama, the seat of the amaMpondomise kingdom. The magistrate, a violent and arrogant man called Hamilton Hope, set off with much pomp, thinking that he was going to be the centre of the ceremony, only to discover too late that the ceremony was about his own ritual murder. My ancestor, who was also a reputable medicine man, conducted the ritual in which parts of Hope's body were to be used as medicine to strengthen his armies. The whole ceremony involved a theatrical performance: Mhlontlo and his people rode back to Qumbu, thirty kilometres away, took over the magistracy and improvised a play where Mhlontlo took the role of Hamilton Hope. Turning over the pages of the big book on the magistrate's bench and adopting a nasal tone in his Anglicised isiXhosa, he mimicked Hope sentencing people.

8

Well, that theatre didn't last for long. The British forces came to arrest Mhlontlo, but he and his followers escaped to Lesotho, where they were given refuge by Chief Moorosi of the Baphuthi clan.

My grandfather was a baby on his mother's back during that long journey of nearly six hundred kilometres. His parents and the hundreds of Mhlontlo's followers felt very safe because he had strong medicine that protected everyone. Both the British and the Boers feared him; he could make their guns spew water instead of bullets and their cannons explode in their faces.

After some time a white trader lured Mhlontlo with new blankets from his Lesotho refuge to the Telle River that bordered South Africa. He was captured by the British troops who took him back to Qumbu for trial. Grandfather never told us the details of how Mhlontlo won the case, but he did. It must have been his strong medicine at work.

Many of Mhlontlo's followers decided against returning to Qumbu. That is why there are many Mdas in Lesotho today. My great-grandfather – Charles' father, that is – the Feyiya Mda who I mentioned in relation to the orchards, decided to cross the Lesotho border back to South Africa and to settle at eKra Village in the Lower Telle area.

By the time I went to live with my grandfather he could no longer remember the story of Mhlontlo. He had become a cantankerous old man who would tap a tyke's head with a walking stick for no apparent reason. We stayed out of his way.

He could no longer work in his fields either. Grandmother did all the farming with the help of the other villagers in work-parties known as *ilima*. But we were spoilt. We were never allowed to work in the fields like other village kids or like some of her older grandchildren. My siblings – who were already staying with my grandparents even before my banishment – and I were greatly distressed that we could not go to the fields. *Ilima* was so much fun – with food, songs and dances. Once we went with people who were taking food to the workers, but grandmother shooed us away.

'Go away,' she said. 'You, children of Solomzi, will be scorched by the sun.'

We took this as a punishment for being my father's children. After all, we had seen how partial she was towards her other grandchildren – especially those who were the children of her daughters rather than of her sons. We had seen how she used to hide chunks of pork in her apron pockets for Cousin Bernard, while we had to eat porridge with peaches. We knew that Bernard's mother, who had left the village for Johannesburg many years ago and never came back, did not send any money for his upkeep. Only my father sent money which my grandmother used to support hordes of grandchildren whose parents didn't bother.

That was why I told my father when he paid us a visit once that we were suffering and my cousins were getting preferential treatment at our expense. That afternoon he went to drink brandy with his friends and came back late in the evening. He was drunk and knocked at grandmother's door, yelling that she did not treat his children well.

The next day he was sober and remorseful. He apologised to grandmother for yelling at her, and then upbraided me for telling lies about his dear mother who was sacrificing so much to look after us.

But that was not the end of that story. When my father's younger brother, Uncle Owen, came visiting from Johannesburg many months later he punched me in the face and kicked me in the stomach even though I was already writhing on the ground, for lying about his mother to my father. And indeed my father's oldest sister, Aunt Nontsokolo, who owned a general dealer's store at 'Musong a few miles away, gave me a few choice words about my lies. Aunt Nontsokolo could afford to be self-righteous because she was the only one of my father's five siblings who did not at any stage dump her children with my grandmother but was bringing them up herself.

How could we not take our prohibition from *ilima* as punishment when we were forbidden even from looking after cattle? Granted, our grandfather no longer owned any cattle since the assassination attempt. Only disused kraals remained as evidence of his cattle-owning days. But we so much wanted to join herdboys from neighbouring homesteads in the fun and games that we knew took place out there in the pastures. As it was, our schoolmates who herded cattle after school and during weekends took us for sissies. Worst of all, we were not privy to their insider jokes and dirty stories whose settings were the great meadows and gorges where the cattle grazed, and the rivers where the boys moulded cattle from clay as the animals drank.

I could only console myself by roaming within the confines of the estate and spelunking the caves that were only a short distance from the rondavels. I was fascinated by the Bushman paintings that were still vivid and I tried to reproduce them in my notebook. This was an illegal act according to my teachers, because notebooks were meant for nothing but notes. I was constantly punished for it – a few whacks on my knuckles with a ruler.

THE REASON FOR RETURNING to this pink mountain is not to relive the past – though one cannot escape a little bit of nostalgia – but to visit the beekeeping project that I started with the village women a few years back. Gugu and I come here occasionally to see the Bee People, as we call them, and to admire the progress they have been making over the years. After taking us on a tour of the hives, especially the two supers that are in an enclosure of aloes between the graves of my grandfather and one of my aunts, we bid the Bee People goodbye and get into my car.

The mountain road is rough and narrow. A Mercedes Benz sedan was not built to negotiate boulders on what passes for a road, and often the rocks that stick out cannot but scrape against the bottom of the car. Fortunately this is not a busy road; otherwise I would be at a loss what to do if another car approached in the opposite direction. I dare not move to the side for fear of rolling down the slope. There are no railings, and already I can see skeletons of cars that must have rolled down over the years. No one could have survived the impact on the rocks hundreds of yards below.

There is a sigh of relief when we reach the village at the foot of the mountain.

It is more like a township than a village really, with modern bungalows, schools and shops. The biggest of the shops belongs to my

Uncle Phakamile, or Press, as we call him. It combines a general dealer's store, a restaurant and a tavern. The villagers call it eRestu. We use it to hold our meetings with the Bee People whenever we visit from Johannesburg or, in my case, from the United States where I now teach creative writing at Ohio University. Sometimes we just hang out to soak in the wonderful atmosphere created by drunken old ladies and various village characters, and by the smell of fish and chips and fat cakes deep frying in oil.

Some of the inhabitants once owned homesteads on the mountain we have now turned into an apiary – at Goodwell. But the Boers – and when we talk of the Boers we actually mean the apartheid government of the time – forced them down from the mountain and resettled them near the Telle River. It would be easier to govern them there and to ensure that they did not hide guerrilla fighters, or terrorists if you like, in their midst.

We branch off to eRestu to say goodbye to Press and his wife as we'll be driving back to Johannesburg. It is a six-hour drive and the earlier we leave the better. I hate driving at night.

'How are the bees doing, son?' Press asks. He is only six years older than me at most, but basks in the glory of being the son of my grandfather's brother. According to tradition, he is a peer of my father's and therefore I am his son.

'The bees are doing fine, Press,' I say. 'Although last winter's snow was not kind at all. The harvest will be small.'

'I do not know why you waste your time doing this honey business from which you gain nothing. You should have invested the money in my shop here. All I need is ten thousand rands to fill these shelves with goods. You would get your money back with a lot of profit.'

He has said this before. We Mdas have worked hard to get where we are. Why should we care about these good-for-nothing villagers?

'It is my time that I put into this honey business and of course my expenses to travel here from Johannesburg occasionally,' I explain to him. 'But many other people have contributed to its success.'

'Johannesburg? But I hear you now live in America,' he says. And he asks one of his daughters behind the counter to give us cold drinks of our choice and some biscuits.

'Yes, I work there now. Just like the migrant workers who go to the mines in Johannesburg. After every few months I return to see my mother. I may as well use that time to see how the Bee People are doing as well.'

Press is a hard-working business man who toiled in the mines in his youth because he did not have any education. To this day he is illiterate. He saved his money, and after a few years he came back to his home village to establish this business. Since he lifted himself up from poverty until he became the richest man in the village, he cannot understand why anyone should waste his time trying to pull others up.

'You see, Press, that beekeeping project will enrich you too,' I say, half-jokingly. 'When the villagers have money they will spend it in your store.'

'I hear you, child of my brother, but still . . .'

'But still we must go now, Press. We have a long way to drive.'

The stretch of dirt road from Qoboshane to Sterkspruit never fails to flood my mind with memories. That is why I turn to look at Gugu and say, 'You know, I am a creation of women. Not only because for nine months I was part of a woman's body, but for the simple reason that every woman with whom I have intimately interacted has contributed something in the moulding – for better or for worse – of who I have become.'

We are driving past St Teresa Roman Catholic Mission about sixteen kilometres from Qoboshane. A minibus taxi in front of us leaves a cloud of dust in its wake, and it remains hanging in the air for quite some time. The buildings look distorted through the combination of dust particles and the heatwaves, creating a very eerie image. I can see twisted nuns in black habits, ghosts of the past, walking silently in the grounds; pacing to and fro; muttering things to themselves; perhaps reading beads on their rosaries.

Among these apparitions I can see Sister Eusebia. She is the only one whose name I can remember, for she was the principal when my father taught at this secondary school from January 1948 to June 1955. She is the one who is still smiling in black and white photographs in my father's album – my only material inheritance from him. That and a number of LPs of Frank Sinatra, Marian Anderson, the Beatles, King

Kong (the South African musical), Ella Fitzgerald, Satchmo, Handel's Messiah, Dark City Sisters, Jim Reeves, the Mormon Tabernacle Choir, the Singing Bells and thirty or so others that he collected when he was a member of a record club from 1963 to 1966. The photo album is the only thing that I still have. The music albums went with my furniture and books when an ex-wife sold my stuff after an acrimonious divorce.

Sister Eusebia, a group of other nuns and the secondary school students in gym-dresses and white shirts still smile at me in black and white whenever I don a surgical mask to page through the photo album. The mask is essential because the dust mites that have accumulated between the pages over a period of more than five decades make me cough and sneeze and cry and itch all over whenever I visit those venerable pages. The mask, however, does not prevent the pain I still feel when I look at the angelic picture of a smiling Father Sahr – he of the Order of Mary Immaculate. His car killed my dog Rex when he drove through Goodwell once. Rex liked to bark at cars that drove on the dirt road in front of my grandfather's estate. And Manqindi – the name we gave to the German Catholic priest because one of his hands did not have fingers, the result of an incident in some world war – did not even stop his car after killing my Rex in cold blood. I vowed I would never own another dog for Father Sahr to kill. Since then I have never had another dog, though of course I have long stopped blaming the poor priest.

What strikes me as I drive past the Catholic mission is that it still looks the same. In fifty-five years nothing has been added; nothing has been taken away. All the stone buildings with red roofs are exactly as I remember them. Even the house where we lived when I was born. My father must have celebrated his new job at St Teresa's Native Secondary School with my conception, for I was born on the sixth of October, 1948, nine months after he joined the staff.

I wasn't born in that house, though, but at Mlamli Hospital a few kilometres from the mission station. My father named me Zanemvula, which has the double meaning of 'the rain bringer' and 'the one who has been brought by rain'. I do not think the heavens opened up and wept when I was born. Rather, I was named after a character in *Ingqumbo*

Yeminyanya, the isiXhosa novel by A C Jordan that was published in 1940 and years later translated into English by the author as *The Wrath of the Ancestors*. It was hailed as one of Africa's finest novels. It captivated readers because of its lyrical prose and its treatment of Western intrusion on the culture of amaXhosa. But what captivated my father most was that the novel was about our clan, the amaMpondomise people.

Father Sahr would not baptise me into the Roman Catholic Church without what he called a Christian name, which had to be a saint's name. But my father, an ardent Pan Africanist, insisted that he would not give me a 'white name', so he opted for Kizito, after the youngest of the Ugandan Martyrs. Although Kizito had only been beatified at the time and was not yet a fully fledged saint (he has since been canonised), the priest approved. My third name, Gatyeni, was my father's way of giving a nod to his ancestors by naming me after one of them.

My earliest memory resides in that house. I was three years old when mother and father came home with two babies in fluffy white. They were the twins, Sonwabo and Monwabisi, fresh from Mlamli Hospital and smelling of Johnson's Baby Powder. They were not my favourite people because they seemed to grab all my parents' attention. These usurpers spent a lot of time crying or sleeping. When they were sleeping and there was no one else in the room I opened their eyes with my fingers and inspected their eyeballs. Then I poked their faces just for the heck of it. This practice continued on a daily basis until I heard the radio telling on me as soon as my father switched it on to listen to the news one evening. It was the same radio that once interrupted Glenn Miller's 'String of Pearls' with ear-shattering static and then ratted on me that I had stolen sugar and condensed milk. Fortunately, on all the occasions it decided to be a tattle-tale no one else paid attention. Both my parents carried on with whatever they were doing as if they had not heard it. But I decided to stop all my criminal activities because I knew that one day the radio's snitching would ring loud and clear in their ears and I would be in deep trouble.

Yes, the grounds of the mission station are exactly as I remember them when I played with my friend Bernard Khosi on our tricycles, and when I followed my father around on a path between the buildings, a

15

newspaper in my pocket. Even though I could not read I always carried a newspaper with me, just like my father. Or a book. Any book from his shelf. It didn't matter that none of its pages was illustrated. The fact that I was walking around with a big book in my hand, just like father did, was satisfaction enough. It could be *Abou Ben Adhem and the Angel*, Shakespeare's *Julius Caesar* or a tome by George Eliot or one of the Brontë sisters that my father taught in his English literature classes, or the William Wordsworth and Percy Bysshe Shelley poetry that he made his students recite. During these walks father would himself recite Mark Antony's oration or something from *Macbeth*. I had no idea what the words meant and he never bothered to explain, but his voice still reverberates in my head: 'Tomorrow and tomorrow and tomorrow, creeps in this petty pace from day to day, to the last syllable of recorded time . . .'

My father was also an ardent gardener, and the staff quarters at St Teresa did not give him the opportunity to consummate his relationship with the soil. So, he rented a house at the nearby village of KwaGcina and we moved there. He cycled to work every morning, and after school he worked in his garden, particularly on those days when he was not conducting the school choir. When he was too tired to water the flowers and vegetables he sat on a chair on the stoep and drew pencil portraits of the twins and me and anyone else who happened to be around. People always marvelled at how he was able to bring out a person's likeness exactly as the person was.

Later, he bought a number of Jersey cows and employed village women to churn butter in big jars that were normally used for bottling peaches. I remember rows of women, some in the red-ochre *isikhakha* attire and big *iqhiya* turbans of the abaThembu people, sitting in front of the hatchery and shaking the jars to the rhythm of four-part harmonies. Occasionally a woman would be carried by the spirit, stand up and flaunt a few oscillations of the waist and shoulder, and then sit down to resume churning the butter.

In the hatchery there were batteries of incubators. Father encouraged villagers to raise chickens for meat. They bought day-old chicks from his hatchery.

When my mother got a job as a nursing sister in another village called Dulcie's Nek my parents employed a nanny to look after us. Nontonje was initially a red girl, which meant she wore the traditional red-ochre clothes, but she was soon socialised into floral dresses that were mostly hand-downs from my mother.

I didn't know of my father's activities besides his teaching and farming. Sometimes he was away for extended periods. We heard adults talking about how he had been banned by the Minister of Justice, C R Swart, from attending any gathering in any place within the Union of South Africa. Then we heard that there was a big problem between him and some local villagers, particularly the village chief, Steyn Senoamali, who was supported by Mr Fihla, the primary school teacher. We never got to know the nature of the problem exactly, but it was somehow related to a civil action in which my father was suing Steyn Senoamali for calling him a communist and the Native Commissioner of Herschel, our district, was in full support of the village chief. Perhaps Fihla was going to give evidence on behalf of Senoamali and the Native Commissioner and tell the court that they were not being libellous since my father was indeed a communist as confirmed by his membership of the African National Congress. Anyone who fought against apartheid was regarded as a communist and was likely to be banned under the Suppression of Communism Act, even if he was as anti-communist as my father was. Most likely, Senoamali and Fihla were being used by the Commissioner to spy on my father.

There was so much bad blood between my family and Senoamali that he haunted my dreams. He was reputed to be a powerful *ixhwele* – medicine man – and I feared that he was going to harm my father with his wizardry. Nontonje, who understood these issues better, kept me and the twins abreast of events, particularly on Senoamali's prowess in the field of magic. She painted a vivid picture of a stick that he used to cast spells, which was also capable of transforming into a snake. His name, which is Sesotho for 'the one who drinks blood' or, even more ominous, 'the blood-sucker', added to my anxieties about the safety of my family.

One night I was woken up by a loud knock on my bedroom window.

And there was Senoamali's stick peeping between the curtains. 'Hello, Kizito,' it said. '*Ndiyeza ngapho* – I'm coming over there.' Behind it out there I could see white horses dancing in the dark, flames raging from their hoofs. The next morning I told Nontonje about the visit, and she confirmed that indeed that was clear evidence that you don't mess with an *ixhwele* of Senoamali's stature. Two decades later I wrote a poem titled 'Dance of the Ghosts' based on the incident. It begins: *I dream/ And my dreams/ Are dreams of ghosts/ I see them prancing/ And gamboling/In the moonlight/ Their eyes glow/ With impish pride/ And their feet dance/ To the rhythm/ Of no music.*

As the days for the court case approached, the dream became recurrent. Until Nelson Mandela came from Johannesburg to rescue me. His presence assured me that Senoamali's stick would be defeated.

He was a lawyer from the firm of Messrs Mandela and Tambo and was instructed by my father to handle the case against Senoamali and the Native Commissioner. I liked him because whenever he visited our house he never forgot to mention how handsome I was. He was quite handsome himself, with finely combed hair parted on the right in what we called 'the road'. That was my father's style too – a style that I often asked Nontonje to do on my head. Alas, my mother never allowed my hair to grow long enough to make 'the road' noticeable.

Mandela was not just my father's lawyer but he was his friend as well. When Anton Lembede died in 1947 my father, a founding member of the African National Congress Youth League, took over as its president. But the following year he had to leave Johannesburg because of ill-health and went to teach at St Teresa. He continued with his presidency and periodically made the trip to Johannesburg to catch up with ANC Youth League business. Later he set up a working committee comprising Nelson Mandela, Walter Sisulu and Oliver Tambo to manage the activities of the organisation in his absence.

Even when we still lived at St Teresa Nelson Mandela would sometimes drive all the way from Johannesburg to consult with my father. One day Mandela came to St Teresa with a briefcase of documents in preparation for some ANC conference where the Youth League was to present its strategy. He was not aware that the Special

Branch cops were following him. When he arrived my father was in his Junior Certificate literature class. Sister Eusebia called him outside, and he and Mandela conferred for a few minutes before Mandela handed him the briefcase. Mandela drove away, but as soon as my father got back to his classroom there was another knock. He opened the door thinking that it was Mandela who had perhaps forgotten to tell him something. But it was the police – both uniformed and Special Branch. They pushed him aside and walked into the classroom. They wanted the briefcase. But it had disappeared and my father did not know where.

'What briefcase?' my father asked.

'We know that Mandela gave you a briefcase,' said an Afrikaner Special Branch officer. 'Where is it?'

My father pretended he did not know what they were talking about. At the same time he really did not know what had happened to the briefcase. The policemen turned the classroom upside down but there was no briefcase. They were fuming because they had hoped to arrest my father with incriminating documents, and then of course arrest Mandela before he got to Umtata where he had clients to defend in a criminal matter.

'Perhaps he didn't leave the briefcase after all,' said a black Special Branch man.

They left in a huff.

No one said anything about the briefcase for three days or so. My father was wary of asking, lest he incriminate himself by admitting ownership of it. One could never be sure whether or not there was a police informer among the students.

One day Sister Eusebia called him to her office.

'Are you not missing something, Mr Mda?' she asked.

Before my father could answer she gave him the briefcase. There was a sigh of relief. She told him that as soon as the students realised that the police were at the door the student in front reached for the briefcase and passed it to the student sitting behind her. It was passed from student to student until the one who was sitting at the window threw it out. Sister Eusebia was there to catch it and hide it.

Some of those students became political activists. Ezra November and Nqabande Sidzamba, for instance, became PAC leaders.

MY MOTHER ALSO KNEW Nel or Nelly, as she and her girlfriends called Nelson Mandela, long before she married my father. She, Albertina Sisulu and Evelyn Mase trained together as nurses. Albertina was the oldest of the girls, and she occupied herself with matchmaking. Thus Nelson ended up courting and then marrying Evelyn, and after about two years my father married my mother.

Nelson and Evelyn were so close to my parents that a few years later they looked after us – me and the twins – at their Orlando home in Johannesburg when politics and then law studies uprooted us from the stability of KwaGcina and our farming activities. At the time the Mandelas had three children of their own: Thembi who was two years older than me; Makgatho, two years younger; and a toddler named Maki. So, three extra kids and their nanny must have been quite a burden, although I never heard anyone complain.

A memory that sticks out during this period is when Nelson Mandela picked us up in his car from Park Station in Johannesburg. We drove to Sophiatown because he wanted to see someone there. In front of us was an old car that looked as if it was going to fall apart any time. It was coughing along and releasing a cloud of black smoke from its exhaust pipe. Our nanny, Nontonje, broke out laughing. I joined in the laughter. So did the twins. Mandela turned to look at us at the back. His face was stern as he said: *Nihleka lemoto yalomntu, kodwa aninayo ne njalo nina* – You laugh at that man's car, yet you don't even have one like that.

That stopped our silly giggles immediately. I had not known that Mandela could be firm. The last time I had seen him was at KwaGcina when he had come for the Senoamali case. He was always smiling and wanting to know what I wanted to be when I grew up. 'Doctor!' I said. He laughed, gave me sweets and said I was going to heal them all.

After that he left in his car with my father, and we didn't see my father for many days. Nontonje looked after us and did very strange things to us. To me and the twins. Especially to me because the twins' bodies refused to cooperate.

When my mother was at work in Dulcie's Nek and the churning women were done for the day Nontonje took us to her room, which was separate from the main house. She told us she was going to teach us a beautiful game that we were going to enjoy very much. First she stripped the pants and underpants off Sonwabo, placed him on the bed and played with his penis. She jerked her hand in a very fast movement, but stopped when she failed to get the desired result. She did the same to Monwabisi. But fortunately for the twins their three-year-old penises stayed limp. Then it was my turn. It didn't take much effort on her part – moving her hand up and down in a fast motion – for my six-year-old penis to get an erection. She lay on her back on the bed and lifted her dress. She was not wearing any bloomers – girls wore bloomers those days, not panties. She placed me on top and guided my penis with her hand into her vagina. To this day I remember the burning sensation that made me jump up and run out of the room. I tried to pee but I could not. The burning sensation blocked me. I could see something red on the tip.

'Let's try again,' said Nontonje. 'You'll see, you'll enjoy it.'

We tried once more. Even though there was no longer an erection she tried to force it. Once more there was the burning sensation. Nontonje never gave up. She tried again on other occasions without success. Always the burning sensation.

I didn't tell my mother when she came back. For more than four decades I didn't tell anybody.

THE DRIVE TO STERKSPRUIT on the dusty road takes us past Dulcie's Nek. I can see the clinic where my mother worked surrounded by gum trees near the road, and the house where Felicity lived. She was about my age, the first white person I ever befriended. Her mother was also a nurse at the clinic. I never saw her exchange visits with my mother, so I doubt if they ever became friends. But Felicity and I played together.

Her mother had this habit of interrupting our play by calling out from her doorstep every day at 10 a.m. and 4 p.m.: 'Felicity, teatime!' Felicity would stop in the middle of any game we were playing, and without a word she would run to her home for the ritual of tea and biscuits. I wondered why my mother never called me for teatime, and why we only drank tea in the morning when we were having bread and peanut butter for breakfast. The only person who drank tea after every meal was my father.

'Felicity, teatime!' the nasal voice echoes in the dust raised by my Mercedes and the minibus taxis that run to and from Sterkspruit. Another voice that echoes is that of Thandeka, the skinny girl who lived across the barbed wire fence from the clinic. She was my first crush, the girl I was playing house with when the barbed wire scarred my face.

I was marked for life chasing a girl.

I can hear her lonely voice singing while she basked in the sun on the red stoep: *Hamba wena juba lami, nguwe olithemba lami. Hamba wena juba lami, hamba juba lam. Kudala ngihlezi estupini, ngilalel'ingoma yakho, nezintsimbi ziyakhala, hamba juba lam* – Go my dove, you are my only hope, go my dove, go my dove. I have been sitting on the stoep, listening to your song, and the bells are ringing, go my dove.

The voice fades with the village behind us. I am wondering why there is no period in my life that I remember with utter joy – a time to which I would gladly return if at all there was such a possibility. I do remember some happy moments, yes, but there was always a gaping hole that could not be filled. Sometimes I am attacked by a profound pain, the cause or origin of which I cannot fathom. Sometimes there is a void.

I do not express these thoughts to Gugu.

CHAPTER TWO

ONCE WE SLEPT IN a ghost hotel. We had gone to see the Bee People at Qoboshane and it was too late to drive back to Johannesburg. So we decided to cross the South African border to Lesotho at the Telle Bridge and drive on the dirt road that winds up and down among fields of withered corn, dry gullies, emaciated cattle grazing on scrappy patches of dry grass, and villages of dilapidated huts. This road soon joins a bitumen two-lane highway to the small town of Moyeni, the headquarters of Lesotho's southernmost district of Quthing.

It is a short distance of fifteen or so kilometres from eRestu, well worth the hassle of going through the scrutiny of border police, and customs and immigration officials. We cross this border so many times that the officials on both sides know us by now and in some instances, depending on who is at the desk, no longer search our car for contraband and don't even ask us to show our passports. They all know my uncle Press because he crosses the border every day to buy groceries from wholesalers in Lesotho to stock his store; much nearer and cheaper than wholesalers in Sterkspruit.

'Oh, you are *Ntate* Mda's visitors,' a policeman says and beckons us to cross the lifted boom barrier. Some have heard of our apiary and want to know how the bees are doing and when the next harvest of honey will be. On the Lesotho side there is always at least one official who was at one stage a student of mine, perhaps at one of the high schools I taught at over the years or at the National University of Lesotho where I was once a lecturer and the head of the English Department.

The hotel used to belong to a Lesotho minister of finance who died a few years ago from complications of morbid obesity. In its heyday it was patronised by local civil servants, businessmen and young professionals. Tourists frequented it because of its location on the crest of a mountain. Yes, this used to be a very busy place. But the first thing that struck us when we drove through the gate that day was the absence of cars in the parking lot. The rough-cast building in powder blue still looked beautiful as I remembered it in years gone by. But the whole place looked deserted, even though the reception door was open.

We stood at the front desk with our bags. There was no one there.

'What next?' Gugu asked.

'Maybe we should check ourselves in,' I said looking at the open register on the desk.

Just when we were about to walk out of the door a woman said, *'Nka le thusa?'* Can I help you? She was standing behind the desk as if she had been there all along.

We checked in; she gave us a key and directions to our room.

The room was clean although it had a musty smell. I turned the television on; there was only snow. We slept with the lights on because Gugu is scared of the dark. But all of sudden there was a blackout,

24

accompanied by the whining sound of a lone mosquito. Gugu panicked. Darkness suffocates her. The lone whine was joined by a second, and a third, and soon the room was whining and buzzing with mosquitoes. I remembered seeing a stump of a candle on the dressing table and I lit it. We stumbled out of the room into the corridor. We knocked at the other doors but none of the rooms were occupied. We were the only guests. The candle flickered in a thin hot draught that came from nowhere. We called out but the only response we got was the echo of our own voices.

We staggered back to our room and opened the curtains, hoping that some feeble light from the stars would find its way in and relieve Gugu's phobia. We got into bed and the mosquitoes began to feast on us. They came through the vents from a swimming pool with dirty stagnant water that we could see through the window.

'What happened to the receptionist?' Gugu asked.

'Perhaps she was Vera the Ghost,' I said, trying to lighten the mood. 'Perhaps we'll wake up in the morning only to find that we spent the night in a cemetery.'

We both grew up in Soweto at different times. Vera the Ghost is one of those stories that link our youth. I have since learnt that there are many Vera the Ghosts the world over – such as the ghost of a high school senior who burnt to death at Cottey College in Missouri. Our Vera was a beautiful girl who lived what our parents referred to as a reckless life. She was a 'good time girl' – a party girl, that is – who was always seen in the various townships of Soweto riding in posh cars with different men. Then one day she was coming back from a shebeen in the current one-night-stand's car and there was a collision. She died on the spot. Since that night Vera the Ghost has haunted the streets of Soweto. Her modus operandi has never changed: a lone male motorist would stop in the middle of the night to give a ride to a gorgeous scantily dressed hitch-hiker. The girl would be so captivating and so open to adventure that in no time the age old question of your-place-or-mine would be answered by an open invitation to her house. Without much ado the couple would be in each other's arms in her plush bedroom. In the morning the man would wake up at Avalon Cemetery. No woman. No clothes. Not even shoes.

Gugu and I did not wake up in a cemetery, though. It was the same desolate hotel with its cold water in the bathroom and an empty reception desk. We loaded our bags in the car and fled, vowing never to return.

THAT IS WHY WE are at the Hilltop Hotel in Sterkspruit tonight. Whenever we visit the Bee People we can only find accommodation in places that are a distance away from the apiary. It may be in the Lesotho town of Mafeteng where some of my relatives live – and that is ninety or so kilometres away – or in this one-street town, which is much closer but slightly out of our way to Johannesburg.

Sterkspruit is one stopover I always find evocative; on the streets of this town and its nearby township of Tienbank walk the ghosts of my past. I came to live here in 1962 after my father completed serving his articles, bought a house in this town and opened his law practice as an attorney. That brought about an end to my banishment in Qoboshane with my grandparents, and also brought back my mother and those of my siblings who lived in Johannesburg. For the first time we all lived under one roof as a family.

Even as I stand in front of the single-storey whitewashed hotel, which is on a hillock, looking down on the main road I can see myself as a spindly fourteen-year-old boy in khaki shorts and black canvas Cats shoes walking past Bhunga Hall and looking longingly at the posters for *Manana the Jazz Prophet*, a musical play by an unknown playwright, composer and choreographer called Gibson Kente. He was to become the doyen of black South African theatre in later years. The play had been produced at the famous Dorkay House in Johannesburg and was touring the whole of South Africa and neighbouring territories. For many months we read about it in such magazines as *Drum*, *Zonk* and *Bona*. We drooled over pictures of actresses dancing half-naked on the stage. We never imagined that one day such a wonderful musical would come to our little Sterkspruit.

But it did. And my father wouldn't let me go see it. He didn't see it either. Nor did my mother, although I suspect she would have loved to attend since most of her colleagues from Empilisweni Hospital, where she worked as a nursing sister, went to see the show. But my father was always buried in his work and never took her anywhere.

I did, however, have a glimpse of the performance on a Friday afternoon on the veranda of Bhunga Hall. A six-piece band of saxophone, trumpet, guitars, and drums played the music and actors presented some scenes from the play as a way of enticing passers-by to attend the performance in the evening. The dancing girls shook their waists in a brisk routine to the howls and applause of street urchins, and then disappeared into the hall.

'If you want to see the rest,' a man announced over a megaphone, 'come to Bhunga Hall tonight. Eight o'clock sharp. Come one, come all!'

It was all too brief for us, but I regard *Manana the Jazz Prophet* as the first play that I ever saw, even though I only had a peek at it. I still do not have any idea what the story was about, but as I stood there staring at the posters of dancing girls plastered on the stone wall I created my own *Manana the Jazz Prophet* in my imagination.

The black elite of Sterkspruit went to the musical. I remember Uncle Owen all dressed up in black tie with a girlfriend on his arm. He had returned from Johannesburg to operate Ndzunga Restaurant and was one of the socialites of Sterkspruit, quite popular with nurses of Empilisweni Hospital, which lies on the outskirts of the town, and of Mlamli Hospital, only a few kilometres away. Mlamli, especially, had a nurses' home that was inhabited by some of the most beautiful trainee nurses from all over South Africa. On any day of the week there were cars parked outside the yard; men who had come to 'check' their girlfriends and mistresses. It was not for nothing that the hospital and its nurses' quarters were referred to as 'the fish pond'. Empilisweni, on the other hand, was not a training hospital and therefore did not have the rich pickings. The nursing sisters and their assistants were mature women with families. Most likely Uncle Owen's partner was from Mlamli.

After the show the socialites went to the Hilltop Hotel for drinks in the bar and the lounge. Of course at that time a boy of my age with strict parents would not witness these activities. He would be at home tucked in bed. But Cousin Mlungisi, who was my age and lived four houses from my home, would be a secret spectator at some of them. His father, Mr Tindleni, was a director in the district education office, and was famous for having spawned many beautiful daughters. His mother was my father's distant cousin, hence she was my aunt and that's how Mlungisi got to be my cousin.

Either they were not too strict at his home or he was sneaky enough to be able to steal away at night and attend events that my mind associated only with adults. He was often caught sneaking into Bhunga Hall to watch the gentlemen of Sterkspruit – teachers, taxi drivers and policemen – and their ladies practise ballroom dancing on Saturday afternoons. The dance instructor finally got tired of shooing him away and let him watch, as long as he didn't invite other urchins into the hall.

'We are not dancing for an audience here, you little twerp,' said the instructor, who was also a teacher at our Tapoleng Primary School.

Cousin Mlungisi was the one who came back with the report of how wonderful it was at Bhunga Hall where he had listened to the whole of *Manana the Jazz Prophet* through the window (he could not see the stage) and of how afterwards he followed the socialites to the Hilltop Hotel and saw Uncle Owen kiss his girlfriend in his blue Opel Kadett. He was close enough to observe that he had actually put his tongue in her mouth, a yucky practice Cousin Mlungisi referred to as a French kiss. He revealed to me that he himself had done it with some of his girlfriends.

I couldn't believe Cousin Mlungisi could sink that low. I knew that he was having sex already; I once caught him in a donga on the way from school on top of a girl and I averted my eyes and took a different direction. I never understood how he got the girls to agree to have sex with him. I was still a virgin, if you don't count my experience with Nontonje at KwaGcina, and such adventures with girls were the furthest thing from my mind. Secretly, I envied Cousin Mlungisi's pizzazz, which resulted in his popularity with girls, but putting your tongue in a girl's mouth was the most revolting thing imaginable.

I didn't know that only a few days later I would experience it.

COUSIN MLUNGISI AND I were walking on the shoulder of the road from the town to our township of Tienbank. We were having a wonderful time infuriating white motorists with political slogans. It was before the road was tarred, but the gravel that was occasionally hurled at us by the speeding tyres did not deter us. We were too much involved in political action to be bothered even by the dust that left our heads looking like our khaki shorts. Whenever we saw a white motorist we raised our thumbs up and shouted, *Mayibuye iAfrika!* This was the slogan of the ANC – Let Africa come back! Sometimes I would add, 'From Cape to Cairo'.

Most motorists ignored us and continued on their journey. But one day we saw a motorist who had zoomed past make a U-turn and drive back towards us. We didn't wait for the burly white man to stop but fled to the nearby eucalyptus and pine woods. The man parked the car on the roadside and got out with pompous deliberation. He didn't come after us though; he just stood there looking in our direction and then got back into his car.

I was relieved.

We could see the white man from our hiding place as he drove away.

'Let's go back and provoke some more Boers,' said Cousin Mlungisi.

'Oh, no,' I said. 'I'm not going back there.'

When he laughed at me and called me a coward who would never be a freedom fighter I had to follow him back to the battlefield. Mercifully, before we got to the road we saw Kili walking back from town with a paper bag of groceries on her head. She was a tall and robust girl, perhaps in her late teens or early twenties, who lived in a village beyond Tienbank.

At the same time, two men in the colourful and shimmering pants of mineworkers known as *phelephatshwa*, matching miners' helmets with lamps and all, and black gumboots, were trotting towards her to the rhythm of the harmonica played by one of them. When they got close to her they stopped and one recited a poem in her honour: *Dudlu! Nongena nkomo uyayidl'inyama, nongena ntsimi uyawudl'umbhona. Nongen'a mazi uyalusel'ubisi. Dudlu! Ide nalomhlab'uhamba kuwo ingath'uthandazelwe! Ndiyakuthanda ntombi ndingazenzisi! O! Vo-*

29

luptuous one! Even those who don't have cattle do eat meat; one doesn't need to have fields in order to eat corn! One doesn't have to own the cow before one can drink its milk. O! Voluptuous one, even the earth you walk on has been blessed! I love you, girl, and I am genuine about it!

Kili looked at them cheekily, arms akimbo, the paper bag balanced on her head, and then walked on towards us. The men merely laughed, performed a small jig to the rhythm of their harmonica and continued with their boisterous journey without looking back once. So much for being genuine. I wondered why Kili did not become outraged that strange men told her to her face that even though she did not belong to them they were entitled to her; that to them she was as good as a piece of meat that could be eaten by anyone who happened to desire it. But girls those days took such uninvited attention in their stride and walked on. Some actually found it flattering.

I would have felt resentful if Kili had rewarded the men's poetry with the slightest smile because unlike the men I had some measure of 'entitlement' to her. Kili was our 'mommy' – mine and Cousin Mlungisi's. Those days cute little boys like us used to have 'mommies'. Older girls approached younger boys and girls and asked them to be their 'babies'. Your 'mommy' bought you sweets and even shared her song book with you, from which you copied lyrics of the latest pop songs into your own song book. 'Mommies' were worldly wise, so you learnt a lot of tricks from them, which you were later going to apply in your own romantic relationships when your time came. I had met Kili some weeks before on the same road to town and she asked me to be her 'sonny'. I agreed even though I did not know who she was. I only learnt later that Cousin Mlungisi was her 'sonny' too.

Kili screeched with joy when she saw her two 'babies'. I for one was happy that she would draw our attention away from our roadside revolutionary mission.

'Come here, my babies,' she said as she put her paper bag on the ground and reached for Cousin Mlungisi. She held him tightly to herself and kissed him. She put her tongue in his mouth and rolled it a few times. His eyes were rolling in a daze, and he staggered a bit when she finally released him from her embrace. Then she reached for me and stuffed her tongue into my mouth. As one would expect, she reeked of fish. It was the custom of village girls to treat themselves to fish and chips whenever they were in town. I could taste the fish in her mouth and could feel the pieces between her teeth. I broke free and ran away, while spitting out a lot of saliva. She and Cousin Mlungisi just stood there, obviously wondering what was wrong with me.

When Cousin Mlungisi came back after walking Kili halfway to her village he had a packet of Bakers Assorted Biscuits, and rubbed it in that I would be munching my own biscuits too if I had not been such a milksop.

I could never live that down. I was the boy who ran away from a French kiss. Cousin Mlungisi made a point of spreading the news in the streets of Tienbank where we played our soccer and at the playgrounds of Tapoleng Primary School where we were both pupils.

Even my girlfriend Keneiloe got wind of the news and that was even more embarrassing. To her, I had posed as a man of the world, and had pretended that the fact that we had never kissed – and here I am talking of an ordinary peck on the lips or even on the cheek – was only because I was protecting her innocence; I was being a gentleman. Now she might suspect the truth; that it was really *my* innocence I was protecting; that I was petrified to ask for a kiss.

I was fourteen and I had never kissed a girl!

Keneiloe was my first love. Not just a crush as before, but a real girlfriend. I actually proposed to her and she said yes. She had made things easier for me by teasing me and singing a song about my knock knees and dancing to it. *Sitshu madolo a jongeneyo, sitshu madolo a jongeneyo* – Alas, the knock-kneed one, the knock-kneed one! So I reckoned she liked me and there was no danger of rejection. Women don't compose songs about your knock-kneed gait if they don't like you.

It turned out she did like me.

She was three years younger and the most beautiful girl in all of Sterkspruit. She came from the rich Mohafa family, just three houses from my home. Her father Teboho owned a fleet of buses, and her mother Hopestill was a nursing sister with my mother at Empilisweni Hospital. They were best friends.

After Keneiloe heard of the incident with Kili she laughed at me on

31

the way from school. As did the hordes of other kids who walked the two kilometres or so between Tapoleng Primary and Tienbank. But I walked on with stoicism with the twins, Sonwabo and Monwabisi, in tow, feeling betrayed that my own Keneiloe was part of the riff-raff that was mocking me.

Yet I spent a lot of time with Keneiloe. Some force drew me to wherever she was, and somehow she found her way to wherever I was. Even though she lived three houses from my home and we saw each other every day we wrote letters to each other. It was during this great romance that I honed my letter-writing skills. My letters became famous for their lyricism and highfalutin imagery. At recess, girls sat under a tree and cheered and laughed and sighed deeply and vented exclamations of envy as she read them one of my letters.

When I passed a group of giggling school girls it was not unusual to hear one of them utter a stage whisper to the rest: 'There he is, the boy who writes such wonderful love letters.'

Every day after school and on Saturdays we played hopscotch, *dibeke*, and rounders in the street that divided our section of the township with its sprawling bungalows and landscaped gardens from the poor side with shacks and dilapidated adobes. We – the children of lawyers, nurses, school inspectors and businessmen – were quite snobbish towards the kids from the ramshackle side of the township and rarely played with them. One of them, a coloured boy named Bomvana, old Page's son, got even by waylaying us with his gang of dirty boys on our way from school and pelting us with stones.

DESPITE THE POOR SERVICE and the rude receptionists who view guests as more of a nuisance than a source of their salaries, the night in the musty bedroom of Hilltop Hotel is much more pleasant than our experience at the ghost hotel. In the morning Gugu and I get into the car and we cruise towards the township of Tienbank. Before we drive the eight hours or so to Johannesburg I want to show her those physical landmarks of my life that may have survived the ravages of time.

Tienbank looks quite shabby today. The luxury homes look rundown and *zimbhatshile*, which means their once-bright colours have faded. Although the Mohafas and the Tindlenis still live here, most of the black elite have long emigrated to the formerly white suburb closer to town. I point out what used to be my father's house to Gugu and we park just outside the gate. Somehow it looks lonely and lost. The thatch on the rondavel looks like a nest that has been abandoned by a mother bird. I wonder what the lounge under that thatch looks like today. I remember the display cabinet with lots of glass and mirrors where my mother kept her special tea set and bric-a-brac and where I once placed my First Class Standard Six Certificate for all the world to see, to the embarrassment of my mother who left it there for a while to humour me and then later gently asked me to remove it so that she could keep it safely for me. Then there were the sofas that she had bought from Bradlows in Johannesburg, upholstered in light grey heavy-duty fabric. Those sofas outlasted my childhood. Many years later when I was a lecturer at the National University of Lesotho they were still at my home in Mafeteng, being used by my ageing parents, in their original upholstery.

I know Johannesburg is a long way and we don't want to reach home at night. But somehow I am unable to will myself to step on the accelerator and drive away. The engine is still running, though. I wonder who owns this place now. Whoever they are, they don't have any appreciation of the work my father put into the garden decades ago. It is overgrown with weeds. I take a long look at the rondavel one more time, and my eyes penetrate through the brick wall.

I can see my mother sitting on the Bradlows sofas with Hopestill, Keneiloe's no-nonsense mother. It was not unusual for the two friends to sit in the living room and gossip over tea and scones.

One day I came back from a gruelling street-soccer game, where I played my usual role of goalkeeper with catlike agility, only to be summoned to appear before the two ladies relaxing – or so I thought – on the Bradlows sofas. I almost wet my pants when I saw what my mother was brandishing in her hand. A letter. The very letter I had written to Keneiloe proclaiming that she was 'the queen of my heart'.

Such a declaration was meant for her eyes only and perhaps for the ears of adoring audiences at those recess-time letter-reading sessions. Not for Hopestill's eyes. Not for my mother's eyes either.

'*Yintoni lento, Zanemvula?*' my mother asked. What is this, Zanemvula?

When she called me Zanemvula instead of Zani I knew that she was not pleased with me at all.

Hopestill was staring directly into my eyes, as if waiting expectantly for an answer that would be some kind of a revelation. Her eyes were bulging, big and round like Keneiloe's. Her gaze did not shift even when she reached for a biscuit on a saucer on the coffee table, delicately placed it in her mouth, and then reached for a cup of tea which she sipped with equal delicacy.

I averted my eyes and looked at the wall. I focused on the round plaster of Paris casts of red roses, thinking what a smart idea it was of my mother's to have round pictures on a round wall.

'I have asked you a question, Zanemvula,' my mother said, forcing me to return my gaze to my tormentors.

Silence. The best defence. She looked at Hopestill helplessly. Hopestill continued with her steadfast gaze. I diverted my eyes to the letter in my mother's hand. I could see very clearly the logo that I had designed which was on every letter that I wrote to Keneiloe. I could see the ornate letters KM, enclosed in a big heart. I couldn't see the smaller letters that followed the big K so that it became the first letter for both Kizito and Keneiloe, nor could I make out the letters that came after the big M, making it the first letter of both Mda and Mohafa. But I knew they were there. This was my logo all right. Keneiloe liked that logo although she laughed at it because she thought I had invented the name Kizito so that I could also have a name that began with K. She never believed me when I told her that I was actually baptised Kizito in the Roman Catholic Church in the name of the Father, the Son and the Holy Ghost.

'I am sorry,' I said, almost in a whisper. 'I will never do it again.'

Even as I uttered these words I knew I was lying. I just couldn't see how I could resist writing to Keneiloe. The highlight of my week was when I received a letter from her. Always short and to the point. Without any flowery language. But the fact that she took the trouble to write to me was fulfilment enough.

The women conferred aloud, both agreeing that I had done a very despicable thing. Hopestill said that she had actually given her daughter a hiding about this letter, and she expected my mother to do the same to me. My mother made a solemn promise that she was going to give me the hiding of a lifetime. My mother was such a beautiful soul that I couldn't see her lifting her hand to me. The only time she ever did was the incident I told you about when I was caught loitering on a store veranda with that knife stolen from her ivory-handled *braai* set in Dobsonville many years before. I knew she would not fulfil her promise to Hopestill, and she never did.

'You write such dirty letters again to my little girl, Teboho will break your neck. You're lucky that Rose has pleaded with me not to show him the letter this time.' That was Hopestill's parting shot.

After this confrontation things cooled a bit between me and Keneiloe. I even got myself another girlfriend, Nombuyiselo Jafta, who lived next door to Keneiloe. But things never really took off between us. Her main problem was that she was not Keneiloe. The fact that her father was a member of the South African Police Force didn't help our relationship. There was a stigma attached to anyone who associated with that family to the extent that we were reluctant to play with their kids, even though the Jafta girls were all so beautiful.

I was glad my father never got to know of my crimes. I don't know what he would have done but we always trod lightly when we approached him. Like my mother, he abhorred corporal punishment. But he knew how to use words that caused invisible weals on your body that would be as painful as the welts of flagellation. He had a way of making you feel not only that you were a disappointment to yourself and your parents, but you had also let the whole continent of Africa down – from Cape to Cairo, Morocco to Madagascar. 'Africa cannot afford to have people who do such things,' he would say.

He was busy with his law practice, spending all day long in his office which was a room in our house with a separate entrance. Or at the magistrate's court in town defending clients in both civil and criminal matters. In the evenings he spent hours in his garden, which had been landscaped by Old Xhamela who had been imported from KwaGcina for that purpose. My siblings and I were resentful that every evening – when all the kids of the township were playing games in the street – we had to go home to work in the garden. We had to draw water with watering cans from the communal borehole just outside our yard and line them up for him to do the watering. He did not believe we were capable of watering his tomatoes, spinach, cabbages and carrots without making a mess of things so he preferred to water them himself. He was so obsessive about watering his garden that even when it had rained, we still had to draw water from the borehole for him to water the plants.

We also had to water his peach trees of different varieties that lined the plot and bore fruit most seasons of the year. Even in winter some trees produced big smooth red nectarines. What amazed the people of the township was that the trees were short, about the height of a man, whereas the peach trees with which they were familiar grew taller than a house. Once or twice a year, depending on the variety, Old Xhamela pruned our trees so well that the fruit they bore was gigantic.

We knew that at night Bomvana and the kids from the poor side of the township stole our peaches, but we said nothing about it. They boasted about it when they waylaid us on the way from school, but we couldn't tell on them for fear of the further violence they would unleash on us.

I liked to watch Old Xhamela work in the garden. Quite often I joined him with my sketch book and crayons, and drew our house from the vantage point of the garden. I loved drawing the red-brick house because its architecture was unique. Whereas the house next door, Nikelo and Xolile's home, was a Spanish-type bungalow with yellow rough-cast walls, ours had a red-brick grass-thatched rondavel that was linked to the rest of the red-brick house by a plastered cream-coloured corridor. It was roofed in black-painted corrugated iron. At the other end of the building there was a porch with a red stoep and a glass door that opened into my father's office.

I never tired of drawing the house from different angles, and Old

Xhamela never tired of giving me his feedback. He was quite an art critic too; in one drawing he pointed out that I had drawn the chimney on the roof even though from the angle where we were standing it could not be seen. You would only see it if you went to the back of the house where the kitchen was located. I had only placed it there, he added, because I knew of its existence from memory, but the drawing was not realistic because I should depict only the things that the eye could see.

His comments were just as useful when I drew the peach trees, the gigantic tomatoes bursting with redness, and the *ujiza* birds – both the blackchested and the brownspotted prinia waving their tails from side to side. Sometimes a pair of thickbilled larks visited and perched on the fence. I painted them, exaggerating their speckled heads and wings. Here again, Old Xhamela noted my misrepresentation. He was a stickler for realism. I never had the heart to tell him that the distortions were deliberate, that I found the birds boring in their natural dull brown colours and thought they needed some vamping up.

MY FATHER WAS A disciplinarian. It was a badge he carried with honour. I often meet his former students – those he taught at Roma College, as the National University of Lesotho was called in the late 1940s; at St John Berchmans Catholic School in Orlando East, Soweto; and the boys and girls, now of course old men and women, of St Teresa. They are always excited to meet AP's son, and gush how they learnt a lot about English literature from him. Some talk about his love of music, and how he conducted mass choirs; others remember how he initiated them into the politics of the ANC, and later of the Pan Africanists. Those he taught at St John Berchmans bring yet another side of him that has to do with soccer. They remember how the present-day Orlando Pirates, one of the leading professional teams in South Africa, was started by his students who gave the team that name because they were reading *Treasure Island* in his literature class. So you see, all these folks revere my father for different reasons. But one thing that they all remember is that AP was a disciplinarian.

The nuns at St Teresa admired him for that reason too. One of the documents in the photo album that makes me sneeze because of the dust mites that have accumulated in it over the decades is a testimonial written by Sister Eusebia, the principal, when my father left the school:

> To whom it may concern: This is to certify that Mr Ashby Peter Solomzi Mda has been employed as assistant teacher at St. Teresa's Native Secondary School from January 1948 till June 1955. Mr Mda has done excellent work as a teacher and educator. He is a man of good character, of outstanding ability, honest, painstaking and self-sacrificing in his duty to a high degree. He is a very good disciplinarian and a first class choir master. In him the school loses a teacher hard to replace.

'AP does not suffer fools gladly,' people said, and they made a point of choosing their words very carefully when they spoke to him. Which explains why we chuckled uneasily at his jokes even when he was all smiles and laughter.

He would call us around the kitchen table, all five of us kids (me, the twins Sonwabo and Monwabisi, our sister Thami and our baby brother Zwelakhe, even though the latter was only six years old), my mother and the 'mother who looked after us' (a euphemism for a maid and nanny). He would then tell us about the liberation struggle. He would sing for us in his mellow tenor: *USobukwe ufun'amajoni, ufun'amajoni, ufun'amajoni enkululeko. Imikhosi yenkululeko, yenkululeko, yenkululeko.* Sobukwe needs soldiers, he needs soldiers, he needs soldiers to fight for freedom. Armies of liberation, of liberation, of liberation.

I saw myself as one of those soldiers. I would one day go out to fight for freedom.

We knew all about Robert Mangaliso Sobukwe. Pan Africanist leaders like John Nyathi Pokela, who was from Hohobeng, a village near our Qoboshane, spoke about him all the time when he visited. He was the president of the Pan Africanist Congress of Azania, known as the PAC for short, a party that broke away from the African National Congress in 1959. My father was regarded as the 'founding spirit' of the PAC, though initially he was not in favour of the breakaway. He believed that the Africanist group should change the ideological direction of the ANC from within. But in the end the young militants who opposed the ANC Freedom Charter – particularly clauses in it that declared that the land in South Africa belonged to all those who live on it – won the day and walked out of the mother organisation.

At the round-table family meetings that my father called to analyse the state of the struggle he emphasised that the PAC had his full support. He outlined to us his philosophy of African Nationalism which he formulated in his famous debates with his friend and roommate Anton Lembede, and which he then developed further when he was the president of the ANC Youth League in 1948. He had initiated Lembede into the politics of the ANC when the latter first came to Johannesburg from Natal. My father talked about the Programme of Action which he drafted and which was adopted as the policy document of the ANC at their conference on December 17, 1949. The fundamental principles of the Programme of Action were inspired by the desire to achieve freedom from white domination and the attainment of political independence. The document did not focus only on the political rights of the oppressed African majority, but on their economic rights and their right to education.

What impressed me most were the cultural rights. My father talked at length about the necessity of uniting the cultural with the political struggle. His unfulfilled dream was the establishment of a national academy of arts and sciences.

When he addressed us on these issues we all had to sit still. If anyone fidgeted or scratched himself my father became quite irritated because that indicated that the culprit was not interested in the proceedings. He was the only one who talked at these meetings, which turned them into lectures rather than discussions. Ours was to listen and punctuate his sentences with *'ewe, tata'* – yes, father – to prove that we were paying attention.

According to my father, the ANC had gone wrong when it fell under the influence of the Communist Party of South Africa, and by extension of the Soviet Union. At that age I couldn't understand why his cardboard boxes were full of books by Karl Marx and Vladimir Lenin – these were never kept in open bookcases as they were banned material – while at the same time he was so much opposed to the Communist Party, which he called anti-revolutionary. Despite his anti–Communist Party stance he was apt to expound on dialectical materialism and to outline in most admiring terms the history of the Bolsheviks in Russia. Of course none of us at the table knew what dialectical materialism was all about. He never seemed to notice or even care if we were out of our depth as long as we continued to repeat *'ewe, tata'*.

When he was not poring over his clients' files and law reports, he was reading *Das Kapital* and quoting from it, or from Friedrich Engels's *Anti-Dühring*. Yet he believed, like the other youths who broke away from the ANC to form the PAC, and like Kwame Nkrumah of Ghana, that Africa should follow a policy of 'positive neutrality', allying herself to neither the Soviet camp nor the American camp. Black people, he said, should determine their own future.

'We can take the best from the West and from the East,' he said. 'And as Sobukwe said in his inaugural speech, we can do that while maintaining our distinctive personality and refuse to be stooges of either power bloc.'

By the East he meant the Soviet bloc and mainland China from which he believed Africa could learn how to run a planned economy. So you see, even though he was anti-Communist Party he was a socialist nonetheless. From Western nations, Africa could learn the establishment and maintenance of viable democratic governance. He completely abhorred what he referred to as totalitarianism in China and the Soviet Union.

My father believed that one day there would be a United States of Africa, which would be a socialist democracy – stretching from Cape to Cairo, Morocco to Madagascar.

And that became our slogan. When Cousin Mlungisi and I wanted to provoke white motorists on the main road I would shout: 'Cape to Cairo, Morocco to Madagascar', and then run away. I doubt if they knew what it was all about. If they heard us at all from their speeding cars they most likely associated the Cape-to-Cairo bit with Cecil John Rhodes.

'Remember, my children, there is only one race on earth; the human race.' That was my father's statement at the end of the meeting.

My siblings and I got a grasp of these issues quite early on because these round-table meetings were frequent, almost weekly. We dreaded them; they took us away from our soccer games in the street, and me from my cavorting with Keneiloe. However, I did appreciate the fact that they left me with greater political awareness than my peers. When there were new developments in the news my father briefed us about them, and how they were going to impact the liberation struggle for better or worse. We were therefore fully briefed when Nelson Mandela was sentenced to five years' imprisonment for leaving the country illegally. Even then my father was already talking of the role of the CIA in his arrest two months earlier disguised as a man called David Motsamai (his client's name) after he had disappeared for seventeen months. It turned out he had visited a number of countries garnering support for the overthrow of the apartheid government.

My mother was quite distraught about the sentence, but my father said, 'Nel is quite fortunate to get such a light sentence.'

Though he and Mandela had taken two different ideological roads, my father was ecstatic that the ANC was finally turning to what he had been advocating since 1948 – the armed struggle.

Of course, he didn't know at the time that the five years would soon become a life sentence for Mandela after the Rivonia Trial. The lightness of the sentence did not console my mother. I had noticed that she had a very soft spot for Mandela, although not as much as she had for Walter Sisulu. Although she spoke of Bhut' Walter with some reverence, she made many jokes about Mandela. I often heard her and her nursing sister friends gossiping about Nel or Nelly. They called him a ladies' man. They giggled about it, which gave me the impression that they were talking of an admirable trait. Although I didn't know what a ladies' man really did, if it was someone as handsome and urbane as Nelson Mandela then I wanted to be one too.

When Uncle Owen paid us a visit from his Ndzunga Restaurant the brothers spoke about the old days in Johannesburg, about the revolutionary activities of the Sons of the Soil, by which they meant the

Pan Africanists. We heard of names like Z B Molete and P K Leballo and other radical youths who were 'organising' all over the Transvaal. Leballo was the secretary general of the PAC, and even then I got the sense that my father didn't think highly of him. He was less of an intellectual and more of a demagogue. My father respected intellectuals like Sobukwe. 'He is a thinker, that Sobukwe,' he often said and then, paraphrasing Rudyard Kipling, he added, 'He is a man who talks with crowds and yet keeps his humility; who walks with kings but never loses the common touch.'

Though my father was an African Nationalist I observed that he maintained his friendship with people who were in different political camps. For instance, his friendship with Oliver Tambo, who used to be his deputy when he was the president of the ANC Youth League, continued at this time and the two kept in contact. Another person whose ideological outlook had developed in a direction that was diametrically opposed to my father's was George Matanzima, a paramount chief of abaThembu. I remember how resentful I was when he visited our home in Sterkspruit to consult with my father. At that time he and his older brother Kaiser were getting a lot of publicity in the media as the leaders of the first Bantustan to be established by the apartheid government in the Transkei. My father had served his law articles under George Matanzima at Engcobo in the Transkei. So had another PAC leader, Tshepo Tiisetso Letlaka, who also occasionally visited and the men would debate in the living room into the early hours of the morning.

At first I was embarrassed that Matanzima came to our house; in my book he was a traitor. But he always redeemed himself with his charm, particularly with his remark when I came to greet him in the living room that I was quite a handsome fellow. He was Nelson Mandela's nephew, and like his uncle he seemed to be appreciative of handsomeness. Vanity won over the little matter of political commitment, and after that I was very comfortable around George Matanzima and laughed at his jokes, even though I had to turn my face so that the adults in the house did not see I was enjoying adult-oriented jokes.

Another regular visitor was Mr Mather, the rich white man who owned a general dealer's store, a wholesaler, a garage with a petrol station, a restaurant and many other businesses in town. People said he owned half of Sterkspruit. Mr Mather was never received in the living room, but in the office, which indicated that he was my father's client rather than a social caller. But still his visits as a white man made us uncomfortable, especially because whenever his car was parked in front of our house township children crowded outside the gate and gawked at the car and at him when he finally left the office. Mather's visits enhanced our prestige with our peers, none of whom would even dream of having a white man visit their homes. But Uncle Owen, who thought himself a radical who once 'organised the masses' with the PAC firebrand Josias Madzunya, saw an inconsistency with Africanist ideals from the visits rather than prestige. Not only was Mather a white man; he was a capitalist exploiter of the black masses. When Uncle Owen raised his concerns in a courteous and cautious manner, as he always did with my father, my father said, 'Well, O, there is something very important that I have in common with Mather. We both belong to the human race.'

THE ONLY OTHER WHITE people who came to my home on one occasion were three boys from the white suburb of Sterkspruit. Cousin Mlungisi and I had met them the previous day when we walked through their suburb playing a game of picking nice houses and cars and claiming ownership of them. Whenever I spotted a beautiful house I would shout, 'I'm picking that house!' It would be the same with the cars that drove by, with their drivers looking at us suspiciously. Cousin Mlungisi would do the same if he saw a house or car he liked. The idea was to be fast in your picking before your competitor picked the property. At the end of the walk we would tally our acquisitions, and the one who picked the most beautiful houses or cars won the game. And of course if you were too fast to pick an approaching car only to find that it was in fact ugly, you couldn't recant. You were stuck with it and it would count against you when the tally was made. I once fought with Cousin Mlungisi because I wanted to 'unpick' a car I had picked before I saw that it was a rickety old model.

The white boys were pushing a bicycle and they told us they were selling it. I had always wanted a bicycle but was afraid to ask my father. The last time I owned anything like that was at St Teresa when my friend Bernard Khosi and I rode our tricycles on the paved path between the houses and the school. I told the boys I wanted to buy their bike. The price seemed reasonable.

'Can you afford it?' the bigger boy asked.

'Of course he can,' said Cousin Mlungisi. 'His father is a lawyer.'

After exchanging names and addresses the boys gave me the bike. The next day they would come for the money. Triumphantly, we pushed it back to Tienbank.

I was crushed when my father told me he would not buy the bike and that I must return it to the owners. It was falling apart, he said, and was not worth the money the boys were asking for it. In any event, how did I know the boys had not stolen it, or that they had their parents' permission to sell it?

The next day the boys came to fetch their money. They were angry that I had changed my mind about buying the bike. But still they could not hide their surprise that *kaffirs*, as they called us, lived in such lovely houses, especially Mr Magengenene's house next door which was more beautiful than most of the houses in the white suburb. He was a school inspector and the father of my friends, Nikelo and Xolile. Mr Magengenene's new and shimmering Ford Zephyr that was parked in his yard exacerbated the boys' anger against me.

'You lied to me,' said the oldest. 'You went against your word. I should be *donnering* you instead of taking my bike back. I should be forcing you to pay me for it.'

'Why don't we? Why don't we?' said the middle one.

'And these *kaffirs* have a lot of money too,' said the small one. 'Look at their houses. Look at their cars. They should bloody well buy our bike.'

But the oldest one had more sense than to start a war in the middle of a black township. Instead he took his bike and the others followed him as he pushed it down our street to the main road that would take him to the town, and then to the white suburb.

I moped about the bike for a long time and buried myself in *Wamba*, an isiXhosa children's magazine with short stories and poems. I also tried my hand at writing my own isiXhosa poems. Most were about the zinnias, dahlias and snapdragons in our garden, but some were about Keneiloe. Things were getting back to normal with her and I resumed sending her letters and an occasional poem. I suppose her derrière was forgetting the hiding it got from Hopestill for fooling around with me.

I shared more than just letters and poems with Keneiloe. She was a reader of a story magazine called *See* and I bought an occasional issue when I had money, or got well-worn copies that my mother discarded, and gave them to Keneiloe after reading them myself. These were love stories told in photographs featuring beautiful white characters in situations of anguish. There was one for black people too called *She*, but its love stories were not as heart-rending and romantic. I still bought it, as I did the more macho story-magazines such as *Samson,* about a strongman in leopard skin trunks who rooted out evil in darkest Africa, and *True Africa* which featured a handsome crime buster in snazzy suits called Bulldog Lawson.

These heroes became so much a part of our lives that when Mario dos Santos, the actor who played the role of Bulldog Lawson, died in some accident in Mozambique my little brother Sonwabo cried. This continued for many days every time anyone mentioned Bulldog Lawson.

The photo story magazine that was most exchanged by my friends, from one boy to another until it was tattered, was *Chunky Charlie* featuring a fat hobo who had MacGyver-like tools (it was decades before the television show *MacGyver*) hidden in his tattered coat. He could use them to extricate himself from all sorts of traps laid by the baddies.

There was, however, reading material that I never shared with anyone: comic books.

Cousin Mlungisi had taught me the art of stealing money from one's parents' wallets and purses in a strategic way so that no one would be any the wiser that some money was missing. He had been doing it for years and was using the money to *bheja* – buying presents of handkerchiefs, sweets and chocolates for his many girlfriends. I learnt the trick, but instead of buying presents for Keneiloe – I would not be so stupid as to *bheja* because that would put her in trouble with her strict parents; she would not be able to explain where she got the stuff – I bought comic books from Mather and Sons. I spoiled myself with DC Comics and Marvel Comics and got lost in the world of superheroes; of Spiderman, of Batman and Robin, of Superman and his alter-ego Clark Kent, of the Incredible Hulk. The last was a newcomer in my collection, having only been introduced the year before. I never really took to this superhero.

But the best for me were not the Marvel or the DC Comics, but the Harvey Comics. Their characters had more fun and were more lovable. There was no heaving and grunting and fighting in Harvey Comics. No Wham! Whack! Pow! Thwip! Even devils such as *Hot Stuff* and ghosts such as *Casper* and *Spooky* were gentle. Though Spooky was an ill-tempered little ghost, he was adorable nonetheless. Casper on the other hand actually went under the title of the Friendly Ghost. These maudlin modern fairy tales appealed to me more than the manly stuff.

Every time I entered Mather and Sons the sales staff would have *Little Lotta*, *Little Dot* and *Richie Rich* ready for me. The last particularly, featuring the richest kid in the world, his butler Cadbury, and his mean cousin Reggie, took me to a fantasy world of splendour and gold-plated limousines and life without pain or toil.

The Mather and Sons people said I was the only black kid in Sterkspruit who bought that sort of rubbish. Only white kids wasted their parents' hard-earned money on comic books. They never got to know that my parents had no idea that I was spending their hard-earned money in this manner, that in fact I was a thief and a scoundrel who sneaked into their bedroom to raid their pockets, handbags and purses to satisfy my addiction.

THE SIGHT OF MY parents' old house is depressing. Slowly I drive away, up the street, past Keneiloe's home. Buses used to be parked in the yard. But today there is not a single one. Only the skeleton of a truck. I drive past the Tindleni residence, and then to Bensonvale College which is about six miles away.

'You know you hate to drive at night, with the lights of oncoming cars shining in your eyes,' says Gugu.

'We'll make it to Johannesburg, don't worry,' I say. 'I just want to show you something.'

But Bensonvale College is no longer there. Only the ruins. I almost weep. The whole college that used to be vibrant with students walking up and down the paved paths is gone. Ivy still covers those walls that have been defiant enough to remain standing. I stop the car on the edge of an open field and get out of the car. Gugu follows. I can hear the voices. At first they are soft, but as if carried by a gust of wind towards me they gather volume and become so loud that I lift my arms in supplication. They are the voices of the beautiful men and women of the Today's Choir. And indeed the choir materialises in the field – women in black skirts and white blouses, men in black pants, white shirts, black jackets and black ties. My father in his black suit standing in front of them. Waving his arms, conducting the choir with gusto. The choir is composed of hundreds. Thousands more people fill the grounds, listening. Many are in school uniform – black gym-dresses and white shirts. Black and white predominates.

I remember how this came about . . . how I was grateful that I had more time to read my comic books and to draw pictures and write stories because for a number of weeks my father was not calling his meetings or demanding that we draw water for his flowers and vegetables. He was busy rehearsing with a mass choir he had named the Today's Choir, which had been assembled from all the choral societies of the Herschel District for the commemoration of the centenary of Bensonvale College.

Although we had some respite from meetings and garden work, one thing he never forgot even when he came back home late at night was to give us our nightly doses of cod liver oil and Scott's Emulsion. That was one assignment he didn't trust even my mother to undertake with the diligence it deserved.

When the day of the centenary celebrations came I joined a group of pupils from Tapoleng – including Cousin Mlungisi, his younger brother Bobby and the twins – and walked to Bensonvale, about six miles from Sterkspruit. We found a place in the open field where the rest of the multitudes had gathered. My mother, sister and baby brother got a ride from the neighbours as my father did not have a car. Speeches were made and the Today's Choir sang Reginald Spofforth's glee *Hail Smiling Morn*. My father's slim frame was dwarfed by the hundreds of singers in front of whom he was standing, fervently conducting them. There were tears in my eyes when the choir sang Handel's *Hallelujah Chorus*, J P Mohapeloa's *Obe* and *Fisherman's Goodnight*. I never got to know the composer of this last one.

There are tears in my eyes as I stand in the grounds among the ruins listening to the ghostly choir. To this day, when I hear these songs I get a lump in my throat and my eyes moisten. The void widens.

AS I DRIVE BACK from Bensonvale I wonder how things would have turned out for me, my brothers and my sister if we had not left Sterkspruit. We would have lived here for the rest of our lives, and become teachers and nurses like everyone else, without the exposure to the world that was a result of the single occasion the Boers came for my father in the middle of the night; a whole contingent of white policemen with bright flashlights. They turned the house upside down, looking for 'terrorist' documents and banned books. My father's Communist books were nowhere to be found. I later learnt that he had earlier that week asked our nanny to bury them underground at her place. How did he know he was going to be raided by the police? He must have got a tip from an insider – maybe from a sympathetic black cop.

They took him away in a *kwela-kwela* police van with bars on the windows. My mother sat at the kitchen table and wept.

The following week was very important for me because I was

representing Tapoleng Primary School in a track meet where Herschel District primary schools were competing. I had outrun all competition in middle and long distance races at my school, and it was time to use my famous long strides to bring the trophy to Tapoleng. But how could I do it with my father in jail? It was not so much for him that I felt sorry, but for my mother. I knew he was strong and could handle any situation. After all, we were all terrified of him. I didn't see how he could fail to terrify the Boers as well. But my mother did not take the arrest well. She worried about how they were treating him in jail and whether they were torturing him or not. Fortunately, she was allowed to take him some food, but never to see him. She cried a lot even as she kept on reminding herself that she needed to be brave for the children.

I lost the race.

The following Monday I went to school as usual, but something unusual happened at the morning assembly. After the prayers the principal Mr Moleko, also known as Mkhulu-Baas, made a speech about the folly of trying to fight against the white man in South Africa.

'There are people who think they can win against the white man,' he said out of the blue. 'That is very stupid. *Umlungu mdala* – the white man is old and wise. What do you think a black person can do to make South Africa a better country? A black person is a baby. If you try to stand up against the white man you will end up in jail.'

I knew immediately that the nincompoop in the threadbare grey suit was talking about my father and I hated him for it.

One evening when we were eating dinner father came home. He was on the run from the police and had come to take a few of his things and to say goodbye.

He went into exile in the British Protectorate of Basutoland, as Lesotho was then known.

We pieced things together later. He was being accused of holding secret meetings all over the Cape, planning the violent overthrow of the state. We had not been aware of all these nocturnal activities because he seemed to be a looming presence at home all the time. A few days after he had been locked up there was a line-up, an identification parade. A certain Mr X was to point out the man who addressed a secret meeting of a PAC cell in a town called Elliot where some acts of sabotage were planned. Mr X was a secret state witness who had attended the meeting, and therefore could not be identified by name. My father knew immediately that the police had already tutored Mr X on how to identify him. He therefore took off his coat and gave it to the man next to him to wear – the people in the line-up were black men picked from the street, and he knew the particular man to whom he gave his coat. He also changed the order of the line-up. Mr X arrived wearing a mask, looked at the men in the line-up and pointed at the man wearing my father's coat.

'That's the man,' he said. 'That's the man who addressed the meeting in Elliot.'

Of course the man would not have held a meeting in Elliot or anywhere else for that matter. The police were angry that their identification parade had been foiled by my father's cunning. They had to release him, but he knew that was only temporary. It would take them hours rather than days to find other ways of getting him. They would never give up. That was why he didn't wait for them to rearrest him but escaped to Basutoland.

Once more we were without a father.

The first place to knell his absence was the garden. Old Xhamela had long gone to work for the South African Railways and Harbours and father's peach trees lost their sculpted shapes. Weeds grew rampant and the seedbeds lay without new seedlings of cabbages, tomatoes and beetroot.

For many days after my father left I could see that my mother's eyes were red from crying. But soon she got used to the idea of his absence. After all, she had lived alone in Johannesburg for many years while he was either serving articles in the Transkei or was travelling the length and breadth of South Africa, first organising for the ANC Youth League and in later years for the Africanists. She kept herself busy by playing tennis at the township tennis courts whenever she was off-duty from Empilisweni Hospital and sometimes I joined her. Until one day she beat me six-love. I gave up tennis for ever.

I must admit that I enjoyed the freedom that resulted from my father's exile. For the first time I was able to build a loft and keep pigeons, which my father would never have allowed. Also, my mother was at work for the whole day most days. Or she was doing night-duty, which meant that I could join Cousin Mlungisi in some of his night-time activities. For instance I could go stand outside Keneiloe's gate and whistle until she came out of the house. Cousin Mlungisi's girlfriends came out to him when he whistled, and then they would repair behind the outhouse toilet to do naughty things. But my Keneiloe could never come to me. Her parents were too strict. She only stood at the door and waved at me so that I could see she had heard the whistling. Then she walked back into the house before Hopestill got suspicious. That was good enough for me; I had 'checked' my girl. I was a fulfilled boy as I walked back home where I had to sneak into my room even though my mother was absent because the nanny was likely to squeal on me if she discovered I had gone to 'check' girls.

When Hopestill visited, she and my mother talked about the hardships caused by my father's absence. They giggled like school girls at something she said to Hopestill. Then Hopestill whispered something back and they burst out laughing. I loved Hopestill at those moments. She was so beautiful. She looked very much like Keneiloe. Then my mother said in a solemn tone, 'But, Hope, I think it's a good thing he left when he did. Look at what the Boers have done to Bhut' Walter and Nel.' She was talking about her friends Walter Sisulu and Nelson Mandela.

Although we no longer had to draw water from the communal borehole for father to water his plants, and we didn't have to stand to attention and repeat *'ewe, tata'* after every one of his admonishing sentences, we still had to work in the house. My mother was no pushover. We had to clean the house, scrub the linoleum floors and apply Cobra Floor Polish. As was the case growing up in Soweto, where there was no distinction between work for girls or for boys and we all performed the same chores, it was the same here in Sterkspruit. That was how our mothers brought us up. I learnt to cook at an early age. I was also an expert at keeping the red stoep outside my father's office gleaming with Sunbeam Polish.

On Sundays my mother insisted that we go to the Roman Catholic Church which was located at Makhetheng Township on the other side of Sterkspruit. Before my father's exile neither of our parents minded that we frequented the Methodist Church instead of our own denomination. Everyone in Tienbank, except us, was a Methodist. So we preferred going to the Methodist Church near Tapoleng Primary with the rest of our friends. After all, it was the church that Keneiloe attended and it gave us the opportunity to walk home from church together. Going to the Catholic Church was quite an ordeal because it was more than an hour's walk just to get there. And another hour back. Taking into account that Mass lasted for one hour, it meant that we had to invest three whole hours on Sunday just to make my mother happy.

I also had to go to the church on some Saturdays because I was training to be an altar boy. A bigger boy was assigned to teach me the ropes, and on those Sundays when I had to wear the red cassock and white surplice I swelled with pride and felt that the three hours were worth it. It was just unfortunate that Keneiloe was not there to hear me chant *Kyrie Eleison Kristu Eleison* or to see me, in the absence of the regular thurifer, wave the thurible with pomp and ceremony, filling the small church with nostril-stinging incense; or, in the presence of the regular thurifer, to hear the ring of my altar bell.

On some Saturdays the altar servers rehearsed the Monody of Gregorian Chants. The rotund white priest whose name I have long forgotten paced the floor in front of us chanting in a shaky voice: *Adoremus in aeternum sanctissimum Sacramentum. Laudate Dominum omnes gentes: laudate eum omnes populi. Quoniam confirmata est super nos misericordia ejus: et veritas Domini manet in aeternum. Adoremus . . .* We will adore for eternity the most holy Sacrament. Praise the Lord, all ye nations: praise Him all ye peoples. Because His mercy is confirmed upon us: and the truth of the Lord remains forever. Let us adore . . .

We repeated the Latin chants after him. But the thurifer was more interested in gossip than in adoring the Sacrament. He whispered to me that the priest was pretending to be engrossed in Gregorian Chants whereas what he was really doing was checking out the thighs of the boys in their shorts for the one he would invite to his room.

'To his room? What for?' I asked.

'Why, to eat him *mawutwana*, of course.'

I didn't understand this eating business so I whispered back, 'What do you mean to eat him? What is *mawutwana*?'

The boys laughed at my naivete but soon shut up when the priest glared at them sternly while continuing with his chants. He walked out of the door, still chanting.

'Where does this one come from?' asked the thurifer staring at me incredulously. 'Don't you know that priests eat pretty boys like you?'

'But this one is a good priest,' said a tiny server in defence of the man of the cloth. 'He does not hurt boys; he only puts his thingy between the thighs. The Father before him put it in the *sebono*.'

'Mama's little boy! Mama's little boy!' chanted the thurifer to the tune of Gregorian Chants. But the return of the priest put an end to the teasing and the banter. The priest was still chanting and had a cane with him, which he gently beat against his hand while looking at the thurifer as a way of warning him and any other server who was bent on chattering instead of focusing on the Chants that the cane would eat into the offender's flesh.

My concentration was no longer on the Monody; it worried me no end that I was ignorant of what the servers were talking about; that I was not in the loop; that I was an outsider who knew nothing about eating *mawutwana*. At least I knew *sebono* was a Sesotho word for anus. Most of the servers came from Basutoland where the Catholic Church was much stronger, so they spoke in Sesotho most of the time. Even the Holy Mass at our little church was conducted in Latin and Sesotho. I would be sure to ask Cousin Mlungisi what *mawutwana* was. He was a man of the world and would know about it, especially since it was associated with *sebono* which sounded quite dirty. Cousin Mlungisi knew all things dirty.

Alas, even Cousin Mlungisi was not worldly enough to know anything about *mawutwana*.

I subsequently learnt from the thurifer that *mawutwana* referred to sex between males and that the eating had to do with engaging in that act with the priest, who then gave the boys nice second-hand clothes that were donated by rich countries to give to the poor. I never experienced any of that myself as no priest approached me. The thurifer said it was because I was always so smartly dressed with new and clean clothes and shimmering black shoes. I was obviously not from a poor family and the priest knew that I didn't need anything from him in exchange for *mawutwana*. Despite this assurance that I was not a good candidate for priestly sex, the thurifer never stopped bugging me about coming with him to the church office when the priest was alone. He assured me that he was going to teach me how to entice him. If I didn't need clothes I could ask for money instead. A fleeting thought crossed my mind. The well had run dry since my father left; I could no longer steal money from his pants at night. I therefore could no longer afford to buy my comic books. My mother was very good at hiding her money. In any event, I would feel very bad stealing from her when she was struggling on her own without my father. What if I took up the thurifer's offer? But I just couldn't imagine myself doing anything of the sort.

I longed for the Sundays when my mother would be on duty so that I could sneak back to the Methodist Church and bask in the Glory of Keneiloe.

One Monday I went to school as usual. At recess I played soccer in the playground in front of the classrooms. I stood between a pile of bricks that we used as goalposts and dived to stop the tennis ball that we used for soccer from passing through. I was about to do one of my catlike lunges when two police vans stopped on the road and a group of armed policemen in uniform jumped out and marched military-style to the principal's office. Somehow I knew they had come for me.

Mkhulu-Baas personally came running and calling out my surname. The policemen were already waiting for me outside his office. Without a word he pushed me to the nearest policeman who pushed me to his superior who pointed me forward. The soccer game had stopped and everybody was watching as I was frogmarched to one of the police vans.

At the police station I was led into a room where an array of white policemen in well-pressed military-khaki uniforms were sitting on chairs as if waiting for a performance. The only black person in the

54

room besides me was Sergeant April, who was my interpreter. They began to question me, at first asking innocuous questions about what I ate in the morning and what subjects I liked best at school. Then they asked me about a white man who went to see my father at home. The only white man I knew who had ever been to my home was Mr Mather and I told them so.

'*Jy sal begin om te lieg, jy sal begin om te lieg,*' they all said in unison. You are beginning to lie. You are beginning to lie.

I was not lying and I was not scared of them. They looked too beautiful to instil fear in me. Somehow they reminded me of the Afrikaans Taalfees that we used to have when I was still in Dobsonville, Soweto, at Lodirile Lower Primary, at Nakhile Lower Primary and at eNkolweni Higher Primary. It was the day to celebrate the Afrikaans language so the students spoke in Afrikaans all day long and dressed up in Afrikaans traditional costumes, with girls in their *kappies* and boys in their bush khakis. We sang Afrikaans songs such as *Hasie, hoekom is jou stert so kort* and recited Afrikaans poems like *Muskietejag, Jou vabond, wag ek sal jou kry.*

The angry policemen reminded me of bit players at an Afrikaans Taalfees. *Jy sal begin om te lieg. Jy sal begin om te lieg . . .* rang in my ears even after they had returned me to school.

My mother worried that something was going to happen to me. Once the Boers have their eye on you, she said, they never give up. They would come back for me even though I was not involved in any serious political activity save to yell *Mayibuye iAfrika* and *From Cape to Cairo* at innocent white motorists. They would make life hell for me if only to get at my father.

'The boy must go stay with his father in Basutoland,' my mother said.

I dreaded those words. What about Keneiloe? What about my friend, Cousin Mlungisi? What about my two friends from next door, from the Magengenene family, Xolile and Nikelo? What about St Teresa? I was doing Standard Six and was looking forward to attending St Teresa Secondary School the following year. Like Nikelo before me. And like Xolile. They had told me so many stories about boarding school life at St Teresa. Please God, let me not be banished to Basutoland. I promise

I'll never do bad things again. I'll never steal and lie again. Just don't let me be banished to Basutoland.

But the only response to my prayers was one catastrophe after another. First, Bomvana and his gang stole my pigeons in the deep of the night. By the time I discovered the theft he was cooking them for dinner.

The second catastrophe: Diza, Mr Magengenene's big black Labrador Retriever, was hit by a car and I was to blame. I had taken it for a walk, in fact just to show it off, on the main road that led to the town and a speeding car mowed it down and never even stopped for a second. I can still see Tapo, Nikelo's mother, walking to the road where Diza lay dead. She was crying and sniffling softly and did not even look at me when I expressed my sorrow. She never spoke to me again after that. I could never forgive myself; this was the second dog associated with me to be hit by a car. I was still haunted by Rex. I wanted nothing to do with dogs ever again.

The third catastrophe was the beating that I got from Teboho Mohafa, Keneiloe's father. A group of us were playing on the road in front of the Mohafa yard. I picked up a stone and threw it at Keneiloe. She ran out of the way and challenged me to throw another one. I thought I would get her this time but she ducked and the stone hit her younger sister, Thabang, on the head. Blood spurted and she bawled in pain as she walked to her home. At first I thought I should follow her and apologise to Teboho and Hopestill. But on second thoughts I knew Teboho would kill me if I went there. So I did the next best thing; I ran home and hid under the bed.

In no time Teboho was knocking at my door holding Thabang's hand. Keneiloe was there too. He told my mother how I nearly killed his daughter. My mother yelled at me and promised him that she would punish me severely. But Teboho would have none of that. He wanted to give me a hiding himself. I stood in the middle of the living room and he took off his leather belt and lashed out at me. Keneiloe cried and told her daddy that we were playing, it was an accident. But Teboho continued to lash out at my buttocks and legs and shoulders. I dared not cry in the presence of Keneiloe, which made Tebobo madder. 'He is a stubborn boy too, a cheeky boy,' he kept on saying.

He lashed out again.

'It's enough, Teboho, it's enough. You will kill my child,' my mother said, getting between me and Teboho. He was so angry he almost lashed out at my mother. But common sense prevailed and he walked out of the house with his daughters in tow.

'You see what the Boers have done?' my mother cried. 'No man would come to my house to beat up my children if your father were here.'

It was my turn to comfort her and to apologise for what I had done.

'I know you were playing,' she said. 'Keneiloe said it was an accident.'

The fourth and final catastrophe happened in December 1963. My friends from next door, Nikelo and Xolile, went to the mountain to be circumcised and initiated into manhood. That would not have been so bad in itself. After all, I only saw them during the June and December holidays since they spent all their lives at boarding schools. But my own Cousin Mlungisi decided to run to the mountain and join their circumcision school. According to custom, when a boy ran to the initiation school he could not leave, even if his parents wanted him back. He had to proceed with the ritual with the rest of the initiates. Not that Mr Tindleni wanted his son back. He was quite pleased that Cousin Mlungisi had saved his family all the trouble of arranging for his initiation at some future date. He was proud that his son was going to be a man, though he had not initially planned for the expensive ritual.

My mother was worried that I would run to the mountain as well. And with my father absent, what would she do? She pleaded with me not to do so. Although I envied Cousin Mlungisi, I decided not to cause problems for my mother. I stayed at home and furiously wrote poems and short stories. I sent some of my stories to Mr Fihla who was a primary school teacher at KwaGcina. I had seen one of his stories published in *Wamba* and I hoped he would advise me on how to get published. Even as I wrote to him I felt like a traitor. Mr Fihla had been one of the supporters of Headman Senoamali in that civil matter in which my father sued Senoamali for calling him a communist to the District Commissioner and Nelson Mandela came from Johannesburg to handle the case. Yes, the haunted times when Senoamali sent his stick to knock at my window at night. Mr Fihla was reputed to be one of the people who had waged a campaign against my father until he left KwaGcina.

Apparently Mr Fihla held no grudges because he replied with a lot of useful advice and I sent my story, *Igqirha laseMvubase* – The Medicine Man of Mvubase – to *Wamba* for their consideration.

After a month or so my friends returned from the initiation school and festivities were organised in their honor. Cattle were slaughtered, and each graduate recited a poem he had composed in praise of himself. There was a lot of singing and dancing both at the Tindleni and Magengenene homesteads. The new graduates were all dressed up in new clothes because they were men and could no longer wear their boyhood clothes. And since they were now men they could no longer associate with me. My own Cousin Mlungisi could no longer be seen in my company because I was a boy.

This isolation was painful.

But just then I received a letter from *Wamba* with a two rand note enclosed. They were going to publish my story, and the money was the fee they were paying for it. The very first money I ever earned for something I wrote.

I no longer gave a damn about Cousin Mlungisi, Nikelo and Xolile. They could get circumcised as much as they wanted and isolate me for ever if it suited them; I would write more stories and get them published.

CHAPTER THREE

THIS IS JUST A coincidence. We didn't know the tourists would be visiting the village today. We came from Johannesburg to see how the Bee People are doing and to buy a few bottles of honey. They are keen to give us the honey for free, but we always insist on paying for it. We want to support their business while at the same time teaching them good business practices. And as we are haggling over the matter on the stoep of eRestu a luxury tour bus arrives and spills out a group of excited young men and women. They are all white, except for their tour guide and the bus driver. Quite a few of them are scruffy, in keeping with how explorers of Darkest Africa should look.

Cousin Bernard suddenly leaves the group of men he was bamboozling with philosophy while partaking of their beer and walks past us towards the bus to meet the visitors. He leaves behind him a whiff from his rich sweat glands. Press, my uncle, told me that he is averse to taking a bath. Often he is forced into the bathroom and hollers and screams as Press scrubs the dirt from Cousin Bernard's body, with two of Press's big sons holding him down so that he does not escape and run out of the house naked. He once did exactly that. People were aghast to see his naked fifty-year-old body running out of the gate screaming that the good people of Qoboshane should come and save him because Press and his clansmen were bent on murdering him with soap and water.

The tour guide wants to protect his charges from the barefoot man in threadbare brown pants and heavy brown lumber jacket. But the man pushes him aside and heads straight to the nearest tourist – a blond, hirsute young man in denim jeans and a heavy backpack.

'Are you a monarchist or a revolutionary sesquipedalian who wants to cannibalise my establishment?' Cousin Bernard asks the astonished man.

'Say what?' asks the man. I know immediately he is an American.

The drinking men on the stoep cheer and laugh. One of them says, 'Oh, yes, Bernard has started with his big English.'

I know all about Cousin Bernard's 'big English'. I am its victim every time I come for my meetings with the Bee People at eRestu. I curse the person who told him that I am a university professor; he always wants to show off to the habitués of my uncle's tavern by bombarding me with his English. I always respond in isiXhosa, at least to the little that I can understand of his rambling sentences, and that always infuriates him. He suddenly remembers another pressing engagement elsewhere and leaves, but not before the parting shot: 'Education has been wasted on you, *wena* Zanemvula.'

Obviously Cousin Bernard thinks the hirsute man is a waste of time, for he goes to a young woman at the very moment she is stepping out of the bus.

'Dot your i's and cross your t's, young lady,' he says.

The tourists gather around the two; they are quite amused because it is clear to them that the man is not quite well upstairs. The hirsute man cuts through the crowd to rescue the young lady, but Cousin Bernard firmly stands his ground between him and the woman.

'He is idiotically inclined,' says Cousin Bernard, making a grand gesture towards the hirsute man for the benefit of the young lady. 'He is not titillated by the tintinnabulation of my grandiloquent gesture of felicitation.'

Though the drinking men enjoy the entertainment, the Bee People and the tourist guide look on with consternation. The Bee People particularly feel embarrassed that their guests are being harassed in this manner by the village madman. They call to my uncle who is inside the store to get Cousin Bernard away. Press comes rushing out, pushes through the tourists and drags Cousin Bernard away from the group.

'*Goduka*, Bernard,' Press says. '*Okanye ndizakufak'ebafini.*' Go home, Bernard, otherwise I'll put you in a bathtub.

Cousin Bernard does not take the threat of a bath lightly. He slinks away. When he reckons he is at a safe distance he stops and shouts back at Press: 'Your antiestablishmentarianism disturbs the peace. With all the possibilities of your hegemony I can only say to you: Fie sirrah! Fie for shame!'

Then he walks on to the cheers and applause of the drinking men on the stoep. I can see from the faces of the tourists that they find the whole scene quite funny, although they are suppressing outright laughter lest their fellows judge them harshly for finding humour in the behaviour of a black person with mental problems.

Later that evening when Gugu and I get to Mafeteng in Lesotho I tell my mother about Cousin Bernard's antics with the tourists and we laugh about it. She laughs even more when I joke that Cousin Bernard was rendered insane by the meat that my grandmother used to hide for him in her apron pocket as the favoured grandchild. I know, I know, it's a cruel joke, but our Basotho people say *lefu leholo ke ditsheho*. This literally translates into 'the biggest death is laughter'. But what it really means is that even in bereavement we joke and laugh.

Actually, what caused Cousin Bernard's mental impairment was his failure to heed the call of the ancestors. He was working as a clerk on the gold mines of Welkom when he first received the call in his dreams to be an *igqirha* – a traditional medicine man, diviner and spiritual healer. Cousin Bernard took up the call with great enthusiasm, following in the footsteps of many of my relatives on my father's side who became traditional healers – beginning with our revered ancestor Mhlontlo who was both a king of the amaMpondomise people and a great *igqirha* who could turn the white man's bullets into water.

Cousin Bernard became an acolyte of a great shaman from the mountains of Lesotho. He attended the *intlombe* rituals, where fellow acolytes with their masters and mistresses beat on the cowhide drums, and danced through the night until they fell into a trance. He learnt how to groan and grunt in the language of the spirits, and how to sacrifice white goats and other beasts according to the needs and demands of particular ancestors. But there was another call on Cousin Bernard; the call of the world out there. It was so overpowering that he left the profession of traditional healing long before he could graduate, while he was still at the *thwasa* stage. This is the stage when the voices of the ancestors still ring in your head, shake your body and demand obedience. He disobeyed and gave up on traditional healing. He went back to work as a clerk on the gold mine and hoped to live happily ever after. When people asked why he left before graduating into a fully fledged *igqirha* he said the demands of the ancestors were too extravagant. He could not afford to sacrifice to them the number of oxen that they required, and did not have any relative who was willing to help him. Well, that was not the ancestors' problem. Their voices continued to ring in his head. Until he cracked, left the job and became a wanderer. Press heard of his plight and got him to return to Qoboshane to stay with him.

Cousin Bernard once confided in me that there is a shitty ancestor who won't leave him alone, even when others have decided to give him some respite. He suspects the vengeful spirit is from his father's side of the family, which he never got to know. His mother, my father's youngest sister, was an unwed mother who abandoned Cousin Bernard and left for Johannesburg soon after giving birth to him. She never came back. Ever. To this day.

Fortunately, the tourists have not been rattled by him. Instead they join us on the veranda and excitedly ask questions about the village. They are from different countries, although the majority is from the United States, Germany and the United Kingdom. They are on the Maluti Trail, a tour that takes them through the Eastern Cape, Lesotho and the Free State. They have come to this village particularly to look at the beekeeping project of the Lower Telle Beekeepers Collective; according to a colourful brochure one of the tourists is reading: *This community-based project was initiated and is supported by Zakes Mda, one of South Africa's leading authors, who grew up in this area.*

When the tourists are introduced to me they are pleasantly surprised to meet in a Drakensberg mountain village this rotund fellow who is a novelist and a professor at an American university. Unfortunately Gugu and I cannot join them for the precarious drive up the mountain to the apiary. We need to be in Mafeteng, Lesotho, by the evening to see my mother, and then leave the next morning for Johannesburg. The Bee People don't need us anyway. They welcome tourists all the time, ever since their project was listed as one of the major tourist attractions of the district. They are happy of course that by coincidence we were there when this particular group of tourists arrived and we have added some value to their experience since they only came to visit the bees, breathe the clean mountain air and, according to the brochure . . . *enjoy a taste of the mouth-watering honey.*

This last bit is not just hype. *Telle Honey* – the brand name with a smiling bee on the label designed by my son Neo, who is an art director at a Johannesburg advertising agency – is reputed to have a unique taste because of a combination of Cape aloes and other indigenous plants that grow only in that region.

Undoubtedly the tourists will also enjoy the view of both the Dyarhom and the eSiqikini Mountains with the steep cliffs, clear streams and white beehives speckling the green mountainside. Imagine if my grandfather's orchard was still there. Imagine. Without anybody to prune them, the trees would have grown in all wild directions and the fruit wouldn't be as large as it was when my grandfather cared for them. But in spring they would contribute a new dimension to the bee food that has made the honey unique and in summer would feed the passers-by with abundant fruit.

Unfortunately, my Uncle Owen would have none of that. He murmured to himself *'amandla ka tata akana'wudliwa ngabany'abantu'* – I'll not have the sweat from my father's brow benefit strangers – as he spent days on end chopping down tree after tree soon after the mountain dwellers were forced down to the lowlands by the apartheid government. When I heard how he chopped down all those fruit trees, I lost all respect for him. The spirit of my grandfather lived in those trees. Besides, I instinctively recoil from a person who is callous enough to chop down a tree – any tree, but more especially a fruit tree – without just cause. I am wary of any person who can be so emotionally stunted as to kill a tree without experiencing something inside him dying with the tree.

Gugu and I wave our goodbyes to the tourists as the Bee People's truck leads their luxury bus up the narrow dirt road. Hopefully the bus driver is good enough to negotiate his way on the steep hill. The tourists had better not look out the windows otherwise they may freak out when they see hundreds of yards away all those skeletons of cars that have rolled down the mountain over the years.

Gugu and I get into our car and drive to the Telle Bridge into Lesotho. From the apiary the tourists will cross this bridge as well. And the tour guide will tell them about its significance in South Africa's history. I noticed in the brochure that the bridge is one of the tourist attractions: *Wind your way down to Telle Bridge, to see the historic border gate where in 1977 Donald Woods, the then editor of the Daily Dispatch, escaped into exile disguised as a priest.* It is a story that was later told in the 1987 Richard Attenborough movie, 'Cry Freedom', featuring Denzel Washington and Kevin Kline, about the friendship between Steve Biko, the Black Consciousness leader who was murdered by the apartheid police, and Donald Woods, a white liberal who was hounded by the police as a result of that friendship. Woods had to go into exile in Lesotho, and later in England.

MORE THAN A DECADE before Donald Woods' adventure – in January 1964 – I crossed the Telle River to exile. I was fifteen years old.

I did not cross at the bridge as Mr Woods did. I wouldn't dare face the South African border police without a valid passport. Instead, I waded in the water following a man who was carrying my heavy trunk on his shoulder. I don't remember who he was. Maybe I never knew who he was in the first place. I only remember him talking to my mother in whispers on the banks of the river. Then I hugged my mother. I didn't want to let go. But the man said to let go; we didn't have all night. Unless we wanted the Boers to catch us. God knew what would happen to all of us if the Boers caught us. I let go and followed him. My mother stood on the bank sniffling.

I was scared of the river, ever since the ice-cold water of a flooded rivulet that we had to cross on our way from Qoboshane to Aunt Nontsokolo's general dealer's store in Mmusong nearly swept me away when I was a tyke. I was saved by my aunt who held tightly to my hand even as the raging waters struggled with her. After heavy rain brooks and streams tend to have the most forceful of waters. Fortunately, that night of my exile the water in the Telle River reached only to my knees and I could wade with ease. And it was not cold at all. The man struggled with the trunk; it was loaded with my clothes and books – I had to leave behind some of my comic books for lack of room. It made me sad to see my trunk bobbing in front of me as the man tried to find a foothold in the sand and rocks under the water. My mother had bought it for me soon after I had received a first class pass in Standard Six. It was the trunk I was going to use for boarding school at St Teresa's. But here now it was crossing the river to a foreign country where I was going to live as a refugee with my strict father and was going to repeat Standard Six because the British education of Lesotho was superior to our Bantu Education.

A short distance away I could see the lights of cars that were crossing the border post at Telle Bridge. I envied those who were going in the opposite direction, driving into the country I was leaving.

I panicked when I saw the light of a torch flashing in our direction. I thought the Boers had discovered us and we'd surely be locked up. Or they might just shoot us dead and let the flowing waters clean up the mess. Boers were known to do such things. But the man with the trunk didn't seem to be bothered. He walked purposefully towards the flashing light. My legs sank deeper as I got closer to the bank on the opposite side, and I slipped on the soft muddy sand and almost fell. The man with the trunk just walked on; obviously he had no time to nurse weaklings. As soon as he got to the shore he placed the trunk down and sighed deeply with relief. I straggled on until I joined him on land.

From a field of maize that ran right up to the river bank a short and solidly built man wearing glasses appeared and walked towards us, torch flashing. The men mumbled greetings and the one who had brought me went back to the river.

'You hold the other handle of the trunk, Zani,' said the man who had come to meet me. He called me Zani, which was what my parents called me. He must be close to my father to know that name, I thought to myself as we walked into the maize.

He told me his name was Ntlabathi Mbuli. He was originally from some village in the Herschel District, but had been a refugee in Lesotho for the past two years or so. I was later to learn that he was a Poqo cadre who was doubling as my father's clerk at his law office. Poqo – an isiXhosa word that variously means 'genuine', 'alone', or 'pure' – was the military wing of the Pan Africanist Congress of Azania, the PAC. Ntlabathi Mbuli was also a poet whose works created a great impression on me. What amazed me most about his poetry was that although the man was a guerrilla fighter his poems were not about war or even about the oppression and suffering of his people. He wrote about love and related passions – hatred, anger, desire, and lust. I also learnt that he was a scholar of the Romantic period. Though his poetry was free verse, you could hear Byron, Keats and Wordsworth in it as loudly as if they were in the room.

We walked uphill over a rocky terrain for what seemed like hours in silence. He spoke only when he asked if I wanted to rest a bit. And I did. The trunk was heavy.

Finally we reached a gravel road. An old *bakkie* – a pickup truck – was waiting for us. We loaded the trunk on the bed and both got into the cab. Without a word the driver, a scrawny man with a goatee wearing blue overalls, pulled away. I asked Ntlabathi if it was okay if I opened the window; there was a stench of beer. On the side of the road I saw a number of bottles of lager. Apparently the scrawny man was having a party by himself while waiting for us.

The road twisted and turned on the mountainside and in the dark I could make out shapes of huts and kraals. But there were no humans at that time of the night. Of the morning, in fact, for it must have been long after midnight. The man opened a bottle cap with his teeth and gave it to me.

'I don't drink,' I said.

'What makes you think I was giving it to you? You want *Ntate* Mda to castrate me?' asked the driver.

Ntlabathi reached for the beer and took one long swig. Then he gave it back to the man who put the bottle between his knees and occasionally took a swig as he negotiated his way along the treacherous bends. He was nursing the pickup so slowly that the folk tale tortoise who won the race because of the hare's over-confidence would have outrun this truck as well.

A teardrop rolled down my cheek. Just one drop. I rubbed it off quickly before the men could notice. I was thinking of my mother. And of my brothers: Sonwabo, Monwabisi and Zwelakhe. And of my sister Nomathamsanqa, who we called Thami for short. I was thinking of Cousin Mlungisi, Nikelo and Xolile. Anger swelled in my chest when I remembered how we used to hang out together and talk about soccer, and how Nikelo used to regale us with his exploits with some of the most beautiful ladies at St Teresa's and then later at Healdtown in the deeper Eastern Cape where he was enrolled for his high school education, how I was no longer part of that camaraderie when the three guys returned from the initiation school. I was thinking of Keneiloe. I was wondering what she was up to at that moment. Of course she was in bed. But what about the next day? And the next? She was likely to find herself a new boyfriend. What song was she going to compose for him? He might not be knock-kneed so the song she'd composed for me would not apply to him. She'd better not sing my song to him. That would be the worst betrayal.

My thoughts constantly returned to my siblings. I regretted that I took them for granted when I was with them, as if they would always be there. There was a big gap of almost ten years between Zwelakhe and me, and I was six years older than Thami. Also, for the most part they lived with my mother in Johannesburg when I was banished to my grandparents' place, so I never got to bond with them. The twins, on the other hand, were only three years younger. They were part of my world because they also lived at Qoboshane for some time. In Sterkspruit we had a lot in common as well. Not only did we sleep in the same bedroom where we played snakes and ladders in the candlelight and laughed at the antics of *Chunky Charlie*, we also played soccer together on the township playground – which was in the street near Keneiloe's home. Whereas my best friend was Cousin Mlungisi, theirs was Cousin Bobby, Cousin Mlungisi's younger brother. We therefore visited their home together and basked in the attention of all those beautiful Tindleni daughters. On Sundays after church – and after a lunch of chicken, dumplings, rice, beetroot, potatoes, spinach, pumpkin, jelly and custard – we played my father's His Master's Voice gramophone and danced to the Manhattan Brothers, Lemmy Special Mabaso, Miriam Makeba and the Skylarks, Spokes Mashiyane, Dolly Rathebe, the Woody Woodpeckers and Dorothy Masuku.

The Boers had smashed all those wonderful days to smithereens. And I had done nothing to deserve this. People were getting killed, arrested or exiled because they planted bombs to overthrow the system. Or they just raised their voices too high in non-violent protest. I was going into exile because I was my father's son. All I ever did was to shout slogans at white motorists.

SOMETIMES THERE IS A VOID.

MY FATHER LIVED IN Quthing – the southernmost Lesotho town where the ghost hotel I have told you about is located. It was, of course, decades before the days of the ghost hotel. In fact, there was no hotel of any kind in Quthing in those days. He rented a one-roomed house from the Moleko family – no relation to that other Mr Moleko, the principal of my primary school in Sterkspruit who preached on the folly of questioning the authority of the white man after my father's arrest.

Quthing those days was just as miserable, although it was not as bustling as it is today. It has grown into a town built haphazardly on a hillside, with motley houses crowded against one another right up to the mountain top where the ghost hotel is located. But in 1964 the landscape was stark and the only ghosts were the grey people in grey blankets teetering on unpaved paths, some driving grey donkeys burdened with grey sacks of maize to the mill or to exchange at the general dealer's store for sugar and paraffin.

As my father was at his office or in court for most of the day one of the grey people from a neighbouring homestead kept me company – a boy in a grey blanket, shoeless feet as hard as a rock with cracks so deep they could hide a one-cent coin, and long matted hair. I shared with him some of the Eskort beef or pork sausages that were a staple at home because my father never cooked even for a single day. I often wondered why my father's mother never taught him how to cook when mine had taught me. We depended on canned sausages and bread during the week and on Sundays he employed a woman to cook a full lunch for us, which was never like the lunch that my mother cooked. I warmed a can of Eskort sausages in a pot of boiling water the way I had seen my father do, opened it and soaked bread in the fat from the can and gave it to the grey boy with one or two pieces of sausage. He chewed with relish, the grease running down his grey arms with abandon.

I didn't have much in common with him and I would have preferred to be left alone to draw pictures and reread the few comic books that I had brought with me, but he insisted on sitting on the doorstep and singing for me: *There was a lady sitting on the corner, and a gentleman smoking cigarettes. Oh, my darling, I am coming. I am coming to kiss you twice.* It was the same song every day – my reward for feeding him Eskort sausages – until I accepted him as a fact of life and appreciated his presence. It served a useful purpose when I decided to compose my own song and try it on him. Mine, of course, was about Keneiloe. I didn't tell you that her name is Sesotho for 'I have been given'. And so I sang: *Keneiloe ngwanana e motle. Lebitso la hae ke Keneiloe. Keneiloe wa me, wa me, ke wa me. Ke mo rata ka pelo yaka yohle.* I have been given (a pun on her name) a beautiful girl. Her name is Keneiloe. She is my Keneiloe; I love her with all my heart.

The grey boy thought it was a brilliant song.

On occasion he overstayed his welcome until my father came home. My father asked him about the health of his parents and his siblings whom he knew by name. He joked with him and teased him about his uncombed hair. If I had hair like that I would have been in big trouble with him, yet here he was pretending to admire it on the grey boy. And the grey boy didn't freeze in his presence as I did. My father and I spent our evenings without exchanging a word. We didn't ask of each other how our day had been, and he buried himself in his files and South African Law Reports as soon as he got home, right until I went to bed. He woke up early in the morning and went to work, even on Saturdays and Sundays. But I realised that he was quite a jolly fellow with the neighbourhood children and was not strict with them at all. They spoke of *Ntate* AP as if they were speaking of a friend.

One morning when my father was at the magistrate's court, or had travelled to another town to defend his clients, I sneaked out of the Moleko yard with the grey boy and he led me along the dirt road among the stalls of women selling various wares and foods, to explore a world with which I was not familiar. A world populated by blanketed men and women chattering in high-pitched tones. In Sterkspruit we did live with Basotho people – even Keneiloe's family were Basotho, although Hopestill was Xhosa – but our Basotho did not wear blankets come rain, come shine. They did not wear cone-shaped grass hats either. I wondered what was cooking in the women's pots in the stalls. Perhaps horse meat. And donkey meat. The Basotho people were reputed to be partial to horse and donkey meat. The smell of meat cooked in onion wafted towards me and I suddenly felt nauseous. Of course it might have been beef or mutton, but in my prejudiced mind it was horse and donkey, animals that were too cute to eat and I felt very bad for them.

70

The grey boy was surprised that all of a sudden I wanted to go back home, even before we had explored further up the hill where the big general dealer's store was beckoning.

As we walked down the dirt road on our way back to the Moleko yard I saw a light-green Wolseley car that looked familiar. When it got closer I noticed that the driver was Mr Mdolomba and the white woman next to him was Mathutha, a name that the people of Sterkspruit gave to Dr Dutton. She was my doctor and the doctor of the multitudes that lined up at her clinics located at various major centres of the Herschel District. Mdolomba, in his white coat, was her driver and her general assistant who also dispensed medicines from the trunk of her car. Dr Dutton had always been my inspiration. When curious adults asked me what I wanted to be when I grew up I immediately said a doctor. I knew that I was going to be a writer, but I didn't think it was something that one could do on a full-time basis. I would need a real job, and medicine would suit me fine, thanks to Dr Dutton. When one of Methodist Reverend Mbete's sons became a medical doctor my resolve was reinforced.

When the car passed I waved frantically. Both Mathutha and Mdolomba waved back. But I couldn't read any recognition in their faces. Children generally waved at them in the villages; perhaps to them I was just one of those children. They didn't see in me the boy who, on his last visit with a bad chest and incessant cough, had black dirt spots on his stomach, a result of shoddy bath-taking. This had embarrassed my mother; she had long stopped inspecting my ablutions thinking that I knew how to wash myself thoroughly. And there I disgraced her in front of the white woman – she, a nursing sister of all people. Later that evening she took a lot of flak from my father about my lack of cleanliness. He took to teaching me how to bathe properly himself . . . yes, at that age! Dr Dutton herself had given me a serious lecture on hygiene that day.

But now seeing her and Mdolomba in this dusty town of blanketed horsemen and donkeys laden with heavy sacks from the mill brought about a searing nostalgia for my disrupted life in Sterkspruit. I thought of my mother and how she was such a beautiful and gentle soul. And my siblings. But my mother most of all. Tears rolled down my cheeks. The grey boy gave me a long, wondering look. I didn't care what he thought of me. I was the older one and I was bawling and I didn't care. I wanted my mother.

It was a number of weeks later that she clandestinely crossed the Telle River to see her exiled men. When there were only the two of us in the room, as my father had gone to his office, I sang her my composition about Keneiloe. She, like the grey boy, thought it was brilliant. Alas, Keneiloe would never hear that cheesy song, or even know about it.

Actually, the main reason my mother had come was to make sure that I was well catered for since I was going to live with the Mafoso family in Mohale's Hoek, a bigger town about forty kilometres to the north of Quthing. My father had got me a place at the Mohale's Hoek Government Controlled Primary School, where I was going to repeat Standard Six, a prospect that didn't sit well with me. Kids my age were already romping about at secondary schools.

OUR USUAL ROUTE FROM the Bee People in the Eastern Cape to Johannesburg is the least convenient one since it goes through another country, Lesotho, where we have to show our passports at two border posts. But it is a shorter route. One of its benefits is that it gives us the opportunity to spend time with my mother in Mafeteng, where she lives with my younger brother Zwelakhe, who is a lawyer in that Lesotho town. When the refugees returned to South Africa after our liberation in 1994 she decided she was too old to start a new life in South Africa. She had lived in exile for too many years and now exile had become home. Another benefit of this route is that we can stop in Mohale's Hoek and visit Willie Mafoso and talk about the old times.

Willie runs a butchery business at the Mafoso estate. He inherited the business from his adoptive parents, Christina and William Mafoso, who died many years ago. One of his specialities is *boerewors* – Afrikaans for 'farmer's sausage'. He has become so adept in the manufacture of this very tasty and spicy delicacy that revellers flock to his shop to buy the sausages for their weekend *braai* or barbecue. He must have learnt the secret recipe from the Afrikaner farmers of Zastron in the Free State from whom he buys his beef cattle and mutton sheep. So, one more reason to stop at Willie's is to buy plenty of his *boerewors* for my mother who is quite partial to it.

Willie is always excited to see me. He remembers the old carefree days when we used to get boisterously drunk on cheap wine or beer. Now in his maturity he drinks for only six months of the year and for the rest he takes a holiday from alcoholic beverages. If my visit coincides with his drinking period he invites me to his living room and offers me passion fruit with tonic water while he drinks twenty-year-old KWV brandy from his stock. That used to be my favourite brandy too before I gave up alcohol altogether; its smooth taste is as good as that of your best Cognac. That is why I find the vapour from his glass redolent and my voice becomes as raucous as if I was imbibing the very product that is distilled from the best white wine of the Cape.

We talk about my mother; how her varicose veins – the bane of many a nurse in her day – and arthritis and hypertension have finally confined her to a wheelchair. I tell him that she can't get over the fact that the friends with whom she worked as a nurse for many years, Albertina Sisulu and Evelyn Mase – Nelson Mandela's first wife – are still going strong on their legs, even though Albertina is older than she is.

Willie and I enjoy looking back in laughter. Sometimes we look back in utter amazement at the stupidity of our youth. We grew up together here in this house, like two brothers. Two doors from the living room where we sit was my bedroom – the first time I had a bedroom all to myself. Willie's home had so many rooms that each one of the residents there – and there were twenty or so of them, including servants – had a space they could call their own.

When my father first took me to live there in 1964 William Mafoso, the patriarch of the family, was already dead. His wife, Mother Christina, was running the businesses which included the butchery; a blacksmith rented out to a smithy, *Ntate* Moholoholo, whose income came mostly from shoeing horses of the Basutoland Mounted Police; and a bakery specialising in bread baked in dug-out clay ovens. The buses that ferried passengers between Mohale's Hoek and Quthing were still there, as was the general dealer's store and café across the street from the Mafoso residence and butchery. But these businesses were no longer owned by the Mafoso family because Mother Christina sold them to the Hlao family as soon as William died. When I first landed here I was fascinated by the extensiveness of the estate, the main house built of solid rock, the many rooms where I thought I would easily get lost, the adjoining houses and rondavel, also built of sandstone. Willie slept in the rondavel, which made him seem more grown-up and independent of the adults in the main house.

What I loved most about those years at the Mafosos was the freedom that I enjoyed for the first time in my life. I could come and go as I pleased. I didn't have to be home by sunset, which had always been my parents' rule. Oh, yes, if any one of us kids returned after sunset we were in for a tongue-lashing. But here at the Mafosos no one cared whether I was there for dinner or not. I would go gallivanting and still find my food in the oven when I returned in the middle of the night. These were indeed the happiest moments of my childhood. I immersed myself in the new life, new country, new language, and rarely thought of my siblings back in Sterkspruit, of my mother, of Keneiloe, and even less so of Cousin Mlungisi, Nikelo and Xolile.

Although I was the same age as Willie he was my new role model. If he had been a scoundrel I would say he was my new Cousin Mlungisi. But, no, he was quite a responsible and diligent bow-legged boy, the antithesis of my carefree irresponsible knock-kneed self. He performed various chores at home, went to assist with the slaughter of animals at the abattoir for the butchery, and helped Phashane – a sinewy young man who whistled incessantly in two-part harmony – knead bread for the clay ovens. On the other hand, no one in the household would let me touch anything by way of work. I only realise now that they regarded me as a boarder; my father paid the family for my upkeep. I therefore did not have any obligation to work. At the time I did feel some pangs of guilt when I saw Willie working so hard while I loitered about.

Willie and I formed a mutual admiration club quite early in our relationship. He admired the fact that I was Attorney Mda's son, I could speak what he thought was impeccable English and could draw pictures that looked like real life; I admired his sophistication and his sense of style. He went out with the best girls in town, the most popular and desired, while I continued with my custom of being afraid of girls. It was enough for me to admire them from afar.

I wished I could be dapper like him, but I couldn't afford it because my father never gave me any money for clothes when he visited. He would demand that I write a list of the items I needed which he would then buy at the local stores. Willie, on the other hand, could order some of the latest fashions from catalogues, particularly from Kays in Johannesburg. He therefore would don the latest Eyre's eight-piece tweed cap, Levi's jeans, Arrow shirts and Bostonian shoes with thick rubber soles – known in those days as 'sticker soles' because shoes were bought with normal soles, but we took them to shoemakers and cobblers to get them to 'stick' on the thick rubber soles. When Bally or the Crockett and Jones shoes came into fashion he was the first one to own them. I learnt from him the cardinal sartorial rule: never wear a black belt with brown shoes or vice versa.

While Willie was out dating girls I spent a lot of time hanging out at the butchery talking to Mapotsane, the striking girl who worked there. She looked out of place surrounded by carcasses of sheep and cattle, or cutting meat and weighing it on the scale for customers. The most attractive thing about Mapotsane, besides her petite figure and her smooth yellowish complexion and white coat that made her look like a doctor, was that she was the only girl in that whole town, at least by my reckoning, who could speak isiXhosa. So we spoke the language that I was missing from home, although I was careful never to do that in the presence of other people. I was ashamed of my foreignness, especially when the neighbourhood kids took to calling me Mothepu, a derogatory name for any Nguni-speaking person. Although the name was originally a Sesotho translation for the abaThembu clan of the Eastern Cape, the ordinary Basotho people used it as an insult to anyone who spoke a Nguni language, be it isiXhosa, isiZulu, isiSwati or isiNdebele.

When my story was finally published in *Wamba* – more than a year after I received the acceptance letter and a two rand note when I still lived in Sterkspruit – my mother sent me a copy of the magazine. I was very proud of this magazine which contained my first ever published work and I wanted everyone in my class at the Mohale's Hoek Government Controlled Primary School to look at my name just below the title 'Igqirha laseMvubase'. But no one shared my excitement. The story was in a strange language that no one could fathom. Also, my name was given as Zanemvula Mda, whereas since my arrival in Mohale's Hoek I was going under the name of Motlalepula, a direct translation of my first name into Sesotho. With a Sesotho name I would not stand out as a foreigner, or so I thought.

At the butchery at least my story had an audience. Mapotsane. I read it to her whilst she cut the carcasses with a hand-operated fine-toothed saw or chopped the stubborn bony parts with an axe. After work I gave her the magazine so that she could read the story for herself at home. She asked me to walk her home, almost three miles away. Outside her home I said goodbye and left. But she called me back, gave me a quick peck on the lips and then ran into her yard.

That night I dreamt of Mapotsane. We were doing much more than just pecking. From then on she became the image behind all my night time self-gratification endeavours.

THE LACK OF PARENTAL supervision was bound to go to my head sooner or later. I never missed school though, because the principal, Mr Mohapi, knew my parents very well and he would not have hesitated to tell them if I played truant. He was once my mother's patient at Empilisweni Hospital, where he was being treated for TB. I suspect that's how I ended up at Mohale's Hoek Government Controlled School instead of any other school in Lesotho. So I attended classes every day even though I was terribly unhappy there. Besides being constantly referred to as a Mothepu by the older boys, I was also called *moketa*. This is a Sesotho word that is used for a cow that is so emaciated that its ribs are showing. Well, I was quite thin, really, and my limbs looked as though they were going to break even as they engaged in the natural act of ambulation.

After school I began to hang out with a group of boys on the veranda of Mafoso's General Dealer's Store across the street from home. It was called that although the Mafoso family had sold the store to the Hlao family many years before. Two of the boys, Teacher and Reentseng Habi, played guitars and we sang and danced the afternoons and evenings away. This was the same Reentseng Habi who joined the army as soon as he completed Standard Six, and then many years later, in 1986 to be exact, became one of the coup leaders, together with the likes of General Metsing Lekhanya, who overthrew the civilian government which had itself been a product of another coup in 1970. As he strummed his guitar on the store veranda no one knew that one day he would be a military councillor and cabinet minister. He never showed any interest in politics in those days.

But that much could not be said about me; I was gradually being drawn deep into the politics of Lesotho. Sabata, one of the boys who sang and danced to the guitars on the veranda, became a very close friend and a fellow political activist. He was the guy who once invited me to have sex with his girlfriend after he had done the deed. I suspect he pitied me for my virginity and wanted to drag me out of that state, screaming and kicking. Fortunately his girlfriend saved me from the shame that would have followed me for the rest of my life by fighting back and telling him that since it was obvious he took her for a *tiekieline* – a cheap woman – he might as well *fokof* – which I suppose is Sesotho for fuck-off. We both did fuck-off and went back to the music of the guitars. He sang a song he claimed to have composed: *Oh, my mother, oh, my father, I didn't know that life would be so difficult. I don't have money, I don't have food, life is so difficult.* Reentseng Habi and Teacher accompanied his sad voice with suitably sorrowful strains of strings.

Besides his eagerness to share his girlfriend with me, Sabata and I had a common passion for the Basutoland Congress Party – the BCP. Willie was also a member of that party, and this was the case with almost every youth in the town.

Those were the heady days of Lesotho politics. The country – officially called the British Protectorate of Basutoland – was on the verge of getting its independence from the United Kingdom and political parties were busy campaigning for the elections scheduled for the following year. Besides the BCP, the other parties that would be vying for power were the Marematlou Freedom Party, which was royalist and enjoyed the support of King Moshoeshoe II; the Basotho National Party, or BNP, which was a threat to the BCP since it enjoyed the support of the Roman Catholic Church in a country with a Catholic majority; and the Communist Party of Lesotho which was the smallest of the parties but had plenty of resources due to the support it received from the Soviet Union. It was natural for me to support the BCP since it was a Pan Africanist party and was in alliance with the PAC in South Africa. PAC refugees generally found a home in the ranks of the BCP. Even the leader of the PAC, Potlako Leballo, actively campaigned for the BCP despite the strict decrees of the British High Commissioner that as refugees we were not supposed to be involved in the politics of the host country.

Lesotho was of strategic importance in that region because it was completely surrounded by apartheid South Africa. That was one of its claims to fame: the only country in the world to be completely surrounded by another country. The second claim to fame was the fact that it is a very mountainous country, hence the sobriquet the Kingdom in the Sky, and also the Switzerland of Africa. Brochures never forget to remind prospective tourists that the kingdom has the highest lowest point of any country in the world. Its position in relation to South Africa was of great concern to the Afrikaners because it was harbouring 'terrorists', namely me, my father and hundreds of other South African refugees from the Pan Africanist Congress, the African National Congress, and even the Trotskyites of the Non-European Unity Movement. The PAC had by far the largest presence, especially after the uprisings in the Western Cape and Pondoland regions of South Africa led by Poqo in the early 1960s.

The South African government was determined to do everything it could to stop the BCP from taking power in Lesotho; otherwise the country would surely serve as a base for further attacks by Poqo insurgents. Earlier in the year the South African prime minister, Dr Hendrik F Verwoerd, had announced that the three British protectorates in southern Africa, namely Basutoland, Bechuanaland and Swaziland, would be better off being ruled by South Africa as Bantustans.

That was what he was negotiating with Britain, and the British would have acquiesced to that had there been no resistance from the people of the Protectorates. In Lesotho, that resistance was led by the BCP.

I was so enthusiastic about the political situation in Lesotho because I saw it as an extension of the political struggle of black South Africans against the apartheid regime.

My political activism started with my helping in the printing and distribution of *Seboholi*, the party organ published by the Mohale's Hoek branch of the BCP. After school Willie, Sabata and I would go to the party offices where some young women typed articles on stencils. These were written by the branch leaders of the party, such as Pelesa Mofelehetsi who was one of my teachers at the Government Controlled Primary School, and Marake Makhetha, a party activist who was one of the numerous sons of the Reverend Makhetha, the local minister of the Paris Evangelical Missionary Society. Whereas the BNP had the unwavering support of the Roman Catholic Church, the BCP was much favoured by the Protestants, and the Paris Evangelical Missionary Society, later dubbed the Church of Lesotho, was the premier Protestant denomination in the country.

After the articles had been typed by the women and edited by Marake Makhetha, it was my task to operate the Gestetner cyclostyle machine and print many copies; Sabata and Willie collated and stapled them. The papers were then sold in the streets by a group of younger boys.

On Sundays, while Willie went to the Anglican Church where he was an altar boy, I sat in my room and drew cartoons that featured on the last page of *Seboholi*. I aspired to be another Bob Connolly, the South African cartoonist whose masterpieces appeared in the *Rand Daily Mail*. But my immediate role model was Mohau Meshu Mokitimi, a famous artist who drew cartoons for the BCP national organ, *Makatolle*. It was my dream that one day my cartoons would feature in *Makatolle*. My famous cartoon that caught national attention was that of Dr Verwoerd as a fisherman who catches a big fish, Chief Leabua Jonathan, the leader of the BNP, with a cob of maize as bait. Verwoerd pulls the line across the Caledon River.

The story behind this cartoon was that the South African government had just donated more than sixty bags of maize to the BNP to buy the votes of impoverished people in the villages of Lesotho. Leabua Jonathan's campaign was focused in the rural areas where he was garnering a lot of support from the peasants who were then being rewarded with rations of maize.

Another of my cartoons that had people talking was titled 'Strange Bedfellows'. It illustrated the King of Lesotho wearing his big crown in bed with a man wearing pyjamas with the hammer and sickle symbol of the Communists, and another man with a stethoscope representing Seth Makotoko, a medical doctor who was also the leader of the Marematlou Freedom Party – the MFP. Here I was playing on the cliché that politics made for strange bedfellows. The MFP, which had been established to protect the interests of the chiefs against the commoners and was supported by the King, was in alliance with the Communist Party of Lesotho. I heard that people in taxis and in shebeens were remarking at my brilliant observation that the Communists were so unscrupulous that to advance their interests they were prepared to work hand in glove with monarchists. The BCP, on the other hand, was against the monarchy and would have preferred a republic, if they could have had their way. They shouted slogans and sang songs that *marena ke linoa-mali, marena ke Marashia* – royals are bloodsuckers, chiefs are Russian thugs.

Marake Makhetha took a shine to me and I was quite often seen in his company. This, of course, increased my stature in the eyes of the other youths for I was much closer to the branch leadership. I was well versed in issues, thanks to my father's round-table family conferences of yore and to my voracious reading of newspapers. I could engage in lengthy debates on Pan Africanism and why it was in the interests of Western powers to keep Africa from uniting.

'You are right, son of Africa,' Marake Makhetha would say. 'The usual divide and rule tactics.'

'But as Osagyefo says, the United States of Africa is inevitable,' I said. 'As peoples of the African continent we share a common history, a common interest and a common destiny.'

We had taken to calling President Kwame Nkrumah of Ghana

Osagyefo, which means 'Redeemer' in his Twi language. He was the leading light of Pan Africanism and ardently supported the liberation of South Africa because, according to him, no African country would ever be truly free until every square inch of Africa was free.

'Yes, son of Africa,' said Marake Makhetha. 'The CIA can kill Patrice Lumumba and any of our leaders, but in the end we'll triumph.'

Then he broke into a song: *Mali a Lumumba rea a batla* – We demand that the murderers of Lumumba pay for his blood. We all joined in the song whose melody was based on a popular Protestant hymn about Jesus' blood, while we churned out the party organ from the Gestetner. These were the most exciting moments in my life; politics was giving me some validation of my worth. Older men like Marake Makhetha were taking my views seriously and engaging with me as an equal. People in the district were reading my cartoons and laughing at the folly of such politicians as Leabua Jonathan, Hendrik Verwoerd, Seth Makotoko, Mmaphosholi Molapo, John Vorster, Harold Wilson and many others whose shenanigans my pen was exposing to the world.

Occasionally I thought of Keneiloe. If only she could see me now. This yearning for her presence, particularly for the purpose of witnessing my greatness, became even more searing when Ntsu Mokhehle, the president of the BCP, drove down from Maseru in one of the thirteen Land Rovers donated by Mao Tse-tung of the People's Republic of China to hold a series of meetings in the southern districts. He was accompanied by Potlako Leballo, the secretary general and acting president of the PAC – the president, Robert Mangaliso Sobukwe, was at that time serving an indefinite term of imprisonment on Robben Island under a special law enacted by the apartheid parliament called the Sobukwe Clause. Leballo introduced me to Mokhehle, and from then on I accompanied the two leaders when they went to campaign in the Quthing district. Mokhehle's driver, Blaizer, became my hero because he was always with the leaders and knew their secrets. He even knew their girlfriends in every port of call because he drove these venerable leaders to their trysts.

The only reason *Moetapele* – the Leader, as Mokhehle was called – needed me in Quthing was to interpret for him when he addressed the isiXhosa-speaking Bathepu (plural of Mothepu) people who lived in that district and who stubbornly supported Chief Leabua Jonathan. Although Mokhehle was popular in the urban areas and his rallies were attended by thousands, in the villages of Quthing only small pockets came to listen to him, and for most it was out of curiosity to see the man who had called their honoured chiefs bloodsuckers and was described by the Catholic Church as the devil incarnate. In a village like Mjanyane there were more people who came from Maseru with *Moetapele* in other Land Rovers, including his bodyguards, than there were supporters of the BCP. Even if there were only forty or so people Mokhehle would make a fiery speech, which I would duly interpret with just as much fire. I often added my own sentiments that the Bathepu's support of Leabua Jonathan was tantamount to treason because he was bent on selling Lesotho to the Boers. Some of them would yell back that Leabua gave them maize. 'What can your leader give us?'

'*Moetapele* will certainly not give you any maize because he is not buying your votes. But if you vote for him he will give you a better life,' I said. 'Popompo (we called Leabua Jonathan 'Popompo' because he was fat) will make you slaves of the Boers. Why do you think he is against our fight for the return of the lands of Lesotho that were conquered by the Boers? Do you know that the whole of the Free State belonged to Lesotho once? That is the Conquered Territory we are talking about. After independence next year, provided you vote for Ntsu Mokhehle, we'll get our Conquered Territory back and your husbands and sons will not have to cross the border to work in the gold mines of the Free State. Those mines will be in Lesotho. They belong to Lesotho. *Ea lla koto!*'

One or two people whose hearts had been won over would cheer, but the rest would jeer and boo. They were Leabua's people and nothing could change that. Their chiefs had commanded them to vote for the BNP and the word of the chief was sacred. That was why we mockingly called them the people of *Inkosi Ithethile* – the Chief has Spoken. Their ignorance embarrassed me because at the end of the day they were my people.

Potlako Leballo, who understood isiXhosa very well, was impressed with my performance. He kept whispering to Mokhehle what I was saying. These meetings had an informal air about them, unlike the rallies of tens of thousands that Mokhehle addressed at the Pitso Ground in Maseru.

After the meeting, while Mokhehle and Leballo conferred with a gentleman who was their point man in Mjanyane, an old woman in the red-ochre skirts and black *iqhiya* turban of the Xhosa people came to me and in very serious tones said, 'Your voice tells me that you are a Xhosa like us, my child. So, what are you doing with these Communists?'

'These are freedom fighters, mother,' I said. 'They are the people who are fighting for our independence from the British without selling us to the Boers.'

'If you say you want independence from the British, where are we going to get sugar? Where are we going to get paraffin? These people you are following like a blind bat are the children of Mao Tse-tung. Do you know that?'

Blaizer, who had been standing next to me, guffawed and said, 'There is no point of arguing with the Bathepu.'

'What do you know of Mao Tse-tung, mother?' I asked.

'Oh, she is a bad woman. Leabua was here last week and he told us all about her. She's the kind of woman who would eat her own children. In her country she has enslaved everyone. If your Mokhehle wins the elections Mao will come here and enslave all of us. It is better to be under the Boers than to be under Mao.'

Mao Tse-tung a woman? I joined Blaizer in his guffaws when I realised that of course to these peasants Mao would be a woman. Mao is Sesotho for 'your mother'.

I HAD HEARD OF Maseru, the capital of Lesotho, from Ntlabathi Mbuli, the Poqo cadre who helped me cross the river and was my father's office clerk. He had moved to Maseru to work at the PAC headquarters where he edited *The Africanist*, the party organ. So, I was quite excited when I went there for the first time.

The bus from Mohale's Hoek took almost the whole day to get

to Maseru – only a hundred and twelve kilometres away – because it moved very slowly on the dirt road and stopped every few minutes to drop or pick up passengers. Halfway through the journey, at Mafeteng, it stopped for a very long time while passengers bought fat cakes and fried fish from the vendors who all surged to the windows as soon as the bus stopped. I didn't know at the time that this dusty miserable-looking town would one day be my home.

Having lived in Johannesburg once, Maseru didn't quite impress me. The only tarred road was Kingsway, the main street. The tallest office building was Bonhomme House, which was only four storeys high. But opposite it was what could be the tallest building in the country: the Roman Catholic Cathedral of Our Lady of Victories, built of solid rock on sprawling grounds with paved pathways and numerous semicircular steps leading to its wide ornate wooden doors. Now, that was an impressive building with its steeples and spires that reached to the heavens. If God lived anywhere at all, it had to be in that cathedral.

Potlako Leballo welcomed me at the PAC headquarters on the fourth floor of Bonhomme House. My friend Ntlabathi Mbuli was present, so were John Nyathi Pokela who later served some years at the Robben Island prison and on his release returned to exile where he became the president of the PAC. Also present was Sipho Shabalala, a highly intellectual cadre who later survived a bomb explosion that had been planted under his car in an assassination attempt.

After giving me a lecture about 'Service, Sacrifice and Suffering' which was the PAC motto, and after a harangue about my father who he accused of 'sitting on the fence' since arriving in Lesotho, Potlako Leballo asked me to raise my hand and, in the presence of the three witnesses, swore me into the PAC. From then on I was a card-carrying member of the party, and not just a person who supported its ideals by virtue of being my father's son.

I enjoyed my brief stay in Maseru, especially hanging out at Sipho Shabalala's house and listening to him analyse our struggle in a manner that was reminiscent of my father. I enjoyed meeting other PAC refugees and seeing how our movement was the dominant factor both in local politics and the South African liberation struggle. The ANC's presence in Lesotho was very low-key at the time – represented by the likes of Joe Matthews and Robin Cranko, both of whom were attorneys practising in Maseru – which some of us mistook for the ANC's universal weakness. On the other hand, our presence as the PAC and its military wing Poqo was quite robust; we strutted around bloviating and showing off, as if we owned the country. And this, by the way, was one of the major things that my father criticised about the PAC's behaviour in Lesotho. He felt that they were being arrogant towards their hosts and were treating them with disdain and disrespect.

The highlight of my visit to Maseru was the discovery of Maseru Café on Kingsway where Ntlabathi Mbuli and I had gone to buy South African newspapers – the *Rand Daily Mail*, the *Sunday Times* and *The Star*. There were some paperbacks on the shelves and this was my opportunity to buy James Hadley Chase's latest potboiler, *Tell It to the Birds*, which would surely make me the man of the moment when I returned to Mohale's Hoek. I was certain that not even Willie and Sabata, who between them had read every James Hadley Chase novel, had read this one since it had only been published a few months back. Oh, yes, at that point James Hadley Chase had crept into our lives and we had become obsessed with his leggy, smart and wily women who manipulated men and made them commit murder. We always knew who the killer was right from the beginning, but what sustained our interest was how the killer would be caught. So, we read and exchanged such titles as *No Orchids for Miss Blandish*, *You Never Know with Women* and *When You Are Dead*. Since we also liked Peter Cheyney's hard-boiled fiction, I bought titles featuring his famous protagonists: Lemmy Caution, an FBI agent, and Slim Callaghan, a British private eye.

We were about to walk out of Maseru Café when something very colourful and familiar attracted my attention. Comic books! My favourites were all there: *Richie Rich*, *Spooky*, *Casper the Friendly Ghost* and all the other Harvey Comics titles. And some DC Comics too. Alas! I didn't have enough money to buy the shelf. Instead I had to make do with one *Richie Rich* and one *Batman and Robin*. I was going to read them over and over again when I got to Mohale's Hoek. Ntlabathi Mbuli was astounded that I had not outgrown such stuff.

'We are in the middle of a revolution and this is what you read?' he asked.

'How is it different from *Jude the Obscure* which you are always reading?' I asked. 'Hardy has nothing to do with the revolution either.'

I was being flippant; he was reading Thomas Hardy for his University of London exams. He only chuckled as we left the shop.

I was just happy that at least I knew now where comic books were sold in Lesotho.

Back in Mohale's Hoek I found that Willie and Sabata had a new hangout: a three-roomed red-brick house on a hill in the woods. This was Dlamini's house. He was a puny balding man who worked as a teller at the Standard Bank and was one of the local activists of the BCP. I don't know why I have forgotten his first name, even though I recall the full names of people who were less significant. I remember vaguely that it was something like Letsema or Leteba.

Dlamini became like a big brother to all of us and we spent a lot of time at his place. We ate many a meal there, spent the evenings playing Crazy Eight and Casino Royale or discussing girls and politics. Marake Makhetha was a regular visitor and there would be a twinkle in his eye as he led us in freedom songs.

At about this time a big conflict was brewing between the BCP and the Communist Party of Lesotho, led in Mohale's Hoek by A S Makhele whose daughter Mphokho had taken my fancy – as usual, nothing came of it because I was afraid to approach her.

The differences between the parties were as much about personalities as they were about ideology. The Communist Party received its financial and diplomatic support from the Soviet Union. But it was quite minuscule in Lesotho although its impact was large because of its resources. The BCP professed to be socialist as well, but in the Maoist vein. Their focus was on mobilising the peasants rather than the working class. There was, after all, no working class in Lesotho except for the small civil service, they argued. Lesotho was pretty much a pre-industrial, almost feudal, state with only one small factory in the whole country – a candle-making and petroleum jelly manufacturing outfit in a small village called Kolonyama. The major export was labour to the mines and farms of South Africa. But as soon as these workers returned to Lesotho they resumed their role as peasants.

The conflict between the two parties, a proxy war between the People's Republic of China and Russia (as we often called the Soviet Union), assumed such proportions that we had to arm ourselves. There were rumours of assassination squads who were roaming the streets of Mohale's Hoek in the guise of respectable citizens ready to eliminate our leaders. People were suspicious of one another. And of their own shadows. Soon a trunk full of handguns was delivered to Dlamini's house. It was a whole assortment of revolvers, derringers and seven-chambered pistols. We looked at them, eyes agog. There was another box full of assorted ammunition. I wondered how anyone would know which bullets belonged to which gun.

These arms and ammunition were kept in a small room that was never locked. We had access to them, but strangely enough none of us boys stole any even though it was obvious that if we took some no one would be the wiser. I don't think even Dlamini or Marake Makhetha ever counted them.

For days on end the trunk just sat there and no one found any use for its contents. Until Tholoana Moshoeshoe came from the BCP headquarters in Maseru. She was a tall woman with a big afro and the long legs of a model. Her face was marred a bit by *chubabas* – the dark spots where the skin had been burnt by the hydroquinone of skin lightening creams. It was nevertheless a pretty face. I thought it would have been more beautiful if she smiled a bit. She seemed to be moping over something all the time.

Tholoana Moshoeshoe spent most of her time in bed. We would arrive at the camp – we had taken to calling Dlamini's house 'the camp' – at midday and she would be sitting in her nightie reading a book, her long legs curled on the bed. We could only imagine what was happening between her and Dlamini at night when we were all gone back to our homes. We envied him the gift that the BCP headquarters had placed on his undeserving bed.

'Do you think she will give us if we ask nicely?' asked Sabata one day. By 'give us' of course he meant 'allow us to have sex with her'. By that time Tholoana Moshoeshoe had been there for almost a month. It was December, schools were closed and our heads were full of nothing but mischief. And this included carnal desire for the much older woman who spent her life in bed. But we dared not approach her with a request for a bout of love-making even though there were only three of us in the house. That would have been disrespectful. So we did the next best thing; we covertly leered at her legs while browsing through Sabata's catalogue of a Durban mail order company flogging love potions. Those days you could trust mail order houses in Durban to sell all sorts of snake-oil – ranging from Mahomedy's who sold cheap clothes and trinkets with magical powers to apothecaries that boasted joint Indian and Zulu ownership, 'tribes well-known for their strong *muti* (potions)'. We wondered which of the potions would be effective on Tholoana Moshoeshoe. Among those we found most attractive were *zamlandela*, a perfume that made girls follow you everywhere at the slightest whiff, or *bhekaminangedwa*, a root that you chewed which compelled girls to pay attention only to you and no one else, or perhaps *velabahleke*, a cream that you dabbed on your skin to make yourself so lovable that when you appeared girls laughed with joy. Alas, we had no money for any of these wonderful concoctions; otherwise we wouldn't have hesitated to order them. If it were not for want of money, Tholoana Moshoeshoe would have been my first experience, if you don't count what happened to me at KwaGcina with Nontonje.

We were sitting at the table whispering and giggling about what we would do to Tholoana Moshoeshoe and all the other girls we fancied if we had the potions.

'Maybe they don't work,' whispered Sabata. 'Maybe it's just a scam.'

'For sure they do,' I said. 'I have seen them work.'

'You have actually seen these wonderful medicines with your own eyes?

'I have actually touched them.'

This was not a lie. I knew of their efficacy from Sterkspruit; Cousin Mlungisi used to order them from Durban, and Cousin Mlungisi was very popular with girls. He used to get small parcels wrapped in brown paper from the post office and he would let me touch the potions as soon as he had unwrapped them. Some were in tiny bottles and smelled like some cheap perfume, others were foul-smelling ointments or herbs. He never shared any of these mixtures with me, though; he said the herbalists who sold them insisted that they worked only for the person who bought them. If he were to let someone else use them their power flew away and returned to the Indian Ocean whence it came.

Tholoana Moshoeshoe broke up our conspiratorial giggles. 'You must be having fun there, boys,' she said and smiled. She had never smiled at us before, so we fidgeted uneasily.

She stood up from the bed and walked to the table. This caught us by surprise and it was too late for us to hide the catalogue. But that was not what she was interested in; she didn't even give it a second look. She wanted to talk to us about a very serious matter, she said.

'Do you know anything about Marake Makhetha?' she asked.

Of course we knew Marake Makhetha. He was like an older brother to us. He was our political mentor. He was the man who sang freedom songs with such a beautiful voice.

Tholoana Moshoeshoe told us Marake Makhetha was not the person we thought he was. He was in fact a spy of the Communist Party who had been planted in our midst to destroy the BCP. She had been sent by Ntsu Mokhehle himself to come to Mohale's Hoek, observe Marake Makhetha closely and then eliminate him. That was her sole mission here, from *Moetapele* – the Leader – himself. It was therefore our patriotic duty to kill Marake Makhetha.

At first we thought she was joking, but she was in earnest. It had to be done that night. There was great urgency because he was planning something that very moment that would destroy the Leader and plunge the country into turmoil. We were the heroes who could save Lesotho. She asked us to select two guns from the trunk and she would help find suitable ammunition for them. Sabata picked a Browning pistol and I opted for a derringer with a white handle.

'That's a lady's gun,' said Tholoana Moshoeshoe, smiling. 'But it will kill him just as well.'

She took our weapons and went into the gun room. We remained behind, debating if we really wanted to kill Marake Makhetha who never harmed us and treated us like his own little brothers. Sabata said that in a revolution one had to suppress all personal emotions about people and do what was right for the good of the country. I had never known Sabata to talk so much political sense before and I agreed with him totally. We were going to accomplish our mission; we were not going to let *Moetapele* down. After all, I knew Ntsu Mokhehle personally. I had toured the Quthing district with him trying to convince the Bathepu people to change from their reactionary ways. He was an avuncular guy with the unruly hair of a revolutionary and a broad dark face that was always ready with a smile. He was dedicated to the freedom of his people from the yoke of the British government and the Boers of South Africa. If Marake Makhetha wanted to harm him, then Marake Makhetha was our enemy. Marake Makhetha must die!

After a few minutes Tholoana Moshoeshoe came back with the bullets and showed us how to load them in the guns. I had touched these guns before, but I had never held in my hand a loaded gun. No one had ever taught us how to shoot. Of course we knew that any fool could aim and pull the trigger. We had seen it all in the movies. That was what we would do. That was all that was required of us. The only lesson she gave us was how to release the safety catch for Sabata's handgun. Mine had an internal safety.

Marake Makhetha's home was at Lithoteng, a township that was about four miles away from our camp. Sabata and I walked silently in the middle of the night to waylay him at a wide donga which he had to cross to get to his home. This was an ideal place because it had rocks and boulders and at that time there would be no witnesses. Before we took our positions behind two boulders Sabata said, 'Maybe after this she will give us.' Trust Sabata to think of carnal pleasures at a time like this. 'Don't you think?' he asked desperately. I didn't give a damn if she gave us or not. I just wanted this thing to be over with so that I could go back to my comfortable bed at Mafoso's. The sooner Marake Makhetha appeared and we blasted his head off, saving Lesotho from calamity, the better. So, who the hell cared if Tholoana Moshoeshoe gave us or not?

'You horny bastard, are you doing this for sex or for your country?' I said as I pushed him behind his boulder and took cover behind mine.

Sabata yelled back at me, 'For both. Why can't we do it for both?'

Tholoana Moshoeshoe was right. She knew exactly what time Marake Makhetha would be crossing the donga. We heard his voice from a distance singing his favourite freedom song: *Boys of Africa rise and fight, girls of Africa rise and fight, in the name of great Africa we shall fight and conquer now. There is victory for us, there is victory for us. In the name of great Africa there is victory for us.*

Damn that song!

As he got closer I drew my derringer and pointed it in his direction. I saw Sabata behind his boulder do the same. I was shaking and couldn't remember how to cock it. My bladder was burning and I wanted to pee so badly.

When Marake Makhetha was about to pass the boulders we emerged from our hiding places and walked towards him at the same time as if we had planned it that way, our guns pointing to the ground.

'Sons of Africa,' he greeted us.

We broke down and confessed that Tholoana Moshoeshoe had sent us to assassinate him because he was a Communist spy.

He shook his head and said, 'Go back to bed, sons of the soil.' And then he continued with his song and walked home without ever looking back.

I DON'T THINK I ever told Gugu about this incident. But as we drive past Mohale's Hoek I remember how it shook me back to my senses. Had we accomplished our mission we surely would have been arrested and spent the better part of our lives first at the Juvenile Detention Centre in Maseru and when we got older at the Mohale's Hoek prison. I would never have known Gugu. My arrest for murder would have come as a shock to my father because he did not know of my political activities, not even of my going to Quthing with Potlako Leballo and Ntsu Mokhehle addressing meetings or my officially joining the PAC. He wouldn't have approved. He wanted me to focus on my education, and indeed this narrow escape made me think twice about my priorities.

I never went back to Dlamini's house again. I heard from Willie that

Tholoana Moshoeshoe disappeared the next morning and no one could trace her. The BCP head office in Maseru had never heard of her. The story went round that she was an agent provocateur working for the Communist Party or the British or the Boers or all of the above. Those heady days one never knew who was in cahoots with whom and to what end.

I often meet Marake Makhetha when I visit Maseru. He is an old man now with grey hair. 'I nearly killed you, son of Africa,' I tease him, and we laugh about it.

In Mafeteng we go to my brother's house to see my mother before we proceed to the border post in Wepener and then drive through the vast flat expanse of the Free State province to Johannesburg. These days she spends all her life sitting in the bedroom, either on the bed or in her wheelchair. She watches endless television programmes and talks of the characters she sees there as if they are real people she actually interacts with in her room. Early in the afternoon she is glued to American soap operas, *The Bold and the Beautiful* and *Days of Our Lives*. In the evenings it is time for the South African soapies, *Isidingo*, *Backstage* and *Generations*. It irks her no end that *Backstage* and *Isidingo* run at the same time at 6:30. Fortunately, both soaps are repeated on weekday mornings and on Saturdays there is an omnibus where episodes for the whole week are played one after the other.

I give my mother some of the honey we purchased from the Bee People and she is happy to hear that the project is progressing well and the women now run it themselves without help from us. In the beginning we had to employ a white farmer from Lady Grey, Aubrey Fincham, to manage it for them while they were learning the ropes.

As we sit with her telling her about the people at Qoboshane and laughing at Cousin Bernard's antics, people from the neighbourhood come to greet her. They sit on the chairs, the bed and even on the floor and gossip about what is happening in the town. They range in age from old men and women of her generation to teenagers. That is how popular she is in the neighbourhood. And they pay these visits every day.

That is proof enough that exile long became home for her. Not just exile. The community of Mafeteng in particular.

We first settled in Mafeteng in 1966 when my father moved his headquarters from Quthing and rented a house from the Thatho family. A few months earlier my mother and my siblings had come to join us in exile and were staying at Mme Mmatladi Maphathe's house, a friend of my mother's who was divorced from the local medical doctor. At the time I was already a student at Peka High School in the northern Lesotho district of Leribe. For a year or so I had continued to spend my holidays at the Mafoso household in Mohale's Hoek, but later we all moved to the green-roofed stone house on the Thatho estate. My siblings were enrolled at local primary schools and once more we lived as a family.

I missed my Mohale's Hoek freedom where I could come and go as I pleased. But the compensation was that I was now with my mother and of course with my brothers and sister. I had to relearn to live with my father's discipline and stand to attention when he spoke and respond *ewe tata* at regular intervals to show that I was paying attention to his elaborate lectures. He now had offices in Quthing, Mohale's Hoek and Mafeteng, and also appeared before the High Court in Maseru. Since he didn't have a car he travelled by bus and spent some nights away in these towns. Those were the days that we really enjoyed Mafeteng. Whenever we came back home from hanging out with friends and found that he had returned from a long trip our hearts sank.

One thing I loved about Mafeteng was that there was a big South African refugee community there and we all lived together as a family, irrespective of political affiliation. Ours was a PAC-aligned family, yet our closest friends were the Mafikeng and Hani families who were staunch ANC members. In fact when my father wanted to escape from clients who bothered him at home he went to work at a café owned by the partnership of Elizabeth Mafikeng, a trade unionist from Cape Town, and *Ntate* Hani, Chris Hani's father. Chris Hani himself, known to us only as Bhut' Thembi, was a leader of the South African Communist Party and a guerrilla commander of *Umkhonto weSizwe* – the Spear of the Nation – the military wing of the ANC. Yet we all exchanged visits, dined and celebrated family occasions together.

All these families returned to South Africa after our liberation in 1994. Only Zwelakhe, the youngest of my brothers, and my mother remained. But there are other Mdas who live in Lesotho and sometimes visit my brother's house to remind us of our origins. They first came here in 1880 as refugees after our revered ancestor killed the British magistrate Hamilton Hope. They were first given succour by King Moorosi of the Baphuthi clan in Quthing, but soon spread to Mantsonyane, a village high up in the Maluti mountain range of Lesotho where they keep goats and sheep. But others live at Taung only a few miles from Mafeteng. Their leader is Bles Mda who once came to pay homage to my father with a large group of his Bathepu people in red ochre skirts and blankets and gigantic turbans soon after we had settled in Mafeteng in 1966. They sat on our green stoep puffing on their long pipes. I remember how we kids were embarrassed by them because we viewed them as uncivilised. Also, they exposed our foreignness to our Basotho friends. I had worked so hard to try to blend into the Basotho culture, to the extent that I had taken the Sesotho name of Motlalepula and had given my twin brothers, Sonwabo and Monwabisi, the Sesotho names of Thabo and Thabiso. And now here were the red-blanketed Mdas sprawled on my stoep with all the passers-by gawking at them.

Occasionally Bles Mda came to visit on his brown and white stallion. He felt very sorry that I, his cousin's son, could not ride a horse and tried to teach me. I was dead scared of the horse and almost peed in my pants when it galloped away with me on its back.

All these are things we talk about when we visit my mother. She thrives on nostalgia ever since sickness confined her to the bedroom.

We also thrive on laughter at the folly of our youth.

CHAPTER FOUR

WHAT I DREAD MOST about driving through Lesotho on my way from the Bee People to Johannesburg are police roadblocks. You are likely to come across one at least three times before you reach the next border post. This would be a good thing if their objective was to catch wrongdoers. The constant police presence would also make you feel safe and protected. But no, they are not there for that. Their main business is to extort bribes from motorists.

Their modus operandi is a simple one: they place a stop sign on the line in the centre of the road and small groups of police officers stand about fifty yards on either side of the sign. They let all Lesotho cars whiz by and stop all those with South African number plates. They ask the motorist to produce a driver's licence and then proceed to inspect the discs on the windscreen, indicators, hooter, and brake lights. If they don't find anything wrong they are bound to manufacture something, as they did once in my case. They inspected the windscreen disc and claimed that it did not state that there could be passengers in the car. It was therefore illegal for me to be with my wife and two minor children in her Toyota Tazz sedan. This, of course, was a cockamamie charge concocted merely to shake down people they deemed to be strangers in the country. When I stubbornly stood my ground and insisted that we had committed no offence and would not pay any fine, they took us to the police station and left us there for the whole day. It was only when another shift came in the evening that we were released. No explanation, no apology. I was proud that I had steadfastly refused to pay a bribe, albeit at great inconvenience to my family. And I was angry that a whole day was wasted and I had missed my appointment with women in the Mjanyane village of Quthing who were interested in starting a beekeeping project similar to the one across the river, the Lower Telle Beekeepers Collective. A whole rural development project which already had prospective donors was destroyed by police corruption. I certainly was not going to subject myself to such treatment every time I had to visit the project, so I called it quits.

I am thinking of this experience when I approach another roadblock of this kind near a village called Peka in the Leribe district. I am still high on my banter with my mother on the high jinks of the various members of the Mda family and am determined that the cops will not spoil my day. But they do. As soon as I get to the first group of officers I stop, but an officer from the second group beckons me. I slow down as I approach the stop sign in readiness to stop, but the officer continues to beckon me. I pass the stop sign and stop next to him.

'You didn't stop at that stop sign,' he says.

'Yeah, because you kept on beckoning me to you,' I say.

'You're supposed to stop at the stop sign,' he says.

'I was following your orders,' I say.

He denies that he gave me any orders. He is going to give me a ticket, he threatens.

'Yes. Go ahead and give me a ticket,' I say.

He asks for my licence, and then checks the discs on the windscreen. Everything is in order. This infuriates him. Also the fact that I don't seem to be prepared to negotiate but instead I demand to be given a ticket that I will defend in court.

'I cannot give you a ticket,' he says. 'You're from South Africa. How do I know you'll pay it?'

'Of course I won't pay it. I'll go to court.'

'How do I know you'll come for the case? I have no way of getting you when you leave this country.'

He looks at me expectantly. He obviously thinks he has a trump card and I am bound to negotiate.

'I don't know.'

'I am impounding your car unless you pay.'

He gives me directions to the charge office and asks me to drive there and wait for him. As soon as I enter the police station I announce quite loudly to the sergeant at the desk, 'A police officer at the roadblock asked me to come here because I refused to pay *tjotjo*.'

The policemen are embarrassed at my blatant use of the Sesotho word for bribery. I tell the sergeant what happened and demand that I be charged even if it means impounding my car. I guess they have never met such a customer before, and the sergeant says he will let me go with a warning.

'I don't want you to let me go with a warning,' I say. 'You can't warn me for doing nothing wrong.'

'Just go, man,' says the sergeant.

'This country depends on tourism,' I say just before I walk out. 'It spends millions advertising in the South African media for tourists to come and enjoy your friendly country. And when they come you treat them like this?'

Back on the road I see the police officer who gave me problems walking back to the police station with two fellow officers. I blow my horn very hard and wave at him. I am fuming inside. I vow never to come back to this country after my mother departs this world. She is the only reason I return here. When she is gone the only thing that will bring me back are weddings, graduations and funerals of my many relatives who still live here. Not just to visit, as I do now. Not just to use the route through Lesotho as a short cut between Johannesburg and the Bee People in the Eastern Cape.

I am sorry that I have to come to this decision because I love this country. I regard it as my home. Which is what I once told King Letsie III, the monarch of Lesotho. He was having dinner with two of his cousins at the Maseru Sun Cabanas one evening when a waitress ushered Gugu and me to a table next to his. The King and I had not seen each other for many years, since I left exile to return to South Africa, and so he was quite happy to see me. What impressed Gugu, on the other hand, was that the King in Lesotho is just like any other guy. There he was having dinner with us commoners in a hotel restaurant without an entourage or even a single bodyguard.

'So, you do visit us sometimes?' he said as we shook hands.

'Of course,' I said. 'This is my country.'

'I am glad that now you feel it is your country.'

'What do you mean "now"?' I asked, rather irritated. 'I have lived in this country almost as long as you have. Why should it be yours and not mine?'

It is true. I came here a few months after Prince Mohato, as he was then called, was born. I grew up here. I had my high school education in this very village of Peka.

I DON'T REMEMBER EVER taking Gugu to see my alma mater even though it is only six miles from the highway we sometimes take when we have decided to enter South Africa from the northern districts of Lesotho. Peka High School looks quite dilapidated now, with broken windows and grounds that are overgrown with grass and weeds. The walls that used to be rough-cast in grey are cracked and the once-green paint has long peeled off the corrugated iron roofs on all the buildings. It was not like this when I was a student here from 1965 to 1969. This boys' high school was the most prestigious in the country, with a one hundred per cent pass rate in the Cambridge Overseas School Certificate every year.

I was very lucky to be admitted here since I had only a second-class pass in Standard Six, even though I was repeating the grade after obtaining a first-class pass in Sterkspruit under Bantu Education. Everyone had expected a first-class pass from me once more, but I knew otherwise. I had spent most of my time in Mohale's Hoek gallivanting with politicians and dabbling in assassinations – albeit attempted ones. I had gone to class only because I had to, and when I was there I didn't pay much attention. I drew pictures while either Mr Mohapi or Mr Mofelehetsi taught and never studied outside class. Most students who were admitted to Peka had a first-class pass or at least a superior second-class with good symbols. My only decent symbols were in English Language and English Literature and I had Fs in Science and Mathematics. But then I was also my father's son, and I am sure that counted for something with the admission authorities at Peka High School. The principal, after all, was Mr Tseliso Makhakhe from Mafeteng – a political activist of the Basutoland Congress Party.

My high school years were generally wonderful, although I cannot say as much for the first few weeks. The first day, in fact, was traumatic, from the time the bus from Mohale's Hoek dropped me at the Maseru bus stop to catch the bus hired by the school. Here the old-comers had a field day ill-treating new-comers. Even as we sat in the bus waiting for more students from various directions to arrive, the old-comers forced us to sing: *Makamara mesemeng'ting, le tla cha mohlang le shoang.* You motherfucking new-comers, you'll burn in hell when you die.

Those who refused to sing or showed the slightest sign of resistance were slapped and verbally abused. I had heard of hazing, but I didn't know it could be this mortifying. It became even more so when the old-comers paid particular attention to me because I was not a Mosotho. They were alerted to this fact by my accent. 'You are not a Mosotho, or if you are then you are one of those fence-jumping Basotho from South Africa.' Then he pressed my nose as if playing the keyboard and demanded that I sing nasally: *Ke lla joalo ka piano. Ke lla joalo ka piano.* I sound like a piano. I cry like a piano.

'Hey, we have a Mothepu in the bus,' he yelled to the rest, and they all laughed, howled and yelped like dogs. To them a Mothepu was a dog.

My mortification became worse when thugs and sundry ragamuffins from the streets of Maseru boarded the bus and were allowed by the old-comers to beat us up and call us demeaning names.

A wiry thug in dirty jeans and a greasy Eyre's cap got on the bus and demanded to be shown who the new-comers were. He was obviously the boss because all the other thugs deferred to him. The old-comers greeted him like an old friend, still showing some diffidence, and eagerly pointed out the new-comers.

'This particular one is very stubborn,' said an old-comer pointing at a cowering new-comer.

The wiry thug gave him a few whacks on the face with the back of his hand. His nose began to bleed. The thug instructed another new-comer to clean the blood with his tongue. When he hesitated the thug dragged him by both ears and shoved his head on the blood that was on the boy's chest. I had never seen such savagery in my life. If this was high school then I wanted nothing to do with it. But there was no escape from the bus. The thugs were blocking the aisle and the wiry one was moving towards me, his eyes rolling like those of a snake about to swallow a rat. He stopped in front of me and stared at me for some time. I fidgeted, expecting a whack.

'What is your name, *lekamara*?' he asked, using the Sesotho corruption of 'new-comer'.

'I am Motlalepula,' I said, already shaking. I was hoping that the Sesotho version of my name would mitigate my crime of being a new-comer and a Mothepu to boot.

'Hey, you motherfuckers,' yelled the thug to the rest of the people in the bus. 'This is my *bitso*.' This meant that we shared the same name. He too was Motlalepula. 'If any of you touch this boy you will have to answer to me. Anyone who as much as makes this boy sing your silly songs will never set foot in Maseru ever again.'

'Why didn't you say so?' asked one old-comer. 'Why didn't you tell us you're Bra Motlalepula's *laaitie*?'

The thug assigned two of the bigger old-comers, Mokitimi – Kittyman to his friends – and Zwanya to look after me.

I was grateful to the thug. Throughout the two-hour journey to Peka High School I was ensconced between Zwanya and Kittyman while my fellow new-comers were singing demeaning songs about themselves and having their tin trunks confiscated and their provisions of chicken and steamed bread devoured in front of their weeping eyes. The two gentlemen, much older than the rest of the old-comers and not participating in the hazing, kept on reminding the rest that I was Bra Motlalepula's *laaitie* – little boy – and therefore no one must even imagine lifting his hand in my direction or utter any profanity while looking at me.

Even after we had arrived at the high school and had been allocated our dormitories the story that I was a *fuzie* – or sidekick – of some bad-ass Maseru gangsters spread even among those boys who were not in our bus but had arrived in other buses from the northern districts or had been brought by parents in their cars. I didn't correct them. I didn't tell them that in fact I had never met the thug before; he merely took a shine to me because of the similarities of our names. I felt like a charlatan. I was benefiting from a name that was not really mine – a Sesotho translation of my real name. You will remember that I named myself Motlalepula in Mohale's Hoek in quest of assimilation and acceptance. But who cared? As long as it gave me protection from barbaric hazing. Why would I correct the boys when this whole misunderstanding enhanced my credentials as this guy who had a personal relationship with the likes of Bra Motlalepula, the godfather of Maseru outlaws and sundry ruffians?

Hazing – euphemistically called 'giving the new-comers treatment' – was relentless for the first few weeks of high school. But thanks to Bra Motlalepula I escaped it all as Zwanya and Kittyman took their assignment seriously. Once in a while there would be some renegade who would be resentful that I was getting off scot-free while other new-comers were being given the treatment. One such renegade was Jama Mbeki, whose uncle, Michael Mosoeu Moerane, was our Latin and Music master. Like me, he was a Mothepu and a refugee from South

Africa. Only the previous year his father, Govan, had been sentenced to life imprisonment on Robben Island together with his comrades Nelson Mandela and Walter Sisulu. Despite this, Jama was a jovial fellow who showed no sign of distress at his father's plight. I admired him for this; I would have been a wreck if my father had been sentenced to life imprisonment.

Although the students called him Mothepu, Jama was quite a popular fellow. The pejorative sounded like a term of endearment when it referred to him. I suppose because of his popularity he thought he could defy Zwanya and Kittyman and give me the treatment. Our dormitories were built like a prison with narrow barred windows just below the high roof. The building formed a square with only one entrance with heavy iron-cast gates. Once those gates were locked there was no escape from the Square. It was at those gates that Jama confronted me and demanded that I sing the famous song about how new-comers were a menace who would end up in hell after death. I stood there and looked at him stubbornly.

'*Bina ntja tooe,*' he yelled. Sing, you dog.

People were beginning to gather and I was mortified. Here was a fellow South African and a fellow Xhosa calling me a dog in Sesotho. Worse still, I could see a glint of pleasure from some new-comers who had come to regard me with awe since I was the only new-comer who never got the treatment. I was going to lose whatever semblance of respect my immunity had afforded me among this miserable lot. This gave me the courage to speak out and be damned.

'You come any closer, *u tla bona lipela lifalla,*' I said, using a Sesotho proverb that threatened one with a dangerous and unexpected encounter. The old-comers who had gathered were having a great time at the prospect of a fight and were chanting: *Bathepu ba batla ho loana. Malinyane a Nongqawuse a batla ho loana!* The Bathepu want to fight. Nongqawuse's offspring want to fight!

I think the fact that the old-comers were not taking his side but instead were looking forward to a fight between the foreigners brought Jama to his senses. He uttered an expletive, opened the gate and walked out of the Square. He turned and looked at me with eyes full of anger and said, 'Beware the Ides of March!' Then he walked away.

A sigh of relief. I had never been a fighter in my life; if he had taken the challenge he surely would have wiped the floor with me.

That was the last time that anyone tried to give me the treatment. By the twelfth of March when hazing was scheduled officially to end, I was long integrated into the life of the high school and anyone would have thought I was an old-comer. I was already spending my free time with the older boys smoking hand-rolled cigarettes at the officially designated Smoking Spot behind the dormitories. Most of my popularity rested on my political experience, which none of my smoking companions could match even though they were much older than me. I was a purveyor of political knowledge, and even distributed the PAC organ, *The Africanist*, and other material. Most students were BCP members or sympathisers, and therefore were comrades-in-arms as fellow Pan Africanists. I was proud that some articles in the *The Africanist* were written by people who were friends of mine: Ntlabathi Mbuli and Sipho Shabalala. So you see, it was no longer because I was a sidekick of a Maseru gangster that I was spared the treatment. I was seen by my peers as a political sage who could, at the slightest provocation, expound on the evils of imperialism and on the goings-on in Addis Ababa, Ethiopia, the headquarters of the Organization of African Unity which had been founded only a year before.

The twelfth of March was an official holiday in honour of King Moshoeshoe I, the founder of the Basotho nation. At Peka High School it was referred to as the Ides of March. It was the day that the new-comers dreaded most because it brought about the end of hazing in a most savage manner. On this day old-comers strutted around threatening all the new-comers against whom they had a grudge, perhaps because they became defiant when they were being ordered around or they became tattletales to the prefects, that the day of reckoning had come.

'Beware the Ides of March,' a boy would yell.

'Yeah, they are come but not gone,' another would respond.

This sent a chill down my spine; I feared that all the old-comers who were not able to give me the treatment because I had gained too much respectability among the most revered seniors would take advantage of the darkness of the Ides of March. Stories were doing the rounds that old-comers would come for the new-comers in the middle of the night dressed in sheets like the Ku Klux Klan and frogmarch them – especially the stubborn ones who, in the two months since the new year began, had become too big for their boots – to the Caledon River that separates Lesotho from South Africa where they would force them, fully dressed in their pyjamas, into the cold water while thrashing them with leather belts and spitting on them.

I was certain that I was one of the uppity ones who was going to get the treatment. And I wouldn't know who was responsible because the culprits would all be in ghostly white. When evening came and there were wolf-like howls all around the Square – 'Beware the Ides of March!' – I was shaking in my Florsheim shoes that I had pinched from my rich Mohale's Hoek friend, Gift Mpho Hlao. I tried to make light of the matter by asking the seniors at the Smoking Spot, 'Shouldn't the Ides of March be on the fifteenth?'

'In *Julius Caesar* maybe,' said Hodges Maqina as he rolled a cigarette of Best Blend Tobacco in a piece of brown paper, 'but for us here it is the twelfth because it's a holiday.'

Although Hodges Maqina was of Xhosa descent he had spent all his life in Lesotho. He was one of the seniors with whom I hit it off immediately because I could hold my own in any political discussion. He was respected by everyone because of his muscular body and the fact that he was a prefect. So, hanging out with him at the Smoking Spot while I was a mere new-comer was something that raised my prestige, for which I was going to pay dearly on this day, the Ides of March. He was well-beloved by all the new-comers because he exuded an air of maturity and authority, and he never got involved in the savage practice of hazing. But of course he wouldn't have been able to save all of us from the Ides of March, even if he had been so inclined.

The spirit of the thug who became my guardian angel by sheer chance at the Maseru bus stop prevailed, and once more Zwanya and Kittyman came to my rescue. I had not asked them for help because I didn't want to impose; they had been a bit distant lately. Perhaps because I had taken to socialising with intellectuals like Hodges Maqina, Phanuel Ramorobi and Kingston Mohapeloa. The last was a particular hero of mine because he was an artist. But none of these sophisticates offered me succour. It was the old stalwarts in shabby coats and unkempt hair who remembered the assignment they were given by a gangster. They smuggled me out of my dormitory and arranged with the Health Prefect to hide me in a small room that served as a dispensary.

Deep in the night I could hear the howls and the wails and the screams. I knew that boys who looked very much like Klansmen were waking their victims up and marching them to the river. 'Where is that Mothepu?' I heard someone ask. 'Damn that Kittyman! Damn that Zwanya! What have they done with that Mothepu?'

When the sun rose I walked out of the dispensary a liberated man. We had all been delivered after the Ides of March. When next I met Jama Mbeki we laughed about our encounter and became friends. Those days the road ahead was still very bleak, and none of us could have suspected that one day South Africa would be free and Jama's brother Thabo would be the president.

After the Ides of March we were all equal.

I could then immerse myself in boarding school life without any reservations. This included bloviating on current events at the Smoking Spot, particularly on the battle for supremacy between the Basutoland Congress Party and the Basotho National Party and participating in the school's official debating society. I soon established myself as an astute debater who converted even the most innocuous of subjects into a political one. Once I was on the affirmative on the topic 'Honesty is the Best Policy' and I started speaking about such freedom fighters as Oginga Odinga who fought for the freedom of Kenya and were honest to their cause despite being jailed at one time, or being promised riches by the British if they gave up the struggle at another time. I won that debate. Dugmore Hlalele, a senior who was on the negative side, claimed that I had invented the story about Oginga Odinga and that in fact there was never such a person. This tended to devalue my great win in the eyes of my peers. Pity the Internet had not yet been invented otherwise I would have 'Googled' the name to prove Oginga Odinga's existence. I had to wait for weeks until his name featured in a newspaper article and I ran triumphantly to the Smoking Spot to show Dugmore that Oginga Odinga was not a figment of my imagination.

This brought me closer to another group of friends, that of Dugs, as we called Dugmore Hlalele, and my erstwhile enemy, Jama Mbeki. Dugs was a good person to know. He was originally from Welkom and his brother-in-law, Jefty Smith, owned 60 Minutes Dry Cleaners in Maseru. Because of Jefty's connections to the underworld of South Africa, during holidays Dugs socialised with the kind of characters we only read about in newspapers – the likes of soccer elites Eric Scara Sono and Chincha Guluva Motaung. He came back after June or December holidays with stories of *braais* – barbecue parties – he had attended in Welkom and Soweto, and of beauty queens he had actually spoken to. For us, me and Jama, it was like Dugs was talking of a different planet; we were exiled in Lesotho and the glamorous world he was talking about was far removed from our experience. The more immediate world was that of politics, particularly of BCP politics. And here, of course, I was the voice they took seriously.

At first I had been reluctant to discuss politics with Jama because I thought we belonged in opposite camps – he being the son of ANC leaders and all – and didn't want to upset the apple cart of our budding friendship. But I discovered that he was as sympathetic to the BCP as Dugs was. I was not surprised though, because Peka High was a BCP breeding ground, and most of our teachers, such as Tseliso Makhakhe and Selometsi Baholo, were BCP leaders. Why, even Jama's uncle, Michael Mosoeu Moerane, talked openly about his support for the BCP. I knew one of Jama's uncles in Maseru, Mofelehetsi Moerane, from the days I campaigned for the BCP in the rural Quthing district. He and the artist Meshu Mokitimi organised the youth wing of the BCP. That's why it would not have been inconceivable for Jama Mbeki's sympathies to lie with the BCP, an ally of the PAC, and not with the Marematlou Freedom Party which was at the time in alliance with the ANC.

My immersion into boarding school life did not only confine itself to academically enriching activities. On some weekends I sneaked out of school bounds in the company of my older friends and protectors, Zwanya and Kittyman, to drink Sesotho beer in the village. I found the beer brewed from sorghum unpalatable with rough malt corroding my mouth, so I only pretended to drink. I was just happy to be in the company of these wise men who were also proud to be with their *laaitie* who was a sidekick of a Maseru gangster. I had to live up to my image.

One day we went to a shebeen at what would pass as the town of Peka – where there were two stores, a café, the post office and one or two other small businesses – about six miles from the school. There were quite a number of us, not just Kittyman and Zwanya. The big boys drank until the early hours of the morning. When we left the shebeen we were all jolly and singing dirty songs. Even though I was the soberest of the lot, the drunkards had infected me with their good spirits. Moss, an older boy from Soweto whose father was a rich businessman there, was a few steps behind us with a drunken village woman he had picked up at the shebeen. Both were singing boisterously and the woman was leading in some of the songs. From time to time they stopped and kissed passionately.

After a while I realised that Moss and the woman were no longer singing. When I looked back I saw that they were having sex on the side of the road. Moss hollered to the boys to join him and soon there was a line waiting to gang-rape the woman. I was horrified, but didn't know what to do. I couldn't stand up for her for fear of being ostracised by the group. I was the youngest and was honoured to have been accepted as a member of this group of popular boys. I didn't think they would beat me up or anything, because of my alleged gangster connections in Maseru. It was being ostracised that I feared most. I decided to walk on. But Moss called me back while Kittyman was busy on top of the woman, who didn't seem to resist but lay there lifelessly.

'Come on,' said Moss, 'it's going to be your turn after everyone has had a taste of her. We are initiating you into manhood.'

When it finally got to be my turn I pretended I was getting on top of her and whispered in her ear: 'Push me off and run for your life.'

She just lay there motionless.

'These guys will kill you,' I said. I was getting frustrated and had to lie. 'I know them. They are my brothers. They have killed before. Just push me and run, I'll keep them at bay.'

That seemed to animate her a bit. But still she didn't have the strength to do what I was asking her. I rolled on the ground, pretending that she had pushed me away. She feebly stood up and staggered away. When the boys tried to stop her I screamed: 'Let her go, please, Bra Kittyman . . . Zwanya . . . Moss, she's not worth the trouble.'

The boys let her stumble away. After all, they had had their fill.

All the way back to school they laughed at me because I had been defeated by a drunken woman and didn't get to have sex with her.

This incident left me shaken and from then I abjured the company of these gentlemen.

However, that was not the end of my errant behaviour. I was quite restless and when bands came to play at our school I left with them as a groupie and a gofer. I did this on two occasions, once with the Leribe Queens, a Lesotho band with singing and dancing girls that played the kind of popular music known as *mbaqanga*, and on another occasion with a soul group from Johannesburg called the All Rounders. I had struck up a friendship with two of its blind singers, Babsy Mlangeni and Koloi Lebona, and travelled with them as they toured Lesotho. I would have gone back to South Africa with them had I not been a refugee.

And all that time my parents thought I was studying hard at school.

I HAVE THIS RECURRING dream: I am in an exam room sitting at my desk staring at a mathematics question paper and sweating like hell because I can't answer a single question. Everyone around me is writing away furiously. They hand in their papers to the invigilator and I am still sitting there. I am completely blank. Often I wake up in a sweat with figures and letters and signs and symbols floating before my eyes, and when I tell Gugu about the nightmare she laughs knowingly. She herself is haunted by the Ghost-of-Mathematics-Past; she gave up her medical studies in the first year because of the damned subject.

As for me, my high school days would have been happier if it were not for mathematics. Though I had one of the most respected teachers of the subject, Selometsi 'Maloro' Baholo, he failed to make any headway with me. He tried to drum into my head all the formulae of Algebra, Geometry, Trigonometry and a horrid subject called Additional Maths which was composed of nothing but Calculus, to no avail. I have no idea why I decided to take Additional Maths since, unlike the ordinary maths, it was not mandatory. But foolishly I did and suffered the consequences for the whole year. At the end of it all I had an F in everything to do with mathematics.

Another subject that gave me problems was Latin, a subject in which I had no business to be hopeless since my father had mastered it in no time when he was preparing for his law studies. Those days in South Africa Latin was a prerequisite for a law degree. I imagined that one day I would follow in my father's footsteps and become an attorney. I therefore needed Latin, and had to stick with it even though it frustrated me.

My first Latin master was Mr A S Mampa. We named him Scutum, Latin for 'shield'. He was a rotund fellow with a balding head. He was always jolly and full of jokes, most of which were a lighter shade of blue. He lived on campus in a four-roomed house with his two sons John and Sammy. The oldest son, Moss, was already at university when I got to Peka, but later his beautiful lyrical poetry brought us together. Even though I became close friends with Sammy and John and spent many hours in their bedroom listening to pop music on Lourenço Marques Radio, I never got to know what happened to their mother because they never spoke of her.

Scutum also taught English, both Literature and Language, and knew how to make his lessons enjoyable. He loved my essays and read them to the rest of the class. He was the first to prophesy that one day I would be a writer.

We all looked forward to his English classes. But, for me, he just couldn't bring Latin to life. The first thing I couldn't wrap my head around was the notion that of the three genders – male, female and neuter – *mensa* which means 'table' was female and not neuter. And then of course there were the silly declensions that we had to recite: *mensa* (nominative) table, *mensam* (accusative) table, *mensae* (genitive) of the table, *mensae* (dative) to/for the table, *mensa* (ablative) by/with/

from the table, *mensa* (vocative) O table! O table? Were the ancient Romans so daft as to address their tables? (Years later I was to catch myself addressing inanimate objects in my own writing in extravagant displays of pathetic fallacy.) And this was only the first declension. There were four more noun declensions that I had to memorise. And all of them presented me with illogical moments of their own.

Thankfully, during holidays I had someone in Mafeteng to help me, especially with translations of Latin sentences into English and vice versa. No, not my father. I wouldn't have dared ask him for help. On looking back now, perhaps he would have been pleased to give his assistance. But I was too terrified of him. In any case he was always busy with his files and law reports and clients. Perhaps I should have mustered the courage as I carried his bag when he walked to Hani's restaurant to hide from those clients who were bent on hounding him even at home, wanting his help for their relatives who were in jail and urgently needed bail.

Help came in the form of Bhut' Thembi, also known as Chris Hani, the guerrilla commander of *Umkhonto weSizwe*. The 'Bhuti' (in full) is from Afrikaans *boet* which means brother. In isiXhosa it is commonly used to address a young man who is older than you rather than the original isiXhosa word *mkhuluwa*.

Occasionally Bhut' Thembi visited his father at the restaurant, and if that coincided with my holiday in Mafeteng he would roll up his sleeves and get to work on my exercise book. He had studied Latin in the Eastern Cape to a much higher level than my junior secondary school grade, so he was able to translate with ease the simple sentences that gave me problems. At first he had told me, 'I am a bit rusty, Zani,' but when he saw my exercises he sailed through them. I tried very hard to follow what he was doing, but with my fuzzy understanding of declensions, I was up a creek. So he ended up doing all the work for me.

The second year of high school Latin got tougher with verb conjugations for all the tenses and all the silly exceptions to the rules. I now had a new teacher, Mr Matebesi, who was one of the three young Xhosa men from the Eastern Cape who taught at Peka High. The other two were Mr Mdutshane, who also taught Latin and History, and Mr Makiwane, who taught General Science, which included Physics, Chemistry and Biology – subjects I did not care about but had to do willy-nilly.

Mr Matebesi's approach was quite different from Scutum's easy-going jolly-good-fellow one. In class he never messed up his well-chiselled face with a smile. He was strict and took no excuses from any boy who had not done his homework. By this time I had mastered all the five declensions but, alas, conjugations still gave me problems. And here we were no longer translating simple sentences but long passages written by Julius Caesar himself. Hitherto I had not been aware of his authorship. I knew him only as the guy who was assassinated in William Shakespeare's play. But there he was, writing about Gallic Wars in his difficult Latin. And there I was, going through hell translating his penmanship into English. And this was only Book 1. By the time I reached the final year of high school, the Cambridge Overseas School Certificate, I would have translated five of his eight books and also some stuff from Virgil's *Aeneid*.

Next time I went to Mafeteng I had my *De Bello Gallico* by one Iuli Caesaris with me. A guerrilla leader was going to translate the damn thing for me at his father's restaurant. We would sit at one of the rickety tables covered with a plaid plastic table 'cloth' and he would render Caesar's warrior words into the Queen's English. Although the book had 52 chapters in all, it was a very slim book. Each chapter was nothing more than a paragraph. I didn't expect Bhut' Thembi to help me with the whole book. Just a few chapters. It would be enough to boost my grade.

Unfortunately, Bhut' Thembi was not there. It did happen like that sometimes because he actually lived in Maseru, although he paid regular visits to Mafeteng. I thought he would come as usual, but his father told me he had been away for almost a month and would not be back for many more. I knew immediately he had gone to fight his guerrilla wars against the Boers and I was left with no one to help me with Caesar's Gallic Wars. I stared at the first lines: *Gallia est omnis divisa in partes tres, quarum unam incolunt Belgae, aliam Aquitani,*

111

tertiam qui ipsorum lingua Celtae, nostra Galli appellantur. Hi omnes lingua, institutis, legibus inter se differunt. The words floated before my eyes, just as mathematical figures and letters and signs and symbols sometimes do in my recurring dream. I struggled on, and could barely make out that the great general and dictator was telling us how Gaul was divided into three parts inhabited by the Belgae, the Aquitani, and the Celts, all with different languages, laws and customs.

Back at Peka High it was test time. June half-yearly exams. I sat at my desk and waited anxiously as Mr Matebesi handed out the question papers. I was quite prepared this time. Not by memorising the declensions and conjugations, but by writing them on a piece of paper that I smuggled into the exam room in my sleeve. This was the famous *koantsanyane* that I had learnt from the older boys at the Smoking Spot. The word refers to a weapon of war of ancient Basotho warriors, but students appropriated it for the prevalent practice of confronting dreaded tests with cheat sheets.

'Why bother memorising mathematical formulae and Latin conjugations when you can just arm yourself with a *koantsanyane?*' a senior called Pilato asked.

I thought it was a great idea. My Latin mentor had gone to war; I was desperate.

Normally I could never complete a Latin exam. The invigilator would announce 'time up' while I would still be struggling halfway through translations. This time I was able to answer all the questions, but not before consulting my notes for each one of them. After about two hours I was one of the last students to hand in my paper. Mr Matebesi took the paper and then said, 'Come here.'

I approached him warily, but not too close. He grabbed my arm and reached for my notes where I had tucked them up my sleeve. He looked at them, shook his head and said, 'You get a zero for this paper.'

And that was all. He said nothing more. I walked out slowly; I thought I was going to pee in my pants. Or even defecate. I was sick for the whole of that day with diarrhoea. I reported to the health prefect and insisted that I needed to go to hospital.

In no time I was in the school kombi on my way to the Seventh Day

Adventist Hospital at Mapoteng, about twenty miles away. I vowed to myself that I wasn't going back to Peka High School. I would not be able to look Mr Matebesi in the eye.

I DON'T KNOW WHY the recurring dream is never about Latin but always about mathematics. After all, no one had any expectations from me in so far as mathematics was concerned. We were a family deeply rooted in the law and the arts. Law ran in our blood, from the days of our revered ancestor Mhlontlo the slayer of magistrate Hamilton Hope who, as King of the amaMpondomise, presided over disputes at his *Inkundla*, to my grandfather Charles who had his own *Inkundla* near the big rock in Goodwell, and then to my father who became an attorney after a stellar career as a teacher. Today, two of my three brothers are lawyers – Monwabisi is the chief magistrate in Kokstad in the Eastern Cape and Zwelakhe is an advocate in Mafeteng, Lesotho. Even Sonwabo, Monwabisi's twin brother, who went to America more than two decades ago and never returned home, read some law and politics. So, it was natural to see myself practising law one day. But here was Latin bent on scuppering my plans of following in my father's footsteps.

No doubt that present and future generations of lawyers in southern Africa are grateful that the mandatory Latin requirement no longer obtains.

After the cheat sheet fiasco I didn't have to worry about Latin or maths or any subject any more. My father took me to Dr Joel Molapo in Quthing to treat me for whatever was ailing me, which turned out to be nothing he could place his finger on, but was obviously not as serious as the typhoid that the hospital at Mapoteng had suspected. I convinced my father that I could only go back to high school the following year.

I had six months to kill, and then I would hopefully go to a different school where there would be no Mr Matebesi.

I spent most of that time with my mentor, Ntlabathi Mbuli, in Maseru. The PAC was renting a big yard with rows of connected single-storey, one-room dwellings from a sympathetic BCP-supporting businessman, Mr Thakalekoala. This was the camp where Poqo guerrillas who were in exile in Lesotho lived. Ntlabathi shared a room there with a group of Poqo men who had led the Pondoland Uprising in the Eastern Cape in November 1960 and had escaped to Lesotho after a country-wide manhunt by the Boer forces. I shared his bed.

This was where my drinking habit started. I was a man among hardened men of war, and it was incumbent upon me to behave like all hardened men of war. Like everyone there I was subject to the military discipline of the camp, which included morning drills, a jog to the soccer field near the Stadium Hotel, about a mile away, and a rough game of rugby on the soccer field. This was my least favourite part; I would have been more at home if we played soccer. Back in Sterkspruit I used to be a star goalkeeper for our township soccer team and I still have scars on my knees to show for it. But, of course, the Poqo people were mostly from the deeper Eastern Cape and in that part of South Africa the predominant sport among black people was rugby, not soccer. The fact that I was the youngest and was the worst rugby player that ever walked on to a field saved me. None of the men wanted me in their team so I stood on the sidelines and chased the ball when it went off the field. And then later, when thirty or so swarthy and smelly men jogged back to the camp, I was in the middle of the group.

The evenings were pretty much free. Ntlabathi and I spent most of them in the shebeens of Maseru drinking brandy. As far as my father was concerned, I was in Maseru to attend art classes at the British Council so he gave me some money for the fees that the white art instructor lady charged and for food. He did not know that I only went to art class once and was soon bored by the still lifes we had to draw. I used the money for brandy and cigarettes. When the money ran out I bought the brandy on credit. My partner in crime had long-standing credit of his own in a number of shebeens at the Location, at Sea Point and at Moshoeshoe II, three of the Maseru townships where we used to drink.

Shebeens were the sites of some of the most heated debates. Here we met some of the leading lights of Maseru, ranging from teachers to lawyers to senior civil servants to nondescript gangsters. Most of the patrons in every shebeen were supporters of the BCP, which had narrowly lost the elections to Chief Leabua Jonathan's Basotho National Party. There was bitterness all round because Ntsu Mokhehle who had fought for freedom over the decades would not have the honour of becoming Lesotho's first prime minister. That honour was denied even Leabua himself because he lost in his constituency of Kolonyama, his home village. The BNP deputy leader, Chief Sekhonyana Maseribane, became the first prime minister of Lesotho. Leabua only took over as prime minister two months later after Mokone Mothepu resigned his safe BNP seat at his Mpharane constituency, making room for Leabua to win it back in a by-election. I had campaigned for the BCP in that by-election, which was in the Mohale's Hoek district.

There was a lot of anger among the elite of Lesotho because the peasants in the villages determined the future of the country by voting for an uneducated chief, and the BCP, a party of the towns and the more enlightened, took only second place with twenty-five parliamentary seats. The party of the country bumpkins ran to the winning post with thirty-one out of the contested sixty. Even if they went into alliance with the royalist Marematlou Freedom Party, which won the remaining four seats, they would not be in a position to form a government. Indeed, the Queen of England through her High Commissioner had called upon the BNP to form a government.

This anger played itself out in the shebeens we frequented. We cursed the apartheid government of South Africa for supporting Leabua Jonathan with maize that he distributed to the villages, as well as South African Afrikaner business tycoon Anton Rupert for pumping money into the BNP campaign. We consoled ourselves that Leabua was too stupid to run a country; soon his government would fall and the more intelligent and learned leader, Ntsu Mokhehle, would take over. As we sipped tots of brandy we laid bets on how long the government would last. I was of the opinion that it would not last longer than six months.

'Who would allow a nincompoop like Leabua in the forums of the world?' I asked. 'Do you think a man like him can be at home in the company of Kwame Nkrumah and Abdel Nasser?'

The shebeen denizens all laughed and nodded in agreement; there was no way these great Pan Africanists whose names I had invoked would be seen dead with a lackey of the Boers like Leabua. I felt great that I was commanding the debate with these professional people when I was nothing but a seventeen-year-old high school dropout. It was never much of a debate, really, because everyone present was a BCP supporter. It was more like venting out after the defeat at the polls. If there was any disagreement at all it would be on the methods that should be used to overthrow the upstart from the seat he had usurped from *Moetapele*, Ntsu Mokhehle.

Ntlabathi and I always returned to the camp in the small hours of the morning in a sodden stupor. We staggered along the streets of Maseru singing Nana Mouskouri or Frank Sinatra or Edith Piaf at the top of our voices. These were Ntlabathi's favourite singers, in addition to Nat King Cole and Sammy Davis Junior. It was not unusual for us to stagger along the streets of Sea Point grating the midnight silence with our poor man's imitation of Dean Martin singing 'Volare'.

Mongrels howled and yelped and growled and barked at our contorted Italian and slurred voices. We paid no attention to them. We were somewhere in Hollywood in the hell-raising company of the Rat Pack. Yes, the very Rat Pack whose barroom brawls and trysts with glamour girls Ntlabathi narrated with relish when he was not talking revolution.

We fell silent as soon as we entered the camp at Thakalekoala's sprawling property. We tittered as we tripped on logs scattered on the ground. We tiptoed into the room so as not to wake up the sleeping soldiers.

On one such occasion I could not even take off my clothes by myself. I was tottering all over the place, and almost fell on the men who were sleeping on mattresses on the floor. Ntlabathi asked one of the men who had raised his head warily to help me undress and prepare my bedding.

'Help him, son of Africa, he is a stranger,' said Ntlabathi as he fumbled with his moccasins.

'How can I be a stranger in Africa?' I asked.

The soldiers cheered. Those who were asleep opened their eyes and were updated by those who had heard my question.

'What did he say?' asked one sleepyhead.

'He said, "how can I be a stranger in Africa?"' answered another. And then they all broke out into fresh laughter.

'He is a true Pan Africanist,' one said. 'An African can never be a stranger anywhere on the African continent.'

Just that question was enough to gain me the men's respect. They were eager to take me under their wing. This made me feel like a real soldier of freedom, although I had some serious doubts about the nature of the war they were fighting.

The doubts had started the previous year, before PK – that's what we lovingly called Potlako Leballo, the secretary general and acting president of the PAC, because his other name was Kitchener – was kicked out of the country by the British authorities under the pressure of the South African government.

He had once sent Ntlabathi to call me to his office at Bonhomme House. I remember him sitting behind his desk puffing on his pipe, which was the trademark of all true African revolutionaries those days. Robert Mangaliso Sobukwe, the jailed president of the PAC, smoked one too. As did a number of the leaders of the ANC. As smoke rings ascended above his head he had reminded me of the oath that I took when I joined the PAC in the presence of witnesses, particularly of John Pokela, who was my father's friend and protégé from the same village of Lower Telle, and of Ntlabathi.

'Azania wants your service in the true spirit of our motto: *Service, Suffering, Sacrifice*,' he had said.

Pride had swelled in my chest. Azania needed me!

Perhaps he wanted me to go and interpret for Ntsu Mokhehle again among the stubborn Bathepu people in the southern district of Quthing. Of course Quthing was not Azania, the PAC name for South Africa. But anything to help Ntsu Mokhehle and his BCP win the elections was a step forward towards the liberation of South Africa. For one thing, if the BCP won, Lesotho would be a base for our Poqo forces to launch guerrilla attacks into South Africa. Yes, most likely PK wanted to send me to the village of Mjanyana in the Quthing district to work with the Mokhehle people in the enemy territory of the Bathepu. I was looking forward to joining my old friends, especially Blaizer who continued to be Mokhehle's faithful driver. This time I was going to drink those wonderful guys under the table; the last time I was with them I was not yet an imbiber of the 'waters of immortality' – as my Poqo comrades called brandy, quoting from a famous isiXhosa novel, *Umzali Wolahleko* by Guybon Sinxo.

But Leballo had soon shattered my daydream of debauchery among the red-ochre Bathepu maidens in the gullied valleys of Mjanyane when he said, 'I want to send you to the Free State.'

I had not been to South Africa since I crossed the Telle River and was whisked into exile by Ntlabathi. Why would the leader want me to go back there?

'You are going there to advance our cause,' he had answered the question I had only asked in my head. 'I want you to get work as a labourer on one of the farms. Many Basotho boys your age cross the border illegally to work as casual labourers especially at harvest time. I want you to join those workers. There'll be others from our forces, but you'll only know them later.'

I remember being gripped by sudden panic as he outlined his cockamamie scheme: he was recruiting me to join his secret force that would kidnap Boer children from the Free State farms to the mountains of Lesotho where he would hold them as hostages for the liberation of South Africa.

I had known immediately that I would not be up to the task. I certainly would not have the heart to kidnap children. But they were enemy children, I had argued with myself as I walked out of Bonhomme House to sunny Kingsway with throngs going about their business. Those kids were going to grow up to be big Boers with hairy arms and FN rifles; they would be kicking down doors of township houses and arresting my people for the crime of being in an urban area without the appropriate papers that permitted them to be there. They would be shooting down peaceful demonstrators as they did in Sharpeville and Langa townships only four years before, on March 21, 1960. At least sixty-nine people were killed in Sharpeville and two in Langa. Our leader Sobukwe was languishing in Robben Island Maximum Security

Prison for leading those demonstrations, so I was still seething inside against the Boers for that and for all the injustices they had committed against my people over the decades. Hell, I was in exile, having left a wonderful life and the most beautiful girl who ever walked this earth in Sterkspruit because of the Boers, while they were having a great time with their children in the South Africa they were bent on denying me. So, why did I have to feel so bad about kidnapping a few Boer children for the liberation of the suffering millions?

I had concluded that perhaps I was a weakling and a sissy.

The more I thought of PK's assignment the more doubt and fear built up in my chest. I was the little twerp who had bungled a simple assassination back in Mohale's Hoek. Where on earth would I find the guts to kidnap innocent kids? Well, yes, they were going to be guilty sooner or later, armed to the teeth and kicking our collective black ass, but at that point in their lives they were innocent. You didn't punish people for a crime you thought they were going to commit in the future. Some of them might even turn out like Patrick Duncan, the white man who had recently joined the PAC, or any of the white people who were actively participating in our liberation struggle.

PK was expelled from Lesotho – which was rather strange to me because he was born there – before he could carry out his scheme, and I breathed a sigh of relief. After that I had doubts about the strategies of the Poqo forces in Lesotho, though I strongly believed in the armed struggle, as did my father as far back as the late 1940s when everyone else was still talking of passive resistance. But it was obvious that I didn't have the stomach to carry it out myself. I would fight in other ways, using my pen. And my paint brushes.

One morning, after a particularly hectic night in the shebeens of Maseru, I was walking down Kingsway to Kingsway Café to buy some fish and chips and fat cakes when I heard a shrill voice call me: 'Hey, *wena* Mda!'

A short fat woman was waddling towards me. I knew exactly what she wanted. My first instinct was to run away. But there were too many people in the street. Maybe some of them knew me. She was going to yell and holler and embarrass me for the entire world to see and laugh. Some might even chase me down the street thinking I was a thief.

'When are you going to pay for that nip of Martell that you owe me?' Martell was the brand name of our favourite brandy.

'Calm down, *Mmamosadi*,' I said with a broad smile. 'I will pay you at the end of the month.' *Mmamosadi* was the name by which denizens of shebeens called every shebeen queen. It translates as 'mother-in-law'.

'Do you think I am stupid?' asked the shebeen queen at the top of her voice. 'You have been owing me for more than two months now.'

Passers-by are always starving for a spectacle. They stood and watched. She grabbed my arm. 'I am taking your watch,' she said. 'You'll get it back when you have paid for my nip.'

It was a Rotary watch that I had got as a present from my father. Everyone who had seen it envied me for it because it was as flat as a twenty-five cent piece. I let her take it without any resistance. I didn't want to give the gawkers more entertainment than they deserved. I was going to retrieve my watch somehow.

I forgot all about fish and chips and rushed back to the camp.

Ntlabathi was sitting next to a mountain of coal in front of one of the rows of houses that accommodated the Poqo freedom fighters, playing draughts with two other men. Some of the Poqo fighters were wood and coal merchants; that's how they earned some money to send home to their families in the Eastern Cape. As soon as he saw me he left the game and came to meet me.

'Hey, where is the fish and chips?' he asked when he realised that my hands were not carrying a greasy paper bag.

'The shebeen queen took my watch,' I said. 'And my father's going to kill me if he finds out.'

'AP would never kill anyone,' he said laughing. 'I bet he has never even meted out corporal punishment to you.'

'Of course, he is not a beater but a talker,' I said. 'But that's not the point.'

He borrowed some money from one of the coal merchants and covertly gave it to me. I immediately went to the shebeen and paid the woman for her damned nip. But she said I should come the next day for the watch because her boyfriend had borrowed it.

The next day I went back to the shebeen. Once again I didn't get my watch back. The shebeen queen gave me another flimsy excuse, something about misplacing it somewhere in the house and she was too busy serving her customers to look for it. I just stood there powerlessly.

'Get out of my house,' she yelled. 'Unless you have money to buy another nip,' she added with a smile.

The men sitting at the table with bottles of Black Label Lager laughed.

As I scampered out of the house and the yard littered with plastic bags, dirty papers and beer cans I knew that I was never going to see my watch again. I had lost an expensive Rotary watch, a gift from my father, for a nip of cheap brandy.

Just then it dawned on me that I was not cut out for the hard-living and hard-drinking life of a revolutionary. I needed to get back to school, get educated and become a lawyer like my father.

THE RUDENESS OF LESOTHO officials to visitors is legendary. It is not just because of one or two isolated incidents that I have decided only an emergency or some really important occasion that has to do with my family will bring me back here after my mother has gone to join the ancestors. But today takes the proverbial cake. We are crossing the Maseru border post back to South Africa in my son's Nissan four-wheel-drive twin-cab truck. My son Neo stops in the parking lot and the three of us – we are with Gugu – walk into the building to have our passports endorsed. After paying the toll fee, completing the immigration and customs forms and having our passports stamped, Gugu and I wait outside near the door while Neo goes to get the truck from the parking lot. There are two young men in police camouflage uniforms armed with AK47s sitting on chairs a short distance away. Gugu and I are holding hands as we normally do when we are together. I see that the police guys are looking at us curiously but I pay no particular attention to them. We just banter as usual. She says something funny and we laugh while I embrace her. One of the policemen stands up and says, 'Hey, we don't do that here.'

We are both taken aback.

'Do what?' I ask.

'Hold women like that in public,' he says. 'We don't do that sort of thing in this country.'

'Says who?' I ask.

'Are you arguing with me?' he asks moving towards me threateningly.

I am getting really angry now. 'I want you to tell me what law says it is illegal for a man to hold his wife in Lesotho.'

At this time Neo arrives with the truck.

'Let's go, Dad,' he says.

'No, I am not going,' I shout. 'I want this man to arrest me for giving my wife a hug.'

I then grab Gugu and plant a kiss on her lips.

'There, now I have committed an even worse crime. Did you see that, sir? I kissed her.'

I don't think she welcomes the kiss. She is afraid for my life and would rather I jumped into the truck and we left. I can sense that Neo is of the same opinion. He is a brawny iron-pumping man in his late thirties and he visits Lesotho regularly enough to know that you don't argue with an armed Lesotho policeman. They once locked him up in prison for a few days for some minor traffic violation.

'Please, let's go, Dad,' he pleads again.

But at this point I am a raging lunatic. Even as I demand to be arrested and taken to jail forthwith I am aware I am being stupid. What if the cop obliges? He will load us into the police van and take us to the charge office where he will have to manufacture some charge because this one of hugging or even kissing my wife won't fly with his superiors. I will finally prevail but only after our whole day has been wasted. So, why don't I just shut up, get into the truck and go? But there is no stopping myself at this point. My people are already in the vehicle and I can see the impatience on their faces. And the fear. Only a fool argues with an AK47. But I demand that they give me a cellphone so I can call my lawyer. It is a bluff, of course; I have no lawyer in Lesotho. Well, my brother is one of the top advocates in the country, but I wouldn't call him for anything. To put it mildly, we are not the best of friends.

The policeman just stands there looking foolish. His partner breaks out laughing. He saves his partner's face by ordering me to go because we are blocking the road. *'Tsamaea, ntate, o koetse tsela mona.'* Obviously he has not come across such a round-the-bend South African traveller before and he would like to see me disappear immediately, especially because I am embarrassing him. He saw our truck's South African number plates and thought we were just tourists whose ignorance of the laws and customs of Lesotho he was going to exploit, only to find that I am making a fool of him. Well, hard luck for him; I grew up here.

Finally, I get into the truck and we drive away. I fume for quite some time while Gugu keeps on saying 'Sorry' as if she was responsible for the conduct of Lesotho cops. I keep on muttering to myself: 'Motherfuckers.' Until Elvin Jones shakes me out of the world of arrogant policemen into another realm with a gong followed by cymbal washes. It is a Radio Metro jazz programme. Jimmy Garrison soon joins with his four-note double bass, with McCoy Tyner on the piano. When John Coltrane comes in with his tenor sax solo I am transported to an age of innocence . . . well, a world of less guilt . . . forty-three years ago. I chant along with Coltrane: *A Love Supreme.*

I am back at Peka High School.

I WAS INTRODUCED TO John Coltrane by Khomo Mohapeloa, who was two classes ahead of me. His parents were educationists and lived in the exclusive suburb of Maseru West, where their house was famed as one of the most beautiful in the city. I had long admired his brother, Kingston Mohapeloa, the artist who also drew cartoons for *Lux Vestra.* I hoped one day I would follow in his footsteps and draw the funnies for the school magazine. Both brothers were tall and handsome with very smooth faces. They were well-groomed and clean-cut. They very much reminded me of Willie Mafoso from my Mohale's Hoek days in the way they paid particular attention to sartorial elegance.

Khomo Mohapeloa played the clarinet in a big band in Maseru, the Studio Orchestra, led by the seasoned bandleader Lesiba Mamashela.

The band played mostly from Glenn Miller's sheet music. At high school he joined Maestro Michael Mosoeu Moerane's orchestra which was composed only of string and woodwind instruments: violins, violas, cellos, clarinets, oboes, and flutes, owned by the maestro himself rather than by the school. It was known as the Peka High School Orchestra, though. In no time he became the bandleader because he was a much more sophisticated musician than all of us put together.

The maestro was one of the leading composers of choral music in southern Africa whose modern classics such as *Sylvia* and *Tlong Rothothang* are sung by choirs in the region even today. Unlike other famous composers of his generation, such as J P Mohapeloa, he had a degree in music and his compositions were not confined to choral music but included orchestral music as well. He is reputed to be the first African to compose a symphony. Although I never heard this particular composition, I heard that it was in four movements.

I was a member of the Peka High School Orchestra too and played the flute. Although the maestro taught us the rudiments of staff notation, it was really Khomo Mohapeloa who taught me the more complicated major and minor scales. The orchestra played hymns on Sundays at the Church of Lesotho services, the Protestant denomination formerly known as the Paris Evangelical Missionary Society, about three miles from the school. But my best moments were when we played at school occasions such pieces as Boccherini's Baroque 'Minuet Célèbre' and Jacques Offenbach's 'Barcarolle' from 'Tales of Hoffman'. The latter was my particular favourite because my flute had a dominant role throughout the piece, albeit a repetitive one.

We practised thrice a week outside the maestro's house or in the school hall and I looked forward to those moments. When the maestro was not there the woodwind guys played jazz instead of sticking to classical music. Khomo Mohapeloa would tell us all about John Coltrane and Dizzy Gillespie and Charlie Parker, also known as the Bird, and Stanley Turrentine and his wife, Shirley Scott, and a host of other jazz cats in all the different idioms. He would then make simpler arrangements of some of the numbers for us to play, and sometimes we would break into crazy jam sessions of bebop.

Here we also dabbled in our own compositions. One composition that still lives in my mind was 'Matebesi's Farewell Blues' by the same Khomo Mohapeloa. Yes, he had written a jazz number for the Latin teacher who was the reason for my deserting school for a number of months after I cheated in an exam. He was leaving Peka High School to study law in South Africa and he had been so popular with the boys that the band was going to play this composition at his farewell concert. And I was going to be part of that band even though I still had a grudge against him. I had returned to Peka High School to find him still there. It was as if the incident had never happened because he never mentioned it. It was a silly grudge anyway, I told myself as I rehearsed with the band, because it was not his fault that I had been so foolish as to be caught with a *koantsanyane*.

Thanks to *Down Beat* magazine we became connoisseurs of jazz and started accumulating our own collections of LPs which we ordered from Kohinoor in Johannesburg. I had albums of Duke Ellington, Mackay Davashe, Count Basie, Dollar Brand, Chris McGregor and the Blue Notes, Johnny Hodges, Thelonious Monk, Early Mabusa, Sonny Stitt, Jimmy Smith, Milt Jackson, Sonny Rollins and Miles Davis. I identified mostly with Roland Kirk because he played the flute so well, in addition to the tenor sax and many other instruments. Later we were to discover Herbie Mann and 'Memphis Underground' became our anthem.

Our tastes were quite catholic though. We also loved the soul music of the time; Booker T and the MGs, Wilson Pickett, Otis Redding and of course Aretha Franklin. And when I visited Scutum's sons John and Sammy at their four-roomed home on campus just a few yards from the Square where we had our dormitories, we listened to the blues of Champion Jack Dupree and to the pop of Tommy Jones and the Shondells.

But of all the different kinds of music we listened and sang to, Coltrane's 'Love Supreme' was sacred. To this day it has a powerful effect on me. I don't go out of my way to listen to it. I don't even own it. But on those very rare occasions when I hear it played I get goosebumps and am attacked by pangs of nostalgia.

I was grateful to have returned to Peka High despite the shame that had made me consider going to a different school. My father would have none of that nonsense, especially because I could not give any good reason why I wanted to change schools. Anywhere else in Lesotho I would not have had the opportunity to immerse myself so much in the world of jazz and classical music – not only as a consumer but as a creator and interpreter through my flute.

One day the maestro heard me play Dvorak's 'Humoresque 7' and he was amazed that I had mastered it on my own even though it was not part of our repertoire.

'We've got to play this together some time,' he said. 'I'll accompany you on the piano.'

I thought he was just talking. But sure enough, months later he called me to his studio in his big stone house and we started rehearsing for the end-of-year concert. He invited Shadrack Mapetla to join us with his clarinet. He had recently taken over as bandleader after Khomo Mohapeloa completed high school and went to the University of Botswana, Lesotho and Swaziland where we heard to our consternation that he had abandoned music for mathematics.

My performance of 'Humoresque' with Shadrack Mapetla and Maestro M M Moerane accompanying my flute haunts me to this day. It was my first public performance and my last – apart from playing the hymns in church. I brought the house down with an instrument that the musically challenged boys never thought highly of because all they had ever heard from it were the trills as it accompanied the 'Barcarolle'. I can still hear the applause and the whistling from a standing ovation.

Years later, when I was teaching at a Roman Catholic high school in Maseru, Maestro M M Moerane came to see me. He talked fondly of the performance and wanted us to play together again, more than just the Dvorak. I was excited about the prospect, though I thought I was a bit rusty. I looked forward to it. As soon as he left I fetched my flute which had been lying idle in some cupboard for years and started playing again. I played the *kwela* music that I used to play on a pennywhistle on the verandas of the stores in Dobsonville when I was a little boy. I also played Dvorak's 'Humoresque'. Over and over again. I could already hear the maestro's piano in the background. Tinkling sounds like drops of rain. I could already see a mesmerised audience, and then the kind of standing ovation that we received at Peka High.

But only a few weeks later I heard that the maestro was dead. I was devastated. It was the death of music. I decided that since I couldn't play with him I would never play in public again.

Today I play only for myself and members of my family.

DECEMBER HOLIDAYS WERE THE best of times and the worst of times, a period of wisdom and of foolishness all rolled up in one hot season, to hijack the opening lines of a Charles Dickens novel the seniors were reading.

It was the worst of times because I was at home in Mafeteng under the strict regime of my father. Though my siblings and I didn't do any chores except water the garden because we always had maids – euphemistically referred to as helpers or workers – we had to help my father find his files in his office for the following weeks' cases. I was always irked by the fact that his filing system was non-existent. His files did not have reference numbers; they were all piled on the floor, each folder fastened with twine. We had to go through stacks of these files looking for specific cases on the list. Then we had to do the same with volumes of *The South African Law Reports* which were also stacked haphazardly on the bookshelves, the table and the floor. Lesotho courts still got most of their precedent from cases decided in South African courts; that's why Lesotho's system was based on Roman Dutch Law even though the country was a former British colony.

I wondered how my father knew which of the volumes to read to get precedent for the specific cases he was preparing for. I never understood why he never had these books bound in leather according to number and volume as other lawyers did in Maseru.

Sometimes we performed this task in the evening, one of us holding a paraffin lamp or a candle while others knelt on the floor reading the clients' names on the folders.

But these worst of times were ameliorated by the fact that we were having a wonderful time as a family, especially when my father was in court, at his office or travelling the country defending stock thieves, murderers and sundry criminals. I was able to spend a lot of time with my mother, the twins Sonwabo and Monwabisi – who were now called Thabo and Thabiso by everybody since the names that I had given them had stuck while mine, Motlalepula, had long fallen into disuse – my sister Thami and the youngest of my brothers, Zwelakhe. The twins had just completed primary school and were going to join me at Peka High School the following year. So, I took pride in playing older brother and giving them back copies of *Lux Vestra* so that they could acquaint themselves with the ways of boarding school.

I never really became close friends with my siblings and we rarely talked about girlfriends and the good life out there in the shebeens. I was not much into girlfriends anyway, and I continued to hanker after Keneiloe. With the passing of the months and the years she had acquired a mythical stature in my imagination, a goddess akin to those of the Greeks and the Romans. I did have a local girlfriend though – Rhoda Mafikeng, the daughter of the trade unionist Elizabeth Mafikeng who owned a café and restaurant in partnership with Chris Hani's father.

Rhoda was very beautiful and the parents on both sides seemed to approve of our relationship. Our mothers could already see in some distant future a marriage between our PAC and ANC families. But I neglected Rhoda and was not an attentive boyfriend because those days I would rather spend my time in the shebeens drinking home-brewed pineapple beer with my friends Peter Masotsa and Litsebe Leballo. So, after an exchange of love letters – even though we lived in the same town – and after a lot of patience from her our relationship fizzled out.

I never got to know Peter's age but he looked much older than us, although he was so scrawny you'd think the wind would blow him away. And he walked as if he was in a constant battle with a gale force wind. His face had razor bumps so he shaved perhaps every day, whereas Litsebe and I had not yet grown a single whisker. Peter was more mature in other ways as well. Whereas both Litsebe and I were still students at junior high schools, he had completed his secondary school education years before and was working full-time as a clerk for the priest at St Gerard Catholic Church. He also ran a pen pal club. He advertised in the classified section of South African tabloids and people sent him money to join the club and be introduced to fellow club members from different parts of southern Africa. Every day he received a stack of two rand postal orders that he cashed at the post office. So we always had a lot of money to buy beer and magazines with half-naked girls in them. When we were not drinking we spent a lot of time reading *Scope*, *Drum* and other magazines of that ilk in the room he rented in a big stone house opposite the Catholic Mission where he worked.

Litsebe, on the other hand, was about my age. Maybe a year older. His father, *Ntate* Ngope Leballo, was a staunch supporter of Chief Leabua Jonathan's BNP and never let anyone forget that his own brother Potlako Leballo, the leader of the PAC, was a disgrace to the Leballo clan. 'When I cross the border to South Africa I get interrogated by the Boers, thanks to Potlako,' he would say. Despite his hostile attitude towards the PAC he was my father's trusted sidekick, a testimony to my father's open-mindedness and tolerance of all those who held different views.

Indeed, colourful characters from all political persuasions – both on the left and the right of the PAC – visited my father at home. Comrade John Motloheloa, the founding secretary general of the Communist Party of Lesotho, would preach his gospel according to Karl Marx and Vladimir Lenin from the doorstep of my home. Passers-by would gather in front of our house to heckle him and provoke him with questions about God. He was a vehement atheist and would shout back: 'There is no God, you fools. Religion is the opium of the people.' People always laughed at this; it was obvious that they treated anyone who denied the existence of God as a joke. It was thanks to him that the only thing that the people of Mafeteng knew about Communism was that it was the wayward belief that God does not exist.

When John Motloheloa was encountering problems in his work as the leader of the Communist Party he confided in my father, even though my father was known to utter hostile statements against Communists. I remember one morning when Motloheloa came to my house fuming that Joe Matthews, the Communist lawyer in Maseru whose main claim to fame was that he was the son of the revered Professor Z K Matthews, had betrayed him. Apparently Joe Matthews had been instrumental in either the establishment or the revival of the Communist Party of Lesotho by providing the money, since he was a conduit of funds from Moscow. But all of a sudden Matthews had turned against his party and was now supporting the Marematlou Freedom Party, whose ideology had nothing to do with scientific socialism. It was in fact a Royalist party supported by the King himself and by most of those chiefs who were not already in Chief Leabua Jonathan's BNP camp. Motloheloa blamed the African National Congress for this turncoat behaviour. They were opportunists who hoped to strengthen their weak presence in the country by throwing in their lot with the MFP because the stronger BCP was already in alliance with the PAC, and the BNP with the apartheid government of South Africa.

My father always gave Motloheloa's rant a sympathetic ear. Often he offered his perspective of the situation for he was known for his insightful political analysis.

But I digress. I was telling you about my high jinks with Peter Masotsa and Litsebe Leballo. I was eighteen so my father let me come and go as I pleased at any hour of the day or night, as long as I reported to him or my mother before I left, and as long as I had performed the only chores that we had, looking for his files and watering the garden. So much for his famous strictness. I am sure he didn't expect that I had gone drinking when officially I was supposed to be discussing creative writing with old man Sebolai Matlosa, the Sesotho novelist who was our neighbour and from whose butchery we bought our meat. His novel *Mopheme*, about scallywags, scoundrels and rogues, was at that time being serialised as a radio play on Radio Bantu and so having conferences with him either at his place of business or at his home across the street made sense. He was a nice, accommodating man though he didn't look anything like I imagined a writer would look.

Usually I only went to Matlosa's place to say hello so that if anyone asked him if he had seen me that day he would say yes, and proceeded to Peter Masotsa's place.

Our bedroom – the four Mda boys' – had a separate entrance that opened to the green stoep of the green-roofed stone house that my father was renting from the Thatho family. I could stagger home in the early hours of the morning without my parents being any the wiser that I had been away all that time. They never caught me drunk.

My father trusted me so much that he did not even believe a report from a certain Rabonne to the effect that one day he found me in the company of thieves who had stolen his meat from a boiling pot. Yet it was true. I was in cahoots with the thief, also known as Litsebe Leballo. You see, during our drinking sprees we often got hungry and bought smiley from the shebeen queens. Smiley was a term of endearment for a boiled head of a sheep which was a delicacy for connoisseurs of home-brewed beer like us.

On this particular occasion we visited Rabonne's shebeen as part of our shebeen crawling expedition. I knew him very well because, like Litsebe's father, he was one of my father's flunkies, some kind of a gofer who was always there for him whenever he needed assistance with something. We found him and a few men who were wearing traditional Basotho blankets in all their colourful splendour playing dice. They didn't pay any attention to us as Peter Masotsa bought a billycan of pineapple beer and took a few gulps before passing it to me. I guzzled it. It was very good as usual. Rabonne's wife had a beautiful hand that knew how to brew, as the Basotho would say. I passed the can to Litsebe. But he was not there. I didn't think much of it; he might have gone to blind the lizard, a Sesotho idiom for taking a leak. So I passed the can to Peter, who passed it to another man sitting on the opposite bench. People share in a Lesotho home-brew establishment. After a while Litsebe appeared at the door.

'Let's go, guys,' he said.

'What's the rush?' I asked. 'Don't you like Rabonne's pineapple?'

'Come on, let's go,' he said. He was already leading the way down Rabonne's many steps.

We went to Litsebe's home, which was only a few houses away. As we sat down on the benches in the kitchen he took out a steaming smiley from under his jacket. He had stolen it from a pot as it was cooking. It had the smell of undercooked meat, but in our drunkenness it was good enough to eat. All we needed was to season it with a lot of salt and we greedily went for the ears and the tongue and the fat that cushioned the eyes. We were not bothered by the taste of rawness. We congratulated Litsebe for his resourcefulness as we masticated the rubbery flesh until our jaws were sore.

We were planning our next move, for the night was still too young to halt our shebeen crawling, when Rabonne burst into the house without even knocking. We had only managed to eat half the head, and the rest was on the table in front of us, jaw bones and all. He was wielding a whip and he looked at the evidence of our crime, shook his head sorrowfully and went straight for Litsebe. He didn't bother with me or with Peter. He lashed out blindly at Litsebe. 'You bloody thief,' he yelled. 'I am going to kill you.'

Litsebe tried to find refuge between the cupboard and the Welcome Dover stove, but Rabonne's sjambok reached him there. He was bawling and asking for forgiveness. We thought it wise to take cover even though Rabonne didn't seem to be interested in us. Litsebe finally found his way to the door and ran out screaming. Rabonne ran after him. But we knew he was never going to catch him.

Some days later Rabonne told my father about the incident. I told my father that I found Litsebe eating the meat when I visited him; I didn't know he had stolen it. He believed me.

The next time I met with Litsebe and Peter we laughed about the matter, even though Litsebe's weals had not yet healed, not even on his face. Our exploits in the shebeens of Mafeteng continued unabated.

We were young and beautiful and shebeen queens loved us. One shebeen queen who was known to have a penchant for young boys was 'Matefo. She was in her mid-forties – about my mother's age at the time – and was petite. She had a *phuza* face – a face ravaged by alcohol. Her method of seduction was a simple one; she fed young boys with a lot of beer then took them to her den where she treated them to her body.

I once tried to have my way with her. I found her in one of our regular shebeens and we shared a bench and I shared my pineapple beer with her. In no time we were fondling each other as the can of beer passed from her lips to mine. The denizens smiled knowingly; I was going to be her victim that night. But as the minutes ticked by I began to have second thoughts.

At about midnight I told her I had to go home otherwise I would be in trouble with my father. I thought that would send a clear signal that I had no plans of spending the night at her den. She offered to walk with me anyway, since we were going the same direction. As we staggered along the footpath she tried to convince me to sleep at her place instead of going home.

'What's the worst thing that your father can do?' she asked. 'You're a big boy now; he's not going to beat you up.'

'You don't know my father; he's going to kill me.'

'Rubbish, everyone knows that *Ntate* Mda is a very nice man.'

It was true. Everyone in Mafeteng knew my father as a compassionate and generous man. But I kept on walking.

'You don't have to spend the night,' pleaded 'Matefo. 'Just one hour, then you'll go home.'

Still, I was going to have none of that. I had to go home. But 'Matefo did not give up.

'Okay, we can do it here on the side of the road,' she said.

It didn't seem like a bad idea; there would be no passers-by at that time except for the drunks who had seen it all and wouldn't give us a second glance. So, we did it. Not quite. I tried to do it but ejaculated immediately after penetration. And then of course I couldn't go on.

She lay there on the ground as I stood and pulled up my pants. I staggered away from her and she yelled after me, 'You messed me up for nothing, *ntja tooe.*'

I could understand her anger; I didn't mind that she called me 'you dog'. I only felt bad that my very first sexual experience – if you don't count the incident with Nontonje at KwaGcina when I was only six years old – was a damp squib. There were no drum rolls, no flares, no fireworks, no flourishes. Nothing.

I blamed my penis for the fiasco; perhaps if I was circumcised it would help. No, not in the isiXhosa traditional manner where boys went to the initiation school on the mountains and came back as men. I went to Morija Hospital, about forty kilometres north of Mafeteng, where a beautiful young nurse shaved my pubis and a white doctor surrounded by more beautiful nurses cut my foreskin in a brightly lit theatre while I was under local anaesthesia. The next day, after the doctor had checked that the stitches were fine, I was discharged from hospital.

My father made such a big fuss of my circumcision, as if it had been the real McCoy traditional ritual, and invited some relatives from Herschel who sat on my mother's Bradlows sofas and told me of the responsibilities of manhood while they chewed meat noisily and drank Castle Lager. I knew this was a charade on their part, just to please my father; according to their customs and traditions I was nothing but a coward to have gone to the hospital for circumcision instead of roughing it up on the mountain where my foreskin would be mutilated with a blunt instrument. But I didn't give a damn because my life was not with the amaXhosa who still valued such customs that in my view no longer had a place in the modern world, but with the Basotho whose educated classes had long stopped the practice. In Lesotho only the illiterates in the rural areas continued with it. With the amaXhosa, on the other hand, right up to this day, most people – even the educated ones with PhDs and professional degrees – still hold the practice dear and send their children to the mountain for circumcision and initiation into manhood.

As soon as the greybeards had returned to Herschel I was back in the shebeens with my friends Litsebe Leballo and Peter Masotsa. At Mamolibeli's shebeen I boasted about my newly circumcised penis to the envy of the habitués. I was not aware that Mamolibeli, an old lady in her fifties but famous in the town for her boy toy lovers, had designs on me. Just when we were leaving she called me to her room and suggested that I spend the night. I told her about my stitched wound which was still far from healed.

'I know,' she said. 'I heard you boast about it. We won't do anything naughty. You'll just hold me and then we'll fall asleep in each other's arms.'

I thought this was quite unscrupulous of her because my mother counted her as one of her friends. I didn't tell her that, though. I wouldn't want her think I was some kind of a mama's boy. Instead I told her that a situation like that was still bound to cause me a lot of pain. What kind of a man would want to be in bed with her and do nothing? This flattered her, I think, and she gave me a broad smile and said that we would try next time when I had healed.

After that I gave Mamolibeli the widest berth possible.

That hot summer my activities were not confined only to carousing. Three women the likes of which we had never before seen in Mafeteng arrived in town and were based at Bereng High School, where they would be teaching. They were American Peace Corps volunteers and were all beautiful in their different ways. Marie Peterson was white and blonde, Patricia Eaton was African American with straight brownish hair, and Lois Saito was Japanese American with jet black hair.

Up to that point, the only Americans we had seen were in the movies or in the magazines that Peter Masotsa bought relentlessly, or in the stories of the escapades of the Rat Pack which Ntlabathi Mbuli used to tell me. But here were live Americans walking the streets of our dusty little town and making friends with everyone without putting on airs.

At first we were wary of these women. I remember one day we were discussing their presence in a shebeen and as usual I was occupying centre stage since I knew all about American imperialism. I was telling the habitués how President Kennedy founded the Peace Corps about five years before to advance the USA's imperialist agenda in the world. This was in line with the Basutoland Congress Party's way of thinking; the party had vehemently opposed Prime Minister Leabua Jonathan when he invited the Peace Corps to work in Lesotho.

'It's one more proof that Leabua is a sell-out,' said Litsebe. His politics was always diametrically opposed to his father's.

'What did you expect from a man who was put in power by the Boers?' I asked. 'He obviously would be in cahoots with their American allies.'

'What do you expect from a man who has only passed Standard Six?' asked another drinker.

Peter said nothing. He avoided political discussions. We knew that it was because he worked for the Catholic priest and was most likely sympathetic to the BNP.

But soon enough the American women disarmed us with their friendliness and we forgot that they were imperialist agents. I found myself visiting the shebeens less and spending more time with these women at their house at Bereng High School. They were in their twenties and were university graduates; I was only a teenager and a high school student, so I never thought of them romantically except in my wet dreams.

Through one of them – I don't remember which one – I discovered a poet called LeRoi Jones. *The Dead Lecturer* was the book and I took it with me everywhere I went. On the occasions when I went to the shebeens with my friends I quoted for them from *The Dead Lecturer* as we passed the can of pineapple beer around: *Crow Jane, Crow Jane, don't hold your head so high. You realize, baby, you got to lay down and die.* In this epigraph to a series of poems about Crow Jane he was quoting Mississippi Joe Williams. These poems became my mantra. *'Your people/ without love.' And life/ rots them. Makes a silence/ blankness in every space/ flesh thought to be. First light,/ is dawn. Cold stuff/ to tempt a lover. Old lady/ of flaking eyes. Moon lady/ of useless thighs.* These lines reverberated in my mind, and in the shebeens of Mafeteng as those on whom they left a deep impression repeated them long after I was gone. Or sometimes quoting from the fifth Crow Jane poem 'The dead lady canonized': *The lady is dead, may the Gods,/ those others/ beg our forgiveness. And Damballah, kind father,/ sew up/ her bleeding hole.*

I didn't know what LeRoi Jones was on about here, but whatever it was I liked it. So did the habitués of the shebeens of Mafeteng. The main reason we found this poetry so evocative was that we were schooled only in the poetry of the Romantics where metre and rhyme reigned and *The Assyrian came down like the wolf on the fold/ And his cohorts were gleaming in purple and gold.* We never imagined that poetry could sound so much like jazz as did LeRoi Jones's.

I have often wondered what happened to Marie Peterson and Patricia Eaton. I know exactly what happened to Lois Saito. She married one of the teachers at Bereng High School, Mr Sebatane, and I was to meet them and their beautiful children many years later when I became a lecturer at the National University of Lesotho. They were both academics there as well.

On Christmas Day – actually from Christmas Eve – all the gallivanting had to stop. I could not visit the beautiful Peace Corps women or shebeen crawl with Litsebe and Peter. My siblings and I all had to be home in our brand new clothes for a big Christmas lunch of rice and chicken and vegetables and beetroot and custard and jelly. After lunch we lounged around listening to Handel's 'Messiah', Bach's 'Jesu, Joy of Man's Desiring', Marian Anderson, the Singing Bells and the Mormon Tabernacle Choir.

A few weeks earlier my father would harness all of us in the house to address envelopes for the Christmas cards that he sent to a long list of friends. He also received hundreds of Christmas cards from them. We hung all these on strings stretching from one wall to the other, forming rows and rows of Christmas decorations. This was one of the few activities that we performed all together as a family. And this was the only time we ever saw my father doing something other than preparing for cases with stacks of files and law books on the table. Actually, I don't remember my father ever being there for my mother. He was either at his office or in court. Whenever he was at home he was still buried in his work. He worked at home a lot and no one could speak to him then. There had to be silence in the house. I don't remember ever seeing my parents sitting down on a sofa having a conversation. Perhaps they did have conversations when they were in their bedroom at night. There were never any public displays of affection. Everything seemed so serious all the time.

This made a lasting impression on me, especially when I visited other families and saw mothers and fathers behaving like old buddies and laughing and ribbing each other.

Another thing that was a source of resentment for us kids was that we seemed to be rather poor for the children of a lawyer and a registered nurse. We were renting our house in the shabby part of town among

137

peasants and blue-collar workers rather than on Hospital Road where all the rich business and professional people lived. We didn't even own a car. I was more resentful when one day a car salesman parked two fancy convertibles in front of our house and tried to interest my father in buying one. But my father wouldn't even look at them. All hope died in me and my siblings that we would ever have a car.

I am not trying to suggest here that we ever went hungry. All our basic needs were taken care of – a roof over our heads, good food and decent clothes. We were certainly better off than our neighbours. But they were not our point of reference. Perhaps even Mafeteng was not our point of reference, but the bourgeois families of Maseru. We thought that our father's attorney-at-law title should have earned us the right to be like those kids who were fetched from Peka High School in posh cars by their mothers and fathers while we had to ride on buses.

Of course as we got older we got to understand our father better. He was totally dedicated to the struggle for the liberation of South Africa and to his clients. He charged the clients very little money to defend their cases, and sometimes no fees at all. Basotho people knew already that if you came with a sob story Mda would take your case for nothing. Yes, he would ask them to promise that they would pay when they got some money, but they never did. In one of the corners of our bedroom there was a folding bed that was left by a client who had promised to retrieve it after paying the fees. He won the case but never came back. My father believed in serving his people, and he did this at the expense of his family. He expected his family to sacrifice just as he did, and would feel wounded if any of us complained. That was why he never had any family time either, with us or with my mother. And that was why he never accumulated any personal wealth.

I remember once when he criticised his colleagues, T T Letlaka, with whom he had served articles under George Matanzima in the Transkei, and Wycliffe Tsotsi, who was in partnership with Letlaka in a lucrative law practice in Maseru. The two attorneys had just bought brand new Mercedes Benz sedans that looked exactly the same. My father felt that they were showing off, which would alienate the people of their host country who couldn't afford such cars.

Oh, yes, my father's key trait, which used to annoy me at the time, was

138

humility. He was also the most generous and the most compassionate of men. Today, of course, these have become my guiding values. In many respects I am now my father. Well, a less smart version of him.

YOU CAN SEE ST Rose Mission from Leabua Highway as you drive out of Peka. Eucalyptus and pine trees surround sandstone buildings that are roofed with red corrugated iron sheets.

'That is the place,' I point it out to Gugu when we drive past on our way from the Bee People of the Eastern Cape. 'That's the place where I was given an anathema.'

At the time I didn't know what an anathema was. I still don't know what it entails ecclesiastically, or whether a small-time parish priest has the authority from the Holy See to give the likes of me an anathema, as did Father Hamel of the St Rose Catholic Church in 1967. At the age of nineteen I carried it on my shoulders with pride and boasted to the boys in our dormitory, 'Hey *majita* (guys), I have the anathema.'

We all broke out laughing about it.

It was only Peter Mofolo who looked at me disapprovingly and told us that it was no laughing matter. I put it down to the fact that Peter Mofolo, a grandson of the great Sesotho novelist Thomas Mofolo, was just jealous because he didn't have an anathema of his own. Or maybe he just wanted to get even after I had tried to embarrass him in front of his friends a few days before. We had just read Thomas Mofolo's novel *Moeti oa Bochabela* (*The Traveller from the East*) which was a set book in our class when I hollered at him: 'Hey Pinky, your grandfather wrote shit, man!'

We called him Pinky because like a lot of his Bataung clan who are descendants of the Khoikhoi he was light in complexion.

'Oh, yeah?' he said. 'And what did yours write?'

That shut me up. My grandfather had not written a damn thing. All he knew was to make shoes.

I liked Pinky a lot, even though he was now being dismissive of my anathema.

This is how the anathema came to pass. I was in church singing

139

hymns and minding my own business. It was not my choice to be there. School regulations forced every student to go to church on Sundays. Although Peka High School was owned jointly by the Protestant Church of Lesotho and the Anglican Church, the authorities were so liberal that they allowed students to attend their own denominations, as long as they were in the vicinity of Peka village. Since I was a Catholic, I walked to St Rose – about ten miles from the high school – for my weekly dose of obligatory religion.

I noticed that as Father Hamel conducted the Holy Mass he kept looking in my direction. After a while he beckoned the catechist and whispered something in his ear, just as he was preparing for the Sacrament. The catechist tiptoed to me and whispered in my ear.

'Father Hamel wants you to leave his church right away,' he said.

'Why?' I asked.

'Because you are from Peka High School.'

He was looking at my green blazer with the yellow badge. The badge was my pride because I had designed it for the school that very year. I took particular pleasure in the open book with a flaming torch and the motto: *Luceat Lux Vestra* – Let your light shine. That's how the priest knew I was from the high school – the green blazer with the yellow badge.

'No, tell him I'm not going anywhere,' I said.

The catechist was taken aback that I was defying his boss. He stood there for a while staring at me. But I did not budge. I focused on the hymnal instead. He tiptoed back to the priest.

The time for the Sacrament came and I joined the line. When it was my turn to receive the body of Christ the priest skipped me and gave it to the next person. 'Well, he can keep his Sacrament,' I said to myself and went back to the pews.

After the service Father Hamel rushed out in full gear, without first taking off his surplice and stole as he normally did. As the congregation streamed out of the church he was already waiting outside the door, a thing he had never done before. He was not in the habit of greeting his congregants at the door after the service.

It turned out he was waiting for me.

'Why did you refuse when I ordered you out of my church?' he asked.

'Because I didn't understand why you wanted me to leave,' I said.

'Because you are a Communist, that's why. I don't want Communists in my church.'

So, that was the reason. I knew immediately that it was nothing personal. I was being crucified solely because I was a student at Peka High School, which was known far and wide as the breeding ground of Ntsu Mokhehle's BCP. The party had been declared Communist by the Roman Catholic Church because it received support from Chairman Mao of China. The Roman Catholic Church had actively campaigned for Chief Leabua Jonathan's BNP, which had contributed to the BNP's winning the last elections. The Catholics were in the majority in Lesotho. The BCP, on the other hand, received most of its support from the Protestant denominations, which were much poorer and smaller. So, it was not only the urban/rural divide that was a factor in the BNP winning those elections; it was also the Catholic/Protestant chasm. Father Hamel was known to preach unashamedly against the BCP in his church at St Rose. That was why activists from the local branch of the BCP once kidnapped him, put him in a sack and abandoned him in the fields many miles away just to teach him a lesson. He became even more rabid after that.

'It is not your church, you don't own it, so I'll be here again next Sunday and every Sunday for as long as I want,' I said, looking down at him. He was a puny man with a bald pate and white tufts above each ear.

Those who had gathered to listen were aghast at my defiance of the man of God. As far as they were concerned this was proof that I was indeed a Communist. Only a Communist would dare argue with a man of God.

On my way back to school I rethought my defiance. Perhaps it was a good thing that I had been expelled from church. I hated going to church anyway but was forced to by school rules. Now I had a good reason not to go.

On Monday I told the principal, Mr Tseliso Makhakhe, what had happened the previous day. I had hoped that he would leave it at that and it would be the end of my Sunday treks to St Rose, or any other church for that matter. But he did not. He ordered me into his Volkswagen Beetle and drove to St Rose. Father Hamel was strolling among the flowers. As soon as he saw us he walked very fast to his office and closed the fine mesh screen door. We stood outside on the steps and looked at him sitting at the desk facing the door.

'Can we come in?' asked Mr Makhakhe.

'No,' said the priest.

I think Mr Makhakhe decided he was not going to demean himself talking to this man from the steps; he walked away. I didn't follow him. I was rather annoyed that Father Hamel should treat my principal like an errant school boy.

'You are very rude,' I said to him.

'You dare talk to me like that?' he said. 'You are beyond redemption. I give you an anathema.'

'What?' I asked in utter amazement.

'You heard me. I give you an anathema.'

'Come on, Mda,' said the principal, already walking back to where he had parked his car around the corner. 'Let's go.'

'If that is a curse at all I'm giving it back to you, Father Hamel,' I said. I was rather annoyed that he didn't respond to this, so I added, 'I give you a hundred anathemas. A thousand anathemas even. So, you take that and smoke it.'

Thankfully, the principal did not hear me utter this curse. He would have been disappointed because he knew me as a quiet respectful boy who would not raise his voice to an adult.

If I thought this banishment from the Roman Catholic Church would bring an end to my church-going days once and for all I was soon proved wrong. As we were driving back to school Mr Makhakhe said, 'We are not going to beg Hamel to take you back in his church. You'll go to the Anglican Church instead. Anyway, their services are almost the same as yours.'

Although this was disappointing it was better than walking all those miles every Sunday. The Anglican chapel was on campus and the lay preacher who conducted the services there was my erstwhile English and Latin teacher, Mr A S Mampa, the one we called Scutum. He preached in English and Jama Mbeki was his Sesotho interpreter. It always amazed me how excellent Jama was in Sesotho even though he was a Xhosa from the Eastern Cape. At the time I was not aware of his deep Lesotho connections: his mother was a Mosotho from the Moerane family. The great maestro that I told you about was his mother's brother. He knew how to translate Scutum's jokes into Sesotho without losing the nuances that made them funny.

Jama completed high school ahead of me, so I took over as Scutum's interpreter when he left. But I could never match his voice that undulated in keeping with Scutum's emotions as he narrated some apocalyptic event in the Bible that had to be taken as a warning lest we went through the same mess if we didn't heed the word of God.

I also led, as Jama had done, in the singing of hymns. The Spirit took possession of me as I sang 'Onward Christian Soldiers' or 'Rock of Ages Cleft For Me'. These were Scutum's favourite hymns and he joined in his basso with gusto as did the all-boys congregation in four-part harmony.

I took a break from these sacred tasks only on those Sundays when our school orchestra was required to play at the Church of Lesotho. There again I would play my flute in praise of the Lord.

It was quite ironic that I, an atheist, was playing such an active role in spreading the Gospel. But then I was not a dogmatic atheist who would have nothing to do with religion. For me, all the rituals of Christianity were an act – a performance – that we could all enjoy in the same way that I enjoyed creating plays, participating in them or just watching them. God and all the members of his family were characters we had created and interacted with in our histrionic routines on Sundays. It was the sense of community that I relished in the rituals of worship, even though I knew that whatever or whoever was being worshipped existed only in our collective imagination. Why not play along if the performance gave one solace and fulfilment?

My scepticism about religion evolved over time. Even as I served as an altar boy years before I was beginning to have some doubts about

God. The question that kept on nagging me even as a child was: if God created the world and everything on it, who created God? And then who created that creator ... ad infinitum? If everything must have a source, what is God's source? Of course I would never raise these questions with my mother, let alone with my father.

And then from the Peka High School library – the very library that had introduced me to such British and American playwrights as Joe Orton, Harold Pinter, Tennessee Williams and Edward Albee – I came across a book on world religions. I immersed myself in the world of Hinduism, Islam, Buddhism, Baha'i, Judaism, Sikhism, Shintoism, Zoroastrianism and a host of others, including some African Traditional and Diasporic religions. It struck me that the adherents of each one of these religions were adamant that theirs was the correct path. Yet all these religions, even those that were monotheistic, professed different philosophies and values. They might have similarities in some of their messages, but they differed significantly in particulars. Sometimes they even worshipped different deities.

I wrote an article for the school magazine, *Lux Vestra*, titled: 'Who Has the Right Path?' What I was really asking, in fact, was what arrogance makes Christians think that they are right and everyone else is wrong? I went further to question the whole notion of God, and came to the conclusion that he was a human creation. When pre-scientific societies couldn't deal with natural forces over which they had no control, and when they couldn't provide answers to the mysteries of the universe, they had to attribute them to some supernatural power.

I shared this article with my father during the holidays. He read it there and then, looked at me and said, 'What is the point of this?'

I was disappointed. I was hoping for praise from this man who had been extremely tolerant even of rigid atheists like John Motloheloa. I thought I was growing up to be an independent thinker, but he was dismissive of the whole effort, which proved to me that like most Christians he was so certain of the correctness of his faith that even raising the kind of questions my article was trying to put on the agenda was foolhardy, if not downright reprobate. And this from a man I had never seen go to church or pray even for a single day.

I began to read extensively, trying to find answers to these nagging questions. I read books that tried to explain and simplify Charles Darwin's theories of the evolution that resulted from the process of natural selection. Surely the world could not have been created in six days!

Later Gordon Tube, another teacher of English Literature, introduced us to *Androcles and the Lion* by George Bernard Shaw which was a prescribed text for drama. My leap into atheism was complete. Our class loved the play, an adaptation of the old story of Androclus, a slave in ancient Rome who was escaping from the cruelties of slavery and took refuge in a cave, into which a lion with a thorn in its paw came. The lion was in great pain and Androclus extracted the thorn. He was later captured and thrown into the arena to be devoured by the lions as a spectacle for the ladies and gentlemen of Rome. When the lion came into the arena it recognised Androclus as the guy who saved it from the thorn and, instead of eating him, it caressed him. Shaw made Androcles a Christian and in his play martyrdom and persecution were portrayed through comedy, some of which I found to be slapstick.

Though we all admired Shaw's humour in the play, it was really the Preface whose polemics captivated me. I was struck by the fact that the Preface was longer than the play. Through a long examination of the Gospel Shaw put Christianity on trial and, after reading it, religious belief, and theism itself, sounded quite ridiculous.

Shaw's atheism gave me permission to be atheistic without any apology. It confirmed what I had suspected all along: there is no God! For the first time I realised that I was not alone in my unbelief when I read:

The first common mistake to get rid of is that mankind consists of a great mass of religious people and a few eccentric atheists. It consists of a huge mass of worldly people, and a small percentage of persons deeply interested in religion and concerned about their own souls and other people's; and this section consists mostly of those who are passionately affirming the established religion and those who are passionately attacking it, the genuine philosophers being very few.

We debated these issues in Gordon Tube's class, and even explored another of Shaw's plays, *Saint Joan*, based on the records of the trial of Joan of Arc by the Roman Catholic Church. Shaw concludes that there were no villains in this matter because everyone acted in good faith – what I later described in one of my novels as 'the sincerity of belief'. This play and its long Preface reinforced what had been planted by the earlier play.

Gordon Tube was the most popular of all the teachers because in his class we debated issues unhampered by convention and taboo. He empowered us with the vocabulary to articulate our ideas. He liked the essays that I wrote and, like Scutum before him, read them to the rest of the class. But what made him most popular with the boys was that he was streetwise and spoke the *tsotsitaal* of Johannesburg. This slang, born of the urban streets and based on a mixture of Afrikaans and other indigenous languages, with a sprinkling of invented words, gave him the sophistication that many of us could only dream of.

I must add that Gordon Tube became my friend and drinking partner. But that was later, after I had completed high school and was carousing in Maseru. At Peka High School he became a mentor who encouraged my writing. After writing my first poem I gave it to him to critique.

Perhaps I should tell you how I came to write this poem since I never really planned to be a poet. In fact, apart from the essays that my teachers read to my classmates, and the articles and jokes that I wrote for *Lux Vestra*, I had not written anything creative since my isiXhosa story, *Igqirha laseMvubase*, in Sterkspruit.

The sleeping muse was awakened by the death of my dear friend Santho Mohapeloa. Don't confuse him with clarinettist Khomo Mohapeloa who taught me a lot about reading and composing music, or with Kingston Mohapeloa the artist who created cartoons for *Lux Vestra*. They were cousins. Santho Mohapeloa was a gifted artist in his own right. We used to sit on the banks of the Caledon River painting landscapes of the Boer farms across the river. I used to tell him, 'One day we'll own those farms.' But he was not interested in politics. Instead we talked about girls. One thing I envied him was his girlfriend Rebecca 'Nau, who at that time was the most beautiful girl I had ever seen. She was herself an artist. We spent our weekends at Scutum's house listening to music in John and Sammy's bedroom. Sometimes I visited his home in Maseru and we socialised with the beautiful girls from St Mary's High School.

Unlike other boarding schools, Peka High School did not have a boarding master. Two students chosen by the principal and staff served as Head Prefect and Deputy Head Prefect and performed all the functions of a boarding master. At this point I was the Deputy Head Prefect – a post that I held for two years – and shared a room in the Square with Lesupi, the Head Prefect. Our room was known as the Cell because it looked like and was as small as a prison cell.

One night there was a knock at the door. It was the Health Prefect with the news that Santho was ill. I was too lazy to wake up so I said, 'Give him an aspirin; I'll see him in the morning.' And I went back to sleep.

In the morning when I walked out of the big gates of the Square I saw Santho accompanied by the Health Prefect. Although he looked pale and drained he was walking without assistance. The Health Prefect told me he was taking him to the Seventh Day Adventist Hospital at Mapoteng.

'How are you feeling, man?' I asked.

He smiled wanly and sang something to the effect that next time I saw him he wouldn't look the same. This was a line from Champion Jack Dupree's 'Death of Big Bill Broonzy'. Dupree had made a promise to his friend Big Bill Broonzy that if Big Bill were to die first, Dupree would write the blues of Big Bill Broonzy, but if Dupree died first, Big Bill would do the same for him. This was comforting because it told me that Santho could still joke about his illness. Whatever it was, it couldn't be that bad.

I responded with another line from the same song.

So, they took Santho away. Later that evening as we were having dinner in the school hall the principal came to announce that Santho was dead.

I was devastated, and I don't think I ever really recovered from this. Not only was this boy my friend and confidant, but he died on my watch. I was gnawed by the fact that I had been too lazy to wake up.

The next day I wrote the poem in his honour, 'Death of an Artist', in the same way that Champion Jack Dupree wrote the blues for Big Bill Broonzy.

But this didn't salve my feeling of guilt. And of loss.

Santho's death relaunched my writing career.

At about that time there was a buzz in Lesotho; Gibson Kente was coming to Maseru with his musical play *Sikalo*. We had read about this play in *Drum* magazine, and *The World* and *The Golden City Post* newspapers and felt honoured that Mr Kente did not forget Lesotho in his southern African tour of his musical. People hired buses from all corners of the country to the Catholic Hall in Maseru to see such stars as Kenny Majozi, Ndaba Mhlongo, Mary Twala and Zakithi Dlamini in live action.

I was in that audience. At last I would make up for Gibson Kente's first play, *Manana the Jazz Prophet*, snippets of which I saw in Sterkspruit years before, but never got to see the whole performance.

I was impressed by Gibson Kente's music and choreography, but I was rather disappointed by the storyline. It lacked substance and was nothing like the plays of Wole Soyinka and Harold Pinter that I read in the school library. The dialogue seemed inane and the acting was too exaggerated. I thought I could write better plays.

As soon as I got back to Peka High I wrote my first play, *Zhigos*, about a gangster of that name. I had fallen in love with the name from the stories that Peter Masotsa told the habitués of the shebeens of Mafeteng about the exploits of a ladykiller called Zhigos who was a student with Peter at Pax Secondary School in Northern Transvaal. Later that year I wrote another play titled *A Hectic Weekend*. Gordon Tube read both plays and declared that they were wonderful works of art. Too bad I can't locate them any more. It would have been interesting to read them today and see what was so wonderful about them. The only thing I remember about them is that *A Hectic Weekend* was a musical for which I composed the music – I sometimes catch myself singing one of the songs, the only one I still remember – and *Zhigos* was set partly in Nigeria. My characters sailed in a love boat from Port Harcourt to the island of Fernando Po. It didn't matter that I had never been to Nigeria. Mphunyetsane Thatho, from whose parents we were renting our home in Mafeteng, had worked there for some years and told me how he used to spend idyllic holidays on the island of Fernando Po. In any event Nigeria was very much alive in many of us, made so by Chinua Achebe's novels and Cyprian Ekwensi's *Jagua Nana* and *People of the City*. For any African literature written in English to be valid it had to be set in Nigeria – or so I thought.

These plays were never performed and I kept the manuscripts for years but, alas, they got lost in one of the many times that I have moved house in my life.

If I imagined these creative activities would take my mind off Santho Mohapeloa it soon became clear that I was deluding myself. He haunted me and I saw him everywhere I went, especially at night. And every time he sang the line from Champion Jack Dupree.

I spent long periods just sitting on my bed in the Cell playing the flute. Or painting portraits of my distant cousin Sibongile Twala, about whom I was obsessing at the time. She was a student at St Mary's High School and through her I had cultivated friendships with some fantastic girls from that school. One of them was Ray Setlogelo with whom I exchanged constant letters like lovers, even though our relationship was platonic. So when I was not playing the flute or painting Sibongile in pencil and charcoal, I was writing letters to Ray.

Sibongile and Ray had become my Muses. But despite their constant presence in my imagination I got no respite from my melancholy and the spectre of Santho Mohapeloa continued its visitations.

To cap it all, at the end of the year Otis Redding died in a plane crash.

CHAPTER FIVE

I HAVE KNOWN GUGU for more than twenty years. Even before we got to know each other well we discovered that we shared common values in a very uncanny manner. As if we had been brought up in the same family. I would utter something and it would sound so familiar to her she would ask: 'Are you sure you're not Josephine's child?' Josephine is her mother. It turned out that, like me, she would insist on buying her kids black dolls – this was long before she had kids of her own – and would never let them play with toy guns. We love the earth and we value all sentient life, a position that led us to become squeamish about meat, even though we came from a strong meat-eating culture. Remind me later to tell you of the ducks that forced us into vegetarianism. We are against the death penalty, and celebrate the fact that our country did away with it, but deplore the lenient sentences that our criminals get from our courts. We are pro-choice in so far as women's reproductive rights are concerned and believe that gay rights are human rights. We celebrate the fact that these rights are enshrined in our country's Constitution, one of the very few in the world that spells out sexual orientation. We believe in these rights so strongly that we have at various times involved ourselves in campaigns whenever they were infringed. Gugu is more of an active gay rights activist than I am and attends LGBT activities on our campus. To crown it all, she has undertaken the arduous task of educating and counselling a neighbour who is the parent of a beautiful gay son but, much as she loves him, is ashamed of him because of his sexual orientation.

We both recoil at homophobia in all its manifestations.

So, we walk into the spacious bar of Maseru Sun Cabanas this particular evening and order a drink. We are both teetotallers so she asks for a glass of water and for old times' sake I order a non-alcoholic passion fruit cocktail that I remember the barmen here mixing so well. We are both bushed after the long drive from the Bee People.

And there is Mr Dizzy sitting in an easy chair counting a lot of coins that he will obviously be sharing with a scruffy partner who is sitting opposite him. The two gamblers must have won the money in the slot machines in the next room. He doesn't see me; he is too engrossed in stacking the coins into two piles. At the same time he is trying to stop his gambling partner from grabbing a stray coin that rolled on the thick carpet and lodged itself near the leg of the coffee table.

'Hey, Mr Dizzy,' I call him.

He looks up and squints his eyes to make sure that what they think they are seeing is indeed what they are seeing. He forgets all about his slot machine winnings and comes over to the bar counter where we are already seated.

'Hey, you Saferi! You Sopete! You Masoba-a-Lieta!' he says, calling me after bumbling cartoon characters whose exploits we used to follow decades ago in *Moeletsi-oa-Basotho*, a Catholic Church newspaper. He is so excited to see me that he gives me a hug and kisses me – smack! – on the lips.

I see the disgust on Gugu's face.

After some small talk – me trying to find out what he has been up to in the years that we have not seen each other and he waffling something that I cannot understand because he is too drunk – Mr Dizzy goes back to the serious business of counting coins.

'*Sies*,' says Gugu. 'He kissed you on the lips.'

'Yes, he did,' I respond. I am quite amused.

'And you seemed to enjoy it,' she says, even more disgusted.

'Yes, I did,' I say. Of course, I did not; the man reeked of beer, although his lips were surprisingly soft for someone so alcohol-ravaged.

I break out laughing because I didn't think she would look so serious about a simple kiss from a friend. I have many female friends who are ravishingly beautiful. There is Nakedi Ribane, for instance, tall and graceful. She used to be one of the two black South African models who attained fame on international ramps and magazine covers some years back. She would have been called a super model if that term had been coined at the time, and of course she has lost none of her looks. And then there is Motshabi Tyelele, one of our leading actresses of stage, film and television, whose playwriting career I have mentored. Whenever I meet these women after I have been away in the USA for an extended period we kiss squarely on the lips. And that has never bothered Gugu. She has actually kissed them on the lips too.

So, why is she aghast at Mr Dizzy's kiss? I don't ask her. But clearly it is because Mr Dizzy is a man and convention dictates that real men don't kiss. We may be anti-homophobia rationally but some of the prejudices of our upbringing may continue to linger under our skin, only to crawl out at unguarded moments.

I FIRST MET SECHELE Khaketla, also known as Mr Dizzy after Dizzy Gillespie and after Tommy Roe's pop song, in the mid-sixties soon after his return from England where his parents had sent him for his high school education. His father was B M Khaketla, the famous Sesotho novelist who was also the secretary general of Marematlou Freedom Party and a member of the King's Privy Council. His mother, 'Masechele Khaketla, was even more famous as a novelist and playwright. She was also the founder and owner of a prestigious private school. They had a palatial home in Maseru West, in the same street where the artistic Mohapeloa brothers with whom I was at high school lived. They were the elite of Lesotho who sent their kids for private piano lessons; hence Sechele and his sister were accomplished pianists. They were the bourgeois kids I felt my siblings and I should have been had our father not nailed his colours firmly to the mast of a proletarian ship.

Mr Dizzy didn't give a hoot for his good breeding. He had no intention of living up to his parents' expectations. Many Basotho people went to England or America for university degrees, especially graduate degrees, but it was unheard of for parents to send a boy all the way to England just for high school. Only the Khaketlas and King Moshoeshoe II did that. But over there Mr Dizzy didn't pay much attention to his studies. Public school was a waste of his precious time. So, he played the piano in skanky nightclubs and bars and drank himself into a sodden mess. No one was surprised when he flunked his A-levels. When his parents got wind of his capers they sent for him. He eluded the emissaries and went underground, sleeping rough with hoboes. It took his father months to track him down and bring him back to Lesotho.

That's when I met him, fresh from his merrymaking in London. What brought us together was art rather than music. He was a wonderful painter and I still have a vivid memory of one particular oil painting of his: an ashtray overflowing with stubs of cigarettes. It was not so much the subject but how it was rendered that fascinated me. The way the old impressionists of a century ago would have done it, using unmixed primary colours to play with light and shadows on the tablecloth, the ashtray and the smoke rising from a smoldering cigarette. I was also impressed by the fact that he could make such a mundane subject interesting. How many of us had seen ashtrays with cigarette stubs and never thought of painting them?

There was a strong community of artists in Maseru those days, led by Meshu Mokitimi whose work had first come to my notice, as I mentioned earlier, in the form of cartoons in the BCP organ, *Makatolle*. It turned out when I got to know him personally that drawing political cartoons was just a sideline for him; he was actually one of the very best painters in oil, acrylics and pastels that I have ever met. I remember earlier on when I was still at Peka High School that he used to give art lessons to a whole bunch of us. There I was with my brother Sonwabo, who was also artistically gifted, and Santho Mohapeloa and his girlfriend Rebecca 'Nau and Mr Dizzy painting murals in the small room he rented at the home of one of our beautiful St Mary's High School friends, Mokone Tlale.

Meshu introduced us to the nuns and monks at Mazenod who specialised in watercolour landscapes of the Maluti Mountains and to another Lesotho landscape realist, Paul Ncheke, whose work of the mountains and rivers and aloes and huts of Lesotho was exhibited internationally. Paul Ncheke was so much impressed with my charcoal sketches titled 'No Peace Without Justice' that he exhibited them alongside his work in Edmonton, Canada. It was my first exposure to the international art world. He brought me some cash from Canada; my charcoals had been bought. I don't remember now how much it was, but it was the first money I earned from my artwork. The excitement reminded me of the first money that I earned from my writing before I left Sterkspruit for exile.

All this art activity prompted Chief Leabua Jonathan – the prime minister that we despised so much for winning the elections against our hero Ntsu Mokhehle – to establish a museum of art in Maseru with Reggie Senkoto as its curator. It housed collections from such South African artists as Father Frans Claerhout, Percy Sedumedi, Dubile Mhlaba and Ephraim Ngatane. These artists also came to Lesotho occasionally to work with us.

Our creativity involved a lot of political activism as well. A war had broken out in Nigeria in 1967 after the Governor of the Eastern Region, Colonel Ojukwu, announced a unilateral secession of the region, then named Biafra, from the Nigerian federation. General Gowon, who was the president of Nigeria, would have none of it, and he sent his federal forces to invade Biafra and bring it back into the fold of the federation.

We were fully in support of Biafra and we held art exhibitions to raise awareness of the plight of the Igbo people.

By 1969 Biafra was under siege from the federal forces and we heard of the terrible famine because Gowon would not let any food supplies into the region. We organised a big art exhibition in Maseru titled 'The Children of Biafra'. I remember oil paintings by such renowned painters as Phil Motsosi of Loretto and Paul Molefe portraying starving children with swollen kwashiorkor bellies. Both Mr Dizzy and I had our paintings in that exhibition.

What was the basis of our support for Colonel Ojukwu? I have often asked myself this question. After all, we were staunch Pan Africanists who believed that one day the continent would unite into the United States of Africa despite the setback the Pan African project suffered when Kwame Nkrumah, the one we called Osagyefo the Saviour, was overthrown in a coup by a bunch of CIA-supported soldiers. We lionised Mwalimu Julius Nyerere for working towards this Pan African goal by uniting Tanganyika, Zanzibar and Pemba into the Republic of Tanzania. We believed that instead of dismantling the colonial borders carved at the Berlin Conference of 1884 by breaking the colonial states into smaller ethnic-based national states, we should work towards uniting neighbouring countries into bigger and bigger federations until we had reached the ultimate goal of a United States of Africa. And Julius Nyerere had shown us how it could be done.

And yet there we were supporting an ethnic group, the Igbo people, when they formed their own ethnic-based state – we who adamantly wrote and preached against tribalism. It dawned on me that our support for the Igbo became apparent as early as 1966 when we heard that they were being massacred by other ethnic groups in Nigeria. And why did we take this massacre so personally when normally massacres are just statistics on the pages of newspapers? Because we identified very closely with the Igbo. It was almost like they were our own people. We knew a lot about them, whereas we knew nothing of the groups that were involved in the conflict with them. The Yoruba, the Hausa and everyone else were just names of ethnic groups, whereas the Ibgo were real people. We had lived in their village of Umuofia and knew of their customs and traditions, we had participated in their ceremonies and rituals, we had eaten their food, and we had enjoyed their proverbs and even greeted each other in their language: 'Umuofia kwenu!' a boy would shout when he arrived at the Smoking Spot, and the rest of the boys would roar back 'Yaaa!' while puffing on their zols or hand-rolled cigarettes. Yes, we were the Igbo people. We were the sons and daughters of Okwonko and the siblings of Nwoye, Ezinma and Ikemefuna. Of Obi and Clara.

It was obvious whose side we would take if the Igbo were at war with anyone, whatever the reason was and whoever was in the wrong. Thanks to Chinua Achebe's *Things Fall Apart* and *No Longer at Ease*, the Igbo were our flesh and blood and Colonel Ojokwu's cause was our cause. We rooted for Biafra's victory and were outraged at the siege. The dream of the United States of Africa could well stay in abeyance if it meant our Igbo people should remain in a federation where they were being oppressed and even massacred.

That's the power of narrative for you. We always sympathise with those whose story we know. Sometimes the cause is good, as I believe it was in Biafra, sometimes it may not be so noble. I remember as kids we watched a lot of Tarzan-type movies in Dobsonville. We always sided with the white hero against the 'savages' because we knew the white hero's story, his family background, his trials and tribulations. The white hero had history; the 'savages' did not. We didn't realise that those 'savages' were us. Narrative manipulated us against ourselves.

The Biafran War was not the only war that we made our business, although it was the only one where we were active in doing something about it. The Six Day War was another one. I remember when it broke out we, the Peka High School boys, were at the bus stop in Maseru waiting in the bus that was going to take us back to school when Mohlomi Ramonate, a former Peka High student who had now gained fame as a newscaster for Radio Lesotho, came into the bus and announced to us that we were on our way towards winning the war. We, in that case, were the Arabs. We were the forces of Egypt, Syria and

Jordan. Remember we were Pan Africanists and the president of Egypt, Gamal Abdel Nasser, was one of the major leaders of that movement. Why, Kwame Nkrumah our Saviour had even married a woman from Egypt to seal the Pan African bond. So, we cheered when Mohlomi Ramonate announced our impending victory. As a newsreader for a national broadcasting station he was an authority on such matters, and throughout that bus journey we sang songs of victory. But only a few days later we heard of the defeat of the Arabs. The Israelis under General Moshe Dayan had captured the West Bank, East Jerusalem, the Golan Heights, the Sinai Peninsula and the Gaza Strip. We cursed Mohlomi Ramonate for promising us a victory he could not deliver.

At the Smoking Spot the intellectual Phanuel Ramorobi said, 'Anyway, you guys know that those Arabs enslaved Africans long before the Europeans and Americans did. They are not our friends.'

I don't know if that consoled us at all.

BACK TO MR DIZZY and me. I often sat in his parents' living room listening to him playing the blues à la Champion Jack Dupree on the piano. Or to his sister, Sekamotho, playing Chopin or Schubert. Here I enjoyed the plushness and the cosiness that was absent in my father's house. It was different here in other ways as well: his mother was the one who did not suffer fools gladly, rather than his father. The mother's strictness reminded me very much of my father. When she walked into the room we all better sit up straight. No slouching. My father exactly.

Mr Dizzy looked out of place in those surroundings.

He was more at home in the shebeens strumming his guitar for appreciative patrons. Often we spent days on end drinking home-brewed beer, be it hops or pineapple, from one shebeen to the next. Because we were always broke his guitar fed our habit. When we walked in everyone was happy because they knew they were going to listen to Mr Dizzy's humorous songs. A denizen would yell, 'Hey, Mr Dizzy, play us "Tell me, tell me why",' by which she meant Jeremy Taylor's 'Black-White Calypso' made famous by the long-running Johannesburg show,

'Wait a Minim!' The denizens, including me, thought it was Mr Dizzy's own composition, and he never disabused us of that notion. Instead he would oblige with relish, rendering in his bluesy voice the song that left everyone in stitches about advertisements in *Drum* magazine for skin lightening creams to make black people white, and in *The Star* for sun tan lotions to make white people black. We all chuckled in anticipation when he got to the next verses about advertisements in *Zonk* magazine for ointments to make black people's curly hair straight, while white people were at the Rosebank Beauty Parlour trying to make their straight hair curly. Everyone in the house would join the chorus that demanded an answer as to why black people wanted to be white and white people wanted to be black. We almost climaxed at the last verse that provided the solution: black and white folks should stop wasting their money on creams and lotions to change their complexion but should instead marry and give each other a little black and a little white in the night. At this the denizens would break into ear-shattering applause and cheers and whistles and then ply us with beer.

For days on end we did not sleep; we merely dozed off on the benches between gulps of the home-brew. We were never bothered by the stench of malt, rotting pineapple fruit, and hops emanating from the cauldrons in the corner of the room or those that were produced by our unwashed bodies. We drank and farted and laughed and sang until the next morning, and then moved on to the next shebeen. Sometimes a shebeen queen would refuse to open for us, especially if all the drinkers had left and she was trying to catch up on much-needed sleep or perhaps on some lovemaking. In that case we staggered on to the next shebeen. You only had to walk a block or two and there would be another.

On looking back, what amazes me is that we never got into drugs at all. Well, once in a while Mr Dizzy would have some LSD and would get psychedelic all over the place. Or sometimes he would have marijuana. I once tried it too, but it did nothing for me. I puffed on and on but didn't get high at all, though I did get the munchies. I decided there was no point; I'd rather stick to my home-brewed beer. As for hard drugs, I never saw them with my naked eye. Only the strips of paper with colourful butterflies and rainbows that Mr Dizzy chewed because they had LSD on them. I never tried them. Not even once. I was scared of the stars and other psychedelic patterns that he claimed he saw after chewing and even swallowing the strips of paper. I've always been dead scared of losing total control of myself.

We saw ourselves as part of the international hippy culture. Make love, not war. Janis Joplin was our chief prophetess. 'Mercedes Benz'. That was my song asking God to buy me the luxury German sedan. The one that I sang as Mr Dizzy strummed the guitar. I never learnt how to strum it myself, so he strummed it for me. And hummed along. Another prophetess was Joan Baez with her folk songs. And the prophets were Bob Dylan and Jimi Hendrix with his psychedelic rock. When we were around the shebeens of Maseru reverberated with some of their music instead of the traditional Sesotho songs that were a staple of drunken sing-alongs. And Mr Dizzy strummed his guitar.

At that point I had told myself: to hell with education. Life was beautiful without it and Mr Dizzy was living proof.

Whenever we were very desperate for money, because even hippies needed to eat, we remembered that we were painters as well. We visited James Dorothy who lived a few blocks from Mr Dizzy's home. James Dorothy was a famous artist who had trained under Father Frans Claerhout in Thaba Nchu where his family originally came from and his style was very much reminiscent of the Catholic priest's Flemish Expressionism. We knew that we would get some art materials from him, and we sat in his living room which doubled as a studio and painted pictures – mostly watercolours and charcoals and pencils. James Dorothy himself was principally an acrylics man.

This was the period in my life when I still had the obsession with my distant cousin, Sibongile Twala. She was a student at St Mary's High School at Roma when I was at Peka High School. But when we were in Maseru we lived with our common aunt, Mrs Kolane, who was married to the Speaker of Chief Leabua Jonathan's parliament. So, most of my paintings were portraits of Sibongile or had something to do with her. I must stress, though, that she was not a romantic interest. Even after all these years my romantic interest continued to be Keneiloe, though her image was becoming blurry in my mind. Sibongile was someone I had idealised as a goddess on some Mount Olympus of my imagination. I had mastered her dimpled face so well that I could draw it without looking at her or at her photograph.

Keneiloe was the one I was going to marry; Sibongile was the Muse who guided my painting and my poetry. And for that I became the butt of all syrupy and mushy jokes among my artist friends.

Living at the Kolanes – the epitome of Maseru high society and political elite – took me from one end of the social spectrum where I slept in a room with rows of sweaty guerrillas on the floor and on single beds, to a grass-thatched cottage in a garden with flowers and sprawling lawns all to myself. I could have my meals in the main house where Sibongile and my aunt's beautiful children would pamper me. What I loved most was that I could come and go as I pleased. I even forgot that I was in enemy territory: my aunt and her husband were staunch members of the ruling BNP – hence he was the Speaker of Parliament – and I was a Pan Africanist who supported the opposition leader, Ntsu Mokhehle. I was too comfortable to feel like a traitor.

When I saw any of the Poqo people in the street I would try to avoid them. If I spied a guerrilla coming down the street I would duck into some back alley. I had been avoiding them like that since the time I went AWOL when P K Leballo wanted to send me on a suicide mission to the Boer farms of the Free State.

One day I was browsing at the comic books shelf in Maseru Café when I discovered they had in stock the new omnibus edition of *Asterix*. I had lately fallen in love with this comic by writer Rene Goscinny and illustrator Albert Uderzo, and I fervently followed the adventures of the tiny Gaul Asterix, and his sidekick Obelix, and all the colourful characters of Armorica, especially the druid Getafix. I particularly liked the premise that Julius Caesar had conquered all of Gaul, except for the Armorican village which was effectively withstanding the might of the Roman Empire, thanks to the concoctions of the druid which gave the villagers supernatural powers through which they always beat the Romans legionnaires to a pulp. I had a few last coins in my pocket and I was debating with myself whether I should buy the omnibus or save my money for a scale of pineapple beer in the evening. The 'scale' was the unit of measurement for home-brew in the shebeens of Lesotho – about one and a half litres in volume.

I was startled by someone tapping me on the shoulder. It was Nqabande Sidzamba. He had just bought the *Rand Daily Mail* and *The World*, the two South African newspapers that we all read to keep up to speed with what was happening back home. He had recently been elected the PAC representative in Lesotho since the party had moved its headquarters to Tanzania after P K Leballo's deportation. I certainly would have hidden from him but now it was too late. I had quite some deference for him, not only because of his position in the party but because he was a close family friend originally from Qoboshane, where my grandfather used to be the chief. He had been one of my father's protégés, in fact. His younger brother Myekeni had been my friend when I was a little boy banished by my parents to my grandparents' custody after my misadventures in Johannesburg, and his older sister had been my teacher at Qoboshane Bantu Community School where she was famous for using the cane on boys and girls at the slightest provocation – to the extent that students named her Ram-Beat-Again. So, you see, I had all the reasons not to want to meet this man at this delinquent stage in my life.

He was more like family than just a leader of our party. He was not staying at the Poqo camp at Thakalekoala's estate, but had a house near Maseru Community Secondary School where he was principal. I had been to his house a few times and had listened to his records of the Manhattan Brothers, the Woody Woodpeckers, the Elite Swingsters, Count Basie, Duke Ellington and a lot of other band leaders of the swing era. I used to tease him that he didn't have any bebop because it was too complicated for him.

He took his responsibilities as a home-boy and a big brother quite seriously. And indeed he did not hesitate to express his disappointment that I was not turning out well and had abandoned the struggle for the 'nice time' of Maseru.

'I have not abandoned the struggle, Bhut' Nqabande,' I said. 'I am fighting it in a different way.'

161

'By vagabonding with that Khaketla boy, getting drunk all over Maseru and disgracing AP?' he asked.

I didn't know he knew I was vagabonding with Mr Dizzy. But then Maseru was a small town and people talked.

'By writing and painting,' I said. 'Art is also an effective weapon of the struggle.'

He was not convinced.

'What do people say when they see you staggering in the streets *unxilile*?'

Instead of answering that, I asked him about some of the guerrillas I knew and had not seen since I left the camp. He told me about those who went on sabotage missions into South Africa and never came back, and those who were smuggled out of Lesotho to the guerrilla camps in Libya and Uganda which PK had established since his expulsion from Lesotho. He also told me that my friend and mentor, Ntlabathi Mbuli, had left the camp for Mafeteng. I wondered why he had gone there. Did my father perhaps invite him back to help him at his office which was what he used to do when I first met him? Whatever the reason, it was comforting to know that once I was back in Mafeteng there would be someone more politically mature to socialise with, in addition to the mindless romps with Litsebe and Peter.

Not that I had intentions of going back to Mafeteng any time soon. The life of a starving and hustling artist in Maseru was too alluring to abandon. I would rather be painting pictures at James Dorothy's apartment with Mr Dizzy than living under my father's strict discipline.

After producing a few paintings and sketches Mr Dizzy and I went to flog them to the tourists at the new Holiday Inn Casino, as the Maseru Sun Cabanas was then called. We had to do these transactions surreptitiously because no soliciting was allowed on the premises of this hotel. We competed with prostitutes for the attention of rich Afrikaners from South Africa at the various bars both inside and by the swimming pool. The Afrikaners were there to sample the delights they were denied in their Calvinistic country where sexual relations across the colour line were forbidden. They were therefore not interested in looking at art, especially expressionist works (I was in my anguished Kandinsky phase) that meant nothing to the eye of a hard-boiled Free State farmer.

We focused mostly on those men who were already safely ensconced in the company of our most beautiful prostitutes. Maseru was a much smaller city then, so we knew most of these women. We knew who their brothers were, or their husbands or their mothers. After all, we drank with some of them at the casino bar after they had scored big with their white johns.

We operated more like small-time drug dealers.

One afternoon, for instance, I was sitting at the end of the long outdoor bar by the swimming pool nursing a glass of water because I couldn't afford beer. Mr Dizzy was cracking jokes with a group of civil servants in suits and neckties a few patrons away from me. Mr Dizzy was always popular with everyone.

I spotted a potential victim in khaki shorts and sandals plying a giggling prostitute with beer. He was an old man, an obvious pillar of the community in some *platteland* town. I wouldn't have been surprised if he were a *dominee*, as the Dutch Reformed Church folks called their pastors. I had encountered quite a few *dominees* in the company of the ladies of the town at this establishment. Whether he was just a *boer* – a farmer – or a man of the cloth it didn't matter; it was enough that he looked like the kind who wouldn't want a scandal to follow him about his shenanigans with black women in this oasis of sin and iniquity, as Maseru was known among the upright white citizens of South Africa. Another thing that made him a prospective customer was that I knew something about the leggy brown lady he was with. I signalled to Mr Dizzy who excused himself from the civil servants, taking a beer they had bought him with him. He pushed his way between our potential customer and his lady of pleasure and whipped out rolled paintings from under his jacket, the lapels of which shimmered with dirt.

'Psss... I have something to show you,' he whispered to the Afrikaner as he unrolled the rubber band that held the paintings together. He had to do all this under the counter so that the bartender and the waiters didn't see that he was peddling contraband to the patrons.

The woman knew Mr Dizzy's tricks and she pleaded with him in Sesotho, 'Dizzy, please don't spoil my business.'

'I've got to survive too, Liepollo,' said Mr Dizzy.

'Then go and get your own white man,' said the woman.

'I don't want to sleep with the guy,' said Mr Dizzy in Sesotho. 'I just want to sell him a painting.'

'Get lost, Sechele,' said the woman. She used Mr Dizzy's real name; she was certainly annoyed and had no time for nickname endearments. The john was also getting restless.

'I don't want any paintings,' he said in Sesotho. 'Please do what the lady is asking and leave us alone.'

I was listening to all this and I chuckled to myself; Mr Dizzy should have known better than to assume he could discuss the white man in his native tongue without the customer getting wise to what he was saying. He must have been one of those Afrikaners from the border farms in the Ficksburg, Ladybrand or Wepener districts who spoke Sesotho like they were born in a rondavel on the Maluti Mountains of Lesotho.

It was time to save the situation. I went to join them.

'Liepollo,' I said in mock surprise, 'what are you doing here?'

She sneered and looked at me in surprise. 'And who are you?'

'Is there a problem, Sweet Pea?' asked the Afrikaner, now getting agitated.

'Sweet Pea?' I said. 'This is my cousin, and now she pretends she does not know me because she's doing something naughty.'

The woman was adamant she did not know me, and the man threatened to call security if we didn't leave them alone. We knew this was a bluff. The rule against soliciting also applied to prostitution. They were sitting there pretending to be a happy couple and wouldn't have liked it if we exposed them as hooker and john.

I ignored the man and said to the woman, 'I bet your mother doesn't know you are turning tricks at the Holiday Inn. I sing with her in the church choir, you know? I may casually mention it at our next rehearsal.'

I didn't sing in any church choir, but her mother did. Her soprano at the Lesotho Evangelical Church choral society was legendary. I didn't know her personally but as a keen follower of choral music, a love I inherited from my father, I had attended a few concerts where I was mesmerised by her voice.

I turned to the man and said, 'You see, this poor man is an artist. He does something with his hands. He doesn't steal, he doesn't rob, he doesn't cross the border to a foreign country to sleep with prostitutes. He's an artist. The least you can do after screwing my cousin is to buy his painting.'

'Hey, I haven't done anything yet with your cousin,' he said.

The woman snapped at the john, 'I am not his damn cousin!' And then she turned to me and asked pleadingly, 'What do you want from me, heh? What do you want?'

'Ask your boyfriend to buy just one painting and I'll say nothing to your mother,' I said.

'This is robbery,' said the man. 'I don't want no bloody painting.'

'You know I can easily go to the reception and phone your mother,' I said.

'How much? I'll buy the painting so that you leave us alone,' said the woman.

'You'll buy no painting, Sweet Pea. I'll buy it for you.'

'Thank you,' I said, and went back to my bar stool to resume nursing my glass of water.

'*Le masepa, lea tseba?*' the woman yelled after me. You're full of shit, you know that?

Mr Dizzy haggled with the man, and finally came back with a twenty rand note, which was quite a lot of money. Remember, those days the South African rand was worth one and a half times more than the American dollar.

We felt like millionaires. A scale of pineapple beer was five cents. We could get four hundred scales from this amount. We could drink this for days on end. But then we also had to buy Russian sausages and chips to sustain ourselves. Even then man did not live by beer alone. That evening we drank at the casino instead of our regular shebeens. With that kind of money we could even afford Scotch whisky. Though I hated the taste – I had always been a brandy or rum or beer or red wine man – it was good for impressing the rest of the patrons, especially the female ones. Soon I was drunk. I staggered home, which was less than thirty minutes' walk from the Holiday Inn.

Early the next morning Mr Dizzy came knocking at my cottage door. I didn't like it when he did that because I didn't think Mr Kolane and my aunt would enjoy the sight of such a dodgy character in their immaculate garden. The way he looked they wouldn't have guessed that he came from a family that had an immaculate garden of their own. As soon as I let him in he told me that he had lost all the money at the slot machines and roulette tables. The fool had also lost the rest of the paintings.

The problem was not what we were going to eat. I could eat at the main house at the Kolanes, and he could eat all he wanted at his home at the other end of Maseru West. The problem was what we were going to drink.

Later in the day, after a long nap, I put a few sketches together and once more Mr Dizzy and I went to peddle them, this time among the commercial travellers and tourists at the Lancer's Inn. The Holiday Inn would have been a lost cause at that time of the day.

After many attempts without anyone showing interest, when we were about to give up and make for the shebeens with our trusty guitar, an old white woman who was standing outside the front entrance as if waiting for someone looked at the works with a beaming face. A black and white pencil portrait caught her eye – the only work of realism in the portfolio.

'I'll buy this one,' she said.

'Sorry, I am not selling this one,' I said.

It was a portrait of Sibongile Twala.

Mr Dizzy glared at me as if I had lost my mind. Or something worse.

'He's just joking, ma'am,' he said. 'We are selling everything here.'

'Not this one, Mr Dizzy. I'll never sell Sibongile.'

'You're not selling your fucking cousin, man. It's a picture and you'll draw another one.'

'Yes, I'll draw another one. But even that one, I won't sell it.'

'Then why did you bring it with you?'

'For luck; she's my Muse. Plus it looks after the rest of my paintings.'

'Muse? Are you crazy? Are you living in some stupid Greek mythology or what? What the fuck is a Muse for an African artist?'

'We'd have money now if you had not gambled it away. I'm not parting with this one.'

All this time the old lady was peering at the two unkempt black kids arguing about a Muse. Finally she burst out laughing and said, 'Okay, okay, I'll buy a different one.'

She only paid five rands for a charcoal sketch; it was better than nothing.

One couldn't stay mad at Mr Dizzy for too long. Soon we were laughing and walking up Kingsway to Lesotho High School to visit our friend Clement Kobo.

Clemoski, as we called him, was an English Literature teacher at the high school and lived in a six-roomed brick house on campus. The youthful elite of Maseru gathered at his house to listen to jazz and soul, and to drink brandy and beer and talk about the state of the world. It was a far cry from the home-brew dives that Mr Dizzy and I frequented. Here we had the more learned citizens – civil servants and teachers. My former English Literature teacher at Peka High School, Gordon Tube, was a frequent guest. It was great to sit down with him and talk about literature in this convivial atmosphere.

In the shebeens the habitués argued about soccer and women; at Clemoski's it was all about politics, jazz and boxing. Muhammad Ali was world heavyweight champion and his rhyming fervour was setting the world alight. Copies of *Ring* magazine were lying all over the living room alongside copies of *Down Beat*.

Sometimes the arguments got so heated that men almost came to blows. Like when Steve Belasco voiced an unpopular view that one of Hugh Masekela's Sesotho jazz numbers about herdboys who must be careful that the cattle they were driving to the veld did not catch cold was shit. Now, Hugh Masekela was our hero, a premier trumpet player who was making his name in the highest echelons of jazz in the United States after being exiled from South Africa. Some of Clemoski's friends took offence, but Steve Belasco stood his ground.

'Shit is shit,' he said. 'It doesn't matter who plays it.'

Two of the guys pushed Steve Belasco outside, but before we could see some fisticuffs Clemoski came between them and stopped the argument. One could smell the bad blood for a while after that.

Steve Belasco was a Peace Corps volunteer. But he was quite different from the normal Peace Corps men and women we had come to know. For one thing, he was not scruffy; he was always fashionably dressed in clean jeans and well-ironed shirts. Also, he knew something about jazz, so we spoke the same language, which couldn't be said of the other Peace Corps volunteers who had never even heard of Dizzy Gillespie or Sarah Vaughn or a host of big-name jazz musicians. Steve Belasco knew them all. But I suppose as a white man from America he had no right not to like our music.

And our local jazz – by which we meant South African jazz – was going through a boom period. Some of the bands came to Lesotho and played at the National Stadium. After the show the musicians would congregate at Clemoski's place or at Tom Thabane's, one of Clemoski's friends who, many years later, held a number of cabinet posts in various Lesotho governments. I remember once sharing a *zol* of marijuana with Gabriel Thobejane in Tom Thabane's garden, after which Thobejane played the African drums like a man possessed by demons and Philip Tabane joined him with his guitar that wailed like a wandering spirit. These were the Malombo Jazzmen who had had a successful concert at the stadium the previous night when we danced ourselves to oblivion.

Thandi Klaasen was another South African jazz musician who would scat like nobody's business at the Holiday Inn. And we would all drink together at Clemoski's place before and after these shows. My prize memory was when the songstress was walking with Clemoski and one or two other hangers-on to her dressing room at the National Stadium, and I was following them carrying her sequinned dresses. The soft velvety and silky dresses were lying across my raised arms like an offering to some kinky deity. The crowd was roaring with anticipation as we worked our way among them to the back of the makeshift stage in the centre of the soccer pitch. I was proud that I was part of the history that was going to be made at that stadium, however minuscule my groupie role was.

MR DIZZY HAS A seizure and his hands are shaking violently. His eyes bulge out and then he shuts them tightly. I can see that he is struggling against the shake-shakes, as we used to call his condition. I am surprised to see that he still has it after all these years. It used to scare the hell out of me when it happened all of a sudden in the midst of our merrymaking. Come to think of it, except for the gaunt face, Mr Dizzy hasn't changed much.

His gambling partner just sits there as if nothing is happening. He gets bored watching the shake-shakes, stands up and leaves; perhaps back to the slot machines.

Gugu looks at Mr Dizzy intently. Perhaps she feels sorry for him. He is a pitiable sight. But who knows? Maybe Mr Dizzy feels sorry for me for having settled for the humdrum life of American suburbia while he continues unabated with the hustling that we were doing when we were boys more than forty years ago. Oh, for the carefree life, unconstrained by the shackles of convention and respectability! Although he doesn't look quite carefree now as he sits in the easy chair, eyes shut.

His shake-shakes subside until they stop. He doesn't make any effort to open his eyes now that the storm is over but just sits there and sleeps.

'*Sies*, you let him kiss you!' says Gugu out of the blue.

'Hey, are you ever going to forget that kiss?' I laugh.

A security guard shakes him awake and drags him out. It is his life. It was our life. Card counting at the casino. Entanglements with the police. Addiction to alcohol and gambling. Nothing has changed with him.

'You know, that could have been me?' I tell Gugu. 'It was just luck that I came to my senses and changed. It's mostly thanks to my father. He was the one who brought me back from the brink.'

MY FATHER GOT REPORTS from such people as Nqabande Sidzamba, the PAC Lesotho representative, that I was living a wanton and reckless life in Maseru and he summoned me to Mafeteng immediately. Mr Kolane asked me to vacate my garden cottage. I think

169

he was relieved that my father had asked him to kick me out; he had tolerated me long enough.

There was no way on earth I could defy my father. If he said I had to go back home, then I had to go back home.

Back in Mafeteng I discovered that he had fallen out with his landlords, the Thathos, and we had moved to a much smaller house that he was renting in the slummy Phahameng Township. It was a small stone building with rusty corrugated iron roofing and no ceiling. It had no indoor plumbing and no electricity. The toilet was a pit latrine outside and we had to draw water from a communal tap a few streets away. My mother and the maid used Primus stoves or a coal stove to cook our meals.

My siblings and I lamented the fact that instead of moving up we were going down the social ladder. We felt that we were the only lawyer's children who lived that kind of life in the whole world. Of course we only said these things among ourselves and would never have voiced them to our parents. Our father would have put us in our place. He would have looked on us as ungrateful children who should be counting their blessings for having been granted political asylum by the Basotho people instead of complaining. His view was that we were of the people and should live with the people. His fulfilment came from serving the community selflessly instead of accumulating wealth.

We felt that our poverty was self-inflicted. To us, it did not make sense that he charged a man who had the means to pay proper fees thirty rands for a divorce case that dragged on for six months at the High Court when other lawyers charged thousands of rands for the same service. What irked me most was that this client, Nthethe was his name, joked in all the shebeens in town that my father had charged him such a small fee. Instead of being grateful, he was laughing about it. But my father continued charging a pittance. And then after that he would be so broke that if there was any emergency he would have to borrow money from friends. Yet he worked so hard. All the time. Until past midnight. And demanded silence in the house, even from our mother. He would yell at our mother as if she were a child if she spoke while he worked at the dining room table in the flickering light of paraffin lamps reinforced by candlelight.

I felt very sad when he yelled at our mother like that. Or even angry. Some of my anger was directed at her. I couldn't understand why she should accept such treatment. Why she should be whispering in her own house, and sometimes even suffer rebuke for the softest of whispers, when he felt he needed absolute silence. We could live with that, we were kids, we could tiptoe our way in silence, but she was a woman, an adult, our mother. She, on the other hand, began to join our little conspiracies. If the twins and I went out to the disco at Hotel Mafeteng until the early hours of the morning we would tell her the truth about it and count on her not to inform our father. Often she covered for us kids when we did something wrong. She would reprimand us, yes, but never inform the old man.

The tradition of family meetings continued. We sat at the dining room table and our father analysed the current events for us, while at the same time giving us lessons on how to be upright citizens with discipline and dedication. Those were his key words. We listened attentively and punctuated each one of his sentences with *'ewe, tata'* – yes father – even if at that time our minds were wandering out there in the dens of iniquity.

Ben Maphathe arrived in the middle of one such meeting and my father asked him to sit down. He was a family friend whose mother gave us accommodation at her house when we first came to live in Mafeteng. His father, then divorced from his mother, was the local doctor who also owned some businesses in Mafeteng and Maseru. I was quite embarrassed to be repeating *ewe, tata* all the time in his presence because this had actually become a joke among my friends. They didn't have such military discipline in their homes. So, I was a bit slack about my *ewe, tata* responses and my father misinterpreted that for lack of interest in what he was saying. He snapped at me right there, in the presence of a visitor. If only the floor had opened up and swallowed me!

Sometimes my father would discuss literature at these meetings. He would ask us what we thought of the set books that we read at high school such as *Silas Marner* by George Eliot, *Great Expectations*, *David Copperfield* and *Oliver Twist*, all by Charles Dickens, and some of the plays of Shakespeare. When he expounded on these works I could see that he missed the days when he used to be a high school teacher and a university lecturer. I didn't tell you that before I was born, in 1947 and 1948, he taught at Pius XII College, Roma, Lesotho.

'What do you think of *Things Fall Apart*?' he asked once.

We all loved that novel. It was the first time in all our education that we were reading a book by an African author for the Cambridge Overseas School Certificate. So, you would have thought I would gush with praise for Chinua Achebe's work. But I instead I said, 'It's just a novel.' This didn't mean much, but fortunately my father didn't press for a forthright answer. You see, I had heard him discuss *Things Fall Apart* with my former principal, Tseliso Makhakhe, a few weeks before when the principal gave us a ride in his car from Maseru. My father had asked the principal the same question: 'What do you think of *Things Fall Apart*?' and the principal had gone all out in praise of the book. I was surprised to hear my father attack the novel as reactionary in its depiction of Africans. It could only serve the interests of neo-colonialists, he said. No wonder the British had deemed it fit to prescribe. And I had thought it was such a progressive novel! I remember making a note to myself to ask Ntlabathi Mbuli next time I met him why my father thought *Things Fall Apart* was a reactionary novel. But Ntlabathi did not know either, since he did not share that view; he could merely guess that perhaps it was because in the book Africans lose their country to a colonial power through their own foolishness. So, when my father asked us at this meeting I was not forthcoming with my answer because I didn't want to say something that would contradict his view of the novel.

One thing I remembered very well even as we read the book at high school was that the main character, Okonkwo, reminded me very much of my father. Not the Okonkwo who is ashamed of his father, for my father was immensely proud of his father, but the Okonkwo who was impatient with failure and ruled his family with an iron rod. Did my father perhaps see himself in Okonkwo, hence his condemning the book?

I was happy to see that my father had taken to drinking some beer on occasion, a habit he had given up decades ago. At least once a fortnight or so he drank Castle Lager as he worked at Hani's restaurant. He came home drunk and was happy with everyone. That's what alcohol did to him. It made him so euphoric that he would be cracking jokes and singing and telling us stories of the revolution. We wished he could stay drunk for ever. But no such luck; the next morning he would wake us up very early, looking remorseful for having been so unguardedly giddy the previous night. 'Wake up, you fools,' he would say. We would then start cleaning up the whole place. Everything had to be spick and span when he was suffering from a hangover.

Fortunately, he never kept us prisoner at home. He allowed us to come and go as we pleased when our chores were done, as long as we reported to him or our mother where we were going and when we would be back. So, our social life did not suffer one bit despite our domestic circumstances. And in Mafeteng social life meant drinking.

My brother Monwabisi had become quite a socialite and was active in organising social gatherings. We went for picnics at the Tsalitlama Lake with the beautiful Mafikeng girls whose mother owned the restaurant with Chris Hani's father, and we drank ourselves silly.

My friends Peter Masotsa and Litsebe Leballo were over the moon that I was back in Mafeteng. They exclaimed that I had gained a lot of weight and I was quite happy about it. Actually the weight gain started in my last year of high school because I drank a lot of *sqo* – the Basotho home-brewed beer made of sorghum and reputed to make people fat. I didn't know that for years to come I would be fighting a losing battle against weight; I was just happy that the guys called me *ngamla*, which meant rich man. No one would ever call me *moketa* again – a name given to a cow so emaciated you could count its ribs. And indeed I carried myself about like the rich man I was supposed to look like.

And this time my ballooning figure did not only strut around in the shebeens but at Hotel Mafeteng. Yes, our little town now had a hotel, owned by a son of Mafeteng no less. Mpho Motloung had been a businessman in Johannesburg where he had made a lot of money. He and his beautiful wife Maggie decided to invest it in his home town by building a hotel. We had watched with anticipation as the octagonal double-storey structure rose from the ground. When it was finally opened we were agape at the kind of people who came from Johannesburg and graced our dusty town. These included such socialites as Dr Joe

Jivhuho and Lefty Mthembu, a big-time gangster whose exploits we often read about in *The Golden City Post* and in *Drum Magazine*. They were all Mpho Motloung's friends and spent many a weekend drinking Bacardi Rum and cavorting with the model-type women in mini-skirts and gigantic afros that they brought with them from the City of Gold. We went to the hotel and watched them enviously and said to ourselves: 'One day we are going to live like that.'

We still patronised our home-brew shebeens because liquor was too expensive for us at the hotel. The trick was to get ourselves drunk at the shebeens first, then later go to the hotel and play big there with one or two beers. Later we would go to dance the night away to James Brown's 'Please, Please, Please' at the disco. Hotel Mafeteng had the hottest disco in the whole country and people even came from as far as Bloemfontein to release tension and taste a little bit of freedom. Remember, it was during the days of apartheid and black people were not allowed in hotels in their own country, so Lesotho became the place to socialise with dignity.

Indeed, life in Mafeteng was so beautiful that I asked myself what the heck I was doing in Maseru where I had to hustle for money when I had it made right here at home with my parents feeding my dirty habits, though they didn't know what I was doing with the 'pocket money' they gave me. To crown it all there was Ntlabathi Mbuli. When I returned from Maseru I found that he had settled in a room he was renting from a local businessman and he was sleeping with a young white Peace Corps lady who had recently come to town and was teaching at the Catholic 'Masentle High School. She was nothing like the three beautiful Peace Corps women who once graced our town: Marie Peterson, Lois Saito and Patricia Eaton. Nothing like Steve Belasco in Maseru who was so sophisticated that you forgot he was Peace Corps.

This one was always dishevelled and her clothes were dirty and her feet were caked black with filth. I often visited her at the tiny brick house she was renting just outside the school premises, and it was always untidy with clothes strewn all over the place and with plates and pots dirty with mouldy food. I felt sorry for the room for I knew it in its heyday when it was clean and fresh. It used to be a café and I would hang out there with Bra Bullet who managed it for his father, Mr Mokhethi.

Ntlabathi only slept with this girl when he was drunk. Invariably in the morning she would come knocking at my door. My brothers and I all slept in the same room and we would be nursing hangovers of our own as she sniffled and complained that Ntlabathi was only interested in sex whereas she wanted a meaningful relationship.

'Why do you allow him?' I asked. I felt bad for her because she was so much impressed by Ntlabathi's intellectual wit and desperately wanted him to take their affair seriously. But he was only interested in what today is known as a booty call.

Ntlabathi's presence in Mafeteng tempered our hedonism with some intellectual pursuits. He was a poet, so some nights we sat in his room reading and discussing poetry. I had written more poems after that one about the death of my friend Santho Mohapeloa, and Ntlabathi would critique them. Litsebe and Peter found such activities a waste of the time they could be spending profitably drinking pineapple beer and sleeping with shebeen queens and their daughters, so they sneaked out. But another friend, Motake Malefane, joined us and read his own poems.

Wantonness was further tempered when Bra Zero Mosisidi completed his BSc at the university at Roma and rented a room in the same township as Ntlabathi. This was another place to hang out and listen to jazz. Bra Zero introduced us to Oscar Peterson's 'Canadian Suite' to which we listened endlessly because we loved it so much. Later Bra Zero was to leave this room to me when he went to work for the government in Maseru. This was the place I lent to Babsy Mlangeni and the All Rounders when they came to town.

Mafeteng was not only the home of drunkards like us; it was also the abode of writers. I have already told you of our neighbour, Sebolai Matlosa, who wrote some wonderful Sesotho novels in addition to being our neighbourhood butcher. But there was also Mosebi Damane, a nationally celebrated Sesotho poet and a scholar of Lesotho history and literature. I discovered in his book *Marath'a Lilepe* that my revered ancestor Mhlontlo featured in the praise poetry of early Lesotho chiefs and kings. So I crossed the road to his house to talk about it, hoping to learn more about Mhlontlo, perhaps some of the things that my grandfather never told me.

Thanks to the oral tradition of Sesotho poetry, and Damane's interpretation of it, I learned that the magistrate Hamilton Hope, who incidentally had been a magistrate in Quthing, Lesotho, before being posted to Qumbu in the Eastern Cape among my amaMpondomise people, had asked Mhlontlo and his people to surrender their guns – part of the British pacification efforts. My revered ancestor pretended that he was going to comply with that order and lured Hope to his Great Place, as a paramount chief's headquarters was known, where he killed him. Damane knew the exact date of these events – October 22, 1880. Mhlontlo escaped to Lesotho and found succour in the village of Phiring near Phamong. I knew both these places. I had been there a few years before when I was campaigning for the BCP with Ntsu Mokhehle and Potlako Leballo. I had goosebumps when I realised that I had walked on the same soil as my revered ancestor who was hiding from the mighty wrath of the Queen of England.

The Sesotho oral tradition further taught me that in Lesotho Mhlontlo was named 'Mamalo and that he was lured back into the Eastern Cape by the white man who owned the store at Palmietfontein who promised him new blankets. That's where he was arrested and taken for trial in Kingwilliamstown. According to Damane, he won that case in 1902. I hoped one day I would find the court records to see exactly how he happened to win a case that was supposed to be so watertight.

Through the Sesotho praise poetry I felt that I was communing with Mhlontlo. This was quite disconcerting because as an atheist I didn't believe in life after death. Yet here I was hearing his voice as Damane recited the poetry. In deep isiXhosa it wove itself in and out of Damane's Sesotho rhythms. 'Heed the ancestral voices,' it said. I could feel that Mhlontlo, he who was given refuge in this very country where we found ourselves once more as refugees, walked with me and expected better of me.

As soon as I walked out of Damane's house I dismissed the thought as so much superstition and went to join my friends at some home-brew joint.

And then Mr Dizzy came to town. And Khomo Mohapeloa. And Choks Masiloane. These were all Maseru bourgeois kids and they looked out of place in our dusty Mafeteng. Yes, city slickers did come to Hotel Mafeteng and its disco, but they always left the next day. There was nothing to stay for in Mafeteng. But here were these guys on an extended visit. They were spending a lot of time with Ben Maphathe. Occasionally I spent some time with them, but there seemed to be some gulf between us. Even with Mr Dizzy. It was obvious they were on some mission they didn't want me to know about.

A few days later I heard that they had all crossed the border and were on their way to Swaziland. So, that was what they were planning all along; to run away from home. I felt very bad that they had not invited me to be part of the scheme. I knew all these guys very well and counted them as friends and yet they didn't even intimate to me that they were planning to run away. I doubt if I would have gone with them; I was too fearful of my father to be a runaway. Plus I didn't have a passport because I was a refugee boy. But all I needed was to be asked. I felt betrayed, especially by Mr Dizzy. It was the same kind of feeling I experienced after Cousin Mlungisi and the Magengenene boys went for circumcision without me, while I remained a boy.

It was cold comfort when reports filtered into the country that the runaways were penniless in Swaziland and had to beg in the streets for survival and Mr Dizzy was busking at some seedy places for scraps of food. I never got to know how true or false these reports were, but a few months later the runaways trickled back into the country. They looked quite miserable and didn't want to discuss their experience with anyone.

I was glad they had not invited me.

CHAPTER SIX

THE BEE PEOPLE ARE very happy to see the visitor from Africa. She is from Uganda, you see, and therefore to these rural folks she is from Africa – as if South Africa is not in Africa. It is the legacy of apartheid where South Africans were isolated from the rest of the continent and were taught by the propaganda machine that they were different and better-off than the hordes north of the Limpopo River who had to wallow in darkness sans the civilising effect of white power.

'She looks just like us,' says Nompendulo Mtlomelo, the secretary.

'Of course she looks just like you. Why wouldn't she look just like you?' I ask.

'I thought because she comes from Africa she would look like people from Africa.'

I want to interpret this conversation for Goretti Kyomuhendo, hoping she will see the funny side of it, but I don't see her in the small audience of beekeepers. She took a walk, I am told, among the rocks and the aloes on the mountain. I was hoping she would stay for the meeting, but I guess the beauty of the mountain was too much to resist. I know because I myself find the place awe-inspiring, especially because for miles around there are no human settlements; just the boulders and shrubs and brooks, and aloes, and birds, and lizards. And caves that used to be occupied by abaThwa people, as we called those who are referred to as the San today. And of course the bees.

Sometimes, when I have steeled myself to drive up the steep and narrow dirt road to this place, I like to stand on a cliff and shout obscenities to the world and listen as they are echoed over and over in diminuendo and before the reverberations die out I shout once again, starting a new cycle of echoes.

Goretti is a novelist from Uganda who is currently based at the University of KwaZulu-Natal where she is studying for a master's degree in creative writing. I am her external examiner, although at this point she is not aware of that. I first met her in Lille, France, where some African writers had gathered to examine ways they could address the Rwandan genocide in their writing. She had written a novel that touched on that subject. When I heard she was in Durban I invited her to my house in Johannesburg where she spent a few days and now Gugu and I have taken her on a six-hour drive through the Free State to the Eastern Cape to show her our rural development project. She is an activist herself in Uganda where she was one of the women who established Femrite, the publishing arm of the Uganda Women Writers' Association. Perhaps after seeing our apiary she may be inspired to expand her activism beyond writers' issues to other aspects of community development.

'You should have told us that you are coming with a visitor,' says 'Makamohelo Lebata, the chairperson. 'What is she going to eat? We have not cooked anything.'

'Are you telling me you folks only eat when there is a visitor?' I ask.

She is mystified by such a stupid question.

'She's going to eat what you eat,' I try to explain myself. I tell her that when I lived on this very mountain with my grandmother there was always food left over in case a stranger came asking for directions. It was our obligation to feed him or her. And this was the practice of every family in the community. It was part of what is known as *ubuntu* – which literally means personhood. The word embodies the values of humaneness, generosity, humanity and compassion.

'So you see, 'Makamohelo, don't blame me for bringing a stranger without warning,' I say. 'Blame yourselves for doing away with such a beautiful custom.'

I am only teasing them. Their beekeeping project gets so many visitors – mostly Europeans and Americans in long tour buses – and they cannot be expected to feed everyone who comes.

The meeting proceeds and we discuss ways of expanding the project. It has always been my wish that they learn to harvest the bottom leaves of the aloes, which end up dying anyway, and then boil them in cauldrons to extract aloe vera. It would be a wonderful income-generating activity for the Bee People between harvests of honey, which take place only twice a year. But we need to get some experts who will make sure that the fumes from the boiling aloes would not have an adverse effect on the hives that dot the mountain. Another problem is that these aloes are a protected species; we would need to convince the government that our activities will not kill the plants. Perhaps if we ask the scientists from the University of the Free State in Bloemfontein to donate their services by making an authoritative study that will put the authorities at ease. We love the environment and want to protect it and are happy that we have a government that cares for it. The villagers too have a very strong conservation ethos.

'What about the essential oils that we spoke about?' asks Nompendulo.

A guest once suggested that the Bee People could reap even greater benefits from their mountain if they harvested essential oils from the shrubs and bushes that grow on the mountain which are used in the manufacture of cosmetics and pharmaceuticals.

'That is another thing we must get the scientists at the university to analyse for us. There are many possibilities on this mountain. But it is important that whatever we do, we should leave the mountain better than we found it, with more vegetation and wildlife.'

After the meeting we look for Goretti and find her strolling alone on the gravel road. The Bee People drive us down the winding and rocky mountain road in their truck to my Uncle Press's store where we had parked our car. We cross the Telle Bridge into Lesotho, and cruise through the Quthing and the Mohale's Hoek districts. After about 80 kilometres or so we are in Mafeteng. We book in at Hotel Mafeteng and then go visit my mother at Zwelakhe's house where she lives. Zwelakhe, you will remember, is the youngest of my brothers. He is an advocate of the High Court of Lesotho and the president of the Law Society.

My mother at this stage spends all her days in the bedroom, disabled by arthritis and hypertension and even varicose veins. I introduce her to Goretti and they pass a few pleasantries. On our way back to the hotel Goretti exclaims: 'Your mother speaks English!'

I am surprised at her surprise.

'If she spoke to you in isiXhosa you wouldn't understand,' I say.

We have always been a multilingual family and I guess I took that situation for granted, as if all mothers the world over, even in the villages of Uganda, speak to their sons, daughters-in-law and visitors in English. It dawns on me that our language situation at home is an unusual one. Even as little kids we functioned in a variety of languages; when we spoke with our father it was almost always in English, with our mother it was predominantly in isiXhosa and when we spoke among ourselves as siblings it was in Sesotho. Our forebears were originally speakers of isiXhosa on both sides of the family – so you can see that mothers are keepers of the heritage.

We spend the night at the hotel. It is now a far cry from the glorious Hotel Mafeteng of my youth which had shimmering bars of glass and mahogany and comfortable lounges with leather-covered sofas. It is now decrepit and the rooms have a permanent musty smell. In the morning there is no water for a bath or shower. The nightwatchman, an old man who has been nightwatchman here for the past thirty years, warms water in big watering cans on the kitchen stoves and brings it to us in the rooms.

The room that I share with Gugu used to be Mpho Motloung's room – the late owner of this place. It used to be where the socialites of Johannesburg, Mpho Motloung's special guests, gathered for private parties. If you were invited to a party at Room Number 4 you knew that you had made it in life.

I remember one night drinking at the bar until I was so sloshed that when I went to the restroom I blacked out on the toilet seat while doing my business. When I finally opened my eyes it was about 3 a.m. and the bar was closed. I was locked inside the building and everyone in the rooms upstairs was asleep. My first instinct was to jump over the counter and treat myself to a bottle of brandy. But common sense prevailed; I bumbled up the stairs to the rooms. Because it was dark I couldn't tell which one was Number 4, so I listened at each door for Mpho Motloung's famous snore. Indeed it did not let me down, it came like a roar and I knocked at the door. He woke up and without any fuss opened the main door for me. I staggered home singing at full volume as though I didn't have a care in the world.

When I tell the women this story at breakfast time Gugu says she is surprised I turned out so well after such rampant and unruly adolescence.

'Turned out so well?' I ask. 'It is true then that love is blind? It makes you not see the scoundrel in me.'

We decide to cross the border at the Maseru Bridge so that Goretti can see a bit of the capital city. We should have known better. This is the worst border post and Gugu has been a victim of the rudeness of immigration officials on the Lesotho side of the border from the days she was a student at the National University of Lesotho and had to cross here often on her way to and from her home in Soweto, Johannesburg. She remembers how the female customs and immigration officials – for it was mostly women who were discourteous, especially to other women – would refuse to serve black travellers if they did not speak Sesotho. The official would not even look at your passport if you answered in English and would say, 'You will stand there until you learn to speak the language.' Only after she had served a number of Sesotho-speaking customers would she take your passport, stamp it and throw it back at you.

On this day we don't get this kind of treatment and our passports are stamped without any incident. But, alas, we didn't count on Goretti having problems on the South African side of the border. They refuse to let her into the country because they claim hers is not a multiple entry visa.

She is fuming.

'What is this African unity that you people talk about if you are giving people from other African countries such problems?' she asks the officials.

I am afraid that if she continues to argue with them they might not let her into the country. Finally they endorse her passport and she is able to enter South Africa.

One thing I notice is that the South African police are polite and courteous even as they explain to Goretti the immigration laws about visas and the like. Very much unlike the Lesotho officials who are abrupt and pompous. Especially the border police. It never used to be like that. All this arrogance began in 1970. Lesotho police and other government officials used to be shining examples of civility.

And then there was 1970. Different governments have come and gone in Lesotho, but none have been able to rein in the legacy of 1970.

LESOTHO 1970. MR DIZZY'S dad wrote a much-touted book with that title. I never bothered to read it though, because I lived through that history.

I had completed the Cambridge Overseas School Certificate in Division Three the previous year, getting credit in only three (English Language, Literature in English and, to my surprise, Latin) out of the seven subjects I sat for. I didn't expect any better because I don't remember ever studying. I'd gone to class, taken notes as the teacher taught, but never looked at them again. While my colleagues were burning the midnight oil I sat on my bed in the Cell and played the flute. I thought I was destined to be Unoka, the flautist from *Things Fall Apart* who did not live up to the expectations of his community and died a poor man.

With that kind of result I certainly would not be going to university any time soon. Perhaps later I would write supplementary exams to improve my symbols. In the meantime I took a job at a night school that was owned and operated by Mr Mahamo, a primary school teacher at St Gerard Catholic School. He rented two classrooms from the poorer and dilapidated Lesotho Evangelical Church primary school and recruited those Mafeteng students who had failed their Junior Certificate to enrol for night classes in preparation for supplementary exams. I taught mathematics – yes, the very mathematics that gave me nightmares – and Ntlabathi Mbuli taught English. Mr Mahamo paid us four rands a month each.

As you can see, Mr Mahamo was quite a resourceful man. As was his wife 'Makopano, who was also a primary school teacher at St Gerard. They ran a very successful shebeen at their house, and Ntlabathi and I drank there on credit. At the end of the month all our night school salary went into paying our brandy debt at Mr Mahamo's shebeen. We were practically working for brandy, and would still owe Mr Mahamo some balance even after he had taken all our monthly salary. Fortunately, I was staying with my parents and didn't want for food, clothing and shelter. Ntlabathi, on the other hand, survived on the monthly stipend that he received through the Lesotho Christian Council as a refugee. So he was also covered in so far as subsistence was concerned.

The patrons of the shebeen were mostly policemen. Even the district commander of the paramilitary Police Mobile Unit *Ntate* Morolong, or Roll-Away as we called him because of his roly-poly figure, spent most evenings there. And then there was Mphahama, a very handsome and delicate-looking rookie whose khaki uniform was always well pressed with his boots shining like a black mirror. These were very sweet guys who carried old 303 rifles that were never fired in anger. The guns were used mostly to scare stock thieves into surrendering. That was the culture of Lesotho cops those days. They were disciplined and functioned within the confines of the law. Once in a while an overzealous cop would stray and torture a suspect to extract a confession. In all such cases the cops would find themselves in the dock charged with a criminal offence. My father defended an occasional policeman who fell foul of the law in his attempts to get evidence. Lesotho cops were generally good-natured guys who were a terror only to cattle rustlers and pickpockets.

That was why we were never uncomfortable drinking the nights away with those uniformed and armed gentlemen. Even those who were on patrol in their Land Rovers would occasionally pop in for a shot of brandy or a pint of beer and then dash out to protect the good people of Mafeteng from criminals. As a senior official I suppose Roll-Away worked only regular eight-thirty-to-four-thirty office hours. I came to this conclusion because he was at Mr Mahamo's shebeen from five on the dot and would sit on his chair imbibing spirits till midnight. He was a very generous man and would not hesitate to share his brandy with us. Mphahama, on the other hand, was always the butt of our jokes because of his fine features. We teased him that he was as beautiful as a girl and that if he were to work in the gold mines of Welkom – where most Basotho men worked for months on end without coming back to their families – he would be some miner's wife. Oh, yes, those days we delighted in homophobic jokes!

The jokes got worse when we heard that he was going through a hard time at home, with a fishwife for a wife who occasionally gave him a beating. None of these rumours were confirmed, but that didn't stop us from making snide remarks as soon as he entered and took a seat at our table. Roll-Away merely cast his fatherly eye over us and then paid more attention to his nip of brandy. I guess it would have been beneath him to make jokes about his subordinate.

One thing that everyone was excited about was the first post-independence elections. We rarely discussed politics at Mr Mahamo's shebeen since Mr Mahamo himself and most of his police patrons were all supporters of the ruling Basotho National Party, and of course Ntlabathi and I were Pan Africanists and therefore Basutoland Congress Party sympathisers. Nevertheless we were indeed looking forward to the change that we hoped would come with the elections. I had not participated in the BCP campaigns as I had done in the first elections in 1965 because Chief Leabua Jonathan's government had been effective in silencing South African refugees. They could no longer participate in Lesotho politics, unless they wanted to be deported from the country. I have told you already how Potlako Leballo, the PAC leader, was deported – even though he was actually born in Mafeteng and should then have been a Lesotho citizen by birth. A few others of our people were forced out of the country in a similar manner. So now we could only be sympathisers of the BCP and not vocal supporters.

The habitués at Mr Mahamo's knew exactly who we were, but that didn't bother them at all because we never commented on political issues. We had been cowed into silence. At least at this particular shebeen. When some leaders of the Young Pioneers came and started snooping around I suggested that perhaps we should start patronising a different shebeen. After all, Mafeteng was a BCP town and in most shebeens we would regain our freedom of expression.

'What can we do?' Ntlabathi said. 'Mr Mahamo is our employer and we owe him a lot of money. We have no choice but to patronise his shebeen.'

The Young Pioneers were the youth wing of the BNP, inspired by the brutal Young Pioneers of Kamuzu Banda's Malawi Congress Party. Not only were they inspired by the Malawians, they were actually trained there. The cosy relationship between Leabua and Banda did not surprise anyone. They had both turned their countries into client-states of South Africa. Banda had gone further than Leabua; he was the only African leader who had diplomatic relations with apartheid South Africa.

The Young Pioneers leaders who had now taken to prying at Mr Mahamo's shebeen were recently arrived from Malawi and carried themselves about with a swagger that told everyone that they were a law unto themselves. We heard stories of how they were going around threatening people that if they did not vote for the BNP they would rue the day.

'They have told you that your vote is your secret, but we have eyes everywhere,' they told prospective voters. 'Our eyes can penetrate the secret ballot.'

After the elections we sat at the shebeen listening to the results on Radio Lesotho. The atmosphere was rather strange because our police companions were nowhere in sight. We took it that they were busy guarding polling stations and generally keeping good order.

According to Radio Lesotho, the BNP and the BCP were running neck-and-neck. Every time they announced a constituency won by the BCP they would announce a constituency won by the BNP. And it dragged on like that, until the announcements stopped. They were replaced by a bouncy song by a South African *mbaqanga* band: *Leabua ke mmuso ngoan'aka*. Whether you like it or not Leabua is *the* government, the group sang in the popular idiom of South African dance music. As soon as we heard the song we knew something was wrong. Not that the song had been scarce on the airwaves before. It was a staple and was played after every news bulletin. But now it was playing over and over again for hours on end. There was some defiance about it. In the Sesotho idiom, it was as if someone wanted to rub something into someone else's face.

Later in the day listeners were warned to await an important announcement. This was followed by martial music. Then Leabua himself spoke. He was declaring a State of Emergency and was suspending the Constitution. He advised the populace to remain calm. There would be a 6 a.m. to 6 p.m. curfew throughout the country until further notice.

It became clear to us that he had lost the elections but was refusing to hand over power to Ntsu Mokhehle's BCP. This was a coup and it was happening right here in Lesotho – a country famous for its greeting *khotso*, which means 'peace'. A country whose motto was *Khotso, Pula, Nala* – Peace, Rain, Prosperity.

We had heard of coups in other African countries; we were still reeling from the overthrow of Kwame Nkrumah, our Pan Africanist leader in Ghana. But we never thought we would actually see one happening right here where we lived. It was a coup of a special kind; the party that lost the elections was refusing to hand over power. Nothing like it had been seen in Africa.

The BNP nullified the elections and refused to release the official results. But we did finally get all the figures based on declarations at polling stations: out of the sixty seats of the National Assembly the BCP had obtained thirty-six, the BNP twenty-three and the MFP only one.

Despite the curfew, Ntlabathi and I continued to teach at the night school. But the numbers of students were dwindling. We got reports that the police had beaten some of them for breaking the curfew. We did not believe these reports. The police in Lesotho were not thugs who beat up people. They would arrest wrongdoers rather than beat them up.

We continued to patronise Mr Mahamo's shebeen and stayed until the early hours of the morning as if nothing had changed. But things certainly were different. All of a sudden our police friends were wearing camouflage uniforms instead of the well-pressed khaki. They were carrying machine guns instead of their World War I 303s. There was the roly-poly figure of Roll-Away hovering over us boasting of his brand new Uzi submachine gun.

'See how this baby shines,' he was saying. 'Direct from Israel.'

He was like a little boy with a new toy.

Even Mphahama showed some braggadocio. When I tried one of our old jokes about his beauty he glared at me cheekily. He had a submachine gun of his own and was showing us how he could dismantle it and put it together again with his eyes closed. The habitués cheered and laughed at his antics, but I was getting quite uneasy. Guns generally make me nervous, perhaps from my early experience when I went out to assassinate Marake Makhetha. What if something went wrong? One couldn't trust these guys with these new Israeli machines. I didn't think they had even had adequate training to use them.

'You're going to shoot yourself in the foot, Mphahama,' I said, half-jokingly.

Another change was that now instead of these guys buying us liquor as before, Mr Mahamo and the other civilian patrons were falling over themselves giving them shots of brandy. And when they were drunk they boasted that Leabua Jonathan's government was here to stay. We learnt for the first time that Leabua himself wanted to hand over power to Ntsu Mokhehle in keeping with how democracies should function, but Fred Roach stopped all that nonsense. Fred Roach was the commander of the paramilitary Police Mobile Unit (Lesotho didn't have an army at the time). He was, in fact, the instigator of the coup.

I was not surprised to hear this from Roll-Away. I knew Fred Roach from my Peka High School days. At that time he was the police commissioner in charge of the Leribe district and he once invaded our high school when the students were on strike. He had surrounded the campus with his troops and had addressed us with a megaphone from the top of one of the police Land Rovers. We had responded with our own song, milling around defiantly, and calling him a British dog born in New Zealand and sent to Lesotho to oppress Basotho children. His men aimed their guns at us and we had to retreat. He successfully suppressed our little rebellion, and later that night his convoy of Land Rovers drove back to Hlotse, the district capital, in triumph. There he was, Her Majesty's subject, subverting democracy in Her Majesty's former colony of Lesotho when the prime minister was keen to hand over power.

I thought the coup would not last, but it did. Ntsu Mokhehle was arrested and King Moshoeshoe II was placed under house arrest. The various radio stations of the South African Broadcasting Corporation came out in support of the coup. Commentators commended Leabua for saving Lesotho and the whole subcontinent from the Peking-supported Ntsu Mokhehle and his Communist cronies. Hennie Serfontein, an Afrikaner journalist who had become Leabua's adviser wrote extensive articles in the Johannesburg newspaper, the *Sunday Times*, in support of the coup.

After classes as we sat at Mr Mahamo's shebeen we often heard women screaming and we knew exactly what was happening. There were stories that the police, the paramilitary guys and the Young Pioneers had gone on the rampage, invading homes without any provocation, beating up the men and raping the women and children. The Young Pioneers particularly were quite merciless. We decided that it was too risky to spend our evenings at the shebeen, so when we finished our classes at the night school, which was at about eight or so, we went straight home. Mr Mahamo got us permits from Roll-Away that allowed us to break the curfew. But still on occasion we had to

189

run for dear life from the Young Pioneers. One day, just after walking out of the school yard, there was a glare of headlights. It was too late to escape and armed uniformed men jumped out of a Land Rover and charged at us.

'Hey, Mphahama, it's us, man,' I said when I recognised one of the men as our dear friend.

'Hey, Mphahama, it's us, man,' he said, mimicking me in a mocking voice. 'You think that because you are educated little fools you can just break the law?'

Then he lashed out at me with a whip. The three men with him took the cue and began to lash out at us as well. Ntlabathi and I took to our heels in different directions. I jumped the school fence back into the yard. I hid among the dustbins at the back. They didn't come after me, nor did they chase Ntlabathi, who had disappeared past the hedge that fenced in the cemetery that used to be reserved for white colonists back in the day. I could hear the cops laughing as they jumped back into their vehicle and drove away.

Oh, yes, the beautiful Mphahama had become so vengefully brutal that from that day on we gave him the widest berth possible.

A few months later Roll-Away was recalled to Maseru because Commander Fred Roach thought he was too soft in a notoriously BCP town like Mafeteng. He was too grandfatherly, so Roach replaced him with a dark stubby man called Potiane who led the raids with a sadistic sneer. Under Potiane's regime we were afraid to walk in the street even during the day. We gave up going to school altogether and Mr Mahamo had to close it. He was quite a buffoon, Potiane, and would march up and down the streets of Mafeteng in full camouflage gear and a bandolier, brandishing an AK47 and an Uzi at the same time. Children would shout: '*Thunya* Potiane! *Batho ba u shebile!*' Shoot, Potiane! People are watching you! This meant that they were spectators waiting for the rat-a-tat-tat thrills. He would smile and wave at them.

To the children he was just entertainment. But to BCP members in the district of Mafeteng he was no joke. He led raids into their homes and commanded his subordinates to shove pokers into their anuses or tie their testicles with wire and tighten the wire with pliers. The soldiers – now the Police Mobile Unit guys called themselves soldiers – boasted in the shebeens how they invaded the home of a prominent BCP-supporting businessman, Mr Malahleha, and forced him to watch as they raped his wife and two daughters. I must add that the elder of these daughters was a very close friend of mine – someone I would have dated had I not been so cowardly in propositioning girls. After ten or more soldiers had had their fun discharging their filth into the women they raped them further with the barrels of their guns, now and then threatening to discharge the bullets. After that they drenched the man's beard with petrol and then set it on fire.

The fearless newspaper of the Lesotho Evangelical Church, *Leselinyana*, reported on this event and many others throughout the country. Later its editor, Edgar Motuba, was murdered.

Mr Malahleha's daughters were scarred for life. The older one became a wanderer, sleeping rough on store verandas and abusing herself so horrendously that it seemed she was competing with the abuse that she had received from the men in uniform with their deadly weapons.

A new culture of brutality was being cultivated right in front of our eyes. Mafeteng had lost its innocence.

A deep sorrow invaded my body and sat inside my chest like a granite rock. It weighed me down and all I did was to sit in the room I shared with my three brothers and grieve. It made no difference that no member of my family was directly affected – we were never invaded, the soldiers stayed clear of our house because politicians of all parties, including the BNP, had this reverence for my father. Mafeteng was bleeding. Her grief was mine. I wanted to escape. But I had nowhere to go. I was already in exile.

Some relief, not quite the escape I yearned for, came in the form of a new temporary job at one of the two local high schools. I was recruited at Bereng High School to take over the classes of the Sesotho teacher, Mrs Mohapi, who had gone on maternity leave. Here I had my first taste of teaching at a regular high school where I interacted with other teachers in the staffroom. The principal was Moses Mampa, Scutum's son – you remember my first Latin teacher at Peka High? We hit it off immediately, especially because he was a poet whose lyrics moved me no end. Especially during those times of war. Another colleague who became a close friend was Mpho Malie. At the time we had no idea that one day he would become an important politician and a Minister of Commerce and Industry in a subsequent Lesotho government after peace had returned.

Those were wonderful times except for the little problem that I was teaching Sesotho Literature and Language, in which I had little expertise. I had studied Sesotho at Peka High School where my teacher was Matlatsa Mokhehle, Ntsu Mokhehle's brother who was also in the BCP leadership in his own right. I had excelled in written essays, grammar and proverbs, but my spoken Sesotho left much to be desired. The students complained that I was teaching them their language in English. Fortunately, they took their complaints to my mother at home rather than to the principal. I think this had become a joke among them. I was relieved when Mrs Mohapi's maternity leave was over after three months and she came back to take over her classes.

I had to say goodbye to my staffroom friends, to my students and, most sadly, to my job. Once more I was plunged into the world of unemployment, of wasting away in the skanky shebeens of Mafeteng, and of dodging patrols of Potiane's Police Mobile Unit and the Young Pioneers who had tasted so much blood that when they didn't find curfew-breakers they created them by dragging targeted men and women from their homes to the streets and then beating them up for breaking the curfew.

I watched at first hand the new culture of impunity that was taking root throughout the ranks of the Lesotho Mounted Police, the paramilitary Police Mobile Unit and the civilian militia of the ruling BNP known as the Young Pioneers. Corrupt politicians used these organs to suppress the populace in the most savage way, and these organs became a law unto themselves.

That was the beginning of what we see today.

EVERY TIME WE RETURN from a visit to the Bee People Gugu and I are brimming with euphoria. Yes, the Bee People and the mountain of

Dyarhom are euphoriants. The joie de vivre of the underprivileged, the scents of the shrubs mixed with the aroma of honey, the crispness of the mountain air, the clearness of the streams, the imposing cliffs, the frolicking of the rock rabbits, cannot but leave their spell on us until we get to the exhaust fumes of Johannesburg. We are also pleased that our guest, Goretti Kyomuhendo, was able to see other parts of South Africa which are quite different from the city of Durban where she lives for the duration of her studies.

Back at my house in Weltevredenpark – a suburb that was all-white during apartheid and mostly Afrikaner; the name is Afrikaans for 'well-contentedness' – I share with her some articles that I have recently written for South African newspapers on issues ranging from crime to criticism of the corruption of some of our political leaders. I have been a frank commentator on the social and political scene and have made quite a few powerful people unhappy.

The next morning we go shopping for groceries at Pick-n-Pay at the Randpark Ridge Mall. Goretti is astonished that we pile our trolley with foodstuffs of all kinds, including varieties of cheese. She marvels at the fact that the black people of South Africa eat cheese. Everyone else in the supermarket – both black and white – is pushing a trolley laden with groceries.

'You people live lives of extravagance here in South Africa,' she says. 'In Uganda we only go to the shop to buy the item we need at that time.'

Later, as we have a meal, she criticises one of my articles on crime for omitting the fact that the guns that were brought into the country by the guerrilla war waged by the liberation movement have contributed a lot to violent crime in South Africa. I see her point, but the focus of the article was on how in urban black communities we grew up lionising criminals, and how that has resulted in the present environment where crime is rampant and the communities are helpless. I wrote in the article that during apartheid the outlaw was the man. He challenged the law. The very law that was vicious towards us. That raided our homes in the middle of the night and reduced our mothers and fathers to whimpering bundles of shame. That locked up our fathers for not carrying a *dompas* – the ID documents that were carried only by blacks to ensure that they were confined to their designated areas. The law that uprooted families, burying them alive in barren places called 'homelands', far away from places of employment. That whipped us and mowed us down with bullets. Yet these outlaws laughed in the face of the law. They spat at the law. They beat the system. They were the enemies of our enemies. They were on our side. The law was our enemy. It was not on our side. We would therefore not have anything to do with anything that had to do with the law. Even if we knew who the outlaws were in our midst and where they were hiding we would not tell. The worst thing any black township person could be was a snitch – or *impimpi*. The snitch was on the side of the law, and therefore the snitch was the enemy. A culture of shielding criminals and giving them succour and lionising them took root and continues to this day, even though the heavy boot of apartheid is no longer on our neck and we are now supposed to be running our own affairs. In my article, published in South Africa's *Mail & Guardian*, I come up with concrete suggestions on how this culture can be rooted out, using the family and community structures that are preyed upon by the criminals.

As we debate this issue, Goretti asks why I decided to live in America when I have it made right here in my country: I drive a late model metallic grey Mercedes Benz, have a palatial suburban home with three garages, five bedrooms, two living rooms, a big dining room, a designer kitchen with all sorts of appliances and gadgets, a study, a gardener, two maids, a swimming pool and a back garden that is as big as a public park with swings, slides and jungle-gyms on which my kids played when they were young. I am obviously part of the new black elite of South Africa, enjoying the fruits of liberation, and I don't need to be in America, she says.

She is not the first person to ask me this question. Friends have wondered what the point of living in the USA is when I return to South Africa every few months to work with the Bee People in the Eastern Cape, with HIV-AIDS infected youths in Sophiatown and with playwrights at the Market Theatre in Newtown in Johannesburg.

'It is some kind of self-imposed exile,' I tell her jokingly. 'Exile of a special kind. One day you'll know what happened because I am going to write about it in my memoirs.'

I tell her that until I took up the professorship at Ohio University I earned my entire livelihood from writing for the stage and television and from my fiction that has an international market. I worked as a full-time writer for seven years, thanks to the fact that dribs and drabs of dollars, pounds and euros become a small fortune when they are transferred to South Africa. But I have other skills for which I am highly trained. I can't practise them in South Africa because all doors are closed by the vast patronage system and crony capitalism that has emerged in my beloved country. Doors were banged in my face, that's why when the opportunity availed itself I left, though it was a difficult decision. We go to where our skills are appreciated first and foremost, and then of course rewarded.

It has everything to do with my outsiderness. I have resisted the centre and have always drifted towards the periphery of things. If you stay with me you'll learn how, because of my being what Nelson Mandela called 'too outspoken', I found myself and members of my family marginalised in our society.

In fact, I always tell my adult children that when they apply for jobs in South Africa they must not mention that they are related to me. I remember drumming it into the head of my eldest son, Neo, a talented painter and a former art director at an international advertising agency, that in the South African job market it is a disadvantage to know me. But he never learns. When he goes for job interviews the question invariably arises: 'Are you related to Zakes Mda?' He always answers proudly: 'Yes, he is my dad.' And then of course they never call him back.

Well, he has the skills and the drive; he does not need a job from anyone. So, he starts his own advertising agency in partnership with some friends from Cape Town. He is a young black entrepreneur and through the government's Black Economic Empowerment programmes there are opportunities for the likes of him. Here again, when he goes for interviews and presentations, the perennial question comes and he answers it honestly.

'As long as you continue to tell them that we are related you will never get any contracts from the government, from parastatals and from the corporate world in general. The people who are unhappy with me have long tentacles.'

'So, you want me to lie, Dad, and say you're not my dad?' he asks.

'No, I don't want you to lie,' I tell him. 'I am advising you to give smart truthful answers. When they ask, "Are you related to Zakes Mda?" simply answer "I'm told we are related" and stop there. They won't ask any further.'

'Told we are related? Come on! I'll be misleading them into thinking that I don't know for sure if we are or not, or I don't even know you personally.'

'If that's what they think that's not your problem because you didn't say so. You can't help it if they make that assumption.'

He shakes his head and laughs.

'I'm told we are related?' he repeats. 'That would be a lie.'

'That's not a lie. You have no first-hand knowledge of your conception. You were *told* that we are related . . . by me and your mother.'

MY SON'S CONCEPTION WAS an accident. It started with my hesitating at a river. It was like going into exile one more time. Exile within exile. Two village men in Basotho blankets helped me with my suitcase and boxes of books, primus stove, pots, plates, blankets and groceries across the raging river. There was no bridge, they told me. The only way to and from the village of Likhakeng is to cross the river. I dread rivers. You will remember that my experience with them has not been a pleasant one. But I struggled on, resisting the force of the water, until I got to the other side.

We walked on a winding footpath among fields of maize and grazing lands until we got to the village. The men took me to a grass-thatched one-roomed house, my new home. The only furniture was a single bed, a table and a chair.

I was the new teacher at Likhakeng Secondary School in the Leribe District, in northern Lesotho.

The following week I met my students, all twenty-three of them. And that was the whole school enrolment. I didn't expect that. In its previous incarnation as Harvey Secondary School it was a relatively big school with a reputation for debauchery. It was closed down after a students' strike when I was still at Peka High School. Now, after a few years, the community of Likhakeng had opened it with this first group of boys and girls who were all doing Form A, as the first year of junior secondary school was called. I was here to teach English – both literature and language.

This is where I met the identical twins, Mpho and Mphonyane Seema. I was twenty-two, they were twenty. We fell in love. Me with both of them, and they with me. They dressed alike and everything about them was similar, down to their voices. For a long time I couldn't tell them apart. But that didn't matter because they were both my girlfriends. I think what initially attracted me to them was the fact that they were much more worldly wise than the ordinary village girls. I had not expected to meet such women in a remote village like that, who even spoke some Zulu. It turned out that they also had a home in Wattville, Benoni, near Johannesburg, where their father and two brothers worked. They spent a lot of time there. Their mother, however, lived in the village of Ha Qokolo, about ten miles or so away. She tended to the fields while the men worked in the factories of Johannesburg.

Initially I had thought that my girlfriend was Mpho, who I later learnt to distinguish as the slightly bigger and more serious of the two. But the girls laid down the law: they had always shared everything, including boyfriends, and I should learn to see them as one person.

'So what are you going to do when you get married?' I asked.

'We'll marry the same man,' they said in unison. They spoke like that quite often, as if each one knew what was in the other one's mind. It was either in unison or they completed each other's sentences. At first this spooked me out, but soon I learnt to like it.

Having two girlfriends was not a bad arrangement for me at all. They liked to cook, and since we were far away from 'civilisation' we depended on canned beef and fish. I learnt from them about a spice called *mixed masala* which could transform the dullest corned beef into a gourmet's delight when fried with tomatoes and scallions. As village girls of Leribe, they knew a lot about all sorts of *masalas* since they had lived with Indians all their lives. The British colonial rulers had confined the Indians to only two of the nine districts of Lesotho – Leribe and Butha Buthe – because they didn't want Indian traders to compete with English traders. In their statutes, of course, they claimed they were protecting small Basotho traders who would be smothered to death by the savvy Indians. But it was the English colonists and not the Basotho traders who had large general dealers' stores throughout the country, and therefore needed protection from competition.

The twins served the corned beef with macaroni, a starch we never ate at home where we were more rice, wheat bread, *pap* and samp kind of people. This was another way the twins found the route to my heart, via my stomach.

I spent most of my time with the twins; I lost all desire for alcohol. The year that I spent in that village I never even got to know where the shebeens were located. It was satisfying enough to imbibe the twins' presence and become intoxicated by it. And to engage in lovemaking with them in nightly turns. Though I suspected that it could not have been that much of a satisfying experience for them because of my old dysfunction – premature ejaculation.

About two months into our relationship the twins wanted to introduce me to their mother. We walked on the village path through fields of emaciated corn and across dongas and rivulets to the village of Ha Qokolo on the foothills. Their mother, Mme Mmapolo, welcomed me with open arms and slaughtered a hen for me which Mpho immediately cooked with her *masalas*. We ate it with the *theepe* wild spinach. I had announced how much I liked it; I had experienced it when I lived with my grandmother at Qoboshane, so Mme Mmapolo sent a little girl to harvest it from the veld.

Neighbours and a few relatives came to see the visitor and I was struck by the fact that many of them were identical twins. I later learnt that Ha Qokolo was a village of identical twins. Every other family had at least one set of identical twins. I met some of them when my twins took me to a general dealer's store owned by twins who were my twins' friends. And each set I came across dressed alike. Even those who were old ladies with *tuba-tuba* scarification marks on their faces – testifying to the fact that they belonged to an earlier world of traditional practices

– wore tired *seshoeshoe* dresses that had similar patterns and colours. Another thing that struck me was that most of these twins were females – I didn't see a single set of male twins. My twins told me that there were some families with male twins but one could count them on the fingers of one hand.

I had never seen nor heard of anything like this before and I wanted to write a magazine article about it. But I never got around to doing it.

We returned to our village quite late.

Some weeks later I got a surprise visit from old friends, people I had not seen for years. At first I did not recognise them because they were wearing heavy Basotho blankets and Basotho grass hats. They looked like any man you would meet in the village. But soon I realised that it was Sabata, the friend with whom I was once sent on an assassination mission by a leggy woman, and Masiu, who I had met at Peka High School. He was doing the final year of the Cambridge Overseas School Certificate when I was doing my first. When I returned to the high school after I had suspended myself for using cheat sheets in Latin, he had already left. The last time I heard of him he was searching for riches up in the mountains, a place called Letseng-la-Terai, where people acquired strips of land from which they mined diamonds.

'What are you doing hiding here when the country is on fire?' asked Sabata. 'Our leaders are in jail and the King has been exiled to the Netherlands.'

'Since when do you care about the King? Are you a Marematlou now?' I asked.

Masiu got to the point. They had come to recruit me for a guerrilla army that the BCP was planning to form to overthrow Chief Leabua Jonathan's illegitimate government. It had been more than a year since Leabua's coup and already pockets of resistance were emerging in some villages where police stations were being attacked. A lot of Peka High School old boys were involved and some of them had been arrested. Even *Ntate* Khoto, the huge man who used to be our school minibus driver, had been involved in acts of sabotage and was in jail.

I began to question myself: what was I doing with my life when my Peka High School colleagues were sacrificing theirs for freedom? Those who were not participating in the fomentation of insurrection had gone to further their education at the University of Botswana, Lesotho and Swaziland or somewhere overseas. Jama Mbeki had gone to study law in England and the BCP had arranged for scholarships for a group of others to study in the Soviet Union. These included Dugmore Hlalele who was studying medicine and my St Mary's High School Muse, Ray Setlogelo. For a while I had kept up a correspondence with her in Kiev where she was studying international law. Later Dugmore and Ray were married and I regretted that I had been too cowardly to express my feelings for Ray during our long years of platonic correspondence. I suspect she had long been ready to take our friendship to a more romantic level. Since the nuns at St Mary's read all the students' incoming letters she had even devised a ruse for me to send her letters to a boy at the neighbouring Christ the King High School who would then take them to her. Why would she do this if she didn't expect the letters to contain something the nuns shouldn't hear? And yet despite the subterfuge my letters had remained innocent, even though in truth I had yearned for her. She must have given up on me as a lost cause. Now she had gone to Russia and Dugmore had married her. And I was marooned in a small village teaching twenty-three students at a nondescript secondary school.

Masiu talked non-stop about Jama and Dugmore and many others, some of whom I didn't know because they were there before my time.

'You seem to know about all the MaPeka . . . where they are and what they are doing,' I said to Masiu. 'How have you been keeping tabs on everyone when you are busy digging for diamonds up in the mountains?'

MaPeka are students of Peka High School – past and present.

'I am active in the underground, that's why,' he said. 'And it's all thanks to you.'

'Underground? I never belonged to any underground.'

He told me that all his years at Peka he had not been interested in politics, until I came when he was doing his final year. He used to listen to me debate at the Smoking Spot and he read some of the pamphlets I used to distribute.

'You won me over,' he said. 'I joined the BCP and the PAC and I work covertly for the organisations even when I am up there digging for diamonds. Actually, part of my mission there is to mobilise the miners against the regime of Leabua Jonathan and his Boer masters.'

Sabata, on the other hand, was quite reserved. As if he was brooding over something. He never used to be a brooder when I knew him back in Mohale's Hoek. He used to be bubbly and was always on the prowl for cheap sex. Now he looked so mature, but in a sad way. I tried to reminisce about some of our escapades in the BCP, especially the one where we botched an assassination mission.

'And you tell me you've never been in the underground,' said Masiu laughing.

'That was no underground. That was Keystone Kops,' I responded, also laughing.

But Sabata did not laugh.

'So what do you say about what we came here for, Motlalepula?' he asked impatiently.

He was calling me by my Mohale's Hoek name. And he had no time for small talk. He was all business. A warrior's warrior. I gathered that he never went to high school but instead worked in the gold mines of South Africa. Gold dust drained him of all flesh and blood, most of which he coughed out in phlegmy fits. Now all he wanted was to go to war against Leabua and his Boer masters.

I was not prepared to leave the paradise I had created for myself with the twins to go fight a futile war.

'I want to focus on my studies so at the moment I have suspended my involvement in politics,' I told them.

I was not lying. I had enrolled for associate membership of the College of Preceptors, a professional organisation in the United Kingdom that offered distance learning courses internationally to teachers who wanted to improve their qualifications. I was focusing on the Teaching of English to Speakers of Other Languages.

This was the good reason for turning them down. But the fact remains that I didn't have the stomach to invade police stations and fight pitched battles with Leabua's paramilitary. I was not ready for suicide. You have already seen in more than one instance that I was not much of a warrior.

My friends and recruiters left the next morning, much disgusted that they had come to my house and all they drank was tea. They had eaten well because the twins cooked their corned beef and macaroni speciality, but I had not offered them a single beer because I had no idea where one could get it in the village. I had not made any attempt to find out because I was nursing my few remaining coins.

Money was the main reason my village paradise did not last. It was tight. The school depended on the fees paid by the twenty-three students and could not afford to pay me the measly thirty-three rands a month. Some months I went without a salary and had to ask my father to send me money for my survival.

I took a new job at Hlotse Secondary School, which was in town – the administrative capital of the Leribe district. The salary at fifty-two rands a month was better than at Likhakeng because the principal, Mrs Ntsekhe, took into account the few courses I had done in the Teaching of English to Speakers of Other Languages, even though she was not employing me for that. I was the new mathematics teacher! Don't ask me how I was always getting myself into such situations.

I prepared painstakingly for each lesson and taught maths with confidence. No one complained. I must have been doing something right because one of the leading mathematicians in Lesotho, Tholang Maqutu, was one of my students at Hlotse Secondary School. Unless, of course, he became brilliant in mathematics *despite* getting his early foundation in the subject from me. Another famous person to whom I taught mathematics at that school was Aubrey Moalosi. Well, he didn't become a renowned mathematician but an actor of stage and screen in Johannesburg.

We discovered that one of the twins, Mpho, was pregnant. Although the conception was an accident I was ecstatic. I had planned ultimately to marry the twins anyway. I had even taken them to Mafeteng one holiday to introduce them to my parents, without mentioning the intention of marrying both of them. That would have been ludicrous to my parents – especially to my father. My mother was quite broadminded about many things. I don't know if she would have been broadminded about polygamy – a practice unheard of in my family even in past generations.

When I brought up the matter of marriage all of a sudden Mpho was singing a different tune. She had realised, she said, that marriage to both of them would not work. She had discussed the matter with her twin sister and they had reached the conclusion that I could only marry Mpho. Well, she was the one who was pregnant, so she had the right to call the shots. The old deal was off; Mphonyane would have to look for her own husband.

When I told my father that I had impregnated a girl and wanted to marry her he was against the marriage. He was quite calm though. He flared up about minor things such as my posture when I sat or walked, yet he remained cool and collected about such a life-changing event in my life. He hoped to make me see reason. I was still young, he said, and there was no reason to rush into marriage. We would support the child, but it was not wise to marry just because the woman was pregnant. For the first time I stood up to him. I was twenty-three years old, I reminded him, and marriage at that age was not unheard of. I was marrying for love, and not just because Mpho was pregnant. He had to relent. He sent his two sidekicks, *Ntate* Rabonne (the one from whom we once stole meat) and *Ntate* Ngope Leballo (my friend Litsebe's father who was also Potlako Leballo's brother) to Ha Qokolo, the magical village of twins, to negotiate for her hand in marriage. Her father had also come from Benoni to be party to the negotiations.

The secondary school allocated me a four-roomed stone house with a red corrugated iron roof on campus. Mpho moved in with me as my common law wife since we had not yet officially married.

A few months later my first son Neo was born. I also named him Solomzi after my father. As was customary, I asked my father to also give him a name of his choice. He named him Ndukumfa after some ancestor I knew nothing about. I thought it was a terrible name that went against everything I stood for. Whereas Neo means 'a gift' and Solomzi means the 'eye of the homestead', Ndukumfa means 'a stick that beats one to death'. I was already developing some peacenik tendencies – well, only intuitively; intellectually, I believed in the armed struggle in a South Africa where black people had no democratic options and every peaceful protest was met with bullets. A name like this made me cringe. But I had to accept it. It was an ancestral name and my father had given it to him. Ancestors were warriors and lived in times when they had to be warriors to survive.

When the second child came two years later – a very beautiful girl – I named her Nomso after a cousin of mine, Nomso Samela, who was the only one of my relatives who bothered to cross the raging river to come and see me when I was teaching at Likhakeng Secondary School and who had met the twins and liked them. Nomso means 'dawn'. This time my father didn't give the child an embarrassing name. He called her Thandiwe, 'the one who is loved'.

By this time I was no longer teaching at Hlotse Secondary School. I got myself a job at Barclays Bank after I wrote an essay on how the otters that were found in Leribe could be bred and harvested for fur, and minks could be introduced as well. Mr Phelps, the British guy who managed the bank, had been so impressed with what he referred to as original thinking that he gave me the job immediately. He announced to everyone that he saw a brilliant banking career in my future since I had the knack of identifying investment opportunities despite the fact that I had zero training in business economics.

This clerical job came with a boost in salary – one hundred and twenty rands a month. No wonder everyone wanted a job at the bank.

I had money to burn so I resumed my old habits of getting sloshed, this time not in skanky shebeens but at the private bar of the Mountain View Hotel. That's where all the senior civil servants and professional people of Leribe spent their evenings. I accumulated a number of new friends, the most regular of whom was Hatasi who had been my junior at Peka. He had a clerical job at the district treasury and always had a lot of money for drinks. And he was quite generous too. When he entered the bar we knew that we were all going to get drunk until closing time without paying a cent. We wondered where he got all that money because it could not have been from his salary. Young civil servants with only high school education earned only thirty-three rands a month. There were rumours that his father was a millionaire who owned thousands of herds of cattle and goats up in the mountain districts. But one day we woke up to hear that Hatasi was in jail. He had been subsidising our bad habits with money he had embezzled from the government. Fortunately, we were not implicated in any way and Hatasi served a few years.

I didn't spend much time with Mpho and the children. Much time? I spent no time at all. I was either at work or in a bar. If I happened to be at home I was always irritable and snapped at everyone. It was the only way I knew how to be a father. I can only imagine how difficult it must have been to live with me.

Though I was an absent father and an irresponsible husband I wasn't unfaithful to Mpho, even though the opportunity availed itself hundreds of times. I am not saying you should give me a medal for that. I am just mentioning it because every one of the guys I was carousing with had a mistress or two on the side. For instance, two of my friends, Teboho and Shabe, often invited me to accompany them to Maryland to have sex with the nuns. Teboho was a salesman who travelled throughout the country selling dress-shirts from a catalogue directly to the customers. Shabe was a civil servant in Maseru. On weekends these gentlemen came to Hlotse and we all drank together at the Mountain View Hotel. After that they went to Maryland, a Catholic mission station just a few kilometres out of Hlotse, and had orgies with the nuns under the bluegum trees that surrounded the campus. They were not the only people who indulged in such orgies. Quite a few guys from Maseru came for escapades with the nuns of Maryland who had gained a reputation for generosity.

I cannot say I was never tempted to join them at Maryland. But I have always been gutless; you know that by now. Or perhaps I would rather occupy the position I have always been comfortable with – that of an eternal outsider. In fact I admired these guys for bonking the nuns and I would have done it too if I had the gumption.

Instead I sat in the bar and made more new friends over Castle Lager. One of them was Mafu Sutu, the District Administrator of Leribe, the political appointee who was in charge of the whole district. He and his wife became fast friends of my family and the only time I socialised with Mpho was when we were visiting them or when they returned our visits. Another friendship that was cultivated in that bar was with Ali Semmelink, a young Afrikaner man who was looking for a new life in Lesotho after escaping apartheid in South Africa. He was not a political refugee as such and could return to South Africa whenever he wanted to.

At first we thought Ali was a spy. Why would an Afrikaner want to escape apartheid when it was created specifically to serve his interests? He spoke freely about his background. He was originally from Cape Town, although he went to university in Pretoria and then worked at the notorious pass office in Albert Street in Johannesburg. He was one of the officials who were enforcing apartheid laws. He became disillusioned when he saw at first hand what the influx control laws were doing to break up families of black people. It was at this office that blacks were endorsed out of Johannesburg to 'homelands' they had never seen in their lives. He was soon disenchanted with his job. He made friends with some of the black people he met there and started visiting Soweto and socialising with folks in the black townships. That was illegal and he feared the law would catch up with him. He needed his freedom and so he found his way to Lesotho.

His family in Cape Town was not pleased with him. After all, they were highly respected in the Afrikaner community and were even related by marriage to Andries Treunicht. You will remember him as the staunch ultra-conservative Afrikaner political leader who was advocating an even more stringent apartheid regime. But Ali paid no attention to them. He had tasted freedom in Lesotho and there was no going back for him.

He got himself a teaching job and married a local Mosotho woman, Tseli.

Ali and I became very close and continued our drinking partnership. It is one of the very few friendships of my youth that have stood the test of time, right up to this day when we are doddering grandfathers. The drinking stopped many years ago, and now we can only look back and marvel at the folly of our youth. But those days of getting sloshed were what defined our manhood.

All this drinking didn't stunt my ambition to be somebody some day. Ali Semmelink and Mafu Sutu gave me their full support when I resigned from Barclays Bank and started an advertising and promotions business of my own. I published brochures with photographs by a famous Lesotho photographer, David Ambrose, who was also a lecturer at the university at Roma, depicting some of the tourist attractions of Lesotho. I also formed a pen-pal club called Bongo International where members from all over southern Africa joined for a fee and then at a later stage when friendships had blossomed undertook a group tour of Lesotho. I rented a suite of offices just across the street from the bank where I used to work and became my own boss.

Life couldn't have been better.

GUGU, GORETTI AND I. We are reminiscing about the bees and the Bee People while having a meal at a restaurant at Cresta, one of the numerous shopping malls that mar Johannesburg's suburbia. A man whose name I don't know, but who I suspect I met at one of my book launches, spots me and comes smiling to greet me. I stand up to shake his hand. He expresses his pleasure that even though I am supposed to have emigrated to America I return to South Africa every year to work with the community projects I founded.

'Well, I don't know if I have emigrated as such,' I tell him. 'I see myself more as a migrant worker in the USA.'

'I am glad to see that you are still proudly South African,' he says.

I am quick to respond that I never said that I am proudly South African or proudly anything.

'My South Africanness speaks for itself. I don't have to decorate it with modifiers. I don't think pride is an attractive quality in any case.'

He looks puzzled. He didn't expect such a rude answer. Obviously he does not understand what could have offended me in what he thought was praise. I can be so brutal in my frankness sometimes, and only later do I think maybe I should have been more tactful.

'South Africanness is just one of my identities,' I continue nonetheless. 'I'm also a human being and I think my humanness trumps my South

207

Africanness any day of the week. If this was not the case I would be saying South Africa right or wrong, just like some American patriots say about the USA. If my South Africanness was the paramount identity, then I'd be a jingoist.'

The poor fellow did not bargain for a lecture. He was just trying to be friendly, that's all. That part of my father that does not suffer fools gladly still lives in me. I am trying very hard to fight against it. Oh, how I'd love to suffer fools gladly like any normal human being!

I have since realised that I am not wise enough to be impatient with foolishness. That is why most times I resort to silence.

The man excuses himself and leaves.

THAT'S WHAT EVERYONE SAID about my father: *AP does not suffer fools gladly*. And sometimes it embarrassed me when he did not mince his words with anyone, including such close friends as *Ntate* Hani and Elizabeth Mafikeng – the two ANC members at whose café he did some of his work. Or even with the magistrate in court. I used to be his interpreter sometimes at the magistrate's court in Mafeteng. The court proceedings were always in Sesotho. My father understood Sesotho very well, but was more comfortable cross-examining witnesses in English. So, when *Ntate* Leboela, the regular court interpreter, was on leave I would be summoned to the court and sworn in as the interpreter for the day.

One day he became so impatient with the magistrate, who kept on interrupting his line of cross-examination of a stock theft witness, that he threw one of his South African Law Reports at him. It didn't hit the magistrate though, but fell just in front of his bench. I was afraid that there would be consequences for this rash action; maybe he would be charged with contempt. I don't know how they sorted this out with the magistrate, but the next day they were laughing about the whole incident.

The magistrate, as did everyone, held my father in great awe.

I always wanted to follow in my father's footsteps and study law. So while I was working for Barclays Bank and then at MDA Enterprises, my advertising and promotions company at Hlotse, I enrolled for a correspondence law degree with a British institution that was preparing candidates for the Inns of Court. I very much wanted to be a Barrister of Gray's Inn. The problem, of course, was that Lesotho was a Roman-Dutch Law country due to its proximity to South Africa. Even though it used to be a British colony, the country did not subscribe to English Law. Yet the whole idea of being a barrister in the English tradition was quite attractive to me.

I decided to transfer my business to Maseru, where I rented an old building on Kingsway and hired a woman from Mafeteng to run it while I focused on my studies. A local attorney, Mr O K Mofolo, gave me a job as a clerk. He advised me to register for Attorney's Admission with the University of South Africa, or Unisa as it was called, because English Law wasn't going to take me anywhere in Lesotho. It was exactly what my father and all his lawyer friends, such as George Matanzima and T T Letlaka, had done, so I happily changed to the Attorney's Admission Examinations course work. It was before South Africa introduced BProc – Baccalaureus Procurationis – as the degree for attorneys.

OK Mofolo had been a society lawyer in Durban and had returned to open his practice on the third floor of the 60-Minutes Dry Cleaners Building just across the road from the Cathedral of Our Lady of Victories. He specialised in third party insurance road accident claims and only went to court when insurance companies contested the claims, which was not often. He trained his chief clerk, Lazarus Mpota, to complete the claim forms and assess the damages, so Lazarus did all the work while OK sat at his desk and dozed away. His practice was bringing in a lot of money because Lesotho is notorious for its road accidents, so he lived very well. His house in Maseru West was a smaller version of the prime minister's palace. He was a staunch supporter of Leabua Jonathan's Basotho National Party, which was normal for an ardent Catholic like him. He once chastised me very strongly when he found a BCP pamphlet lying on my desk.

One of my weekly tasks was to take a packet of candles to a rotund

Mosotho priest at Our Lady of Victories Cathedral for his blessing. Every afternoon before we closed the office OK left a burning candle on top of his office safe. We extinguished the flame the next morning when we started work at eight-thirty. I never knew why he did that but I think he believed that God would give him more money. But then the only way God could give him more money was if God created more road accidents so that OK could lodge claims for the casualties. The more serious the accident, the more money he made. Road deaths brought more money for the heirs, and OK took quite a big share of that, in addition to the fee that the insurance companies paid him for lodging the claim. I wonder how other lawyers in Lesotho missed out on such a lucrative, effortless business. My father, for instance, had to drudge, going to court defending thieves and murderers for a pittance, while OK just dozed at his desk, Lazarus and I completed the forms, and money rolled in.

Every time I went for the candles to be blessed I found the rotund priest shooting doves with a pellet gun. He strolled on the paved path around the cathedral and when he spotted a dove he aimed carefully and fired. Thankfully, he was not a crack shot; he missed quite often. But he was getting better all the time and sometimes a dove would be cooing happily one moment and spinning in the air until it crashed on the ground the next. The priest would almost dance with glee as he reached for the dead bird. I wondered how a man of God could enjoy killing birds. If I arrived while he was aiming his rifle with strained concentration I would will the dove to fly away. 'Fly away, little bird, fly away before he pulls the trigger.' I said this under my breath. The dove would heed my warning and fly away. The priest would then look at my smirk, reach for the packet of candles in my hand, make the sign of the cross around the candles and then give them back to me. That was all it took for them to have the sacred power to be the guardian of the riches in OK's safe.

One day I came back from the priest with a packet of newly blessed candles and I met Sibongile Twala outside our office building. She was with two very handsome and fresh-looking boys. They were well dressed in expensive-looking jeans and shirts. Sibongile, my cousin and Muse, had matured into a very beautiful and sophisticated lady. I reckoned the boys were fellow students at the university where she was studying for a Bachelor of Science degree. I had not seen her for years, not since the days we lived at my aunt's in Maseru West and I was prancing around Maseru with Mr Dizzy.

She looked at me and I saw pity in her eyes. Or maybe I just imagined it. I was self-conscious about my threadbare clothes and especially my shoes. They were in tatters and the soles were held together with wires. I was ashamed that Sibongile saw me like this. She smiled, kissed me, and left with her beautiful friends.

Things had not been going well for me financially. OK Mofolo was only paying me twenty-five rands a month even though I worked for him full-time.

'You are here for the experience because you want to be a lawyer,' he said. 'Anyway, you have your own business.'

Well, I didn't have it any more. I had had to close my business because it went bankrupt for lack of proper attention.

I was renting a one-roomed flat from the Sehlabo family in a township called Qoaling on the outskirts of Maseru where I lived with Mpho and our two children. Sometimes I didn't have money to buy them food and I had to borrow twenty-five cents from a neighbouring shebeen queen to buy them a loaf of bread. Whilst I was at it, I would also drown my sorrows in pineapple beer which the shebeen queen gave me on credit. I only went home to sleep, stinking like a sewer.

One day Mphonyane, my wife's twin sister, arrived with two guys in a black Valiant, a car much beloved by taxi drivers and mine workers. The men didn't go into the house. They parked the car in the street some distance away but I could see it from the window. The twins conferred outside for some time and when Mpho came back into the room she told me that she was accompanying Mphonyane. She did not tell me where Mphonyane was going or why she needed to be accompanied.

'Who are the two guys?' I asked.

'They are Mphonyane's boyfriends,' she said.

I had heard that line before. When we were still staying at Hlotse and I was running MDA Enterprises at Kokobela Building I once passed

Mpho standing with a boy on a path near the woods. She looked glorious in a pleated mauve dress I had bought her from a mail order house in Johannesburg where I purchased her special clothes. The two were talking animatedly and giggling like teenagers. They saw me but didn't seem to mind. I didn't think much of it at the time and went off to work. After about two hours I left my office for a pub lunch at Mountain View Hotel. Mpho was still standing by the woods with the boy. Still I said nothing. When I asked her later that evening who the boy was, she said he was Mphonyane's boyfriend. I took her at her word, although I wondered what she was talking about with Mphonyane's boyfriend for more than two hours.

Here now, again, I was looking at Mphonyane's boyfriends through the window.

'Both of them? And why are they out there? Why are they not coming in?'

She didn't answer.

The twins left and I stayed home with the kids. That night Thandi, the daughter, was crying for her mother. I held her in my arms and paced the floor with her and sang a lullaby. That didn't stop her. She bawled even louder for most of the night, until her voice was hoarse.

In the morning she whimpered, and then was quiet for some time, and then she sighed, and then cried again. I raised the volume on the portable radio to listen to the morning news. A police station had been attacked at Mapoteng in the Berea district. Masiu's body was found nearby riddled with bullets. It could have been me, I thought. Thanks to my resistance to insiderness I was still alive.

Mpho did not return until the following evening. And nine months later she had a baby boy. We named him Dini, which is isiXhosa for 'sacrifice'.

CHAPTER SEVEN

THE BEE PEOPLE ARE very angry. We are sitting on the grass in Uncle Owen's yard. I am here at the Bee Place – that's what we now call Qoboshane village – without Gugu; it is as though a limb is missing. But I am here for an emergency meeting. I came as soon as I received a telephone call from 'Makamohelo Lebata, the chairperson of the beekeeping collective, and now we have before us the shame-faced elder Morrison Xinindlu. He is tall and wiry in his neat grey pants, woollen skullcap and a heavy sweater despite the heat. He has to endure the humiliation of answering to us, we who could be his children and grandchildren.

213

Upbraiding an elder is not something I relish. But Old Xinindlu deserves our wrath. Two days ago he took off in the project's Toyota pickup truck and drove to Sterkspruit. He was utterly drunk. When he sped past St Teresa the vehicle was zigzagging all over the dirt road, and soon after Dulcie's Nek it capsized into a roadside donga. Fortunately it did not roll over the rocky slope; otherwise we would not be having this meeting today but a wake instead, and the truck would have been totalled. Still, the truck needs panel-beating which will cost the Bee People thousands of rands.

'There is no point in behaving like the wronged party here, Tat'uXinindlu,' I tell him as he stares at me sulkily. 'These women are the wronged people. You had no business driving their truck while drunk. It was very irresponsible of you.'

'I think he has heard, *Ntate* Mda,' says 'Makamohelo, addressing me. 'It was a mistake. Let us forgive him. He is our father.'

The rest of the Bee People are mumbling their agreement. My Uncle Owen does not say anything. I know why. He is Morrison Xinindlu's friend and age-mate – both are in their eighties – and like Xinindlu he is quite partial to his brandy. It could easily have been him instead of Xinindlu.

'What do you mean we should forgive him?' I ask.

'He will not do it again,' says 'Makamohelo.

'How do you know he will not do it again? Did he say that? Did he ask to be forgiven, or are you so generous with forgiveness you want to dish it out free?'

I hate to be so hard on the old man, but his obstinacy angers me.

He and my Uncle Owen were the two men who accepted the beekeeping idea with great enthusiasm when I first introduced it in the village. As an elder he was a councillor to the headman Xhalisile, a descendant of the man who tried to assassinate my grandfather and left him mentally unstable. Thanks to Xinindlu's advocacy the villagers gave us the mountain and soon our beekeeping project was under way. He was one of the few men who were members. They have all fallen by the wayside – some just giving up when the benefits were slow in coming and others dying of AIDS. Now the Bee People are all female, except for the two elders, Uncle Owen Mda and Morrison Xinindlu.

The women are soft-hearted. They insist that the old man should be forgiven. I am against the idea because the elder has not apologised. All he said was 'I didn't do it on purpose.' That's not an apology. Also, I feel there need to be consequences for such irresponsible behaviour. But I am outvoted, although there is no formal vote. It is obvious to me that the consensus is that we should just let the matter rest, so I give up. They don't say so, but I suspect that they are fearful of alienating the old man lest they lose him as a driver. I have been urging the women to take driving lessons so that they can drive their own truck instead of depending on the men, but they are afraid. Perhaps it is not out of self-interest that they want to forgive the old man; perhaps they are just being respectful towards the elder as young women who have been brought up in the isiXhosa and Sesotho traditions.

'I don't see how you can run a business this way,' I tell them nevertheless, trying not to appear a sore loser. 'When it comes to the affairs of your business you are all equal. We continue to respect each other as is the custom, but in the boardroom there is no man or woman or child or elder. We have the same voice, equal to everyone else's, and the fact that we are elders does not give us the right to do things that will end up destroying our project. Now a lot of your money will be going towards repairing the vehicle just because an elder has behaved like a delinquent. That's a few steps backwards for your business.'

I am quite ashamed of upbraiding the elder like this. Quite embarrassed, in fact. But I feel that it has to be done.

After a brief discussion on housekeeping matters I go to greet my Uncle Press at his general dealer's store, otherwise known as eRestu by the villagers because it is also a restaurant and a tavern. He'll be coming soon, I'm told, so I while away the time looking at the items behind the counter. It is a well-stocked shop. The shelves are full of various items of groceries ranging from canned meats, fish and vegetables to household utensils. There are drums of paraffin, stacks of white bags of maize meal and bread flour, cans and bottles of cooking oil, and packets of candles. There are also shelves that are stacked with the fluffy white blankets each with a single black stripe that the men wear

215

during traditional ceremonies such as initiation rituals and ancestral feasts. On the counter there are basins full of fat cakes, fried fish and salted dried *snoek* fish. The store supplies all the needs of the villagers and they don't have to go to Sterkspruit just for groceries. Uncle Press has done well for himself, although I have never seen him work behind the counter. His wife is at the cash register come rain or shine, and his sons and daughters serve the customers.

When Press arrives I notice that he is wearing single strings of white beads on his wrists and on his head. He even has anklets of a single strand of white beads. I know immediately that he has been called by the ancestors and is now a diviner and shaman, or *igqirha*. I had no idea that he had undergone the *thwasa* process, the first stage of the calling. He managed to keep his calling a secret known only to members of his immediate family. No wonder he had been absent lately. Sometimes I would come to the village and leave without seeing him and no one wanted to talk about his whereabouts. He was undergoing training and initiation into the world of spirits and now he is a fully fledged traditional healer.

I congratulate Press on his entry into the world of healers. He seems to be shy about it. Or even embarrassed. I don't think this is something he wanted for himself. He must have been forced into it by some physical illness or some mental dis-ease. That's what the ancestors do to you; they drag you kicking and screaming into serving them. That is what the believers say.

It is like that with many of my people. A number of close relatives have become diviners and traditional healers. I told you about Cousin Bernard who didn't complete the training and was therefore rendered insane by the ancestors. I have other cousins at 'Musong who are traditional healers. My revered ancestor himself, Mhlontlo, was known for his magical powers. He even turned the white man's bullets into water. Others, such as Cousin Nondyebo, may not necessarily be fully fledged healers and shamans but they are adherents of isiXhosa traditional religion and whenever the family gathers they want to introduce rituals that have to do with paying homage to the ancestors.

Usually this does not go well with those of my relatives who have found Christ. And I have quite a few of those too. In fact, members of my family – both immediate and extended – are finding Christ all over the place. Even my younger brother Monwabisi, a magistrate who used to be a hedonist of the first order, is a lay preacher at his church. My nephew Dumisani, my sister's only son, is doing youth ministry work in the United Kingdom where he married an English rose. My sister-in-law Johanna and some of her children are saved and born again, and when I visit her she does not hesitate to tell me about prophecies of the end of the world which is always just two years away.

I respect their choices and love them dearly, as long as they don't assume the arrogance of thinking that theirs is the right path and everyone else is wrong. I value both the ancestor-venerating and the Christ-worshipping sides of my family as long as they don't try to convert me into subscribing to the weird notion that mythologies – especially foreign ones in the case of Christianity – are objective reality. My people should grant me the right to go to hell, if that is where unbelievers go after death.

In the same way that I am tolerant of those who believe differently, and I am even not averse to participating in their rituals if it makes everyone happy, I expect them to grant me the same kind of tolerance. As an atheist, I don't have rituals of my own for them to participate in. I just need to be left alone with my beliefs. But it is difficult for some of them to understand this because Christianity, like the rest of the Abrahamic faiths, is a very intolerant religion. You are either with them – their brand of Christianity – or you fry in hell. Period. Strangely, the only Christians who were ever tolerant towards my unbelief were a bunch of American Catholic nuns with whom I worked at Mabathoana High School in Maseru some years back.

MABATHOANA HIGH SCHOOL WAS named after the Archbishop of Lesotho, the Right Reverend Emmanuel Mabathoana OMI, the first black Roman Catholic archbishop in southern Africa. It was run by nuns of the Holy Names, most of them hailing from Canada and the United States of America. They were more liberal than the local nuns we had come to know so well. For instance, at Mabathoana there was no morning assembly before school started where prayers and announcements were made. When the bell rang in the morning students went straight to their classrooms and lessons began without any prayers. All announcements were posted on the bulletin boards at both the senior and the junior blocks. This was very unusual for Lesotho where schools of every denomination, including government-controlled schools, had a tradition of morning assembly with prayers and readings from the Bible.

Another unusual thing about Mabathoana was that all the cleaning of the classrooms and the surroundings was done by employees. After school in Lesotho girls had to take turns to sweep the classrooms and boys kept the school grounds clean. The Basotho teachers at Mabathoana, especially the older female teachers, complained that the American nuns were spoiling Basotho children who needed to be brought up under the strict discipline of prayer and work – *ora et labora*. But the nuns were adamant that the children had not come to school to work but to study, and if they wanted to pray at all they could do it at their homes or in church. Religious education, they insisted, should be left to the parents and the priests, except in those instances when it was taught in the classroom as a subject for those who opted for it.

I was impressed by this philosophy when I joined the school as a teacher of Literature in English, following in the footsteps of short-story writer Mbulelo Mzamane, who had taught there after completing his BA degree at the University of Botswana, Lesotho and Swaziland at Roma and my younger brother Monwabisi – the one they called Thabiso – who had taught there immediately after obtaining his secondary teacher's certificate at the Morija Training College.

The first time I met Mbulelo Mzamane I was buying a loaf of bread at Maseru Café. It was already sliced and was neatly wrapped in cellophane, which was quite a new way of packaging bread because before this we bought bread unsliced and unpackaged. I heard a voice behind me, 'Hey, don't you have a bread knife at your place?' I didn't even know who this tall guy was who had just pounced on me asking me this silly question. I bet he didn't know who I was either, and I resented his forwardness. He was with some guys I knew, the Lebentlele brothers who were jazz musicians. He was introduced to me as one of the talented young South African writers exiled in Lesotho. He turned out to be such a lovable guy after all. He was quite an activist in organising cultural events, and some of his students at Mabathoana had formed a band, the Anti-Antiques, led by a scrawny boy called Semenkoane Frank Leepa. This was the band that later became Uhuru and then gained international fame as Sankomota. Now Mbulelo Mzamane had resigned from the high school because he was going abroad for higher education.

My brother, on the other hand, had left the high school after he had been at loggerheads with the nuns on some matter that I never got to understand. That helped him because he went to university to study law, and at that time he was doing his LLB degree at the University of Edinburgh in Scotland.

In February that year, 1976, I had completed a distance-learning degree with a Swiss private fine arts academy that had started as a learned society but was then offering courses for artists who wanted to qualify for its membership. The International Academy of Arts and Letters has, unfortunately, long since closed down with the demise of its major funder, the International University Exchange Fund (IUEF).

I had been studying law, as you might remember, while working for the attorney OK Mofolo. Because of the measly salary he was paying me I had gone back to painting and flogging my works to tourists at hotels with Mr Dizzy and sometimes with James Dorothy. I had found myself spending more time painting and less time studying law. I had also re-established relations with the older artists such as Meshu Mokitimi, Paul Ncheke and Phil Motsosi. Most of us were starving artists, but to me the life of a starving artist was much more fulfilling than the life of the lawyer I was going to be on obtaining my Attorney's Admission. I decided to give up on law altogether. I did not tell my father about it because he would have been very disappointed. Although he had always been careful never to push me into law, or in any other direction, he had been proud that at last I was making something of myself, especially in a noble profession that had become a family tradition.

Unlike my fellow artists who were happy just being artists, I yearned desperately for a formal qualification. It didn't matter what it was or how much recognition it had, as long as it allowed me to put the letters after my name. That was one reason I had previously attempted the courses of the College of Preceptors in London – on qualifying I would have been an Associate of the College of Preceptors, or ACP, and would continue with them until I became a Fellow, with an FCP after my name.

I came from a family of learned people where degrees were valued for their own sake. Even if I were to sell lots of paintings and make millions of rands, there would still be a gaping hole in my life that could only be filled by a university degree. And of course I was not making the millions. I could barely survive. Once in a while I would sell a painting but the money would not be enough to pay rent. I was still renting a room on the outskirts of Maseru, at Qoaling, where I lived with Mpho and the kids. Occasionally I had to borrow money from my mother who was then working as a registered nurse at Holy Cross Clinic, a Roman Catholic mission station in southern Lesotho. I was too ashamed to ask for assistance from my father.

One day an artist from Pretoria, an old white man called Walter Battiss, paid a visit to the Lesotho Museum that Leabua Jonathan had established in Maseru. What impressed me about him, besides his very unconventional looks with his mane of white hair and flamboyant style of dressing – a flowing white caftan – was the fact that he was not just an exuberant abstract painter but a scholar of art. Indeed, he had retired from a professorship of art at the University of South Africa a year or so before. I was in awe of artists who were also academics because they were not the sort of people one usually met in our circles. He was a Fellow of the International Institute of Arts and Letters (IIAL), a learned society in Switzerland, and I wanted to see letters of that type follow my name as well. So, Walter Battiss introduced me to artists in Switzerland who were operating the distance learning International Academy of Arts and Letters. They were financed by the International University Exchange Fund which was in turn funded by the Swedish government.

You may remember the IUEF as the organisation that was infiltrated by the South African master-spy Craig Williams in the 1980s

– long after my association with them, I must add. He had inveigled the Swedish director Lars Eriksson into appointing him to the staff, and reached the high position of deputy director where he was able to gather information on the South African students whose scholarships were being sponsored by the organisation. He was also able to carry out a wide operation of bombings, kidnappings and assassinations of South African refugees and political activists in Europe from the offices of the IUEF. When he was exposed as a spy of the apartheid government, the IUEF had to close down. But that is another story, and if you want more of it visit the documents of the Truth and Reconciliation Commission.

The Lesotho representative of the IUEF was a friend of my father's, Abner Chele. He handled the funds and paid all the fees for South African refugee children who were attending the various high schools in Lesotho and the local university. He recommended that the IUEF in Geneva pay directly to the Swiss academy and I was able to study while I struggled to make a living. At least the IUEF purchased all the art materials for my school projects, but of course most of the materials were used for the paintings that I peddled to the tourists.

On completing my studies, Sister Arnadene Bean, the principal of Mabathoana High School who hailed from Oregon in the USA, gave me a job as an assistant teacher of Literature in English. The salary was two hundred and forty rands a month, a far cry from the twenty-five rands a month I was earning from OK Mofolo. I had never had so much money in my life, and of course I immediately put it to good use drinking with the civil servants at Lancer's Inn and at some of the more up-scale shebeens, rather than at the pineapple and hops home-brew joints I used to patronise with Mr Dizzy.

In addition to Mr Dizzy and Clement Sima Kobo – the Lesotho High School teacher we called Clemoski – my circle of drinking buddies increased to include Thabo Sithathi, an aspiring lawyer who was reviled by everyone else as a South African spy while they continued to associate with him, Sol Manganye – Bra Sol – who taught commercial subjects at Lesotho High School and was also a PAC activist exiled from Lady Selbourne in Pretoria, and Mxolisi Ngoza, a thoroughly gay man who

221

was my colleague at Mabathoana where he taught mathematics. These were my Maseru friends.

Whenever I visited home in Mafeteng I continued my drunken association with Litsebe Leballo, Peter Masotsa and my mentor Ntlabathi Mbuli.

The other two Mafeteng guys who had been promoted into my ever-widening circle were my brothers, the twins Monwabisi and Sonwabo. But Sonwabo, also called Thabo, was at the Lerotholi Technical College in Maseru studying technical drawing and Monwabisi, as I said, was in Edinburgh. My other siblings, my sister Thami and the last born in the family, Zwelakhe, were still living with our father in Mafeteng, but I did not socialise with them when I was there because there was quite a wide age-gap between us and we didn't have much in common to talk about. In any event, I didn't have a reason to go to Mafeteng that often, especially with my mother now living seventy kilometres away at Holy Cross; I had it made in Maseru in my new job and I wanted for nothing.

The nuns gave me a fully furnished four-roomed house next to the junior block and opposite the convent of the Sisters of the Holy Names. I moved in with Mpho, our four-year-old son, Neo, our two-year-old daughter, Thandi, and our three-month-old son, Dini.

A few weeks after we had taken occupation of the house my mother came in a van with her driver from Holy Cross to see the child. We could host her now that we had a decent house with an electric stove, a fridge, a bathroom with a geyser for hot water.

I was having a beer with Thabo Sithathi in the living room when my mother and Mpho joined us. My mother took the baby in her arms and marvelled at how beautiful he was.

'He doesn't look like your other kids,' she said.

'Are you saying my other kids are not beautiful?' I asked, laughing.

'They are beautiful in their own way,' she said. 'This one has fluffy hair and is light in complexion like a Coloured.'

'Maybe he takes after your people, mama,' I said. 'You are light in complexion because you are a descendant of the Khoikhoi people. We all know that we Mdas are not easy on the eye, but you and your people are very beautiful.'

We all laughed about it, including Mpho. But Thabo Sithathi didn't think it was a laughing matter. He looked at us pityingly and said, 'My friend has been cuckolded and you people think it is a joke?'

I was surprised that Thabo Sithathi should make such a statement because I had never discussed anything of the sort with him. I also felt deeply offended that he should be so brazen as to mention something that Mpho and I never talked about. We had gone on with our lives as if nothing had happened. We glared at Thabo Sithathi in unison, and then turned our attention to the baby and talked baby language with him, extolling his beauty.

I wasn't about to make a song and dance about anything.

I THINK I UNDERSTAND why Press is a bit shy about his new calling. He sees me as his brother's son (I am actually his first cousin's son in the strict Western sense) who has accumulated so much knowledge from the land of the white man and would therefore be ashamed to be associated with a relative who is a servant of the divine ancestral spirits. He does not express anything of the sort, but I know him so well I am certain I am correct. I try to make him perish the thought by congratulating him once more for responding so positively to the call.

'It's an honour to have an uncle who is *igqirha*,' I tell him. 'When I am ill or have evil spirits that bother me I'll know where to go.'

'*Khawundenz' umntu, mntak'a Bhut' Solomzi*,' a grating voice startles me. Make me into a person, son of Solomzi. You may remember that Solomzi is my father's name, and therefore these words are addressed to me. I know immediately that the ragged old lady uttering these words is asking me for a favour. It is how words are used by my people. When someone needs help from you she is in fact asking you to make her into a person. We are not people, my grandmother used to instil in us, until somebody makes us into people by being generous towards us. When we are born we are animals. We are no different from the rock rabbits that urinate on the cliffs and boulders of Dyarhom Mountain, making them slippery. Until someone makes us people by showering us with acts of kindness. The more acts of generosity and compassion we receive from others, the more human we become. In return, we become generous and compassionate to others, making them human as well. When we do that, our own humanity is enhanced. When you make others human, you enrich your own humanity as well. Thus goes the cycle of humanity and humaneness. Thus it expands as we make one another human. It is for that reason that the forebears composed the saying: *umntu ngumntu ngabantu*. A person is a person through other people.

When a whole gang of us grandchildren lived with my grandmother and the resources were scarce, it was difficult sometimes to be kind towards others and to share whatever little we had. The first instinct was to hog and hoard for even harder times. Whenever my grandmother discovered such selfishness she would shout at the culprit, *'Awungomntu!'* You are not a person! Why? Because only those who are generous and compassionate have reached the state of personhood. That was what *ubuntu* as practised by the villagers was all about.

'When you say I must make you a person, grandma, are you not yet a person?' I ask the old lady.

Press sneaks away. He has no patience with fellow-villagers who beg.

'Sukundigezela,' the old lady says. Don't ask me a silly question. 'How can I be a person when you have not made me a person?'

'You are old,' says my aunt behind the cash register. 'How many people have been making you into a person all these years?'

What she means is that the old lady has been a beneficiary of the kindness of others for such a long time that by now she should long have attained the state of personhood.

'You are the last person to say that,' says the old lady mournfully. 'You know the problems of this village.' Then she turns to me and says: 'The problems of poverty, my child . . . they have stripped people like us of all personhood. Your aunt is a person because she is married to your uncle who is rich. Now she does not want us to be people too.'

'So how do I make you into a person today, grandma?' I ask her.

It is very simple. All she wants is a quart of beer. Normally I don't indulge people who ask me for beer, a request one gets a lot when one walks into a bar here and in Lesotho. I always tell them that I cannot spend my hard-earned cash subsidising their drinking habit when I myself gave up drinking many years ago. But I make an exception with this grandma. She is old and she might as well have a blast in the few moments that she has left. The irony is not lost on me that I am making her into a person by helping her get drunk.

My aunt gives her Black Label and I pay for it. She walks to some corner where no one will bother her asking for a sip, and enjoys her process of becoming human in a spirited manner. Press returns, perhaps because it is safe to do so now.

'I tell you all the time that you are spoiling these people,' he admonishes. 'We work hard for our money and we cannot be dishing it out to people like these who do not want to work.'

I don't respond to this. It is futile to argue with Press about such matters. He is living proof that the rich among us are more often than not the first to dismiss *ubuntu* as a touchy-feely philosophy of losers that has no place in our ruthlessly acquisitive and competitive South Africa. On a broader national level, crony capitalism rules supreme, killing whatever had stayed with us of the values of *ubuntu* instilled in us by our grandmothers.

On the other hand, the oppressed cling to *ubuntu* because for them it is the only way to move from victim to survivor. The perpetrators have no need for that.

Ubuntu was displayed by the people of Lesotho when they welcomed a flood of new South African refugees into their country. In Sesotho culture the philosophy exists as *botho*, which means the same thing.

IT BEGAN A MONTH or so before I joined Mabathoana High. I was having fun with the two beautiful women who worked at Badul's office. Badul was a lawyer from Durban who had recently opened a practice in Maseru. Thabo Sithathi, the aspiring lawyer who often pretended to be a real one to those who did not know, had introduced me to him and we spent a lot of time just hanging out at his office. Obviously, my heart was still in the legal field.

Badul had two secretaries, even though there wasn't much business since he was new in town and prospective clients did not know of him yet.

So there I was, horsing around with these lovely women when one of them received a telephone call from Soweto where she originally came from. All of a sudden I heard her scream: 'They are killing our children in Soweto!'

It was June 16, 1976, and police had responded to the students demonstrating in Soweto with bullets, killing some of them. At the time we did not know the extent of the uprising that later engulfed most of the country. Later, we heard of young leaders like Tsietsi Mashinini and Khotso Seatlholo and other members of the Soweto Students Representative Council who were leading the resistance, first against the forced introduction of Afrikaans as a medium of instruction for black students and, at a broader level, against apartheid and all its race-based institutions. We also lamented the death of Hector Peterson whose young body in school uniform in the arms of Mbuyisa Makhubo flashed across the newspapers of the world, courtesy of a photograph by Sam Nzima.

The developments in South Africa had given us exiles a lot of hope in recent years with the advent of the Black Consciousness movement. The philosophy had captured our collective imagination. This political reawakening happened after an internal political lull since the Sharpeville massacre and the incarceration of such leaders as Robert Mangaliso Sobukwe; and then later the Rivonia Trial that resulted in life sentences on Robben Island for the likes of Nelson Mandela, Walter Sisulu, Jama's father, and others of their revolutionary colleagues. It was during that lull that some of us began to forget about these leaders while they worked in the quarries of Robben Island, though my mother never forgot to mourn Bhut' Walter, as she called Walter Sisulu, even though he was not dead. Hope bloomed in us once more when we heard of what the fearless young leaders who were emerging out of the universities were doing through the South African Students Organisation and, of course, the mass organisation, the Black People's Convention, one of whose leaders was Albertina Sisulu, Bhut' Walter's wife.

June 16 brought a new flood of refugees into Lesotho. Some of them became my students at Mabathoana High School and spent a lot of time at my house. I was both their bigger brother and their political mentor. I remember particularly three of them who became close to my family: Buti Moleko, Nelson Mogudi and Steve Tau. Steve got into a very serious relationship with my younger sister Thami, to the extent that we were certain they would marry.

Buti wrote plays and composed music. He invigorated the theatre scene in Maseru by establishing a theatre group along the lines of Gibson Kente's touring companies. Thami got her first taste of acting in *Life Is Like a Wheel* by Buti. Like Kente's, Buti's plays were naïve – not intentionally so – both in form and content, and were replete with dance and songs he himself had composed. It was not the most brilliant theatre, but the important thing was that people were watching plays and young Basotho actors who hitherto had no opportunities to express themselves artistically were becoming ardent thespians.

The new arrivals revitalised exile and all of a sudden there was a lot of cultural and political activity. These young men and women had been nurtured by the Black Consciousness Movement which had reintroduced the view held by my father when he was president of the ANC Youth League that politics and economics were not the only important sites of the struggle; culture had a crucial role to play as well. That was why my father mooted the establishment of the African Academy of Arts which, unfortunately, never took off.

Poetry readings were organised at such venues as the British Council Hall and at a restaurant called Fat Alice. I remember a drunken and rowdy Mandla Langa singing the praises of Joe Slovo at one such affair at the British Council and threatening that he would *vala le zozo* – bring the house down and close the whole event – if people continued to read reactionary poetry that ignored the heroes of the struggle. Mandla, of course, has since become one of our leading novelists in South Africa. After being forced off the stage by some of his ANC comrades he sat down and cried. He used to cry a lot when he was drunk, and that endeared him to me because it told me that he was a sensitive young man.

What was wonderful about these events was that they availed me the opportunity to read some of my poetry, which I had been writing and then storing away since I didn't have any outlet for it. At Fat Alice I read my poems to the sounds of jazz – guitar, double-bass and saxophone – played by the Lebentlele brothers and other Maseru musicians.

The poetry scene was set ablaze when Duma ka Ndlovu came into exile, which was months after others had been there already. He had gained a reputation as a journalist on *The World* newspaper but, more importantly, he was a founding member of Medupe, a group that was famous for its poetry performances. Duma came into exile after Medupe, *The World* and many other organisations were banned and after he had been detained and then later released by the apartheid government.

Before Duma came our poetry readings were sleepy affairs. He brought much flair and pizzazz. His booming voice filled the venues as he recited: *Re ta bagunda, re ta bagunda, re ba bolaya*. We'll hit them hard, we'll defeat them, and we'll kill them. This was highly charged poetry that gave us goosebumps and assured us that we were marching towards victory in South Africa. He was an imposing figure in his dashiki robe as he moved among the electrified audience to the stage where he performed to the rhythm of the drums. Duma became an inspiration to us all. Not only him, but other fiery poets from Soweto who were not in exile *per se*, but were able to smuggle themselves across the border to add more fire in our bellies: Ingoapele Madingoane of *Africa my beginning, Africa my ending* fame, Mapalakanye Maropodi, Matsemela Manaka and Jaki Seroke. They came to perform their poetry, but most importantly to give us information of what was happening in the struggle back home and to get material, mostly books that were banned in South Africa. Franz Fanon's work was at a premium and we couldn't get enough of his books for the demand back home.

It was wonderful to be alive those days. For once, the void was filled.

To cap it all, Sister Arnadene Bean and her fellow Sisters of the Holy Names promoted me to deputy headmaster after the incumbent,

Ezra November, a PAC exile formerly from my ancestral village of Qoboshane, went to further his studies at the University at Roma. At the same time, Sister Arnadene resigned and went back to the United States. She was replaced by a Canadian nun from Manitoba, Sister Yvonne Maes – she of the *triste* eyes.

I was acting headmaster for some time while we were waiting for Sister Yvonne. When she came into the office for the first time I was sitting at the principal's desk doing some paperwork and a beautiful petite woman called Tholane, a colleague who taught biology and general science, was bending over getting some coffee and creamer from a low cupboard. She was wearing the tiniest tennis skirt imaginable and frilly white panties. Her tennis racquet was on the floor. She had been on her way to the tennis courts when she had decided to come to my office to treat us both to a cup of coffee. I saw this young white woman in brown tunic and white veil standing at the door. She had a horrified look on her face. I tried to signal to Tholane to stand up and look decent, but she didn't notice. Instead she uttered a mild expletive because she couldn't find the coffee and the water was boiling.

I stood up quickly to greet the nun.

'I'm Yvonne Maes, the new principal,' she said.

Tholane was blasé, while I was embarrassed that the new principal had seen her in the principal's office bending over in my direction. She most likely thought there were worse things that I did in that office.

'She just came to make coffee,' I said after introducing Tholane. 'She is on her way to the tennis court.'

This last bit of information was necessary to explain why her lacy panties were hanging out of her teensy-weensy white skirt. But Sister Yvonne just walked out without another word. Perhaps she thought she had been assigned to Sodom and Gomorrah.

'What's it with you guys and nuns?' asked Tholane.

'We guys? Me and who? And what are you talking about anyway?'

'I saw the way you were looking at her. You desire her.'

I didn't know it had been that obvious. Although 'desire' was quite a stretch, I thought she was quite attractive. If I had any lustful look at all it must have been a reflex reaction.

229

Sister Arnadene used to tell me that where she came from nuns did not wear the habit, whereas in Lesotho they were forced to be in tunics and white veils. Sister Yvonne was the first nun I saw in civvies. I was at the Maseru Holiday Inn Casino minding my beer at the bar counter while watching Mr Dizzy minding the slot machines, where he was losing a lot of coins that would otherwise have been useful in filling our stomach with beer and our heads with giddy mischief. And there was this beautiful white woman with a wistful look smiling at me. I smiled back even though I didn't recognise her, though she looked vaguely familiar. It only registered later when she was walking out of the casino that she was none other than my new principal, Sister Yvonne Maes. What she was doing at night in civvies at the casino I never got to know.

I have often wondered what happened to those beautiful nuns. Well, today you can look people up using any one of the search engines, and I did so for the purposes of this story. I discovered that Sister Arnadene Bean is still going strong as a nun in Oregon, minus the habit. She ministers to female prison inmates. But Sister Yvonne Maes is no longer a nun. She has written a book titled *Cannibal's Wife: A Memoir* in which she tells the story of how she was sexually abused repeatedly by a priest who was her retreat director in Lesotho. When she reported the matter to the Catholic Church it was covered up and the priest was transferred back to England whence he came. Yvonne resigned from the convent and the church, after thirty-seven years as a nun, and now advocates for survivors of sexual abuse in Canada.

I didn't know this had happened to my principal. But I can easily believe it because the whole environment of the Catholic Church in Lesotho was sexually charged, sometimes perversely so and at other times in ways that were absolutely exhilarating. I have told you already about the pilgrimages of some of my pals to Maryland for orgies with the nuns. I watched as an outsider when these things were happening. But in two instances I became either an insider, or almost one.

When I went to the shops or to the shebeens at the Location I passed through the premises of St Bernadette Primary School which was just across the fence from Mabathoana High School on one side and Lesotho High School on the other. From there I walked on the pristine stone-paved grounds of Our Lady of Victories Cathedral, where I used to take Attorney OK Mofolo's candles for the blessings, between the imposing sandstone cathedral and a double-storey sandstone house that I figured served as the offices of the priests and the bishops.

One day a friendly priest with sparse white hair and a white goatee approached me just when I was passing the steps of this building.

'What is your name?' he asked.

I gave him my first name.

'You were baptised with that name?'

I don't know why he assumed I was Catholic or even Christian at all. Perhaps he expected everyone who made these sacred grounds a thoroughfare to be at least a member of his faith.

'No,' I said. 'My church name is Kizito.'

He seemed to find this quite fascinating. He told me he was Father Villa. He was an Italian, just arrived from Malawi where he had been working as a priest for many years. He was quite impressed to hear that at my young age I was the deputy headmaster at a prestigious Catholic school.

After that, every time I passed by he would pop out of nowhere to talk to me. I began to dread passing there because I found the small talk a waste of time. But it was the shortest route to my destination. I don't know how he knew I would be coming past because I didn't keep regular times. Maybe he was spying on me from the window upstairs and could see me from a distance. He was like a spectre that haunted me.

Then one day he invited me upstairs to show me something that he said would interest me. I followed him through the office where a middle-aged secretary was typing mechanically as if in a daze and then climbed the stairs to the rooms upstairs. It turned out that one of these was his bedroom. There was a single bed covered in a blue Basotho *lesolanka* blanket as a bedspread, a small dressing table with a number of newspapers on it and a nightstand with a lamp and book. On the bed was a pile of rosaries.

Father Villa took a newspaper from the dressing table and showed it to me. It was from Malawi, he said, from the diocese where he ministered.

231

'Don't you think it's a wonderful newspaper?' he asked, coming very close to me.

It was just your standard Catholic paper and I didn't see anything wonderful about it. He started to breathe very hard and began to caress my thigh. I removed his hand and moved back a little. He came closer still and his body touched mine. His hand was busy on my thigh again. I pushed him away. He started to whine, I think overcome with desire.

'You can choose any rosary you want,' he said, almost out of breath. 'I can give you as many rosaries as you want. Look at this one.'

At this he went to the bed and picked one rosary with shimmering red beads.

'Isn't it beautiful? Come and get it.'

The old bugger was dangling the rosary, trying to entice me to come closer to the bed. But I was not about to do that. So he leapt at me by the door, grabbed me and breathed into my ear.

'You know my car?' he asked.

I had seen the white Volkswagen Beetle parked outside and on a few occasions I had seen him driving it in town.

'I can give it to you ultimately if you come here occasionally and we do fun things,' he said with a naughty glint in the eye. 'I can do wonderful things for you.'

He reached for me and tried to plant a kiss, but I turned my head. Then I pushed him away so hard that he fell on the bed. I heard him moan 'Kizito, please Kizito' as I walked out of the room. Downstairs in the office the secretary was typing away, seemingly oblivious of what was happening upstairs.

As I walked away I wondered how many young men – perhaps some of them children – he had lured into his lair with his trusty rosaries.

In the evening I was sitting at 'Mamojela's shebeen with Clemoski and Mr Top, whose real name was Thabang Thamae. He was the Principal Secretary in the Ministry of Finance. I had taken to patronising this particular shebeen lately because it was just across the road from my high school. Clemoski, who had become my best friend more than anyone else, was a regular there since he was sleeping with 'Mamojela behind the back of her regular boyfriend. Also, I had been terribly savaged by dogs one night on my way home from the distant shebeens at the Location. I could stagger back from 'Mamojela's to my house in the small hours of the morning without some mutt getting ideas about the taste of my flesh.

So there I was, sitting with these honourable gentlemen guzzling Castle Lager and telling them of my close encounter with Father Villa.

'Rosaries! How cheap does he think you are?' asked Clemoski.

'Well, he did raise the stakes and offer me his Volkswagen Beetle. "Ultimately" I would own it, he said. It means I'll have to be his permanent mistress before I get it.'

Everybody laughed at this.

'You don't have a car,' said Mr Top. 'This was your chance to own a car.'

'Well, he should make the offer to Mxolosi,' I said.

Mxolisi Ngoza was our thoroughly gay friend who taught mathematics at Mabathoana High School. The 'thoroughly' part stems from the fact that most of the gay guys we associated with in Maseru, some of whom were senior civil servants, were either bisexual or lived a lie. They even married women to give a semblance of 'respectability'. Though Mxolisi never broadcast his sexual orientation to anyone he did not pretend to be anything but gay.

The exhilarating moments were the result of Sister Cathy's magical company. She was a nun of the Sisters of the Holy Names in a well-pressed grey tunic and snow-white veil, a beautiful Mosotho woman, quite big in stature, full-figured, with a large bosom that heaved wistfully when she sighed. And she sighed quite often when she was with me.

Sister Cathy taught Bible Studies at Mabathoana High and ran a girls' club where they got together and sang and talked about Jesus and how to live a clean, sin-free life.

I spent a lot of time with Sister Cathy, to the extent that I neglected my duties as deputy headmaster. I sat on the veranda with her and listened as she played her guitar and sang for me. Sometimes I brought my flute and we played together. These were very simple ditties, the type that she sang with her girls.

Often I would open my cupboard in the staffroom and find cookies wrapped in paper serviettes. I knew immediately that Sister Cathy had brought them for me from the convent. From the cookies we graduated to the missal wine that she stole for me from the cathedral every Monday. In most instances it would just be half a bottle, but on one or two occasions it was a full bottle of red wine, sealed. I feasted on the cookies and on the blood of Christ when I got back home after school. I told Mpho, my wife, that the treats were from the convent but she didn't see anything to be suspicious or even jealous about.

I must say that I was absolutely smitten with Sister Cathy. If I had not been married to Mpho at the time I would have asked Sister Cathy to elope with me. I toyed with the idea. I don't know if I would have made any headway. She was married to Jesus. Unlike Jesus' love, mine was not pure and innocent. It was dripping with sinful lust. I imagined Sister Cathy in all sorts of ungodly positions. Our relationship, however, was never consummated, except in a play that I wrote many years later, *The Nun's Romantic Story*, that had its premiere at the Johannesburg Civic Theatre. What I feared most was that I would arouse the devil in her and leave her unfulfilled. Remember the little problem? So, all we ever did was to hold hands, gaze into each other's eyes, smile and then peck quickly and shamefacedly. She would then strum her guitar furiously as her bosom heaved in one sigh after another.

We sat for hours on the veranda of the junior block where the staffroom was located, until Sister Yvonne Maes looked at us with stern and disapproving eyes. Then we took refuge in the school library and sat there and gazed at each other while pretending to be reading. Even there, Sister Laurent-Marie, the aged librarian, displayed her disapproval with a stern gaze of her own.

After my daily encounters with Sister Cathy I needed a cold shower. But instead of taking one, I either went to 'Mamojela's shebeen or to the Lancer's Inn. I never gossiped about Sister Cathy even when I was with my boisterous drinking buddies who boasted of their conquests. I felt ours was a sacred relationship. It could not be tainted by cheap gossip.

On Fridays I would go to poetry readings at the British Council. At least there, in the midst of the rhythmic voices promising a forthcoming

234

victory over the Boers and the drums throbbing like AK47s, I was able to forget about Sister Cathy. When there was no poetry reading organised on some Fridays it was just good to be with the dynamic guys from Soweto. Many of them were teetotallers, dedicated only to the struggle and to poetry. I drank less or not at all when I was with them.

I remember one day I was hanging out with Duma ka Ndlovu in front of Maseru Café when Chris Hani came hobbling along on crutches after yet another assassination attempt on him. His house at Qoaling on the outskirts of Maseru had been set on fire by a petrol bomb, but he and his family were able to escape. It amazed me that Chris was hobbling about town without even a bodyguard so soon after the bomb attack.

'Hey, I heard the Boers almost killed you,' Duma said, teasing him. 'This wouldn't have happened to you if you had me as your bodyguard.'

'You'd be the first one to kill me,' said Chris Hani.

It was a joke of course and he chuckled after saying that. But it might also have been a parapraxis – the ANC harboured a lot of distrust towards those Black Consciousness firebrands who had not chosen to join the ANC in exile. And Duma ka Ndlovu was hardcore Black Consciousness. Not all of the new exiles stayed faithful to their original philosophy though. Most of them joined the ANC, with a smaller number joining the PAC. In fact the ANC now had a much stronger presence in Lesotho than the PAC, which used to be the dominant South African movement in the country. The ANC now had many vibrant young activists and no longer depended on the Communist lawyers like Joe Matthews and Robin Cranko to represent its interests. In fact both these lawyers had left Lesotho some time back. Robin Cranko for sure was deported by Leabua Jonathan's government. I don't remember how Joe Matthews left, but we heard he was now living in England.

The young exiles – be they aligned to the ANC, PAC or Black Consciousness – gathered together to create poetry and theatre. No one cared what ideology the individual artists espoused. Even local Basotho artists became part of the mix.

I was never so energised in my life, and I was forever grateful to the Class of 76 – as these new exiles were called – for coming to Lesotho to recharge our batteries which had almost gone flat.

Culture was not only invigorated by the new exiles, but a lot of overseas acts came to Maseru to garner South African audiences. These artists couldn't perform in South Africa due to the cultural boycott. Stars like Sarah Vaughn and Eartha Kitt became the regular nightly acts at the Maseru Holiday Inn. As one of the cultural elites of Maseru – a big fish in a small pond – I was invited to meet them all. I remember wasting the afternoons away with Jimmy Witherspoon drinking beer at the Victoria Hotel beer garden. And when Jane Fonda – a hero of ours because of her position against the war in Vietnam and her general opposition to what we regarded as American imperialism – came to visit I was invited by her promoters to have dinner with her at the Maseru Hilton Hotel, an association that paid great dividends years later when I was stranded in America and she came to my rescue. I'll tell you more about that in the next chapter.

All this flurry of activity revived my creative juices and I started writing plays again. My three plays that were later published by Ravan Press in a collection titled *We Shall Sing for the Fatherland and Other Plays* were written during this period. The 'other plays' of the title were *Dark Voices Ring* and *Dead End*, the earlier version of which I had written when I was at Peka High School and then put away in a trunk full of all the junk I was hoarding.

One day I read in the *Rand Daily Mail* about a new competition for playwrights in southern African, the Amstel Playwright of the Year Award, sponsored by the South African Breweries. I mailed the manuscript of *We Shall Sing for the Fatherland* to the address in Johannesburg and forgot all about it. I was surprised to get a letter a few weeks later informing me that the play had been granted the Merit Award of the Amstel Playwright of the Year Society, which was in fact a runner-up prize to the joint first prize winners John Pank and James Ambrose Brown.

Mpho went to Johannesburg to accept the prize on my behalf at a gala event. She came back star-struck after spending the evening with the South African celebrities we only got to see in newspapers and magazines. She also brought me the prize money – a cheque for two hundred and fifty rands.

Maseru was further energised by the arrival of another South African playwright who was not really a political exile but came to Lesotho in quest of creative freedom. He was Dukuza ka Macu and I had read about his plays – such as *A Matter of Convenience* and *Heaven Weeps for Thina-Sonke* – in the newspapers. It was a thrill to be working with him, helping revive a Lesotho production of *A Matter of Convenience* with some of my students acting in it. Dukuza was a new breed of playwright who had moved away from the influence of the Gibson Kente musical and was creating a highly intellectual yet entertaining kind of theatre, replete with symbolism and metaphor. I was impressed by his mastery of the language. What amazed me most about him was his history; he had never been to school in his life. He grew up looking after goats and cattle in Natal and taught himself how to read and write. He developed into a voracious reader, not of comic books like me, but of great works of philosophy by the likes of Kant, Nietzsche and Wittgenstein.

Some of the best acting I have seen in my life was in Dukuza's production of *The Park*, an adaptation to a South African setting of Amiri Baraka's play, *The Dutchman*. Dukuza himself performed in this play with an English woman who was my colleague at Mabathoana High School, Sarah Walton. Amiri Baraka was the new name of LeRoi Jones, the African-American poet who had captivated and influenced me in a new direction of poetry a few years back.

One day a stranger came to my house at Mabathoana High School. He was a white man from South Africa called Nicholas Ellenbogen. He invited Mpho and me for dinner at the Holiday Inn where he had booked for the night and told us that he was the founder of the Amstel Playwright of the Year Award. He had come to negotiate for the rights to have my play performed professionally in South Africa. But because it was a one-act play he wondered if there were any other plays I had written so that *We Shall Sing for the Fatherland* could be presented as a double-bill. Indeed, from my junk trunk I was able to dig out *Dead End* and *Dark Voices Ring*.

We Shall Sing for the Fatherland was first produced by the Federated Union of Black Arts as a double-bill with *Dead End* – a two-hander about pimps, johns, and abortion. It was the least political of the three plays. *We Shall Sing for the Fatherland*, on the other hand, looks at the life of the veterans of the liberation struggle who are now marginalised in the new society they helped to bring about. It is the most enduring of my plays and continues to enjoy revivals by various groups in South Africa and abroad to this day. In post-apartheid South Africa they call it prophetic because the marginalisation I was writing about has come to pass. It was not difficult to be 'prophetic' about post-liberation South Africa. Remember, I was living in an already independent Africa where some of these things were already happening. It was obvious to me that the dominant black classes in South Africa would hijack the liberation project to serve their own class interests, as they had done in Kenya and in other independent African countries.

The plays were directed by Benjy Francis and opened at the Diepkloof Hall in Soweto. However, I doubt very much if the people of Soweto enjoyed them because they were not the kind of theatre they were used to – with songs and dances *à la* Gibson Kente. Nevertheless they received extensive coverage in all the newspapers of the time. John Mitchell wrote in the *Rand Daily Mail*:

> Lesotho-based playwright Zakes Mda claims a special love for the work of Tennessee Williams and Joe Orton, an affinity apparent in his play 'Dead End'. But perhaps his work is closer to Samuel Beckett – if, indeed, we can draw comparisons between Western and South African black writers.

It is true that I was much enamoured of the work of the Absurdists, although I didn't subscribe to any notions of the meaninglessness and hopelessness of life. My plays aimed to show that the struggle for liberation was not futile.

Later, the plays were transferred to the Market Theatre with Nicholas Ellenbogen himself as the new director. The Space Theatre in Cape Town mounted its own production of *We Shall Sing for the Fatherland* on a double-bill with *Dark Voices Ring* directed by Nomhle Nkonyeni and Rob Amato. Amato was also the director of Matsemela Manaka's plays.

The success of these plays gave me a new voice. And a new political purpose. I no longer felt guilty for not taking up arms when some of my comrades had gone to join the guerrilla forces. I still strongly believed in the armed struggle – in *Dark Voices Ring* I actually present the armed struggle as the solution – but I was going to fight with words while others took the guns.

That was exactly what I told some Peka High School old boys, the so-called MaPeka, when they came to my house under cover of darkness and wearing heavy Basotho blankets to recruit me for combat, as the late Masiu had done when I was teaching at Likhakeng Secondary School a few years earlier. The armed wing of the BCP, the Lesotho Liberation Army (LLA) that had been formed in 1974, was finally preparing to launch guerrilla attacks inside Lesotho to topple the illegitimate government of Chief Leabua Jonathan. Its commander was Sekamane, a fine-featured, light-complexioned and well-heeled man I never imagined as a fighter. But there he was leading blanketed Basotho men, some of whom were my high school friends, to war. I had met Sekamane a few times before but was not on first-name terms with him. The person I knew very well was his sister Limpho, who was Clemoski's girlfriend. This was before Limpho married Chris Hani.

Sekamane and his LLA forces had trained under the auspices of the PAC in Libya and other African countries where the PAC had military camps. The MaPeka who came to recruit me never forgot to remind me of that fact, hoping it would arouse my interest.

'Even your friend Jama Mbeki is one of us,' they told me. 'We all trained together with the APLA forces.'

APLA was the Azanian People's Liberation Army, the PAC military wing that replaced the more peasant-based Poqo.

No wonder Jama went to Botswana after completing his law studies in England. There was a big community of BCP exiles in Botswana, including the leader Ntsu Mokhehle himself, and his deputy Tseliso Makhakhe. You will remember Tseliso Makhakhe as my Peka High School principal who went with me to confront the Catholic priest, Father Hamel, when I was given the anathema. The command structures of the LLA were in Botswana.

My enthusiasm for the PAC had waned at this point. But that was not the reason I turned MaPeka down. They should have known by now that I was not prepared to be a warrior. Perhaps they thought I had cultivated more guts since the last time Masiu approached me. But I was not in a fighting state of mind. Even more so now than ever before because I was getting all this new recognition as a writer. My work was getting good reviews and had now been published in a book.

The Ravan Press publication of my plays was my very first book. I was so proud of it that I took it with me everywhere I went. But the Publications Control Board of the South African government had other ideas. They banned the book, which meant that anyone could go to jail for possessing it. I first learnt of the ban when I chanced upon an article in the *Rand Daily Mail* with the headline: *Black writers lash ban on book*. The African Writers' Association was quoted as saying: *We view the banning of Zakes Mda's book as naked kragdadigheid* (brutal force) *against another umpteenth black man's voice through literature. Another view into the black man's world has been sealed.* An article in *The Star* was headlined *Ban on book 'a show of force'.* In the article the president of the writers' association, Nape Motana, encouraged black writers to disregard the Publications Control Board when they set about writing, adding that: *We are proud of Zakes, one of the most prolific breed of young playwrights to emerge in southern Africa. We say to him courage brother, a worthy soldier dies in his boots.* In the same newspaper Mike Kirkwood of Ravan Press said *We Shall Sing for the Fatherland and Other Plays* was the first Ravan Press book to be banned. 'The ban was completely unjustified,' he added.

I was encouraged by all this support and saw myself as a soldier for freedom who was now using other weapons than the AK47, bazooka and grenade.

I began to take my writing more seriously than my painting. In any event, I was earning good money as the deputy principal and didn't need to hawk my work to the tourists to make ends meet. I was painting less and less while spending more time at Lancer's Inn or at 'Mamojela's. With the recognition I was getting as a playwright I began to focus on writing more plays. I stopped drinking during the week. I sat in the staffroom and worked on play scripts after school. I wrote longhand,

and then typed the manuscripts on a typewriter that was placed in the staffroom for the use of teachers. It was slow going because I never learnt to touch type; to this day I use only two fingers, even as I write this book.

Sometimes Sister Cathy brought me cookies and missal wine and laughed at me, saying that I typed like a hungry hen pecking at scattered grains of corn. She could only pop by in the afternoons because Mother Superior expected her to be at the convent after school for her chores or prayers or whatever nuns did in their cloister.

One person who spent a lot of time with me was Tholane. You remember the science teacher who was making tea in the principal's office when Sister Yvonne first arrived?

Tholane was different from any woman I had known. She spoke her mind, laughed freely without any of the decorum expected in the staffroom of a nun-run Catholic school. She was indeed a free spirit with an impish sense of humour. There was some tomboyishness about her which made her very sexy. I called her *Fana*, which means 'boy'; she called me *Fana* too.

A passionate and tempestuous relationship developed between us. Unlike my relationship with Sister Cathy, this one was very sexual. I started spending my evenings at her house. Then the nights. This was a very dumb and cruel thing to do because she lived only two houses from the house I shared with Mpho and our three kids. I was blinded by lust for this woman who was so sure of herself, who knew what she wanted and how she wanted it. Through her patience and guidance my 'little problem' was cured without much effort and I found myself going all night long with her. And all day long. And all weekend long. Without venturing out. We just couldn't have enough of each other. It was like I was making up for all the years I had been celibate or had short-changed my partners.

I was healed! Thanks to Tholane I was healed! I would have turned cartwheels if I could. I would have danced in the clouds. In my mind I did. So this was what I had been missing all along?

I wrote a poem about the sweet stenches of sex.

I had never gone for professional counselling when I consistently

241

ejaculated prematurely. But years later, long after I had been healed, I got an opportunity to analyse myself and the roots of my dysfunction. I traced it back to the sexual abuse I suffered as a six-year-old child at the hands of our housemaid Nontonje. I told you that when she grabbed my penis and forced it into her vagina I felt a burning sensation, and after that I couldn't pee for hours. For days I would pee with difficulty. On looking back, it became clear that my penis had a memory of that pain and every time it had to face a vagina it associated it with the agony and defended itself by ejaculating immediately and then dying. That was how it saved itself from any prolonged stay inside the inferno. Somehow Tholane had managed to make it trust the darkness inside and to coax it into staying longer and longer until it realised that it was safe and warm and comfortable and very pleasurable. When it was convinced that not all vaginas were as deadly as Nontonje's it wanted to frolic in there forever.

There you have it: I was damaged by a woman; I was made whole again by a woman.

Mpho was bound to find out about my scandalous affair. She yelled and pleaded and threatened and cajoled and cried, and I promised it would stop forthwith. To assure her of the security of our relationship I decided to marry her officially in a civil ceremony after many years of a common law union. On December 22, 1978, we appeared before the District Administrator in Maseru and took our vows. Her twin sister, Mphonyane, and my brother Sonwabo were the witnesses.

You would have thought after this I would settle down and be a good husband and father, but no, I could not resist sneaking into Tholane's house after pretending I was going for a drink with my friends. But of course Mpho was not a fool. She could see what was happening and went to Tholane's house one night and set her bed alight through an open window. Fortunately when this happened neither of us miscreant lovers was there. We were at Clemoski's house at Lesotho High School making love in one of his three bedrooms. We had taken to camping there for freer romps.

The nuns didn't take kindly to their burnt bed. What if the whole house had burnt down? Sister Cathy, especially, looked very disappointed in me. She didn't say anything. But she no longer gave me cookies and missal wine, and she avoided me. We no longer played innocent ditties together. Sister Yvonne Maes didn't say anything either, but looked at me as if I stank. The whole atmosphere at Mabathoana High was fetid. And I was responsible for all that. I resigned after serving a month's notice because I had been promised a job teaching art at the National Teacher Training College. But on the day I was supposed to report for duty I was told the job was no longer available. Apparently the nuns of Mabathoana had given a very bad report about me to the principal of the Teacher Training College. I rented two rooms at Qoaling on the outskirts of Maseru where I moved with my battered family. I went back to being a hustler with my paintings, hoping to get a new job with the Protestants since I had dirtied my name with the Catholics.

Tholane also resigned from Mabathoana and set off to improve her qualifications. She only had a Secondary Teachers' Certificate so she went to study for a BSc degree at the National University of Lesotho where she met a law student, fell in love with him, and forgot about me.

Mpho and Mphonyane took a job with a Danish non-governmental organisation that established kindergartens in Maseru. They worked at a kindergarten that was just over the fence from the rooms we were renting.

If I thought this was the time to rebuild our lives I was dead wrong. Mpho decided that it was time to avenge herself for all the hurt I had inflicted on her. She and Mphonyane started partying really hard with the Danes. She did not come back home for days on end. But I would see her at the kindergarten during the day. I would wave at her, hoping she would come back home. When she finally did come we had an altercation that almost became physical. She packed all her clothes and the children's in suitcases and left. She set herself up at the kindergarten next door and sent the kids to live with her mother in that wonderful 'village of the twins' that I told you about. I later obtained a court order, thanks to my pseudo-lawyer friend Thabo Sithathi, and got all three kids back and sent them to live with my mother at Holy Cross Mission in southern Lesotho. We were both so irresponsible that we simply dumped our kids with our parents rather than dutifully raising them ourselves.

Thus I separated from Mpho, without officially divorcing. We had been in a common law union for slightly more than six years and our civil marriage had lasted less than a year. Later I heard she had gone to Haifa University in Israel to study for a certificate in early childhood education.

I DIDN'T KNOW ANYTHING about this German boy. No one told me he would be coming. But of course the Bee People don't have to tell me everything they do at their apiary, even though when there are problems they expect me to solve them. I don't mind pitching in with advice occasionally as long as they realise that they are the final decision makers. It took them a long time to reach this stage where they see themselves as the owners of the project rather than employees. Because I initiated the project, for a long time they couldn't get used to the idea that I was not their boss. I am not even a shareholder in their business, and all the hives, the buildings, the equipment in them and the truck belong to them and them only.

The German young man – his name is Christof – is a student back in his own country. He is here as a volunteer to help the villagers in their rural development project. Perhaps it is for credit in some college class. He knows nothing about beekeeping; he majors in development studies or something along those lines. He stays at Morrison Xinindlu's house. The elder is proud that there is a white man staying at his house. This has increased his prestige in the village.

The women tell me that Christof is a hard worker. He climbs the mountain with them on foot and carries the heavy supers down to the building where the women extract the honey from the combs, heat it so it doesn't crystallise and then bottle it.

But his enthusiasm for the project has placed him at loggerheads with some of the community members. He is not aware that he is being used in local power struggles. I am told that at one stage my Uncle

Owen threatened to beat him up because he believed he was inciting the Bee People against him. But what has brought me to Xinindlu's house to talk to the young man has nothing to do with petty disputes. It has to do with the fact that his zeal has gone too far and I need to find a way of restraining it.

Apparently he has been spending his evenings writing down rules for the Bee People. As he was working with them he observed problems that in his view were constraining their progress, and he was devising ways to overcome them. He already had a list that included instructions on what time work should start in the morning, and when the women should take a break for lunch and who among them should supervise which aspect of the production process. Worse still, he had written a constitution for the organisation; from now on everything should be run according to this document. What riled the Bee People most was that now they were supposed to elect a new committee to meet the requirements of this new constitution drawn up solely by Christof in the solitude of Morrison Xinindlu's bedroom. Because he is a white man these rural folks see him as some authority figure who must be obeyed.

'We don't do things that way,' I tell him after we have been introduced and I have taken a seat in front of Xinindlu's house.

I can sense that he is resentful. He sees me as an intruder.

I try to explain that he can't just draw up a constitution for an organisation that he knows nothing about. He can't just make his own rules either. He admits that he is not familiar with South African laws governing non-profit and community-based organisations. But, according to him, that makes no difference because a constitution is a constitution in any country.

'Did you ever try to find out about this organisation's founding documents?' I ask.

'They told me they have no constitution. They can't operate without a constitution.'

'Do you know why they have no constitution?' I ask. 'It is because they are a Trust. The Trust Deed is their constitution. They are not just a makeshift organisation; they are registered. In any case, even if they didn't have a constitution, you can't just write a constitution by yourself and then impose it on them. That's not how things are done here.'

He becomes angry and starts yelling that he came all the way from Germany to help these rural people because they don't know anything and now I am trying to stop him from doing his job.

'To help people is a good thing,' I tell him. 'To help them help themselves is even better. We aim for self-reliance. But you are not helping them when you come here and start behaving like their boss and impose rules on them and even appoint people to positions and assign duties in their own business. You can table ideas for discussion, you can make suggestions, but you are not their boss. We have tried to cultivate a democratic culture here. We need to maintain it and enhance it.'

He is not listening. He is visibly angry. He obviously sees himself as a dispenser of wisdom and doesn't seem to understand that he is here to learn as well. He is a white man come to civilise the natives and now here is an equivalent of a native chief resisting the generosity of his knowledge. He angrily grabs his papers from the bench and snatches from my hand the constitution I was reading which was so naive you would have thought it was written by a high school kid.

Gosh, I lose it!

'Who the fuck do you think you are, man?' I yell as I stand up to face the impertinent numbskull.

But the Bee People gently push him into the house to talk to him about manners.

THAT HAS ALWAYS BEEN a problem with me, the short fuse. It used to happen in the classroom too in my early days as a teacher. But, thankfully, in the long run I was able to overcome it, although occasionally my irritation does show. What can I say? I am my father's son.

But my father could be very diplomatic too. And wily. I saw this when my kid brother was arrested by the Boers and was sent to Grootvlei Prison in Bloemfontein.

It all started when Limpho, Chris Hani's wife, tried to smuggle a group of young men out of Lesotho for military training in the ANC camps in other African countries and abroad. The group was composed of my former Mabathoana High School students – Buti Moleko, Nelson Mogudi and my sister's boyfriend Steve Tau. The fourth young man was my brother Zwelakhe. I was quite surprised to hear that he was in this group because his sentiments were strongly PAC. It was the case with the other young men in the group as well. But then those days things tended to get blurred sometimes and ideology and party loyalties became secondary to the goal of liberating South Africa. I have told you, for instance, that Limpho's brother Sekamane was a commander in the Lesotho Liberation Army which trained under the auspices of the Azanian People's Liberation Army – the PAC military wing – in Libya. Actually, Limpho herself used to be strongly pro-BCP, an ally of the PAC, when she was still Clemoski's girlfriend before she married Chris. Well, don't even try to sort that out.

My brother told me later that what was uppermost in these young men's minds was to get higher education abroad. It didn't matter under the auspices of which one of our liberation movements.

But they had not reckoned with the Boers. When they were crossing the Maseru border post with Limpho and the driver in the guise of a family going shopping in Ladybrand, they were arrested. Someone had snitched on them. Limpho and the driver were released after questioning because they were Lesotho citizens and there was no evidence at the time that they were not who they claimed to be. Their Lesotho passports were genuine. But the young men were clearly South Africans who carried false Lesotho passports. There was evidence that they had crossed the border illegally when they took refuge in Lesotho. They were taken to Bloemfontein where they were fortunate enough to be sentenced to only one year in prison.

It worried my father no end that his last-born was in the hands of the Boers. The Boers, on the other hand, had their own ideas about Zwelakhe. They wanted to use him as bait to get my father to cross the Caledon River so that they could arrest him. They sent emissaries to Mafeteng with the message that they were willing to negotiate for Zwelakhe's release if my father would meet them on the South African side of the border post. My father insisted that they meet by the river on the Lesotho side. He was accompanied to the meeting by Sechaba Kalake, a Mafeteng youth whose father was serving a long term on Robben Island, and by my brother Sonwabo. He instructed them to stand a few yards behind him as he negotiated with an Afrikaner police captain. The two young men pretended that they were armed in case the captain grabbed my father by force with the view of dragging him across the border.

'You know, Mr Mda, we have nothing against you,' my father later told us the captain had said. 'We know that you've not been doing anything subversive since coming to Lesotho. Come back to South Africa. No one will do anything to you.'

The captain promised that they would release Zwelakhe if my father undertook to return for further negotiations about his safe passage back to South Africa. My father promised he would return for further negotiations if they released Zwelakhe first.

A few weeks later Zwelakhe was released from Grootvlei Prison, but my father never kept his word to the Boers, despite their gesture of 'goodwill'.

The next time I met Chris Hani I confronted him about this.

'Bhut' Thembi, how can you guys take my kid brother across the border without our knowledge?'

'AP knew,' he said.

I was quite surprised. Was Chris just trying to shut me up?

I still don't believe that my father would allow his son to be taken out of the country for military training by the ANC. But then you never know. My father, though a Pan Africanist and a champion of African nationalism, had a very open mind and even affection for his old organisation.

After his release from prison Zwelakhe gave up all ideas of going for military training and went to study for an LLB degree at the National University of Lesotho.

At about this time John Nyathi Pokela was released from Robben Island after serving thirteen years. He was my father's protégé from the village of Qoboshane – the Bee Place. While he was in transit to

Tanzania to take over the chairmanship of the PAC he stayed at Bra Saul Manganye's house at Lesotho High School. Bra Saul was another friend of mine who taught commercial subjects at the high school and had come to Lesotho some years back as a refugee from Lady Selbourne in Pretoria. Lady Selbourne – and the neighbouring Pretoria townships – was the headquarters of jazz in South Africa, so one of the pleasures of hanging out with Bra Saul, besides his nostalgic reminiscences about launching the PAC in Pretoria, was listening to jazz. Also, he was the only person I knew who had a TV in those early days of South African television.

I went to Bra Saul's home to pay my respects to Pokela. He looked fine despite the years he had spent working in the lime quarries on Robben Island. I remembered him from his youthful days at eHohobeng, which was the name of his sub-village at Qoboshane, and then when as a refugee he taught at Maseru Community School. He was present when Potlako Leballo swore me into the PAC. He was very happy to see me and remarked that I had not changed one bit. He was being nice, of course; I had gained quite a few kilograms since the last time we met. I paid him the same compliment. He told me that my plays were smuggled into Robben Island and he and his comrades from all the political parties had staged readings of them. *Dark Voices Ring* resonated particularly with them. I was quite moved to hear that my work was giving hope and solace to those who had been condemned to spend their precious lives behind bars for our freedom.

'We of the PAC boasted to the rest of the prisoners that these plays were written by one of our cadres,' he said.

I didn't have the heart to tell him that I no longer saw myself as a PAC cadre, despite the fact that I never officially resigned from the party. I was more inclined towards the ANC line of thinking. When I had mentioned this to Bra Saul he thought it was because of the influence of the ANC guys who had become my drinking buddies. Top among them was Zingisile Ntozintle Jobodwana, or Jobs as we called him, who had his law practice in Maseru. Even though these ANC guys were his friends too, Bra Saul dismissively called them Charterists because they subscribed to the Freedom Charter, a document that was adopted by the Congress of the People at Kliptown, Johannesburg, in 1955. This document had played an important role in bringing about the final split that resulted in the formation of the PAC.

I was disillusioned with the PAC, though I still believed in two of its three guiding principles, namely continental unity and socialism. It was with the leadership's interpretation of the third principle, African nationalism, that I had a problem. It was quite different from the way my father used to outline it for us at one of his family meetings. His was not a narrow nationalism. It was all-inclusive of all South Africans who identified themselves as Africans and paid their allegiance first and foremost to Africa. But the way my PAC comrades understood the concept it became clear to me that that the rights of citizenship of a future Azania, as they called South Africa, would be limited only to black people of African descent. In the meetings that we attended, especially when I was staying at the Poqo camp, the leaders did not make any bones about that. I, on the other hand, did not think any modern race-based state was viable or even desirable. I saw this position as a misrepresentation of the tenets of African nationalism as propounded by my father.

The PAC wrote extensively against tribalism; African nationalism was essentially about embracing Africans regardless of which cultural, linguistic or ethnic group they belonged to. But our PAC and Poqo cadres in Lesotho, who were predominantly amaXhosa, had a negative attitude towards their Basotho hosts. They viewed themselves as naturally superior to other ethnicities. I used to get very embarrassed when I met one of these cadres late in the afternoon and he would greet me by saying: *molo, mAfrika, yazi oko kusile ndiqal' ukubon'umntu ngawe.* Greetings to you, African, you are the first person I have seen this whole day. Obviously, according to him, the rest of the people he had been interacting with throughout that day were not really people because they were Basotho.

Another thing I observed was that the PAC promoted chauvinistic and patriarchal values in the name of Africanism. The movement had a very static view of what it meant to be African – an archival one that advocated for a return to some glorious pre-colonial past. Culture meant the way Africans used to live, rather than the way they live today.

What scared me most about my comrades was their social conservatism particularly on gay rights – 'homosexuality is unAfrican' – on reproductive rights – 'abortion is unAfrican' – and on the issue of the death penalty – 'an eye for an eye'. These were positions they shared with the American right, the Catholic Church, fundamentalist Protestants and fundamentalist Muslims. It seemed to me that the PAC were birds of a feather with these intensely patriarchal, retrogressive and conservative organisations. But of course I continued to like what the PAC used to stand for: pan-Africanism (which the ANC appropriated so effectively), identification with the peasants and their struggles, and the concern for the return of the land to its rightful owners.

On the other hand, from my discussions with the likes of Jobs it became clear to me that the ANC was much more progressive on these issues and was more inclusive in its definition of both Africanness and of South Africanness. Thabo Mbeki's post-liberation 'I am an African' speech is a product of that tradition of inclusiveness. I found the values enshrined in the Freedom Charter – the very document my Africanist comrades were derisive about – quite attractive. It was obvious to which camp I naturally belonged, although I would never officially join a political party again. I was too much of a free spirit to toe a party line.

'Whatever happened to you, son of Africa?' Bra Saul would ask whenever I took Jobs' side in a debate on these issues. 'Jobs has made you a Charterist.'

'Don't blame Jobs,' I would reply. 'Blame my sensibilities and sensitivities.'

The wonderful thing about the Lesotho exile was that we talked across party and ideological lines as we quaffed large quantities of alcohol. There were no recriminations.

For me, the swilling combined very well with what my friends cutely called womanising. I was renting what the Americans would call a mother-in-law apartment in a large and modern stone house belonging to the Lebotsa family. I was wifeless since parting ways with Mpho, though not divorced, and my three children were staying with my mother at Holy Cross Mission in southern Lesotho. I could go on the rampage as I pleased at 'Mamojela's, at the Lancer's Inn, at Clemoski's, at Bra Saul's. At my apartment the rampage included women. Motena

251

Mokoae, a daughter of a cabinet minister in Leabua Jonathan's government, was a very special girlfriend. But there were many others who came to my house, mostly the Soweto girls who were students at various schools in town. I have only a vague memory of most of them. I was almost always in an alcoholic and sexual daze.

But I do have a memory of Nono. She was a tall and slender Mosotho woman I met at the bar in Mafeteng. We soon hit it off even though she told me she was married to a white man. She used to drive to Maseru every week and we made furious love. She would phone me on a daily basis and tell me how much she missed our lovemaking. (Well, she didn't put it in those words, but, you know, I must go easy on any X-rated language; my kids will be reading this book as well.) Even when I was in Mafeteng visiting my father she would come and snatch me away, to my father's consternation, and would only bring me back in the morning. Obviously to Nono and the rest of the women I had become quite a stallion. They didn't know that it was because I was a late bloomer. I was still marvelling at the wonders of sex and at what I had been missing all the years I had been encumbered by Nontonje's enfeeblement.

One December morning Nono arrived unannounced and found me in bed with Motena. The room had the stench of the night and of beer. She just sat on a sofa next to the bed and engaged in some small talk as if nothing had happened. Then she said goodbye and left. She got into her brown Opel Kadett, drove away and never came back.

I missed Nono, but life had to go on. Plus Dizzy was in town. Not my Mr Dizzy who was a feature of Maseru, but Dizzy Gillespie. He came to headline a jazz festival at the Maseru Stadium. With him were the Jazz Professors from Rutgers University as his sidemen and Marc Crawford, who was a professor of creative writing at Rutgers. But he was more famous as a staff reporter for *Life* magazine who also dabbled in public relations for B B King and Johnny Mathis.

Dizzy Gillespie and the Jazz Professors held jazz clinics for us and Marc Crawford conducted a creative writing workshop at the Maseru Holiday Inn. I had never been in a creative writing workshop before and didn't even know that writing could actually be taught. Crawford made us gaze into each others' eyes for a minute or so and then furiously write anything that came to our mind. After that we read to the rest of the workshop participants what we had written and giggled at the silliness of it all. I don't know if we gained anything from the workshop, but I for one was quite satisfied with the fact that Crawford read my poems and told everyone that they were great. He even read one of the poems to the group.

I don't think we benefited that much from the jazz clinics either. Well, maybe the Lebentlele brothers who were advanced players did. It was just great that we got to hang out with Dizzy Gillespie, the Jazz Professors and Marc Crawford. Dizzy Gillespie talked a lot about a prophet called Bahaullah from whom he drew his strength and hope for humanity. I had not known that he was of the Baha'i faith. He told us that one could not play great jazz if one was not spiritual, whatever form or religion that spirituality took. For him jazz was an expression of spirituality.

You may wonder how I found time to write with all these goings-on, particularly the unbridled promiscuity. But I did. I had started writing a play about migrant workers titled *The Hill* when I was still at Mabathoana High. I had gone to stay on the hill opposite the high school where men from all over Lesotho spent their nights in the Caves of Mpokho waiting for contracts to go to the mines of South Africa. I had also read a pamphlet titled *Another Blanket* written by an ecumenical organisation that investigated the problems of these migrant workers from the time they left their villages, the humiliation they suffered at the recruitment centres where labour recruiters demanded bribes before they would sign the men on, the months they spent in Maseru scrounging a living doing 'piece jobs' and raiding the dustbins of wealthy Maseru West, right up to the degradation they suffered in the mines. My play was largely based on my experiences interacting with these men.

It won the Amstel Playwright of the Year Award in 1979. André Brink and Barry Ronge were the judges. The Lesotho government granted me citizenship so that I could qualify for a passport and go to accept the award in person. My father was concerned that if I returned to South Africa I would be arrested; I had left the country illegally and I had been involved in politics in Lesotho, and of course the Boers had eyes everywhere and knew exactly what I had been up to. But the deputy prime minister and minister of the interior, Chief Sekhonyana 'Maseribane, who had been urging my father for years to take up Lesotho citizenship, assured him that nothing would happen to me because with Lesotho citizenship I was under the protection of the Lesotho government.

'Your son has brought pride and honour to Lesotho,' 'Maseribane, who I regarded as an odious character because it turned out he was the first member of Leabua's government to join Fred Roach in instigating the savage coup of 1970, told my father. 'He must go accept his prize as a Mosotho. Have no fear of *Maburu*.'

I believed him. His government was in bed with the Boers – or *Maburu* as he called them in Sesotho – and the apartheid government would not want to upset an ally by bothering with small fry like me. After all, I was not involved in any direct guerrilla action as other exiles like Chris Hani were. I was a mere talker and writer.

My father reminded me that the apartheid government had banned my book, which meant that they had a file on me.

'Those fellows have a long memory,' he said. ''Mascribane must give us some guarantee that nothing will happen to you.'

I was prepared to take the risk, but dared not defy my father and go to South Africa without his blessing. Chief 'Maseribane kept his word and contacted my father with a message that he had it in writing: the *Maburu* had given me temporary indemnity, so I must go there and represent Lesotho and continue to put it on the map.

In November 1979, after fifteen years as an exile, I went back to South Africa as a Lesotho citizen to accept my award. I thought returning to South Africa after all those years would be a big deal, but I was preoccupied with the award I was going to receive rather than the fact that I was back on South African soil. Perhaps if I had returned by road, crossed the border post in Maseru and rode in a taxi or bus through the Free State I would have had time to ruminate and interact emotionally with the land and the people. But I took a plane from Maseru to Jan Smuts International Airport, which was just a one-hour flight. Once my passport was stamped and I walked out of the terminal building I found Nicholas Ellenbogen and a bunch of journalists waiting for me. They interviewed me as we drove in a Kombi to the five-star Hotel Braamfontein in the city, and once again I had no time to take in the fact that I was actually in a South Africa I had left all those years ago because of apartheid, and that I was now back but apartheid was still in place. I was only able to stay at this hotel in the city because it had been granted 'international status' by the government and therefore 'foreign' blacks like me could be accommodated and served there.

I knew nothing much had changed in South Africa since my family left. Therefore nothing surprised me about that first visit. I interacted with South Africans all the time in Lesotho, those who were in exile themselves and those who came as visitors and returned home. I had been interacting with South African culture, not only through the visitors, but also through music, art, newspapers, the radio and other media, since my arrival in Lesotho. My return, therefore, did not present me with any culture shock. In any event, I was returning as a 'celebrity' who was surrounded by theatre people and journalists – both black and white – in an artificial non-racial bubble that was far removed from the realities of the Soweto of my youth which was still the Soweto of the day. Only now there was more resistance, more deaths from police bullets and, as the Black Consciousness artists – Matsemela Manaka, Maishe Maponya and Ingoapele Madingoane – who came to see me at the hotel and at the awards ceremony emphasised, more poetry and theatre and art in the bloody streets that both rallied the people to more action and gave them hope that a new day was bound to dawn soon.

The day after the ceremony the headlines in *The Star* screamed: *Lesotho teacher wins play award*. The newspaper wrote of the play as a 'poignant, witty observation of the South African migrant worker situation'.

The play was first produced at the people's Space Theatre in Cape Town to rave reviews. It was directed by Rob Amato and featured Nomhle Nkonyeni (now regarded as the doyenne of the South African stage), Sylvia Mdunyelwa (now an acclaimed jazz singer) and Natie Rula (who later became an enduring actress of soap operas). When the play went to the Market Theatre in Johannesburg it was greeted by the *Sunday Times* headlines: *The mountain comes to the Market – Award winner 'The Hill' is in town.* Another newspaper in the same stable, the *Sunday Times Extra*, had the headline: *'The Hill': best since 'Sizwe' and 'Island'.* This was a reference to the plays created by Athol Fugard, John Kani and Winston Ntshona – *Sizwe Banzi Is Dead* and *The Island*. Rob Amato made a point of seeing that the play came to Lesotho and it was performed at the Hilton Hotel and at the National University of Lesotho.

Now that I had a passport and could go to South Africa I was able to reconnect with Keneiloe Mohafa, my childhood sweetheart from Sterkspruit. This, in fact, is what helped to rein in my rampant behaviour. She was the woman I had been yearning for all those years. I had continued to write poetry about her, even as her memory was fading in my mind. Now there she was, as beautiful as ever with her big round eyes, though now she was quite overweight and very much concerned about it. She was now a social worker, having qualified with a bachelor's degree in the field from the University of the North in Turfloop some years before, and was working for the Johannesburg Child Welfare Society. She was renting a back room in Alexandra Township.

She drove all the way from Johannesburg in her Volkswagen Golf to visit me in Maseru, and I took a plane from Maseru to Johannesburg to visit her in Alexandra Township. I could afford to do that because I had by then secured employment with the American Cultural Center on Kingsway as a Cultural Affairs Specialist. The Center was part of the United States Information Agency and ran a library and resource centre.

Keneiloe, quite a heavy drinker in her own right, used to take me to some of the famous night spots for black people in Johannesburg. I got to know of Ha Kolokoti, a famous shebeen in Orlando, through her. She also took me to a nightclub that was always in the papers because it was patronised by the black elite, the Pelican, and introduced me to Kelly Michaels who owned and operated the place. Gugu tells me that she was one of the kids I saw peeping through the fence gawking at the celebrities who patronised the Pelican. I didn't know then that one of those urchins would one day be my wife.

Keneiloe also took me to Mabopane near Pretoria to visit her friends Alpheus and Mamathe Mosenye. I fell in love immediately with this couple because of their humour and the easy-going way they related to each other. I hoped Keneiloe and I would be like that, because surely we were meant to be together and, though I didn't express that to her, we were going to marry and live happily ever after. Alpheus was one of the best artists I had met. I gave him all the poems I had written; most were about Keneiloe and my longing for her. He illustrated each poem. Years later I published the poems and the illustrations under the imprint of my own publishing company, Thapama Books. By that time I had lost contact with Alpheus Mosenye and he never got a copy.

CHAPTER EIGHT

WE ARE RELAXING OUTSIDE our grass-thatched chalet at the Riverside Lodge in Aliwal North. This splendid holiday resort is situated on the banks of the Orange River, and from where we are sitting we can see the brown water flowing lazily around the bend. It hasn't rained for quite some time so there are islands of sand and pebbles in the river. We can see the bridge that crosses to the Free State province floating in the fog. We rest our eyes on the distant hills that appear in grey and blue patches in the white mist.

This Eastern Cape town is famous for its hot springs, but that's not why we are here. Our destination was Lady Grey where we had a meeting about the finances of the beekeeping project with Aubrey Fincham who had been appointed by the Kellogg Foundation to manage their donation to the project. His wife was a goldsmith in the tiny town situated in the foothills of the Witteberg Mountains. We also wanted to talk to the local hotel that stocks the honey to find out what their guests think of it. We were pleased to see bottles of *Telle Honey/Ubusi baseTelle*, which is the brand name under which the Bee People market their honey, on display at the reception. Aliwal North is only fifty-five kilometres from Lady Grey so we decided to drive here and spend the night.

'It's a beautiful town and a wonderful view,' says Gugu.

'It's a nice lodge too,' I say. 'But my memories of this town are not about the beauty. The only time I was ever arrested by the Boers was in this town.'

THABO SETHATHI, MR TOP and I had come to Aliwal North for Clemoski's funeral. He died of liver cirrhosis, as did a number of our alcoholic friends before him. Great warriors fallen at the altar of Bacchus. He originally came from this town, from its black township of Dukathole, to be exact. He had initially gone to Lesotho to attend the university at Roma, then known as Pius XII College. After his Bachelor of Arts degree and Postgraduate Certificate in Education he got a job teaching English at Lesotho High School and decided to stay permanently. But in death our people believe we must all return home, to our places of origin, and be buried on the stomping grounds of our ancestral spirits.

Thus I had crossed the border using my newly acquired Lesotho passport to pay my last respects to my dear friend with whom I had spent wonderful drunken moments at his Lesotho High School house. Or at the shebeen owned by the woman who was also his secret mistress, 'Mamojela. Now Clemoski was gone, leaving us dispirited and dismayed. He was also leaving his six-year-old son Bataung, his estranged wife 'Mabataung, and two or three other children he made with various girlfriends over the years. One of the children, Kefuoe Molapo, now a big man who is an actor and film maker in New York, subsequently became a protégé and a friend. You'll get to know how in later years this same Kefuoe retitled my novel from *Ululants* to *The Heart of Redness*, and how I have lived to regret that ever since.

At Clemoski's funeral I met Thabang Mohafa, Keneiloe's sister. She told me she was a teacher at one of the schools in the town. I had not seen her for many years, since the days we used to play *dibeke* in the street in front of her house in Sterkspruit. I reminded her how I had hit her on the head with a stone and her father had frogmarched me to my home where he lashed me with a belt in the presence of my mother. We laughed about it. She invited me and my pals – Thabo and Mr Top – to her house where we had drinks. Soon more people came from the township and we had a jolly good time getting drunk. She introduced us to her teenage daughter or niece, I don't quite remember. I think it was a daughter though.

As we were imbibing and reminiscing about Clemoski's greatness and telling the locals how the man they called Abuti Sima, using his birth name, had been my mentor from the days I was at Peka High School, a young man sauntered into the room. One of the locals at the table told us he was the teenager's boyfriend from the Coloured township. He demanded that the teenager go with him, but the girl said she would not because it was late. It was already after midnight and I wondered what parent would allow a girl that age to go out with a boy at that time. The young man became abusive and started dragging the girl by the arm. Thabang and another woman, who had been introduced to us as her housemate, yelled at the young man, asking him to leave the girl alone. The young man responded by slapping the girl.

That was enough for me. I stood up and hit the young man on the jaw with my fist. He fell down and I kicked him on the head and in the stomach. Soon the other people in the house, particularly the local women, joined the assault. I just couldn't stop myself even though the guy was bleeding all over the place. I think it was Mr Top who stopped the mayhem and helped the young man up. He staggered away crying and vowing that his *broers*, or brothers, would come and give us a taste of our own medicine.

'He will never even dream of assaulting another girl again,' said Thabang, as we went back to our merrymaking. I felt like a hero when she said that. But soon, even as I joined in the banter, I wondered at the violent streak in me, the existence of which I had not been aware. I was never a fighter. I could rant and rave when someone made me mad, but it would never deteriorate into a physical brawl. How did it come to this? How did *I* come to this? Even in my drunken state I began to worry that there was a thug hiding in me waiting to burst out.

The next thing I knew the battered young man was back with four white policemen and a whole lot of angry folks from the Coloured township.

'There he is,' he said pointing at me. 'And this one too,' he added, pointing at Thabang's housemate.

The policemen arrested us and loaded us in the back of a police van. They did not handcuff us though.

I don't know where they took Thabang's housemate, but I was locked up in a cell with a bunch of petty criminals who were so nice that they shared their lice-infested blankets with me. There were no beds or bunks in the cell, so we rolled the blankets and sat on them. For a toilet there was a bucket in the corner. Up on the high ceiling was a naked bulb that was on all the time.

I sobered up very fast in that cell. I was regretting my rash action. In two weeks' time I was supposed to go to America to study for a Master of Fine Arts degree in playwriting. While working at the American Cultural Center organising cultural exchanges between Lesotho and the USA I had come across an advertisement in a theatre journal for the Ohio University School of Theater Playwriting Program and had immediately applied, sending them my banned book of plays. I had been fascinated by the fact that it was possible to do a master's degree in playwriting, a field in which I was already proficient, by all accounts. I had not even known that there was such a degree anywhere in the world. I was from the British tradition where university education in literature and drama meant studying the English canon, not writing plays. When the head of the playwriting program, Seabury Quinn Junior, responded offering me a place on their three-year MFA program and a tuition waiver I was ecstatic. It had not mattered to me how I was going to survive in

America. All I needed was a one-way ticket. I had then approached a cabinet minister in Leabua Jonathan's government, Desmond Sixishe, for assistance. I had known Desmond from Sterkspruit where he had been a taxi-driving playboy and one of the older guys we looked up to. I had not known at the time that he was born in Lesotho. Then later I had trained him on how advertising agencies functioned on commission from the media when he started his own advertising agency, patterning it on my old company MDA Enterprises. His business had become more successful than mine had been, but he left it when he was appointed Minister of Information and Broadcasting. Now he returned the favour by approaching the National Manpower Development Secretariat to give me a loan for my one-way air ticket. They emphasised that was all I was going to get from them; no full scholarship for me because according to them I was going to study something that would not contribute to national development. The ticket was good enough for me and I was looking forward to flying to America in a fortnight's time.

But here I was languishing in a South African jail for some stupid act of violence.

These thoughts of recrimination were interrupted from time to time by prison guards who opened the iron doors and ushered us out to squat on the ground while a stern Afrikaner warder shouted our names for roll-call. We each responded 'Yebo Nkosi!' Yes, Chief. And then we were ushered back to our cells. The same happened when we were being fed. I didn't eat the pap and vegetables that the guards slid along the floor to each of my five cellmates. I was given fish, chips and Russian sausages that I assumed Thabang had brought for me. They did allow awaiting-trial prisoners to receive food from outside. But I had no appetite even for that. I gave it to the other prisoners.

In the cell I listened to the petty criminals boasting about the housebreakings they had committed. One was a habitual criminal who specialised in the theft of car batteries. He was looking forward to being sentenced and sent to prison where he would meet his old friends. He was already planning his life there and the other prisoners were contributing their wisdom as to how to handle particular situations, especially with prison gangs. When it came to my turn to relate my crime I told them I had beaten someone almost to death and I was likely to be given a life sentence. It was necessary to stress the violent nature of my crime and exaggerate it a bit so that none of these grubby guys should think I was a pushover who could be raped at will.

On the third day I was taken out of the cell to another building where I was interrogated by a team of white policemen, both in civvies and in uniform. They did not ask me anything about my crime, but were interested only in my activities in Maseru and in the people I associated with. I could see the glee in their eyes. Obviously they had initially thought they had caught a petty ruffian who had been engaged in a drunken brawl, but had discovered that I was someone who wrote books that were banned by the government and that I associated with the kind of people they would like to lay their hands on.

'We know that you know Chris Hani,' their chief interrogator told me.

I couldn't lie and say I didn't know him.

'Yes, I know him. But I don't move in the same circles as he does or any other political figure.'

I was lying on that score because people like Jobodwana and other ANC activists were my close friends and drinking partners. And before them I had that intimate connection with Poqo and lived with them and trained with them and was even sent on a botched mission with them. I was hoping the Boers would not have any of that information in their files. They should continue to view me as some small fry son of a PAC man who had been rendered ineffectual. I was hoping that if there was any information at all in their files about the Latin lessons with Chris Hani they would not interpret them as a code for something more sinister that would be a threat to the whole Afrikaner race.

Fortunately they did not go there at all. Instead one of the officers told me, 'Do you know the boy you assaulted is in a serious condition in hospital? He may die any time and when that happens you'll face a murder charge.'

I suddenly wanted to go to the toilet with a running stomach. It didn't occur to me that when the victim of my violence came with the police to point me out he didn't look anything like a walking corpse.

'If you cooperate with us we may make things easy for you,' said the officer.

They left me sitting in the interrogation room for a while, supposedly to think things over. I passed the time by looking at pictures on the walls. Most were maps of Angola and Mozambique with yellow and red pins indicating the location of ANC guerrilla camps. I had no idea what distinguished the yellow from the red camps.

After three days without making any headway, because in truth I had nothing to cooperate about, the chief interrogator said, 'We have decided to release you on condition you report to Brigadier Cornelius van Wyk at the Maseru Bridge next week.'

I said I would certainly do that. They gave me the day and the time I was required to report to the police at the border post. On my word of honour, Thabang's housemate and I were released from jail. She told me they just kept her in the cell with other female prisoners and only interrogated her once – not about the assault, but about me and what I was doing in Aliwal North and who I had associated with when I was there.

I wondered how these Boers could sacrifice justice for the guy who was assaulted, especially if he was dying in hospital as they claimed, but I learnt from Thabang that the guy had not been that seriously hurt at all. He was seen walking about in town with nothing more than a slight limp and a bruised face.

All I wanted was to disappear from that town, especially because I heard that the thugs from the Coloured township were gunning for me. I took a train to Wepener and from there got a minibus taxi to Maseru without even going to Mafeteng first. I was not aware that my father knew about my arrest. I only learnt when I got to Maseru that Thabo Sethathi and Mr Top had sent a message to Mafeteng as soon as they arrived in Lesotho.

I heard that my father was furious with me. He had instructed a firm of lawyers in Zastron called Snyman and Malherbe to defend me. They were the lawyers who, years back, were pitted against Nelson Mandela, who was my father's lawyer in the case where my father had sued the headman Steyn Senoamali and the Native Commissioner of the

Herschel District for defamation. And I didn't even have the decency to go home and inform him that I had been released. When I finally went to Mafeteng he had a few choice words for me about my irresponsibility and ingratitude.

Back in Maseru, the American Cultural Center also had their say about my arrest. I was summoned to the American Embassy where I was subjected to further interrogation by a woman I assumed was a CIA agent. I had never seen her before in the few times I had gone to the Embassy about visas for our candidates for exchange programmes. Or when I had gone to get our fortnightly salary cheques since we were paid from the Embassy. She must have been posted, maybe from the American Embassy in Pretoria, to interrogate me. She wanted to know why exactly I was arrested. When I told her it was on account of some drunken altercation she didn't believe me.

'That cannot be true,' she said. 'How do you think we got to know you were arrested?'

How indeed? I hadn't told anyone at work that I was in jail. I merely reported that I was delayed by circumstances beyond my control.

When she started asking me about my family background and about my father I thought I would draw the line. I told her my father was not anybody's business.

'I can understand why the South Africans would be interested in my father. But what business is my family to the Americans?'

Instead of answering my question she asked, 'Why were you sponsored by the International University Exchange Fund?'

'Because they funded South African refugee families. I wanted to study art and no one else would fund that.'

'The South Africans would not arrest you for nothing,' she said. 'You must be a terrorist.'

I flared up.

'Whose side are you on?' I asked. 'I went through interrogation with the South African police and I must go through interrogation with you too? You think just because I work for you, you have the right to bully me. I am not answering any questions from you and I resign.'

At this, I stood up and left the Embassy. I only went back to the

American Cultural Center to clear my desk and to say goodbye to my colleagues.

I knew that I had kissed my job with the American Cultural Center goodbye, which shouldn't have really mattered because of my pending trip to the USA, but then I started worrying that perhaps the trip itself might fail. I was supposed to get a visa from the very guys I had pissed on, and I was not prepared to go back to that Embassy with the proverbial tail between my legs. I was not even going to try applying.

I flew to Johannesburg with all my bags packed for the USA. Keneiloe took me to the American Consulate in the city where I applied for a visa. They turned me down, saying that they didn't understand why I hadn't got the visa in Maseru since I had a Lesotho passport. I told them I lived in Johannesburg with my fiancée, namely Keneiloe. On a second attempt and a third they still turned me down. I wanted to give up and return to Maseru to the good life of a starving and drunken artist, but Keneiloe was persistent. She took me to the American Consulate a few more times, at one time finding Gibson Thula, the Inkatha Freedom Party Johannesburg representative, there and enlisting his help. Thula had been a social worker at some stage and Keneiloe knew him from those circles. He was at the Consulate for his own visa and his Zulu Bantustan organisation was in the good books of the Americans, so Keneiloe figured they would listen to him if he pleaded my case. I was angry with her and told her, 'I'd rather not go to America if it means I get a visa through the assistance of people like Gibson Thula.'

I don't think Keneiloe understood my vehemence against Thula because to her he was just a guy she socialised with in Johannesburg whereas to me, coming from my tradition of politics, he was a Bantustan sell-out.

The Americans finally relented and stamped my passport with a visa. After promising Keneiloe that I would make sure she joined me at Ohio University I flew to the United States.

ATHENS, OHIO, SEPTEMBER 1981. My first culture shock was that there was no jazz in America. I expected the air to be permeated by the trumpets of Miles Davis and Dizzy Gillespie; the saxophones of John Coltrane, Sonny Rollins, Eric Dolphy, Sonny Stitt and Charlie Parker; the double bass of Art Davis and Charles Mingus; the flutes of Roland Kirk and Herbie Mann; the xylophone of Milt Jackson; the guitars of Barney Kessel and Kenny Burrell; the pianos of Thelonious Monk and Oscar Peterson; the drums of Art Blakey and Max Roach; and the demented scats of Sarah Vaughan, Lorez Alexandria and Ella Fitzgerald. But no one I met in the college town of Athens had heard of any of these cats. All the radio stations played country music. Not even soul music. Not even rhythm-and-blues. Just the bluegrass and other mountain sounds that whined in my ear like an irritating mosquito. Even my new African American friend, Reggie from Dayton, had never heard of the names. Except for Ella Fitzgerald, who was getting a lot of airtime on television doing a commercial for Memorex. I couldn't get over the fact that Reggie had never heard of Ella Fitzgerald before the Memorex commercial. The only jazzmen we used to admire growing up in Lesotho and South Africa who were known to Reggie and most of the people in the town were Ray Charles (whom I saw in Maseru as well) and Quincy Jones – only because they were crossover artists who practised in more popular genres as well.

Jazz or no jazz, the quaint little town with red-brick buildings dating back to its foundation at the turn of the nineteenth century and the red-brick paved streets captivated me immediately. Life had its pace here, easy-going and unrushed. A direct contrast to the hustle-bustle of Johannesburg. Even Maseru had more of a rat-race atmosphere to it than Athens. This suited me well; I was burnt-out from all the fast living.

I immersed myself in student life and became a regular at the Graduate, a bar on West Union Street. The first few months were a struggle because I had neither a scholarship nor a job. But fortunately the head of the School of Theater, Bob Winters, and the head of the playwriting program, Seabury Quinn Junior, did their best to see to it that I got a small stipend from the university and arranged for my accommodation at the Convocation Center where I shared a room with a Japanese student.

Ohio University was the first university I attended on a full-time basis – to date all my education after Peka High School had been by correspondence. I was admitted here on the strength of my published and performed plays, rather than my art education with the now defunct Swiss academy.

My mentor, Seabury Quinn Junior, was a cantankerous but lovable man with a moustache and a bow-tie. He was cynical about everything. But for some reason he liked me and we spent a lot of time together. He had many questions about South Africa and seemed to be fascinated by the fact that there were white people who were either so foolhardy or so brave as to live in Africa. He invited me for his Thanksgiving dinners where it would be only the two of us facing a whole turkey stuffed with cranberries and a huge pumpkin pie that could feed a family of five. He lived in a log house in the woods, just off Richland Avenue, and I got the feeling he was a very lonely man. Maybe he was not lonely at all. Maybe he was just a loner.

It was only after his death – years later – that I learnt from Joanna Perry, who was my fellow playwriting student under Seabury's tutelage and now makes films in Hollywood, that our Seabury had demons of his own that were haunting him.

'He adored you, but he was a troubled soul,' Joanna told me.

'I thought he was just a grumpy old man,' I said. 'I didn't know he was a troubled soul. What was troubling him?'

'It could not have been easy being a gay man in a time when gays were reviled in this country,' she said. 'And Seabury was grumpy for a reason that he once told me which was the shadow of his father, the writer, who he felt he could not live up to. He had a lot of old feelings that were never resolved in his psyche, I think, as we all do.'

I didn't know of Seabury's sexual orientation and I felt very angry at his culture that was and unfortunately largely still continues to be intolerant. I knew about his father, Seabury Quinn, the famous author of the *Weird Tales* series featuring the occult detective Jules de Grandin. But I didn't know that our Seabury had issues about being his son. He never mentioned his father to me.

I was glad that Joanna told me this because I now understand Seabury better. Our friendship endured even after I had left Ohio University. We continued to correspond over the years, right up to his death, but it was always about work – about my novels and plays. He kept up with what I was doing and read every novel I wrote. Sometimes I would tell him of my play being translated, say into Catalan and being performed in Barcelona, and he would say something bitchy like: 'Well, you know, every little bit helps.' As if it was no big deal to have a play in Spain in a regional language!

But that didn't bother me because it was Seabury being Seabury.

I never attended any of Seabury's playwriting classes or workshops, so I have no idea what his students did there or if they learnt anything at all. All my playwriting lessons with him were independent study. I wrote plays and gave them to him. He looked at them, chuckled a bit here and there, and gave them back to me with an A. For the three years he was my teacher and mentor I learnt nothing about playwriting from him. But that was fine. I had not come to learn anything about playwriting anyway. I had come to get a degree.

I also took his history and criticism classes, from which I did learn a great deal, though in many instances without realising it. I particularly liked his European Theatre classes, and also classes on American Melodrama, which he conducted in a laid-back manner. We just sat around and had casual conversations about the plays. We all enjoyed his whimsical and farcical humour, which was nevertheless quite deadpan.

Though he never gave me any feedback on my plays he must have liked them because I often heard him being brutally frank to others about their plays. I didn't see any reason why he should save my face by keeping quiet. At the same time I didn't understand why he didn't praise them outright if he thought they were good. But he did produce and direct one of them as my thesis work. *The Road* was performed at the Little Theater at Kantner Hall.

One thing Seabury was always grateful about was that I made him aware of African theatre. He had not known that there was such an animal. His only encounter with Africa was through the tunnel-vision of American media whose reports on Africa comprised only war and famine. For my history and criticism credits I devised an independent study course on African theatre with a long reading list of such playwrights as Robert Serumaga, Femi Osofisan, John Ruganda, Ama Ata Aidoo, Wole Soyinka, Efua Sutherland and many others. He had to read these books in order to supervise and grade my essays. This independent study also helped me by introducing me to many African playwrights whose work I wouldn't otherwise have read.

Seabury enriched my life in other ways too. I worked with him when he produced Derek Walcott's plays *The Joker of Seville* and *O Babylon!* It was a great event when Derek Walcott himself came to town to direct his works. It was the first time I had closely observed a professional director at work. You will remember that my own plays were produced and performed in Johannesburg and Cape Town in my absence; I never even got to see them, except for *The Hill* which went to Lesotho. Athens was so honoured by Walcott's visit that he was given the key to the city. I haven't heard of anyone being given the key to the city of Athens since. I wonder what happened to that practice.

My life as a student at Ohio University, however, was not only confined to the activities of the School of Theater. In fact most of it was out there in the town with the many African students who became my friends. Besides my sojourns at the Graduate, a bar popular with international students, I spent a lot of time at Wilson Abok's house which was a gathering place for some of us. He and his Motswana girlfriend, Tebogo Molefhe, were always gracious hosts. We sat in their living room until the early hours of the morning and had heated debates on how to rescue Africa from its malaise. And of course such debates could only make sense when accompanied by huge quantities of Miller or Michelob.

I don't remember the name of the Japanese student who was so kind as to let me share his room, but I owe him an apology. He was a pleasant, quiet guy who minded his own business and I took advantage of that. Like him, I was a nice guy. But only during the day. In the evenings I went to Abok's and came back in the middle of the night with my South African friend Simphiwe Hlatshwayo, and held long drunken debates in the room, disregarding my host whose sleep we were disturbing. Then I phoned Keneiloe in Johannesburg at 3:00 a.m. and sighed and laughed and giggled while my roommate was trying very hard to sleep.

270

With this kind of behaviour I wouldn't have lasted that long at the Convo. The guy didn't kick me out, but his attitude made it obvious that I was no longer a welcome guest. I moved out and shared an apartment with two white American girls whose hygiene was not of the best. They washed their hair in the kitchen sink, which was unheard of where I came from, and kept a small bucket in the kitchen where they dumped their used sanitary pads and tampons. They just left the bucket by the sink for weeks on end until the contents were black in colour and smelled like a dead rat. I have no idea why neither of them thought of dumping it in the dustbin outside. I never saw the girls' rooms but I can imagine how untidy they were, judging from the fact that some of their clothes and frilly undergarments were scattered all over the floor, even in the corridor and on kitchen floor. They had a well-fed cat that pooed all over the house even though there was a cat litter box in the kitchen. I had to be very careful when I walked in the corridor and in the kitchen. And yet these beautiful girls were talented artists who produced some of the most wonderful intaglio at Siegfried Hall where they were students.

I wanted to leave and find an apartment of my own but I couldn't afford it. The stipend from the School of Theater was too small for such a luxury. I couldn't even afford food sometimes and had to sell my blood for a few dollars to survive. On two occasions my blood was rejected. They didn't tell me why. I had become anaemic and suffered from dizziness. Maybe I was harvesting too much plasma in order to buy my favourite subs at Rax Beef Sandwiches. Or a few items of groceries and toiletries at the Super Duper Store on Stimson Avenue.

It was at this time that I remembered Jane Fonda. When we had dinner at the Lesotho Hilton she had said to me, 'Next time you are in the United States do see me.' Normally people say such things to be nice, you know, just to make small talk. But I told myself that I didn't give a damn if she meant it or not, I was going to take her up on that. I had kept her postal address and telephone number in Santa Monica where she lived with her husband Tom Hayden.

So, I got in touch with her and told her of my predicament. She told me that in fact I had contacted her at the right time because she was planning to make a movie set in South Africa and was looking for the right property. She immediately engaged my services as what she called a script consultant, and sent me a cheque in advance.

With her money I was able to rent myself a nice basement apartment on East Carpenter Street from Professor Gifford Doxsee. It was fully furnished with a big kitchen, a living room, a bedroom and a laundry room with a washer and a dryer. I lived like a king. I was even able to send flowers to Keneiloe occasionally through Interflora. Now I could entertain as well. Abok had long completed his studies and returned to Kenya. But I had a number of friends from Africa. There was Baratang Mpotokwane from Botswana who was doing her PhD in Education; Zanele Mfono and Simphiwe Hlatshwayo, both from South Africa and both doing African Studies; Mike Kirubi and Macharia Munene both from Kenya and doing PhDs in International Business and History respectively. Another special friend was Augustin Hatar from Rwanda. Hatar is the only one who I met later in life on African soil. He had been the head of the Rwandan broadcasting services during the period that led to the genocide. He was able to escape and found refuge in Tanzania, where he continues to live and teach at the University of Tanzania. He and his wife once visited me at my house in Johannesburg.

I remember all these people very fondly because we had such wonderful carefree times together, which were nevertheless very intellectually stimulating. I felt for the first time that I was becoming a real scholar. Here my promiscuity ceased, my excitement at discovering sex so late in life had waned, and the only vice that remained was drunkenness.

In the meantime the South African establishment got to hear that Jane Fonda was planning a movie set in South Africa and became hysterical. Alden Library at Ohio University subscribed to the *Sunday Times*, published in Johannesburg, and one day I saw the headline: *Though not fond of it, Jane wants SA's story*. A columnist by the name of Adrian Monteath wrote:

> I have news of quite extraordinary gravity this morning. Jane Fonda, the famous ageing banshee, wants to write, produce and direct a film about . . . South Africa. Since her views on the world are only

marginally less extreme than those of the crazed Redgrave woman, I shudder at the possible result. She has been obsessed with the project since her 1981 visit to Lesotho, when she was 'held' at Jan Smuts. There is yet no story for the film, which is still very much in the planning stages. But it is known that she wants to make it in Lesotho.

Jan Smuts was the airport in Johannesburg, now known as O R Tambo International Airport. I hadn't known that Jane Fonda had been detained there by the South African authorities when she was in transit to Lesotho.

The article went on to express the hope that since Fonda had engaged my services as a consultant I would help with the authenticity of the script.

And this paranoid diatribe was from a supposedly liberal South African English newspaper! You can only imagine what the conservative Afrikaner newspapers were saying.

There were other things that were happening in southern Africa besides the paroxysm over Jane Fonda. The African students at Ohio University, especially those from the subcontinent, were outraged when they received reports that on December 9, 1982, South African commandos crossed the Mohokare River into Lesotho just before dawn and massacred a number of South African refugees and Lesotho nationals. They called the raid Operation Blanket and claimed it was a pre-emptive strike against ANC terrorists who were preparing a raid of their own into South Africa. For a long time we were in the dark as to who had been killed. I worried about my ANC friends, especially Jobodwana. Newspapers from South Africa only reached us after two weeks, via the Alden Library. I was shocked by the *Sunday Times* headlines that extolled the raid even though twelve of the forty-two people who were killed were Basotho people who had nothing to do with the ANC. Some of these were women and children, including a woman we grew up with in Mafeteng when her father worked for the education department before he joined the diplomatic service and then became a cabinet minister in Chief Leabua Jonathan's government. The woman, 'Matumo Ralebitso, allegedly fell from the window when

South African soldiers barged into her flat near the Victoria Hotel, guns blazing, looking for Limpho Hani. The rest of the casualties were South African refugees. Apparently the agents of the apartheid government pointed out what they believed to be houses occupied by the so-called ANC insurgents all over the town and its outskirts. A lot of their information was either wrong or outdated and many innocent people died.

When I read in the *New York Times* that a Lesotho government spokesman said, 'The only reason why South Africa invaded Lesotho was Lesotho's rejection of apartheid', I knew that the romance between Pretoria and Maseru had come to an end. This was apparent even before the invasion when Chief Leabua Jonathan established diplomatic relations with the People's Republic of China, the Soviet Union and North Korea. He even invited North Korea to train his paramilitary force. As a bonsella they built him a brand new stadium.

This was a one hundred and eighty degree turnabout for Leabua and Lesotho, and some of my comrades and I applauded it. In our view he was now taking a progressive direction and needed our support. We were prepared even to forgive him his brutal coup of 1970 when he refused to hand over power to Ntsu Mokhehle who had clearly won the elections. Lesotho was now plainly on the side of the ANC. BNP members, including the much-feared BNP Young Pioneers, saw themselves as revolutionaries. They accused the BCP and its armed wing, the Lesotho Liberation Army, of being reactionaries who were secretly supported by South Africa and the American CIA.

But there were some of my old MaPeka comrades who were adamant that Leabua Jonathan's government was illegitimate; they were determined to overthrow it at all costs. My brothers, the twins, who were regarded as MaPeka themselves although they did not matriculate at Peka High School, wrote me letters updating me on the events in Lesotho. They told me that the LLA was launching more attacks into the country from bases at Qwa Qwa, the Bantustan in South Africa designated for South African Basotho people. This gave credence to the claim that there was some South African collusion in the incursions, which surprised me no end because the BCP I used to campaign for was

274

vehemently anti-apartheid; its *raison d'être* was the return to Lesotho of the land conquered by the Boers more than a century before. Leabua Jonathan had been the South African stooge, now all of a sudden he was on the side of the angels and Ntsu Mokhehle was the alleged South African lackey!

I was shocked to hear that Jama Mbeki, my friend from the Peka days, had been killed by the Police Mobile Unit. I had no idea what Jama had been doing in Lesotho at that time. The last time I had heard of him he was practising as a lawyer in Botswana where a number of his BCP comrades were in exile. Of course, I had known that he was a member of the LLA from the MaPeka LLA members who had tried to recruit me into the guerrilla force in earlier years. I was greatly saddened by Jama's death and recalled all our high jinks at Peka High School. It had been an age of innocence where there was a clear line of demarcation between politics and death.

Although I was thousands of kilometres away in Athens, Ohio, and therefore physically cut off by distance from these events, I couldn't insulate myself emotionally. It was obvious to me and my fellow African students at Ohio University that South Africa's arrogance knew no bounds and that something had to be done about it.

We therefore immersed ourselves in anti-apartheid campaigns. I worked closely with my fellow South African Simphiwe Hlatshwayo, who was an ANC member. I myself, as I have already indicated, was not a member of that organisation although I totally agreed with its philosophy. I could work with its cadres, but it was important for me to jealously guard my freedom to speak my mind without being constrained by party discipline. Another student who joined our activism and became the president of the African Students Union was the Rwandan Augustin Hatar.

Our campaign focused on disinvestment and divestment. With the latter we aimed to force universities, including our own, which had shares in companies that operated in South Africa to dispose of those shares. Disinvestment was targeted at the companies themselves to withdraw all operations from South Africa. We campaigned against Ronald Reagan's policy of 'constructive engagement' which was devised and strenuously defended by his undersecretary of state for Africa, Chester Crocker.

We invited people like Congress Mbatha, who had been an activist of the ANC Youth League from its formation in the late 1940s, to address us. Mbatha, a member of ANC president Oliver Tambo's three-man Syndicate of old, was Simphiwe's professor when he was doing his undergraduate degree at Syracuse University.

We also worked closely with Dennis Brutus, the poet and former Robben Island prisoner who had founded the South African Non-Racial Olympic Committee (SANROC) which was achieving great success in getting South Africa kicked out of international sport. He was a master campaigner and he came to Athens to rally us to put pressure on our university to divest. I went on the road with Dennis Brutus to a number of campuses in the United States. My play, *The Road*, became the rallying tool. Extracts from it were performed at campus rallies to give the spectators an idea of what apartheid was all about since the American media had its own prevarications when it reported on Africa. A full production of the play was mounted at the Loeb Theater, Harvard University, in Cambridge, Massachusetts, directed by Gerard Fox who has since become a film maker in the United Kingdom.

When I arrived at the Loeb I was told that Dennis Brutus, who had been there two days before, had left me a message. 'We must now wage a campaign against Athol Fugard,' the note stated. The reason he wanted Fugard to be boycotted was that Fugard had been making statements against our campaign, especially the cultural boycott aspects of it. He claimed that sanctions, be they economic or cultural, would bring about a lot of suffering, not to the white ruling elite but to the black masses. Our position, of course, was that the black masses were already suffering. They were prepared to suffer a little bit more if it led to the overthrow of the apartheid system.

The cultural sanctions were my focus even more than the sports boycott and divestment and disinvestment work. It was my domain because I was a cultural worker myself – as artists were known those days. I therefore felt I would be more effective in that area.

I could understand why Fugard's advocacy for cultural engagement with South Africa infuriated Brutus. It infuriated me too. He was at the time regarded as one of the most important playwrights in the English language and his word would carry weight against what we were trying to achieve.

But I disagreed with the boycott of Athol Fugard. I thought it would be counter-productive, and I told Brutus so when I phoned him that evening after a successful performance of my play.

'Old Warrior,' I said, 'we'll be fighting against our cause if we do that. We'll be alienating a lot of our liberal supporters who think highly of Fugard and see him as an anti-apartheid playwright. Our campaign in the West – and we know that Western governments are the mainstay of the apartheid system – depends on the liberals, whether we like it or not.'

Brutus agreed that we depended very much on the support of the liberals although at the same time we had contempt for them. But if Fugard got to know of our displeasure and saw the pickets outside his shows he might change his tune or at least shut up.

'We are spread too thinly, Old Warrior, to be focusing on people like Fugard,' I said.

Although Brutus was not totally convinced by my argument, he gave up the idea of actively campaigning against Fugard because he realised that it was best to utilise our resources against the apartheid government and the American companies and universities that made it possible for that government to ride roughshod over the black population and to invade such weak neighbours as Lesotho. That was good enough for me. It was for that reason that I had opposed the picketing of *Umabatha*, the Zulu adaptation of Shakespeare's *Macbeth* by Welcome Msomi. The musical suffered greatly from the boycott both in London and in New York because my comrades felt that it and its creators shied away from politics and also played a public relations role for the apartheid state. Although I had not seen the play, I felt sorry for Msomi and didn't agree that South African works abroad should be condemned for lack of politically correct content. In my view, we were doing exactly what the apartheid government was doing to our own works in the country – banning them and jailing people for reading them, as they had done with my anthology of plays. I felt that only those South African works that actively promoted apartheid should be targeted. We should not campaign against art by South Africans solely on the basis that it was silent on apartheid and merely addressed social and personal issues as did the earlier work of Gibson Kente. Dennis Brutus disagreed with me very strongly on this position. He was a by-any-means-necessary kind of guy when it came to the overthrow of the apartheid state.

In some respects, but to a lesser degree, I was like that too. I was once invited to make a speech at the College Green at Ohio University on Martin Luther King Day. It was at a time when we were still fighting for the day to be observed as a federal holiday. I upset the American liberals when I started outlining why in South Africa we had opted for an armed struggle instead of the non-violent path mapped out by Martin Luther King Junior and Mahatma Gandhi before him. It was the wrong occasion for such a speech and the more mature members of the audience – faculty, staff and townsfolk – were not impressed at all. Most of the students, however, thought it was quite a brave and revolutionary speech.

On the personal side, things were looking up. Keneiloe was admitted to the MA International Affairs Program and had resigned from the Johannesburg Child Welfare Society to join me in Athens. And for a while life was great. Her only disillusionment was that there was no rhythm-and-blues in Athens. Just as I had been the envy of my friends when I left Lesotho because I was going to the home of jazz and would therefore be in the company of some mean cats, she had boasted to her friends in Johannesburg that she would be attending live concerts by the likes of Teddy Pendergrass. Alas, there was no Teddy Pendergrass in Athens.

But her disillusionment was with more than Mr Pendergrass's absence. It was with me. And with the city of Athens and its student population. She had come from Johannesburg where she was a high profile social worker socialising with the black elite of South Africa. Your lawyers and your doctors and your businessmen. Here, she was confined to this small town where our only entertainment was to sit in my apartment and drink beer or visit her friend Baratang Mpotokwane or my friends Macharia Munene or Mike Kirubi and drink ourselves silly. There were no nightclubs and no socialites in expensive Mercedes Benzes and BMWs. I didn't even have a car, whereas in Johannesburg she could get into her Volkswagen Golf and raid the Pelican Club or Kolokoti's tavern any time she felt like it. The only one of my friends here who had a car was Simphiwe, but even with his Volkswagen Beetle there was nowhere for a woman like Keneiloe to go. In Alexandra Township where she lived, and in Soweto where she was a regular, she could attend *stokvel* parties on Saturdays where she could eat her favourite fermented *ting* sorghum porridge with pulled beef. But in Athens she was a prisoner to our lack of imagination. She began to despise me for being satisfied with the life in Athens.

I would hear her phone her brother Tseko in South Africa, or one of her social worker friends, complaining that I was an absolute failure.

'At least Tseko has a truck and is making money even though he has no education,' I once heard her say to a friend on the phone. 'Zanemvula with all his education has nothing.'

There was the week she was invited to join South African students in Lansing, Michigan. When she came back she was even more dissatisfied with Athens. They had partied there in South African style, a thing that we didn't know how to do in Athens. She kept on boasting to me that in Lansing they knew how to live, whereas in Athens we were all dead alive.

Obviously my life in Athens, Ohio – particularly my poverty – did not meet her expectations of the hot-shot playwright she had been reading about in all the major newspapers in South Africa.

One thing that troubled her most – and understandably so for a woman who had been independent all her life – was the fact that she had no income of her own when she was here. As a professional woman who always had her own money, the dependency bugged her no end and she then took it out on me. At the time I couldn't understand what the farce was about since we wanted for nothing and I had even made her a joint-signatory to my bank account, but now I do. She never touched my account even though she had access to it. We tried to get her a scholarship and by the time she got it from the United Nations it was too late. She had already left for South Africa after her father, Teboho, died. I knew she wasn't coming back and that would be the end of my lifelong dream to marry my childhood sweetheart.

The disillusionment with Athens was not peculiar to Keneiloe. I saw it many times with some of the South Africans who came here. For instance there was Danisa Baloyi and Tselane – I don't recall her last name – who came to Ohio University on scholarships and were so disgusted with the place that after only a few months Tselane gave up her studies and returned to South Africa. Danisa was too smart to do that. Instead, she got a transfer to Columbia University in New York where she completed her degrees. I bet she was more at home in New York. Today she is one of the new Black Economic Empowerment millionaires in Johannesburg. I never heard of Tselane again.

But there were other South Africans who made the best of their stay in Athens. Simphiwe was one of them. After his PhD at Ohio University he became a professor somewhere in Pennsylvania. Then there were Audrey Molise and Zanele Mfono. Both stayed in Athens without any fuss, with Audrey returning for the second time to complete another degree. Zanele did not even have a scholarship. She had to work at all sorts of menial jobs to pay for her education. I admired her because she was quite different from your spoilt black South African student who had it all made thanks to anti-apartheid donor funding. Today Audrey is another leading Black Economic Empowerment business woman in Johannesburg, while Zanele is a leading academic at Fort Hare University.

After Keneiloe left I was crushed for a while. But life had to go on. My poverty was relieved by a Fulbright award. I was invited to Ronald Reagan's White House and to the Capitol with a group of other southern African Fulbright scholars where we were given tours and listened to talks on how the American government functioned.

My life changed when a new group of students from Botswana arrived to do their master's degrees at the Ohio University School of Education which had established ties with the University of Botswana. It was like being back in Lesotho again because culturally there are many similarities between Basotho and Batswana. Once more, in the company of Ruth Monau, Itah Kandji and Sis' Dudu, I gradually forgot about my doomed love for Keneiloe.

On the rebound, I fell in love with Ruth Monau.

She was a true lady, Ruth. A no-nonsense slender woman who was not only a teacher but looked like one. It didn't take long for us to move in together in the basement apartment I had shared with Keneiloe on East Carpenter Street. We had a wonderful time together and I thought I had undoubtedly found my mate for life. Only a few months into our relationship I asked her to marry me and she said she would, provided my parents went to Botswana and asked for her hand in the traditional manner. I knew my father would never do that. Not only was he a refugee in Lesotho, but he was disgusted with my promiscuous ways and with, especially, my separation from Mpho. He would not even entertain the idea of sending relatives to Botswana after what I had put the family through. It would be like encouraging my wayward behaviour. And I told Ruth this, but she insisted that she would never be able to live with herself if we didn't go through the cultural route.

'We are both adults,' I said. 'And both of us have been married before. Surely we can marry right here in Athens and inform our parents later.'

She had told me about her previous marriage, and I had seen photographs of her beautiful children, a boy and a girl. I had shown her photographs of my three beautiful children too.

'I'm a Motswana girl,' she said. 'My parents would never forgive me if I did that.'

What stays in my mind about Ruth is something that I am so very ashamed to narrate. Although we lived a life full of love and fulfilling intimacy, sometimes we quarrelled about extremely petty things. In most cases, it was my own childish irritability coming to the fore. One day we quarrelled over an iron. I wanted to use it first but she was holding on to it because she wanted to use it too. As we struggled over it the ironing board fell and hit my toe. I lost my cool and slapped her. Yes, me who was once jailed for beating up a man who had slapped a girl! Immediately, I knew it was something that would haunt me forever. Even though she forgave me and that very evening we were in each

281

other's arms, I knew I was stained forever; from then on I could never truthfully say, 'I have never raised my hand to a woman.'

I lived happily with Ruth until I completed my MFA in Theater, with the focus on playwriting, and then went on to do a second MA with the School of Telecommunications, focusing on radio and television, with special emphasis on scriptwriting for film and television.

I was with her when I was inducted into the International Understanding Honor Society with Charles Ping, who was the president of Ohio University.

I was also with her when I got the news that my play *The Road* had won the Christina Crawford Award of the American Theater Association.

The award was established by Christina Crawford, the actress who wrote *Mommie Dearest* in which she portrayed her mother, actress Joan Crawford, as an overbearing and cruel alcoholic who abused both Christina and her brother. In 1981, the year of my arrival in the USA, the book was made into a movie starring Faye Dunaway. With some of the royalties Christina Crawford set up the award and there I was winning it in 1984. Unfortunately, Ruth couldn't come with me when the play received a staged reading at the San Francisco Hilton during the annual conference of the American Theater Association because Professor Christian Moe who was running the competition could only pay for one ticket. I enjoyed the experience nevertheless, especially interacting with all those hundreds of American theatre practitioners. Crawford was there in person to give me the award which was a five hundred dollar cheque and a handwritten letter congratulating me.

Every time I hear of the movie *Mommie Dearest* my eyes get moist with gratitude; I gained materially from its success.

After the summer of 1984 it was time for me to return to Lesotho. After teaching playwriting at the School of Theater for one quarter, I mailed my books through the post office – they still had surface mail then – packed my bags and left my close friends Simphiwe and Hatar who were continuing with their PhD studies. I suspected Simphiwe would not be returning to South Africa even after graduating. He had married Sandy, a lovely lady from Guyana, at the Galbreath Chapel and they planned to make their lives in America. Munene and Kirubi had long since departed for Kenya where they were academics.

I also left Ruth with the promise that I would see her when she got back to Botswana and we would take up the issue of marriage then.

Back in Lesotho my father was beaming with pride, telling everyone that I had returned with a double-master's. He rented the hall at Bereng High School and organised a big party to which friends and relatives from all over Lesotho and the Eastern Cape were invited. I made a speech wearing my academic regalia and thanked everyone, ranging from the people of Mafeteng to Desmond Sixishe, the cabinet minister who had made it possible for me to get the air ticket to America. But I forgot to thank my father. And even my mother, of all people. My father had spent so much money on this feast and he didn't get a single mention. Did I perhaps take for granted these wonderful parents without whose guidance I would be nothing?

Shame dogged me long after the feast.

CHAPTER NINE

UNCLE OWEN HAS MARRIED one of the Bee People and his daughter Nobantu is not amused. I am told she came all the way from Soweto to express her rage, not towards her father but towards the woman. She stood outside the new couple's house and shouted for the entire village to hear that the woman was a shameless gold digger who was young enough to be Nobantu's daughter. The elders of the village came to calm her down. They took her to Uncle Press's general dealer's store, known as eRestu by the villagers because – just to remind you – it's both a restaurant and a tavern, so that she could get some comfort and sympathy from her own relatives.

I am not aware of this marriage and its repercussions when I drive into the village. Uncle Owen never warned me about it. In fact, I was not even aware that there was something going on between him and any woman since his misadventure when he was still in exile in Mafeteng: his house was once invaded by the brothers of a young woman with whom he had made a baby. They beat him up and confiscated the baby who had been in his custody for months. I wouldn't have imagined that at his mature age his friskiness continued unabated.

I have merely come to see the Bee People as I often do when I need a break from my writing. I innocently call at Uncle Owen's house as I usually do when I am in the village. I notice that he has added another room to the house and there are construction materials in the garden – tools, bricks, sand, and bags of cement. I find the village madman, my Cousin Bernard, pacing the ground in front of the house mumbling something to the effect that Uncle Owen now thinks he is better than everyone else since he has suddenly become rich.

'Where is Uncle Owen?' I ask.

'He's gone to Sterkspruit with that whore he calls his wife,' says Cousin Bernard.

'His wife? He has a wife?'

'They've gone to eat his money. And he can't even give me ten rands. You know Nobantu was here? He didn't even give her a cent. His own daughter coming all the way from Johannesburg for nothing. And here he is, an old man of eighty-one, five months and three days, spending his money on *idikazi* who is young enough to be his great-granddaughter.'

He carries on in this vein and doesn't even notice when I walk away, get into my car and drive to eRestu. I don't know why Cousin Bernard is taking Uncle Owen's behaviour with the woman he calls *idikazi*, or whore, so personally. And what are these riches that he is talking about? The last time I was with Uncle Owen his sole means of survival was the meagre old-age monthly pension that he received from the government – which couldn't have been more than six hundred rands a month at the time.

I learn only later when I meet some of the Bee People at the gate of eRestu how Uncle Owen suddenly got rich. He received a lump sum of money from the government for being a veteran of the cadres who fought for the liberation of South Africa. Although Uncle Owen was a PAC activist and was exiled in Lesotho, I never knew him to belong to any guerrilla army. But he qualified for the pension because the Special Pensions Act of 1996 states that any South African citizen who made sacrifices for the liberation of the country, thus making the establishment of a non-racial democratic constitutional order possible, is entitled to a means-tested grant. The recipient, the law states, should have been active for at least five years on a full-time basis in the service of a banned political organisation or should have been forced to leave the country, banned or banished, imprisoned or detained, for a minimum of five years. Dependants of those who died in the political struggle also qualified. The law emphasises that this is reparation and not welfare. Uncle Owen obviously met some of these requirements to receive the pension.

I myself meet all the criteria for this Special Pension, as do my siblings. But we never applied for it. I have the means to make my own livelihood and don't think it would be ethical to exploit my involvement in the liberation struggle for personal gain. This does not mean I do not support the establishment of this Special Pension for those who are more deserving of it than I am. I know, for instance, that my mother did apply for it and she does deserve it.

I don't know exactly how much Uncle Owen has received but I think it is not less than two hundred thousand rands, judging from what other people have been getting. I remember he has been going to Johannesburg a lot lately, staying at Nobantu's house in Chiawelo, one of the townships of Soweto, and she took him to Pretoria to fight for the pension. It is good that he finally got it, but sad that it has caused a rift between him and his beloved daughter who assisted him in getting it in the first place.

The Bee People tell me that Uncle Owen has bought a big-screen television with a satellite dish, a set of sofas, a dining room table and six chairs, and a gas stove with a big oven. He has even added an extra bedroom to his house. He really means to spend his remaining time on earth in comfort.

As soon as I walk into eRestu my aunt, Press's wife, says, 'I am glad you are here, Cesane. One of your Bee People has caused a scandal in the village.'

Cesane is one of our clan names – we of the Majola branch of the amaMpondomise clan.

I look at Uncle Press sitting next to his wife by the till, hoping he will elaborate. But he just sits there staring into empty space.

'Which one of them?' I ask.

'The one called Weli,' she says.

The name doesn't register because I only know those Bee People who are on the committee as I meet them on a regular basis whenever I visit their project.

'What scandal did she cause?'

'She married your Uncle Owen.'

I burst out laughing. She didn't see anything funny.

'Why would it be a scandal to marry a nice gentleman like my Uncle Owen?'

'Because she is a child. Your Uncle Owen is an old man of more than eighty and she is only a baby in her early twenties.'

'But why is it her scandal and not his?'

'There is more than fifty-five years difference between them.'

That doesn't tell me why *she* is to blame for this relationship and not him. But then among my people it's always the woman's fault.

Press just sits there silently. He is a brooder ever since he became a traditional healer. Sometimes his head moves rhythmically up and down as if it is responding to the drums of the ancestors that are throbbing in it. He adds nothing to the discussion so I don't know if he views the marriage as scandalous or not.

As for me, I don't see any scandal and I tell my aunt and the Bee People so. If the two people are in love and don't give a damn about their age difference then it is their business. They are adults and their marriage is lawful. They don't need anyone's permission, and none of us can force them to divorce. My aunt is adamant that this has nothing to do with love. Weli is only interested in Uncle Owen's filthy lucre.

'Even if that is the case it has nothing to do with us,' I tell her. 'It has nothing to do with Nobantu either. Her father has all his mental faculties intact. If he is stupid enough to spend his money on a gold digger, as you call her, then that's his own lookout.'

Everybody is disappointed at my reaction. They had thought that I would bring some sanity into this matter, and perhaps even tell Weli where to get off. Part of me can sympathise with Nobantu's concerns. Her father has a history with young women. The only marriage of his that was deemed respectable and was recognised by his people was with Nobantu's mother in the late 1940s. His wife, a nursing sister, died while giving birth to Nobantu in the early 1950s, leaving Uncle Owen with two older boys and the newborn. His life of instability began soon after that. He married and divorced many times, and had numerous girlfriends with whom he made children. He has no idea where some of his children are.

I remember that my mother used to tell us – me and my siblings – that she hoped none of us would ever make Uncle Owen our role model. 'I hope you'll marry and have stable families as your father and I have tried to have,' she used to say.

But that stability has eluded me and my siblings.

AFTER MY RETURN FROM the United States I hoped to bring back stability in my life by marrying Ruth. That was why I was on a train from Cape Town to Kimberley. I was returning from a successful visit to the Drama Department of the University of Cape Town where I registered for a PhD degree. I had also met Professor Mavis Taylor who was going to be my supervisor. UCT was the oldest university in South Africa, having been founded in 1829. It was also the highest ranked university in Africa. The Drama Department was established in the 1940s and yet I was going to be its very first PhD candidate. Until I came along it had only offered certificates, postgraduate diplomas, bachelor's and master's degrees.

I have always loved train journeys, since the days I used to travel with my siblings and our mother from Zastron to Johannesburg via

Bloemfontein where we changed trains. The grinding rhythm of the wheels on the rails never fails to lull me into a blissful sleep. On this particular journey the experience was enhanced by high expectations. I was going to see Ruth. It was almost two years since we parted at Ohio University. She had completed her Master of Education degree and had returned to the University of Botswana where she was teaching in their Primary Education Department.

When I left her in Ohio I returned to Lesotho, although initially Lesotho had not been my preferred destination. I had hoped to work for the Zimbabwe Broadcasting Corporation instead. I was an admirer of Robert Mugabe and his progressive policies and thought working for his government would advance the liberation struggle in southern Africa. He had only been in power for four years then, and I had no way of knowing that he would turn out to be one of the most despicable and corrupt dictators in Africa.

Another thing that made Zimbabwe very attractive to me was the fact that a number of Zimbabweans who had lived in Lesotho over the years and worked at the university at Roma had gone back home to build the country soon after Mugabe took over. I knew and admired some of them, such as Stan Mudenge whose beautiful and highly refined wife was Kgokgo Mamashela. I knew Kgokgo very well because she organised a few conferences for Lesotho writers. She was also Lesiba Mamashela's sister. You may remember Lesiba as Khomo Mohapeloa's bandleader during my Peka High School days. So, it would have been wonderful to be with those guys in a new Zimbabwe. The country was just teeming with joyful and productive activity, and it beckoned those of us who hoped South Africa would follow its path after attaining liberation.

I was looking at my old files the other day and I chuckled to myself when I read a copy of my application to the Permanent Secretary of the Ministry of Information, copied to the Chairman of the Zimbabwe Broadcasting Corporation. After outlining my qualifications I went on to say:

My guiding philosophy on radio and television in the Third World is that these media should not only serve to inform and entertain, but should be used to attain nation building and other national objectives . . . Broadcasters in Africa usually claim that it is cheaper to do mass importation of American and British programs than to produce their own. That may have a lot of truth to a great extent. However I can prove that local programs can be produced very cheaply, and more so they will be more entertaining and relevant to local tastes, they will be contributing to the cultural upliftment of the nation, and to achieving political, social, economic and cultural national objectives as laid down by the government.

I was indeed a true ideologue. I instinctively cringed when I got to the as-laid-down-by-the-government part. I was actually applying to be Robert Mugabe's propagandist.

Who could argue against lessening dependency on foreign programmes and meeting the needs of local tastes? As an advocate of the New International Information Order, I thought a progressive Zimbabwe under pan-Africanist Mugabe was the right place to put into practice some of the theories that were designed to counter Western cultural imperialism.

But I am eternally grateful that the Zimbabweans ignored my application. I would have been part of the 'nation building' that later smothered all opposition and killed thousands of the Ndebele people as part of the 'national objectives' for 'unity' and 'social cohesion' that were 'laid down by the government'.

Having been snubbed by my Zimbabwean heroes I had no choice but to return to Lesotho and work for Chief Leabua Jonathan's government. Though he was still a dictator who brooked no opposition, he was no longer the enemy he used to be because he was now on the side of South Africa's liberation struggle and had built a strong alliance with the ANC. This was the year Chief Leabua declared that Lesotho was at war with South Africa, condemned apartheid at the United Nations and the Organization of African Unity, and gave succour to Umkhonto weSizwe combatants. It would not be a bad idea to work for a man like this.

His government paid for my passage from America. And I was able to ship to Lesotho hundreds of books that would become useful in my research for the PhD.

Before taking up my new job I spent a few weeks with my mother and three children at Holy Cross Mission. The children had grown quite a bit and I was very grateful that my mother had looked after them so well. I was also happy to see that on the wall in her bedroom the calendar that I had sent from Ohio with a colour picture of her and the three kids occupied pride of place. In the picture the kids are wearing the new clothes I sent them from America. My mother had the picture taken by the Catholic priest and sent it to me. I then sent it to the calendar company that enlarged the picture and printed it on the calendar. I was told the kids were very proud to be part of a calendar and there it was on the wall, even though it was two years out of date and therefore no longer served any practical function.

My mother told me that Mpho – who had by then returned from Israel and was working at a kindergarten in Maseru with her twin sister, Mphonyane – often visited the kids, sometimes spending up to two weeks when she was on leave from her job. I loved the way my mother had a soft spot for Mpho. She told me that she didn't care whether we chose to divorce or not, Mpho would remain her daughter-in-law for ever.

'Because both of you will live for ever,' I said, chuckling.

Back in Maseru I was employed as the Controller of Programmes at Radio Lesotho, a title that scared me a bit. And indeed my job involved controlling all programmes, seeing to their quality and also to their content. They had to be in line with government policy, which meant that every magazine or documentary programme had to extol the virtues of the government, to feature Chief Leabua Jonathan or, at the very least, his senior cabinet ministers. My friend who had organised the government loan for me to go to America, Desmond Sixishe, was still the Minister of Information and Broadcasting. But I only saw him when he had something to complain about; for instance, when he was aggrieved because Chief Leabua's speech was not broadcast in its entirety, having been edited to make room for other items, or because the host of a magazine programme forgot the protocol of mentioning the guests in their proper order of importance at a meeting addressed by Chief Leabua. Most of these were sins of omission, and I was able to get the staff to correct them without any problem.

Although the news was outside my domain, I noticed that it was also governed by the same philosophy: all the news that's fit to broadcast must have something to do with the prime minister or at the very least with one of his ministers. Every news bulletin led with 'The Prime Minister of Lesotho, Dr Leabua Jonathan . . .' He was now referred to as 'doctor' after some honorary degree from an American university.

One of the most important items in my job description was the introduction of a television service in Lesotho. I drew up the plans for the setting-up of a new station and for training staff. There were already some cameras and editing suites and two or three cameramen and editors. I occasionally sat with them to look at their footage and to make sure that they showed Chief Leabua in the most flattering angles in the documentaries of his *pitsos* – or public rallies – that they shot. I use the word 'documentaries' very loosely. They were just images of Chief Leabua making speeches and the crowd ululating and shouting slogans and singing songs in his praise. These reels would go on for hours because it was a sin to edit any speech. There were no subtleties or sound bites. Everything had to be faithfully recorded and broadcast, including the speeches of the cabinet ministers who introduced him, extolling his virtues as the great-great-grandson of King Moshoeshoe the Great, and a revolutionary of the first order who freed the Basotho people from the yoke of the British and was also going to free the black people of South Africa from the yoke of the Boers. He was going to achieve this with the help of his North Koreans. And at this women would ululate and that had to be included in the 'documentary'.

After working on this kind of material I felt dirty and had to take a bath as soon as I got home to the luxury flat that the government was renting for me near Victoria Hotel. It was the same block of flats that was stormed by the Boers when I was still in Ohio where they killed a number of South African refugees and innocent locals, such as 'Matumo Ralebitso.

I wouldn't have lasted in such a job. Much as I was in total agreement with the sentiments of liberating South Africa, and with the policies of the ANC, and therefore wary of alienating an ally like Chief Leabua Jonathan, I was never cut out to be a propagandist. Especially in such a crude manner. I resigned, losing the privileges of the use of a government vehicle with a driver who transported me eighty kilometres to my home in Mafeteng every afternoon and fetched me there every morning before I was allocated the fully furnished flat, and who took me around to places in Maseru and other districts any time I felt like it. And of course I had to vacate the flat. I went to live in the servants' quarters of my sister-in-law Johanna, who was teaching at the National Teachers' Training College and was staying in the staff houses there.

All this was a world away. I was on a train to see Ruth. I would deal with my homelessness and joblessness when I returned. At that moment all that mattered was that I was going to see Ruth.

The train stopped briefly at a small station in the Karoo and urchins came running to the windows shouting 'Dankie Auntie! Dankie Auntie!' Passengers threw apples, oranges, cookies and other foodstuffs to the ground. The children scrambled for the food and fought each other over scraps of steamed bread and chicken bones as the train pulled out. This was the incident that inspired my next play, *Dankie Auntie*, which was directed by Mavis Taylor and opened at the National Arts Festival in Grahamstown in July 1989.

In De Aar, a town in the Northern Cape famous as the second most important railway junction in South Africa, I changed trains. I bought the *Sunday Times* at a newspaper stand before boarding the train to Kimberley. Between Cape Town and this junction I had shared the compartment with a guy who was so conscious of his dark complexion that he kept on reminding me that although he looked like me he was actually a Coloured. His accent proved his point, although a lot of Batswana and Xhosa people of the Northern Cape are Afrikaans first-language speakers and have the same accent. But now, from here to Kimberley, I was alone in the compartment and had time to think about what I was going to do with my life. The only option open to me in Lesotho was going back to teach at a high school. Once more I had come full circle, despite my two graduate degrees: an MFA in theatre and an MA in telecommunications.

My only consolation after resigning was that Jane Fonda's movie project would take off and I would be occupied with script editing and perhaps even get a job as a consultant of sorts on the movie set. But even that dream had been smashed when I received a letter from her telling me that she would no longer be proceeding with the project. I still had her letter in my bag where she wrote: *I have abandoned my efforts to develop a feature film on South Africa for lack of a strong story that was more artful than a political docu-drama. Alas!*

She went on to say that if it was at all possible I could use the money she had advanced me to support a humanitarian endeavour of my choice in Lesotho or South Africa.

Between counting the telephone poles that were passing the window at a tremendous speed and being awestruck by the barren yet breathlessly beautiful landscape, I browsed through the pages of the *Sunday Times*. I was suddenly struck by the headline: *Fonda, thankfully, cans movie on SA.*

I quickly went through the short article. It was the same old South African 'liberal' hysterics about Fonda being some loony leftie who wanted to besmirch their country.

From Kimberley the wheels of the train ground their way to Mafikeng, from where I took a taxi to Ramatlabama border post in Botswana. This was my first visit to Botswana and I was amazed at how the ambience and the people were very much reminiscent of the Lesotho towns. In the bus to the town of Lobatse it was as if I was in a bus from Mohale's Hoek to Mafeteng. The only difference was that here the land was flat, and among the vendors who were selling fat cakes, fish and other home-cooked foods at the bus stop in Lobatse some women were selling Botswana currency. I had South African rands in my pocket so I bought a few Botswana pula notes. I had never seen money being sold this way before. In Lesotho all such transactions were done at the bank.

In Gaborone I booked in at the President Hotel and phoned Ruth. I was sitting in the bar having a beer when she came in the evening wearing a big black floppy hat and a broad smile. As we kissed there were tears in my eyes. I had missed her so much all those months. She didn't go home that night. It was as though we were back in our basement apartment in Athens, Ohio, again.

During the next few days she was due to travel to northern Botswana, right up to Francistown, with three of her university colleagues, to visit schools where some of her students were doing practical teaching or some kind of internship. So she took me along in their Land Rover and I got to see much of the country. She even took me to her home village, Mochudi, and introduced me to her parents and to her two kids. From there she took me to Serowe to meet Bessie Head, a South African writer who had made her home in that village after being exiled in Botswana some years back. Alas, after greeting her we couldn't get anything coherent out of Miss Head! She was very drunk and was more occupied with shouting invective across the fence at the woman from next door. A pity, because I would have loved to discuss a few things with her. Although I was now an ANC supporter, I still had a strong kinship to PAC people, and from what I had read she was a member, or a strong supporter, of that organisation. My affinity with PAC folks – which continues to this day – was understandable because I was from a PAC family.

Once again, I raised the issue of marriage with Ruth. And once again she said there was nothing she wanted more in the world than to marry me, but she still insisted that this would only be possible if my parents went to Mochudi, her village, to ask for her hand in marriage in the traditional manner.

I spent a few blissful days with Ruth, and went back to Lesotho with a heavy heart knowing that she would never be my wife.

Back in Lesotho I buried myself in writing plays while scouring newspapers for teaching jobs, which was the only thing I could do, or perhaps the only kind of job available to me other than the civil service. And I had already had my chance and had blown it there.

The German Embassy came to my rescue by commissioning me to adapt Bertolt Brecht's *The Caucasian Chalk Circle* for six characters. The play – directed by Wonga Matanda, a Trotskyite who was a refugee from Port Elizabeth and a student at the National University of Lesotho – was performed at the Victoria Hotel to great acclaim. One of the actors was 'Maseipei Tlale, an old crush of mine from when we were kids in Mafeteng. Her father had been our local doctor in the town and she and her sister Nonkosi were popular girls who were the fantasy of every boy. Their father brought them up reading scientific journals, and they both followed scientific careers when they grew up. Their brother, Moabi, became an engineer, Nonkosi became a medical doctor, and 'Maseipei studied in Ireland and became a medical laboratory technologist at the Queen Elizabeth II Hospital where her sister Nonkosi was practising as a doctor.

'Maseipei loved the theatre and did a lot of amateur acting. But while we were rehearsing the play she revealed to me that she was in the process of training to be a diviner and traditional healer – what in Lesotho is known as *ngaka-ea-Sesotho* or a *sangoma* in the more common parlance of South Africa. She had been called by the ancestors and had responded by going for training in the Leribe district under the mentorship of a woman she had been shown by the ancestors in a dream or vision. She had walked on foot all the way from Maseru to Leribe, a distance of more than a hundred kilometres, beating a cowhide drum, until she arrived at her mentor's house. She had never been there before, but had been led by the ancestral spirits. She stayed there for training for a number of weeks, and was now an acolyte who would soon be a fully fledged *ngaka*.

I was fascinated by her story. Somehow I had this affinity for traditional healers and shamans. If they were not my relatives they were my friends and even my crushes. I also marvelled at the cheek of the ancestors. They didn't give a hoot that you were brought up in a superstition-free home where science reigned supreme and that you had followed a career in the sciences; when they called you, you had to respond.

It was from 'Maseipei's experience that I was to create my character Misti in my second novel, *She Plays with the Darkness*, years later.

Another commission came from the National University of Lesotho. Dr John Gay who taught African Development asked me to write a play for his class to perform. There were no particular guidelines as to what the play should be about. I wrote a play in verse titled *Moroesi*, which was performed to a full house at the Netherlands Hall at Roma. It was directed by a former Peka High School colleague, Mare Tsiki. I don't really remember the details of this play since I no longer have the script, but I know vaguely that the protagonist was a young woman called Moroesi – I had always liked that name – who led her people to victory against foreign conquerors and oppressors.

From these commissions it became clear to me that writing was taking over from painting as my main occupation, or perhaps as the final resort to put food on the table whenever unemployment struck.

After seeing an advertisement for a teaching post at Sehonghong Secondary School, I applied. I got the job and discovered that Sehonghong was a village high up in the Maluti Mountains. There were no roads in the village and people who grew up there had never seen a car except in pictures. Transportation from one village to another was on horseback, donkey cart or sleigh pulled by a span of oxen. Travelling between Sehonghong and the lowland districts was only by a single-engine aircraft from and to an aerodrome in Maseru. Villagers looked forward to the arrival of the plane because it also brought mail, mostly from husbands and fathers who worked in the mines of South Africa.

I rented a one-roomed, grass-thatched house from a young widow who lived next door, where she engaged in nightly sessions of noisy sex with miners who landed at the airstrip. Besides these nocturnal disturbances of a poor celibate man trying to get a good night's sleep, she was a nice landlady who didn't bother me. I would have had a pleasant stay in her house even though I didn't have a bed but slept on a mattress on the floor, if it were not for the little fact that there was no toilet anywhere in the house or outside in the yard. To relieve myself I had to walk to a donga about a hundred yards behind the house. I could only do it under the cover of darkness, although this also meant there was the likelihood of stepping on someone else's fresh pile. This was the worst part about my stay in this village, the lack of sanitation facilities. Even the school did not have toilets for the students. They had to walk down the hill to the dongas in the valley.

But somehow I had to make myself at home here. I had brought some of my books and journal articles on mass communication, especially those that focused on development communication, which I had shipped from Ohio because I knew I would not readily get such materials in Lesotho. I had already determined that my thesis, as the final doctoral document is called in South Africa, was going to examine the use of theatre as a medium for development communication. Since I had already enrolled at the University of Cape Town, I thought my stay in this godforsaken village would avail me the opportunity to study and even write part of the thesis.

In my thesis I wanted to pay special attention to what development communication scholars of those days called folk media, by which they meant traditional performance modes that could be used as channels for developmental messages. I had always been interested in Sesotho traditional theatre, by which I mean any performance mode that encoded messages (and these may or may not be in the form of narrative) that could be decoded by those who were privy to the code.

I had heard of a ceremony called *pitiki* that was done a few weeks after the birth of a child. A sheep or a goat was slaughtered, beer brewed and a small feast was made to thank the ancestors for the gift that was the child. While relatives and friends gathered to enjoy the meat, the women locked themselves in a house and performed a theatrical ritual which they refer to as the real *pitiki*. The word itself means 'to roll'. I very much wanted to see this ritual, but men are not allowed where it is performed. It is the kind of theatre that is performed by women for women – but only those women who have experienced the joys and the pain of birthing.

'I hear there is going to be a *pitiki* in the village this weekend,' I told my landlady one day when I found her sitting on her stoep on my return from school. 'I want to attend.'

'I'm sure you may attend,' she said. 'You know that everyone is welcome at a feast.'

'No, I want to go into the room of women, where they do the real *pitiki*.'

She laughed; she thought I was joking. Why would any man want to see an all-female secret ritual? Unless, of course, he was a pervert.

I told her about my doctoral research and how it was essential to see things before I wrote about them.

'You'll see big things if you go into a *pitiki*,' she said. 'You'll go blind.'

'I'm willing to take that risk.'

She just laughed and went into her house.

The next day I knocked at her door so that she could see that I was serious. When she came out I begged her once more to take me to the *pitiki*. She would be doing this for the good of *thuto* – education – I told her. I desperately wanted to see that performance so that people in Lesotho and in other countries could see how wonderful Sesotho culture was.

'It is not my *pitiki*,' she said. 'What do you want me to do?'

'Smuggle me in. I'll disguise myself as an old woman.'

She broke into laughter. She still did not take me seriously and I was getting desperate because there might not be another *pitiki* again for a long time, maybe not until after I left the village. I even thought of offering her some money but I knew I wouldn't feel too good about myself after that. It would be like I had cheapened her with a bribe.

The next day she told me she would help me attend the *pitiki*, as long as I didn't ever mention her name in whatever I would be writing, since the women of Lesotho who still valued such secret rituals would regard her as a traitor.

On Saturday, the day of the *pitiki*, she gave me an old blue *seshoeshoe* dress to wear, a red *doek* – head scarf – with blue and yellow paisley patterns on it, old tennis shoes worn with pantyhose that had a few runs, and a plaid shawl over my shoulders. All of a sudden she was more enthusiastic than me about this whole adventure. I, on the other hand, was beginning to doubt its wisdom. I knew right from the beginning that there was nothing ethical about it, but I was going to do it all the same, if only to satisfy my curiosity. But then again, doubt was beginning to gnaw at me.

'I don't think I want to do this,' I said.

'You said you wanted to do it,' said my landlady. 'You cannot change now. Not after I have gone to all this trouble.'

She was getting more fun from this charade than I was, and giggled at my ridiculous appearance. I was worried that she wouldn't be able to contain herself at the *pitiki* and that she would burst out laughing. I didn't want to think what would happen to me if the women found me out. Not only would they beat the hell out of me before throwing me out, but the men enjoying beer and meat outside would certainly hit me with sticks and stones for seeing their wives in a way that they themselves had never seen. On top of that, they would frogmarch me to the chief who would levy a heavy fine for my perversion.

I used a walking stick as we trudged along the footpath to the *pitiki* on the other side of the village. I was a highly arthritic and osteoporotic old lady. As we met groups of villagers they greeted us as was the custom, but I did not respond lest my voice betrayed me. My landlady explained to them that I was her grandmother who was deaf and dumb from old age. This was the excuse we would give at the ceremony for my silence.

Our destination was less than fifteen minutes away. As we approached the homestead – a cluster of three rondavels and a four-walled grass-thatched house – I saw young girls whose ages ranged from anything between four and twelve shaking their little waists in a vigorous dance. Older women were singing and clapping their hands to provide the rhythm. The young girls were doing the famous *ditolobonya* dance that I had seen performed for the entertainment of guests on state occasions and at political rallies in Maseru. I stopped to watch but my landlady didn't want me to spend any time outside lest I was found out. She led me among men and women who were sitting outside near one of the rondavels eating meat and samp from big basins into one of the bigger rondavels.

I took a seat near the door next to two cowhide drums, hoping not to draw too much attention to myself. My landlady introduced me to the woman sitting on the bed with a baby in her arms. She was covered in a fat *Qibi* blanket. She was the owner of the *pitiki*. I merely nodded. Other women began to stream into the house singing and clapping their hands. Soon the door was closed and bolted from inside.

An old woman with strings of white beads on her arms and legs began to dip a short broom into a small basin of water and to spray us with it. I think she was the *ngaka* or shaman of the group. The water had been mixed with the juice of aloes so it tasted quite bitter when I licked my lips where some drops had fallen. She made certain that most of the spray was directed at the mother and the child. Another woman began to beat the drums. The rest of the women – including the mother on the bed – undressed and remained wearing only very short pleated skirts. Some were so short that their undergarments showed. They were all topless, for they threw even their bras on to the pile of clothes on the floor. They stamped on the cow-dung floor with their feet and shook their waists in a fast rhythm. This was the *ditolobonya* dance I had seen the little girls doing outside, but these women gave it the weightiness of a ritual. Like the young girls outside, there was still some playfulness in their steps and a naughty gleam in some of their eyes, but there was also purposefulness. Their dangling breasts from which countless babies had suckled added more acoustics as they flapped against their bodies and swooshed in the air only to come back again to hit their stomachs. When they did this the women became gleeful. Some even giggled in the midst of song.

The women mimed in pairs and in the course of the dance performed what I interpreted to be courtship, and then marriage. Then they danced closer to the bed while the mother laughed with a naughty glint in her eyes. At the same time she pretended to be shooing them away, as if she didn't want to have anything to do with them. They began to chant: *Re bonts'e he, u ne u etsang, u ne u bapala joang, ha ho tla ba tje.* Show us, what were you doing, how were you playing when things resulted into this. The cowhide drums added to the din and to their shrieks of joy.

The mother sprawled on the bed facing upwards and rolled the baby on her stomach. That's where the name of the ritual came from – to roll the baby. She began to mime a sexual act and as the dance of the women became frenzied so did her act and her moans of pleasure. This happened until it peaked with a mimed orgasm. All of a sudden there was silence. The women had stopped their dance and were looking at the mother expectantly. And then the mother mimed pregnancy. In all her actions throughout the performance the baby was the prop. What amazed me was that throughout all this it did not cry. Even in her performance of pregnancy she rolled it on her stomach for it was now a prop for a fetus and it merely prattled in baby talk.

The drums began again as did the *ditolobonya* dance. She mimed the pain of birth and then the ecstasy after the child was born.

301

Everyone laughed and congratulated one another on the performance. I signalled to my landlady that we should leave; I had seen enough.

'So, did you see what you wanted to see?' asked the landlady as we walked home.

'More than I thought I would see. I don't know how I can thank you.'

'You can thank me by just shutting up about it.'

I didn't ask her what the purpose of seeing it would be if I was just going to shut up about it. As soon as I got to my house I jotted down a few notes titled '*Pitiki*: the Theatre of Re-Birth.' I was to write about it later in my doctoral thesis.

This adventure did not bring me any closer to my landlady. She continued her life of noisy sex with travellers and I continued with my teaching of junior certificate English and reading for my thesis. I interacted more with members of the community, especially the abaThembu who were proud that there was one of them – by which they meant me – who was a teacher. There was quite a big community of these isiXhosa-speaking people and none of them had any formal education. I visited their homes and encouraged them to keep their children at school. They could afford to spare their daughters and send them to school. But their sons had to look after cattle, sheep and goats. And when they reached the age of manhood, after the necessary initiation rites, they had to cross the border to work in the gold and coal mines of South Africa. But then it was like that throughout the villages of Lesotho; girls went to school and boys went to work. That is why today there are more women than men who have formal education in Lesotho. Even as a teacher I observed that there were more girls than boys in my classes. There are more female university graduates than there are male ones.

At the end of the month I took the plane to Maseru to unwind with my friends. They were all curious to hear about this strange place I had chosen as my hermitage. You would have thought Sehonghong was somewhere in China.

Two of the friends I met occasionally were Mpho and her twin sister, Mphonyane. Mpho and I were not officially divorced, although we had been separated for a few years. I often visited them at their house at Ha Thamae Township and we talked about the old times. Mpho confessed to me that when we were still together she and her twin sister had continued with an affair with a Catholic Brother – a Brother is a Jesuit monk who has not been ordained as a priest – that had started long before I met them. I remembered that they used to talk about this Brother, and I had just taken it as an innocent friendship. I had no hard feelings about it; I was just glad that finally we were being honest with each other although it was too late to save our marriage. But I knew that we would remain friends for ever. I still kept many boxes of my documents at her house since I had no place of my own in Maseru.

Mr Dizzy was still in town. He had a steady job as an illustrator for the study materials produced by the Lesotho Distance Teaching Centre which conducted correspondence classes for junior certificate students throughout the country and for those Basotho people who were working in the mines of South Africa and wanted to advance their education. We went out to drink; this time not at the home-brew joints but at Lancer's Inn or the Maseru Sun Cabanas, as the old Maseru Holiday Inn was now called. We were now moneyed gentlemen and didn't have to sing for our beer or peddle our paintings to tourists. Or I was the moneyed gentleman who bought him the beer. He was always broke because he paid shebeen debts and gambled all his money as soon as he received his salary.

Other friends had dispersed to other parts of the world. Litsebe Leballo had completed a junior degree at the National University and was a hard-drinking and hard-living civil servant in Maseru. Peter Masotsa was no longer in Mafeteng working for the priest at St Gerard but was now working for the Catholic printing press at Mazenod. My brother Monwabisi had completed his LLB degree in Edinburgh and was working as a lawyer in Maseru while also lecturing at the National University of Lesotho's law school. His twin brother, Sonwabo, was at my alma mater at Ohio University where he had been admitted for an MA International Affairs degree. He had left four beautiful children with his wife Johanna, who was teaching at the National Teacher Training College. I stayed with them when I was in Maseru from Sehonghong.

Ntlabathi Mbuli, my Poqo friend and mentor, was in the United Kingdom doing an MA degree at the London School of Economics. He was extremely unhappy there because his professors despised Marxist theory and were a bunch of laissez-faire free marketers who didn't even want to listen to his arguments. This bothered him so much that he wrote many letters to me about it. After a while he stopped writing and I heard that he was hearing voices calling his name in the streets of London.

One place I never failed to visit whenever I flew in from the mountains was Lesotho High School. Although Clemoski was long dead, Bra Saul was still there. And Mxolisi Ngoza, my thoroughly gay friend who used to be my colleague at Mabathoana High School, was now teaching at Lesotho High School and had a house on campus. We all drank at his house or at Bra Saul's. Bra Saul was still a stalwart of the PAC and at his place I socialised with some of the leaders of the movement, even though my political orientation was now different. One of them was Thami Zani, a famous Black Consciousness leader and former colleague of Steve Biko's who joined the PAC in exile. I had a few drinks with Thami at Bra Saul's while we listened to jazz. Although he was the PAC representative in Lesotho he didn't confine himself to diplomatic work but was a hands-on guerrilla. I was saddened to hear later when I was back in the mountains that he and five of his comrades had been killed in an ambush by Chief Leabua's Police Mobile Unit while they were smuggling arms and explosives. You may remember that this was the same paramilitary force that killed my friend Jama Mbeki.

Every time something like this happened I felt very guilty and very depressed. Not only because I knew the guy so well as a kind-hearted and generous gentleman, but mainly because someone else died for my freedom while I fooled around with women, alcohol and jazz. Someone else took up arms for my liberation while I only wrote about liberation. But what could I do? I didn't have a strong enough warrior gene. I was becoming more and more squeamish about anything that smacked of violence, even though intellectually I knew that our armed struggle was essential. My whole emotional make-up was leading me towards the path of pacifism despite myself.

In Sehonghong my depression continued unabated. Until one day Mr Ndumo, a colleague at Sehonghong Secondary School, took me to the Cave of Barwa. We walked from the school down a steep rocky hill until after an hour or so we got to a stream of clear water running on smooth sandstone. Just above the stream was the mouth of a big cave, the home of the Bushmen of old, referred to as Barwa in Sesotho. I was enthralled by the paintings on the walls, but was saddened by the names of people who had visited the cave and then signed their names with chalk for posterity. Some of these names were even signed across the paintings themselves. I could recognise some of them. They belonged to important people in the government and the church. I couldn't understand how they could indulge in such acts of vandalism solely for the vanity of having future visitors see that they too once trod these sacred grounds.

Thanks to the man who introduced me to the Cave of Barwa, I made regular pilgrimages there and sat in the cave for many hours just meditating. I could feel the presence of the ancient people, which made me question my non-belief. The Cave of Barwa could not but make me talk in terms of a spiritual connection. At the same time, I knew that the brain was capable of creating magic to palliate the pain of the present. We draw within ourselves to comfort our sorrows and to heal our pain and we call it God. We are the originators of our own spirituality. Yes, I am a spiritual being, thanks to the power of imagination. The Cave of Barwa had a calming effect on me. When I wrote my second novel, years later, I recalled my communion with the cave. Part of the novel, titled *She Plays with the Darkness*, is set in Sehonghong even though I don't use that name in the story.

It was after the novel had been published that I learnt something of the history of the great cave, which would otherwise have featured in my novel and would have taken my fiction in a different direction altogether. What I learnt was that the cave was also called Soai's Cave after a Bushman chief of that name. Chief Soai was killed by Chief Joel Molapo's men who accused the Bushmen of cattle theft in 1871. The cave was then occupied by a Bushman chief called Sehonghong – after whom the village was named. But Chief Sehonghong himself was murdered by Chief Jonathan Molapo in 1873. I would have brought these murdered chiefs back to life in my narrative, if I had known about them at the time.

You'll note that I keep referring to these vanquished people as the Bushmen instead of the politically correct term that is used for them today, the San people. The reason is simply that these people never called themselves the San. They had no generic name that encompassed all of them. They merely referred to themselves as 'people' in the various languages of the tribal groups. The clans or tribes did indeed have names: the !Kwi, the /Xam and so on. The San label has the same weight as Barwa or abaThwa or Bushmen; it was what other people called them. They were called the San by the Khoikhoi people (who did call themselves the Khoikhoi) and the name referred to those people who were vagabonds and wanderers and didn't own cattle. The Khoikhoi even called fellow Khoikhoi who were poor and didn't have cattle San. So the name, though generally accepted, has derogatory origins.

Anyway, this is just a little digression from my story. After discovering the Cave of Barwa I spent close to three months without going to Maseru. I didn't find the need to socialise with my human friends because I got satisfaction from socialising with the spirits of the cave. When I finally did fly to Maseru and visited Lesotho High School I discovered two new teachers who had come to Lesotho as refugees from Uganda. I took to John Zimbe, who taught science, and Patrick Nkunda, who taught history, immediately. Nkunda had actually trained as a lawyer but couldn't practise in Lesotho. I don't know if I have mentioned this before, but I have always had a great affinity for Ugandans, even though I've never been to their country. Perhaps it is because of my Ugandan name, Kizito.

I had noticed that the Ugandan fellows were close friends with a very beautiful local woman called Sebolelo Mokhobo. But I had never met Sebolelo, though I had seen her from a distance. So, one day I was drinking at Chinese Palace with Zimbe, and maybe Nkunda, I don't quite remember. I was thinking of how beautiful their friend Sebolelo was and how I would like to know her better. I decided there and then to send Zimbe to her house to call her. I don't know what gave me the

306

bravado, or even conceit, to think that I could just summon a woman from her house to come and talk to me, a stranger, at a bar. But lo and behold! Zimbe came back with her and we sat at the bar and had a few drinks. Later she told me that she came because she was quite intrigued by my chutzpah.

Sebolelo, or Sebo as she was generally called by her friends, became a close friend. In fact, she became one of the landmark women in my life. These are the women who shaped my life for better or for worse; who had such a profound impact on my life that I would have been a different person without them. They begin with Sis' Rose, the nurturer who gave me life, the beautiful and munificent daughter of the Cwerha Gxarha clan, descendant of the Khoikhoi people. I am talking here of my mother. She was followed quite early on as a landmark woman by Nontonje, the red woman who sexually abused me when I was but a tyke. Other landmark women followed after that: Keneiloe, my childhood sweetheart; Mpho, my wife and mother of my three children; Tholane, the one who healed Nontonje's damage; Ruth, the Botswana woman who left me with wistful memories.

Now here was Sebo. We became inseparable. She was very popular with the guys because she was just like them. Except for the fact that she was smarter by far than all of us. She was a teacher at Life High School and was well read in literature. I was at home discussing my writing with her. But I also felt comfortable baring my soul to her. Though I was an open book to her as far as aspects of my life were concerned, one page was always closed to her, the page that contained all my feelings for her. It was an unrequited love.

When I met Sebo she was already married. Her husband, Zukile Nomvete, lived in Ethiopia, where he was an aircraft engineer for Ethiopian Airways. He was a refugee from South Africa and an activist of the ANC. I envied Nomvete for having a wife who could hold her own in any company and commanded attention when she spoke about any topic, and was incredibly beautiful to boot. I wished I had met her before he got to know her.

One thing I had in common with Sebo was that we were both ANC people – she a member and I a supporter – who came from PAC families.

Her father, a medical doctor in Mmabatho, had been a staunch PAC man before he joined the Bophuthatswana government as one of Lucas Mangope's cabinet ministers.

One thing we knew how to do expertly with Sebo was to pub crawl. She introduced me to watering holes I wouldn't have visited by myself. One of them was a shebeen owned by the jazzophile Moruti Mphatsoe, and there we drank and talked literature, jazz and politics till the wee hours of the morning. Because we were always together many people thought we were lovers. But we were not. Not in the normal sense. We were buddies. I wasn't seeing anyone at that time and didn't even wish to be in a romantic relationship, and she had a husband who was many countries away.

So, we kept it platonic and partnered each other on social occasions and in community activism. For instance, she would be with me when Frank Leepa, the genius founder and guitarist of the band Sankomota, invited me to prison when the band was playing there. I think Frank got the idea of playing free for the prisoners when his brother was arrested for car theft and sentenced to a term of imprisonment. Sebo and I visited Maseru Central Prison with Sankomota to keep up the spirits of the prisoners as part of some rehabilitation programme. I remember exclaiming to her that I was not aware that some of the guys I used to know and had not seen for years, were hiding themselves in prison.

I felt sorry for these guys, though I knew that most of them were there for some criminal activity. At that very time my own Aunt Nakiwe, one of my father's four younger sisters, was serving five years in prison in Kroonstad for drug dealing. She and my cousins had been smuggling dagga from Lesotho and Swaziland and selling it in Cape Town. As with these prisoners that I visited with Sebo and Sankomota, I could only imagine what my aunt was going through, much as I deplored her crime. I occasionally sent her money to make life a bit more comfortable for her.

Sebo and I also founded a theatre company in Maseru. Lesiba Players, according to a write-up in *New African* magazine, attracted some of the country's best talents. These included Wonga Matanda, who came from Port Elizabeth where he had been a member of Athol Fugard's Serpent Players, and Julian Borger, who had been a member of Oxford University's Experimental Theatre Company in the United Kingdom. My Ugandan friends, Patrick Nkunda and John Zimbe, were also members. The latter brought his lighting designing skills from his experience working with various East African theatre companies. There was also Thabo Moholi who had gained tremendous experience in television camera work and cinematography in Swaziland, but was quite useful in aspects of theatre management. Lesiba Players' first production was *The Road*, the play that premiered at Ohio University under the direction of Seabury Quinn Junior. In this two-hander about race relations in South Africa, Wonga Matanda played the role of the Labourer and Julian Borger was the Farmer.

Back in Sehonghong I yearned for Sebo's stimulating company, but also for the camaraderie of the Lesiba Players. Even the Cave of Barwa was no longer a fulfilling experience by itself. I wished I could spelunk with Sebo.

At about that time Professor Andrew Horn, who had been teaching drama and theatre at the National University of Lesotho, resigned to take up a professorship in the Fiji Islands. I had known and admired Andrew Horn for his theatre-for-development work for quite some time. He had invited me to Roma to observe some of the plays he created with his group of students. He also invited me to a big conference that he organised in Maseru in which theatre-for-development prac- titioners from Botswana, Swaziland, Zimbabwe, Zambia and Malawi participated. This experience had introduced me not only to these practitioners and scholars, but also to the very concept of theatre-for- development which later became my specialisation as a practitioner and the subject of my doctoral research.

I applied for Andrew Horn's job at the university and got it, despite the opposition of an influential Catholic priest in the English Department, Father Dermot Tuohy. I think Catholics have long memories, especially if you have been their employee and then you started messing around with nuns and female colleagues.

Finally, I came down from the Maluti Mountains to be an academic at the National University of Lesotho at Roma, following in the footsteps of my father who taught there in the late 1940s when the institution was still called Pius XII College.

Finally, a promise of stability. Unless I botched things up again. I was determined not to.

CHAPTER TEN

WE ARE WITH THANDI this time. She is not only my daughter – you remember, Mpho's second child? – but she is also our very close friend. Gugu's and mine. Sometimes we take her along when we visit the Bee People so that on our way back she may see *Makhulu*, as she calls my mother. Thandi is a beautiful dark-complexioned thirty-something and we laugh a lot when we are together because she has a way of seeing the funny side of things even in serious situations. We like to tease her about her taste in fashion; often she looks like a gypsy queen in garish jewellery and studded shoes. But the joke is sometimes on us when the shoes we have been laughing at become the vogue two years later.

As we drive into the town of Mafeteng Thandi mentions something about looking forward to the opening of her Uncle Zwi's hotel when it finally happens.

Zwi is Zwelakhe's nickname.

'Hotel?' I ask. 'What hotel?'

She looks surprised that I don't know my brother has a hotel. Gugu doesn't know either. Thandi offers to take us to a township called Motse-Mocha on the outskirts of Mafeteng to show us the hotel. The dirt road has gullies and potholes full of muddy stagnant water. It is difficult for our Mercedes Benz sedan to negotiate its way but I drive on slowly until we stop next to a light green single-storey building roofed with tiles. There are chalet-like side-buildings with grass thatch roofs. The impressive structure looks out of place in this obviously low-income township.

'That's your brother's hotel,' Thandi says. 'It's called Roseville after *Makhulu*. It's been standing here for two years, complete. I don't know when Zwi intends to open it.'

I wonder why he chose this type of location for what looks like a nice little holiday resort. When we were kids these were wheat fields. Low-income houses have since mushroomed in a haphazard way without any proper planning of the streets and without infrastructure. That is why the roads are better suited for a four-wheel-drive vehicle. Now here is this hotel standing like a shimmering brand new German sedan in a junkyard.

A hotel is a big deal, and I know nothing about it. It's been here for two years now and I have been coming to Mafeteng all that time and no one ever mentioned it to me. This tells you at once the kind of relationship I have with my brother, the last born of the family.

He is the only one of my siblings who remained in Lesotho when we returned to South Africa after liberation. He is well established here as a respected lawyer; his colleagues regard him so highly that they elected him the president of the Law Society of Lesotho, a position he has held for many years. He is a genial fellow, well-beloved by the whole town of Mafeteng. One beautiful thing about him is that he interacts with everyone in the town without any discrimination or prejudice. He has no airs about his status as one of the leading advocates in southern Africa. His friends range from the top judges and political leaders of both the government and the opposition to the unemployed youths of Mafeteng. Yet there has been a chill in my relationship with him over the years, and for the life of me I can't trace its source. There has been an occasional chill between him and my other siblings as well, but often it warms up and they become friends again, only for it to freeze up again over some minor issue. But between me and him the temperature has remained at a constant low.

We are an estranged family. My favourite brother Monwabisi, or Thabiso, the one who is the Chief Magistrate of Kokstad, once said that we have developed into a dysfunctional family of high achievers. For instance, I know nothing of my siblings' lives since we went our separate ways. We never share any news of our triumphs and defeats, our achievements and frustrations. We continue regardless, as if we all sprang from a stone and were not at one time occupants of the same womb, albeit at different times for some of us. Even Monwabisi who is much closer to me than the others leads a life that I know very little about. I remember being introduced to his new wife and child for the first time when I visited him in Kokstad. It was an awkward meeting for me because no one had told me that he had divorced the wife I knew, had remarried, was widowed and then remarried once more.

His twin brother, Sonwabo, or Thabo, also lives a mysterious life in Columbus, Ohio, and I have never been to his place though I live in Athens, Ohio, which is only eighty miles away. He does come to my house when I or Gugu invite him over. But for us his residence is out of bounds. We have no idea why. We don't even know his address in a city we frequent almost on a weekly basis. We only contact him via email. He left his wife, Johanna, and four children in Lesotho more than twenty years ago and never returned from the USA. The children – Limpho, Solomzi, Thembi and Mpumi – are now adults making their mark in the world. The alienation continues even with my sister Thami, who has moved from Johannesburg to Mafeteng, where she is a fashion designer specialising in designing suits and gowns for the legal community in Lesotho.

313

Uncle Owen calls what is happening between Zwelakhe and me sibling rivalry. Perhaps it is, except for the fact that I have no idea what the content of our rivalry is. He has nothing that I want and I don't think I have anything that he envies. I keep my distance from the affairs of the family so as to minimise chances of conflict. Except when I am invited. As in one instance when I was summoned by him all the way from Johannesburg for a family meeting in Mafeteng – a six-hour drive. I thought something earth-shattering had happened so I went. When I found that he had also invited two of our cousins from Qoboshane I got worried that perhaps it was more than earth-shattering. It was universe-shattering.

A family meeting was held in Zwelakhe's living room to resolve a dispute between him and Monwabisi about my mother's Special Pension. I didn't know anything about this so I listened with interest. None of them had ever told me that my mother had received a Special Pension from the South African government or how much it was. So I just sat quietly at this meeting, and did not participate in the proceedings. My mother did not participate either. She just sat there with a pained look.

After the meeting my mother sat in her bedroom and wept. I found her there when I went to say goodbye. 'What will happen when I am dead?' she asked me.

I could not answer that question. I am the ultimate outsider even in the affairs of the Mda family.

I recall this incident as we park in the street to admire Zwelakhe's hotel.

'I'm surprised you didn't know about his hotel,' Thandi says.

'You know *mos* Thandi that I'm in the dark about everything that affects my siblings' lives.'

'What happened? How did it come to this? When I was a little girl I thought you were close to Uncle Zwi.'

Everyone thought so, especially when I didn't give my car to his older brothers, Sonwabo and Monwabisi, but to him when I went to the United States. It was a Fiat jalopy that I bought after winning the Amstel Playwright of the Year Award for *The Hill*. I don't know what ultimately happened to it. Maybe he sold it for junk.

I am unable to answer Thandi's question because I don't know the answer. I just know that there has been so much tension between us that once he banned me from coming to his house to see my mother. When I said I would not go into the yard but would stand outside the gate and ask my mother to come out, my sister-in-law Johanna warned me against that because she said it would be provocation. I suspected she was merely repeating what Zwelakhe said.

'The first time I became aware of any tension was some years back when I had just joined the National University of Lesotho as a lecturer. He was already practising as a lawyer. He was also a playwright at the time, and had his own theatre company here in Mafeteng.'

One day I was passing by the Thomas Mofolo Library at the university and saw posters for a play by Z Mda that was going to be performed at the Netherlands Hall.

EARLY 1986. I WALKED into the BTM Lecture Theatre, National University of Lesotho, to teach an undergraduate African Poetry class. But before I began the lesson I told the students that the author of the play that was going to be performed that night was not me but my brother Zwelakhe Mda. One of my students, Ouma, who was known as an ANC activist asked why I felt it was necessary to tell them that.

'Because the posters all over campus have the author and director as Z Mda. I just want to make it clear that it's not me.'

Ouma was the most argumentative student in my class. I had once met her husband, Ngoako Ramathlodi, when Sebo brought him and a few of his ANC comrades to my house in the Maseru suburb of Florida. At the time no one had any inkling that he would one day be the premier of the Northern Province after the liberation of South Africa, and Ouma would be the first lady.

Ouma wouldn't let the matter rest but pressed on, 'Could it be that you don't want to be implicated in case the play is embarrassing?'

'Could it be that I want to take credit for my own work and tonight's author should take credit for his own work? Some students this afternoon were telling me they were looking forward to seeing my play tonight. Admit it, you, too, Ouma thought it was my play.'

She didn't respond to that, but another student told me that indeed they had thought it was my play. Many people would be attending under the impression that it was a Zakes Mda play. 'We have read so much about your work in the South African newspapers and now finally we'll see one of your plays!' an excited girl had told me earlier that day.

'Why didn't your brother use his full name? Could it be that's the result he wanted?' asked Zandile, who was also from South Africa.

I couldn't answer that one because I had no idea what my brother's motive was. I hate to assign motives. But next time I met Zwelakhe I raised the matter. He told me that his name was Zwelakhe and Z was his legitimate initial which he would use any time he felt like it. That was the end of the discussion. I did not ask him why he felt it necessary to use only his initial in this case when in all other instances he used his full name. After all, it was his initial and he could use it whenever he felt like it. If it confused people that was their problem not his.

That might have been the beginning of mistrust between us. Or even distrust because it seems to me we regard each other with suspicion.

I never saw the play, but was told by a colleague who was sitting next to me in the university bus in which we travelled between Maseru and Roma that she and her friends who saw the performance were grateful that it was not my play. I didn't want her to elaborate further so I quickly changed the subject to the inconveniences of our daily commute.

There was no reason for me to complain about the commute. It was my choice to live in Maseru, forty kilometres away from the campus. The university had houses on campus at Roma and indeed I had been allocated one of them when I joined the university a few months back. But I couldn't last there. Life was too quiet on campus. There were bars, yes, such as the Staff Club, open only to those who worked at the university and their guests, and Mzalas, which was a student bar. But the problem was that one socialised only with one's colleagues there, and you know how boring academics can be. So I asked to be transferred to Maseru where the university had a number of houses in different suburbs. I was allocated a house in Florida which became the headquarters of some first class hedonism.

Through the university car scheme I bought a brown Toyota Corolla which I used to travel between Roma and Maseru and at weekends between Maseru and Mafeteng. But it was cheaper to take the university bus sometimes; especially because one was required to go to the campus every weekday even when one didn't have a class.

Besides my bosom friend in Maseru, Sebo, I had a new girlfriend. Her name was Bolele and she was a trainee nurse at Queen Elizabeth II Hospital in Maseru. I heard that this relationship irked quite a few girls who were students at Roma. Zandile from my impudent African Poetry class once asked me, 'We hear you're going out with a student nurse. What is wrong with us?'

'And why should my going out with a student nurse be an indication that there is something wrong with you?' I asked.

'Are you intimidated by Roma girls?' she said.

Now, don't be surprised by such a question from a student. It was the norm at that university for students to have affairs with lecturers. I am not talking of clandestine relationships here. They were public and accepted by everyone as normal and respectable. Indeed, quite a number of lecturers, both male and female, had spouses who were once students there, sometimes who were even in their classes. In Sesotho they had an idiom for the practice: *u ja mohlapeng*. You eat from the flock. The university didn't take issue with any of these relationships because in their view both the students and the lecturers were consenting adults. No one came up with any argument on power relations that favoured the lecturer over the students in such romances, or possible abuse of power to gain sexual favours.

At first I did not engage in such relationships because I thought I would find them uncomfortable. For the first two years or so teaching at Roma my world revolved around Sebo and Bolele and I shunned any social life at the university. I was busy enough in Maseru, mostly with my Ugandan friends Patrick Nkunda and John Zimbe rather than with Mr Dizzy or the jazz crowd. I was not seeing much of Mr Dizzy because he had gone back to his old ways of spending his life in skanky shebeens. He had even lost his illustrator job at the Lesotho Distance Teaching Centre. Occasionally I would find Mr Dizzy at the Lesotho Sun Hotel or Maseru Cabanas where he would take over the piano without the permission of the management and play the blues à la Champion Jack Dupree before the security guards kicked him out. Quite often they came after he had earned a few banknotes as tips from appreciative guests.

Every weekend the Ugandans were at my house with their girlfriends from the Nurses' Home drinking beer and roasting meat. They referred to my three-bedroom university house as 'the stadium'. It was at these binges that I introduced Nkunda to Palesa Thoahlane, a trainee nurse who was Bolele's friend. They later married and emigrated to Canada where Nkunda is a successful immigration lawyer and Palesa is a registered nurse. Zimbe emigrated to Canada too, but I never heard from him after that.

Nkunda and Zimbe both had nice staff quarters at Lesotho High School. You know already that Lesotho High School was my playground, from the days of the late Clemoski and then of Bra Saul and of Mxolisi Ngoza. Now with Nkunda and Zimbe, particularly with Nkunda who was much closer to me, I had even more reason to hang out there.

One day I was at Nkunda's place drinking Castle Lager. There were quite a few of us in the small living room. Pressed next to me was a striking young lady who knew who I was though I didn't think I had met her before. But what impressed me about her was her vulgarity. She uttered earthy expletives at the slightest provocation, which made her very desirable. Before I knew it we were covertly fondling each other and giggling.

I learnt that her name was Nzwakazi and that even though she had an isiXhosa name she was originally from Mohale's Hoek. She taught Sesotho at the high school, hence the ripeness of her language.

That evening we staggered to her house where I spent the night. I left my car parked outside Nkunda's house. We did that a few more times. Sometimes she would pay a quick visit to my Florida house. It was a clandestine romance because she had a fiancé who was studying in

318

Australia and didn't want to keep rumour-mongers busy. The nocturnal visits did ultimately cease.

My life also revolved around my children and my doctoral studies. I often drove to Mafeteng to see them where they continued to live with my parents. My mother had given up her job at the Holy Cross Clinic and was running two small cafés in Mafeteng. Neo was thirteen and had started at Masentle High School. Thandi was eleven and Dini was eight. Both were at St Gerard Primary School. I was grateful that my parents continued to look after them. In fact, my mother would not part with them even though I wanted them to stay with me in Maseru since I now had a stable job and a big house. She didn't even want to hear of that.

As for my research, I was able to do most of it at Roma because my case studies were mostly my own theatre work. I had taken the job of Professor Andrew Horn who had established a theatre-for-development project at the university. With his group of students who were doing a Practical Theatre course he created plays on social issues and had them performed in the villages around the Roma campus. I took over teaching that course and continued with the theatre work he had started. This grew into a permanent theatre company that continued the work beyond the scope of the course – the Marotholi Travelling Theatre. *Marotholi-a-pula* means 'raindrops' and I got the name in Francistown that time I visited Ruth in Botswana. She had taken me on a tour in the northern part of the country where I was impressed by an arts and crafts and textile manufacturing establishment called Marothodi – the Setswana spelling of Marotholi. It was the name itself that I loved rather than the store, and I was glad to find so apt a use for it.

After establishing the travelling theatre company I raised funds from donors in Europe and Canada and bought a brand new Volkswagen Kombi that the troupe used to travel far beyond the Roma Valley, to other districts throughout the country. We experimented with various modes of theatre, ranging from Brechtian epic theatre to agit-prop to Augusto Boal's theatre-of-the-oppressed to other models that evolved in the course of our performances in some of the most inaccessible villages in the country. Sometimes we had to leave our vehicle miles away and travel on foot and on horseback to performance venues. My doctoral thesis, therefore, would examine the efficacy of the various modes of theatre and hopefully emerge with a theoretical framework for the analysis of such work. Although I was doing most of my research and writing in Lesotho I had to go to the University of Cape Town occasionally to meet the university's residential requirements and also to consult with my supervisors.

The first time I went to Cape Town it was by bus that took me through the Transkei. That was the occasion I took the train to Botswana to see Ruth. Now that I had my Toyota Corolla I drove to Cape Town. I went with Sebo who helped with the driving and navigation since she was a more seasoned traveller than I was. I wouldn't have managed to drive all twelve hundred kilometres by myself that first occasion, but later on I made that trip many times on my own.

We were booked at Serengeti self-catering apartments in Mowbray, one of the suburbs of Cape Town within walking distance of the main campus in Rondebosch. However my campus, the Hiddingh Campus, where the departments of fine arts and of drama were located, was in the city. I had to negotiate my way in the busy multi-lane traffic of Cape Town to get there. It was at that campus that Sebo introduced me to Richard Esterhuysen who was a student in the drama department. He is the fellow who later became a famous British actor under the name Richard E Grant. Sebo was at school with him at Waterford Kamhlaba College in Swaziland where Richard was born of South African Afrikaner parents. On the main campus Sebo also introduced me to Zindzi Mandela, Nelson and Winnie Mandela's daughter, who was a student there. I had only read about her and her older sister Zenani because when I stayed at Nelson Mandela's house Zindzi was not yet born – and her father was still married to Evelyn. We spent a lot of time hanging out at the home of Herbert Vilakazi who was a sociology lecturer. Both Zindzi and Herbert provided stimulating company, Herbert making intellectual observations about life in Cape Town and Zindzi offering a street-smart perspective of the same. All this to the smooth flow of Boschendal Chardonnay and the philosophical *Whispers in the Deep* by Ray Phiri and his band Stimela.

Even though we were sharing a one-bedroom apartment my relationship with Sebo remained platonic. Of course I cannot pretend I didn't have ungodly thoughts. What warm-blooded man wouldn't with a woman like Sebo?

After consulting with my supervisor, Professor Mavis Taylor, and making arrangements for a much longer stay next time, Sebo and I drove back to Lesotho.

I continued to go to Cape Town every few months.

One day Chris Hani paid me an unexpected visit. He was with his two little daughters, as if it was a social call. He told me that my father had mentioned that I would be going to Cape Town that week. He asked if I could carry a small package for him to Cape Town. I had done something like that once before for Wonga Matanda of the Non-European Unity Movement, an organisation I didn't give a hoot about. I was just doing Wonga a favour. I was quite happy to do the same for Hani, a man who was not only a family friend but a representative of an organisation whose principles I supported. My Toyota Corolla was parked outside, so I gave him the key and asked him to hide the package in the car. I did not want to know what was in the package or where it was hidden. This was important, because if I was searched by the Boers at the border post or anywhere else in South Africa I would truly not know what they were searching for or where it was hidden.

I gave him the address where I would be staying in Mowbray and he told me someone would come for the parcel.

The trip to Cape Town was a thirteen-hour drive and since I was driving alone without Sebo I was quite exhausted on arrival. I parked the car in the underground parking garage and went straight to bed in my apartment. In the morning I waited for a while but when Hani's contact didn't arrive I went about my business at the university. This time I had brought some books for Mavis Taylor. I had mailed her my reading list so that she could catch up on the scholarship of what I was working on, but unfortunately she couldn't get most of the books. I had them all because I had brought them from the United States for this very purpose. I had suspected that most of them would not be available in South Africa.

In the evening I was having dinner by myself when there was a knock at the door. I opened it to a bald-headed Coloured man who was well dressed with a whiff of Aramis about him. I knew that scent because it was the cologne I had used at some stage. He told me his first name and showed me his ID document. I didn't bother to look at it because it didn't mean anything to me.

'You have something for me from Maseru,' he said.

'I don't know what you are talking about,' I said.

I put the car keys on the table in front of him.

'Brown Toyota Corolla with Lesotho number plates,' I said as he took the keys.

'I know,' he said and left.

A few minutes later he came back holding a foolscap-size jiffy bag. He put the keys back on the table.

'Tell them in Lesotho that we're still alive,' he said as he walked out of the door.

I drove the car a few times in the city before the long journey back to Lesotho. For a while I hoped the car would not explode while I was driving it. You never knew with the Boers. What if they had intercepted Hani's communication with his contact person and the Coloured man was not Hani's contact but a member of the notorious South African Bureau of State Security? When nothing happened after driving a few times between Mowbray and the campus in the city I soon relaxed and forgot all about my role as courier.

Back at Roma, I was walking one day from the Oppenheimer Building, where my office was located, to the BTM Lecture Theatre. Suddenly a woman running towards the building that housed the offices of the Dean of Humanities caught my attention. Perhaps she was late for something because she looked quite flustered. I was struck by her dark complexion and her features which looked more like those of West African beauties. I have always been partial to dark beauties. The second thing that struck me about her was the hairdo. The hair had not been treated with chemicals or straightened in any way. It was a natural finely combed afro. She reminded me of the Angela Davis of the 1960s. A darker-complexioned Angela Davis. The hair spoke of progressive political consciousness. I detested the fashion of frying the hair with chemicals in order to straighten it because I thought it smacked of self-hate. In my view, it ranked with skin-lightening creams in the black people's quest for whiteness. So, to see a woman with an afro or dreads or braids in the midst of all the straightened hair on campus was an inspiring sight.

I said to myself: *That woman is going to be my wife.*

I didn't know who the woman was. I had never seen her before, and had no idea I would ever see her again. But I somehow knew she was going to be my wife. She went her way and I went to class to teach African Drama.

I didn't give the woman another thought until one day, two weeks later, she walked into my office. She told me that her friend Phaee Monaheng was a member of my travelling theatre troupe and she was wondering if there might be a vacancy for her. Unfortunately, there was no place because I only took those students who had done my Practical Theatre course. But of course I couldn't let her go without finding out who she was and if there was any chance of seeing her again.

She told me she was Adele Mafoso. That surname in that form, a Sesotho corruption of the Nguni Mavuso, was not common in Lesotho. Surely she would know Willie Mafoso, who had been more like a brother to me when I lived at his home in Mohale's Hoek in my early years in Lesotho.

'Yes, Willie is my brother,' she told me.

'Willie is my brother too, sort of,' I said. 'We grew up together in Mohale's Hoek. We did many naughty things together.'

I thought she would at least chuckle at my lame joke; she didn't find any humour in it and just looked stern.

In Western culture, Adele would be referred to as Willie's first cousin; their fathers were brothers. But in the Basotho culture he is her brother. When I lived at Willie's she was one or two years old and lived with her parents in a village in the northern district of Leribe. That was why I did not know her.

Soon Adele and I began to see each other quite frequently. She had a boyfriend, a young man from the blue blood House of Molapo. This was the family of the ruling classes of Lesotho. One of its leading lights was the prime minister Chief Leabua Jonathan. But she began to see less of the Molapo boyfriend and more of me, until he faded out of the picture.

Some days she drove with me in my car to spend the night at my house in Florida. I was taken by the very idea of dating Willie's sister. I regarded him as a brother even though we were not related at all. But here was the opportunity to strengthen our ties and become relatives; we would be brothers-in-law if I married his sister. I know that is a stupid reason to marry anyone but, hey, I am quite prone to stupidity sometimes. I didn't believe that I would be marrying her just for that reason. Actually, at the time I didn't think Willie had anything to do with it at all. After all, I had decided she was going to be my wife long before I knew who she was. It was only on looking back and trying to analyse what contributed to my rash decision that it became clear to me that Willie had been a factor. At the time I believed there was genuine love between us. Indeed, quite early on in our relationship we began talking of marriage.

I discovered that she was humourless and had no time for my silly jokes and childish pranks. But that didn't bother me. Her positives far outweighed that little flaw. She was serious and ambitious and solid and would certainly bring stability to my life. She also had a very strong sense of family.

What bothered me was her political outlook. She was a staunch BNP member even though the rest of her family, including Willie, were BCP members or supporters. This on its own wouldn't have bothered me. After all, we had come to accept the BNP as a de facto government which was in alliance with the ANC. It was no longer the old BNP that was supported by the apartheid government, but had actually come out blazing against South Africa, to the extent of declaring that Lesotho was at war with the apartheid state. At that stage, therefore, I wouldn't have viewed her BNP membership as a cardinal sin. But what brought fear to me was her membership of the BNP Young Pioneers, then just known as the Youth League, which was armed. It was trained by troops from North Korea which were stationed in Lesotho for that purpose.

The Youth League used its North Korean training effectively by making every civil servant toe the party line. This was the group that marched senior civil servants out of their offices at gunpoint and up and down Kingsway, the main street of Maseru, shaming them in public with searing insults and threats of removing them from the face of the earth if they didn't display their support for Chief Leabua Jonathan. This happened a lot to those civil servants who shunned Chief Leabua's political rallies. Quite a few of them were seen being frogmarched and whipped in the streets of Maseru by the Youth League. I once saw the governor of the Lesotho Central Bank, a fellow I knew well from my youth in Mafeteng, suffer the same fate because the youths felt he was becoming too much of an independent thinker.

Adele was surprised that I didn't have a gun in my house.

'How do you live without a *thoboro*?' she asked.

She called it a *thoboro*, an onomatopoeic term of endearment for a machine gun. She thought I was a sissy when I told her the sight of guns, never mind touching them, made me cringe. The last time I touched a real gun with my hands I was a teenager who was being used by adults to commit their dirty acts of assassination. Even when I lived at the Poqo camp I never messed around with guns because whatever arms and ammunition was there was hidden so that the police didn't find them; the camp was in an urban environment and everyone in town knew about it. There were never any arms lying around there.

'Maybe you're right, I am a sissy,' I said. 'But I don't want a gun in my house. I hate guns wholeheartedly. Even our kids, when we have them, will not play with toy guns.'

Those were the days when I thought I could lay down the law!

The next time I visited Mohale's Hoek with Adele I expressed my reservations to Willie about his sister's involvement with Chief Leabua's lawless bands of armed youths. He didn't seem to take it that seriously because he thought it was just a phase that was influenced by her relationship with the Molapo boyfriend. Now that I was in her life, he said hopefully, she would give that up. I took his word for it. But I didn't take comfort in the fact that when we sat down for lunch he teased her about the activities of the Youth League and they laughed about it as if it were a joke.

Although Adele continued to be a staunch BNP member she stopped participating in the activities of the Youth League. She also had to accept that she was now involved with a man who would have nothing to do with *thoboro* or any other weapon of death.

Nevertheless, I was very proud of Adele and I wanted to introduce her to all my friends. I once took her to meet Ntlabathi Mbuli – my Poqo friend and mentor. The last time I told you about him he was losing his mind in England where he had gone to study for an MA degree. He did complete the degree at the London School of Economics and returned to Lesotho to work for the Lesotho Christian Council while he was trying to get a lecturing job at the National University of Lesotho. He had built himself a nice concrete block house in one of the townships on the outskirts of Maseru where he lived with his wife and children. I don't remember exactly how many children he had but I think there were three. Adele knew his daughter from a previous relationship in Mafeteng; she was a fellow student at the National University of Lesotho before the daughter went to study medicine at the University of Cape Town. She was therefore quite keen to meet her friend's father.

We found Ntlabathi running up and down his living room with his arms outstretched; he was 'flying' like an aeroplane and making the appropriate sounds. He stopped long enough to express his joy at seeing us and to acknowledge the woman I introduced as Willie's sister, and then he resumed his 'flight'. His wife Karabo came to join us and asked him to settle down and attend to his visitors.

He told us about the voices that kept calling his name. They started while he was in England battling with conservative dons who were dismissive of his Marxist approach. Now the voices had become worse. I didn't say this, but it was obvious to me that if he were a believer in African traditional religions he would have interpreted these as a call from the ancestors to become a diviner, a *sangoma* or an *igqirha* – a traditional healer. But unfortunately as an unbeliever he had to settle for a mundane diagnosis – that of schizophrenia. That of course was my own *tiekieline* diagnosis which I shared with Adele on our way back home. I don't think he had sought any medical advice since he didn't see that there was anything wrong with him. He had become paranoid and we listened while he told us of enemies who were bent on destroying him.

Before we left he gave me manila envelopes of his manuscripts – most of them true manuscripts since they were in longhand. But there were some typed pages too. These were his poems and short stories. I didn't want to take this material because I didn't know what to do with it. But he insisted. Later, when Ntlabathi returned to South Africa after our liberation in 1994 and was teaching at a high school there, he sent me another envelope of manuscripts. They were accompanied by a letter listing a number of attempts he had made to get the material published and asking me to keep them and maybe in future he would self-publish them after getting my comments. I still have all that material. I never gathered enough courage to read it after I got the news that Ntlabathi had died from an undisclosed illness. I am hoping to give all this material to his heirs when I get around to attending to that.

My relationship with Adele was tempestuous from the word go. I played some part in creating the initial storm. For instance, one day I was on campus with members of my theatre company, most of whom were also her friends. When she arrived to join us the first thing that struck me was her new hairdo. She had obviously come straight from a hair salon because her hair was relaxed and set in some fancy style.

I called her aside and said, 'What did you do to your hair?'

Even before she could answer, I added, 'I can't go with you when you are like that.'

She was perceptibly shocked by my outburst and looked very hurt. I knew immediately that I had been tactless and insensitive. But she didn't say a word in her defence. Instead of apologising immediately I went back to my troupe and continued with whatever I was talking about. Her friends didn't make things any better for my feelings of guilt when I overhead them admiring her new hairdo and asking which salon she had been to and which particular hairdresser, so that they might go there themselves. I heard her tell them sadly, 'He doesn't like it. I did it for him but he doesn't like it.'

I only apologised when we got to my house later that evening. But the incident haunted me for a long time. Just like the slap on Ruth's beautiful face. It was a good lesson for me. Even today, I marvel at the arrogance of thinking I had the right to tell a woman she should look or dress or do her hair in a manner that met with my approval just because she happened to be my girlfriend or even wife. Today I am reluctant to give an opinion even when it is solicited. There is no question I dread more than 'How do I look in this dress?' All right, I am exaggerating; there are worse questions. But still I have feelings of trepidation about that one because it forces me to lie.

Although I thought we had made our peace about that particular gaffe, our life was mired in conflict. For instance, when Sonwabo's children came to visit me she became very jealous and would mope and not even talk to them for hours on end. I told you that my brother Sonwabo had gone to the United States to study for an MA degree in International Affairs and never returned. We heard from Ohio that he was no longer a student there. He left before completing the degree and no one seemed to know where he was. So, for these children – Limpho, Solomzi, Thembi and Mpumi – I was the only father they knew.

One day they came to visit and we went for a walk around the suburb of Florida. When I came back Adele didn't want to talk to me. I only realised then that maybe I should have invited her to join us on the walk. She felt left out when I was with these kids. But then I had thought she would understand that I saw these kids only once in a while and I needed to give them all my attention just for those few hours of their visit. It was essential for that time to be just with them.

My own children were still in Mafeteng in the care of my mother. Occasionally they visited me in Florida, and if Adele happened to be there she would be unhappy about it. I hoped she would learn to love them, especially if she was going to be my wife.

Sometimes I could not understand Adele's logic. She still had her room at one of the residences at the university, although she visited and spent the night in Florida whenever we had made such an arrangement. One day my brother Monwabisi, who was practising as an attorney in Mafeteng, visited and we went out to my neighbourhood shebeens to drink ourselves silly as was our habit. When we returned at night Adele was waiting outside.

Immediately she saw me she attacked with: 'You locked me out of your house! You locked me out!'

328

I would be angry too if someone had locked me out of the house, but I had not.

'Did he know that you'd be coming?' asked Monwabisi.

'No, he did not,' she said.

'Then he didn't lock *you* out of the house. He locked the house because that's what you do when you leave a house unattended.'

She had no answer for this, but she was still fuming.

But there were also moments of pure joy, when she was such a sweet person that I would soon forget about the stormy moments. I would convince myself that the turbulent times were an aberration, and that when we were married things would settle because neither of us would have reason to feel insecure.

In the meantime the university decided to promote me from lecturer to senior lecturer. I had not applied for this promotion. It just had not occurred to me that my work merited a promotion and I should take steps to bring it to the attention of the university senate. Positions did not mean anything to me; I was just happy teaching my students, writing plays and articles for journals and organising the work of the Marotholi Travelling Theatre.

I also had outside interests that kept me busy when I got to Maseru. These included a company called the Screenwriters Institute which I had established at Mothamo House. I had bought cameras and editing suites and was producing videos on various social development subjects. Entities such as UNICEF, the Ministry of Health and the International Labour Organization engaged our services to produce VHS videos for their workshops. Some of these were dramas on such topics as HIV/AIDS and TB. I employed the services of freelance camera people and editors each time I had a project. I remember one of them, Lineo, a petite and outspoken young lady, who would regale us with stories of her adventures as we travelled in a Land Rover to the mountain villages of Lesotho shooting footage for a UNICEF documentary. She had travelled with King Moshoeshoe II and Archbishop Morapeli of the Roman Catholic Church between Paris and New York in a Concorde, the British-French supersonic jet. The four of us in the Land Rover – our driver, 'Mamotsepe the UNICEF Representative, 'Mope our second cameraman and I – had never been in a Concorde so we listened with fascination as Lineo brought the experience to life for us. But what we found even more titillating was her detailed description of how she was planning to seduce the Archbishop whom she was eyeing all the time they were relaxing in the first class cabin of the supersonic flight. She outlined for us how she would strip off his robes one by one until she got to the undergarments and what she would do to him when she finally had him at her mercy, stark naked like the day he was born. She lamented that she had missed her opportunity on that journey to New York but vowed that she would still get her chance since when these big shots travelled they quite often engaged her services to record their expeditions on video for posterity.

Alas, one day we had to part ways with Lineo as she went to seek better opportunities in South Africa. The last time I heard of her she was directing the soap opera *Generations* which was screened every weekday on SABC 1. And then she died. I don't know what killed Lineo, but I hope she got her heart's desire before she died.

I continued my work for UNICEF and other agencies with other freelancers. There was only a short lull in our activities when the government of Chief Leabua Jonathan was overthrown by the paramilitary on January 24, 1986. I was at my house with Patrick Nkunda when we first heard of the coup. We walked to the streets to witness what was happening and saw convoys of soldiers driving up and down the streets of Maseru and thousands of people dancing in the street waving branches of trees. Cars were blowing their horns and there was jubilation all around. We heard that General Metsing Lekhanya had taken over the reins of government. Without wasting any time, he had set up a Military Council that would manage the affairs of the state. He was the Chairman. One of the members of the Military Council was the fellow to whose guitar playing we used to dance in Mohale's Hoek, Reentseng Habi. Now he was one of the most feared people in the country.

Patrick Nkunda had seen some coups in his life, particularly the one that removed Milton Obote and put Idi Amin in power. Blood did flow in the streets of Kampala and Entebbe, and indeed Mr Amin's regime was a bloodthirsty one.

'The Basotho people never cease to amaze me,' said Nkunda as we walked back home. 'The King has no special title; he is just called *Ntate*, same as the labourer who digs the road. A cabinet minister can be seen standing in the queue at the bank just like everyone else. And here now is a coup where no one is killed or arrested and people just sing and dance.'

Well, no one was killed, but he spoke too soon about arrests because although Leabua Jonathan and his cabinet were never arrested, some military officers who opposed the coup were locked up by General Lekhanya.

Although we had not expected this coup, it was a culmination of strange events that had been happening during the past few weeks. It started with harsh words being exchanged between Chief Leabua Jonathan and the South African government. The main issue was the strong Communist presence in Lesotho, as represented by the North Koreans. Chief Leabua had also kicked out South Africa's allies, the Taiwanese embassy, and had established diplomatic relations with the People's Republic of China. Another sore point with the South African government was the strong presence of the ANC in the country.

Clearly, according to the apartheid government, Chief Leabua was becoming too big for his boots. He was their creation and now he was turning against his creators. They pounced on him with a vengeance. First there was a general blockade and no food or fuel was allowed into the country. You will remember that Lesotho is completely surrounded by South Africa and a blockade like that could cripple the country since it was dependent on South Africa for all its supplies. Local newspapers had observed that before the blockade petrol tankers had been parked at the American Embassy, which meant that the Americans knew there was going to be a blockade. Without oil and gas most of the country was at a standstill.

And then the coup. And then the sadness when, a few weeks later, General Lekhanya and his government deported most of the ANC refugees and some PAC ones as well from Lesotho. Many of these were my students at the National University of Lesotho. Fortunately Lekhanya did not hand them over to South Africa but made transit arrangements with his new friends in Pretoria, and many of them landed in Zambia where the ANC was headquartered. My friend Jobs was one of those who were deported, leaving his law practice to a local partner.

I despised Lekhanya for this.

That same year of the coup the arrival of the Gonzalez family injected new energy into the cultural life of Maseru – just as the June 16 youths had done a decade earlier. Albio Gonzalez, his wife, Teresa Devant, and their two kids, Adrian and Sara, came from a sojourn in Botswana where they had been cultural activists. Albio was born in Cuba. He and his family had lived in Sweden for many years. He worked for the Swedish International Development Agency which sent him first to Botswana as a town planner and then to Lesotho in the same position. In Botswana both Teresa and Albio were highly involved in the activities of Medu Art Ensemble which was founded by the South African poet in exile in that country, Mongane Wally Serote. Some Medu members were leading South African exiles, such as the musicians Hugh Masekela and Jonas Gwangwa, novelist Mandla Langa, poets Willy and Baleka Kgositsile, puppeteer Adrian Kohler and artist Thami Myele. You may know the last as the artist killed along with other ANC refugees in a cross-border raid into Botswana by the South African army in 1985.

Teresa was a theatre director and Albio was an artist and designer. They had worked with Medu creating theatre and organising art exhibitions and poster-making workshops. When they arrived in Maseru and didn't find much happening along those lines – Lesiba Players had gone defunct long before and Marotholi Travelling Theatre was confined to theatre-for-development work in rural Lesotho – they decided to establish their own theatre company, Meso Theatre Group. Two of its members who became my close and lifelong friends, besides the Gonzalez family, were Kefuoe Molapo and 'Maseabata Ramoeletsi. Kefuoe was the son of Clemoski, my late and lamented friend, although I didn't know that at the time. It was only after we had known each other for some time that we both realised that we had a bond that went deeper than the theatre that had brought us together. 'Maseabata, on the other hand, was a Mosotho woman who would have been called Coloured in South Africa because she was the product of a white father

332

and a black mother. Her day job was that of a pharmacist at Queen Elizabeth II Hospital, but she loved the theatre so much and was such a wonderful actress you would have thought that was her full-time occupation.

Meso Theatre Group specialised in producing my plays. Their first production was *And the Girls in Their Sunday Dresses*, a two-hander about corruption in the food aid programmes. It also looked at the oppression of women both by the political system in Lesotho and South Africa and by cultural patriarchy. The play was so successful in Maseru that it went to the Edinburgh Festival and then went on a tour of Spain. It was the first play from Lesotho to be performed abroad. Although the two actresses who performed in it didn't have any formal training in theatre – Tokoloho Khutsoane was a journalist and Gertrude Mothibe a pharmacist – they acquitted themselves well and received wonderful reviews both in the United Kingdom and in Spain. The following year Meso produced another of my plays about the liberation struggle in South Africa, *Joys of War*, which they performed in Maseru and in various cities in Botswana and Zimbabwe.

After the performance of *And the Girls in Their Sunday Dresses* I was astounded when I was confronted by a woman in the street who accused me of writing about her sister. Mpho Mofolo was a local lawyer and the daughter of OK Mofolo, for whom I worked when I was studying to be a lawyer. She claimed that the prostitute character in the play, who falls in love with an Italian chef while she was at university and then leaves for Cape Town with him, was based on her sister. I was quite amazed because I knew nothing about her sister. In fact, I didn't even know she had a sister at all. My character was not based on anyone I knew, and I told her that. But she wouldn't listen. Instead she threatened, 'I'm going to sue your pants off.' I had no idea why her lawsuit would involve my pants, but I was quite satisfied that I had created characters from my imagination who were so believable that intelligent lawyers saw their relatives in them and were prepared to take me to court about them.

'Once again, Mpho, I have no idea who your sister is or what she did,' I said, walking away from her increasing fury. She repeated her threat of a lawsuit. Some inquisitive middle-aged women who had stood close by hoping for a shouting match were disappointed. I knew the type; they were junior civil servants – secretaries and receptionists – who should be at work serving taxpayers. But they were out scouring the street for morsels of gossip. I heard one who had joined them late ask what the problem was. Another one explained that I had written dirty things about OK Mofolo's children.

I had to stop and listen to this while Mpho Mofolo walked away, still fuming.

'I know him,' said the woman. 'He's the son of *Ntate* Mda who is a lawyer in Mafeteng. His brothers are lawyers too. It is part of the wars of lawyers. I think his family is jealous of the Mofolo family because they are making more money and are wealthier.'

That was Maseru for you. Everyone thought he or she knew everyone else's business. When they didn't have the facts they made them up. I continued with my interrupted saunter to the post office on Kingsway.

'You think you can just ruin other people's lives?' one of the women called after me. 'You think just because your brothers are lawyers you can write dirty things about other people's children?'

I was not going to waste my breath on the busybodies. If only they knew that if there was any lawsuit at all my brothers would be the last people I would resort to for help.

FROM MY BROTHER'S HOTEL we drive to his house to see my mother. I am not going to ask him anything about the hotel. If he wanted to tell me he would have done so already, especially because I hear it has been standing there for years now. Is he fighting battles about getting a licence perhaps? I don't think I'll ever know.

My mother is in her bedroom as usual. But this time in addition to the neighbourhood people who like to hang out with her in her bedroom there is a young man, perhaps in his twenties, who is holding a big Bible. He is in the middle of prayer, and we stand quietly until he completes it. My mother introduces him to us as the pastor of the Universal Church.

'Oh, so it's true that you now belong to the Universal Church?' I ask her while the pastor massages her legs because the Good Lord has vested him with hands that heal.

Yes, she says, she was introduced to the Universal Church by a neighbourhood woman who used to be my father's secretary and typist, Cousin 'Maletsatsi. She thinks that the prayers are doing wonders for her arthritis and hypertension and varicose veins. So does the blessed physiotherapy. Since she can't walk to the church the pastors come here to hold a service for her, a thing which the Roman Catholic Church cannot do. I am quite surprised to hear her praise another denomination like this because she used to be a committed Catholic. When I was a kid I remember her pride in her black skirt and purple blouse and cape which were the uniform of the Legion of Saint Anna and Saint Cecilia. Now she has joined the Universal Church of the Kingdom of God, a Pentecostal denomination founded only three decades ago in Brazil and which has taken Lesotho by storm. I never thought she would leave the Catholic Church for any other church in the world.

I tell Thandi that's what people said about me too: *we never thought this devoted altar boy would leave the Catholic Church for anything.* I was a third generation Catholic. Before that my people were Anglicans, as were most people in the village of Qoboshane. My grandfather converted to Catholicism because the best schools in the region were owned and operated by the Catholics and he wanted my father and his siblings to get places at those schools. But he was drawn to the liturgy and became a firm believer. My grandmother remained in the Anglican Church, so they went to separate churches on Sundays. I admired this because it showed how open-minded my grandfather was. Remember, that was in the early thirties and women were by law minors since males were recognised as the sole heads of the family. They laid down the law and one would have expected that my grandfather would insist that his wife should follow him to his new church, especially because his new church did not tolerate the kind of arrangement he had in his family where he and his children were the only Catholics and the wife belonged to some renegade church born of a King's adultery. Either my grandfather was open-minded or my grandmother was strong-willed and independent.

335

When I was a kid I visited my grandmother's church on one or two occasions. I thought my grandfather had made a smart choice because the rituals of his church had more colour and pizzazz. But I have since changed my mind.

Before the Universal Church pastor leaves he shakes my hand and says, 'I hope we'll see you in our church soon.'

I don't tell him that he'll have a long time to wait. After his departure I tell Thandi that if I were to be a Christian again and wanted to be part of organised religion I would join my grandmother's Anglican Church instead of the Catholics or any of your right-wing charismatic churches. The Anglicans are the most progressive of the mainstream denominations; they have produced such fearless champions of human rights and justice as Desmond Tutu, Njongonkulu Ndungane and Trevor Huddleston. But most importantly, they have female and gay clergy – both priests and bishops – despite the protestations of the conservative African segment of the church.

'The Zion Churches have always had female pastors, maybe you should join those,' says Thandi as we drive on Leabua Jonathan Highway towards Maseru.

It is true that the African Independent Churches, collectively known as the Zion Churches, have always had female clergy. In fact, most of them are led by female bishops and archbishops, and indeed were founded by women. Occasionally there may be a male prophet who gains universal fame, but most of the revered prophets in these denominations are women. This does not come as a surprise to me because even before Christianity was introduced to my people, when they still adhered to African traditional religions, most of their spiritual leaders were women. In the courts of our kings and queens the chief advisers were diviners – or *amagqirha, inyanga, izanuse, izangoma,* as they were variously known – who were not only healers of ailing bodies but also served a spiritual function. Most of these traditional healers were women.

'I agree,' I say. 'Religious patriarchy was brought to these shores by our erstwhile colonial masters.'

Then we talk about other things. Just reminiscing on how life used to be when we still lived in Lesotho, and how we think that since we tasted other lifestyles we wouldn't be able to survive in Mafeteng. The place looks dull, like a once-bright floral dress that has run out of colour.

Then somewhere between Morija and Maseru I slow down and drive to the side of the road. I park the car under a tree next to the remains of a building that have been fenced in by sagging strands of barbed wire.

'This was our Jerusalema,' I announce grandly.

'What happened to our Jerusalema?' asks Gugu. 'How did it come to this?'

Yes, our Jerusalema is in ruins. At least the tree is still there, although it looks emaciated and forlorn.

WE NAMED IT JERUSALEMA because of its architecture. The white building was in the style of buildings we had seen in illustrations of biblical stories. It was a church of one of the African Independent Churches – the Zion Churches. It looks so ghostly now, but it used to be teeming with life when in 1989 Gugu and I adopted it for our little trysts. Not the church itself, but the tree just outside the yard.

I first saw Gugu Nkosi at a *braai* party at Tom Lynn's house. Tom was the lovable head of the English Department at the National University of Lesotho who was famous for his drunkenness. He occasionally organised parties at his house where he invited staff and students to eat barbecued meat and drink wine and beer. He was very popular in the department because the people said that although he was from the United Kingdom he did not have the snootiness of the British. Gugu was one of the students who attended. I didn't pay any particular attention to her that day, though I did notice that she did not touch any of the alcohol whereas her friends were getting quite tipsy and therefore quite loud.

I saw her again a few months later when she enrolled in my African Poetry class. She was one of a group of students from South Africa in my class. I learnt that she was from Soweto and that her sister Smangele had been in my earlier classes. I had not left a favourable impression

337

on her sister because she thought I was a hard taskmaster who gave students a lot of work and demanded more rigorous scholarship than they were used to from other lecturers. Gugu, therefore, must have taken my class with trepidation. But she had no choice because it was a required course. She told me later that to her surprise she enjoyed the class and gained skills in the analysis of poetry that she used when she became a high school literature teacher in Swaziland. What I remember about her in that class was that as a speaker of isiZulu she became very useful when we studied poetry from the South African workers' movement. Three of the favourite poets were Nise Malange, Mi Hlatshwayo and Alfred Qabula, the trade union stalwarts who were based in Natal. They composed and performed poetry on issues affecting the workers. Although we studied this oral poetry in English translation, it was necessary for the students to hear how it sounded in its original isiZulu. I would ask Gugu to read it for us and we all looked forward to the scintillating cadence of her isiZulu accent.

I got to know that Gugu was from Armitage Road in Orlando West, a township I knew very well. Her home was a street away from Vilakazi Street where Nelson Mandela and Desmond Tutu had their houses – reputed to be the only street in the world with two Nobel Peace Prize laureates. When I lived with the Mandela family, however, it was long before they moved to Orlando West. After they moved from Orlando East my family visited them at Vilakazi Street, never knowing that only a street away was the home of the woman who was to be my mate.

I gradually became friends with Gugu and two of her fellow classmates, Xoliswa Vumazonke, who was from the Eastern Cape, and Gugu Mkhonta, who was from Swaziland. I often took them for long drives in my theatre company's Volkswagen Kombi. Once I took them to Mafeteng to introduce them to my mother. She was happy to meet them. When we left she gave me provisions of steamed bread which she knew I liked very much and Gugu teased me that I was 'mama's boy'. I liked her ribbing; it gave her company a very homely quality. Unfortunately my father was busy in court. I would have loved it if my friends had met him. It would have made Xoliswa's day because she was a PAC supporter and knew of him as the founding spirit of that organisation. That's how PAC adherents referred to him – the founding spirit – as if he was already dead and people communed with him through prayers or ancestral rituals.

After the visit we went to relax at Hotel Mafeteng and had mixed grills and a few drinks. The women were teetotallers so none of our drinks was alcoholic. This was the kind of company that inspired sobriety in me. I was finding Gugu increasingly intoxicating the more I spent time with her, even though at this point it was always in the company of her girlfriends who had become my friends as well.

But Adele did not find anything amusing about my association with Gugu. She heard stories that I was spending a lot of time with her; she and her group of friends were often seen in my Kombi in Maseru at Mothamo House where my company, the Screenwriters Institute, had its offices and production studios. She also heard that I had taken this bevy of beauties to a concert I organised and promoted at the Airport Hotel for the American hard bop and soul jazz organist, Rhoda Scott. I was hosting Ms Scott through the auspices of the American Cultural Center.

Adele confronted me about Gugu and I told her Gugu and I were only friends. This was true only to a point because even though at that moment we were strictly not lovers it was obvious to me, and hopefully to Gugu, that the friendship was gradually assuming a much more romantic tenor.

'I forbid you to see her again,' said Adele.

'Oh, no, you can't forbid me,' I said. 'You have your own friends too and I don't forbid you to see them.'

I should have added that those friends included the Molapo young man who seemingly had not given up hope that he would win her back. But I didn't because I didn't want to rub it in.

'What do you see in this Gugu anyway?' she asked.

'She makes me laugh.'

She gave me a puzzled look.

'Why do you want to laugh?'

Why indeed? I couldn't provide her with an answer. But still I knew that I needed Gugu and I desperately needed to laugh. As it turned out the feelings were mutual – between me and Gugu – although it took me some time to realise that.

I did not have much time to dwell on the pickle in which I had put myself with women. There were other pressing demands. Not only was I running the Screenwriters Institute in Maseru which was producing video and radio programmes and comic books on health and community development issues, I was a UNICEF Consultant on Social Mobilisation. My focus was on child survival and development and I travelled to many African countries attending meetings and conferences and holding workshops on how to use various media to promote the cause. During these trips I was also in search of theatre, particularly the traditional pre-colonial performance modes that were extant in various African cultures. I was also observing theatre-for-development practices in other parts of the world.

My work with UNICEF took me to Zimbabwe to participate in the International Symposium of Writers, Artists and Intellectuals for Child Survival and Development in Frontline States and Southern Africa – dubbed the Harare Symposium. The Symposium was attended by one hundred and forty delegates from twenty countries. Its objective was to mobilise African and international writers, artists and intellectuals for child survival and development, and to focus international attention on the plight of children in the Frontline States of Southern Africa. The frontline states were those countries that were directly affected by apartheid policies either because they shared borders with South Africa or they hosted the liberation movements. For instance, Tanzania was a frontline state even though it did not share any border with South Africa. Zimbabwe, of course, was in the frontline in many ways. It hosted the liberation movements and had emerged only eight years earlier from a liberation struggle of its own that we still regarded with awe for its bravery and achievements. It also shared a border with South Africa that was often violated by raids of apartheid's covert forces into the heart of Harare.

Besides me, the delegation from Lesotho was composed of Prince Mohato – who later became the present King Letsie III – and Fine Maema, his private secretary.

One of my greatest joys at the Harare Symposium was meeting some of my compatriots who had been strewn all over the world by exile. These included Miriam Makeba, our songbird also known as Mama Africa, and Oliver Tambo, the president of the ANC. I sat with Mr Tambo at the Sheraton Hotel auditorium where he talked to me about my father as we watched a ballet company of children brought from Mozambique by Graça Machel perform *Swan Lake*. It struck me that the ANC leaders continued to hold my father in high esteem even though he had left the organisation. Mr Tambo told me that he continued to be in contact with my father and often asked for his counsel and had even once asked him to write him a speech. I didn't know about all this and was surprised that my father had never spoken about it.

'Pass my greetings to AP of Old,' he said when we parted after the show.

Graça Machel, who was Minister of Education in Mozambique at the time, introduced a number of children who testified to the delegates gathered at the Sheraton on how they had been turned into soldiers by the MNR. The MNR (Mozambique National Resistance, also known as RENAMO) was the political organisation that was fighting to overthrow the FRELIMO (Front for the Liberation of Mozambique) government in Mozambique. It was created by the Rhodesian intelligence during the liberation struggle in Zimbabwe. It was led by a man called Alphonse (Afonso) Dhlakama and was heavily supported both financially and in terms of manpower by the South African government.

I remember in particular twelve-year-old Isaac, who told the gathering how the MNR bandits raided his village in a remote part of Mozambique, captured him and trained him as a soldier. In the many battles that he fought against the government forces he killed two FRELIMO soldiers. He was such a brave fighter that he became a commander of a unit that raided villages, looting food stores, burning down houses, raping women and killing everyone in sight after the deed. He led quite a few massacres of innocent civilians. He told us that all the time he was yearning to escape. One day an opportunity availed itself; he killed two MNR soldiers and escaped and handed himself over to government forces. He was undergoing rehabilitation at one of the centres established by the Mozambican government for child soldiers.

Isaac was just one of the former child soldiers from Mozambique, Angola and Zimbabwe who gave testimonies of their harrowing experiences to the delegates.

The delegates included writer Ngugi wa Thiong'o, actress Cicely Tyson, playwright George Wolfe, musician Manu Dibango, *New Amsterdam* news editor Wilbert Tatum, anti-apartheid activist Allan Boesak, French first lady Danielle Mitterrand, academic and theatre practitioner Chris Kamlongera, singer Harry Belafonte, who was also UNICEF Goodwill Ambassador, and the president of the Swedish Committee for UNICEF, Lisbet Palme, the widow of slain Swedish prime minister Olof Palme.

Robert Mugabe hosted us at the State House for a banquet and a cocktail party. His wife Sally was as gracious as ever. Mugabe himself struck me as a very down-to-earth and humble man. I remember that when I walked with him down the steps at the Sheraton to an outdoor event – traditional dancing in the grounds of the hotel – ordinary people approached him. He clapped his hands in humility in the Shona manner of greeting. I was highly impressed by Mugabe and his wife Sally who attended to us at their official residence as if we were old friends.

Towards the end of the Harare Symposium we elected a Pan African Planning Committee and Advisory Council on Child Survival and Development, which included people like Graça Machel, Chinua Achebe, Sally Mugabe, Miriam Makeba, Ali Mazrui and the exhilarating Mozambican artist Malangatana. I was elected to chair the literature sub-committee that resolved to establish a magazine for children whose content would be produced by the children themselves in their own languages with translations in English, Portuguese and French. We also resolved to publish an anthology of stories, poems and plays to be edited by George Wolfe, Botswana poet Barolong Seboni, and me. Its royalties would go to UNICEF for the rehabilitation of the child soldiers.

I must add that none of these resolutions was implemented; it all came down to distance between the implementers and lack of funds. But long after the Symposium I continued corresponding with Graça

Machel and she sent me photographs of dancers that I published in my newsletter, *MTT Report*. This was after I had told her that to me a dancer is a god or, better still, a goddess.

On my return to Lesotho I wrote an article for a news magazine called *Southern Star*. At the end of my article I made the following observation:

> Finally, I must state that in many respects the Symposium was a great success, and in the four days a lot was achieved particularly in focusing international attention on the plight of children. However, something did leave a bitter taste in the mouths of some of the delegates *(I was really talking about my mouth and Chris Kamlongera's mouth)*. The Symposium was a successful media event, graced by 'stars' of all types. It was a celebrity showcase. We enjoyed ourselves in all that gloss, glamour and glitter. We sipped champagne and ate caviar. We attended nightly cocktail parties. All in the name of the starving children of Africa.

All the time I was in Harare stuffing myself at Robert Mugabe's State House banquets on behalf of the hungry children of Africa, I caught myself thinking more and more of Gugu and how I would have had an even greater time had she been with me. It was the laughter that we shared that I missed. I resolved that as soon as I got back to Roma I would take her out to spend quality time alone with her away from the rest of the world.

My first outing with her, without her girlfriends, was a long drive up steep and winding roads to the Oxbow Skiing Lodge in the Maluti Mountains of Lesotho. I rented a comfortable chalet for us. Although there were all types of skis for rental we did not venture on to the snowy slopes. We spent a couple of days there, sitting by log fires or out on the rocks admiring the imposing mountains and the gorges and rivers that we could see in the distance. And of course we made love for the first time.

After this trip we had a few dates, mostly to my hometown of Mafeteng, because I had to see my mother and my kids quite often. We stayed at Hotel Mafeteng. My mother liked her very much and would ask after her on those occasions when I visited by myself.

I took her out to the Lesotho Sun, a luxury hotel on a hilltop in Maseru, for her twenty-first birthday. We had dinner from their wide-ranging buffet. I gave her a present of African-themed jewellery and a West African style dress specially designed by *Ntate* Jabbie, a West African man who lived in Maseru. *Ntate* Jabbie designed and made all my Afro-shirts and was Bintu Jabbie's father, another beautiful woman who became my friend when we both worked for the Department of Information and Broadcasting. Bintu was the one who introduced me to her father in the first place, which resulted in my unique style. The brown dress he made for Gugu's birthday was especially elegant with its ornate embroidery.

Adele got to hear of the birthday present from some of the gossips at Roma and she drove from Maseru to the university to confront Gugu. She threatened Gugu with violence if she did not hand over the dress and jewellery. Gugu, of course, had no intention of risking life or limb for material objects, however sentimentally valuable they might have been. She meekly handed the gifts over to the bigger and more aggressive woman. I was very embarrassed when Adele returned from Roma and showed me the items she had confiscated from Gugu.

That evening Adele phoned Josephine, Gugu's mother in Soweto, and told her that her daughter had stolen her husband. I don't know how she got Josephine's number. But she had her mysterious ways of investigating things and finding information. I could not vouch for this, but I suspected that her strong Youth League and ruling party connections had something to do with it.

Next time Gugu went home for a short holiday she was in big trouble with her mother. She was only twenty-one but was already stealing other women's husbands. As if that was not bad enough, the woman whose husband she had stolen was related to her; Adele's mother was from the Nhlapho family, which was also Josephine's family. This meant that, according to Josephine, Gugu was practically Adele's sister. It became obvious to Gugu that Adele must have had a long conversation with her mother. Josephine yelled at her so much that she didn't even have the chance to explain that Adele had lied about my being her husband.

When Gugu returned to Lesotho things cooled a bit between us. I think Josephine's voice was still ringing in her ears. But as soon as the sound began to fade the old attraction returned and we began to see each other again. But this time we had to be careful lest Adele's spies saw us. The best times to see her were during the rehearsals of my theatre group which took place at the Netherlands Hall at the university. As the group went through their paces Gugu and I got into my new white Toyota Cressida and drove about twenty kilometres from campus in the direction of Maseru. When we got to Masianokeng, instead of turning right towards Maseru we took a left turn and drove on past Mazenod in the Mafeteng direction until we got to the church which we named Jerusalema. We parked outside the yard under the tree and just sat in the car and talked the kind of nonsense that lovers talk and sang to Queen's 'Radio Gaga'. The members of the congregation walked in and out of Jerusalema in their blue and white uniforms wondering what Sodom and Gomorrah was happening under their sacred tree.

WE LOOK AT THE ruins of Jerusalema and we giggle. Thandi wants to know what is so funny about a withered tree and a heap of bricks and mud. If only that tree could talk. If only she could see what I see – ghosts in white and faded blue walking in and out of the building, stopping from time to time to stare at the car under the tree, faces scowling. Our Jerusalema.

THE SECRET OF JERUSALEMA could not last forever, but Gugu was an opiate I could not give up. I did not know where this would lead, but Adele was still very much in my life. She had graduated from the university and was a civil servant in Maseru. She lived with me at my university house in Florida. At this time my daughter Thandi, who was a student at St Mary's High School at Roma, was staying with me. She commuted in a minibus taxi that transported students to and fro between Maseru and Roma, a distance of about eighty kilometres.

The two women did not get along at all. Every day I would be fielding complaints from Adele about Thandi: one day it would be about Adele's perfume which Thandi allegedly used even though Thandi denied it; the next day it would be about Thandi who had allegedly gossiped about her to her friends . . . and so it would go on and on like that.

I decided to take Adele with me to Cape Town when I went to consult with Mavis Taylor about my PhD thesis so that I could buy her a graduation dress at one of the exclusive boutiques in the city.

The day I took her to the underground Golden Acre Mall she quarrelled with me because as we were walking I would stop to look at something attractive in a window display. I would point it out to her, only to find that she had walked on. On realising that I was no longer by her side, she would stop and look back at me quite furiously, arms akimbo. I would have to gather speed towards her to save myself from the embarrassment of being yelled at. After buying the dress she liked we returned to our accommodation at Serengeti self-catering apartments in Mowbray.

I don't know what was on Adele's mind, but as soon as we entered the living room she put the shopping bag on the carpet and sat down on the glass coffee table. Maybe she was tired or just too furious to realise what she was doing. The glass cracked. I was horrified, but she looked unperturbed.

'We'll tell them we found it like this,' she said.

'They know we didn't find it like this. They were here just this morning to clean,' I said.

'Precisely. The cleaners must have done it. They have no evidence that it's us.'

I didn't want to argue, though I knew that I could not go along with her plan. The cleaning woman might be fired for something she had not done.

'They can't prove it's us. We'll deny it,' she repeated to make it clear that she would tolerate no dissent. I said nothing. I didn't want her to think I was a traitor or to start another quarrel.

346

While she was freshening up I went to the manager's office and told her that I had inadvertently broken the coffee table and would like to pay for it. She added the cost to my accommodation bill and Adele never got to know that I squealed. To this day she thinks she got away with breaking the Serengeti coffee table. This episode worried me. I was seeing a side of her that I had not known before. And it scared me.

But I didn't have time to dwell on this. I had come to Cape Town primarily to attend to my thesis. At the university my supervisor was having problems finding someone with the right credentials to co-supervise my doctorate with her. My research was on how theatre could be used effectively as a medium for development communication. Mavis was a professor of theatre who specialised in training students in voice, movement and directing. She had no knowledge of theatre-for-development, which was my specialisation. But that could easily be remedied because she was well read in theatre-in-education and with all the books I had brought with me from the United States she could read up on theatre-for-development. The problem was the communication side of things. The University of Cape Town did not offer any field of communication studies and therefore there was no one appropriate who could supervise my work which was interdisciplinary, encompassing theatre, interpersonal communication and what was known in those days as mass communication. There was, however, what was referred to as the Professional Communications Unit that was headed by Mr M L Fielding. I didn't know what exactly the Professional Communications Unit did, but it did not offer any courses. Although Mr Fielding only had an MA degree he was appointed as one of my supervisors. I later discovered that he was studying for his own PhD at Rhodes University at the very time he was supervising my PhD. He enriched my thesis by advising me to ground it on mass communications and interpersonal theories, beyond just my Marxist approach to communication-for-development. However, it seemed to me that every time he learned something new from his professors at Rhodes he wanted to impose it on my thesis. In most cases these would be outdated communication theories that had no relevance to my work. We argued a lot about this and on many occasions Mavis Taylor had to intervene. Mavis, on the other hand, was fine because she was willing to learn and I spent many evenings at her house discussing the work of Augusto Boal on the theatre of the oppressed, Keir Elam on the semiotics of theatre, Penina Mlama, Chris Kamlongera and David Kerr on theatre-for-development in Africa. Even though I would have liked to discuss communications theorists – especially development communications theorists – with Mr Fielding, he didn't think it was necessary and never availed himself of the opportunity. I was fighting these battles at the university and would then return to fight other battles with a morose Adele.

My stay with Adele in Cape Town, however, was not only confined to the petty battles in my life. There were other bigger battles of national proportions. It was 1989 and the struggle was at a turning point in South Africa. We attended some of the rallies that were organised by the United Democratic Front in Cape Town. At one of these demonstrations we managed to march up to Greenmarket Square but the police sprayed the protesters with purple dye, giving birth to the slogan *The Purple Shall Govern*, a play on the words of the better known slogan *The People Shall Govern*. The intention of the police, of course, was to identify all the people who were stained purple as the culprits marching against the state and demanding the release of Nelson Mandela and other political leaders.

We were part of the thirty thousand plus who marched into Cape Town – the very first successful march into a major city by demonstrators. I could see the glint of pleasure in Adele's eyes as we sang and danced and marched in Adderley Street – the main street in Cape Town – as Desmond Tutu, Allan Boesak and Gordon Oliver led us to St George's Cathedral. Gordon Oliver was the liberal white mayor of Cape Town who had convinced the police to allow the march, hence our continuing right up to the Cathedral without being sprayed with purple rain.

We went back to Lesotho for Adele to attend her graduation ceremony and take up a new teaching job at a middle school in Thaba Nchu in the 'homeland' of Bophuthatswana – one of the reservations designated by the apartheid government as the natural home of black people where they could exercise their political rights. I had to return to Cape Town for an extended stay to complete the thesis, bind it and then submit it. Because I was going to be there for a few months it would have been too expensive for me to stay at the Serengeti apartments. My Afrikaner friend Ali Semmelink, who I had first met in Leribe, Lesotho, and had continued my friendship with him when he moved to Roma to teach at Christ the King High School, had now returned to Cape Town which was where he originally came from. He told me that his sister-in-law, Elsa Semmelink, who happened to be the daughter of arch-conservative white supremacist leader Andries Treurnicht, would help me find accommodation. Elsa, obviously a rebel who didn't share her father's political views, knew which hotels in the city would give accommodation to a black person. She located a nice hotel within walking distance of the Hiddingh Campus, the site of the Drama Department. This was rather expensive accommodation for me, as you can imagine, but fortunately Mavis Taylor came up with some money to assist me. She said it was from an anonymous donor who liked my work, but I suspected that it was really from her. I played along and asked her to thank the donor for me. Actually, I kissed the dear heart and asked her to transfer that kiss to the donor.

I completed the PhD at the end of that year. I was used to the American system where candidates had to defend their dissertations and was surprised to discover that there was no defence at all. I heard that Mr Fielding had not been happy with my final work because I had not used some of the theories he had suggested. But if the defence system had been applied I felt that I would have been able to argue my case quite effectively. However other committee members, those from the Drama Department, prevailed and on June 29, 1990, I walked on to the stage at Jameson Hall to be capped by Chancellor Oppenheimer. My mother was in the audience. So were my brother Zwelakhe, my sister Thami and my girlfriend Adele. Even from the stage I could see my mother's eyes gleaming with tears of pride. When the choir broke into *Gaudeamus Igitur* and the whole hall thundered into the commercium hymn that celebrates the bacchanalian mayhem of academic life, I knew I had arrived. Everyone in my party was visibly moved.

In the evening we went to Langa Township where one of my cousins, Zanemali Mtshula, had organised a very big party to celebrate my graduation. People from the township gathered in his small house and garden and speeches were made about how I was an inspiration to the youth to work hard and reach for the sky. It was wonderful to be among my mother's people and to meet a number of her relatives I knew nothing about. She sat there between Thami and Adele beaming with pride. My mother's people fell in love with Adele immediately. She was pleasant and beautiful and dutiful. They said: this is the right *makoti* for us; we look forward to the day you marry.

A few days later we drove back to Lesotho. The fourteen-hour road trip was just as enjoyable, with Zwelakhe having us in stitches with his humour.

But of course the fun had to end when we got back to Lesotho. It was back to the grind: me to the teaching job at the university, Adele to her teaching job in Thaba Nchu, Zwelakhe to his legal practice, Thami to her fashion designing and seamstress job, and my mother to her cafés in Mafeteng. We all went back to being ourselves.

A few months later I received a letter from the Vice-Chancellor of the National University of Lesotho, Professor Adamu Baikie. I had been promoted to a full professorship, even though I had not applied for the promotion. I was told that Baikie had argued at a Senate promotions meeting, and then at a Council meeting, that with all my publications and my performance as a teacher I should have been made professor a long time ago.

When the university did not renew Tom Lynn's contract for reasons that I never understood – Tom was one of the most valuable teachers I had ever known and he had also created an effective communications skills programme for first-year students – I was appointed head of the English Department. This was a position I had not asked for and did not relish. It made me an insider despite myself. It also interfered with my off-campus work with the Marotholi Travelling Theatre and the Screenwriters Institute. Before this promotion I had spent a lot of time in Germany, Spain, Denmark, France and the United Kingdom giving talks at universities and holding theatre workshops and seminars. Now all that would have to change. I would have to spend my life sitting in a gloomy office doing boring administrative work.

However, I still continued my work with UNICEF. For instance,

I attended one memorable event in Bamako, Mali, where African intellectuals and artists gathered to discuss child survival and development. In many ways it was reminiscent of the Harare Symposium that I have told you about, but with less star-power. What made it memorable for me was the round-table we had with Julius Nyerere who had just stepped down as president of Tanzania. When my turn came to give a talk and ask questions I commended Nyerere first for his literary work in translating some of Shakespeare's plays into Kiswahili, and secondly for his political work in supporting our liberation struggle in South Africa and for peacefully stepping down from power to let others take over the leadership in Tanzania. Then I asked him if he had any thoughts as to why his fellow heads of state in Africa were allergic to democracy, why they wanted to stay in power forever, and why there were so many coups where democratically elected governments were overthrown. Everybody around the table froze. This question obviously embarrassed Nyerere especially because at that moment he was sitting next to Moussa Traore, the president of Mali who had attained that position through a bloody coup. The Zimbabwean woman who was chairing the round-table unceremoniously moved to the next speaker.

As soon as I walked out of the room I was confronted, not by Traore's soldiers, but by journalists from Mali and other African countries who accused me of showing disrespect towards both Nyerere and Traore by asking Nyerere an embarrassing question. After that I was shunned by the delegates. No one wanted to talk to me, not even at a goat barbecue in a remote village where we had been taken to witness some wonderful traditional performances. Instead, they abandoned me in that village while I was talking to some kids. Fortunately I got a ride from a Frenchman who was passing through. The next day when they saw me at the hotel they pointed fingers at me.

'That's him,' I heard a journalist say. 'That's the guy who asked our Mwalimu rude questions.'

'Didn't you say you left him behind at the village last night? How did he get here?' asked his friend.

'I don't know. But he deserved worse for insulting President Traore like that.'

Right there and then I knew why Africa was in such deep trouble.

On my return to Lesotho I went straight to Mafeteng because I wanted to share my Malian experience with my father. I found that he was busy with a visitor I had not met before, but I had heard that he often infiltrated the country from his headquarters in Tanzania to consult with my father. He was Sabelo Pama, the commander of the Azanian People's Liberation Army – which you may remember as the armed wing of the Pan Africanist Congress. I knew that he was trying to lure my father into relocating to Tanzania to deal with the crises in the PAC leadership and perhaps take over as president, which would certainly have been welcomed by all the members of that organisation. I also knew that Sabelo Pama would fail because my father had made up his mind a long time ago that he would rather be the 'back-room boy' of the political struggle, by which he meant the thinker who gave those in the forefront ideological direction.

People were always trying to lure my father into taking more prominent positions than his humility allowed him. I knew, for instance, that for many years successive Lesotho governments had been knocking at his door trying to persuade him to become the Chief Justice of Lesotho. He always politely turned down such requests.

When Sabelo Pama stayed at my home in Mafeteng he was treated just like us kids. He performed chores like all of us and was yelled at by my father as if he was his own kid. I, on the other hand, was in awe of this young man who had so much power that he sent men and women to kill and be killed. He held meetings with my father into the night on military strategies, but during the day he was just like one of us kids. When my father went to hide himself from his clients at *Ntate* Hani's restaurant Sabelo carried his bag for him. He sat there and had food and cold drink while my father attended to his chamber work. I wondered what would happen if Chris Hani came in and found Sabelo Pama sitting there in his father's restaurant. What would these guerrilla leaders of rival forces talk about?

I was able to talk briefly with my father to tell him about Mali. He thought my sentiments were correct but that I was tactless in expressing them. You don't tell a dictator to his face in his own country, where he has the power of life and death over you, that he was allergic to democracy, especially when you are a stranger in that country. But he commended me for taking a position fearlessly. I thought he was contradicting himself but I said nothing about it.

He congratulated me on my latest book, *The Plays of Zakes Mda*, published by Ravan Press, but did not mince his words about the Introduction by Professor Andrew Horn. You may remember Horn as the academic whose place I took at the National University of Lesotho who had also founded the theatre-for-development project there. Horn wrote that my work questioned the basic tenets of the PAC as represented by my father who had 'joined Anton Muziwakhe Lembede in resisting the dominant ANC trend towards a class analysis of South African society, and promoted a rather narrower race-based pan-Africanism, much influenced by Marcus Garvey, within the ANC Youth League'.

This, of course, did not accurately represent my father's politics and I could understand his anger. My father believed that in a free and democratic South Africa there would be only one race, the human race. He spoke of non-racialism as opposed to multi-racialism long before it became the trend in South Africa and wrote against 'narrow nationalism'. Race as defined by the social engineers of the apartheid state came into play when he discussed the intersections of class and race. Even ardent Communist leaders like John Motloheloa came to him for his class analysis of the South African situation. Although I am not an authority on my father's writings, as people like Robert Edgar and Luyanda ka Msumza are, I'll be so bold as to say Marcus Garvey never featured in any of them. Well, in all our meetings I had never heard him mention Garvey even once. To make sure I was not wrong about this I asked Luyanda ka Msumza, one of the young leaders who used to be mentored by my father and was with him a lot of the time, who angrily shot back in an email:

This is garbage of the century . . . AP's Nationalism is well articulated in two statements, 'African Nationalism: is it a Misnomer?' and a series of articles published in *Inkundla* entitled 'African Nationalism'. I think he published two or three in a series. AP's

African Nationalism is very clear and unambiguous but liberals and radical liberals (Communists) find his positions too correct [*I am not sure what Luyanda means here*]. AP's positions debunk their non-scientific *and* dogmatic approaches. In articulating his brand of African Nationalism he actually pooh-poohs Marcus Garvey's notion of 'Back to Africa' and 'Drive the White Men out of Africa'. These scholars know that, they deliberately seek to demean AP and African Nationalism and Pan Africanism.

It suffices to say my father's Pan-Africanism was inclusive rather than narrow.

'I respect the rigorous research of American academics,' my father told me, 'but this Andrew Horn is a disappointment.'

I knew that when he was talking of American academics he meant Gail Gerhart and Robert Edgar who had researched his life and politics extensively.

I apologised for Horn's inaccurate descriptions. I felt guilty because they were in my book. I feared that he would never be proud of that book because it contained such inaccurate statements about him. I felt like a traitor.

While in Mafeteng I paid a visit to Mpho who was running a chicken farm in one of the townships. My father had given me a piece of land that he had bought some years back, hopefully to build his own house but decided against it. I had built a house on the land and established the chicken farm, as my father had done before me when I was a kid back at KwaGcina in the Eastern Cape. But this one was not a hatchery like his. Mpho ordered day-old chickens, raised them for eight weeks and then sold them as broilers. I saw that the business was not doing badly, though it would bring better returns if she extended it and ordered more day-olds. We discussed our divorce. We had separated years ago; it was high time that we were officially divorced.

And indeed we were. It was a very amicable divorce presided over by the Chief Justice of the High Court of Lesotho, Mr Justice Peter Brendan Cullinan. Lawyers on both sides were family friends. On her side was Attorney Winston Churchill Matanzima Maqutu and on my side was Advocate Semapo Peete. The hearing did not last more than fifteen minutes. The judge gave me the custody of the three minor children with reasonable access to their mother. But he added a clause where he gave 'care and control of the children to the parents of the plaintiff'. I was the plaintiff. The house and the chicken farm went to Mpho. All these arrangements were amicably agreed upon even before the hearing, which merely formalised them.

Even after the divorce I was still in a pickle with women. I saw myself as an utter failure in relationships. Adele worked more than a hundred kilometres away in Thaba Nchu. I had given her my Toyota Corolla and she could drive to Maseru any time she felt like it. But it was obvious that neither of us saw any future in our relationship, so she stayed away for most of the time.

However, I was able to spend more time with Gugu, not only at our Jerusalema this time; she also visited my house in Florida. I often sent my driver, *Ntate* Lelosa, to pick her up from Roma to spend the weekend with me.

One thing about Gugu was that she hated cigarette smoke so every time I wanted to smoke I had to go outside. This was too much trouble for me so I decided to stop smoking altogether. This was a year after I stopped drinking. Oh, I didn't tell you that on New Year's Eve in 1989 I had drunk myself to an utter stupor, hoping that after a serious hangover on New Year's Day I would be so sick that I would hate liquor and therefore stop drinking altogether! And indeed it happened that way. It would not be accurate to say that I hate alcohol, though; I am actually a wine collector. I just don't drink it myself. Now, thanks to Gugu, it was time to give up another vice. For her I stopped smoking and have never touched a cigarette with my lips again.

On February 11, 1990, Nelson Mandela was released from prison. We watched on television as he walked out of Victor Verster Prison hand in hand with Winnie Mandela. Other stalwarts of the liberation struggle such as Govan Mbeki, Walter Sisulu and Ahmed Kathrada had been released a few months earlier. We were moving towards achieving what we had been fighting for for so many years. Gugu went home to Soweto to visit, taking her friend Xoliswa Vumazonke with her. When she came back after the brief holiday she was excited because she had met Nelson Mandela who was her neighbour in Orlando West. This was before Mandela moved to the formerly all-white suburbs. She had shaken his hand and joked that she felt the 'Madiba magic' running through her arm like an electric current.

By this time I was spending so much time with Gugu that I was convinced she was the woman I was going to marry. We looked out for each other as good couples did. When I was worried that I was getting vitiligo because I developed some white spots on my body she took me to a Nigerian doctor at Queen Elizabeth II Hospital who had made claims to the invention of a concoction that banished that skin disorder. Even though the doctor was working for a government hospital he charged privately for this remedy. It tasted like Beano, and I think it was a scam. I only took it once and then dumped it in the dustbin. The white spots disappeared on their own. I, in turn, took Gugu to Ingo's mom when she was bothered by period pains. Ingo was a young German man who repaired televisions and installed aerials in Maseru. His mother made claims that she could cure most ailments using herbs that she got from the Bavarian forests. She had also learnt a few tricks from Basotho herbalists. We sat with Ingo's mom on her veranda as she prepared her medicine. She advised Gugu to wear only cotton underwear, which she did in any case. When we got home Gugu tasted the mixture and it was awful. We poured it down the drain.

So, you see, we have had our share of herbalists and their concoctions.

Alas, that year Gugu completed her degree and went back to Soweto. We spoke on the phone occasionally. Then she got a teaching job at Mhlosheni in Swaziland, at the high school where she had done her Cambridge Overseas School Certificate. I once drove to Swaziland, my first and only visit to that country, to see her. Her house was on the campus of a very strict Protestant mission school and I spent the two days hiding in her bedroom so as not to be seen by the school authorities. Her mother, Josephine, came to see her and I had to sit quietly in the bedroom so as not to alert her to my presence. Remember, Josephine did not approve of our relationship from the day she got that telephone call from Adele claiming that Gugu was messing around with her husband. Thankfully, I was not discovered either by the school authorities or by Josephine before I drove back to Lesotho – after Gugu had taken me for a drive to see Mbabane and Manzini, the two bigger towns of Swaziland.

The following year I went to Durham, England, as a writer-in-residence at the Cathedral there. I was the guest of an organisation called Lesotho-Durham Link which was itself linked to the Anglican Church. My brief was to write a play that would be performed in the Norman Cathedral as part of its nine hundredth anniversary celebrations. I was based at St Chad's College just across the street from the Cathedral and I spent a lot of time taking long walks along the Wear River. It was during these walks that my character Toloki was born. This was after I had read J M Coetzee's *Age of Iron*, which had just been published. In this novel I fell in love with a character called Vercueil who had the 'stench of death'. I was fascinated just by that fact. I said to myself: if Coetzee can create a character that stinks like this, so can I. But mine, of course, had to stink for different reasons, while maintaining the important status of 'angel of death'. Mine would be a professional mourner. At the time I didn't know that there were cultures that have or had professional mourners. I thought I was inventing a new profession in the name of absurdity. I took pains to create the details of this character, even though I didn't have a story for him. I thought that one day I would use him in a play.

I wrote to Gugu constantly when I was in Durham, sending her humbug sweets which she liked very much. The British brands were much more minty and richer in flavour than the South African humbugs. I also sent her music cassettes and beautiful life-like bridal dolls that I discovered being sold from a wagon in the town square. She wrote to ask: 'Do these dolls mean what I think they mean?' She had decoded the message of the dolls and I responded positively. I waited for a *yes! yes!* for a long time, but all I got was silence.

I was supposed to be in Durham for a few months – I don't remember how many months exactly – but I cut my stay short because I developed an anal fissure and the British health system put me on a waiting list for months for the surgery. In the meantime the pain was killing me. I also received a letter from my mother telling me that Dini, my last born, was developing some behavioural problems. I flew back to Lesotho to address that, and then drove to Johannesburg for the surgery.

I completed the play I was supposed to write in Durham as soon as I was settled at Roma. It was a verse play titled *By Way of the Rock* loosely based on the history of the Durham Cathedral and the relations between that region and the Kingdom of Lesotho.

My return coincided with a period of great change in South Africa. Negotiations were going on between the apartheid government and the liberation movement for the establishment a new democratic non-racial and non-sexist South Africa. The *New Nation*, an independent newspaper edited by Zwelakhe Sisulu, one of the sons of Walter and Albertina Sisulu, organised a big writers' conference in Johannesburg at which South African writers, some of whom had been in exile for decades, were invited to participate. There were also writers from the African diaspora of Britain and the United States, and those writers and scholars who were in solidarity with our struggle from countries as far off as Japan. This was where I first met my friend Keiko Kusonose who is a professor of African literature at Kyoto Seika University. This was also where I first met young South African writers like Zaccharia Rapola and Raks Seakhoa who were on some of the organising committees of this conference. I had not known of them because my only contacts in South Africa were theatre practitioners like Gcina Mhlophe, Matsemela Manaka and Maishe Maponya. And of course the writers I met in Lesotho such as Ingoapele Madingoane and Duma ka Ndlovu.

I was accommodated at the Johannesburger Hotel in the city with other writers. The first thing I did was to phone Gugu in Swaziland. I wanted her to come and join me in Johannesburg to see some of the writers whose works she loved, such as Ngugi wa Thiong'o, Dennis Brutus, Ngugi wa Mirii, Lewis Nkosi and many others who were in South Africa for the first time. I had met most of these writers before in my travels abroad, but for South Africans it was a new experience. I phoned the office at Gugu's school, and the secretary answered. She told me Gugu was nearby and she called her to the phone. Gugu didn't sound pleased to hear from me.

'Hey, I am in Johannesburg at the *New Nation* Writers' Conference and I'd like you to come over and join me,' I said.

And then the line just went dead. She had hung up on me. I dialled again and once more the secretary answered.

'May I speak with Gugu?' I said.

The secretary hesitated a bit, and I could hear whispers in the background.

'She's not here,' the secretary said.

'But I was speaking with her only a few seconds ago,' I said.

The line went dead again.

I knew then that Gugu did not want to speak to me. There could be only one reason, she had found someone else and wanted to end our relationship. She didn't have the courage to tell me.

A fleeting thought crossed my mind: I could go to Swaziland and fight for her if my instinct that there was someone else was right. After what we had gone through, both the bad and the wonderful times, I would most likely prevail. But I certainly would not demean myself. I made a decision right then that I would let her go. I would not go to Swaziland to try to make her change her mind. Instead, I would go back to Lesotho and mend fences with Adele. Adele was a more solid, family-values person. She was also Willie's sister.

My sister Thami had a flat in Hillbrow at the time. It was only a few streets away from the Johannesburger Hotel. I skipped some of the conference events and visited her. I needed to speak to someone other than a bunch of writers. Thami liked Adele but had never met Gugu. When I told her what had happened between me and Gugu she said it served me right. She took it upon herself to call Adele even though I kept telling her that I didn't think she would want to have anything to do with me since our relationship had gone cold. I did not want to resuscitate a relationship with her on the rebound, but would rather wait until I returned to Lesotho.

'You and Adele were made for each other,' Thami said. 'She is family already; she's Willie's sister.'

I spoke with Adele on the phone and she said she would come to Johannesburg immediately. And indeed the next day she was there. We attended the sessions of the *New Nation* Writers' Conference together, and throughout that period she was a very pleasant and lovable person. She did not yell at me once or start a quarrel about some petty thing. We joined the writers' tours to Soweto and the surrounding informal settlements. Normally she was stern and unyielding, but in the city of lights she was relaxed as we goofed about in my hotel room.

A child was conceived at the Johannesburger Hotel.

After the conference I returned to the university at Roma. I had made up my mind that it was time to return to South Africa. I was only coming back to the university to serve my notice.

I applied for the job of Chief Executive Officer at the Community Arts Project in Cape Town which had been run by the famous cultural activist Mike van Graan, who had resigned to take on other challenges. I flew to Cape Town for an interview, which was successful. The *Weekly Mail* trumpeted my impending return with the headline: *Mda puts some snap into Cap. Playwright Zakes Mda is coming home to the city he loves – and bringing with him a wealth of knowledge on development theatre and some challenging new ideas for the Community Arts Project in Cape Town.*

You can understand then why I felt like an utter turncoat when it turned out that I would not be taking this job after all. The reason for disappointing the people of Cape Town who were so much looking forward to my taking the reins of this premier arts and cultural organisation was that I had received an invitation from the renowned historian Leonard Thompson to join his Southern African Research Program at Yale University as a Research Fellow. This came out of the blue because I had not applied for the position. But I could not turn Yale University down even though I loved Cape Town so much. So, with sadness, I wrote to Bulelani Ngcuka who chaired the board of trustees of the Community Arts Project informing him that I would not take up the position and apologising profusely for wasting their time.

I had just one more European trip before packing my bags for the United States of America. I accepted an invitation from Teresa Devant and Albio Gonzalez, who had since left Lesotho and returned to Sweden. Teresa was continuing with her work of producing and directing my plays in that country. On this occasion, through the auspices of the Swedish anti-apartheid movement, she invited me and Mandla Langa to tour Sweden. Mandla Langa was at the time representing the ANC in the United Kingdom. Teresa and Albio presented my play *The Road*, first at the Kulturhuset in Stockholm and then at the Backa Theatre in Göteborg.

One thing I remember about this tour was that at one time Mandla and I were stuck in Umea, which is in northern Sweden. Everything was covered in snow and we were marooned in our hotel rooms for days, cold and miserable. I joined Mandla in his room and watched him as he sat there and drank whisky. He was quite disgusted with me because I wouldn't join him in demolishing the bottle. He lamented the fact that I had changed from the brandy and beer swilling reprobate of his Maseru days.

I gained a lot of love and respect for Mandla in that hotel room. I discovered that he was quite a sensitive soul. I believe sensitivity is an essential ingredient for great art. Let me quote from a letter I once wrote to the writer Aryan Kaganof who had expressed embarrassment at being so sensitive that he had been hurt by some of my very mild criticism of his work:

Sensitivity is a baggage that comes with being an artist, Aryan. It is because of the very sensitivity that as an artist you observe and give us insight to things that other people take for granted. The more sensitive you are, the greater an artist you become. It comes with the job. And I suspect it makes one a better human being. Not necessarily a stronger human being but a better one; a more compassionate and caring one.

In that hotel room in Umea I discovered that this could easily apply to Mandla Langa, though not because of any criticism I had made of his work. He was just a sensitive soul generally. Maybe that's why he drank so much. One had to suppress the pain somehow, even if temporarily. Or one had to relieve it through some artistic expression.

We talked about our lives, our families, our loves and losses. In the name of the struggle he had gone through a lot of hardship and even lost his brother at the hands of his own comrades. Yet he continued with the struggle because it was bigger than him and his personal loss. Mandla sat there and cried. I admired him immensely as a hardened guerrilla fighter who nevertheless was sensitive enough to cry.

Those were some of the humbling moments of my journey. There would be many of them in the future. They could not but transform me. But none of them could completely fill the void. I returned to Lesotho after a successful tour of Sweden and after performances of my play that was well received by audiences. Yet the void continued.

Often on my way to see my children and my mother in Mafeteng I drove past the church by the highway. Already the walls of our Jerusalema were crumbling and the tree was beginning to go flaccid. I slowed down a bit, and wistfully recalled how it used to be.

CHAPTER ELEVEN

WE ARE ON THE road again. Gugu and I. To see the Bee People in the Eastern Cape and my mother in Lesotho as usual. We are still in the Gauteng Province, driving towards the border with the Free State Province when I stop under a highway bridge to pick up a hitch-hiker. I have this dangerous habit of giving rides to people stranded on the road, especially if they look indigent. I have been rightly warned against it by my family and friends, and I have often promised that I would stop doing it. The concerns for my safety are legitimate because we know of instances where motorists have been robbed and even killed by hitch-hikers. In this case, the hitch-hiker is a thirty-something white man, a bit unkempt though his blue jeans and shirt are clean. He is on a journey, yet he is not carrying a bag or anything else, which is rather unusual.

'Where to?' I ask.

'Welkom,' he says.

Welkom is a gold mining town many kilometres off the N1 freeway in a different direction from where we are going.

'We are taking the Bloemfontein route,' I tell him. 'But we can drop you off at Kroonstad.'

'Kroonstad will be fine,' he says. 'You'll have cut my feet still.'

Cut his feet? That's a Sesotho proverb for shortening someone's long journey by giving him a ride up to a point. And yet the man speaks with a heavy Afrikaans accent. He obviously has been interacting with the Sesotho language so much that he now subconsciously transliterates it into English, or perhaps into his native Afrikaans. I keep this observation to myself.

We are silent for some time as we drive into the Free State. In the rear-view mirror I can see that he has a startled expression and turns his gaze from the road to Gugu to me and then back to the road. After a while I ask him where he has come from and why he is hitch-hiking.

'I'm from Sun City,' he says.

I think he means the famous gaming resort in the North West Province and ask him if he has been gambling there and lost everything.

He chuckles and says, 'Gambling? I was serving a sentence.'

It turns out the Sun City he is talking about is the Diepkloof Prison in Johannesburg. He served fifteen years for killing his friend in a drunken brawl. He was released that morning without any money or any means of getting back to his home in Welkom, three hundred and fifty kilometres away. I can see that Gugu is worried; we have a killer in our midst. I give her hand a reassuring caress. The man has been honest enough to tell us that he has been in jail; I don't think he will kill us. He could have lied; he could have invented some mishap that portrayed him as a victim. I trust this man.

I am curious about prison life and how he coped there as an Afrikaner in an establishment with an overwhelming majority of black inmates.

He is reluctant to talk about his experiences there, except to say that he had never lived with blacks before but after fifteen years he has become one of them.

'In what respect?' I ask.

He does not respond, so I press on again, 'You've become one of them, you say. Is that good or bad?'

Still he does not respond. He only shakes his head. After a while he says, 'I don't know if my people are still there in Welkom. Or if they'll talk to me. No one ever came to see me in prison. I don't know if they want to see me,' he says.

Before I drop the man on the outskirts of Kroonstad I give him two hundred rands in bank notes. He is taken aback.

'Who are you, boss?' he asks.

'Never mind who I am. Just go and enjoy yourself, but don't kill anybody again.'

He is so moved that he wants to cry.

'I never had so much money in my life,' he says.

As I drive away he just stands there looking after my car as if mesmerised.

Gugu doesn't say a thing about any of this. She knows and accepts that's how I am. She herself is a giving person. If I were with Adele I wouldn't have been able to assist the hitch-hiker with money. Or I would have had to hand it to him furtively.

ADELE AND I WERE on a road trip to Mafeteng. We were going to inform my parents of our decision to marry. We were both ecstatic about it. I had banished all thoughts that our relationship had been largely toxic before this, and was looking forward to a happy future with her. She was the dark beauty who was carrying my child and I loved her. Also, she was a hard-working woman who would build our family. I was playful and whimsical; she had no time for frivolities. Maybe her sternness and serious approach to life was exactly what I needed to bring stability into my life. She was very nice to other people, and I had no doubt that she would learn to be nice to me too when she was secure in the knowledge that we were married. To crown it all, she was Willie's sister.

Somewhere between Bloemfontein and Wepener I saw an old couple and a boy standing on the shoulder of the provincial highway. The woman's *seshoeshoe* dress used to be blue, but had now become an uneven grey colour from the unforgiving sun. The old man's and the boy's khaki pants and shirts had patches of different coloured cloths. The three of them looked like farm labourers, perhaps from one of the farms through which the highway ran. The old lady feebly flagged down my car and I stopped. She came over and asked for a ride for the old man and his grandson. They were going to another farm in the Wepener area to attend the funeral of a relative and didn't have enough money for the bus. Although I could see in Adele's face that she was not happy about this, I gave them a ride. When we got to Wepener I bade them goodbye and good luck, and gave them a hundred rand note. The old man thanked me profusely. With eyes lifted to the heavens, he asked the Good Lord to shower me with more blessings.

'What did you do that for?' asked Adele as we drove towards the border post.

'Just a helping hand for the funeral,' I said.

'Whose funeral? You don't know those people.'

She was much more practical than I was. Much smarter. She was certainly going to bring stability and good judgement into my life.

'Yes, I don't know them, but that's not a good reason for not helping them.'

'So now you're a do-gooder bleeding-heart, are you? You are just doing it for your own selfish reasons, so that they can talk about you and spread the news that you gave them money. You're buying your own fame.'

She said this with so much venom that I was taken aback. And we had been so ecstatic just a few minutes before. Inwardly, I cursed myself for my habit of generosity to strangers. But still I had to defend myself.

'Buying fame, eh?' I asked. 'How is helping those people going to make me famous? They don't know who I am. I didn't give them my name; I don't see how they are going to spread it among the miserable farms where they work that I am a bleeding-heart.'

Although she was wrong about the fame part, her position was a rational one. You cannot dish out your money to all and sundry while you remain poor. Become Warren Buffett first, and then you can afford to be a philanthropist. In any case, as Oscar Wilde observed, philanthropy recreates the problem it tries to solve. But what the heck – I am a sucker, and happily so! It was also true that my generosity was for selfish reasons. I was not a true altruist because I got something back from giving – joy and satisfaction. It made my day when I made someone else's day. Just the look of utter amazement and thankfulness in the eyes of the receiver gave me something akin to an orgasm, although in this case it was not of a sexual kind. Let's call it a platonic orgasm. After an act of generosity I became effervescent for the rest of that day. So, you see, it was for my own happiness that I gave.

But that's not what I told her. I had to make peace with her before we got home to Mafeteng so I patiently explained to her that I gave for religious reasons. By giving, I was hoping that God would give me more. I was banking on the fact that she had no idea that I was an atheist. I was hoping as a Christian woman herself who professed the Catholic religion she would get off my back about doling out money. God can be a convenient tool even for atheists.

I reminded her of this sacred reason every time I got the urge to be generous to my fellow human beings in her presence, although in the long run she stopped buying it. I had to develop clandestine ways of generosity.

When we got to Mafeteng my father was watering his vegetable garden. We all went into the house and took our seats at his dining room table. My mother was not there. I think she was working at one of her two cafés. I announced to my father that Adele was pregnant and we had decided to marry. He congratulated us and then asked us to kneel down. The three of us went on our knees on the hard linoleum floor. He prayed, asking God to guide and protect us and the baby. We had his blessing to marry.

It was strange to see my father praying because he rarely did it.

Well, perhaps in private he prayed quite often, I wouldn't know about that. Although he never went to church – at least not since the days he was a teacher at St Teresa's Catholic Mission and conducted the church choir – he was clearly a believer. I remember on one occasion when I was about to undertake a long journey – perhaps it was when I went to America for the first time – we knelt down and he prayed for me.

When we left Mafeteng Adele was elated. She said that for the first time she felt welcome in my family, thanks to my father's prayer. On the road to Johannesburg I made certain that I didn't pick up hitch-hikers lest I spoil the good mood.

The following week we went to Leribe to the village in the hills where Adele was born. Her parents, *Ntate* Thesele and MaNhlapho, or Hlapho in short, were a wonderful loving couple who tilled the land and kept a few animals in the kraal in front of the homestead which comprised a rondavel and a flat-roofed house built of solid rock. Most of their livelihood came from the old-age pension they collected at the end of every month across the border in the South African town of Ficksburg. It was the same with thousands of citizens of neighbouring countries who survived on old-age and disability government grants meant for South Africans, but that the foreigners were able to access because they either once worked in South Africa and acquired the old South African reference books known as the *dompas* or had fraudulently obtained South African identity documents that qualified them for such pensions. *Ntate* Thesele and Hlapho fell in the former category; they once worked in South Africa in their youth, and now were part of the refrain that could be heard in the border towns of Lesotho and Swaziland, and to a lesser extent in Botswana: 'It's the end of the month; we're crossing the border to eat Mandela's money.' As a result they were quite well-off compared to their neighbours.

They were particularly proud that the wedding would be at their homestead.

On the wedding day a marquee was constructed in front of the homestead. That's where the wedding took place. Adele and I were dressed in isiXhosa traditional clothes: she was in a red *isikhakha* dress and a black *iqhiya* turban, and I was in black pants and a red Afro-shirt made from the rough calico of the *isikhakha* dresses, and embroidered with the black patterns that are normally found in *isikhakha*. The hundreds of villagers who gathered were astonished that Adele was not wearing the customary white with a veil and I was not in a stuffy suit.

I heard *Ntate* Thesele tell his friends, 'That's what I like about these Bathepu people, they are proud of their customs. Even when they are so highly educated like my son-in-law here they still wear their traditional clothes with pride.'

My Uncle Owen represented my father. He was the only member of my family who attended my wedding. My brothers and sister were not there. Even Zwelakhe whom I had personally invited in writing did not attend, nor did he respond to my letter or send a message of any kind. My mother was the only one who told me she would have come but her health was beginning to deteriorate. A number of my friends from Maseru and my colleagues from the university did attend though, and we all had a wonderful time with villagers performing traditional dances.

What impressed the guests most, besides our wedding attire, was the fact that we did not go to church to make the vows but the priest came to *Ntate* Thesele's homestead to officiate under the marquee.

'He must be a very important man, this man who is marrying Thesele's daughter, for the priest to come all the way from Maseru to conduct his marriage,' I heard one villager tell the others. They did not know that it was not because of me that the priest came. He was Adele's friend. The Reverend Father Khasoane was based at Our Lady of Victories Cathedral in Maseru but got permission from the Maryland parish under which Adele's village fell to conduct the wedding. What almost presented a problem, though, was the fact that I was a divorcee. As far as the Catholic Church is concerned once you are married you are married for ever. I was still married to Mpho in their eyes because they did not recognise our divorce.

'It doesn't matter,' I said to Adele. 'We can have our marriage solemnised by civil authorities. The District Administrator will gladly do it for us.'

But Adele didn't want a civil ceremony. She wanted to be married by a priest of the Roman Catholic Church. She was an ardent Catholic who had converted to that denomination for the purposes of schooling but became a true and firm believer in their doctrine in the process.

Fortunately Father Khasoane discovered a loophole in my first marriage. It had not been solemnised in the Catholic Church but by civil authorities. Mpho had not been a Catholic either but belonged to some Protestant church. Therefore the Catholic Church did not recognise it as a marriage at all. Presto, I had never been married before!

Father Khasoane looked beautiful in his white and gold Roman Catholic regalia when, on February 22, 1991, he solemnised the marriage of a happy couple in red traditional isiXhosa costumes under a marquee in a homestead in a remote Lesotho village.

Soon after the wedding I took Adele to Qoboshane village in the Eastern Cape to introduce her to my relatives. They knew her quite well because she had been there before. But now of course she was officially my wife so it was necessary that Uncle Press and his wife and my grandmother's people, the Mei family, meet her in her new status.

Adele, as a family-values person, was happy that I had taken this step. She was particularly pleased when they called her MaMiya. That was her clan name where she came from. It's always been like that with my people, and in fact with all the Nguni people of southern Africa. A woman was called by the clan name of her own father; she didn't adopt the clan name of the family into which she was marrying. The practice of women taking the surnames of their husbands was introduced to my people by the British with their patriarchal colonialism. Remember, we did not have surnames in the Western sense before we were colonised. Men were identified by both their fathers' names and their clan names. For instance, my great-great-grandfather was Mda son of Gatyeni, my great-grandfather was Feyiya son of Mda, my grandfather should have been Gxumekelana son of Feyiya, my father should have been Solomzi son of Gxumekelana, and I should have been Zanemvula son of Solomzi. The over-arching familial identity of all these generations would have been the clan name, the Cesane branch of the Majola House – uMajola kaCesane. But as you can see, we got stuck with the

Mda surname – and some of our relatives got stuck with the Gatyeni surname – when the British forced us to have the kind of surnames that they could understand, that were passed from generation to generation.

Similarly, the wives had to come from different clans, and they kept their clan names in marriage. After colonisation the British made laws that forced women to adopt their husband's surnames. But my people retained the practice of calling the women by their clan names and it continues to this day. That was why my relatives in the villages called Adele by her clan name, MaMiya. This was an indication to Adele that they gave her full recognition and honoured her as a daughter-in-law of the Majola kaCesane clan.

Back in Maseru, a pregnant Adele was the sweetest person ever. We became inseparable and walked in town hand in hand. I had found happiness at last and the void had been filled. I was never ever going to be unfaithful to her, and I was happy that she was always around.

Even when I went to rehearsals of a one-man play I had written and was directing, *In Celebration of our National Arrogance*, she was with me.

The play looked at the corruption in the public sector in Lesotho and the culture of impunity that resulted in the second highest per capita number of road accidents in Africa. I had written it especially for Lesotho's premier actor of the time, Gonzalez Scout, who performed it to music provided by guitarist Mafata Lemphane – who has since emigrated to Canada – or sometimes to Sam Moeletsi's piano. Sam Moeletsi was a well-known piano teacher in Maseru. In my work as director of this play I was assisted by my old friend 'Maseabata Ramoeletsi, who stage-managed it and also acted more in a producer capacity. I had been close to 'Maseabata from the time she was with Meso Players, Teresa Devant's group that specialised in my plays. Another person who became quite close to me was Deborah Mpepuoa Mokitimi. She had assisted me in my office at the Screenwriters Institute. I used to hang out with her a lot, and enjoyed her company. She had a lot of stories to tell about her neighbours and friends, some of which found their way in the early novels that I was to write. I later learnt that Deborah was the daughter of Kittyman, my protector from savage ill-treatment at Peka High School. That brought me even closer to her.

I never noticed any jealousy from Adele about my association with these women. I took it that she understood that I had a history with them, and what brought us together was nothing more than theatre.

She was still teaching at Thelejane Middle School in Thaba Nchu, but we spent every weekend with each other, alternating between Maseru and Thaba Nchu.

The baby was born at Pelonomi Hospital in Bloemfontein. We named him Zukile, an isiXhosa name whose meaning combined 'serenity', 'tranquillity' and 'grace'. I was pleasantly surprised at the kindness of the nurses at this public government hospital. I was used to the nurses in Lesotho who were always rude and talked to patients, especially to birthing mothers, in a rough and inconsiderate manner. If a woman as much as moaned during the process of giving birth they yelled at her, 'You shut up; we were not there when you were enjoying it. Didn't you know that the child comes out where it got in?' But in South Africa things were different. The nurses were very kind, and everyone went out of their way to be helpful. And they didn't even know who we were. It was just their regular kindness and compassion.

A few days later, after transporting my books and some household effects to Adele's home in Leribe where her father had offered to store them for us, I flew to the United States to join the Southern African Research Program at Yale University. I was not alone. I was with Dini, the youngest of my three kids with Mpho.

I MISSED ADELE TERRIBLY when I was at Yale. In my basement apartment in New Haven, Connecticut, I wrote her anguished letters professing my love for her and how life was impossible without her. She responded with her own letters, also professing her love for me and how she and the baby missed me. All this was snail mail correspondence because it was before the prevalence of email. I looked forward to the day she was going to join me in a few months' time. She had a few things to do first in Lesotho, such as selling my truck which I had bought for my business at the Screenwriters Institute and raising money for her ticket and Zukile's. I felt guilty that I could not help her with all these tasks, but she was a strong and resourceful woman and I knew she would cope.

My anxieties were relieved by the demands of the Program. There were a number of scholars in various fields attached to it, and every Wednesday we gathered under the chairmanship of Leonard Thompson and critiqued that week's presentations. These were papers that were assigned to us the previous Wednesday. I enjoyed discussing papers by such organic scholars as Achmat Davids who wrote extensively on the origins of the Afrikaans language. I marvelled at the copies of old documents with the first ever Afrikaans text – written in Arabic script. It was, of course, written by the early Cape Malay scholars who were Muslims.

One thing that made Achmat Davids even more attractive was that he had a wife who simply loved to entertain. She cooked some of the most wonderful Cape Malay dishes that titillated our taste buds and sent our collective imagination wafting to the Cape Town suburb of Bo-Kaap where they had their home. Scholars of the Program looked forward to Mrs Davids's invitations. So did Dini, who became their regular visitor.

One thing that Leonard Thompson's Program taught me was robust and rigorous multidisciplinary scholarship. I am normally not forthcoming in a big group of people where I am called upon to criticise others; I simply hate to hurt people's feelings in public. I have always lived in my own namby-pamby-land and am comfortable there, thank you. But at Yale the environment encouraged brutal frankness and I relished the challenge. After all, I was my father's son and he was known not to suffer fools gladly. I hated it when this characterisation was used with regard to me and therefore chose to withdraw into my cocoon. Until the Program forced me to come out.

I remember on one occasion when I was the main discussant for Colin Bundy's submission – a number of chapters which were part of the biography he was writing of Govan Mbeki. You may know Colin as the eminent historian and Rhodes Scholar who is currently the Principal of Green Templeton College at the University of Oxford. At the time he was based at the University of the Witwatersrand in Johannesburg.

I went to town on his paper because just as we were about to sit down for the seminar he whispered to me: 'I hope you didn't find my paper onerous.' I thought that was rather patronising and I said to myself: *Onerous? I'll show him onerous.*

My role at the seminar was to provide an assessment of the paper, raising questions that would stimulate debate. First, I noted that Colin's was a very interesting study and I enjoyed reading it tremendously. It certainly would be a valuable contribution not only to our understanding of some aspects of the South African situation, but also to the body of work of the 'life-history' genre, which in South Africa was dominated by autobiography rather than biography. But I went on to point out that throughout the paper, which was supposed to be on the childhood and education of Govan Mbeki, I looked very hard for Govan Mbeki but did not find him. For most part, the paper presented a sketch rather than a portrait of Mbeki. Colin told us of African education in the Cape in the early twentieth century, and gave us a well-researched picture of various institutions, but there was very little about the man and his interaction with those institutions. Mbeki was not foregrounded in relation to the institutions, even though this was supposed to be about his life, and not that of Healdtown or Fort Hare.

Most of the weaknesses of this paper, I asserted, were due to the fact that Colin was dealing with a period of childhood which would present any biographer with problems in selection and interpretation. He depended solely on literature and archival material for his sources, and as could be expected there was very little on Mbeki's childhood from such sources. Oral reminiscences could be effective, I pointed out, if one was able to sift mythology from fact. I advised him to use the techniques of participant-observer in addition to historical record. After all, some of Mbeki's peers and contemporaries were still alive at the time.

I felt that the paper was an over-impersonal treatment of Mbeki since Colin did not recreate his private life. The biography was therefore more of a study of the period than of the man. Critical debates as to whether formal biography should include little homely details were settled in the seventeenth century, and since then it had become the practice even in political biographies to present the subject as a rounded character. Mbeki was a public man, but he still had aspects of a private life that impacted on the public life. He was a political animal, but he was not the one-dimensional figure that was being portrayed by Colin. He too was once a child with a childhood and a mother who played a role in his life. He fell in and out of love, and suffered all the petty pleasures and pains of daily life.

Colin was visibly shaken. I think I had savaged him too much and I felt very bad about that. After my presentation no one else had anything to say. Even the most argumentative scholars were silent. When we were walking out of the building Leonard Thompson congratulated me and said mine was the best critique of biography they had ever heard at the Southern African Research Program. I didn't thank him for the compliment because I didn't understand why he was telling me this privately and hadn't said it at the seminar. But as I walked home I cursed myself: I had acquired the pettiness of scholars. I was one of them now and was just as obnoxious and vindictive as the best of them. I would rather be an artist than an academic. I would rather create than destroy others as scholars are wont to do.

A few days later Colin asked for my notes and I made copies for him of all twenty handwritten pages.

Scholars from elsewhere sometimes attended our seminars. Among them were Simphiwe Hlatshwayo, with whom I was a student at Ohio University, and Mbulelo Mzamane of my old Maseru days. Simphiwe was a professor at some university in Pennsylvania – I just forget which one now – and Mbulelo was a professor at the University of Vermont. Steve Kalamazoo Mokone also came to visit. He was a professor of psychology at the University of Rochester, but was better known as the first black South African to play professional soccer in Europe in the 1950s. He played variously for teams in Barcelona, Italy, England and Holland. A street is named after him in Amsterdam. He was quite a sensation with many hat-tricks to his name. Towards the end of his

375

career he played for teams in Australia and Canada and then moved to the United States where he was arrested at his Rutgers University office and served nine years in jail for domestic violence. He was keen that I write a movie script about his life.

One of the regulars at our seminars was Bethany Yarrow. She had the most beautiful eyes I had ever seen on any human being and was dazzling overall. A friendship developed between us and I spent many a magical evening at her apartment. It was a platonic yet intoxicating relationship, at least for me. My days as a philanderer were over; I loved Adele and wanted my marriage with her to work. So, I sat in Bethany's bedroom and admired her collection of paintings that she brought with her from Cape Town. She herself was a painter and a film-maker. She inspired me to paint again after many years and I created many pastel works with her.

Bethany invited me to her elegant home in Manhattan, New York, and introduced me to her father, Peter Yarrow. I remembered him from the days of Peter, Paul and Mary, and he was amused when I told him that 'Puff the Magic Dragon' was one of my all-time favourite songs. There is something beautifully sentimental about it. He reached for his guitar and played the song for me. But of course without Mary and Paul it was different. But I was happy to have had a command performance just for me by one of the three greatest folk music heroes of all time. Well, at least in my estimation!

Sometimes Bethany would have screenings of her films in her father's living room. After she completed editing a documentary she had shot in Cape Town titled *Umama Awethu* she invited me to one such screening. I in turn invited Steve Kalamazoo Mokone thinking that he would enjoy seeing some aspects of South Africa on the screen since he had not been in the country for decades. The movie was set in some informal settlements in Cape Town and looked at how women coped despite the problems of poverty and apartheid oppression.

As we walked to the subway after the screening Kalamazoo expressed his unhappiness with the film. Not the quality or the production. It was quite good, he said. But he despaired at the fact that portrayals of South Africa in the West, even by such liberal and radical film-makers as Bethany, had prevarications. All they ever showed were 'squatter camps', poverty and suffering. No other aspects of South Africa were ever shown. One wouldn't know that there were clean and beautiful cities in South Africa that compared with any in the Western world, and middle-class black folks who drove luxury cars and lived in posh houses in such townships as Dube Village and Diepkloof Extension. Even in the ordinary townships and villages of South Africa people lived, laughed, sang and danced. Kalamazoo told me that he was done with watching such films because they reinforced the American stereotype of South Africa. You see one of them, you have seen them all. The message was a simple one: the whole of South Africa was one massive squatter camp.

I apologised for having invited him. I could see his point, though in Bethany's defence she made a film about a subject that touched her most – women's resilience in the face of adversity.

I met Kalamazoo a few more times during my stay in New Haven. I was writing a film script about his life and I visited him and his wife Louise at their New Jersey home to get more material, especially the documents pertaining to his court case and prison term. I had interested some folks at 40 Acres and a Mule Filmworks, Spike Lee's production company in New York, in taking a look at it. A soccer movie, they thought, might sell well to investors since the FIFA World Cup was going to be held in the USA in three years' time, in 1994. Alas, Kalamazoo read the first draft and was very unhappy with the manner in which I portrayed him. I was interested in a story of a fall from grace and then redemption; he wanted me to paint him as a hero through and through who was a victim of the system and didn't have any flaws of his own. I gave up on the project, and our relationship soured.

Every time I went to New York I had to return to New Haven the same night because I had left Dini alone. Although he was fifteen years old I didn't think he could cope on his own.

I had rented a piano and enrolled him for piano lessons. He was doing well at school, although he was struggling with spoken and written English. He had spent all his life attending schools where Sesotho was the language of instruction in the early grades. But unfortunately I couldn't afford to get him a tutor. With the measly stipend Yale was giving me I could barely survive. As was always the case when finances were tight, I fell back on my paintings. I found a gallery in a sombre part of New Haven that was willing to exhibit them and sell them on my behalf for a percentage of the price.

After I had taken the paintings to the gallery I didn't hear from them for a few weeks. I took a bus to the suburb where the gallery was located and found that it was closed. Through the window I could see my paintings displayed all over the shop. I went there many times, but the gallery was still closed. I was not going to give up, however, because my valuable paintings were in that shop. One day a passer-by told me that the owner of the gallery had gone bankrupt and it would not open again.

How the hell was I going to get my pictures? I had no contact information other than the physical address of the gallery and the telephone number. I didn't even know the name of the owner. I stood there for a long time looking longingly at my paintings. Some of them were intaglio that I had done almost ten years before when I was a student at Ohio University. I would never be able to create those again.

I was sitting on a bench at the bus stop waiting for the bus and brooding about my paintings when a well-dressed and well-groomed African American gentleman sat down next to me.

'You are not from here,' he said.

Normally people could tell from my accent but I had not uttered a word. And my manner of dress was not different from that of the natives.

'How did you know?' I asked.

'You smiled,' he said. 'You looked at me and smiled. Black folks here don't smile. They carry a big chip on their shoulder. They think smiling is a sign of weakness.'

I had been so deep in the doldrums I had not been aware that I had smiled at him.

Letters from home were always a source of great joy, especially those from my mother and my children. My daughter Thandi was at Bereng High School in Mafeteng, still staying with my parents. She was seventeen years old. My son Neo was at FUBA Academy in Johannesburg studying visual arts. He was nineteen. He was staying with my sister Thami in her flat in Hillbrow. Thami was working for the mining company Anglo American at the time. I was getting letters from her that the boy was giving her many problems and that I was not sending enough money for his support. And this was true. Some months I didn't send any money because I didn't have any. She couldn't understand how it was possible not to have money when I was working in America. I couldn't understand it either, but there it was, long before the end of the month the Yale stipend was gone. People who knew said I should have negotiated a better deal for myself before accepting their offer. I was so dumb I didn't know one could negotiate about these things.

One question I dreaded in my mother's letters: *Have you found Sonwabo yet?* I had not found him. You will remember that he left almost ten years before for Ohio University, and never returned. None of us, including his wife and four beautiful children, had heard from him for years. I contacted people I knew in Athens, Ohio, and they told me that he was indeed once there but he left before completing his degree. They had no idea where he had gone. Cosmo Pieterse, the Namibian/South African playwright teaching in the English Department at Ohio University, told me that to his knowledge Sonwabo had been an ANC activist in America and after the release of Nelson Mandela and the return of exiles he was recalled to South Africa by the ANC. I contacted Lindiwe Mabuza, who was the ANC's United States representative, but she knew nothing about him. Thobeka Mda, one of the lovely daughters of the highly esteemed lawyer Mda Mda, had met him when she was doing her PhD at Ohio State University. At least that gave me some idea that he was somewhere in the Columbus area. I used the missing persons bureau of the Salvation Army who tried their best but came back with the response that they were able to find only those people who wanted to be found. I informed my mother of all these attempts. In one of her letters she pleaded: *Please, Zani, try very hard to find my son. I must see him before I die.* I wrote back to say: *Come on, mama, you're not going to die any day soon. You will see your son before then.*

I enjoyed letters from my friend 'Maseabata. I had left her in

Lesotho managing Gonzalez Scout in our one-hander, *In Celebration of Our National Arrogance*. Now Gonzalez was at Durham to complete my residency there. He was rehearsing my Durham play, *By Way of the Rock*, which he was going to perform in the Cathedral as part of the nine hundredth anniversary celebrations of that majestic Norman building. Scout was bombarding me with letters about the lousy time he was having. 'Maseabata on the other hand had also moved to Britain, not for theatre this time but to study for a master's degree in pharmacy. She wrote about her experiences in England and how she missed theatre.

The greatest source of joy, however, was the arrival of Adele and Zukile. I couldn't contain myself when I took a train from New Haven to meet them at JFK Airport. The boy was only two months old and looked very much like me in pictures when I was that age. I made up my mind that with this kid and any other kids I had with Adele I would never again be an absentee father. I would make up for all the sins I committed in bringing up my older kids, who had very little of my guidance. I would be a hands-on father. I would also be a loving and faithful husband.

Although this was the first time she had been in the United States, it didn't take much time for Adele to adjust and settle. I had made it clear to her even before she came that our living conditions would not be the same as in Lesotho where I had a big four-bedroom house provided by the university and servants who cleaned and cooked – though even in Lesotho I preferred to do my own cooking. She therefore didn't complain about the basement apartment. Though it was small it was like a love nest for us. We were happy. I told her once that I was the happiest I had ever been in my life. Not only did I have a beautiful family, but I was also having a fulfilling time at Yale, writing and presenting papers that were critiqued by my peers at the weekly seminars. I had just presented a paper titled 'Politics and the Theatre: Current Trends in South Africa' and *Theater*, the prestigious journal of the Yale School of Drama and Yale Repertory Theatre, was keen to publish it. The seminars inspired more creativity in me.

Up to that point I had written all my papers and plays in longhand, and then typed them later or gave them to someone else to type for me. I could never compose on the typewriter. It was necessary to draft something first and then type it. I had never used a computer either, although it was 1992 and the whole world was already computer literate. I decided that it was high time I got into the technological age. Actually, this decision was brought about by the fact that I saw in a student newspaper an advertisement for a used computer that a student was selling. I immediately phoned and asked her to deliver it to my apartment.

It was an old IBM computer that took up all the space on my desk. But it still had its manual which would be helpful in my learning how to use that monster of a machine.

On Christmas Day that year my wife went to church about two streets from our apartment. I was home with four-month-old Zukile. Dini was visiting friends. Since the baby was not giving me any problems, I thought perhaps I could fiddle about with my computer and learn how it worked. With the baby on my lap, I read the manual for a program called WordPerfect and then pecked at the keys with my two middle fingers. It was easy enough. The first sentence I wrote was: *There are many ways of dying.* I didn't know where it came from but I liked it. Since it was about death it brought to my mind the character I had created when I was a writer-in-residence at the Cathedral in Durham – Toloki, the Professional Mourner. I had initially planned to use him in a future play, but what the heck, whatever it was that I was writing demanded his presence. But whose death would he be mourning? Duh! The deaths that were prevalent at that time in South Africa.

It was during the period of transition and we read in the papers of senseless killings that were happening all over the country: gunmen would walk on to trains and mow down everyone with AK47s; in the townships hostel dwellers supporting the predominantly Zulu Inkatha Freedom Party marched down the streets beating up people and killing those suspected of being Xhosas, and by implication ANC supporters; and many other incidents of what was termed black-on-black violence. Later, it was discovered that most of the violence was instigated and supported by the apartheid state to derail the changes that were sweeping the country. Those were deaths that were ready-made for Toloki the Professional Mourner.

By the time Adele came back from church I had the first two pages of what became my first novel, *Ways of Dying*. I was amazed at myself because I never thought I could write sustained prose and be descriptive. As a playwright I was a dialogue person. I had written a PhD thesis (that's what it's called at South African universities, not a dissertation) that was mostly descriptive, but it had not been easy going. Actually, it had been agony writing that thesis in hotel rooms in Cape Town. I never thought I would want to write anything akin to prose ever again. But there they were: my first two pages of creative prose! And all those sentences had come in such a playful manner, with Zukile in his baby talk taking part in the conversation I was having with the IBM monster, and with the words as they flowed so easily. Even the bells that were ringing, presumably at Adele's church, found their way into those first two pages. The events of the fiction were happening on Christmas Day because I was writing them on Christmas Day. And, wonder of wonders, for the first time in my life I had composed something directly on a keyboard without drafting it first!

As I continued writing what I had then decided was going to be a novel, I was surprised by the fact that I enjoyed the actual process of writing prose. I looked forward to waking up in the morning and sitting at the computer interacting with my characters. When I was writing plays I never enjoyed the writing process. It used to be agony, and then there would be relief and fulfilment when I got to the final period. But in that basement apartment writing *Ways of Dying* was sheer ecstasy.

I went to the library at the university to peruse South African newspapers – the *City Press* and the *Sunday Times*. I read about the horrendous deaths that were happening in my country. It seemed South Africa was slowly killing itself. Then I went back to my basement apartment and recreated those deaths. Every death Toloki mourns in my novel was a real death that I read about or I knew about personally because it affected family or friends. The very first death in the novel was based on an incident when my Cousin Nobantu, Uncle Owen's daughter, went in search of the corpse of her brother who had met a violent death, and she finally found him being buried by another family elsewhere.

After I had written the first chapter I mailed it to my mother in Lesotho and gave another copy to Adele. I watched her read it expressionlessly and I waited anxiously for her feedback. She shook her head as she gave me back the copy.

'This is useless,' she said.

'What exactly is useless?' I asked.

'This whole chapter.'

'Everything about it?'

'It has too many characters. No one will want to read this stuff. If only you wrote like Mbulelo Mzamane.'

Mbulelo Mzamane was her favourite writer. She had read his short story collections, *Mzala* and *My Cousin Comes to Jo'burg*, over and over again.

I continued to write, but I did not try to write like Mbulelo Mzamane. I could only be myself. And I didn't give my chapters to Adele again. A few weeks later I got a response from my mother. She enjoyed the chapter. She particularly loved the character I had invented, Toloki the Professional Mourner. She also felt affection for Noria and hoped that I would foreground her more. I sent her every chapter I wrote and she sent me her feedback. I felt as if I was writing this novel for her. When I created an event or a character I caught myself saying: *I think my mother will like this*, or *Let me use this or that expression because it will make my mother laugh.*

I had never written a novel before, so feedback was crucial. Perhaps that is why workshops serve such an important function. I had no workshop to resort to. In fact I had never been to a single workshop all my life – except the one I have told you about that was conducted by Rutgers Professor Marc Crawford in Lesotho. That was why I took the first three chapters with me when I went to France to speak and read at the Grand Amphitheatre at the Sorbonne University with a number of South African writers such as Nadine Gordimer, André Brink, Zoë Wicomb, Wally Serote, Peter Horn and Malcolm Purkey. Afterwards, Mike Nicol and I went on a train journey to Grenoble where Jacques Alvarez-Pereyre had invited us to attend some events.

In the train I gave the manuscript to Mike Nicol who showed so much enthusiasm for it that he asked if he could publish the first chapter in a journal called *New Contrast* which he was editing. He also advised me to go easy on the adjectives and rather use adverbs if I needed modifiers at all. That was my first lesson in creative writing.

In Grenoble, Jacques read the manuscript and dismissed it outright, saying, 'It's a pity because you are such a wonderful playwright.'

My first attempt at novel-writing was getting mixed reviews. But I had faith in what I was doing. I was going to go with my mother and with Mike Nicol.

I completed the novel on April 1, 1993. All Fools Day!

The completion of my first novel, and its positive reception by my colleagues at the Yale weekly seminars, seemed to me to be cause for celebration.

And then I heard on the *MacNeil/Lehrer NewsHour* on PBS that Chris Hani was dead. He had been assassinated by two right-wingers, Polish immigrant Janusz Walus and Conservative Party Member of Parliament Clive Derby-Lewis. I saw Tokyo Sexwale in a tracksuit in front of Hani's house. He was crying like a child. I wailed like a child too. Adele rushed in to find out what was happening.

'Those motherfuckers have killed Bhut' Thembi,' I cried.

I feared there were going to be riots in South Africa. The whole country was going to be in flames. I followed news reports closely and phoned home. My brothers told me that the ANC leaders were able to calm the situation. I was impressed by their restraint and that of the people. If I were a believer, I would have thanked God for their maturity. You see, that's the problem when you are an atheist; you don't know who to thank.

I embarked on a campaign to get the novel published. Mike Nicol had given me the contact details of his agent in New York, but she told me she was not interested in African literature. Yet she represented Mike Nicol who wrote African literature. Or perhaps to her because Mike Nicol was a white South African his work was not African literature. My best bet was Heinemann Books, African Writers Series. A person called Adewale Maja-Pearce wrote back to say the work was feminist diatribe. I must admit, I was offended that a publisher who had published so much rubbish in much of the later African Writers Series novels was dismissive of my book in those terms. I sent the manuscript to Skotaville Press in Johannesburg but they did not respond. I put it away and worked on a play, *The Dying Screams of the Moon,* set in the period of transition in South Africa; a story of a woman who was demanding back her family's land that had been confiscated during apartheid.

I had forgotten about the manuscript when I received a letter from Oxford University Press in Cape Town. They were compiling an anthology of plays for schools and were enquiring whether I had any unpublished play that I wanted to submit. I wrote back to say I didn't have any new play but I had a novel. They asked me to send them the novel, and a few weeks later I signed a contract with them. Mary Reynolds, the commissioning editor, thought we had treasure in our hands.

That same year, 1993, Zed Books in London published my PhD thesis as a monograph titled *When People Play People: Development Communication Through Theatre.* The Swedish International Development Agency in Stockholm came across it and decided it was so useful they wanted to buy hundreds of copies and send them free of charge to scholars, universities and theatre practitioners throughout Africa. They asked me to compile a list of anyone I thought deserved a copy.

One day I came back from the university and found a fuming Adele waiting for me at the door. She was waving some papers. We had been so happy since she arrived, without a single quarrel; I hoped I had not done something stupid to take us back to where we used to be in Lesotho.

'What is this?' she asked.

'Oh, that's a list of names and addresses of people who will receive my book from SIDA,' I said innocently.

'So, it's you and Gugu again?' she said, tapping her finger on the list.

Oh, gosh! I had put Gugu's name and address on the list. The book was free and I had thought, what the heck, she might enjoy it. There was nothing more to it than that. But Adele was not convinced. She started yelling that I was a rotten cheat and nothing in the world would save me. I told her that there had been no communication between me and Gugu since we broke up. I was not even sure if the address I had for her was still current. This was true. There had been no contact between us. I heard from a Zimbabwean colleague before I left Roma that Gugu was married to some guy in Swaziland. But Adele didn't want to hear any of that. She was yelling for the entire world to hear. Zukile didn't understand what was happening and was crying on the bed. I thought she would stop when Dini returned from school, but she continued to call me names in his presence.

That was the beginning of the end of our marriage.

The tension continued throughout our stay in New Haven. We went for counselling and the first thing she told the marriage counsellor was: 'This man likes women too much!'

Without getting my side of the story or asking for details of what happened, the marriage counsellor said, 'Maybe he can't help it. Maybe he has a problem. Some men are addicted to sex.'

Did she think she was helping me? There was nothing more I could say there. I just sat and listened to them as they analysed me and my addiction. The marriage counsellor never even got to know that the whole thing started with my placing Gugu's name on a list.

The Basotho people say: *ditsietsi di latela ditshotleho*. When troubles come, they come in legions. The English also have a similar expression: it never rains but it pours. I was attacked by a sickness that the doctors didn't understand. They thought it was arthritis because all my joints, especially at the waist and the knees, were sore. But they didn't know why it had attacked so suddenly and so severely when there had not been even a hint that I had arthritis. I suffered searing pain when I walked, but because I didn't have a car I had to slog by foot to the doctor and to the Wednesday seminars. When I walked in the street with Adele she would be impatient with my snail's pace and would leave me behind. After a few hundred yards she would stop and wait, clearly annoyed. When I finally caught up to her she would tell me that I was wasting time.

Another trouble in the legions of troubles: a letter from my mother that my father was ill and had been taken to a hospital in Bloemfontein. This was his first trip to South Africa since he had gone into exile in

1963. He was going there to die; a few days later I received a telegram saying that he had passed away on June 22, 1993.

I couldn't go to the funeral. Not only was I flat broke, but my waist and my legs were killing me. I wouldn't have survived the eighteen-hour flight.

With the end of the academic year my contract with Yale had also come to an end. I was looking forward to returning to South Africa, but Adele wanted to do a master's degree in America. Mbulelo Mzamane came to our rescue. He was resigning from the University of Vermont to take up the position of Rector and Principal of Fort Hare University. I was pleasantly surprised when I received a letter from the English Department at the University of Vermont, offering me a position as Visiting Professor for one academic year to replace him.

The family moved to Burlington, Vermont, towards the end of that summer. I was grateful for my time at Yale which had been very productive: I had completed a novel and a full-length play. And I had not even known that I could write a novel!

I taught African Literature, African Theatre and Pan African Literature at undergraduate level at the University of Vermont. The Pan African Literature course had been devised by Mbulelo and it consisted of literatures from Africa and the diaspora – mainly the Caribbean, African-America and Latin America. I thought it was a brilliant course and I taught it lock-stock-and-barrel including the prescribed texts, just as Mbulelo had designed it. Since I was not familiar with some of the texts I spent the remaining part of the summer reading them.

I had not received my salary cheque, so Dini and I took to the streets of Burlington hawking my paintings. We didn't have a permit to do this, and I am sure if we had applied for one it wouldn't have been granted. Hawkers and peddlers were not allowed in the streets or in the town centre. But we sat defiantly on a bench and displayed my paintings. It was either that or my baby would die of hunger.

Some people looked at us curiously, but others were fascinated by the art. We did this on two occasions, each time displaying the paintings on the sidewalk and on the bench for an hour or two and then removing them quickly before they caught the attention of the authorities. On both occasions we sold a painting a few minutes after spreading them out and got enough money to last us until the end of the month.

Adele enrolled at St Michael's College for a Master of Education degree. She got a job at a local IGA Food Store. Dini enrolled at a local middle school and got a job at McDonald's. They had not been able to work in New Haven because they didn't have employment authorisation from the immigration people.

Alas, the bickering between me and Adele continued unabated. Gugu continued to be the subject, even though she was thousands of miles away in Swaziland raising her family. Another subject was 'Maseabata whose letters to me Adele was intercepting. And all these letters were about theatre and her studies in the United Kingdom. There was not an inkling in them that there was a romantic relationship between us. Yet Adele yelled into my ears, accusing me of having an affair with her. She even wrote her a letter ordering her to stop writing to me. She wrote back to say that the person she could order around was me not her.

The third subject was Gcina Mhlophe. Now, this is new to you because I have not mentioned her before. She was an actress and a playwright from Johannesburg and I was compiling a scrapbook of newspaper and magazine articles about her. I first met Gcina in 1986, long before I met Adele, when I was invited by the African Writers Association in Johannesburg to hold playwriting workshops. Gcina was one of the participants, together with such playwrights as Matsemela Manaka, Gamakhulu Diniso and Maishe Maponya. She was involved in a group called Thakaneng with Gamakhulu. We began to date at that time, but our relationship did not go anywhere because of distance and the fact that I was having problems entering South Africa on some occasions despite the temporary indemnity I had received from the apartheid government through Lesotho's Deputy Prime Minister and Minister of Home Affairs, Chief Sekhonyana 'Maseribane. The Johannesburg newspaper, *The Weekly Mail* (later to become the present-day *Mail & Guardian*), reported:

Lesotho playwright Zakes Mda was barred last week from entering South Africa by South African police at three different posts. Travelling to Johannesburg from Lesotho to see actress Gcina Mhlophe, Mda first went to Peka bridge, where he was searched and kept waiting for the whole day. The same thing happened at Maputsoe and Maseru border posts. At Maputsoe his passport was defaced by the police.

Because of police action the course of true love did not run smooth. But Gcina did come to Maseru once to spend some time with me and perform *Have you Seen Zandile?*, her autobiographical play, with Thembi Mtshali at the Maseru Sun Cabanas. After that it became impossible to see each other again. Our relationship just fizzled out in the long run. I did write to her when I got engaged to Adele informing her that I was getting married.

'So, why are you keeping her scrapbook if there is nothing between you?' asked Adele.

'I'm her fan, that's why.'

And that was Gospel, if you'll allow me to borrow from the vocabulary of the believers.

She never mentioned Gcina Mhlophe again, perhaps because for some reason she did believe that there was nothing between us. But she kept on hammering me about Gugu. When she felt like making me worse of a scoundrel than I really was, she would throw 'Maseabata's name into the mix as well.

One day I received a letter from Zwelakhe. He never wrote to me normally, so I knew immediately that there was something drastically wrong. The letter was on his official letterhead and he had attached a photocopy of a letter that Adele wrote to my mother. I had no knowledge of this letter, but I was shocked by its contents. I could deduce that Adele's letter was a response to a letter my mother wrote to her enquiring about a radio that I had left with Adele to give to my eldest son Neo. Adele had allegedly given the radio to her sister instead and my mother was trying to get it back for her grandson. In her letter Adele gave my mother a piece of her mind, telling her that she was being judgemental of her; even though she was poor, she would not steal a radio. In any case, she would pay for that radio as soon as she got a job. She added that she would like to live in peace with my mother but it seemed they were both failing in that regard. At the end of a long tirade she asked: *How is Ntate Mda? We heard that his health is not so well. Hope he recovers sooner than later.*

Zwelakhe took great offence at this letter, but I think what infuriated him most was this last line. Adele knew that my father was ill, yet she wrote this kind of letter to my mother. By the time my mother received it my father was dead. She was reading Adele's rude letter in her bereavement. After outlining his grievances against Adele, Zwelakhe concluded his letter to me thus:

In view of the fact that Adele is demonstrably vicious and malicious towards my mother she will always cause her great harm if her behaviour is not properly checked and monitored. Consequently, I have decided that she should not communicate with her in any manner whatsoever neither is she to come anywhere closer to her – physically or otherwise. At this juncture I should disclose that other members of the family associate themselves entirely with my decision. Finally, I wish to underscore the fact that I will readily act, and promptly so, in protection of the best interests of my mother, whenever the circumstances so dictate – especially now that my father has been laid to rest; I am her sanctuary. This should not in any way be misconstrued as any form of an indictment against you. But I have considered it wise to make our position clear without equivocation.

It was not lost on me that in his letter Zwelakhe was talking of his mother and his father as if these people had had no part in creating me. I did not respond to his letter; instead I wrote to my mother apologising for Adele's letter and relating to her the kind of life I was living with her.

Adele became the martyr in this matter. She told me that she knew all along that my people hated her.

'And yet you are keeping your rubbish in my father's house,' she added. 'You must go and take your rubbish from my father's house.'

The rubbish she was talking about were the books and some household effects that her father had agreed to store for us during our sojourn in the United States.

Adele became nice when she wanted help from me. Like when she was invited to give a presentation on South Africa at the county prison and she asked me to come along with my paintings and talk about art, which I did. We presented a united and loving front to the inmates. What amazed me about this prison was that half the inmate population was African American. Yet you could walk in Burlington for the whole day without meeting a single African American. Where did these inmates come from? Was that where they kept their African American population – in the county jail? I was impressed by the fact that this seemed to be a co-ed jail. In the canteen where we held our presentation there were both male and female inmates. We were told, though, that they were locked up in different wings of the prison.

One young man, barely out of his teens, told me that he was particularly happy to meet us because he was a Zulu. Just as we were becoming excited about seeing someone from South Africa, we learnt that he had never been to South Africa. None of his parents or grandparents had any South African connection. They were descendants of slaves.

'But my father told me that we were Zulus back in Africa,' he said proudly.

It would have been cruel to burst his bubble. His was part of the sad African American search for an African identity.

Back at our house – not a basement apartment this time but a three-bedroom house – the bickering resumed. I moved out of the bedroom to sleep in another room. Dini could not bear it any more. He moved out to stay with a friend's family in the neighbourhood. Although I had never met the family I couldn't stop him because I knew that the atmosphere at home was toxic. When he came to visit and Adele was at school there would be tears in his eyes as he expressed his sorrow that his father was subjecting himself to this kind of treatment. He just couldn't understand why and how I could stand it.

'Well, Dini, I'm paying for all the women I have mistreated in my life,' I said jokingly. 'Now it is my turn to be mistreated. It is payback time, my boy.'

For a moment I believed myself. She must have been sent to me as an avenging spirit for all my misdeeds in my long career as a failed lover. This was some kind of atonement. Perhaps it would pass when I had paid the price and there would be peace and happiness again in the home. On second thoughts, this was bunkum, influenced by that part of my subconscious that still yearned for spiritual solutions.

The truth of the matter was that I felt trapped. I went to see a divorce lawyer but his fees were too high. Also, I didn't meet the residency requirements of the state. I toyed with the idea of a Las Vegas divorce. I heard that Reno required only six weeks' residence. That still would have been too expensive for me. I took to reading the classifieds in tabloids looking for cheap non-residential divorces in foreign climes.

I got some form of therapy from the second novel that I was writing. Titled *She Plays with the Darkness*, it was based on my experiences working with the Maseru lawyer OK Mofolo, who specialised in third party insurance claims for motor vehicle accidents. My main character was an ambulance-chasing charlatan who didn't have any legal qualifications. The novel was also informed by some of my experiences in the mountain village of Sehonghong. One of my major characters was a woman called Tampololo who was in many ways a fishwife and a harridan who bullied her husband; a lot of her dialogue came directly from Adele's utterances towards me. I found it healing that every time she yelled at me I would use that in my novel. At least her insults were good for something.

My mother read each chapter of *She Plays with the Darkness* and as usual sent me her feedback. She loved the Tampololo character and had her suspicions on whom she was based.

The academic year was coming to a close, and South Africa was preparing for its first democratic elections. Fortunately, in Burlington we could get the Canadian television stations which, unlike the USA television channels, covered the events of the world. On CBC we saw some of the election campaigns. I remember looking at Nelson Mandela talking to a group of people at a rally, many of whom were children. He was making promises, as politicians are wont to do: 'All of you here will get houses if you vote for the ANC. Each one will have a house.' He was laughing when he said that, as if it was a joke. I began to despair.

Why was he making these extravagant promises when he knew that they would be impossible to keep? Why was he raising expectations that would certainly not be fulfilled?

On election day I took a train to Canada and went to vote at the Ukrainian Center in Montreal. Every South African of voting age, whether a registered voter or not, qualified for two votes: one for the national government and the other for the provincial government. If you were voting in a foreign country you could choose any province you liked. I cast my national vote for the PAC on behalf of my father, even though I was an ANC supporter. He had died only a year before, without seeing this day. He would have voted for the PAC. I chose Natal as my province so as to stop the Inkatha Freedom Party and cast my provincial vote for the ANC.

Back in Burlington, things were getting worse between Adele and me.

A saviour came in the form of Professor Ian Steadman, the Dean of the Faculty of Humanities at the University of the Witwatersrand in Johannesburg – or Wits University as it is generally known – who offered me a position as a Visiting Professor in the School of Dramatic Art. This was the chance to return to South Africa I had been yearning for. And I grabbed it with both hands. My intention was that as soon as I got back to South Africa I would initiate the divorce.

Adele said she would stay in Vermont to complete her degree but insisted that I should take Zukile with me. Of course, it was easier for me to take Zukile, given that Adele was studying and I had a support system in South Africa, but he was eighteen months old at this time and was still breastfeeding. I begged her to wean the child so that he would not give me problems crying for his mother's breast when I was travelling with him on the plane. But she said she would not do that. It would serve me right if he gave me problems on the plane. This was her final revenge.

Dini also decided to stay with his friends and continue his studies and his job at McDonald's.

I left Burlington, Vermont, with my little boy and took a train to New York, and then a plane to South Africa. I had bought a lot of fruit juice which I gave to the boy every time it seemed like he would cry for his mother's breast. But he did not cry. Throughout that long flight he did not cry. Not even once. Not even when I was changing his diapers in the toilet. It was as if he knew that his daddy was in trouble and he didn't want to make things worse for him.

CHAPTER TWELVE

WE PAUSE AT VENTERSBURG as usual. It is a pit stop on our way to or from the Bee People. We are regulars here to the extent that the women who work at Steers have got to know us and look forward to our visits and our liberal tips. At first they were surprised to see black folks who did not eat meat. We always ordered vegetarian burgers and they felt very sorry for us because they thought we were suffering from a deprivation imposed on us, perhaps by some religion or weird belief. They praised us for having the willpower to resist the temptation of meat. Gugu patiently explained that we didn't need any willpower at all to stay away from meat. We are squeamish about it and if we were to be forced to put it in our mouths we would throw up. They have come to accept us as their nice weird customers who look like them and speak like them and are therefore of their culture, and yet have the bizarre custom of not eating anything that had a face or that once had a mother – which is how Gugu explained it to them.

One of the women is an ardent listener to Lesedi, the Sesotho radio station of the South African Broadcasting Service. She says she often hears me commenting on the political situation of Lesotho and South Africa.

'How do you do it when you are so far away in the USA?' she asks.

'The SABC phones me whenever they want my opinion on the various issues,' I say.

'I know they phone you. I have heard you commentate on the American elections, which I can understand because you live there. But how do you comment so incisively on what is happening in Lesotho or in South Africa when you live so far away?'

'I'm here now, am I not? And I have just come from Lesotho.'

'But most of the year you are in America.'

I have heard this question before, even from my brother Zwelakhe. The answer is simply that with all the technologies and the media that are prevalent today, including social networking, it is possible not only to know what is happening in any part of the world but to be an active participant in the dialogue that shapes the events there. I was an occasional SABC Sesotho service radio commentator long before I went to the USA. Since I left, whenever they think they need a brutally frank opinion on a specific issue which is within the scope of my expertise they continue to phone and interview me.

While I am explaining this to her, and Gugu is ordering our favourite burgers, a distressed woman comes to enquire if anyone may have found her purse which she forgot in the ladies' bathroom. She is with her daughter who is about eight or so. The purse has all her money and credit cards in it. She only realised after filling up with petrol and wanted to pay for it that she didn't have it with her. She remembers placing it on the floor next to her while sitting on the toilet seat. Apparently when she was done she just stood up and left, forgetting about the purse.

Gugu and I know immediately that the chances of getting her purse back are next to nil. Unless she is extremely lucky and it is found by someone with enough decency and honesty to hand it over to management. But up to now no one has done so; the woman had better forget about it.

She is panicking. What is she going to do? How is she going to get home? Johannesburg is more than two hundred kilometres away.

'We must help her,' Gugu says.

'Don't worry, *'m'e*, you will get home,' I tell the woman. 'And as soon as you get to Jo'burg report your cards to the bank so that they stop payment.'

I pay for the petrol and give her extra money so she can buy some food for herself and her little girl. She thanks me and drives away in her gleaming late-model BMW.

She never got to know who the stranger who helped her was.

A STRANGER. THAT'S HOW I felt. Though in reality I was flying into my own country. I was a bit apprehensive of Johannesburg. Remember, I had not lived there since I was a little boy in Orlando East and then in Dobsonville. I had visited occasionally after getting the temporary indemnity to receive an award or to hold playwriting workshops for the African Writers Association and later for the Congress of South African Writers. But this was different. Now I was here to stay. I had lived in many countries, and in all of them I was viewed as a foreigner. Even in Lesotho, where I had practically grown from a child to a man, where the leaders had given me citizenship and a passport in order to represent the country, where the Lesotho Ambassador, Mr Reggie Tekateka, had declared me a national treasure during one of my European tours, I was still seen as an outsider, as a Mothepu. Even though everywhere I went I was proud to say I was a Mosotho from Lesotho. Now, for the first time in my life I was not a foreigner. I say 'for the first time in my life' advisedly because even though I had lived in South Africa until I was in my mid-teens, during the days of apartheid the South African government regarded me and all black people as foreigners in our country of birth. According to them, we all belonged in some barren patches of land they called Homelands or Bantustans. Now I was flying into my own country, where no one would call me a foreigner.

But why did I continue to feel like an outsider?

Through the plane window I could see palatial homes, all with swimming pools shimmering blue in the sun. I pointed them out to Zukile: 'One of those is going to be ours,' I told him. Of course he didn't understand what I was talking about.

I was met at the airport by Maishe Maponya and Jerry Mofokeng. I had met Maponya a few times before on my previous visits. He was one of the two most revered playwrights of the Black Consciousness generation; the other was Matsemela Manaka. I had not met Jerry before, but had read that he was one of the hottest new theatre directors in South Africa. He came to my attention particularly when he directed Vusi Kunene in my play *The Hill*. It was Vusi Kunene's first experience as an actor, and today he is one of the premier South African actors of screen and stage. Both of these guys were lecturers at the School of Dramatic Art at Wits University and were going to be my colleagues.

Maishe and Jerry couldn't get over the fact that I was on my own with an eighteen-month-old baby. How was I going to cope?

'Will you be taking him to your mother in Lesotho?' Maishe asked.

'Oh, no, I am going to raise him myself,' I said.

We were still at the airport when my eldest son Neo arrived. He was now a man rather than the boy I used to know. I was grateful he responded to my call. He was going to help me to take care of the baby. Zukile looked very much like him.

I pushed Zukile to the parking lot in a stroller while Jerry, Neo and Maishe helped with the luggage. It was July 1994 and I could see the euphoria of the new South Africa reflected on the faces of the people – especially the black people. I was going to be part of it. I was getting infected by the elation already. I was going to play my role in making the new South Africa a success story. I was returning home at last and I had skills that would contribute in whatever small way to building the great country that the progressive policies of the party that had won the election, the ANC, were bound to bring about. I was going to be part of the reconciliation that the new president, Nelson Mandela, was talking about.

I could have kissed the ground I was walking on. But I was not the Pope.

My friends drove me to my new quarters – a splendid university house in Parktown in the vicinity of the Wits Business School. This was temporary accommodation for the first two months or so, until I found a place of my own.

When Thandi arrived from Lesotho a week later I was a totally fulfilled man. I was with two of my sons and my daughter – just the four of us – and I was going to make up for the years I had spent without the two older ones. Neo was still at FUBA Academy studying visual arts and Thandi soon joined him there to study drama. The founder and principal of FUBA was the renowned novelist and poet Sipho Sepamla. As soon as he heard that I had returned to Johannesburg he roped me into joining the board of trustees of the school.

Neo liked to push Zukile in his stroller to the Pizza Hut in Jorissen Street where we stuffed ourselves on the buffet. Young university women would stop and exchange some baby-talk with Zukile and congratulate the father on having such a cute baby and for being such a doting father. And of course in this case the father was none other than Neo. The two looked very much alike so it was quite logical to see them as father and son. Neo did not correct them. I guess it was fine with him to use his little brother to attract the attention of the ladies.

I was Visiting Professor at the School of the Dramatic Art, which was headed by a very pleasant and helpful man, Fred Hagemann. I taught Theatre in Education and African Theatre. Wits University was still largely white and only a small number of my students were black in the broader sense that includes the Indians and the Coloureds. Some of the white kids had an attitude towards black lecturers and were quite resistant to learning anything from them. One young white lady made it her business never to pay attention when I was teaching. Instead she held conversations with any white student in her vicinity. I called her to order in class and made it clear that I would not tolerate her distracting behaviour. I was pleasantly surprised when she came to my office to apologise. She told me that she had never had any contact with blacks before, except for her maid, the washerwoman and the gardener. She never knew that there were blacks who were intelligent, had university degrees and actually taught at universities, let alone at a white university like Wits.

Although her apology was adding insult to injury, I accepted it. She was obviously brought up in some cocoon in the northern suburbs. She had a lot to learn about her country and her compatriots; it was only a few months after the first democratic elections.

When the time came for me to vacate the university house Maishe Maponya drove me around in his car helping me find accommodation. He took me to Ponte City after I had seen an advertisement about some apartments there. With fifty-five floors and a hollow core throughout its entire height, Ponte is the tallest residential building in Africa, and at one time in the southern hemisphere. But immediately I saw all the dodgy characters that were walking in and out of the building, some milling about in the reception area, I told Maishe this would not be a place to bring up a child. A lot of them looked like prostitutes and their pimps, and later I learnt that my observations were indeed correct. I don't know why Maishe hadn't advised me against the place if he knew its reputation.

Through the classifieds in *The Star* I finally found a beautiful furnished three-bedroom townhouse in Westdene, a suburb that bordered Melville and Triomf – as old Sophiatown had been named by the apartheid government. Maishe helped us move there. I set up a desk in my bedroom and began working on the finishing touches of *She Plays with the Darkness*. I sent the manuscript to my mother for her final feedback. As soon as I completed this novel I started writing a novella for youth, *Melville 67*. Melville 67 was the bus that I took every day to the university and back. My story was mostly set in the bus and my characters were based on the people I observed every day travelling to and from work.

That bus was our main link with the outside world. Neo and Thandi told me many stories about what happened in it on their way to and from the FUBA Academy in Newtown. Thandi was blossoming into a lovely young lady and I hoped that the course in acting she had chosen would help take her out of her extreme shyness. I was very proud of her and thought my mother had done a wonderful job bringing up her and her brothers. She became my friend, and I enjoyed her company and her humour.

I took her with me when I was invited to the launch of Nelson Mandela's *Long Walk to Freedom*. The event was held at the mansion of an Afrikaner multimillionaire in Sandton. Thandi and I sat at the edge of the stage, just in front of the ANC elders. I was able to introduce Thandi to both Mandela and Walter Sisulu. They were happy to meet AP's granddaughter. Sisulu was more interested in finding out how my mother was and what she was doing. But Barbara Masekela would have none of that. She was in charge of the proceedings and was as strict as a headmistress. She told us all, including the elders, that we were disrupting the proceedings. We all shut up.

One day I received an unannounced visitor at home. His name was Albert Nemukula and he was the owner and managing director of Vivlia Publishers. He told me how he had established his publishing house a few years before. He used to work for Juta, a highly respected academic and legal publishing house. He used to deliver royalty cheques to Afrikaner authors who had written school textbooks and was astounded by the large amounts these writers were earning. One day he delivered a one million rand cheque to a certain Meneer van Schalkwyk who had written a textbook that was prescribed nationally by the then Department of Bantu Education. He asked himself: *if this one author is making so much per year from this one book, how much more did the publishing house make?* There and then he decided to start his own publishing house. He identified gaps in the market and recruited writers. While he was going about his work for Juta he was also running his publishing house from the boot of his car. That's how Vivlia Publishing was born.

When Albert Nemukula came to see me about submitting any manuscript I might have, Vivlia Publishers was a well-established and respected company. I was impressed by his resourcefulness and by the fact that his was a black-owned company that he started himself from scratch. He was not given equity in a well-established multinational on a platter by some white capitalists in return for political favours, as was the case in most of the Black Economic Empowerment deals one heard about. I agreed immediately to give him the manuscript of *She Plays with the Darkness*. He told me he was going to have a race with Oxford University Press and release the novel before they could publish *Ways of Dying*. That's why the two novels came out in the same year, in 1995, with my second novel coming out before my first novel.

When I completed *Melville 67* I gave it to him as well.

My return to South Africa received tremendous publicity in the media. The *Sunday Times* carried the headline: *The Legend Comes Home to Play*. Yet I had hoped I would sneak into the country and quietly go about my work! The theatre establishments in Johannesburg, under the leadership of Walter Chakela who was the chief executive officer of the Windybrow Theatre, decided to hold a festival of my plays. The Windybrow produced two of my plays: *You Fool How Can the Sky Fall*, which I had written in Vermont during the times of domestic turmoil, and *We Shall Sing for the Fatherland*. What I found particularly sentimental about the latter was that it was directed by Kefuoe Molapo, the son of my late Maseru friend, Clemoski. *You Fool* was a world premiere and was directed by Peter Se-Puma. The Johannesburg Civic Theatre produced *The Nun's Romantic Story* directed by my friend Jerry Mofokeng, with music composed by Tu Nokwe. The Market Theatre produced a revival of *The Hill*, directed by Philiswa Biko. The Wits University Theatre produced *Dead End* directed by Jojo Mei. Even a city that was hundreds of kilometres away got into the spirit of the festival: the North West Arts Council in Mmabatho produced *The Dying Screams of the Moon*, directed by Siphiwe Khumalo.

My work was getting wall-to-wall reviews and write-ups in the press.

About two weeks later I went to the Civic Theatre and demanded that they close their production of *The Nun's Romantic Story*. Although Jerry and Tu had worked so hard to come up with a wonderful production of the play, I felt that the management had not done anything to publicise the play, with the result that it was performing to empty houses. They had not given my play the same kind of treatment that they gave the overseas productions that were their main focus. They were taken aback because they had never met a playwright who demanded the cancellation of his own play. But they complied. It was only later that I regretted my rashness. I had put actors, including the greatly talented Yael Farber who was playing the lead with such touching delicacy and gracefulness, out of work. I had thought only of myself and my reputation, which was rather selfish of me.

I found that all of a sudden I was in great demand in Johannesburg; people of all sorts wanted a piece of me. I was so naive that I did not see through those who were merely using me for their own ends. For instance, a group of white women commissioned me to write a play that would be used on the gold mines to educate miners on issues of safety. They promised me a substantial amount for the script. They had successfully pitched the project to the mine bosses but the final approval would only come if the trade union liked it as well.

I went to the gold mines of Welkom in the Free State with three of the women where they had a meeting with members of the National Union of Mineworkers. I was introduced to these unionists as the author. I became uneasy when the women kept referring to me as if I was the face of the project, or indeed had a key role in initiating and running it. The unionists had never heard of me, of course, but it was good enough for them that there was black participation in the project.

The women got the contract, but two days or so after we returned from Welkom I received a letter from them. They were dropping me from the project because they realised that they could actually write the play themselves; it was not the kind of play that needed my refined and internationally acclaimed playwriting skills. I had wasted my time going with them to the Free State and attending a long dreary meeting, and those who know me will tell you how much I hate meetings. I had not yet signed any contract with the women because I had relied on their good faith. It was my loss.

But, you know, I am a bit dim-witted because I never learn. The same thing happened again with a company called Blue Moon, which was then white-owned and operated. Choreographer Robyn Orlin and I were engaged to create a production for the relaunch of *Drum Magazine*. I realised too late that I was their black front, so as to qualify for the black empowerment contract. I attended the initial meetings, giving a semblance of black participation and as soon as Blue Moon clinched the deal and signed the contract with the company that published *Drum Magazine* they told me that Robyn Orlin would rather go it alone.

I didn't want to pursue the matter further in any of these cases; it was far below my dignity to do so. I put it down to experience. I would be smarter next time. I was in the cut-throat world of Johannesburg where there was no such thing as good faith or a gentleman's agreement.

I was strolling around the Market Theatre one day when I came across Barney Simon, the director who was revered by every theatre practitioner in South Africa. He was one of the founders of the Market Theatre and continued to work there as an artistic director.

I decided out of the blue to pounce on him.

'Hey Barney,' I said, 'I want to know why you guys don't produce plays by black playwrights here at the Market.'

'We've produced your plays,' he said, chuckling a bit at my impudence.

'Yeah, but I'm not the only black playwright in South Africa, am I?'

I had not realised that Aubrey Moalosi, an actor who had been my student many years before when I taught mathematics at Hlotse Secondary School in Lesotho, was following me and overheard my attack on poor Barney.

'That's telling them, Bra Zakes,' he said.

'Find me the black playwrights and I'll produce them,' said Barney and left.

Where the heck do I find black playwrights? I remembered Dukuza ka Macu with whom I worked in Lesotho. I respected and loved his work but I didn't know where he was. The last time I saw him he was shacking up with some white woman in one of the southern suburbs and they were both totally sloshed. The Black Consciousness stalwarts

Matsemela Manaka and Maishe Maponya were not producing new work. Maishe was focusing on academic life and Matsemela had shifted his focus to painting. His had invited me to his house in Diepkloof once and it was like a gallery. Later he opened his own gallery at Southgate Shopping Mall.

Well, if we can't get any established playwrights maybe we can create some.

That was the beginning of my long relationship with the Market Theatre.

Soon after the death of Barney Simon, actor and managing trustee of the Market Theatre, John Kani, employed me as a dramaturge and writer-in-residence, fulfilling Barney's wishes. I accepted a nominal monthly retainer for my services. Although I was a member of the artistic team that decided on the theatre's programme, my main interest was in the development of new writers for the stage. I held regular workshops at the Market Theatre Laboratory, and both aspiring and established writers attended them.

On Zukile's second birthday I drove to Lesotho and took him to see Adele's parents in Leribe. I had a long meeting with her father, *Ntate* Thesele, outlining the problems I had with her and informing him of my intention to divorce. He didn't talk me out of it, although I had hoped for his intervention, but told me that whatever happened between us I would always be part of his family since I was the father of his grandson.

I then drove to Mohale's Hoek to see Willie. I had written to him about my problems and he had not responded. Even now he was not of much help. All he said was: 'Maybe you guys should live separately for a while. Things will work themselves out.'

In Mafeteng, my mother was glad to see Zukile. She praised me for taking care of him so well. I told her I wouldn't have managed without the help of my two older kids, Neo and Thandi. She recommended a neighbourhood woman who would be a good nanny. She was sad that I had not been able to find Sonwabo. I promised that I would not give up.

The next day I drove back home with the nanny.

Back in Johannesburg I was writing prolifically for newspapers, commenting on current political, cultural and media issues. My articles were being published in *City Press*, *Sunday Independent* and *Sunday Times*. I was treading on people's toes and making enemies. Philip van Niekerk, the editor of the *Mail & Guardian*, employed me as a regular contributor to his newspaper. I wrote articles ranging from the conflicts within the ANC in a small Free State town to the marginalisation of qualified blacks in government and parastatal jobs in favour of political pals in the crony capitalism and patronage system that was beginning to take root in South Africa. I wrote on crime: why it was prevalent and how it could be reduced; and on how and why the penal system should be reformed. These articles created a lot of debate and I featured as a guest on radio and television talk shows.

I was also writing academic articles and getting published in such journals as *Theatre and Performance in Africa* published by Bayreuth University in Germany; *Theater*, published by Yale University; and the *Journal of Southern African Studies*.

At about this time Wits University Press also published my collection of plays titled *And the Girls in Their Sunday Dresses: Four Works*. Besides the title play, the book contained *Joys of War*, *Banned* and *The Final Dance*. The last was a cine-poem that was never produced and *Banned* was a radio play that I wrote for the BBC which had been broadcast the previous year.

At the end of the academic year Wits University was very keen to convert my visiting professorship into a permanent position but I had tasted the life outside academia and it was much sweeter. I was able to earn a decent living writing, which meant that I could work at home and spend more time with Zukile. Vivlia Publishers were giving me more work as well. I was reviewing novels that had been submitted to them and editing those they had selected for publication. With all this independent work that I could do lying in my bed, I turned Wits down even after Professor Willy Malegapuru Makgoba, the new deputy vice-chancellor and the first black to hold such a high position at that university, held an urgent meeting with me in his office begging me to stay because there were very few senior black academics at the university. I was sorry to let Willy down because I liked him very much, but I needed the freedom. As a full professor I would have no choice but to be on all sorts of committees and be part of the activism for the transformation of the university to an institution that reflected the values of the new democratic South Africa. All I wanted was to create. This was becoming a very productive period for me. There were so many stories to tell and so little time.

Philip van Niekerk, in his capacity as a film producer, commissioned me to tell one of those stories. He and Mark Newman of Phakathi Films had devised a new television series titled *Saints, Sinners and Settlers* in which such historical figures as King Dingane of the Zulus, Dutch colonist Jan van Riebeeck, apartheid founder and former prime minister Hendrik Frensch Verwoerd and many others were being tried in a contemporary courtroom for their historical crimes. I was commissioned to write an episode on the prophetess Nongqawuse who would be tried for making false prophecies that resulted in the death of thousands of amaXhosa. This mass suicide enabled the British to finally subjugate the amaXhosa people once and for all.

The prophecy was that the ancestors would come back from the dead bringing with them new cattle and new crops, provided the amaXhosa people killed all their existing cattle – which were ailing with lung disease in any case – and destroyed all their crops in the fields and silos. Some people believed the prophecies and killed their cattle, but there were those who doubted them. They refused to kill their cattle and destroy their crops. There was great conflict between the believers and the unbelievers. If the unbelievers did not obey the prophecies, the believers believed, the prophecies would not be fulfilled. The believers therefore tried to force the unbelievers to kill their cattle, and when they didn't the believers invaded their kraals at night and did it for them.

The appointed day came and passed without the fulfilment of the prophecies. Many amaXhosa people died as a result of the famine that followed.

Like every Xhosa person, I knew this story quite well. In Lesotho I was even blamed for being Nongqawuse's child by ethnic chauvinists. But I didn't know many of the historical details that I read in Jeff Peires's book, *The Dead Will Arise*, which I was given by Phil. The author himself was appointed my consultant by the producers and I learnt a lot from him about that period. They also arranged that I drive to Qolorha-by-Sea in the Eastern Cape and visit the area where Nongqawuse lived with her uncle. That was where she was supposed to have seen some visions and a number of miracles took place on the banks the Gxarha River – a river named for my mother's people, the Cwerha Gxarha clan, descendants of the Khoikhoi.

Driving on the winding roads of the Eastern Cape I was struck by the beauty of the land and the colourful villages. I had never been in that part of the province before. I said to myself: *This place is so beautiful it deserves a novel.* I didn't know what the novel was going to be about, but I knew that as soon as I completed the screenplay on Nongqawuse I would write it.

My contact at Qolorha was Rufus Hulley who owned a trading store in the village. His family had lived there for generations and he was an expert on the history of the area. He was not at the store when I got there, but one of the clerks asked a young lady, perhaps in her late teens, to take me to him at his house which was behind the store. The young lady introduced herself as Boniwe Yako. She was a cleaner at the store. She showed me Rufus's house but before she left she said, 'I am not married.'

I didn't know how to respond to that statement. I just stood there looking foolish.

She went on to say: 'You may *lobola* me if you like.'

Then she giggled and ran back to the store. She was just teasing, of course. I knew immediately that whatever novel I was going to write I was going to base my main character on her. On my subsequent visits to the village I sought Boniwe Yako out and she gave me a lot of information about the life of a young woman in the village. She even took me to her home and I met her mother, uNoManage.

But on this first visit my focus was on Rufus Hulley who took me to various places of historical interest in the village. I knew then that although my novel would focus on the present it would have to be about the past as well – the days of Nongqawuse. Boniwe Yako could easily have been Nongqawuse. I loved her spunk. My novel would have to illustrate that the past is always a strong presence in our present.

I drove back to Johannesburg highly inspired by the Eastern Cape and by the story I was going to write. As soon as I completed writing the screenplay and submitted it to the producers I embarked on writing the novel titled *Ululants*. The story shuttled between the present and the past. The past was informed mostly by Jeff Peires's *The Dead Will Arise*. I did look at other historians who dealt with the period generally and with the Cattle Killing events in particular. But Jeff's treatment appealed to me most, and suited the kind of magical story I wanted to tell because it was very romantic. I knew that some of his conclusions were questioned by some of his peers. But that was not my concern. I was writing a novel, a work of fiction, and not history. I was going to go with Peires's version of history because it suited my fiction. Historical record was important in my storytelling, but the oral traditions of my mother's people were crucial as well. They gave the history the magical environment that became a comfortable home for my fictional characters. I went out of my way to interweave my narrative with Jeff's account in my historical segments of the novel, but most importantly with some of Jeff's primary isiXhosa sources. The contemporary segments, however, were based solely on imagination. For instance, I created a new conflict between the believers and unbelievers, but now on more contemporary issues such as the protection of the environment and the preservation of the people's heritage. In reality, I found no believers and unbelievers in today's Qolorha.

I was quite happy with the end result and I submitted it to Oxford University Press who had already paid an advance after I had submitted the first chapter.

Kate McCullum, the managing director, phoned me to say that she didn't like my title, *Ululants*. There was no such word, she said. Well, there is, although at the time I couldn't defend myself because I thought I had invented it. According to Merriam-Webster Online Dictionary it dates to 1855 and it means 'having a wailing sound'. In my novel there are groups of people who ululate and the title referred to them. But Kate was insistent that no one would know what it meant and therefore she would not be able to sell the book. I told her I would think of a new title.

One day I was at the Market Theatre having a drink with a few friends at a bar called Kofifi. One of them was Kefuoe Molapo,

Clemoski's son. I told them of my dilemma about finding a new title for my novel. Kefuoe had read the manuscript and he said, 'Why don't you call it *The Heart of Redness*?'

All the drunkards agreed it was a catchy title even though they had not read the book.

'That will work,' I said, even though I was the only sober one among them. 'After all, the book is set among the red people, a reference to the so-called backward people. When they talk of *intliziyo yobubomvu* – the heart of redness – they mean a place where people are still 'backward' and practise their old customs and smear their bodies with red ochre and wear clothes dyed with the same ochre.'

'Precisely,' said Kefuoe. 'I'm a genius.'

'Yes, you are a genius,' I said.

Everybody agreed and applauded his genius.

I have regretted that incident ever since. That title has invited associations with Conrad's *Heart of Darkness* which, by the way, I have not read up to this point. I have heard of papers that have been written on the intertextuality between the two texts. I do not dispute that there may be such intertextuality because you can find parallels between any two texts if you look hard enough. Writers write about life, and the human condition is the human condition in any culture or clime. The only intertextuality that I was conscious of was with Peires's *The Dead Will Arise* and Jordan's *Ingqumbo Yeminyaya* – the *Wrath of the Ancestors*. On reading the last chapter of my book, where I wrote of 'pacification', I could hear some influence from Achebe's *Things Fall Apart*. But that does not mean there can't be other intertextualities. Many of these would be unintended. For instance, whereas the intertextuality with Jeff Peires's work was overt and intended, Jordan's and Achebe's influences just found their way into my work uninvited, solely on the basis that they were works I read and loved during my formative years.

When a graduate student told her supervisors at one Italian university that I claimed I had never read *Heart of Darkness*, the professors laughed derisively. 'How can he say he has not read Conrad?' they said. 'Everyone has read Conrad. Even Chinua Achebe has commented on Conrad. And Mda is a professor in an English Department to boot.'

I am sorry to be boasting of my ignorance. I may be from an English

Department but I teach creative writing and world literature courses that have nothing to do with Conrad. Not everyone in an English Department has read Conrad. I grew up in Lesotho and South Africa, and Conrad was not part of the canon there. At high school I read Achebe, who put me off Conrad. And then I wrote *The Heart of Redness* and there was all this talk of intertextuality with Conrad. I decided I would stay ignorant of Conrad for a while so that instead of saying 'I had not read *Heart of Darkness* when I wrote *The Heart of Redness*', I can safely and truthfully say 'I have not read *Heart of Darkness*'. Period. Of course, I have no intention of staying ignorant of this canonical text for ever. One day I'll read it and marvel at the intertextuality between Conrad's great novella – I've heard some call it a long short story – and my humble novel.

That was a digression; I have no intention of writing a polemical autobiography. I was telling you of how productive my return to South Africa was turning out to be. Through my workshops at the Market Theatre Laboratory I was making it productive for others as well. I had some of the most wonderful and talented playwrights and I meant to fulfil Barney Simon's declaration: if you find me black playwrights I'll produce them. But the participants in my workshops were not only black South Africans; there were Afrikaner writers such as Neil Sonnekus and Jaap de Villiers as well. Some of my writers had already made a name for themselves internationally. Bongani Linda, for instance, had his own theatre company called Victory-Sonqoba based in Alexandra Township; it had become a staple in European theatre festivals. It had also travelled to the Far East and Australasia. All the plays the group performed had been penned by him. Xoli Norman had also written some plays before and came to these workshops with a degree from the prestigious Wits University School of Dramatic Art. Xoli announced at one of the workshops that he had learnt more at my workshops than he had learnt in all the four years of his degree. Ntshiyeng Sithe was a talented woman who had written a runaway success at the Market Theatre titled *Umdlwembe* before she joined my workshops. Yet she felt the need to sharpen and refine her skills.

If only Barney Simon were there to see what had resulted from my flippant question.

One thing I cherished about the workshops was that they became a forum for debate on some of the contentious issues in the new South Africa. Some views were shaped and long-held prejudices eliminated. For instance, one of my favourite participants was a young man from Soweto called Mpumi Njongwe. He no longer lived in Soweto though; he had been cast out by his own people at an early age because he was gay. He shared a flat with an older white lover in Hillbrow. I got to know the couple well and they sometimes visited me at my house and took a dip in my swimming pool.

At the workshop Mpumi was writing a play based on his experiences as a young gay man growing up in the highly prejudiced environment of Soweto. Bongani Linda, a proud Zulu man, had no sympathy with people like Mpumi. He thought that homosexuality was a trend and a fashion statement of the new South Africa. It was an abomination that no true African man should tolerate.

'It is one of the terrible things that were brought to Africa by the white man,' he said.

I had heard this argument before, advanced especially by Africans from other parts of Africa, that our progressive laws on gay rights were a result of Western influence. I reminded Bongani that the new human rights culture was not introduced by whites or by the West in South Africa. There were no human rights in Africa under Western colonialism. Instead, we had patriarchal, racist and sexist dictatorships where the word of unelected colonial officials was final. Under the West as represented by white English and then white Afrikaner power, South Africans were the most oppressed people in the world. Gay people were the lowest on the social rungs. There were strict sodomy laws and many homosexuals suffered dehumanisation and imprisonment for loving each other. In fact, the sodomy laws that prevail in most African countries were enacted by the colonial masters. In Western countries they persecuted and prosecuted their homosexuals relentlessly. Ask Oscar Wilde, if you don't believe me. You say that's the past. Okay, ask American gays in the military and in states where they can't exercise their human right to marry and be miserable like the rest of us.

In 1994 a black majority government undid all those oppressive laws for the simple reason that we fought against oppression for centuries and we were not going to turn around and oppress others. When we put sexual orientation as a protected right in our Constitution we were not mimicking the West because none of their Constitutions had such a clause. We realised that gay rights were human rights, a lesson we learnt the hard way during the struggle from those comrades who happened to be homosexual. They helped us banish our own prejudices.

Mpumi told us about his life: how he suffered as a child not understanding why he felt different from other boys, his first crush on a boy, how he was chased in the streets of Soweto and called such derogatory names as *setabane*, how his own parents condemned him as a cursed child who would go to hell, and how he left home in his teens to be free to love. Bongani came to the conclusion that gays were born that way; no sane person could subject himself to all that pain and humiliation for a trend or a fashion statement.

I was grateful that my playwriting workshops were playing such a crucial role in transforming staunch homophobes into more tolerant people.

I intended to nurture Mpumi into the artist he yearned to be. I took him to arts events. I remember once taking him to a book event at a restaurant in Newtown – I think they were giving some writer a prize, but that's not what I remember about the occasion. What I do recall is that I met author Miriam Tlali and her daughter Moleboheng at this event. I had not seen them for many years, not since Moleboheng was a statistics lecturer at the National University of Lesotho and was my neighbour in Florida. She and her boyfriend lived an enviously carefree life and one day Miriam Tlali arrived unexpectedly and found them totally smashed. She blamed me for not looking after her daughter and for not guiding her into responsible adulthood. She did not know that those years I was just as irresponsible as her daughter, if not more.

But I was telling you about Mpumi. He went on to become an actor. He was part of a team that made a television documentary on pre-colonial homosexuality in South Africa. Most people learnt for the first time of women who married other women in some of our ancient kingdoms and of institutionalised homosexuality in some of the *sangoma* traditions among our spiritual healers and diviners.

I mourned Mpumi for a long time after he died of AIDS.

Another significant event in my association with the Market Theatre was the creation of the play *Broken Dreams* whose performances continue to this day. It has been seen by millions of students in the Gauteng Province, but also in many other provinces of South Africa.

The play came about as a result of the concerns of a pharmaceutical company called Glaxo that their drugs for the treatment of TB were no longer effective in South Africa because of HIV and AIDS. They financed the Market Theatre Laboratory to create a play that would mobilise people against both TB and HIV/AIDS. A nurse who was employed by Glaxo – shamefully, I forget her name now, and none of the people I worked with can remember it – identified child sexual abuse as one of the major problems in South Africa, cutting across all races and all social classes. It was one of the causes of the spread of AIDS among children. She wanted the play to link the three subjects: TB, HIV/AIDS and child sexual abuse.

I put together a team of actors which included Keke Semoko, who had been my student at the Wits University School of Dramatic Art and has since become one of the leading actresses in South Africa and who has appeared in many international movies; Kefuoe Molapo, Clemoski's son who you are beginning to meet quite often in this story; Sello Motloung, another actor who has since done well for himself and has been seen in international movies; and a woman called Rosetta who would have gone far if she had pursued her acting career as rigorously as the others did.

I sent the actors out to the townships and suburbs of Johannesburg to find out about child sexual abuse. They interviewed children, teachers, social workers and parents. They came back from these expeditions and told harrowing stories of young lives destroyed mostly by men – and an occasional woman here and there – who preyed on them. And in most cases these predators were in the family – fathers, brothers, uncles – or neighbours.

As we sat there in the rehearsal room creating a play from these stories we related our own experiences of abuse. Rosetta, for instance, had her own disturbing stories from her childhood. I had mine too. I told them about Nontonje, the red woman who abused me sexually when I was a small child. It was the first time I had talked about this. Even when I was healed through my relationship with Tholane when I was at 'Mabathoana High School, I had never told her about it because I had not associated my sexual problems with it. I had never told anyone until that day when I sat with my actors and we wept at some of the stories we heard. I realised for the first time how that sexual abuse at KwaGcina – that I had even forgotten about until then – had had such a great impact on my life and how it had resulted in my dysfunction as a man, husband, father and human being. I had not realised this because I never had flashbacks about it, I never had nightmares. Right from the beginning I had dismissed it as water under the bridge. Yet subconsciously it took its toll on me.

Here was theatre acting as psychotherapy in a very practical sense.

After every hectic day I went home to my four children in Westdene. I didn't tell you that Dini had returned from the United States and was staying with me too, in addition to Zukile, Thandi and Neo. I was living a fulfilling celibate life. Occasionally I thought about Gugu. I wondered where she was and what she was doing. One day I decided to write to her. I addressed the letter to the old address that I used to know. If she had moved they would forward it to her. I told her about my life with Adele, and that I was planning to consult lawyers about a divorce. I would wait until she returned from the United States though, so that I did not burden her with extra worries while she was busy studying for her MEd degree.

A few weeks later I received Gugu's response. She was still in Swaziland and was happily married with a beautiful daughter called Nonkululeko – Mother of Freedom. She advised me very strongly not to divorce Adele. It was the easy way out. I should remember that we had a child and we should try to work out our problems for the sake of Zukile. In any marriage there were bound to be problems, she went on to say, but running away from them was not the solution.

There was a lot of sense in what she was saying. Divorce was the coward's way.

CHAPTER THIRTEEN

THE TWO RESEARCHERS ARRIVE at Gugu's apartment at the Twin Oaks townhouse complex in Randpark Ridge, Johannesburg. Bob Edgar is a professor at Howard University in Washington, DC, but spends a lot of time in South Africa because that's his area of scholarship. He even has property in Cape Town. He is usually pushing his handicapped son Leteane in a wheelchair. He adopted him in Lesotho when he taught at the university there as a Fulbright Scholar many years ago, which was where I first met him. But Leteane is not with him today. Bob is an authority on my father; he and Luyanda ka Msumza, my father's former protégé, are compiling and editing a book of my father's writings.

The second researcher is Dorothy Steele, a sweet elderly lady from Cape Town who is writing my literary biography for a master's degree she is doing with the University of South Africa. I have known her for a number of years now and she has become close not only to my immediate family but to my distant relatives as well. She has been to the Bee Place and spent some time with the Bee People, has been to KwaGcina where I was violated and she has spoken to Reuben Mkhwentla, one of the elders who knew my father well. She has gone to Kokstad to speak to my brother Monwabisi, and my cousin Nondyebo, who lives with my brother. She has also spoken to my ex-wife Mpho and to all our children, and has even attended some of the workshops I conduct for playwrights at the Market Theatre. She is quite thorough in her research, and is a beautiful kind soul to boot.

Today Gugu and I are taking these scholars to Orlando West, Soweto, to visit my Aunt Ella. She is my father's younger sister and was a PAC leader in Soweto in her own right. I love visiting her because she reminds me of my father; she resembles him so much you'd have thought they were identical twins. Bob wants to interview her about her memories of growing up at Goodwell at my grandfather's estate – the present-day Bee Place.

Aunt Ella's house is only three streets away from Armitage Street where Gugu grew up, and two blocks from Vilakazi Street, where Nelson Mandela and Desmond Tutu had their homes. When we arrive we are welcomed by two of her daughters who are just as robustly built as she is. They tread on the floor with gravitas as they usher us into the living room. My aunt joins us and does not reprimand me for bringing visitors without warning. That's how things are done among our people; you don't call before, you just visit. If people happen not to be there it doesn't matter, you'll come unannounced another day.

Bob wants to know about my grandfather and how life used to be those days on Dyarhom Mountain, which today I call the pink mountain. But my aunt is more interested in talking about the great work that Robert Mugabe is doing in Zimbabwe redistributing farms to the previously dispossessed and how South Africa will undergo an uprising if the ANC does not follow Mugabe's example and reallocate the land to the masses. She says that Nelson Mandela sold out the African people. That is why he is the darling of the West. He has always been a sell-out from the days she knew him as a young man and neighbour. That was why he took the side of the Communists against the African Nationalists in the 1950s. Now he and the ANC are selling out the African people to corporate interests.

I chuckle at the irony of a Communist selling out to capitalist interests. Then I remember that this is South Africa; some of our biggest black capitalists profess socialism and some of the leading members of the Communist Party are involved in the rampant accumulation of personal wealth. It was the same in Zimbabwe; Mugabe and his cronies were big on socialist rhetoric while they distributed hotels, farms and factories among themselves, without ever addressing the land question among the poor for all those years. It was only when there was a threat of real opposition that they started rendering their country ungovernable and throwing due process out of the window in a wholesale land grab, not only from the white settler community, but from those black Zimbabweans who did not support the ruling party. My son-in-law, Limpho's husband, worked hard at McDonald's in South Africa until he attained a management position.

He bought his parents a farm in Zimbabwe which was duly confiscated by Mugabe's 'war veterans'. And, guess what, my son-in-law was not a white settler but a black Zimbabwean.

Anyway, let me leave Mugabe and Zimbabwe alone and listen to Aunt Ella and her guests. I am aware of her sentiments because she has expressed them to me before. Although I don't agree with her, especially when she praises Mugabe and condemns Mandela's reconciliation efforts as a Western plot to deny the African people justice, I never argue with her. I become an unresponsive sounding board. I understand her anger and pain; one of her sons, Cousin Mzwandile, was a casualty of the liberation struggle. So were many others – friends, neighbours and relatives. And now she and her people have nothing to show for it. Instead, they are faced with escalating costs of utilities, discontinued water and electricity services, and chronic unemployment, while a minority of politically well-connected black fat cats is riding on what in South Africa is referred to as the gravy train – if you don't mind our mixed metaphors. She reflects the anger that we often hear among our black people in the townships and in the rural areas where I work with the poor.

I ask that Gugu and I be excused from the meeting. While they continue with their interview, we take a sentimental tour of the township. We go to the nearby Hector Peterson Museum and talk to the vendors of arts and crafts, and to a PAC stalwart called Ali Hlongwane who runs the museum. We drive past Gugu's former home at Armitage Street and wonder who owns it now. Her parents sold it some years back. Gugu's friends and playmates of old still live next door, but unfortunately they are not home today. We decide to buy *spykos* – or junk food – of fried dough cakes known as *amagwinya* and the pickled mango called *atchaar*. I never leave Soweto without tasting the *spykos*. This one is particularly meaningful because we buy it from the same little café which we used to patronise when we were kids – albeit in different years. Those days we would also have added fish crumbs and battered fishbone. But now, of course, we wouldn't buy that even if they still sold such fare.

We always find Soweto – particularly Orlando West and Orlando East, and for me Dobsonville – very inspiring. It takes us back to our childhood. This is the area and the youth that I captured for posterity in my novel *Black Diamond*. These were also my father's stomping grounds during his ANC Youth League days. The Mda Street that we drive through is named after him.

After about two hours we go back to pick up Bob and Dorothy. I don't know if their trip has been fruitful. For me and Gugu, just breathing the air of this part of Soweto is satisfying enough.

ONE THING I REGRETTED about leaving the Wits University School of Dramatic Art was that I would not be able to continue my visits to Soweto with my students. As part of our Theatre in Education course, which I subverted by adding elements of Theatre for Development to it, I had started a programme where once a week I took the students to Dobsonville to work with township kids who were members of the Dobsonville Arts Association, which was led by its founder, Maswabi Legwale. At first my students, who were mostly white and had never been in a black township before, were apprehensive about venturing into a foreign world that conjured only images of crime in their collective imagination. But soon they were enjoying it and were looking forward to the visits, first in Legwale's own backyard and later at a cultural centre called Kopanong. Though I would no longer be going with my students, I hoped to keep my connections with the group.

I couldn't keep to that undertaking on a regular basis because my time was swallowed by efforts to make a livelihood as a full-time writer. Not only was I reviewing and editing manuscripts for Albert Nemukula's Vivlia Publishers, but occasionally I undertook some writing projects for television. I also continued to express my views in the columns of newspapers.

The *Sunday Times* engaged my services to write a weekly column called 'On the Small Screen' reviewing programmes on South African television. Since I travelled abroad extensively I also commented on overseas programming in comparison with South African television. My columns did not only confine themselves to television, but I used them as a springboard to comment on social and political issues affecting broader society. For instance, President Nelson Mandela was shown on television lamenting the death of Sani Abacha of Nigeria. He said his death was a great loss to Africa. I wrote a scathing column attacking Mandela for being 'economical with the truth'. He was being 'an African statesman' in a situation that demanded honesty and not glib diplomacy, I wrote. Africa would not miss Sani Abacha one bit because he was a dictator, a murderer and a thief. I think I was even more biting in my article because two and a half years before this same Sani Abacha killed a dear friend of mine, Ken Saro Wiwa. Ken was a Nigerian writer, television producer, environmentalist and political activist who I had met on a few occasions in Europe. South African poet Don Mattera and I had spent wonderful moments with Ken in Bayreuth, Germany. We admired him for his relentless struggle against the oppression and exploitation of his Ogoni people in particular and of Nigerians in general.

Many people commented on what they regarded as my 'attack' on Nelson Mandela. Some noted that this was not the first time I had been critical of the great leader. When the Deputy Speaker of Parliament, Baleka Mbethe, a woman I admired very much for her poetry and her leadership in the liberation struggle, was accused of obtaining a driver's licence through fraudulent means in the corrupt Mpumalanga Province, Mandela had come to her defence even before he knew the facts of the case, calling her a woman of integrity. I criticised him for his blind loyalty to his comrades, which led to the condonation of corruption.

I had also featured on a BBC radio programme where I expressed fears about the deification of Nelson Mandela. I commended him in that programme because he did not go along with that, and in fact opposed any notions that he was a saint. I went on to say that most of the problems that we had in Africa began with the deification of our political leaders. They had fought for our liberation and as soon as they took over government we gave them such titles as the Messiah and the Redeemer. Why would they not have a Jesus complex? Megalomania developed, cultivated in them by us. We the intellectuals became useful idiots in the service of the petty dictators. When they began to loot the coffers of the state we turned a blind eye. They deserved a little reward for the decades they suffered on our behalf, some spending years in colonial prisons and in exile. Soon they thought they could do no wrong. They became all-powerful and all-knowing without becoming all-loving. No one could touch them. They inspired nothing but fear and became even worse than the colonial masters they replaced. They jailed and murdered even the mildest of opposition. They became agents of neo-colonialism, selling the riches of their countries to the West for their own self-aggrandisement.

I went on to say South Africa showed promise of going against that trend. We resisted the deification of the leaders. Staunch members of the ruling party were the first to go out in the streets to demonstrate against their own comrades in the government when they did not make the right decisions or did not perform to their satisfaction. We had a very strong civil society and a robustly free press which was always vigilant. Hopefully, things would stay like that and the gains we had made would be safeguarded.

My column in the *Sunday Times* became very popular. The English Academy of Southern Africa awarded it the Thomas Pringle Prize for 1998. I had to give up the column, however, because I was becoming increasingly involved in producing television programmes. I could not be a referee and a player at the same time. Also, it was becoming very difficult for me to hurt other people's feelings, especially the young producers and directors and even actors, who were doing their best and were wary of this mean person with a powerful pen who was always ready to pan their efforts. Another thing was that I was tired of fighting battles with the sub-editors of the *Sunday Times* who were ready to mess up my copy with their bad English and ignorance of historical and political facts.

At this time my novels and plays were also garnering some awards in South Africa. *Ways of Dying* received the M-Net Award, *She Plays with the Darkness* was awarded the Olive Schreiner Prize for Fiction and *The Nun's Romantic Story* won the Olive Schreiner Prize for Drama. *Ways of Dying* also got a Noma Award Honourable Mention. This in itself would not be worth mentioning, except for the fact that the judge was none other than the publisher who had turned the novel down as 'feminist diatribe'.

I was quite happy with my writing life, and with the fact that I had reconnected with my friend Sebolelo Mokhobo, or Sebo. She and her husband now lived in Johannesburg where she worked for a government department in the education sector. I occasionally met her for a drink at one of the pubs in Randburg, and she was surprised that I had become a teetotaller. She was still on to her beer, and I remembered fondly the old days when we used to pub-crawl in Maseru. I still had a very soft spot for her and I was sad when she told me how unhappy she was even though she had an important government job. I convinced my publisher Albert Nemukula that he should commission her to write the study notes for my novella for youth, *Melville 67*. The cover of the book was a painting by my son Neo, as was the case with the cover of *She Plays with the Darkness*.

Happy as I was as a writer and dramaturge at the Market Theatre, I also had other skills that I thought would serve my country well if only I could get into a position where I could use them. *Matsoho mohomeng*, the Basotho people say. 'All hands on the hoe' is the direct translation. All hands on deck! All hand to the pump!

My hands were needed on the hoe to eliminate the weeds that had resulted from decades of apartheid's absurdities. I owed my country that. That was the main reason I was back here. I could write my novels and plays anywhere in the world, but I needed to contribute more, in practical terms, at a physical workplace where I could make a difference. I had returned home with qualifications and experience that my country would certainly find useful. *Matsoho mohomeng!*

I therefore started applying for positions that were advertised in the local press. In all instances I was shortlisted for interviews. After the interviews the interviewers expressed their satisfaction. But then I would never hear from them again. I applied for various advertised positions at the South African Broadcasting Corporation, at the Independent Broadcasting Authority, at the various government and parastatal agencies that needed someone with mass communications, telecommunications and media arts skills. In all instances I was interviewed, and in all of them someone else with fewer qualifications but with strong party affiliations was employed. In many cases the people who ended up getting those jobs had no qualifications in the field at all, save for the fact that they were close relatives of important people in the government or were known ruling party apparatchiks.

In one instance, after an interview for the position of the director of a government communications agency for the Gauteng province, one of the interviewers – I won't tell you her name because she's going to be victimised; she's still in government – told me when I met her some days after the interview: 'It was the best interview ever; you are getting this job. We were unanimously impressed with you.'

I didn't hear from them for months. The woman who had told me I had the job avoided me whenever I saw her at a social event. One day I cornered her and she admitted that she was embarrassed I didn't get the job after giving me the assurance that I would. She shouldn't have done that before the appointment had been ratified by the presidency. The presidency had vetoed my appointment.

I told her not to worry, it was not her fault. But I wondered why civil service appointments had to be approved by the presidency. Who exactly in the presidency made such decisions and what clause in our Constitution gave them such power? Shouldn't the presidency rather be concerned with heavy matters of state than with keeping little me from serving my country?

I began to investigate this phenomenon and discovered that there were some highly qualified black people who were leaving the country because they could not get jobs. I wrote an article for the *Mail & Guardian* about it, mentioning the names of those who had left and also those who were still in the country but were being sidelined because they didn't have the approved party affiliation.

I also discovered that the patronage system extended to the corporate world which had become a big network of crony capitalism. The ruling party was able to 'deploy' its people even in the private sector where they implemented the unwritten policy of exclusion against those whose names did not resonate with the powers that be. Their tentacles were so long that they had the final word even in scholarships and research bodies and independent trusts and foundations. I wrote about that too.

The last straw was when I was nominated for the board of the South African Broadcasting Corporation. As was the practice, I had to be interviewed by members of parliament, those who were on the portfolio committee responsible for broadcasting. I flew to Cape Town for the interview. In parliament I fielded questions from the Honourable Members who represented the different parties. The hearings were chaired by Saki Macozoma of the ANC who I respected as the man who could advance the Mandela legacy – judging from some of the articles he wrote in the newspapers. The questions ranged from the mundane, such as Pieter Mulder of the Freedom Front asking me which was my favourite sitcom (it was *Seinfeld* at the time – I had read somewhere that it was his too) to more serious questions from Suzanne Vos of Inkatha Freedom Party about my views on provincial broadcasting for both radio and television. I supported it, of course, in the same way that I supported community broadcasting. It gave the people at local level a voice, which was stifled, often inadvertently, by the SABC since as a national broadcaster it focused on national and international issues. The SABC was dominated by events in Johannesburg and, to a lesser extent, in Cape Town – both news and entertainment – as if these metropolises were the whole of South Africa. I knew at the time that the ANC was wary of provincial broadcasting because it advanced the federalist ambitions of the Inkatha Freedom Party and would give that Zulu-based party a mouthpiece in KwaZulu-Natal which was under its rule. So, the ANC's opposition to provincial broadcasting at the time was political rather than principled. Nevertheless, after the interview I received an ovation from all the members present – including those of the ANC and PAC.

And indeed a few days later my name was on the list of those who had been chosen by the South African parliament to be on the governing board of the South African Broadcasting Corporation. The list was published in all the newspapers. I received congratulations from staffers at the SABC and other colleagues. Some even said they suspected Nelson Mandela would appoint me chairman of the board. 'Don't jump the gun,' I told them. 'He still has to approve the list chosen by parliament.'

I was right. A few months later when the final list was published in the newspapers my name was not there. Nelson Mandela had vetoed it. It was not an amorphous presidency this time but the president himself.

Many months later an Afrikaner woman came to my house to discuss a television series the script of which she wanted to commission me to write. She was one of the well-known Afrikaners who had been with the ANC even before liberation. As we sat in my lounge sipping coffee she asked, 'Who was your father and what did he do to Madiba?'

Many young ANC members don't know who my father was and what role he played in their liberation. But I was surprised that this woman – who must remain nameless because I don't want her to be marginalised for my sake – should ask me about him and should also imply that he must have done something to displease Nelson Mandela.

'My father was one of the founders of the ANC Youth League. As far as I know, he and Madiba were friends. Madiba has said as much in his autobiography. When my father was the president of the Youth League, Madiba was on his executive committee.'

She told me that Carl Niehaus, another ANC Afrikaner who was a close adviser of Nelson Mandela's at the time, had told her that the president had vetoed my name from the board of the SABC because, firstly, I was too outspoken, and secondly, my father betrayed them when they needed him most. I burst into laughter because it all sounded so silly. Was it not a virtue to be outspoken? As for the sins of my father – namely that he supported the Africanists who broke away from the ANC – was I going to be crucified for that? And by a man who forgave his oppressors and jailers and extended a hand of reconciliation to them? Why was his reconciliation only between black and white, and not between black and black?

Yes, Nelson Mandela spoke of inclusion and compassion and reconciliation, but I was seeing something different from his government. I was seeing black South Africans being excluded from participating in the development of their own country by a patronage system that was centred solely on greed and on rewarding the comrades for past services to the party. Many months later, on December 28, 1997, I wrote him a long letter.

After a few pleasantries wishing him a bountiful and healthy 1998, I got to the point. I wrote:

> Sir, I am writing you this letter to voice my concerns about the corruption, nepotism and cronyism that have found their way into the South African civil service and parastatals. Accompanied by a burgeoning patronage system and the greed that has taken over our lives, these threaten to destroy the wonderful country that you and your comrades have created for us all. They threaten the great gains that the ANC government has achieved.

I apologised for bothering him with such matters when he, as president, was obviously busy with many pressing issues – what with the whole world wanting a piece of him. But we were sitting on a powder keg, I said. I continued:

Like you, sir, I love this country, and I do want to save it from the impending doom. I do not want to see it becoming another Nigeria (*sorry to my Nigerian friends, but that's what I wrote to Madiba*) where bribery and corruption rule every aspect of the people's lives in all sectors of society.

After relating some anecdote that happened in the 1950s when I was a kid staying at his place I assured him that I was not writing to rekindle old relationships. I wrote:

I am not the type that hobnobs with the high and mighty – especially politicians – even when they are the world's statesmen that are universally admired. I am a humble writer who wants only to write his novels, plays and film scripts.

I think I should just reproduce the rest of the letter here verbatim rather than summarise it as I have been doing. Of course in parts it repeats some of the concerns I have stated elsewhere in these memoirs, but I think it is important for you to get its tone and intent directly:

Before I decided to be a fulltime writer I had great ambitions of serving my country in any capacity in which I might be useful. I had no doubt that my qualifications and experience would be useful in the development of a new South Africa. After all, I was coming home with masters and doctoral degrees in varied fields such as mass communication (radio and television), development communication, development studies, theatre, and film making. I was coming home as an international expert who was consulted on a regular basis by international organisations such as UNICEF (on social mobilisation), World Health Organisation (on using popular media in health education), USAID (on using radio drama in family planning campaigns), International Labour Organisation (on participatory communication in worker education) and the Lesotho government (on rural development strategies, the Institute of Land Use Planning, Village Water Supply etc). I was coming home as an author of a book on development communication that was prescribed at universities in such countries as Austria, France, USA, Ghana, Zimbabwe and South Africa (*since writing this letter that work is used even more widely*). Surely my country would find me useful!

But I was wrong. For reasons that I still do not understand I was sidelined at every turn. I diligently applied for employment, but people with less qualifications and no experience were employed instead. Why was I denied the right to serve my country by your government, sir? Why was I accused at job interviews by the awestruck bureaucrats of your government of being too educated for the post, of being too experienced (have you ever heard of such poppycock?), or of being overqualified? How is it possible to be overqualified? Is education not a good thing? Then why was I penalised for acquiring too much of it? These jobs (and I can name them if you like) were subsequently given to people who had zilch training or experience, but who were close relatives of ANC party loyalists – what I have referred to elsewhere as the Liberation Aristocracy.

Before I go any further, let me make it clear to you that I am not looking for a job. I do not want a job. I am happily working for myself as a writer and filmmaker, and I continue to share my skills with the international community which consults me. I therefore earn a good living for myself and a lot of foreign exchange for South Africa. The market for my activities is an international one. I also create employment for fellow South Africans. For instance a British company with British finance will be shooting a movie of my novel worth millions in South Africa in the course of 1998, using South African talent and crew; next week I am sending a crew of South African camera and sound operators to Ethiopia to work on a German documentary production there etc.

It is not because I want to boast of my achievements that I am mentioning these projects. I am only trying to assure you that my motives to write to you about nepotism, patronage and corruption in your government are not based on self-interest. I have nothing to gain from raising these issues. I have no personal axe to grind. I am mentioning my personal experience of being sidelined as proof to you that these things do really exist in your government.

But this is not only my experience. It is the experience of many other South Africans. I have actually interviewed and written about a number of highly qualified black people who have since left their country to work in America, the Far East and other African countries because they did not have the necessary party credentials to get jobs in South Africa. I have written about these things, after which I have been contacted by numerous others who have suffered the same plight. Many are still in South Africa, squirming in their bitterness. They can easily be dismissed as whiners and whingers by your fat bureaucrats, but the fact of the matter is that your government is busy cultivating a field of bitterness from which our children shall reap crops that will not be palatable at all. Things began like this in Nigeria. Before we know it we shall be swimming in a similar quagmire, for we seem to be determined to emulate some of the most unsavoury aspects of that society.

I repeat: when you discriminate against black people you are creating a lot of unnecessary bitterness. And it is not only me who is saying that. There is a lot of unhappiness out there, and people are talking. Recently an African woman wrote in the *Mail & Guardian* (December 24, 1997 to January 8, 1998): 'The future is decidedly bleak for black and white who feel they are being excluded from making a contribution to the government of the country, without the requisite struggle credentials, or at the very least, membership of the ANC.'

Indeed many victims of discrimination by your government have 'struggle credentials'. I met them all over in Europe and America actively participating in demonstrations against apartheid, organising local communities for disinvestment campaigns and sports and cultural boycotts. Only they were doing these things outside the structures of the ANC. Even inside the country people participated in mass actions, were shot at and died, without necessarily being members of the ANC. I lost relatives in this way, and some of them were not members of any political party. The struggle in South Africa was not the sole preserve of ANC members. I myself have a struggle record that speaks for itself in my numerous writings and campaigns in Europe and America, even though I was never a member of the ANC.

However even if these sons and daughters of South Africa had not actively participated in the struggle, by virtue of being South Africans who are keen to contribute their skills in the development of their country, they must not be discriminated against.

After all, you and your comrades have forgiven your jailers. You have embraced people who tortured you, kept you away from your families for thirty years, exiled you, and murdered thousands of your compatriots. Surely it is reasonable for black people to expect you to show the same magnanimity towards them, even if they did not actively participate in the struggle, or even if they participated in other ways and in other organisations that were not necessarily ANC aligned.

I have said before that every government in the world must have political appointees. For instance no one expects your spokesperson or political adviser to be a member of the PAC or NP. It must be somebody who shares your political vision. In any government there will be a few of such sensitive political positions. However every South African, irrespective of political affiliation, must have a place in the sun.

Lest you think that my concerns are only for the elites who have returned with degrees from foreign lands, let me hasten to add that I do a lot of work in the communities in the townships. I talk with the youth in community centres in Dobsonville and Alexandra. I create theatre-for-development with them – a concept of using theatre as a vehicle of a critical analysis of the problems that beset the community – and all the time they express their disillusionment at what is happening in South Africa today. I have a play, created with the actors and produced by the Market Theatre Laboratory, that has been touring the townships of Gauteng for the past three years. The play is on child and spousal abuse, TB and AIDS. But invariably when the time comes to discuss the issues raised in the play, the youth will mention the corruption and nepotism that is prevalent in the country.

The youth have a perception that generally our political leaders are thoroughly rotten. Many of our youths are despondent and have lost hope. The older ones talk of having been used as cannon fodder in the struggle, yet now they are forgotten while 'the leaders ride on the gravy train'. They believe that since they do not come from families that have names that count they have no future in the country of their birth. All doors are closed to them. The concept of the Aristocrats of the Revolution has taken root.

The youth are beginning to talk of violence. They put blame on everyone: politicians, white people, 'exiles', members of the chosen families – all of whom they believe are responsible for their woes. When Jon Qwelane and Thami Mazwai wrote in the *Sunday Independent* (December 21, 1997) of the *gatvol* factor that has built up among the youths of our country, to the extent that they are threatening to 'meet them (recalcitrant whites) bullet for bullet', I knew what they were talking about. I have come across these sentiments myself out there in the communities. Only they are not just directed to whites. They are directed at all those the youth feel have failed them . . . all those who have closed doors and are dispensing favours only to the favoured ones. When you try to dissuade them from such thoughts, and show them the great gains that this government has made, they laugh at your face. It is a reality they refuse to see, for what is dominant right now in their perceptions is the corruption and nepotism in the government. Now, we can easily blame the media for these perceptions. Indeed the media does make great song and dance about government weaknesses, and nary a word about its great achievements. But, however misguided some of the sentiments expressed by these young people may be, there is a grain of truth somewhere there, especially in matters pertaining to nepotism and corruption, as I have personally experienced them myself.

The democracy that you fought and suffered for, that a lot of South Africans died for, is working, sir. That is why I am able to write you a letter of this nature. There is no doubt that we live in a wonderful country. I have lived in many countries of the world over the past thirty years of exile, but never have I had such a wonderful lucrative time as I am having in South Africa today. That is why I am fearful that this dream will not last if the corruption and nepotism prevalent in your government is not nipped in the bud. I do not want my children to inherit a country that has been wrecked by greed and stupidity. The decay has begun to set in. Only you, Madiba, can stop it!

Do not ignore my pleas to you, sir. I am one of the millions of South Africans who voted for the ANC, even though they were not card-carrying members of that organisation. But that is not the reason why you and your government must not sideline me and those who are like me. The reason is a simple one: I am a South African. Even if I had voted for the NP, the PAC, the Inkatha or the DP, I would still ask that you heed my call. I would still demand not to be sidelined in my country. I would still say that I have the right to serve South Africa!

Nelson Mandela did not write back. No. He phoned. He told me that he had received my letter and somebody would call me to arrange for a meeting with some of his ministers so that I might outline to them these problems I was talking about. And indeed after about two weeks or so I got another call from the presidency. Whoever I spoke with there – maybe a personal assistant or a secretary – told me that reservations had been made at Sahib Indian Restaurant in a Pretoria suburb where I would have lunch with three cabinet ministers: Joe Modise, Minister of Defence, Penuell Maduna, Minister of Minerals and Energy Affairs, and Zola Skweyiya, Minister of Public Service and Administration. I could understand why Mr Mandela had chosen Zola Skweyiya to meet me; I had complained about the public service and the patronage system that had emerged particularly in doling out jobs for pals and political cronies. But I had no idea why the military guy and the energy and minerals one were part of this. Even though I didn't have any idea what the agenda was going to be, I agreed to the lunch.

On the appointed day two ministers were there promptly, Maduna and Skweyiya. They conveyed Joe Modise's apologies. He had been urgently summoned by the president because of the Meiring affair.

'The Meiring affair? What is it exactly?' I asked.

'You'll hear about it soon enough,' said Maduna. 'It's bound to be in the papers this week.'

If I was a newspaper reporter I would be digging further for a scoop, but I let it rest.

Skweyiya struck me as a very quiet guy; he did more listening than talking. Maduna on the other hand was garrulous. Once more I outlined my position as already stated in my letter to Nelson Mandela. Skweyiya did not say much on the issues I raised. He just looked at me sadly. Perhaps he thought I was making a fuss over nothing. He didn't say so, though; it was just my own impression. Maduna, on the other hand, was clearly dismissive of my concerns. Instead he tended to lecture: the youth must pull themselves up by their bootstraps. He

432

presented himself as an example; he came back from exile with a law degree from Zimbabwe. He didn't just sit there but went back to school. He continued his education even when he was already a minister until he got a PhD from Wits University.

'As we speak, I've enrolled at RAU for a diploma in energy and in transportation so that I don't depend on experts and consultants in my cabinet portfolio,' he said. 'I need to be an expert in my own right.'

RAU was the Randse Afrikaanse Universiteit, which has since become the University of Johannesburg.

I admired Maduna for his resolve and dedication, though he didn't strike me as a likeable fellow. There was a tinge of arrogance in his attitude.

'You are indeed a good example that all South Africans – not just the youth – should follow,' I told him. 'I like people who pursue education as relentlessly as you do.'

After the lunch I drove back to Johannesburg. I didn't know what the meeting had achieved. I wondered what the ministers were going to tell Madiba, or if they were going to report back to him at all about it. It looked like a public relations exercise to me. Nothing changed in the areas that I complained about; today patronage and cronyism are worse than ever before. We are overtaking Nigeria. Worse still, blatant racial arrogance – 'closing ranks' – and a culture of impunity have developed among some of the ruling elite who have obviously taken good lessons from the laager mentality of the Afrikaners of yesterday.

Perhaps the meeting was just a way of shutting me up. Well, I shouldn't complain; in other countries they shut you up by imprisoning you if you're lucky, or by feeding you to the crocodiles instead of feeding you sumptuous Indian cuisine of vegetarian biryani, assorted pickles and chutney, served with garlic naan.

The Meiring scandal broke in the weekend newspapers. General George Meiring, who had been inherited from the apartheid era, was the commander of the South African National Defence Force. He presented what he claimed was a military intelligence report to Nelson Mandela that an organisation called FAPLA – Front African People's Liberation Army – was plotting a coup to assassinate Mandela and overthrow his government. What made the story even juicier was that FAPLA was alleged to be composed of well-known ANC loyalists, including the president's ex-wife Winnie, the deputy chief of the defence forces Lieutenant General Siphiwe Nyanda, former MK guerrilla Robert McBride, and politician General Bantu Holomisa and a host of black soldiers. Don't laugh now, but even pop star Michael Jackson was implicated in the plot. One hundred and thirty names in all were listed in the report. Nelson Mandela appointed a judicial inquiry which concluded that the report was utterly fantastic. It was the work of what was referred to in the press as the 'third force' of the old guard security operatives who were bent on provoking uprisings and mayhem. Meiring resigned in disgrace.

Adele returned from America. I was happy to welcome her back. I had stayed celibate all the time she was away, hoping that on her return we would start afresh and build a family. I was not going to give up on this marriage that easily. I resolved to have more patience and not be abrupt or brutally frank. I had to realise that my views, and indeed my values, were not sacrosanct; there were other views that might be opposed to mine but were just as important. I also had to learn not to respond to every little provocation, and accept the simple fact of life that things would not always go my way because I was not the alpha and the omega but a simple human being replete with flaws.

When she was still in Vermont I had sent her information about a vacancy at Vista University and encouraged her to apply. When she returned there was a job waiting for her at the East Rand campus of the university.

For a while she commuted by train from the Johannesburg station to Daveyton, Benoni, where the campus was located. It was very inconvenient because she had to take Melville 67, the metro bus, which had its bus stop across the street from our townhouse, to downtown Johannesburg, then walk to Park Station, as the Johannesburg station was known, for the train. She felt very unsafe. A month or so later she bought a brand new Toyota Tazz hatchback, which made her commuting easier. I was impressed by her resourcefulness so soon after she had arrived in Johannesburg – she just went to a Toyota dealership, selected the car she wanted, the dealership got a bank to finance her, and in a day she had a car. I had never thought it was that easy. I would have got a car for myself long before if I had just thought of doing what she did. Or if I had even thought of getting a car at all. So, I followed her example and got myself a new Mercedes Benz.

Our life at the townhouse in Westdene was cordial, though one could feel the tensions bubbling beneath the surface. I tried very hard not to tread on her toes. Zukile was also happy to have his mother with him at last. But he was the only child who was pleased with her presence. Dini moved out and I heard he was staying with a group of gardeners his age who were employed by a neighbouring townhouse complex. He dropped out of the Roosevelt High School in Roosevelt Park where I had enrolled him after his return from the United States. He told me he was now working as a gardener as well. I tried hard to persuade him to come home and return to school. He told me he had been very much traumatised by our bickering when we were in Vermont, to the extent that he had moved out and gone to live with friends. He remembered vividly the names that Adele called me in his presence, referring to my genitalia in a degrading manner. He did not want to experience that again.

'People can change,' I pleaded. 'Give us a chance.'

He was not prepared to go along with that. This was a dilemma. I wanted to work things out with Adele, but in the process I was losing my son.

The two older kids, Thandi and Neo, stayed however and continued with their schooling at FUBA Academy.

I spotted an advertisement for the post of director of a non-governmental organisation called L-MAP in Bloemfontein. The organisation produced materials on language training methods and conducted workshops for language teachers. I advised Adele to apply and she got the post. This meant that she had to move to Bloemfontein, a city in the Free State Province, four hundred kilometres from Johannesburg. She rented herself a flat in the city centre.

I often visited her there and we had a great time. Her brother Willie told me that now that we were living apart our marriage had a chance. But the harmony was not to last. When she visited our townhouse in Johannesburg she used to spread her files and work papers all over the dining room table and everywhere else in the house. The whole place looked very untidy when she was around and it made me very uncomfortable. I have always been a neatness freak. One day after she had been working at the table she just left everything there. I wouldn't have minded if it was only for a day or so, but she was returning to Bloemfontein and would only be back after two or three weeks. This meant that the room would be in a mess for that long.

In a situation like this my old self would have said, 'Please remove this mess from the table. I am trying to keep the room clean.' But, as I have already told you, I was trying to tread lightly to keep the peace. So, I said, 'Do you mind if I take these papers and store them away in my drawers until you come back?' She was at the door carrying her bags, about to get into her car. She turned around and exploded in a tirade about my reproductive organs that you wouldn't want me to repeat here. I felt so small, more so because she said these things in the presence of my niece Limpho, who was visiting from Lesotho. I yelled back at her, telling her how peaceful it had been for everybody before she came back into my life.

'You dare touch my papers, you'll know me,' she said.

'I know you already,' I said. 'And I don't like what I know.'

She stormed out. I was so mad that I took all those papers and put them in a garbage bag. But I did not dump them. I put them under my desk in our bedroom; she would find them next time she came.

The next time she fired the young girl we had hired from her village in Lesotho as Zukile's nanny. Her crime? I had enrolled her at a dressmaking school in the city. The objective was that when Zukile was at pre-school she would not just be idling at home but would be learning a trade so that she would not have to spend her whole life working as other people's maid.

'Why would you be interested in sending this girl you don't even know to school if you were not sleeping with her?' she asked.

There had to be some prurient reason for my charity. That was always the problem in our relationship – she assigned motives and in her mind they became fact even if there was glaring evidence to the contrary. She held to them firmly and refused to change her mind. The more sordid the motive she invented, the more stubbornly she held to it. I created one or two characters like that in my future novels as a way of trying to understand her.

This new round of hostilities was followed by a period of truce. We were going to make it. For the sake of Zukile, we were going to make it.

We bought a house in Weltevredenpark, a previously all-white and mostly Afrikaner suburb of Roodepoort, one of the satellite towns of Johannesburg. It was a big brick house roofed in brown tiles, with three garages, five bedrooms, three bathrooms, two living rooms, a big kitchen with modern gadgets and a small dining room. We were doing so well that we were able to furnish the whole house all at once and pay in cash. She, for instance, paid in full for a custom-made living room suite. She was a homemaker and didn't hesitate to splash out on household items and even pay extra on the mortgage so that it would be fully paid long before the period stipulated by the bank.

I enrolled Zukile at Popeye Nursery School in Weltevredenpark and Thandi at Allenby Film School, which was in Randburg.

The truce did not last long. When she came home from Bloemfontein the bickering resumed. I wrote her a long letter expressing my grievances and suggesting divorce was the best solution. We were in Maseru on an outing to discuss an amicable divorce when Adele told me that she was pregnant with our second child. Neither of us seemed happy at the thought of another child when our marriage was so rocky that we were contemplating divorce.

During the nine months that we were expecting this baby Adele was the sweetest person I have ever known. I looked forward to the weekends when I would be driving to Bloemfontein to be with her. Sometimes she drove to Johannesburg to see me and Zukile.

I took her to Paris and we sailed on the River Seine and visited the Louvre and Musée D'Orsay and La Defence and the Eiffel Tower and did all the silly tourist things one does in France. We joked that this was our honeymoon, since we had never had one.

The sweetness continued until our baby girl was born. I named her Zukiswa, which was a female version of Zukile. I also named her

Moroesi, which was the name we had always said we'd use if we had a baby girl even when we were still at Roma in Lesotho. The name had actually become a joke among her friends. They would ask: 'When is Moroesi coming?' I don't know what the name means, but in Sesotho fairy tales Moroesi is always a very beautiful girl. I once wrote a play titled *Moroesi*, about a beautiful young lady who saved her village from foreign forces that were threatening to take it over and subjugate her people. Adele suggested we also name the child Zenzile after my grandfather – the one who was a chief of Goodwell, the present-day Bee Place. That's the name that stuck and everyone called her Zenzi.

Zenzi stayed with Adele in Bloemfontein and I stayed with Zukile in Johannesburg. I took Zukile with me on some of my travels abroad. We went to Barcelona, Spain, to visit Teresa Devant and her husband, Albio Gonzalez. Teresa had directed and produced a number of my plays in Barcelona. She had recently directed *La Romántica Historia D'Una Monja*, the Catalan version of my play *The Nun's Romantic Story*, translated by a revered Catalan translator and writer, Carme Serrallonga and presented at the Sala Muntaner during the Grec 98 Festival by Associació d'Investigació I Experimentació Teatral.

On this occasion I was there to give a lecture on Bertolt Brecht at the University of Barcelona and just to spend time hanging out with the family. Teresa's two kids, Adrian and Sara, immediately fell in love with Zukile. I, on the other hand, became much captivated by an older woman, Julie Wark, who lived in the same building as our hosts. She was originally from Australia but had lived in Barcelona for years where she worked as a translator. I liked hanging out with her because she had wonderful stories to tell about her former lovers, one of whom was a great African poet and scholar who I knew very well but who shall remain nameless because the intention of my memoirs is not to gossip about others but about myself and those who were unwise enough to get involved with me. Some of Julie's stories were about her association with guerrillas in East Timor and Papua New Guinea. She made those places come to life for me and I decided that one day I would go there to write a book. She really made revolution sound very romantic.

At a restaurant in Barcelona people at neighbouring tables stared at Zukile as he struggled with a knife and fork and even with a spoon. He was sitting next to Albio and I was sitting at the opposite end of the table. He was four and a half years old yet his hands could not grasp anything. Back in Johannesburg I had been trying to correct that with the help of physical therapists. I was the cause of the problem. When I was bringing him up on my own, having never brought up a child by myself before, I became too protective of him. During meals I fed him instead of letting him eat by himself; I pushed him in a stroller at all times instead of letting him walk. I did everything for him instead of teaching him independence. Now Barcelonans were staring and giggling as he struggled to eat with his soft hands. I hated them for gawking so shamelessly. But I could do nothing to help him.

At night we slept in one of the kids' bedrooms under an original painting by Thami Myele, the South African artist who was murdered by the South African Defence Force in Botswana during the bad days of apartheid. The whole house, every wall, had paintings by various South African artists, including some of mine, which Albio had collected over the years. Zukile spent what seemed like hours gazing at Thami Myele's painting. Even in the morning when we woke up his eyes were on the painting. He told me that it was an X-spray.

'Do you know what an X-spray is, Daddy?' he asked.

'No, I don't,' I said.

'It's a man or woman who dies and becomes an alien.'

I thought it was an interesting interpretation of Thami Myele's painting.

Zukile grew up surrounded by paintings. Not only mine, but those of my friends who were artists or art collectors. One artist I got to know during this period was Theo Gerber. He was the most awe-inspiring artist I had seen, whose paintings combined aspects of Surrealism and Lyrical Abstractionism. His work was breathtakingly sated with allusions and eroticism. He came originally from Basel in Switzerland, but lived in the south of France. He and his wife Susi came to South Africa quite often because they had been in solidarity with South African artists during apartheid. They worked with many of our artists, such as Nhlanhla Xaba and Matsemela Manaka, both in South Africa and in the south of France.

On one occasion I was on a literary visit to Aix-en-Provence in France with a number of South African writers like Njabulo Ndebele, Mandla Langa, André Brink, J M Coetzee, Antjie Krog, Gcina Mhlophe, Sindiwe Magona and Ivan Vladislavić. I decided to take my family with me, so I was there with Adele, Zukile and Zenzi. Zenzi used to have tantrums in those days – you wouldn't believe it if you saw her now because she's the sweetest girl you'll ever meet – and she made a lot of noise both in the plane and at the hotel where we were staying. I started to regret having taken her along.

After my reading sessions at the Cité du Livre I decided to take my family to visit Theo Gerber. I had heard from Susi that he was not well, but I wanted to introduce him to my wife and kids because on the occasions that he had visited me in South Africa only Zukile was there. Theo lived in a castle in a small village in the south of France. Susi came to pick us up in her car from our hotel in Aix-en-Provence. That ancient castle, which at one time was a monastery and then a convent, had seen many of our artists work there. Some of the great works of Matsemela Manaka and of Pitika Ntuli were created in that castle. But it had also seen some wonderful theatre performances by such doyennes of the South African stage as Sibongile Khumalo.

'He'll be happy to see you,' said Susi. 'These are his final moments.'

He lay on his bed surrounded by his giant paintings and a rooster. And by me and my wife and my children and Susi. The mistral was blowing outside, ruffling the feathers of his pet emu. And Theo Gerber was dying in his castle. I held his hand as his breath slowly slipped away. He looked at me and smiled.

When I returned to South Africa I wrote about that experience in the *Sunday Independent*.

Theo haunted me for a long time. Many months later I was at a beachfront restaurant in Durban sharing paella with Yvonne Vera. We were participating in a literary festival called Time of the Writer with, among others, Wole Soyinka, Abdourahman Ali Waberi and Breyten Breytenbach. Though I had long known and loved her work, I met Yvonne for the first time at that festival and we hit it off immediately. We went swimming in the sea at dawn. I introduced her to paella which had been introduced to me by my friends in Barcelona. She couldn't have enough of it, although for me it was inferior to the paella that Teresa had cooked in Barcelona.

So, we were sitting there, stuffing ourselves and looking at the sea when I pointed at the waves.

'You see those waves with the surf,' I said. 'They look like a Theo Gerber painting. Look, look, they actually form an image of a human head. It looks like Theo Gerber. And it is smiling.'

She didn't understand what I was talking about. Her full-time job was managing an art gallery in Bulawayo, so she was keen to know more about Theo Gerber.

'You see him over there,' I said. 'Right there!'

But other waves came and swept the image away. I hope Yvonne didn't think I was crazy. I was just being haunted by Theo Gerber.

As I was preparing to write this chapter my eyes popped out of my head when I discovered that Theo Gerber was alive and living in South Africa. Could I have dreamt his death? No. That was just a coincidence. The two were not related in any way. The South African Theo Gerber I saw on the Internet was a much younger man who painted ordinary still life.

DEBE MORRIS IS A gorgeous film director from Toronto. Brown, tall and slender with a hint of a Caribbean accent. She came to my house in Weltevredenpark to negotiate for the rights of *And the Girls in Their Sunday Dresses* for performance by the AfriCan Theatre Ensemble in Canada. Now I am on the N1 South freeway in my metallic grey car driving her to Lesotho to visit the Royal Family. She has been corresponding with the Queen Mother, 'Mamohato, for some time since the death of the Queen's daughter, Princess 'Maseeiso, who had been a close friend of Debe's when the princess lived in Canada.

We hit it off with Debe immediately and I offer to take her to Lesotho. I'll leave her there and proceed to the Bee Place in the Eastern Cape. Then I'll pick her up a day or two later and drive her back to Johannesburg.

On the road I pick up some hitch-hikers – my dangerous habit that you already know about. It is a white couple and they are on their way to Cape Town. They have been on the road for days, they say, and hope with the kindness of strangers like me they will ultimately reach their destination. They look scruffy, which can be expected of anyone who has had no access to a shower and clean clothes for an extended period.

'We are hoping in Cape Town life will be better for us,' says the man.

'What is your line of work?' I ask.

'I fix things. I can do anything. I am a handyman.'

'Jobs are scarce, are they?'

'It's this affirmative action of the new South Africa. It has no place for us poor whites.'

I let that go. I could have told him it has no place for me either, black as I am. These folks had sheltered employment during apartheid by virtue of being white and, most importantly, Afrikaner. I turn to Debe and we talk about her experiences with Princess 'Maseeiso. They used to have wonderfully wild times together. From the high jinks Debe tells me about, which are none of your business, she must have been a fun person to be with.

In Ventersburg I stop for gas and I buy everyone burgers from Steers. The hitch-hikers opt for dagwoods with everything on them: bacon, eggs, steak, sausage patties, tomatoes, lettuce, the works. Debe orders a tiny tomato and cheese sandwich. We share a table and the hitch-hikers wolf their food like people who haven't had anything to eat for days. The man keeps looking at us uncomfortably. He seems to make Debe a bit nervous. I am sorry that I have to subject her to this. The woman has her eyes fixed on one spot on the floor as if she is ashamed that they have been reduced to depend on the charity of strangers. Worse still, black strangers.

Back on N1 we drive quietly for about two hours until we get to the Verkeerdevlei junction. We drop our hitch-hikers there because Debe and I are branching off on the R703 to the small town of Excelsior. We drive among vast farms of deep yellow sunflowers in full bloom. When we get into the town I first take Debe to the street where the Dutch Reformed Church is located and I point it out to her from some distance away.

'That's the church where my Afrikaners worship,' I say.

She knows that I am talking about the Afrikaners in my yet unpublished novel, *The Madonna of Excelsior*. She has read the manuscript and has given me wonderful feedback on it.

She is quite excited to see small-town South Africa and is clicking away with her digital camera. It is quite different from Johannesburg or Cape Town where she has spent some time. I take her to the town hall where the town council meetings of both my fictional characters and of the real-life town councillors of Excelsior are held. She photographs the walls, the ceiling, the curtains and everything else that I describe in my fiction. She says my descriptions make her feel as though she has been here before. I then take her to Mahlatswetsa Location to the home of Senkey Mokhethi who is one of my important sources for the history of Excelsior. He lives in a solid four-roomed concrete block township house. He is one of the town councillors of Excelsior and part of my novel is based on his life story and that of members of his family. After a brief visit with him I take Debe to see Senkey's mother. She lives in a corrugated iron shack and is lying on her bed. She is on this bed most times I visit her because she says her health is no longer what it used to be. We also meet her daughter, Tiisetso. She is called a Coloured in South Africa because she is of mixed race. Her father was an Afrikaner policeman for whom Senkey's mother worked. I am surprised to find Tiisetso here because she is supposed to be at school in Bloemfontein. I pay for her tuition at a private college where she is studying office management. Senkey tells me that she is under the influence of her boyfriend who keeps taking her out of school. I threaten to stop paying her fees if she is not serious.

Debe tells me that the whole scenario reminds her very much of her native Caribbean island. 'She looks like some grandmothers I know,' she says of Senkey's mother.

It was really a chance meeting that brought me to this family when I first came to this colourful little town in search of a story.

I RECALLED A SCANDAL that broke out when I was in my final year at Peka High School. A group of Afrikaner men and black women appeared at the magistrate's court in a small Orange Free State town called Excelsior charged with contravening the Immorality Act which prohibited sexual relations between blacks and whites. There were many such cases throughout South Africa, but what made this one different was that the men were pillars of the Afrikaner community and included pastors of the Dutch Reformed Church and leaders of the ruling National Party – the very political party that introduced a lot of the discriminatory and oppressive race-based legislation in the country, and actually coined the word *apartheid*. The miscegenation came to light when the police discovered a number of Coloured or mixed-race children in the town, and the culprits were rounded up and imprisoned. The case received so much publicity in the local and overseas media that it embarrassed the South African government. Percy Yutar, the attorney-general, was instructed to withdraw the case, and he did. That was supposed to be the end of it. Indeed, the people of Excelsior thought the past was dead and buried for ever.

But not for me. One day, as I sat in my house in Weltevredenpark, I wondered what had happened to the people of Excelsior; the black women and their Coloured children, and of course the Afrikaner men – those who had not committed suicide because some of them did or had attempted it. What were they doing and how were they coping in the new South Africa? I got into my car and made the four-hour trip through the rich farmlands of the Free State to the small town of Excelsior.

I discovered that the people of Excelsior did not want to talk about the past. They resented the fact that I was trying to open old wounds. The white people I asked pretended that they knew nothing about the scandal.

The owner of the hotel where I had booked my accommodation told me: 'We bought this hotel long after those events which you say happened in 1969 and 1970. We know nothing about them. Ask the man who runs the liquor off-sales outlet next door. He might know. He has lived here all his life.'

At the off-sales outlet a group of black men were sitting on the low window sill drinking beer from quart bottles. They overheard my enquiry directed at the white man behind the counter and one of them stood up and said, 'I know what you are talking about. One of those women was my mother.'

That was Senkey Mokhethi. He was one of the town councillors of Excelsior and one of the men sitting drinking with him was actually the mayor of the town and was married to one of the Coloured children who had resulted from the scandal. Senkey took me to his home and introduced me to his family: his wife, his mother and his Coloured sister, Tiisetso. He also introduced me to a number of the townspeople who had had some involvement in the scandal, including the Afrikaner lawyer who defended the men, a black woman who was a town councillor for the National Party and personally knew some of the women and their Coloured children, and an old one-eyed Afrikaner farmer who was one of the accused who had attempted suicide. He had his missing eye to show for it.

I wrote a story about my Excelsior experience for the *Mail & Guardian*, and decided that it would also be the basis of my new novel, *The Madonna of Excelsior*.

It was about this time that we had our second elections in South Africa. I became a voter for only the second time in my life. The first time, you'll remember, I cast my vote at the Ukrainian Center in Montreal, Canada. This time I was doing it in my country. Unlike the first time, when I split my vote between two parties in honour of my father, this time I voted for the ANC. Even though I was not satisfied with the corruption and nepotism that I wrote about to Mandela, I felt it was the most progressive and most inclusive of all the parties. I liked its foreign policies – this was before the Zimbabwe debacle – especially because the ANC leaders refused to be dictated to by Western powers and stubbornly maintained strong relations with heads of state the Western world did not like but who had supported us in our struggle when the West was propping up the apartheid regime. I liked their insistence on human rights for everyone, including homosexuals, transgender and intersex people. I also liked their pro-choice position in matters of reproductive rights and their abolition of the death penalty. These were human rights issues I felt very strongly about. I did not like the economic policies of the ANC, particularly the party's fiscal conservatism – which was a big surprise to me because the ANC had communists in its midst. But at least it was slightly more to the left of the two major opposition parties – the predominantly Zulu-based Inkatha Freedom Party and the predominantly white Democratic Party. The PAC, on the other hand, had become more of a conservative party than the pan-Africanist and progressive one of the glorious days of Mangaliso Sobukwe. Its Africanism meant the conservation of values of a romantic Africa of some imagined past. Some of these values were chauvinistic, patriarchal and homophobic.

The ANC won the elections with an increased majority and Thabo Mbeki, the party's president, became the new president of the Republic of South Africa. For his inauguration, a famed Italian composer and conductor, Carlo Franci, was commissioned to compose some kind of opera using orchestra, singers and dancers to tell the story of the African Renaissance. I was commissioned to write the libretto in the form of poetry. The performance on the evening of June 16, 1999, at the State Theatre in Pretoria was attended by a number of heads of state who had been at the inauguration during the day. In the audience I could see Yasser Arafat, Muammar al-Gaddafi, Kofi Annan and Fidel Castro relishing my words brought to life by Franci's music as the revered South African actor Sello Maake kaNcube performed a particular poem of mine titled 'Birth of a People'.

I attended the day's events and the evening performance with Adele and she was overcome with emotion when she met and shook the hand of Winnie Mandela. She had always been a fan. She once told me that some of her friends said she looked like her.

After the performance I saw the doyen of South African television and movie producers, Mfundi Vundla, and the musician Caiphus Semenya, who is also regarded as an elder statesman of the arts and culture in South Africa. They were outraged that a composer was imported from Italy to create an opera for the inauguration of an African president when South Africa was replete with world-class composers of all types of music. These artists were right. I felt like a traitor for having collaborated with this betrayal of South African composers.

At the inauguration I met Thabo Moerane again after many years since we parted at Peka High School and introduced him to Adele. He was Thabo Mbeki's cousin, the son of the maestro Michael Mosoeu Moerane who had been such a great influence in my life. He told me he was now based in Geneva where he worked for some UN agency and played the piano at some of the jazz venues there.

I was sad that Jama Mbeki, my late Peka High School friend, was not there to see his own brother become the president of a free, non-racial and non-sexist South Africa.

Another person that I was always sorry never got to see the new South Africa because he died only a year before its birth, was my father. I know he would have been very critical of some aspects of the country, particularly the so-called Black Economic Empowerment which did nothing to empower the ordinary black people but was aimed at creating a new capitalist class among the hand-picked ruling party 'deployees'. But still it would have been interesting to get his always insightful analysis of the situation. I wished I had paid more attention to him when he was still alive. I should have relished the round-table family meetings instead of being disdainful about them because they took me away from friends and play. I would have learnt a lot and would have become a better human being.

These were the thoughts that preoccupied me when Adele and I drove to Mafeteng for the unveiling of his tombstone. The event was held at Zwelakhe's house. He had always been the pillar of the family. Not only was he there when my father died – I was away in America and couldn't even attend his funeral – but he was the one who looked after our mother, helped financially of course by me and by the old age pension from the South African government and the lump-sum Special Pension for former refugees and freedom fighters. I was grateful to him and I expressed my gratitude in the dedication of my novel *She Plays with the Darkness*. He had read the novel and loved it; he could identify some of the people and events I was writing about.

We booked in at Hotel Mafeteng and went to Zwelakhe's house to assist with the preparation for the event the next day. Adele was busy helping the women who were cooking when my sister-in-law Johanna came and told me that Zwelakhe sent her to tell me that Adele should go away since he had made it clear in his letter to me when we were still in America that she should never set her foot in his house or come close to my mother. I was taken aback that Zwelakhe could hold a grudge for so many years. I was also offended that he hadn't discussed the matter with me personally but had sent Johanna instead.

'I am not going to tell Adele to leave,' I said. 'If you people don't want her here you'd better tell her yourselves.'

Johanna finally did give her Zwelakhe's message, but Adele refused to leave. She sat there and continued to help the women. I knew she was daring him to make a scene in public and physically kick her out. He did not take the challenge. Instead he became very angry with me, without confronting me personally. Johanna became his emissary, and through her I got to know that I was a persona non grata at his house even though my mother lived there as well. All because I was supporting my wife. My mother was saddened by this episode and assured me she had no part in it and would like Adele to be around. She had long forgotten and forgiven the conflicts of the past.

The next day the unveiling ceremony went without a hitch. Both Adele and I were at the graveside as speeches were made by various members of the community, including leaders of the PAC and the ANC, about my father's contribution to the liberation struggle and how those who were in power today thought they could wipe him off the pages of history. After the ceremony we went into the house to greet my mother and then left without participating in the feasting that followed.

There was a bitter taste in my mouth as we drove back to Johannesburg.

CHAPTER FOURTEEN

I FEEL THAT MY visits to my Aunt Ella bring me closer to my father, who I miss very much. Her face is a replica of my father's. She is one of his two surviving siblings. The other is Nontombi, the last born in the family, but we have not seen her since she left Qoboshane more than fifty years ago and never returned. We only hear of her from those who have seen her. They tell us she lives somewhere in Orange Farm, one of the former informal settlements of Johannesburg. She is the mother of Cousin Bernard, the village madman I told you about earlier.

Gugu and I are coming from Mofolo where we have paid a brief visit to her sister, Sis' Pat Mphuthi. Even if Aunt Ella's house was not on our way we would have branched off to see her and imbibe more of her A P Mda aura. She waddles from her bedroom where she now spends most of her life, just like my mother, and joins us in her living room.

She is a political animal and she complains that the government of Thabo Mbeki is no different from that of Nelson Mandela in marginalising Soweto. The cost of electricity is very high and the government is not subsidising the poor people enough. Some have to go without the necessary utilities.

Then she wants to know about 'my' bees.

'You got your knack for beekeeping from my father,' she says.

I am surprised to hear this because I never associated my grandfather with beekeeping. Even when we were kids staying with my grandparents we never saw or heard of his bees.

'At that time my father was already old and had given up on beekeeping,' says my aunt.

But before that, when Aunt Ella was a girl attending Qoboshane Bantu Community School and being taught by Mr Nyanginstimbi who also taught me many years later, my grandfather was a beekeeper at the very spot where my present-day Bee People keep their bees. That would have been in the late 1920s – two decades before I was born. My aunt is surprised to hear that I didn't know of my grandfather's beekeeping. She had assumed that I had established the apiary on Dyarhom Mountain knowingly following in my grandfather's footsteps.

'Were you not doing it because he had done it before?' she asks. 'Was it not under his influence?'

'Not at all. It's a great coincidence. I had no idea that my grandfather was a beekeeper, let alone that he kept them at the very spot where I later became a beekeeper.'

'There is nothing like a coincidence. You were led there by the ancestors.'

She tells me that my grandfather used to harvest many buckets of honey. Mr Mather of Mather and Sons used to drive from Sterkspruit to purchase all the honey which he resold at his store. I tell her that the present-day Bee People sell some of their honey to the descendants of Mr Mather at Mather and Sons.

THE BEEKEEPING PROJECT STARTED from a quest for a story. One day I was sitting in my house in Weltevredenpark when Phyllis Klotz of Sabikwa Theatre arrived with two guys from a Netherlands theatre company called De Nieuw Amsterdam Theatergroep – DNA. They wanted to commission me to write a play set in South Africa and the Netherlands about a subject or theme of my choice. They suggested that I might write about slavery in the early Dutch colonial days at the Cape. But a historical subject didn't interest me. I wanted to write on a more contemporary theme.

As part of this commission I went to stay in Amsterdam for a couple of months observing the work of the DNA Theatergroep and getting to know some of the actors and directors. But since I was going to set my play in that country and I had never been there before I needed to learn more about the people, the food, the rituals and other aspects of the culture – sort of put the natives under a microscope. Besides spending a lot of time being mesmerised by Dutch masters and modern artists at the Rijksmuseum, the Van Gogh Museum and the Stedelijk, I paid a number of visits to a great South African scholar who had settled in Holland, Vernon February. He told me stories of South Africans who were exiled in the Netherlands during apartheid and how life used to be those days. I learnt of a particular woman he knew who originally came from the Eastern Cape. She had a very difficult time in Holland and I thought I would write a play based on some of her experiences. But I would have to find her first; she had since returned to South Africa.

Aram Adriaanse and Gerrit Wijnhoud of the DNA Theatergroep took me to the city of Amersfoort where I saw the college where some of our Afrikaner theologians of the Dutch Reformed Church had done their higher degrees. I also saw Long John, the famous bell reputed to be located at the centre of Holland.

In Amsterdam I frequented a number of jazz cafés listening to both unknown and famous jazz musicians. It became clear to me that jazz had migrated to Europe. I was surprised at the number of American jazz musicians who were living permanently in Amsterdam and other European cities. They told me that they couldn't make a living in America.

One evening as I sat at the Waterfront Jazz Club listening to Terence Blanchard's wailing trumpet, the play crystallised in my mind. It was going to be set in Amersfoort and would involve the famous bells, an Afrikaner *dominee* or pastor who had been an apartheid security policeman and a black woman anti-apartheid activist exiled in Holland. It would address issues of peace, justice and reconciliation.

Back in South Africa I went in search of the woman I had been told about at Vernon February's house. She came from Herschel which was a district I knew very well. My search pointed to Qoboshane Village in the Lower Telle region which, as you know by now, is my ancestral village. I had not been there since I was a little boy staying at my grandmother's home. I was struck by the beauty of the place. It was spring and the mountain was pink with aloe blooms. But I was also struck by the poverty that I saw in the village. Men who used to work in the mines of Johannesburg and the Free State had been retrenched. There was hardly any income-generating activity in the village. The land was parched and rocky, so it wasn't good for agriculture. There were patches of subsistence farming among dongas that marred the beauty of the landscape.

As I was driving back to Johannesburg I said to myself: *That mountain cannot be beautiful for nothing. It's got to yield something that will give life to the people.*

In my mind, the flowers on Dyarhom suggested bees, and the bees suggested honey. But I knew nothing about beekeeping. As soon as I got to Johannesburg I bought the *Farmer's Weekly* and there, in the classifieds, was a beekeeper called William Dinkelman on the outskirts of the city – a place called Kibler Park – offering beekeeping training. I immediately enrolled for a two-week course at his Blessed by the Bees Apiary. The course was hands-on and quite intensive. We worked day and night, having lessons and getting practical experience on the very rudiments of beekeeping, on how to care for the bees and how to feed them in times of drought, how to catch bees from the wild, how to rear the queens in order to create new swarms, how to harvest honey, how to heat it and then bottle it, and how to market it. We also learnt about the diseases that often assail bees and how to treat them.

The following month I went back to the village and asked the headman, Chief Xhalisile Nombula, and his councillor Morrison Xinindlu to give me back the land that used to belong to my grandfather on the mountain so that I could start a beekeeping project with those villagers who might be interested. The headman could not make such a decision on his own. He had to call a meeting of all the villagers. I had brought bottles of honey from Blessed by the Bees and I displayed them at the meeting as I addressed the villagers showing them the benefits of beekeeping to the community.

After a long debate, with some villagers objecting because the mountain was used for the initiation of boys into men at certain times, and others because everybody who used to have property on that mountain would want it back if I was allocated the land that used to belong to my grandfather. But finally a consensus was reached. After all, the mountain was very big. Boys could still be initiated on other parts of the mountain that were more remote than the place I wanted for beekeeping. Also in my favour was the fact that I didn't want the mountain back for my own personal gain but for the good of the community.

The next step was to establish a cooperative society of all those who wanted to be part of the beekeeping project. About forty men and women registered their names.

It took me a long time to raise funds for the project. Our major electricity utility company, Eskom, had a foundation that funded development projects throughout South Africa and they approved our application. They were willing to fund the training of ten of our members who would then train the rest on site. They also funded the necessary equipment such as overalls, helmets, veils, stainless steel smokers, supers, frames, containers and hive tools. In addition to all this, the Eskom Foundation paid for the first forty hives with swarms that we purchased from Blessed by the Bees, which was where the group of ten also received their training.

Since it had taken me months to raise the money, many villagers who had initially registered had lost interest. We remained with about twenty, including Morrison Xinindlu and my Uncle Owen. It was good to have Uncle Owen in the group because he was the most educated of the lot and could handle the records and correspondence. The meetings were held at his house. I heard that in my absence he tended to be a dictator and pretended his word was final, whereas in fact the project was owned and operated by its members through the office bearers they had elected and no single member owned it and could have the final word. I called him to order as soon as I got the report.

Part of the funds from the Eskom Foundation was used to initiate literacy classes for those members who could not read and write. We also got the services of the Mineworkers Development Agency to hold classes on small business management.

At the Kellogg Foundation offices in Pretoria was a woman who had read my novel *The Heart of Redness* and had liked my ideas on rural development. She told me that they had funds which they could allocate to us, provided they were channelled through a well-established agency with a track record of handling a sizeable budget. I discovered the Herschel Development Agency based in Lady Grey and went into partnership with them. Indeed, the Kellogg Foundation gave us one hundred thousand United States dollars. The money was used to construct two buildings on the mountain, to purchase a truck, furnish the buildings, and buy equipment for extracting the honey from the combs, heating it and then bottling it. We also bought the bottles and printed the labels that William Dinkelman had designed. Dinkelman delivered more hives with swarms and trained the members to catch swarms from the wild. The Herschel Development Agency gave us a Lady Grey farmer, Aubrey Fincham, to manage the project while training the members to operate it themselves. The Department of Agriculture of the Eastern Cape provincial government was approached by Uncle Owen and they assisted by fencing the part of the mountain that had our hives and buildings.

That was how the brand *Telle Honey/Ubusi base Telle* was born. The honey that the project produced soon gained a reputation among connoisseurs of honey for its unique taste, which was the result of the fresh unpolluted air of Dyarhom Mountain and the indigenous herbs, bushes and aloes that grew on that mountain.

I learnt a lot about bees and beekeeping from this project, and I used that knowledge in the novel I was writing at the time, *The Madonna of Excelsior*. Bees play a big role in the development of some of my characters' conflicts. So you see, there is a symbiotic relationship between my writing and my community activism. My trip to Qoboshane in search of a story gave birth to a community project that is changing people's lives; the community project gave birth to aspects of a novel.

Let me add that even though I never found the woman I was looking for – she had moved to other places – I did write the musical play titled *The Bells of Amersfoort* and it was a resounding success. Directed by Aram Adriaanse, it toured Holland and South Africa, and was presented at the National Festival of the Arts in Grahamstown and the Baxter Theatre in Cape Town. Because the powers that ran the Market Theatre at the time refused to present it there despite the fact that I was their dramaturge, in Johannesburg it was performed at the Theatre on the Square in Sandton. I never got to know what the Market Theatre's problem was with Phyllis Klotz who was co-producing this musical with the Dutch. Nevertheless the play was performed to full houses and standing ovations in Sandton, which was the Market Theatre's loss.

I composed all the music for this play, except for one number which was a traditional wedding song.

The play was later to be published by Wits University Press in a collection titled *Fools, Bells and the Habit of Eating* – my earlier plays *Mother of All Eating* and *You Fool, How Can the Sky Fall?* were also in this anthology.

The writing of *The Madonna of Excelsior* proceeded well, with Debe Morris and Sara – Teresa Devant's and Albio Gonzalez's daughter in Barcelona – giving me wonderful feedback. I was having a great time narrating my story through the paintings of Father Frans Claerhout, a Flemish expressionist I once visited with my daughter Thandi, and nieces Limpho, Thembi and Mpumi – my brother Sonwabo's kids – in Tweespruit, a small town about twenty kilometres from Excelsior. We were all inspired by the priest and his paintings.

During this period I also travelled abroad extensively, giving readings and lectures and participating at literary festivals. For instance,

I took a group of writers to Reykjavik, Iceland, where we attended and conducted workshops on writing for children with writers from Norway, Denmark, Finland and Sweden. Since I was organising this event I made a point of having writers who roughly represented the demographic groups of South Africa. One of the writers was my former colleague at the National University of Lesotho who was at that time a civil servant in Bloemfontein, Mpapa Mokhoane. Together we wrote *Penny and Puffy*, which I illustrated. It was published by Aeskan in Reykjavik. We repeated these workshops in Cape Town, with most of the writers participating again.

Among the many countries I visited was the United Kingdom where I was on tour with other writers, including Ama Ata Aidoo whose short stories and plays I enjoyed when I was a high school student. I had been with her before in Germany with Ngugi wa Thiong'o, and somewhere else, I don't recall where exactly, with Miriam Tlali and Buchi Emecheta. Maybe it was Germany again on another occasion. Come to think of it, I have been to many places with these more mature and more powerful African women writers. Somehow organisers of literary events always harnessed me with them. But what makes me recall this particular case with fondness was an incident that took place in Bath where we had a reading.

When we arrived at the venue we found that there were posters all over the place of a charity organisation that was asking for donations; the funds would be used to educate the children of Africa. I was quite uncomfortable with this, though I said nothing about it. When we were about to take the stage the organisers told us that, before we began, the charity organisation would like to make a brief speech asking for donations. I found it very embarrassing that they were using us for fund-raising purposes when they had not told us anything about it. When they invited us to their festival they hadn't mentioned anything about fund-raising. But I would not have said anything; I would just have gone along with it, even though I was unhappy about it. I wouldn't have wanted to be ungracious to our hosts. But not Ama Ata Aidoo. She put her foot down and said no, we hadn't come to England to beg for anyone's money.

'But it is for a good cause,' said the white-haired lady from the charity. 'We pay for many children who would otherwise have no opportunity for education . . . especially girl children.'

Ama Ata Aidoo was not impressed.

'Why don't African governments educate African children?' she asked. 'Why should that be the role of English people?'

I could have kissed her. But, of course, that would have been too forward. We treat our elders with respect. We don't just grab them and kiss them, even when they have said something brilliant.

'African countries are poor,' said the woman frantically. 'They don't have enough money for education.'

'Oh, no, they have the money, but they don't spend it on education because they know that you are there with your charity,' she said. 'You will educate their children for them.'

She knew what she was talking about, this wonderful Ama Ata Aidoo. She had been the Minister of Education in Ghana. She knew of the millions that went to the military instead of to education and health services. And of those other millions that went into the Swiss bank accounts of corrupt leaders. She couldn't last as a cabinet minister because she was too honest and frank to be a politician.

Thanks to Ama Ata Aidoo, we did not become writers with begging bowls that evening. She was indeed an African leader after my own heart. I had written extensively – and also in my book *When People Play People* – against the dependency mentality that had been created by Western aid to developing countries. I am not talking here of humanitarian assistance when there are disasters and occasional catastrophes, but of regular aid that went into the day-to-day survival of the country. I have noted in some of my writings, and in the same book, that food aid from America and the European community has smothered to death the agricultural sector in a country like Lesotho. The peasant farmers have no incentive to produce food from their patches of land because more food will come from America or from the Food and Agricultural Organization of the United Nations.

Another trip that stands out in my mind was to Chile, where I was on a literary tour of Santiago, Valdivia and Valparaiso with South African writers Nadine Gordimer, Wally Serote and André Brink; Chilean writers Ariel Dorfman and Antonio Skármeta; and Australian writers Peter Carey, Helen Garner and Roberta Sykes. In addition to these writers, we were accompanied throughout the tour by a man who was introduced to us as Gordimer's official biographer, Ronald Suresh Roberts.

During this tour we were entertained by government ministers and presidents of universities. We spent some time at the home of the late poet Pablo Neruda and also visited Salvador Allende's wife, Hortensia Bussi Allende, and their daughter, Isabel Allende – not the Isabel Allende who is the author of magical realist novels. I stress this because when I came back to South Africa and wrote an article about this trip for the *Mail & Guardian* the woman who was editing it argued with me, saying that I was wrong, the magical realist novelist and the Allende daughter I met were one and the same person. Yet I was the one who had met these people in Chile! I knew what I was talking about. When the article was published the editor had left out the contentious relationships. The main thrust of my article, however, was the Mapuche people, the natives of Chile, and their struggle to regain their land. I met a Mapuche writer in Valdivia who told me how his people were marginalised by the broader Chilean society and how they had suffered under General Pinochet, and continued to suffer under the new democratic government.

One thing that moved me on this trip was a visit to the Avenue of Memory at the General Cemetery where the remains of Salvador Allende had been transferred in 1990 after lying for almost twenty years in a private grave in Santa Ines Cemetery at Vina del Mar. The General Cemetery is truly the city of the dead with towering tombs, some of which are multi-storey. We stood at Allende's grave and observed a moment of silence. People came, prayed for him and left. But one man broke down and cried. Ariel Dorfman reached for him and embraced him. They sobbed in each other's arms. Ariel didn't know who the man was, nor did the man have a clue who Ariel was. They were just two Chilean men sharing their grief at events that happened two and a half decades ago, but that had left untold suffering that would be felt in Chile for generations. Some of the writers standing around Allende's tomb, including me, couldn't help but shed tears as well.

It is one of the images that lived with me long after I returned to South Africa.

When a Chilean cabinet minister visited South Africa I was invited to the banquet given for him in Pretoria. That's where I had a very brief chat to Nelson Mandela. We didn't talk about the letter that I wrote him or some of the snide remarks I made about his being 'economical with the truth' in his statements in praise of a dead Sani Abacha. Instead he asked me: 'Tell me, Zakes Mda, are you one of the twins?'

'No, the twins are my younger brothers, Sonwabo and Monwabisi,' I said.

'Oh, yes, you were the quiet one,' he said. I thought he would add: *how did you become so vocal?* But he didn't.

Obviously, I had not made much impression on him when I lived at his house forty-four years before, but the twins had. I can understand that; I was a reserved, introverted little boy.

Now, let me tell you how I had a falling-out with my publishers, Oxford University Press. It started when I wanted to have an agent after a Japanese publisher to whom I had submitted *Ways of Dying*, hoping he would get it translated and published in Japanese, advised me of an agency in London, Blake Friedmann, which represented a number of South African writers. I wrote to one of the partners, Carole Blake, who told me her company was keen to represent me. In fact, she said, a member of the agency, Isobel Dixon, had approached Oxford University Press enquiring as to whether I didn't need their representation, and my publishers turned her down. I was offended when I heard this. Who the hell did they think they were to turn an agent down without consulting me? Did they think they owned me or something?

I immediately engaged the services of Isobel Dixon as my agent. My publishers opposed the move because they said they were capable of looking after my interests without an agent. I only realised at that point that they owned all the rights to the two books they had published, *Ways of Dying* and *The Heart of Redness*. I owned nothing of those books. They wanted to continue in the same vein with all the books I was going to publish with them. The contract that I had signed with them placed me in their bondage, so that they had the right of first refusal for my next book, and it was going to be like that for each book I wrote in perpetuity. That's what happens when, as a new writer, you are just happy that a publisher is interested in your work and you sign a contract blindly. You may not even be aware that the terms are always negotiable, it is never a matter of take it or leave it, and you don't have to sell your soul to get published. I had sold mine and they were the sole decision makers on my work.

No wonder they didn't want me to have an agent.

I had a protracted email correspondence with Daphne Paizee, the publishing director of Oxford University Press, which ultimately turned very acrimonious. She was adamant that they would not tolerate my having an agent because that would eat into their heavy investment in me and my work, and I was insisting that an agent would in fact broaden the market, bringing in greater returns for their investment. She told me that my prospective agent had 'painted a rosy picture' because there was nothing she could do for me that they were not already doing. And yet they were not able to market my work abroad. Even the French and Spanish translations of *Ways of Dying* were due to my own efforts when I was travelling in Europe. I wrote:

> You people failed to market my work even inside South Africa! Every day I get phone calls from people who are looking for my books in the bookstores but can't find them. I don't think you know how to deal with the book trade. I think your expertise begins and ends with the academic trade.

There was this sort of back and forth for months, with Paizee at one stage telling me that I seemed to be ungrateful for all they had done for me. I took great offence at that because I didn't think they had done me a favour. Publishing my work was a business deal from which they benefited. I was getting desperate because I wanted to see my work all over the world. I offered them a 50:50 split if they agreed that the two novels, for which they held all the rights, be represented by an agent. Paizee finally wrote:

We will agree to an agent taking over the sale of UK and USA English rights as well as the remaining translation rights on *Ways of Dying* and *The Heart of Redness*. We also accept your offer of a 50:50 split on income from the sale of these rights as our costings assumed additional rights income and the agent you have appointed charges quite a high commission.

I responded with a tinge of bitterness:

It is a pity that you only agreed to engage this agent after offering you a 50:50 split – an unheard of thing. But it is fine with me. As long as my books, which certainly deserve a much wider readership than you have been able to muster, reach the important markets.

I had learnt a hard lesson that I hope new writers will also learn from reading this. It is a cut-throat world out there and, whatever happens, make sure that you own the rights to your own work. Today I own the rights of all my novels except *Ways of Dying* and *The Heart of Redness*. Someone else who doesn't have my interests at heart owns those. For instance, many translators and local publishers have been keen to have *The Heart of Redness* published in Afrikaans, but the owners of the rights of my novel have consistently refused to give them the rights because they say it is not in their interests, even though it would be in my interests as a writer to have Afrikaners read my work in their language.

When the agent, Isobel Dixon, who originally came from the Eastern Cape but now worked in London, visited Johannesburg I sent my son Neo to pick her up from Melville in my car and to bring her to my house for lunch. I was dazzled by her beauty and her youthfulness, and I told her so. She got a bit worried that perhaps I thought because of her youth she might not be able to handle my business.

'Oh, no,' I said. 'That's not what I mean. In fact, I think you'll do excellently. I am a man of art, I love beauty. It will be my pleasure to work with you.'

She had already read some chapters of *The Madonna of Excelsior* and she told me frankly that she didn't think it would do well. People did not want to read about the apartheid period, she said. She was, instead, looking forward to *The Whale Caller*; I had told her of my plans to write it, but I had not yet written a single line.

I was not deterred about *The Madonna of Excelsior*. I knew I was on to something there. It became the only one of my novels to be on the South African best-seller list. I was right. Isobel later sent me an email to admit that she was wrong. This is another lesson for young writers: always take the advice of others to heart, be they ordinary readers or experts in the literary field. But when you have faith in your creation do not be deterred. I had only written a few chapters of the novel when I received discouraging comments from my well-meaning agent who was looking after my interests and wanted me to be the best that I could be. I could easily have given up on that novel right there. But I was confident that I was on the right track, and it did finally pay off.

Acquiring this lovely agent was one of the best things that happened in my life as an artist. Yvonne Vera, who had fallen deeply in love with *The Heart of Redness* and called it 'our novel', told me that her books were published in America by Farrar, Straus and Giroux and were doing well. I asked Isobel to contact them immediately, and in no time she had clinched a deal with them. At the time I didn't know they were such a prestigious publishing house. They were going to publish *Ways of Dying* and *The Heart of Redness*. I was honoured when a New York editor, Paul Elie, and his wife came to my house in Johannesburg to finalise things. I took them to the Market Theatre, but I don't remember what play we saw.

If it was a local play you can be sure that I had something to do with the process of its development. I was continuing as a dramaturge of this great theatre, and enjoying working with writers to develop their plays for production. I worked with Xoli Norman, a younger writer who was also a trumpeter, who had shown much talent in my workshops, and with the Tony Award winning actor John Kani, who I convinced to write his own play after a series of collaborations with Athol Fugard which were wrongly being attributed to Fugard alone. There was also Ntshiyeng Sithe, a young woman who was making her name with her brutally honest plays, and Percy Mtwa. You may remember Percy as a co-creator of some wonderful theatre with Mbongeni Ngema and Barney Simon. While working with him on his new play, I discovered that he was quite a sensitive soul. His theatre was far more intelligent than Mbongeni Ngema's; that's why Percy was less successful.

But even outside the structures of the Market Theatre I continued to work with playwrights. I helped, for instance, in the development of a single-hander by our award-winning actress Motshabi Tyelele, which she continues to perform at various venues to this day.

I was also involved in television production at this time. I had established a company called Thapama Productions in partnership with a musician who had a long-running radio show on SAfm, *The African Connection*, on music from Africa and the diaspora, and a former PAC cadre who had been exiled in Kenya where he became involved in a number of Hollywood movie productions that were shot in that country. Thapama produced *The African Connection* as a successful television show for the South African Broadcasting Corporation. But I am afraid we ran the company like a *spaza* shop – a township tuck shop. The musician partner travelled abroad extensively, spending weeks on end in France getting videos he could easily have sourced from South Africa. When the SABC paid out for a season he doled out all the money to us – with the lion's share for himself – as 'dividends', without keeping proper books or investing some of it in the company. And, stupidly, I just sat back and let him do that. Soon the company was in debt and there were no new contracts forthcoming from the SABC because I had put my foot down that we would not pay the bribes that the commissioning staff of the national broadcaster demanded from producers.

But I didn't give up on television altogether. I wrote scripts whenever I was commissioned to do so. Shane Mahabier and his partner Saths Cooper commissioned me to write scripts for a police drama series titled *Behind the Badge*. I was surprised when the thirteen-part series was screened that I was not credited as the writer but as some peripheral person. Clearly South African television was another cut-throat industry that was not for the likes of faint-hearted me. I gave up on the production company and on all television work.

But I didn't give up on transferring scriptwriting skills to others. I established the Southern African Multimedia AIDS Trust – SAMAT. I found a venue at the Trevor Huddleston CR Memorial Centre at the Anglican Church in Sophiatown and recruited a number of HIV-positive people from all over Gauteng to participate in creative writing workshops. Some came from as far as the Eastern Cape and KwaZulu-Natal to tell their stories as part of peer education and to learn how to write them as short stories, radio plays and film scripts. The European Union funded our activities.

I didn't give up on other forms of community involvement either, even though some of them left me disillusioned. I was drafted on to the committee that was planning the Apartheid Museum at Gold Reef City. The committee was composed of architects, cultural workers and business people. This was a project of a gaming company called Akani Gold and it was created in order to win a bid for a casino licence in the area. The major movers in this company were the identical Krok twins, Solly and Abe, who had made their billions manufacturing skin lightening creams for black people who were eager to be white during the days of apartheid. They had a company called Twins Pharmaceuticals that manufactured and sold throughout southern Africa the *Super Rose Lotion*, *Aviva* and the *He-Man*. These skin lightening creams and lotions had high levels of hydroquinone that left many women and, to a lesser extent, men blemished for life. I had written about the damage of skin lightening creams in my earlier play, *And the Girls in Their Sunday Dresses*, and I found it odious to be working with these super-rich characters who had caused such damage in the name of profit. Some of the meetings were held at the twins' sprawling estate called Summer Place in one of the northern suburbs of Johannesburg; it had once belonged to the Italian oilman Marino Chiavelli but was purchased by Solly Krok in the mid-1990s. I saw all the excesses of wealth and lamented the skins of black women who were fried with hydroquinone and were now hard and caked for ever.

One morning I got a call from Reuel Khoza, a leading black businessman who was also the chairman of Eskom. He was part of the Akani Gold conglomerate and was in fact the one who had invited me to join the Apartheid Museum Committee.

'We have an urgent meeting at Nelson Mandela's house in Lower Houghton this afternoon,' he said.

I drove to Lower Houghton and was almost late for the meeting. We sat on the sofas in one of the living rooms of Mr Mandela's mansion and he joined us while Zelda le Grange hovered around protectively. It was not the whole committee that met, but just a hand-picked few. They were all white except for me and John Kani. I sat next to Solly Krok as he outlined to Nelson Mandela the plans for the Apartheid Museum. Although I had no idea what the agenda for this meeting was, it became clear at once that Solly Krok wanted Mandela's endorsement. I learnt from their discussions that they were buddies and that the Krok brothers had given him a few million for his projects, which were at that time the building of schools in the rural Eastern Cape. But he was demanding more from Solly Krok.

'You know, every time I see you, I see money,' Mandela said. 'Give me more money, Solly.'

It was as though somebody had tickled the puny Krok twin; he giggled and promised that he would give more money.

Mandela didn't seem to be paying much attention to the details of the museum. He turned to me and started telling me the problems he had had some years back, perhaps in the 1950s, with a stubborn Mda Mda when he was trying to convert him from the Unity Movement. I had nothing to do with Mda Mda, though I knew him as a respected lawyer in the Transkei and my father's friend. He was the father of the dynamic Mda women – Lizeka who is known as a fearless journalist, and Thobeka who is a brilliant academic at the University of South Africa. But I had no idea why Mandela was telling me about Mda Mda. Had he perhaps forgotten which Mda I belonged to? But, of course, an elder cannot be denied the indulgence of his memories. We chuckled politely at his adventures with Mda Mda, took photographs and left.

It became clear to me what my role was at this meeting. The impression was being given to Nelson Mandela that I was an important cog in the Apartheid Museum project. Yet I was not. I was just one of the many irrelevant committee members. The movers and the shakers of the project were all white. I was a black face who was merely a front to show the great man that black folks were participating actively in the project. It took me back to what happened with Blue Moon, when I was taken all the way to Welkom as a front. It was the same with a number of Black Economic Empowerment deals where white capital found some black faces to front for it.

That was the last meeting of the Apartheid Museum committee that I attended. But John Kani had more patience than I had. He continued with the committee and today he is the chairperson of the Board of Trustees of the Museum.

As for the Kroks, I wrote about them and their history in one of the chapters of *The Madonna of Excelsior*.

My queasiness about the twisted world of business evinced itself once more when I became part of another Black Economic Empowerment deal. This time I was recruited by my actress friend Motshabi Tyelele, who had put together an empowerment group called Salungana with television producer Duma ka Ndlovu. We were part of Island Television, a bigger consortium that was bidding for a free-to-air commercial television licence. It was led by Makana Trust, a group of millionaires who were former apartheid prisoners. Most of them had served years on Robben Island where one of the Xhosa heroes of the early colonial times, Makana, was once imprisoned; hence a synonym for the prison is the Island of Makana. These former prisoners had turned into suave businessmen who already owned radio stations and other media-related corporations. They would be the majority shareholders if we got the licence and we and some orphanages and women's groups would own a tiny minority share. Our presence as shareholders served mostly to convince the Independent Broadcasting Authority (IBA), who would decide which bidder would be granted the licence, that Island Television would empower the disadvantaged.

I attended a few of the meetings where the documents of the bid were debated. They had been compiled with the assistance of Malaysian experts who would also be shareholders. At one meeting I was chosen to be one of the representatives who would defend the bid in front of the IBA. I told the meeting that my presence would disadvantage the bid because in my *Sunday Times* column I had been very critical of some of the processes of the IBA and of the woman who would be chairing the hearings in particular.

'Why would you be critical of people who put bread on our table?' asked Peter-Paul Ngwenya, the chairman of Makana Trust.

All eyes turned on me admonishingly. I was a disappointment to the human race. I knew immediately that I was in the wrong place. If I carried on with these types my voice would be stifled for ever in order to appease the powerful forces that gave us a livelihood.

Someone else was chosen in my place to defend the bid. The next meeting that I attended was the report-back after the IBA had made the decision. Island Television did not get the bid. But I was surprised when Mr Ngwenya told the meeting that in any event they knew that they were not going to get the bid. Thabo Mbeki had informed them that the television licence would be given to another group. Makana Trust's turn would come when bids opened for another important venture. I wondered why we had gone through that laborious process if our leaders knew already that it was just for show, that we would not get the licence. This was what 'managed democracy' as it existed in Russia was all about, where the president had his dirty finger in everything. There was a semblance of fairness and openness, whereas in fact decisions had already been made behind closed doors. The chosen people were going through the motions knowing quite well whose turn it was to be doled out favours. So, you see, we had mastered that game quite early in our liberation. This was the typical patronage and crony capitalism I had been railing against, and there I was finding myself in the middle of it.

Many years later I was to fictionalise these events in my novel *Black Diamond*.

One little irony worth mentioning: the consortium that won the bid of what later became a successful commercial television station called e.tv was founded by a group that included me and my friend Melanie Chait. It was called Vula Television and Melanie was the leading figure. She and I spent days working on its programming at her house in Melville. We resigned from the group when our insistence on quality programming was rebuffed by the rest of the partners. That's how I

467

lost out becoming one of the owners of a television network. Island Television was my second attempt at becoming a 'black diamond' and it proved that I was not cut out to be one. I lacked the necessary gumption.

I was destined to be a poor itinerant artist and scholar.

Things started going bad in my personal life when Adele decided to return to Johannesburg. On the weekends she visited from Bloemfontein our relationship was generally cordial, although there would be occasional flare-ups of anger from both sides of the divide. She felt it was a strain to live so far away from her home and family, which was quite understandable. But what was she going to do about the job in Bloemfontein where she was the director of L-MAP? She told me that the board of trustees had agreed that she could operate from Johannesburg where she could focus only on fund-raising for the organisation.

'Are you giving up your job as director?' I asked.

'No, I am not. I'll still be director but only focusing on fund-raising here in Johannesburg because that's where all the big donors are located,' she said.

'Then who is going to run the organisation when you are here focusing only on fund-raising?'

'Buti will.'

Buti was her assistant in Bloemfontein.

'Will he agree to do your job without the title and salary of director?'

She became livid, and accused me of not wanting her to stay with me and her son in Johannesburg. There must be things that I was doing in that house with women; that's why I didn't want her to return. She would come back whether I liked it or not because it was her house too, she added.

'I was merely asking because I don't see how the board of L-MAP can approve of moving the office of director to Johannesburg. The people of Bloemfontein are very proud of L-MAP. Won't they be suspicious that they are losing it to Johannesburg?'

I surprised myself. I was not usually this cool when she made false accusations. I usually yelled back.

The following weeks she hired a construction company and built a high brick wall around our house. I objected to this because our house distinguished itself by being the only one in our street that was not surrounded by a high wall, and that spoke of our confidence and fearlessness. But she wanted a wall, so she got a wall. Then she converted one of the three garages into an office. She furnished it and bought some office equipment. She told me that she was using funds that had been approved by the board of L-MAP to do all this construction work.

As soon as all the work was completed, but before she could start working in her new office, the board of L-MAP summoned her to a meeting in East London. I was at the National Arts Festival in Grahamstown when she called me to say she had been summarily fired. I asked her to come to Grahamstown and I spent the rest of the festival with her, trying to comfort her and to assure her that she was a highly qualified woman and would surely get another job soon. But in the meantime I would help her sue L-MAP for unlawful dismissal. She would have none of that, she said, the L-MAP people could take their job and stuff it where the sun didn't shine. Though I didn't know the details of her dismissal, I suspected that it was not unlawful. Otherwise why didn't she want to contest it?

She got another job with the Technical College of South Africa in Roodepoort. She didn't last long there either before moving to a job with the Department of Education in Pretoria dealing with adult education.

In the meantime, auditors came to our house when she was at work and asked me about the wall and the other improvements that had been made on our property. I told them what Adele had told me: it was funded by L-MAP as part of the costs of her moving to Johannesburg. Since she would be using her property as an L-MAP office, these costs would go towards the rent the organisation would be paying for the office space. After the auditors came the police, with the same questions.

I later learnt that Adele had been charged with the embezzlement of L-MAP funds and the theft of the company laptop. She was not taken into custody, but was asked to appear before the magistrate at the Roodepoort Magistrate's Court. She engaged the services of a brilliant attorney, Raymond Tucker, who had made his name defending anti-apartheid activists during the bad days. For two days I attended the trial in her support. That's how I got familiar with the Roodepoort Magistrate's Court which later featured in *Black Diamond*.

In their evidence the members of the L-MAP board denied that they had authorised the expenditure. She, on the other hand, insisted that it had been authorised, and denied any knowledge of the laptop. The magistrate was the final judge and she acquitted her on all the charges.

This trial soured our relationship further. But it is possible we could still have survived it if other events had not intervened, mostly connected with what I felt were my responsibilities. Limpho, my brother Sonwabo's first born, came to live with us while she did part-time jobs waitressing with the view of saving money for her education. Adele resented her presence in our house. She told me that she was already tolerating the presence of my two children Neo and Thandi – Dini had gone to live with his mother somewhere on the East Rand. Now I was burdening our lives with yet another child. All these kids were already adults, so I sympathised with her position. She had a point, but I am an African father; I had to help my children until they were on their feet. It didn't matter that they were in their twenties; they were my children still. Limpho didn't make things any easier for me because she was very helpful in the house and pampered me in a way that I was not used to. For instance, immediately I walked into the house from work she would ask, 'Uncle Zakes, may I make you some tea?'

And, of course, I wanted the tea. No one had ever asked me that kind of question before. If I wanted tea I either made it for myself or asked the maid. So, Limpho made me tea and this riled Adele no end. She finally put a stop to it when she told Limpho: 'This is not your husband; you have no business making him tea. You are spoiling this man and soon he'll expect me to make him tea.'

But things came to a head when she discovered that I had been helping to pay the school fees of Limpho's younger siblings. You will remember that their father deserted them when they were babies and toddlers. Their mother Johanna was struggling to educate them. In most cases she was able to cope, but once in a while she would be behind in

470

the payment of fees and the principal of the high school they attended in Wepener in the Free State would threaten to expel them. I would then drive to Wepener to save the situation. I never told Adele about this because I knew she would give me hell for it. But she discovered the receipts and drove to Lesotho to confront Johanna. I am told that she accused her of sleeping with me.

'Otherwise why would he be paying for your children?' she asked.

It got worse when these children visited me, which was always for very brief periods. She grumbled about them and claimed that they were displacing her in her own house.

Limpho finally had to move out of the house. As did Neo at some later stage. They were followed by Thandi and her son. I didn't tell you I was already a grandfather at this time. Thandi had gotten pregnant by some boy she met at Allenby College where I had sent her to study film-making. Instead of coming home with a diploma, she returned with a baby. I joked with her that we should name the child Diploma. But she named him Wandile instead. So Thandi and Wandile went to live with her mother Mpho at Etwatwa, which I discovered when I visited them was a sprawling shantytown in Benoni on the outskirts of Johannesburg. It looked like the pictures of the favelas I had seen in Brazil. They lived in a corrugated iron shack.

I certainly could not have my ex-wife, my daughter and my grandson living in a shack. I gave Mpho money to pay a deposit on a three-bedroom house with servants' quarters in the previously Afrikaner suburb of Welgedacht in one of the satellite towns of Johannesburg called Springs. I also signed as surety on the mortgage bond. They all moved into the new house and I had peace of mind.

But I didn't have peace at home when I told Adele about it. This was too big to be hidden. In any event, she had a way of discovering things because I was such a lousy liar.

I remember one day I was having coffee with a friend of mine, Keke Semoko, at some restaurant in either Sandton or Rosebank. She is the actress I had directed in the Market Theatre Laboratory production of the TB/AIDS/child sexual abuse play, *Broken Dreams*. I was telling her about my problems at home because I had helped my ex-wife buy a house. She told me straightaway that Adele was right. She herself would kick her husband out if she discovered he had bought a house for his ex-wife.

'No woman can allow that,' Keke told me.

She was right, of course. But I had already done it, and was not sorry for it. In any event, my marriage was already irretrievably broken even before I saved my ex-wife from the favelas.

Another thing I recall about my coffee with Keke, who had by that time become a household name in South Africa thanks to her recurring role in a television drama series called *Isidingo*, is that we discussed the child sexual abuse about which we created *Broken Dreams* and how it was still playing to thousands of school kids throughout the province. We ended up talking about my own sexual abuse by Nontonje which, unbeknown to me, had left me shattered for a great part of my life.

'You must write about this,' Keke told me. 'Men don't normally talk about such things. They like to pretend they are all strong and macho and unbreakable. You're a different kind of man who openly talks about how he was abused by an older woman, which resulted in his sexual dysfunction, and how he was healed by another woman. If you wrote about this it would be a lesson to many other men.'

So, there, I am writing about it, Keke. Thanks to you.

African Theatre Ensemble produced my play *And the Girls in Their Sunday Dresses* in Toronto and I flew to Canada for the opening night. I enjoyed Rhoma Spencer's direction of the play. I also had a wonderful time with Debe Morris and my friends from the old days in Lesotho, Patrick Nkunda Kabeteraine and his wife, Palesa Thoahlane. Patrick was one of the Ugandan refugees I used to party with in Maseru. I was the one who introduced him to Palesa during those wild days. He was now a very successful immigration lawyer in Toronto.

From Toronto I went to England on a tour of the literary festivals there. I think I was gone for about three weeks. When I came back earlier than expected I found that Adele had accommodated a couple from Swaziland in our house. They had been there for a week when I arrived home. The wife was sick and the man had brought her to specialists at the Sandton Clinic. This was not just Adele's kindness to strangers, which would have been a breath of fresh air. The woman was a stranger to her but the man was not. He had been her boyfriend when she was a student at Roma and she had assured me before we married that they had broken up. I had not been aware that they were in contact again.

I said nothing to her about it. Instead, I went to greet the man as he sat in my living room and to wish his wife a speedy recovery. I told him they were welcome to stay at my house for as long as they wished. I had my suspicions about him, but I wanted to give him and Adele the benefit of the doubt. I was already good at giving her the benefit of the doubt. One night, at about midnight, a barman at Maseru Cabanas phoned me all the way in Johannesburg to tell me that she was at the bar cavorting with some man. I told the barman it was not his business and he should never again call me about such things. The next time I met Adele – she was still staying in Bloemfontein then – I asked her about it and she told me she was not with a man but with three men who were her cousins. I gave her the benefit of the doubt, especially because throughout our marriage, stormy as it was, she had never given me the slightest reason to doubt her fidelity.

I was surprised when I came back from the Market Theatre the next day and the couple told me that they were leaving because they had found accommodation closer to the hospital. They thanked me for my kindness and drove away. I never raised the matter of the ex-boyfriend again.

Even after all my kids and niece had vacated the house our relationship didn't become any better. But in public we were seen together and pretended that nothing was wrong. When my friends Nakedi Ribane or Motshabi Tyelele or Keke Semoko visited they never forgot to say what a happy family we were and how lucky I was to have such a nice wife. When journalists came and interviewed us for magazine articles she told them what a great husband and father I was and how I cooked everyone great vegetarian dishes. She was telling the truth. Because I did all my writing at home, and only went to the Market Theatre to hold workshops with the writers on Saturdays, I was more of the househusband. She worked in Pretoria and left very early in the morning and came back late in the evening. I took Zukile and Zenzi to school and for their piano lessons and swimming lessons and everything else.

When I made a feast in Qoboshane for the unveiling of my grandfather's and grandmother's tombstones she was with me. My father's people saw nothing but a happy couple. She was beside me when I made a speech to the villagers to tell them that I had bought the tombstones and erected them because I dreamt of my grandfather. He was lying down and his rotting flesh was peeling off his thighs and falling on the ground. The elders had said that the ancestors were talking to me, telling me that my grandparents needed tombstones. They had never had any since they were buried decades ago. Obviously, my father and Uncle Owen didn't bother about such things. I didn't tell the villagers that I went along with appeasing the ancestors not because I believed in life after death, but because such ceremonies and rituals brought relatives together and contributed to social cohesion.

When President Thabo Mbeki invited me to a gathering of black intellectuals and opinion leaders at Mahlamba Ndlopfu, the presidential residence in Pretoria, I went with Adele. Under the huge marquee we shared a table with Sudanese poet Taban Lo Liyong, his wife and some senior civil servants and their spouses. Taban and his wife told us what a charming couple we were. We listened to the speeches about the African Renaissance and danced together to the music of the Soweto String Quartet. No one was any the wiser of the hostilities brewing within us.

The only two things worth mentioning about that event was that as I was greeting some folks who were excited to see me and were congratulating me on the Annual Steve Biko Memorial Lecture that I had given to a standing ovation at the University of Cape Town, I spotted Keneiloe Mohafa. Yes, Keneiloe, my childhood sweetheart. There she was, sitting with her friends who were pointing at me, obviously gossiping about me. The last time I saw her was when she left me in Ohio for her father's funeral and never came back. I went to greet her. I was glad to see that she was doing well and seemed to be very happy. She was my first love.

The second thing was meeting Tony Yengeni, the former ANC chief whip who served time in jail for corruption. I must admit that I have always had a soft spot for Tony Yengeni, not only for the suffering he went through during the struggle but because he was Chris Hani's friend. I always thought he'd had a bum rap going to jail for getting a big discount from Daimler Benz on a Mercedes Benz when a lot of his comrades were getting away with corruption worth millions every day. Tony told me that Limpho Hani would have liked me to write Chris Hani's biography because I knew him more than most people.

'It is true I knew Bhut' Thembi very well,' I said, 'but only at a personal human level, rather than at a political level.'

'You can always research the political level,' said Tony. 'We are here, we'll tell you.'

I felt it would be a daunting project that would take me away from my fiction for more time than I could spare. But I knew that Limpho Hani's instincts were correct. My book would have been more credible than the life stories of politicians that I have read in South Africa which pretend that the subject lived a purely political life and had no father or mother or friends or family who contributed, for better or for worse, in shaping the subject into what she or he became.

On our way back from Pretoria we reverted to our ugly selves. This time it was about some woman I smiled and waved at. I remember before we married my mother once called Adele for a private meeting where she tried to talk to her like mother and daughter. She had warned her against jealousy which she said could destroy our marriage. It had happened already and was the bane of my life.

The following week I went to Lesotho to see my mother. I made a point of visiting her at least once a month and taking her some money. Her health was deteriorating to the extent that she had not been able to read the manuscript of *The Heart of Redness*. The neighbours who always gathered in her bedroom had read it to her. My mother was as beautiful as ever, sitting in her wheelchair in her bedroom. She cried immediately she saw me. I held her in my arms. She told me, in the midst of sniffles, that the ANC government had forgotten my father's contribution to the struggle. There was no mention of him anywhere, as if they were the only ones who fought for freedom, as if he never existed at all. It was like that with her those days, something would trigger the memory of her husband and she would get all emotional.

'Don't worry, mama,' I said, 'history will remember your husband. They cannot rub him off its pages, however hard they may try.'

She seemed a bit comforted.

I gave her the perfume that I had bought for her in Paris and spent the whole afternoon with her. I could see that she was becoming forgetful of many significant events in her life. But I didn't take her sporadic loss of memory seriously.

On my way back I stopped in Maseru to see Deborah Mpepuoa, Kittyman's daughter who worked for me when I still had the Screenwriters Institute at Mothamo House. She was very distraught because her husband was in hospital in Leribe.

I decided to take the Leribe route on my way to Johannesburg to see the guy, though I had never met him before. After all, Kittyman looked after me when we were students at Peka High School and saved me from savage hazing. I was walking between the buildings at the government hospital in Leribe when an excited man came running towards me, calling my name. When he got close I saw that it was Dugmore Hlalele in a white coat with a stethoscope hanging around his neck. But he looked strange. He was thin, almost skeletal, and his rubbery muscles clung desperately to his bones. I suspected AIDS. Many of my friends in Lesotho were dying of AIDS. One of Dugmore's friends, Nthethe, who was a lawyer in Mafeteng had also died in the pandemic. Dugmore was certainly a dying man, yet he still worked as a doctor, healing others.

He brought his hand forward reluctantly, as if he feared I would rebuff it. I didn't take his hand. I reached for him and embraced him. His face cracked into a dry smile. We talked briefly of the old times as he walked with me to the ward I was looking for. He knew Deborah's husband because he was his patient but he had not known the guy was Kittyman's son-in-law.

'I'll take special care of him because Kittyman was a good man,' he said.

I thought he himself needed someone to take special care of him. I didn't ask him if he was still with Ray, nor did I tell him how much I used to love Ray, and how jealous I was of him when I heard he had married her when they were students in Russia.

He walked me back to my car and just before we parted he said, 'I am glad to see that you're not like the other MaPeka who are trying to isolate me.'

'Come on,' I said. 'Why would anyone isolate the popular Dugs?'

'They are accusing me of killing Jama.'

He was not smiling; he meant it. I didn't know that anybody had accused him of killing Jama Mbeki, and I told him so. He told me that the Peka High School old boys who were Jama Mbeki's comrades in the BCP were spreading lies that he sold Jama out to Leabua Jonathan's Police Mobile Unit who then kidnapped and murdered him.

'He did come to my house that night, disguised in a Basotho blanket,' he said. 'But he left. I don't know what happened to him after that.'

It seemed he desperately wanted me to believe him. I had not heard any of those details nor of the rumours that he was being blamed for betraying his friend, who apparently was on the run and had come to him for assistance. I drove away feeling sad for everyone: those who died for some elusive cause and were buried underground, and those who died but continued to walk among the living as living corpses.

I later heard that Dugmore Hlalele died soon after that chance meeting.

It was a Wednesday morning towards the end of April 2001. Adele was at work and the kids were at school. I was in my back garden near the swimming pool being interviewed for television by a striking South African Indian woman. She was irritated that I was giving elaborate nuanced answers to her questions and she kept on interrupting me. 'We need sound bites. Give us sound bites.'

In turn, I was getting increasingly irritated that she was irritated with me.

'I am an intelligent person,' I said. 'I don't speak in sound bites.'

I was about to unclip the microphone from my jacket and call the whole interview off, but the cameraman and the sound woman pleaded with me. They needed the footage for the news that evening. I had won the Commonwealth Writers' Prize for the Africa Region for *The Heart of Redness* and would be going to Ghana to receive my award and perhaps, if I was lucky enough, to get the overall Commonwealth Writers' Prize which would only be announced at the ceremony. The novel had also won the very first *Sunday Times* Fiction Award, so it had caused some sensation. The woman wanted to know what I would tell the Queen of England at the reception if I won the overall prize. I thought it was a silly question and I was in the process of giving her an equally silly answer – that I would ask Her Majesty to facilitate the return of King Hintsa's head which was taken to England by her ancestors who were famous headhunters, and while she was at it she should return all the heads of my ancestors that had found their way into the museums of England – when she pleaded for sound bites again.

'If she wants sound bites she must harvest them from my answers,' I said, addressing the cameraman and the sound woman. 'I am not going to speak in sound bites. I am not some stupid politician.'

I was saved by the arrival of a messenger who was led to my back garden by 'M'e 'Mathabang, my helper. A helper is a South African euphemism for a maid. The messenger had my three novels, *Ways of Dying*, *She Plays with the Darkness* and *The Heart of Redness*, and a message from Charlayne Hunter-Gault that I should sign them for President Bill Clinton. Ms Hunter-Gault was the CNN Bureau Chief in Johannesburg, but also a well-known figure in the history of the civil rights movement in the USA. I think she is great fan of my fiction because she has introduced it to many of her celebrity friends. I once received an email from David Shaw, Glenn Close's husband, telling me that Glenn Close had fallen in love with *Ways of Dying*, to which she had been introduced by Ms Hunter-Gault, and she wondered if she could option the rights to adapt it as a movie. Unfortunately, at that time the novel had been optioned by a British film company, which never exercised the option. In this case also, Ms Hunter-Gault thought

478

my novels would be an appropriate South African gift for Mr Clinton who was already in South Africa on a private visit after shedding the shackles of power earlier that year.

The messenger also delivered an invitation to meet Mr Clinton at a reception to be given by Nelson Mandela that Friday. Alas, I had to turn the invitation down. I had two trips that week that were already clashing. One was the trip to Ghana for the Commonwealth Writers' Prize. The other was a long-standing engagement in Nyon, Switzerland, where I was going to be on the jury of Vision du Reel, a highly esteemed international documentary film festival. It did not worry me that I was not going to meet Bill Clinton, though as far as American presidents went I thought he had been the very best. I had met him and Hillary Clinton before when they visited the Market Theatre. I liked them at once, especially the man who had an easy-going manner about him despite the flurry of Secret Service men and our own police who had cleared the place, including the vendors who sold arts and crafts in front of the theatre building.

The Market Theatre is a historical establishment. All the celebrities stop there whenever they visit Johannesburg. I have seen guys like Denzel Washington and Danny Glover going there to see plays or to dine at Gramadoelas, a restaurant known for its South African cuisine.

I decided I wasn't going to Ghana for the prize ceremony. I was going to Nyon instead because I had made that commitment long before they announced that I had won the prize. I went looking for Sello Duiker, who had won the Commonwealth First Book Prize for his novel *Thirteen Cents*. He would be going to Ghana for his prize so I thought he could grab mine as well. I had never met the guy before so I went searching all over Yeoville and found him living in a garret in some old building. He agreed to represent me in Ghana. That was how our friendship started. I became part of his troubled life. But that is a story for another time.

I didn't regret my choice of taking a rain check on Bill Clinton's party and on the prize-giving ceremony in Ghana. I had a wonderful week in Nyon watching some of the greatest documentaries from all over the world. By the end of that week I was drained since I had sat in the cinema for hours on end watching one full-length documentary after another. I heard when I visited friends in Geneva that Peter Carey had won the overall Commonwealth prize for his *True History of the Kelly Gang*. I didn't begrudge him; it was a damn good novel. He wrote to me to say he had been looking forward to meeting me in Ghana, which had been his very first trip to Africa.

With this Nyon trip I didn't only miss partying with the high and mighty, I also missed an important visit that took place at my house during my absence. My mother had come to visit from Lesotho, and when author Elinor Sisulu heard that she was around she brought her parents-in-law, Walter and Albertina Sisulu, to see her. Walter and Albertina Sisulu were at my house and I was not there to welcome them. I could have kicked myself. I would have missed the Nyon Vision du Reel Festival for Walter and Albertina. Integrity is not part of the make-up of politicians, but these two had it in abundant doses. I don't normally hero-worship human beings, not even the deified Mandela, but these two are my heroes. Of course, they had not come to see me; they had come to visit my mother.

My mother was still there when I returned from Europe and she had been rejuvenated by the visit.

Fortunately, Elinor was kind enough to take me to the Sisulu home in Linden, a suburb of Johannesburg, to see her in-laws. Walter had many stories to tell me about my father, how they used to be in awe of him as a thinker and a debater and how they learnt a great deal from him. He was disappointed that he wrote to him and to my mother a few times when he was on Robben Island but he never got any response. I don't know why my parents did not respond to those letters, if indeed they received them at all. Walter told me that if my father had been in Johannesburg at the time instead of the Eastern Cape, the young militants who formed the PAC wouldn't have left the ANC. He believed in a stronger ANC that could be reformed from within.

After talking to Walter Sisulu I missed my father very much and regretted the time I wasted avoiding his company. I could have learnt so much.

480

Adele told me that she wanted to do a PhD in the United States. Even though there was no love lost between us, to the extent that we were no longer intimate though we shared the same bed, she wanted me to help her get there. She wanted me to get a job at one of the universities, even if only on a short-term basis, so that she could have her foot in the door and then stay and continue with her PhD while I returned to my sinful life in South Africa.

I thought it was a good idea. I would have done her a good turn while at the same time separating myself from her – for good, this time. In any event, I reasoned, a PhD would make her even more marketable and she would be able to look after our kids very well since she was certainly going to have custody of them after our divorce. The divorce was now a certainty and we talked about it all the time. I certainly would not want to stay in America. I was not doing badly as a full-time writer, I had my pet rural development project with the Bee People, was a dramaturge at one of the most prestigious theatre houses in the world, and had my HIV-positive friends at the Southern African Multimedia AIDS Trust.

The poet Willy Keorapetsi Kgositsile was working in the United States at the time and I asked him to spread the word that I was looking for a short-term position anywhere in the country. He wrote back to say he would be returning to South Africa soon, but he would spread the word. In no time, I heard from Mbulelo Mzamane informing me that my alma mater, Ohio University, was looking for a Visiting Professor in Anglophone African Literature for one academic year. Mbulelo, ever so resourceful, had come to our rescue again just as he did when I had completed my contract at Yale University and had nowhere else to go. Remember, he had recruited me then for his old position at the University of Vermont. A one-year Visiting Professorship was an ideal job. I applied and was interviewed by the head of the English Department, Ken Daley, and the Director of African Studies, Steve Howard, on the phone. I got the job.

Adele was ecstatic. She was unemployed again after having lost the Department of Education job. We put things in motion to apply for visas. I wanted Thandi to join us as well so she could go to school.

I thought that finally Adele would be nice to me since I was sacrificing my good life in Johannesburg for her. But instead I was suffering a lot of verbal abuse from her. I stubbornly continued to assist my nieces and nephew financially on one hand, and my children on the other, and that of course exacerbated the situation. Sometimes when we were in bed she would wake up and start yelling at me. I yelled back at her and called her a fishwife when she did that. I would wake up, get dressed, and attempt to leave the room. She would stand at the door and say, 'You are not going anywhere until I am done insulting. I'm going to insult you until you walk slowly.' Here I am making a direct translation from Sesotho. In Sesotho that last statement has more impact. It is very ominous.

She knew I would not hit her. I was too scared of jail. In fact, she challenged me to hit her so that she could lay a charge of domestic abuse with the police. Nevertheless we would struggle until I managed to push her away from the door. I would walk out of the house to the garage, with the view of getting into the car and driving away, maybe to book in at a hotel. But she would follow me and force herself into the car. I should have driven away with her to the nearest police station but I didn't. Instead, I went back to the house and listened to her verbal abuse until she finally fell asleep.

Things came to a head and I started looking for a townhouse for myself in the neighbourhood. My main worry was who would give my children their medicine if I left.

One day I was sitting in my study which was next to our bedroom. I was looking at old files. In a shoe box – yes, a shoe box – I found the letter that Gugu wrote me seven years before, in response to mine, encouraging me to stick it out in my marriage with Adele. I wondered where she was and what she was doing. I put the letter away and went to play with Zenzi on the lawn.

'You know, Daddy, I wish I was a boy,' Zenzi said.

'Yeeech! A boy? Why would my pretty little girl wish to be a boy?' I asked.

'Because Mommy told me that when I am big I'm going to have a period.'

'Of course you're going to have a period. That's no reason to wish to be a boy.'

'She told me that it's terrible and it's not pretty and it stinks. I don't want to bleed, Daddy.'

She was really scared. I didn't understand why her mommy didn't realize it would frighten a five-year-old girl like that, or if it was even the right age to tell the child about menstrual problems. I tried to calm her fears and told her how great it was to be a woman.

That evening I went back to the shoe box. I heard Adele yelling at the maid and just sat there staring at the shoe box. Then I went to sleep.

I dreamt about the shoe box. In my dream I opened the box and a misty face emerged like a genie. It turned out to be Gugu's face as it was when we sat in my Toyota Cressida under the tree at our Jerusalema.

The next morning when it was just me and the maid at home I went to the shoe box. I took the letter out and resolved that I was going to write to Gugu. Something inside me told me: *Don't do it! This is dangerous! You're playing with fire!* My heart began to pump faster and faster. It was like I was standing on the railway line and I could see the train coming at full speed, but I could not move. I did not want to move. I was going to write to her and damn the consequences. They might be bitter, but I was too far gone to care. The train was almost here; there was no avoiding it.

I wrote a brief letter. I asked how she was and what she was doing. I wished her well. I drove to the post office and mailed the letter. I hoped the old address I had was still her address, or if it was not that whoever received the letter would forward it to her.

I carried on with my life and forgot about the letter. I was completing the final chapters of *The Madonna of Excelsior* and preparing to start on the first chapter of *The Whale Caller*.

A few weeks later I received a letter from Gugu. It was even briefer than mine. She asked: *Ukuphi? Wenzani? Nabani?* Where are you? What are you doing? With whom?

Then there was her phone number.

That was all I needed. I called her there and then. After all those years her voice was like balm to my scalded soul. She told me she still lived in Swaziland and taught at a high school in a town called Nhlangano. Her parents lived in Piet Retief, a South African town a few kilometres from the Swazi border. She would go visit them the following weekend and we could meet if I drove up there.

I drove to Piet Retief in the Mpumalanga Province, about four hours from Johannesburg, and booked in at the Waterside Lodge. The next morning I sat on the porch of Mr Fries, a fast food place just in front of the lodge, and waited for her. And she came along wearing orange slacks, a white blouse and a white cap. She had not aged one bit since the last time I saw her more than ten years before. I know that's what we say to women to flatter them, but in this case it was true. If only she knew how often I had thought of her, that when I used to write my column for the *Sunday Times* or my articles in the *Mail & Guardian* I hoped she read them and could hear my voice in them, that when I was at a literary festival in Adelaide, Australia, I read to a multitude that had gathered outdoors as if it was a rock concert the poem I had written about our Jerusalema and actually sang Queen's 'Radio Gaga'.

As I suspected, her marriage had gone to the dogs too. I didn't think she would have agreed to meet me there if it had not. I didn't want to know the details but she intimated that for a long time she had felt like a soccer widow; her husband was a FIFA referee and spent his life on the soccer fields of the world. She told me about her three children: Nonkululeko, a girl a year younger than my son Zukile, Simphiwe, a boy a year younger than my daughter Zenzi, and a baby daughter called Gcinile.

'Now that I've met you again I am inspired,' she said. 'I know I'll go back to school; I'll do a master's degree.'

That evening we made love. I had broken my vow never to be unfaithful to Adele despite the terrible life I was living with her. I had kept my vow until then. Now I had broken it; there was no going back.

I gave Gugu the manuscript of *The Madonna of Excelsior*. Some days later I was to get her feedback.

I drove back to Johannesburg with my head buzzing with excitement.

Gugu applied to Wits University and was admitted for an honours degree and then for an MA in Forced Migration Studies. She lived in Braamfontein and I saw her quite often. Adele was bound to hear about it, ironically from the same gossip-monger who had told her about us when we were still at Roma, Lesotho. History repeats itself.

In the meantime we finally decided to do something about our divorce. Adele insisted that I should be the one who initiated it. Her logic was: 'You have done it before and you'll do it again. You are experienced in divorce.'

She promised not to contest it because she wanted out of the marriage as much as I did. We therefore consulted the same lawyer.

'I can only work for you both if it's a consensual divorce and all we are doing is to draw up an agreement,' he said.

We both agreed.

'But you tell me you are going to America together,' said the lawyer. 'How are you going to live together there when you are going through a divorce?'

She wanted to go to school, so she said we certainly could live under the same roof even though we were not together conjugally.

But it turned out that she wanted half of my royalties from all my books as part of the settlement, even those I wrote long before I knew her. Obviously I was going to contest that. I was not going to share any of my royalties with her when she had discouraged and disparaged my work from the word go. It was no longer a consensual divorce. She consulted her old lawyer who had defended her in the theft and embezzlement case, Raymond Tucker Esq., and I consulted different lawyers from Rosebank, Alet Beyl and her husband, Mark Anthony Beyl.

My lawyer lodged the divorce case and summonses were issued. Her lawyer lodged a counter claim. The battle-lines were drawn, but it was going to be a protracted affair as contested divorces normally were in South Africa. Since the case could only be heard in the High Court our attorneys would have to brief advocates. We would leave for America while the matter was pending. At some stage we would have to come back for the hearings.

Under the circumstances my association with Gugu became quite open. I went with her to my reading events where we would, with Sello Duiker who was almost like my son, tease the woman we called Mama, novelist Miriam Tlali, about her new unpublished work titled *Bleeding Shoulders*. We laughed our lungs out at the jokes we made about the title. I took her to the Bee Place where I introduced *The Heart of Redness* to my grandfather at the graveside. I stood there while Gugu watched, next to the polished marble tombstone that I had erected, and spoke with him about the book, and gave it to him by leaving it on top of the grave, telling him I hoped he would enjoy it. I had done the same at my father's grave in Mafeteng.

Don't be surprised at this; some non-believers do have strange rituals which edify them and fulfil a yearning even when they know there is nothing beyond the grave, and that the friend they are talking to is imaginary. Remember: *sometimes there is a void*. That's why we created God and all the other deities in the first place. Humans don't want a vacuum. I was creating my own spirituality.

After this invented ritual I introduced Gugu to the Bee People, who became her friends as well. Then I took her to Kokstad in the Eastern Cape, a ten-hour drive away, to meet my favourite brother, Monwabisi, and his family. We had a relaxing holiday with him and my cousin Nondyebo, away from the mess I had caused in Johannesburg.

On our way back we saw a road sign for the town of Estcourt in KwaZulu-Natal. I remembered the beef and pork sausages that I used to eat with my father when I had joined him in exile in Lesotho. We drove to the town and looked for the factory that manufactured them. I was going to buy them in memory of my father. But we learnt that they no longer manufactured that brand. No wonder I no longer saw them on the shelves.

I took her to Mafeteng to meet my mother. They had met before when she was still a student at Roma fourteen years before. She hit it off with my mother immediately. She told me just before we left: 'I can see you're happy at last, Zani.'

I asked Gugu to join me for a few days when I was invited to the University of Cape Town as a visiting writer, a few weeks before I left for America. She was there when I had a showdown with my publishers.

Mary Reynolds, the commissioning editor at Oxford University Press, was a very charming lady and we got along famously. But I was not happy with the woman who was editing *The Madonna of Excelsior*. I had a history with her because she was the one who had edited my very first novel, *Ways of Dying*. She had changed a modifier I had used and had substituted it with 'enchanting'. I hated that word in my book because I felt that if the situation I had portrayed was enchanting at all it should just enchant without instructing the reader to be enchanted. It was as if you had a magical realist situation and then you wrote 'the characters magically floated in the air'. That would be ridiculous. Strange and unusual events in the book should be deadpan without calling attention to themselves through silly modifiers. But it was my first novel and I had to go along with what that editor wanted. Now, in this new novel she was insisting that I change the portrayal of the Afrikaner characters and explain things and psychologise the characters when I wanted to write a naive novel in keeping with the naive paintings of Father Frans Claerhout that I had harnessed in my storytelling. I was no longer a first-time novelist and I knew my rights. I demanded that they fire the editor from working on my novel. Mary Reynolds came to my office at the University of Cape Town with the editor to plead with me not to fire her. The editor assured me she would stop trying to put her own stamp on my novel. I agreed that she could go ahead and complete the job. After all, she did have some useful suggestions. For instance, I had made the Afrikaner pastor wear a dog-collar. She corrected that because she knew that in the Dutch Reformed Church pastors did not wear dog-collars. I hadn't known that.

I might add that the editor did have her revenge. Many years later when a Yale University history student accused me of plagiarism in *The Heart of Redness* because he didn't understand the workings of intertextuality, he quoted this woman as the Oxford University Press editor who told him that I was stubborn and was not amenable to correction by editors; otherwise the plagiarism could have been avoided.

Anyway, this is a digression. I was telling you about me and Gugu. It was as though I was born again. Not in the crass Christian sense. In the sense of: *Hey, I didn't know that there could be so much laughter in one lifetime!* Even my daughter Thandi said, '*Ntate*, Sis' Gugu has done wonders for you. You are no longer an angry man. Your face is open and bright and shines with joy.'

My ex-wife Mpho agreed with her.

CHAPTER FIFTEEN

FROM THIS POINT, THE past has collided with the present. They have merged into one. We are today's people, and our collective life unfolds in the present.

WE ARE MET AT the Columbus International Airport by a young man, a graduate student at Ohio University, who tells us he has been assigned the pleasure of driving us to Athens. We are in America and the kids are excited about it. They have heard so much about the country from the South African entertainment media which tend to paint it as some kind of paradise. Zukile has long forgotten that he was once in Connecticut and Vermont.

We wanted to bring Thandi as well, but the American Consulate refused to grant her a visa on the basis that she could not be my dependant since she was over the age of twenty-one. What I didn't like was the attitude of the consulate official who, when I tried to plead Thandi's case, threatened that he would deny us all our visas if I didn't shut up and be grateful that he was kind enough to process our applications. I thought that was insulting and I exploded right there in front of everyone.

'I have my own country which is free and beautiful,' I said. 'If you don't give me the visa I don't care. I'll just stay in South Africa and enjoy my beautiful life.'

Every visa applicant present was aghast. No one talks to an American consulate official like that. They were dying to be granted visas to America and here I was playing with my chances. To tell you the truth, I was already having second thoughts about going to America. I hoped he would throw the papers back at me and say, 'Fuck off then, I am not granting you a visa.' Then I would happily drive back to my house in Weltevredenpark and resume my life. If Adele pestered me about going to America I would smile and say, 'Sorry, but the Americans don't want me in their country.'

But he didn't. He just looked at me and shook his head. He processed the papers and told me to come for the visas the following week.

We load our ten big suitcases and bags in a fifteen-seater bus; I had specifically told Ken Daley, the head of the English Department, that I was coming with my whole tribe and its baggage. We have just driven out of Columbus on Route 33 when Zenzi spots a familiar fast-food place and exclaims, 'Look, Daddy, they have McDonald's in America too.'

The freeway from the airport to Athens doesn't look familiar at all. There have been lots of improvements since the last time I was here, eighteen years ago. We pass through more built-up areas during the almost two-hour drive. I never thought I'd be back here. I never thought

490

I would be back in the academy. Period. After seven years as a full-time writer I was enjoying the freedom. I could come and go and travel the world as I pleased. Now I am going to be restricted by university schedules and some of the silly meetings that I had come to dread the last time I had formal associations with a university.

It is getting dark already but the kids' excitement is unabated. Adele is talking with the driver who is curious to know about Africa. It is obvious that his view is that it is one big jungle out there. But I am not paying attention to their discussion. I am thinking of an email that I inadvertently sent to Ken Daley. After he had made his offer I wrote to Mbulelo Mzamane who had alerted me to this post: *Before I respond to the Ohio University people: do you think this is a reasonable offer? The figures you gave me in your previous email were for a semester rather than an academic year. I have no problem in accepting it provided it is reasonable by American standards because I do not want to be taken as cheap labour from Africa.* But foolishly I sent the email to Ken Daley instead of Mbulelo. That's what happens when you click 'send' without making sure that the mail is addressed to the correct person. I only realised my mistake when Daley responded to the effect that they regarded the offer as especially generous for a one-year appointment – *far more than any other one-year term person is making here and more than many of our permanent faculty.* I was embarrassed, although it was good to know that I was not cheap labour. I wrote to apologise and to explain that the letter was not intended for him, and also that I was glad to accept the offer.

After I had told Mbulelo about my gaffe he encouraged me to take the post even if I were not satisfied with the offer because it was just for one year. *It's all right to take it up Zakes for the leverage we can get out of it, not least because of Adele's case.* Like me, he was very concerned that Adele should get a place and do her PhD.

Anyway, I am here now and there is no turning back.

Once in Athens the driver first takes us to Kroger to buy groceries and then delivers us to our new apartment. It is a fully furnished double-storey red brick duplex, one of two buildings that look similar. A wall separates us from an Indian family comprising a young man who, we later learn, teaches at the business school, his wife and their three-year-old son.

It is a comfortable apartment, but it is nothing like our grand home with its sprawling garden and swimming pool in a quiet Roodepoort suburb. I hope Xoli Norman will take care of our house. He is the playwright who attended my workshops at the Market Theatre. I helped him develop his play *Hallelujah!* for the stage. He has agreed to stay in our house and take care of it for the year I'll be away. Resentment begins to build in me. Not only about my house, but about the beekeeping project in the Eastern Cape, the Southern African Multimedia AIDS Trust in Sophiatown, the Market Theatre, and all the opportunities that could be accruing to me by virtue of being a black man in a new South Africa. I chuckle to myself at this last bit. I am not part of the politically connected black elite. I have no such opportunities in the first place. Instead, the rulers of South Africa, even those that are most revered by the world, go out of their way to marginalise me. But still, despite their attempts to slam all doors in my face, I had created my own life as a full-time writer for seven years, and now I am giving all that up.

I hope Xoli Norman will look after my original artwork on the living room walls and the two wooden sculptures in the front garden. One is a woman standing like a tree and the other is of a stylised Chris Hani lying prostrate on the ground. I only knew that it was Chris Hani because there was the word *HANI* carved out on the chest. I bought them from an artist in Newtown and it took a heavy-duty truck to deliver them.

The driver brings me back to the present.

'These are the Ridges,' he tells us. 'These houses used to be the doctors' quarters for the famous mental hospital that used to be here. The place is reputed to be haunted by the ghosts of inmates who died here. Up the hill there's a cemetery where they are buried.'

I don't know if it's wise to be telling us about ghosts; this is our first night in a strange house.

On the second floor there are three bedrooms and a bathroom. Adele and I agree that we will share a bedroom so that the kids can have one each. Nothing conjugal is happening between us at this stage, which has

492

been the case for a while now. We are – or at least I am – used to it. The first thing we both notice is that there is no en suite bathroom or walk-in closet, which is what we were used to at our house in Roodepoort. For me, this is no big deal. Remember, even though my father was a lawyer, I grew up on the poor side of town. Some of the houses my parents rented didn't even have running water.

It is night already so we gather in Zenzi's room and look out of the window. We switch off the lights so that we can see outside without being distracted by our own images. I tell them that I am hoping we'll see one of the famous ghosts. Our backyard is a public park. In the distance we can see the lights of cars on the road. A group of animals comes prancing into the yard.

'Daddy, look! The buck-like creatures in our garden!' said Zukile.

There are two adult creatures and a young one.

All the resentment that has been building in me about being here from the time we arrived at the airport begins to dissipate. We live with the buck-like creatures and my children are thrilled about it. Perhaps things are not that bad after all.

The next morning John, our Indian neighbour, and John, his little son, tell us the buck-like creatures are in fact deer.

That day I go to East Elementary School where the kids had already been admitted and meet the principal, Mr Denny Boger. The kids will travel by bus to and from school. He personally comes in the school bus the next morning to make sure that Zenzi and Zukile know how to change buses at Morrison Elementary and take the correct bus to their school. I am quite amazed to see a principal who takes such a special interest in the students. Where I come from principals don't give a damn. They just sit in the office and pretend to be important. I see Mr Boger after school helping students cross the road to their buses, and even cleaning one of the buses. What dedication!

When the kids have settled at their school I go to mine and try to get settled as well. The English Department is on the third floor in Ellis Hall. I have been allocated the office of a professor who is on sabbatical for the whole academic year. I meet Ken Daley but we don't talk about my gaffe. He is a very nice, helpful man who even invites my family to his house out there in the woods. I meet my colleagues and find that they are a decent bunch of people, many of them dedicated scholars with national and international profiles. But, of course, like every university, one does come across instances of pettiness, people guarding their little empires with their lives, and a fair amount of backstabbing and backbiting. There are those who take themselves seriously to the extreme despite their meagre contribution to scholarship and creativity. This situation, however, is not an aberration; it is inherent in academia the world over. I have found it at every institution of higher learning with which I have been associated in Africa, Europe and the Americas.

My friend the ex-model Nakedi Ribane once told me that I have a reputation of aloofness out there in the real world. My outsiderness continues unabated. I do my job to the best of my ability as long as everyone understands that I am not your conventional professor. I just want to teach, consult with my students for individual tutoring and advising, and then go home to write and paint. I am not looking for anything more from the academy. I don't want to be the head of the English Department one day, and then the dean, and then the president of the university. I just want to teach and create and be left alone.

And at the moment I am writing the second chapter of *The Whale Caller*. I wrote the first chapter in Johannesburg. I am much enthused because my two novels, *The Heart of Redness* and *Ways of Dying*, have been receiving great reviews in newspapers throughout the United States. *The Heart of Redness* even featured as a cover story in the *New York Times Book Review*. Both books become the Editor's Choice. They are also featured in the weekday *New York Times*.

I am allocated a graduate fiction class to teach, which I think is baptism by fire. These are PhD and master's students who have done workshops all their university lives and I have never been in a creative writing workshop, let alone taught one. I am not counting the one conducted by Marc Crawford in Maseru during my wild days. When I tell my students that I have taught some playwriting but never fiction, they are even more enthusiastic about my classes. I find that they are prepared for me, and most of them have read my novels. Some have only read the reviews. But they think it is wonderful to be taught by someone who has not been 'polluted' by the workshop system.

'Yours is a fresh approach,' one of them, John Kachuba, tells me.

I realise that some of my students are highly experienced as writers. For instance, Elly Williams has a novel – under the pseudonym E W Summers – for which she received a one hundred thousand dollar advance. I have never received a hundred thousand dollar advance. John Kachuba has also published widely and has an instructional book on how to write humour. I am wondering, what are these guys doing here learning how to write?

These two in particular become more than just students, but friends. They are so enamoured with my style of teaching that they take other classes of mine which have nothing to do with creative writing. One such class is titled *Narratives of Memory, Truth and Reconciliation: South Africa and Rwanda*. I introduce them for the first time in their lives to the works of other writers outside the United States such as J M Coetzee, Antjie Krog, Njabulo Ndebele, Veronique Tadjo, Goretti Kyomuhendo and many others. Later, I supervise Elly's PhD.

My teaching does not confine itself to the Ohio University campus. I fly to Switzerland to conduct workshops on Fiction in the Classroom for the Swiss Association of Teachers of English in Zurich, Switzerland. Here I am hosted by a wonderful couple, Ulrich Gerber and his wife, Doris. I am impressed by their love for each other. But they also love *The Madonna of Excelsior* and South Africa. They have many stories to tell about the country, which they visit every other year.

I also tour the United States, courtesy of my New York publishers, promoting my two novels and reading at the Miami Book Fair, at the Tisch School of the Arts, New York University, and at the Du Bois Center at Harvard University.

To the consternation of my publishers, I have to cancel other venues that they have already booked because Adele decides to return to South Africa to complete a project she was doing for a private company as a consultant in educational programming for the SABC. She also tells me that she has to consult with her lawyers about our divorce. I look after the kids until she returns after a month or so.

One of the first things we do after buying an old red Nissan is to drive to Columbus in search of my brother Sonwabo. Thanks to Bob Edgar's Internet detective work, he discovered through some letters to

495

the editor of the *Columbus Dispatch* which Sonwabo wrote on some local political issue, that he was living in Columbus. My mother is glad to hear that at least he is still alive, and asks me please to look for him. I am going to persist this time and will not give up as I did on my previous sojourns in the United States. I have written to him via the *Columbus Dispatch* and he has responded, so now I have his address.

The house is next to the Ohio State University campus off High Street. We meet the landlord who is sitting on the porch supervising some workmen sawing wooden boards. He tells us that Sonwabo has left and he has no forwarding address. Our spirits are dampened. We drive back to Athens. I later learn from an African American woman who writes to me about visiting her school to talk about South Africa that she knows Sonwabo and that he works for a soccer team called the Crew as a custodian. Through this connection I trace him to a conservative think-tank organisation where he works as a political consultant. The Crew job is a part-time one. We finally get in touch and he comes to Athens to visit and to meet Adele and the kids. He mentions something about his plans to return to South Africa soon, but I know it's just empty talk. Why should his desire to return to South Africa happen only when he sees me? He has been here for years without writing even to his children, let alone to his wife and his mother.

The divorce is moving very slowly. The lawyers from the opposing sides are involved in protracted negotiations. Raymond Tucker, Adele's lawyer, makes it clear in his letter that they do intend to drag the matter out because the divorce may have some effect on the visas of Adele and the children which are dependent on my visa. His fear is that the divorce may affect their right to remain in the United States. Adele, who has been admitted for a PhD in media studies, has been granted a tuition waiver by the university on the grounds of being my wife, and therefore the divorce may affect that as well. They also want me to continue to pay the mortgage on the house in Weltevredenpark, but the property must be transferred to Adele. I should continue to pay the mortgage on Adele's property even after our divorce until it is fully paid up. I, on the other hand, will take possession of some property in the Eastern Cape – 'the Herschel property', as Tucker's correspondence refers to it. She is demanding half of all my royalties from my books. She also wants custody of the children and maintenance for herself and the children of a ridiculous amount that exceeds my entire salary at Ohio University before taxes.

This is obviously not going to be an amicable divorce. I instruct my attorneys to respond that indeed she must have custody of the children. It is my belief that children of this age should be with their mother, as long as I get reasonable visitation rights. But of course the maintenance will have to be reasonable, an amount that I can afford rather than her current demand which is beyond my means. The 'Herschel property' is a myth she has concocted so that she can have our property in Weltevredenpark, and I must not get a single cent from it. The 'Herschel property' does not belong to me but to the Lower Telle Beekeeping Collective Trust, the Bee People, and it cannot be part of the dispute. She knows that as well, but she brings it into the mix to muddy the waters and give the impression that I have more assets than I really do. The only solution I am prepared to accept is that we sell the property in Weltevredenpark and divide the proceeds equally, after paying off the mortgage.

As for the royalties, here I am prepared to fight to the last man. She will not get a single cent of my royalties because she has never supported my writing. Instead, she disparaged it quite early on in our marriage and later lost all interest in it. The only time she paid attention was when I got a bad review, and these were few and far apart. Most of the reviews were glowing with praise. But once in a while there would be a scathing one. And then she would become animated, make copies of it and send it to her friends and to those people in South Africa who she thought were interested in my work. For instance, when a writer called Norman Rush savaged me in the *New York Review of Books*, accusing me of the literary crimes of not featuring AIDS in my novels and of not being previously known by him, she was so gleeful that she distributed the article to all and sundry in South Africa.

The last time I was in South Africa Dorothy Steele, my biographer, told me that she had received Norman Rush's review from Adele and added, 'Thank her for me and please ask her to send me the good reviews too, such as those from the *New York Times Book Review* and the *Washington Post*.'

I wish I could get more bad reviews so that there is more sunshine in her life.

That notwithstanding, I am determined not to share my royalties with her. It's a matter of principle.

When Raymond Tucker insists that she must have sole possession of our Weltevredenpark house because I have the 'Herschel property' I state my position thus:

The property was never part of any dispute because it belongs to the community of Herschel. It is a Trust and I am only one of the Trustees. Raymond Tucker and I are both Trustees of the Market Theatre. Why doesn't he mention the Market Theatre in this dispute? Why doesn't he include it in the spoils that must be given to Adele?

Since we both stand our ground on these issues it is clear that our divorce will not be resolved in the near future. Yet I am desperate to be free. I ask my attorneys to explore the precedent set in the case of Nelson Mandela and Winnie Madikizela-Mandela – which had been successfully followed in the case of Barry Davidson versus Sally Davidson – where the court granted a divorce without having settled the financial issues between the parties.

While my lawyers are exploring this line of action and her lawyers are opposing it, life in the family is living hell. The children are affected because there is perpetual tension between us. I think she is angry that she is not getting her way and she wants to take it out on everyone. In the morning she wakes up and struts around in her undergarments yelling at the children. It is her way of teaching them how to take their bath and clean their teeth and prepare for school. I lie in my bed frozen with fear lest she turns her wrath on me. But she never does, until one morning when I cannot take it any more and I ask her to cool it a bit.

'You are a teacher by profession,' I say. 'And a very good one by all accounts. I am sure you don't teach your students by yelling at them. Zuki and Zenzi will learn better if you go gently on them.'

'You shut up,' she says. 'These are my children. What do you know about bringing up children when yours are failures who have achieved nothing in life? You left them with your useless mother to bring them up for you; now look how they have turned out.'

I know already that every time we disagree about something she brings up my older kids – Neo, Thandi and Dini – and drives her point home that I have no right to say anything because Mpho and I did a botched job of raising our children. Her running mantra is: 'I don't want my children to grow up to be like your children.'

But I think she does see my point because when the kids come back from school she apologises for her morning behaviour. She blames it on the stress of living with me. But the next morning she does it again.

I can understand her point about the stress of living with me. I have my own stress of living with her. I would be having a similar breakdown too if I didn't have an outlet, namely my creative writing classes and *The Whale Caller*, which I have resumed writing. But I don't write it at home. I wake up early in the morning and go to my office at the university where I work furiously for the whole day, until late in the evening. Colleagues see me and praise me for my dedication. They don't know that I am an exile from a poisonous home environment.

I don't want to medicalise Adele's anger, turning it into something pathological, but I feel very strongly that she needs help. I suggest that we both go for counselling as I need help too. She opposes it because she says counselling will not do her any good; I will lie about her to the counsellors as I have always lied about her all my life. But I suspect that she does go for medical advice privately. I am hopeful that things will be better, not between us as such, but between her and the children.

They never are. They worsen instead. Zenzi is a relentless painter and a very talented one. She is certainly going to be a great artist one day. Some of her paintings have inspired mine. She uses every free moment she has to paint a picture. Her mother starts a new campaign of destroying Zenzi's paintings. I do manage to save some and hide them in my office. They are still there to this day. But I am not always there for the rescue. Sometimes I find her crying because her mother has destroyed a prized work. All I can say to comfort her is: 'Don't worry, my child, you'll paint another one.'

'But it won't be the same again,' she says sniffling.

She is right. You can only create a work of art once. Even a performance of a play in the theatre cannot be repeated. It can run for every night for months on end, but no performance will be the same as any other performance. I can tell you proleptically at this point that in the next novel I write after *The Whale Caller* I create a character who destroys her daughter's works of art. Adele has indeed inadvertently given me many ideas for characterisation in a number of my novels, beginning with *She Plays with the Darkness*, as I have already told you. Her habits are coming in quite handy in my creation of some aspects of my main female character in *The Whale Caller*, which I am currently writing.

Maybe I do owe her royalties after all!

For me, relief comes from my travels. And from my varied literary activities in America and abroad. As you may have noticed, literature has taken over completely and I don't do much painting these days.

I feel giddy when I am away from the rancour that pervades the homefront. *The Heart of Redness* wins the Zora Neale Hurston/Richard Wright Legacy Award. I ask Robert Edgar, the Howard University professor who writes about my father, to represent me at the awards ceremony because I am at Philips Academy in Massachusetts where the students are performing my play, *The Bells of Amersfoort*. I composed the music for this play so their director wants me to teach them how to sing the isiXhosa songs properly.

When *The Heart of Redness* is published in Dutch and in Swedish I go to those countries to read and sign books. When Salman Rushdie writes to me inviting me to do more readings in New York I gladly attend the PEN World Voices Festival where I am on the panel with Ngugi wa Thiong'o and Tsitsi Dangarembga. I read for the full-house public about a man who is mating with a whale in *The Whale Caller*, which is still a work-in-progress. Ngugi tells me he is mesmerised both by the reading and the content.

'Even though there is no revolution or class analysis in it, *Mzee*?' I tease him.

I call him *Mzee*, which is a title they use for elders in his country. I find these older writers inspiring and I like to hang out with them. That is why a month or so later I fly to Basel, Switzerland, to visit writer Lewis Nkosi and his partner Astrid Starck. There I debate with the Yiddish writers who gather in his small living room about fiction and politics. It is a pity, though, that I can't join them in guzzling the vast amounts of hard liquor that seem to oil good conversation. Lewis is still a heavy drinker as I have always known him to be. He has no sympathy for the likes of me who have chosen to walk the lonely path of temperance. The thought of going back to Athens could easily have driven me back to drink. But, thankfully, I no longer have the stomach or the head for it. The problem when you become a teetotaller is that you can't postpone your problems by postponing sobriety.

Good company that makes you forget your problems is found not only in Basel, but in Barcelona where I pop in occasionally to be with Teresa, Albio, Sara and Adrian. And in Toronto, Canada, where I read poetry at the International Festival of Authors at the Harbourfront Center. It is not so much the reading but the meeting of old friends that I relish. There is the couple Patrick Nkunda and Palesa with whom I enjoy reminiscing about the old wild days in Maseru. Just to remind you, Nkunda is a top-notch immigration lawyer and Palesa is a nurse in the city. There is also the attractive film director Debe Morris, with whom I reminisce about her South African visit. She is the lady I took to Lesotho to see Her Majesty Queen 'Mamohato.

I remember that on that trip, after Debe was done with her royal visit she decided to take a minibus taxi to the Basotho Pony Trekking Centre up the very steep mountains where she hoped to hire one of the famous Basotho ponies and ride to the Maletsunyane Falls. It was already afternoon and I worried that she would not be able to get a taxi back, in which case she would be stranded in the mountains. I went to Lesotho High School to get my friend Mxolisi Ngoza, the mathematics teacher, to accompany me. I drove up the winding road that ascends steeply for more than forty kilometres past Molimo-Nthuse Lodge to the horse breeding place. We waited there for only a few minutes before Debe arrived on horseback. We drove back with her, stopped briefly at the Lodge for a few drinks, drove on and then stopped again at the most dangerous part of the road, the Bushman's Pass.

'This is where two former cabinet ministers of Chief Leabua Jonathan's government and their wives were murdered,' I told Debe.

I was talking about Desmond Sixishe, the Minister of Information who helped me get to America that first time in 1981, and Vincent Makhele, Minister of Foreign Affairs. They were abducted from their homes with their wives. Their bodies were found at this mountain pass riddled with bullets. This happened soon after the 1986 coup when General Metsing Lekhanya overthrew Chief Leabua Jonathan in what seemed at first to be a bloodless coup. It was not until 1990, after Lekhanya had been overthrown by fellow officers, that two senior members of the Lesotho Paramilitary Force, who were also relatives of the King, were convicted for these point-blank executions of two men who were political rivals and two women whose only crime was that they were married to the men.

Debe took photographs of the horrid place.

In Toronto, we recall the blood-soaked mountain and the rest of the journey. Debe says her strongest impression of the trip is being in awe of me and my generosity and kindness. I am rather flattered by it all. It is not every day that women tell me they are in 'awe' of me. I know of one in Athens, Ohio, who thinks I am the worst scumbag ever to walk this earth. But I do not tell Debe about my miserable situation back home. One doesn't burden friends with one's afflictions, especially when they are self-inflicted – yes, I was not forced by anyone to be in this situation, I walked into it with my eyes open. A sane person would ask: then why don't you just walk out of it? Good question. And when people say that, you know immediately that they don't have a good answer. I don't know if you'll buy it if I tell you the children have something to do with it. You will buy it even less when I tell you I feel I have an obligation towards her. But take it or leave it, that's how I feel.

The greatest relief comes when I return to South Africa during the summer months. South Africa means the bees and the Bee People. It also means the comforting presence of Gugu in Johannesburg and of my mother in Lesotho.

I rent a townhouse in Sandton and Gugu and my daughter Thandi join me there. We travel to the Bee Place and find that the Bee People are still as determined as ever to make their project a success. Only women remain in the project now, the men having given up long since. One of those who left is Morrison Xinindlu, the elder we once upbraided for wrecking the car in his drunkenness. But others have been forced out of the project by death. One of these is my Uncle Owen. I heard of his death while I was in the United States, but I couldn't come for the funeral. My children Thandi and Neo and their mother Mpho represented me.

The only retrogressive step that I find among the Bee People is that they still haven't learnt how to drive. They tell me that they did enrol two women at a driving school in Sterkspruit but neither of them made any headway because they were so fearful of driving. Now they have to employ one of Uncle Press's sons, Sandile, to drive their truck whenever they have to deliver their honey in Sterkspruit or Lady Grey and he charges them exorbitant amounts as if they were hiring his own vehicle filled with his own petrol. I try to give them more pep-talk.

'This is now a women's only project because you are more persistent and have more patience than men,' I say. 'You have proved that you can be successful without men. In fact, in your case it is likely that you are successful because you do not have any men running things here. That is all the more reason why you must learn to drive your own truck. This guy you employ as a driver is robbing you blind. You should be doing your own driving.'

They promise that they will try to banish their fears and return to the driving school. But their eyes tell me that none of them have any intention of doing so.

From the Bee Place we drive to Lesotho to visit my mother. Her health has deteriorated and she is beginning to lose her memory. She is grateful to the Lord that I finally found Sonwabo and she hopes that she will see him before she dies. I admonish her for talking as if she is at the mouth of the grave and promise that I will persuade Sonwabo to come back home, even if just to visit and see his mother, his siblings, his wife and his children who are now three grown women and one giant of a man.

Back in Johannesburg we launch *The Madonna of Excelsior* at Exclusive Books in Hyde Park. Kader Asmal, the Minister of Education, is present. I am glad that he came when he heard I was launching a book even though he was not specifically invited. He is a true lover of literature and a supporter of my novels in particular, though he has told me that he does not agree with my political position in *The Heart of Redness*. I tell him that I am particularly proud of *The Madonna of Excelsior* because I own all the rights, thanks to my beautiful agent Isobel Dixon.

An eavesdropper whose book I have just signed asks, 'What has her beauty got to do with it?'

I laugh and say, 'I know, I know I am being sexist and all that jazz. But I am a man of art, I love beauty.'

Gugu and I pay a long overdue visit to Nadine Gordimer in Parktown. Today she is all alone in her huge house. We relax in her tastefully furnished but subdued living room and she offers us brandy. Alas, we are wet blankets because we are teetotallers. She treats herself to a shot nonetheless. She is a very disappointed woman. One of the icons of the struggle, Mac Maharaj, has just been accused by the *Mail & Guardian* as having been involved in some financial scandal. I never really get to know what it is all about because I am really corruption-fatigued; there are too many such stories in the papers.

'What do you think happened to our comrades?' Nadine keeps on asking.

But I don't have any answer. I can offer some cliché like 'power corrupts', but it does not provide us with any insight into the specific problem of her comrades in her party, the ANC, who always occupied the moral high ground during the liberation struggle and who sacrificed careers and families in pursuit of justice, fairness and equality, but whose snouts are now buried deep in the troughs of corporate crony capitalism.

'If the domination of business by government is socialism and the domination of government by business is fascism,' I offer unhelpfully, 'in South Africa we have these opposites in an unnatural coexistence. This breeds the double-dosage of corruption and patronage we see in our country today.'

I know that my characterisation of our system and my definition of the '-isms' are simplistic, but they do serve my anger at the damage that our leaders are doing to my country. Nadine thinks I am making the situation sound bleaker than it really is. I think she still has faith in her ANC comrades. I lost it long ago. When I wrote to Nelson Mandela I still thought the situation could be saved. I gradually lost hope with the next administration. Now, of course, there is wholesale plunder.

Nadine wants to know what I teach in America and when I tell her that I teach creative writing she laughs and says, 'But you know that creative writing cannot be taught. You and I were not taught.'

I don't think she is correct on either count. The craft and techniques of writing can be taught, just as those of painting or acting or singing can be taught. What cannot be taught are the flair and the artistic vision. Raw talent alone is not of much use if it is not refined, polished and channelled in the right direction. When Nadine says we were not taught, she means that we did not go to any formal class or workshop to learn how to write. We are self-taught. But self-taught writers are taught by other writers whose work they read and emulate. They are also taught by friends, family, neighbours and school teachers who read their work and give them feedback. And, by the way, that's what a workshop does, albeit in a more formal, organised and distilled environment. So, Nadine and I were taught after all.

The following week Gugu and I go to the National Arts Festival in Grahamstown to launch *The Plays of Zakes Mda*, which have been translated into isiXhosa, isiZulu, Southern Sesotho, isiNdebele, Setswana, Siswati, Xitsonga, Northern Sesotho and Tshivenda. This is where we meet a poet called Natalia Molebatsi who works for my publishers, the University of South Africa Press. We fall in love with her and establish a strong friendship. She encourages us to adopt a vegetarian lifestyle. I have always been inclined towards vegetarianism even as I devoured huge chunks of pork. I have always felt bad for the animals I was eating but did not have the courage to do anything about it. Even after Natalia has given us encouragement we don't do anything about it and continue cannibalising other creatures unabated.

It is only on a subsequent visit to South Africa that something happens that forces us to think twice about eating meat. Gugu has moved to Twin Oaks, a townhouse complex in Randpark Ridge. I buy a plump duck that I first steam for her. I then bake it after basting it in a mixture of ginger, cloves, cinnamon, nutmeg, white pepper, soy sauce and honey. After I have done the job it looks really good and we are looking forward to eating it. Just as we are preparing to serve the meal we hear some quacking sounds outside. When we open the door there is a mother duck and her ducklings standing on the doorstep looking at us admonishingly. We quickly close the door.

'There's no way I can eat this meat now,' I say.

'Nor me,' says Gugu.

We dump that whole duck into the dustbin. From that day we stop eating meat altogether. In fact, Gugu had started earlier by giving up pork after she saw on television how pigs were slaughtered. She had kept only to ostrich, chicken and fish. But after the visit of the ducks we decide to stop eating all creatures of the sea or land or air.

We are committed vegetarians but we don't proselytise about it. Ours is a live-and-let-live attitude. I, for one, do recognise the fact that for humanity to survive the harsh environment of past eons it was necessary to bludgeon each other to death and to eat other sentient beings. That's how we evolved to be what we are. But I think now we have reached a stage where some of us have evolved to such a high level that our warrior gene has diminished and we have become squeamish about death. We can therefore survive quite healthily on the non-sentient bounty of the earth, without visiting acts of violence upon each other and on those creatures we deem to be of a lower order.

After completing my one year contract as Visiting Professor I decide to stay, this time not reluctantly but because this is the place for me. I have nothing to go back to in South Africa because all doors are closed for me there. I was surviving by my writing before I came to America, but I don't need to be physically there to write. And I can continue to contribute to the development of my people through the beekeeping project, the workshops I hold for writers at the Market Theatre and my work with the HIV-positive people, while living in the quiet and peaceful environment of Athens, Ohio. I handle a lot of the work while I am here, thanks to the Internet, and spend a few months each year working directly with the people in South Africa. I have discovered that here I am able to write undisturbed by the demands on my time in South Africa where people seem misguidedly to think that I am some kind of a celebrity. Here, in rural Ohio, I am a nobody and am able to lead a quiet life. Even those people who may know that there is an international writer of sorts in their midst don't associate that writer with me.

The most important reason I decide to stay is that my children have fallen in love with their school and I am going to feel very bad if I uproot them once again and take them back to South Africa. Zenzi actually does ask me not to take them back to South Africa.

The third reason is that I begin to smell a story after attending a party at Steve Howard's house. He is the head of African Studies. At his party I find myself being an audience to an argument about the distinction between the Mulengeons and the WIN people. I learn that the Mulengeons are descendants of the Roma people, the so-called Gypsies, whereas the WIN people are tri-racial, descending from Whites, Indians and Negroes. A film professor called Charles Fox tells us stories about his own family which is WIN. I decide there and then that I want to pursue the WIN people. There may be a story there somewhere.

I apply for a vacant position in African Literature and go through the motions of interviews and job talks. But before I can take up this post, a creative writing professor called Jack Matthews retires and I am offered his position. This, for me, is a much better job than the African Literature one and I take it without hesitation. In South Africa I had thought I was done with academia for the rest of my life, but thanks to Adele I am in Athens, Ohio, as a Full Professor in the English Department.

But life is not getting any better with her. There is too much strain on us because the divorce is not through yet. There is very little communication between us even though we live under the same roof. I moved out of the main bedroom long since and have confiscated Zenzi's room. She now sleeps in her mother's bedroom. Adele and I rarely talk but communicate our frustrations with each other through email. As a result I have a box full of hundreds of emails that will be fodder for researchers one day. I'll only quote a few lines from some real mild ones in this book, otherwise you'll think I'm being vindictive or tasteless or both if I blurt out those with X-rated language directed at me and my body parts.

Out of the blue she writes: *I am trying by all means to make our lives easy but you seem to be trying your level best to create a hostile environment around us. I am and shall continue to be nice to you as much as I can for the sake of the children.* I am happy that she undertakes to be nice to me for the sake of the children, but in reality I never see the niceness. I respond: *Although I don't know what hostile environment I created lately I apologise. It is obvious that just seeing me around fills you with anger. Throughout I have been quiet and keeping very much to myself. I have no intention of creating any hostile environment.*

I finally decide to move out. We reach a verbal agreement that she will have custody of the children and they will visit me every other weekend. That's all the visitation I need. I leave her with the Nissan while I buy myself a Chrysler PT Cruiser. I will also continue to pay the rent and all their living expenses. I pack my bags and book into a hotel for a few days, until I find a two-bedroom apartment on Pomeroy Road on the same side of town as the Ridges where Adele and the kids live. I furnish every room of my apartment and set up a workstation in my bedroom with a laptop and resume writing *The Whale Caller*. I teach only two days a week and on the other days I write the novel.

But when it's the weekend visitation with the kids I stop all the writing and spend the time with them. I take them to amusement parks and theme parks in neighbouring cities and states. It is like I am making up for the rest of the time I am not with them.

I finally complete the novel. It is the only one of my novels that doesn't draw from specific historical events in southern Africa. It was suggested to me by a real-life incident, though; a newspaper story about two kids in the Western Cape who stoned a village drunk to death because they were bored. I created my own Bored Twins who do not in any way share a history with the original killer girls. The novel was also suggested by a story I saw on television about the whale crier of Hermanus. The television story gave me the impression that the guy, in black tails and tricorne, blew his horn and the whales came sailing towards him. On a visit to the University of Cape Town I asked my biographer Dorothy Steele to take me to Hermanus to see the magical whale crier. We spent the whole day in the town, my first visit there. I was disappointed to discover that the whale crier did not call whales at all, but tourists. He blew his kelp horn to inform tourists about the presence and location of the whales and the tourists could interpret the meaning of the staccato of his horn decoded on the sandwich board that he wore. I said to myself: *if this whale crier cannot call whales, I am going to create my own who can.* My second visit to the town was with Gugu, and here I was consolidating the geography of my novel vis-à-vis that of the town and the surrounding villages.

The names of the characters in the novel were suggested by Zenzi when I was playing with her in her room in Weltevredenpark. I asked her to think of a name, any name. And without any hesitation she said, 'Sharisha'. That sounded like the name of a whale to me and therefore I was going to have a specific whale character called Sharisha. If Zenzi had not thought of the name there would have been no such character. My fictional whale crier would be blowing his horn for whales in general. I asked her to think of another name and she said 'Saluni'. Mind you, these were just names that she invented. There are no such names in our culture, or in any culture that we knew of. I decided that Saluni would be the village drunk.

Now the novel is complete. It has drained me emotionally to such an extent that when I get to the final period I break down and cry. I cry for a long time.

At about that time my New York publishers, Farrar, Straus and Giroux, publish the American edition of *The Madonna of Excelsior.*

It receives great reviews from all the major papers. Later it wins the second prize of the Hurston/Wright Legacy Award and is also selected by the American Library Association as one of the twenty-five notable books of 2005. Of course, I am absolutely ecstatic about this. Do you know how many books of all types, not just novels, are published in America every year? Thousands. If your book is chosen by a group of people whose lives are books as one of the best twenty-five out of the thousands, you have no right not to wet yourself with joy.

The next summer I go to South Africa as usual to work with the Bee People and, of course, to see my mother, Gugu, Neo, Thandi and all of Sonwabo's children. During this time I also teach my regular playwriting workshops at the Market Theatre and creative writing workshops with HIV-positive people at the Anglican Church of Christ the King in Sophiatown.

I get a message that my sister Thami is seriously ill and I go to Mafeteng to see her only to find that I am too late. She is dead. It turns out that she died of AIDS. But Gugu and I know that she really died of denial. We have experience enough of working with HIV-positive people to know that they can lead normal lives with the virus for years, as long as they protect and take care of themselves. After her Master's degree in Forced Migration at the University of the Witwatersrand, Gugu did a postgraduate diploma in the Management of HIV-AIDS at the Workplace at the Medical University of South Africa in Pretoria. Following a stint organising campaigns for Amnesty International, she now works for an organisation called Love Life which aims to educate the youth on HIV-AIDS. I, on the other hand, work with HIV-positive people in the organisation that I founded in Sophiatown. In Lesotho, where my sister lived, HIV-AIDS still carries a lot of stigma, even though it is so prevalent that every weekend in a small town like Mafeteng there are at least five funerals of its victims. We still believe that if my sister had undergone tests early on, and had then taken the necessary treatment, she would be alive today. Gugu and I test quite regularly and we advise our relatives to do so as well. Thami resisted any testing. She said that she would rather not know. When she was forced by the illness to test it was too late. She already had full-blown AIDS and she died.

At the wake, her son Dumisani, who is a missionary in Germany and the United Kingdom, gives a moving sermon, and at the funeral I take the opportunity to preach about HIV-AIDS. People are impressed that we do not hide the fact that our sister died of AIDS as families usually do. We use her death as a teaching moment. My mother is very distraught. 'We don't expect children to die before their parents,' she keeps on saying.

Later that summer Gugu and I go for HIV tests at our doctor's office in Melville. We invite Thandi to come along. We get the results immediately. Gugu and I are both negative but Thandi is positive. She is distressed and flustered. We are there for her, and we are both good counsellors. We assure her that we'll be there every step of the way. Gugu teaches her how to take care of herself, what kind of food she should eat and what exercises she should do daily. She follows the regimen and she continues to be a very healthy woman taking care of her son to this day.

Back in America, Adele starts to harass me with telephone calls, accusing me of stealing the documents that prove that I own the beekeeping property in the Eastern Cape. But, strangely, she does not report the theft to the police. She is lying, of course, because there were never such documents in the first place. When I point this out to her, advising her that she can always apply for duplicates of the documents she claims I have stolen, she threatens me with death. She does not say she will kill me herself, but makes some vague prophecies about my impending demise. I take her threats seriously and report the matter to the police. Not the university police this time, since I no longer live on a university property, but to the city police. She claims that all she said was 'your dirty heart which is full of cruelty and spite will kill you soon'.

Well, we all leave it at that.

When I go to fetch the children at the weekend, she refuses to let them come with me. She says that from now on I must give her two weeks' notice before I can have them for the weekend. She stands at the door and says I cannot come in to pick them up, nor can they come out to join me. I do not want to create a scene. I have no choice but to go back to my apartment without them. I sit down at my computer and write her an email giving her the two-weeks' notice for the next visitation, and notices for all the subsequent fortnightly visitations for the next six months.

On the appointed day she does release the children to me but tells me that she rejects all the notices that I have given all at once because they are not two-week notices. I must give one two-week notice at a time.

When I return the kids on the Sunday evening she is very angry with me because I took them to my office and I walked on campus with them. She warns me never to do that again, otherwise I will not have the children again.

'You have no right to stop me from seeing my children,' I say. 'Why should I not see them when they are here in this country because of me and I am their sole support?'

'You are not our sole support,' she says.

I don't know what she means by that. As far as I know she is not working anywhere. I discover only much later that she has propagated a story at the university and elsewhere in town that I have abandoned her and the children and they receive no financial support from me. Apparently I did this after meeting another woman since coming to Athens, Ohio. She, who used to be a staunch Catholic, has now joined a charismatic church which is known for its charitable works among the destitute. She has sold the pastors her woeful story and they begin to collect donations for her. That is why I am no longer their sole support.

Ours is a small town where gossip travels fast. She gets a lot of sympathy from the townspeople, and even from some of my colleagues in the English Department, because she is supposedly a poor African woman who resigned from a lucrative job in Johannesburg and accompanied her husband to America to support his career, uprooting the children from their school in the process, only to be abandoned by the unscrupulous husband for another woman. Worse still, the husband has allegedly deserted his children as well, leaving them without any means of support. Even East Elementary School buys into this narrative.

I discover that my children are getting free lunch at school because their mother is destitute and their father does not provide any financial support.

No wonder she does not want me to be seen with the children on campus. My frolicking around with happy children messes up her neat narrative.

She has no choice but to let me take Zenzi for her figure skating lessons on Tuesdays and Thursdays. She is at school at those times and cannot do it herself. Those who see me with her at the Bird Arena begin to doubt at least some aspects of the narrative. But they never ask me because they want to pretend that they don't want to get involved in other people's business.

Adele makes a new rule one day when I come to fetch the children. She is sitting on the stairs that lead up to the bedrooms and is holding a broomstick. She says the kids are not going anywhere with me because I didn't give her adequate notice. From now on she wants one month's notice. I can hear Zenzi crying upstairs. She has been looking forward to spending the weekend with her daddy. But obviously her mother wants to cut me off totally from my children. Her narrative to the sympathisers of Athens must be seen to be true at all costs.

At least I will see Zenzi twice a week when I take her for ice skating. If I am lucky, I'll see Zukile standing outside and I'll wave to him. Zenzi is rehearsing for an ice show. She is one of the kids in *Charlie Brown*. I know she will do well, although she is a bit nervous about it since it is a bigger role than last year's when she was a fairy in *Neverland*.

I consult a local attorney, Claire Buzz Ball, for advice on how I can get reasonable access to my children. That's all I want. Not custody, but to spend every other weekend with them. But Buzz tells me that since the divorce proceedings are in a different jurisdiction, namely South Africa, the family court in Athens, Ohio, cannot decide on custody and visitations in the matter. He advises me to withdraw the case from South Africa and initiate a new one in Athens. Only then can the court in Athens address questions of custody. His advice makes sense. After all, the case in South Africa has stalled. Adele's lawyer, Raymond Tucker, died in a car accident and his office had transferred her file to a new firm of lawyers. I instruct my attorneys in Johannesburg to withdraw the case immediately, and they do so.

Buzz is a sharp lawyer. He used to be a politician and a member of the State House of Representatives for the Republican Party, so he knows his way around the system. He files a Complaint for Divorce and Temporary Orders for Visitation Rights in the Court of Common Pleas Domestic Relations Division, Athens County. Again, you can see that even at this point all I want are my visitation rights and nothing more. Adele does receive these documents through certified mail and signs for them. Later she is to claim that she never received them.

On Thursday I go to the Ridges to fetch Zenzi for the final dress rehearsal. The show is on Saturday and I know she is looking forward to it. She was very excited when I took her for her costume fitting two days before. I knock at the door but there is no response. It is strange because the red Nissan is parked outside and the curtains are not closed. I wait for a while. And then I drive to the Bird Arena where the show will be held, hoping that perhaps Zenzi's mom took her there. She is not there. I go back to the Ridges and wait outside. It gets dark but still there is no sign of Zenzi, Zuki or Adele. I drive back to my apartment. I call Adele's place repeatedly, hoping that she is back with the kids from wherever she had taken them. No one answers and I leave voice messages. The voice messages become frantic as the night progresses. Early in the morning I return to the Ridges and still no one is there. By this time I am a nervous wreck. What could have happened to my children?

That morning, April 8, 2005, I file a missing persons report with the police at the university. An officer accompanies me to the house. Since this is a university house he has the keys. Inside we find that things are in a mess in the living room and the kitchen. It does not look as though anyone lives here. Upstairs in the bedrooms everything is topsy-turvy. But their clothes and suitcases are not there. I go to the bedside telephone and replay the messages. I hear my pained voice: *It's ten o'clock now and I'm getting worried. Zenzi and Zukile, please call me as soon as you come back.* Sometimes it is just a sigh and: *Oh, my God!* If you wondered who atheists call to when they are in trouble

514

you now know. One of my many messages: *It's eleven-thirty and I've been calling every thirty minutes to find out where my children are.* But there are messages from other people too. There is a message from the principal of East Elementary School where the kids are students: *Zakes, this is Denny Boger at the school. Please call me this morning.* I don't know why he called me on Adele's number. Maybe he doesn't have my number. There are three such calls from the principal, one even asking me to call him at home. But the message that renders my bowels loose is from a woman I don't know: *Adele, this is Nadia. I got your call. Please call me before you go back to South Africa.*

Adele has abducted my children to South Africa! She obviously got my application to the court for reasonable visitation, and instead of having the kids visit me every other weekend, which is all I want, she'd rather steal away with them so that I have zero access!

The first thing I do after seeing my kids' principal, who confirms to me that Adele has withdrawn the children from school and has returned to South Africa, is to engage the services of a private detective called Phillip Smith in Johannesburg. Buzz also files a Magistrate's Temporary Order granting me custody of the children.

The private detective locates Adele in Johannesburg. She and the children are squatting with the tenants in our house in Weltevredenpark. She has enrolled the children at Panorama Primary School in the same suburb, which used to be Zukile's school when we still lived in South Africa. My private eye secures some emails, which I can quote here because they are part of open court proceedings. The correspondence is between Adele and officials of Ohio University, the pastor of her Athens Community Church, and Ann Leeman, who I learn is the woman who assisted her to flee with the children, and drove them to the airport. There is even an email from a colleague of mine in the English Department, Linda Rice. All these people knew of her plans to abduct the children to South Africa. For instance, Adele wrote to Linda Rice: *Arrived safely in South Africa and trying to get kids into school. Shall email you once I am settled. Thank you for everything.* And Linda Rice responded: *Very good. I was wondering but not wanting to ask around as I knew things might be tenuous. But well; I'm praying for you and your family and God's will in your life! That it be made known clearly and that you have inner peace and feel grounded with support and friendship.* Pastor Jeff of her church promises to pray for her in her difficult times. *Whatever we can do for you, we are here to serve,* he writes. Many of the Athens people encourage her to keep her strength in Jesus. Even her PhD supervisor assures her that she will be in his thoughts and prayers throughout *her ordeal.* Ms Leeman, on the other hand, is reporting to her on my activities in my attempts to get the children back. She tells her when I have been to the police, to court or to the children's school. She writes jointly with someone called Stacy Lee in one of the emails: *I need to tell you Zane* (that's me) *went to the school on the Friday after you left and said that you were not legally allowed to take the children and that the sheriff has a warrant out for your arrest. I think he was just talking because I haven't seen anything in the paper and Mr Boger has not been contacted by the police asking questions.* I still don't understand how this woman becomes privy to the discussion I have with the principal of my children's school. You may make your own deductions.

There is all this flurry of activity around me and my children and I was ignorant of it all. All these people have become players in the drama of my life and I didn't even know it. I understand their concerns. I would do the same too if I were in their position; I would help an abused woman in whatever way I can so that she escapes the abuser. They are trying to rescue a poor African woman whose life has been made hell by her husband and whose only way out is to escape with her children back to her home country. She has sold her narrative very effectively.

The most revealing of the emails is from her attorney in Johannesburg, Nicholls Cambanis. He writes: *There is also the question of your residential status in the U.S. Your instructions were that the divorce should be delayed as long as possible, so you could have rights in the U.S. as his wife for as long as possible. Presumably this is still applicable.*

Now, finally, I get it. That is why our divorce has dragged on for almost four years to date. She and her lawyers are playing delaying games so that she obtains permanent resident status as my dependant

516

when I change my immigration status. And, of course, each delaying tactic takes more paperwork, which means mounting legal fees.

I get a bill from the university for Adele's general fee and I decide that this time I am not going to pay it. She will have to settle it herself now that she has abducted my children.

I am supposed to perform at the Calabash Literary Festival in Jamaica and then after that at the Northrop Frye Literary Festival in Moncton, New Brunswick, on the east coast of Canada. I write to poet Kwame Dawes, who is one of organisers of the Calabash and a participant at the Northrop Frye, to convey my apologies. I ask John Kachuba, who is now an adjunct since completing his degree, to take over my classes. Because now I know that Adele has spies everywhere, including the English Department, I don't tell anyone except the head, Joe McLaughlin, that I am going to South Africa to get my children back.

But before that I must get her stuff out of the university house and hand the key back to the housing authorities. I ask my brother Sonwabo to come down from Columbus to help me pack in boxes the clothes and household effects and children's toys that are strewn on the floor in every room, and take them for storage. It takes us the whole day to clean up the house. After all that, I drive the abandoned Nissan to my place.

I take the next available flight to Johannesburg where I instruct an attorney, Reon Marais, to make an urgent application for the return of my children. Because in South Africa only the High Court – rather than the magistrate's court – can hear divorce and custody cases, Reon briefs an advocate who quickly draws up the papers. On April 26, 2005, the Honourable Judge Jajbhay of the High Court of South Africa issues an order giving me temporary custody of the children and orders Adele to hand them over to me together with their passports and visas. He also orders the Sheriff of the Court and the South African Police to physically take possession of the children and hand them over to me. He further issues a *Rule Nisi* calling upon Adele to show cause in court two days later why this order shouldn't be confirmed with costs.

It turns out that the Sheriffs of the Court are the Visagie brothers –

Jeremy and Andre. I go with them to my house in Weltevredenpark in the evening when we surmise Adele and the children will be home. The Visagies press the buzzer at the gate but no one opens. They jump over the gate and rush to the house. They burst into the house through the kitchen door. They are in there for a few minutes, and then they come out with the kids and their passports. I am standing outside the gate of my own house all that time. They hand the children to me over the gate which is still locked. I am very much impressed with the efficiency of the Visagie brothers and I like their last name. I decide that one day I am going to have characters in a novel who are called the Visagie Brothers. But mine will be outlaws instead of enforcers of the law. Indeed, a few years later I write a novel titled *Black Diamond* with the Visagie Brothers, Stevo and Shortie, as the lovable thugs – well, lovable to me even if some readers may not think so.

I am using Gugu's car and I drive the children to the Holiday Inn in Braamfontein where I have booked for a few days. I don't want Adele to know where I am with the kids. Who knows what she is capable of? In Johannesburg thugs are two a dime and any unscrupulous person can hire them to do any dirty work for him or her. The kids are shaken by all this drama, as can be expected of a thirteen-year-old boy and nine-year-old girl. I am so sorry that we have to put them through all this crap. All their clothes were left in Weltevredenpark so I take them to the Cresta Mall to buy them a few items of extra clothing.

Two days later we appear in court. Adele is there with her sister 'Mapolao and her attorney, Sanjay Dava Jivan. I am there with my attorney Reon Marais, and the advocate he has instructed to argue the matter before the judge. Adele's lawyer argues that the court in Athens, Ohio, has no jurisdiction over the children because they are South Africans and have returned permanently with their mother to live in their home country, and *this was done with the knowledge and consent of the plaintiff* – meaning me. But my evidence – including the divorce and custody documents from the Ohio court, the letter from East Elementary School, the report from the police in Athens – contradicts her story. This is where the emails that I told you about came into play. In one of them – and my attorneys got them through an arrangement called 'discovery' where each side in the dispute must submit all the documents pertaining to the case to the opposing side – she tells the university authorities that she is suspending her studies because she has *an assignment outside the US.*

The court assigns a social worker to interview the children. They tell her that much as they love their mother dearly, they want to go back to the USA with their father. Zenzi mentions how miserable she is at her new school. Zukile is the silent one. He says nothing about his new school but expresses his eagerness to return to America.

The judge issues an order confirming my interim custody of the children, pending the outcome of any custody dispute between Adele and me, whether in the United States or in South Africa. The children are ecstatic at this order, and we return to the hotel.

I buy new air tickets for them and while we are waiting for the departure date we move to another hotel. I don't want us to stay at any one hotel for too long. I prefer those hotels that are on the outskirts of the city where no nosy journalist will spot me and start asking me questions about this or that book or what I think of the latest corruption scandal that has been exposed by the newspapers. Gugu and Thandi accompany us on our odyssey from one hotel to the next and from one arcade to the next amusement park to keep the children entertained.

I ask the kids, 'Guys, why didn't you tell me you were going to South Africa with Mommy?'

'She took us from school without any warning,' says Zukile, 'and Mrs Leeman drove us straight to the airport.'

Zenzi says her mommy told them that *Ntate* Thesele, her father, was ill and they had to leave for South Africa without telling me because I would stop them, and if *Ntate* Thesele dies without their being there it would be their fault. It is best not to say anything about this. I don't even ask them if they found *Ntate* Thesele ill or not. I'd rather not involve the children in our skulduggery.

The night before our departure I get a phone call from Reon.

'I hear that the order giving you interim custody has been rescinded by the judge,' he says.

'On what grounds?' I ask.

'Your wife's lawyers convinced him that they will be instituting divorce proceedings in South Africa and the judge has given them three days to do so.'

'I have not been served with any such order, so I'm leaving tomorrow as planned,' I tell him.

I know that lawyers are experts at dragging things out indefinitely as they have deliberately done in my South African case with Adele. I have already seen how Adele instructed her lawyers to delay matters for months on end – for almost four years. I will prevail in the end, but it will be after months and after numerous court processes. In the meantime what happens to my job at the university? And how do I pay the legal costs? That is exactly what they want and I am not going to give them the pleasure.

The next day I board South African Airways with Zenzi and Zuki on a flight back to the United States. It is only when I am in the plane that I am able to breathe a sigh of relief. This is just an adventure to the kids.

We finally get back to Athens and to my apartment in Pomeroy Road. The next day I take the kids back to school. Their friends and teachers are happy to see them. Thanks to the magic of 'discovery', I know now that the next day the pastor writes to Adele: *I hear the children are back in the area. I know that this has been and continues to be very difficult for you. Know you are loved and missed.* And Ann Leeman writes: *Sam and Maria burst into the door today after school saying that Zenzi and Zukile were at school! Are you in Athens? What happened? Please call me so we can see each other. Let me know if you need help with taking care of the kids or anything.*

Unfortunately, their friend is not here. She is in Johannesburg, South Africa, mapping out her next strategy.

CHAPTER SIXTEEN

THERE IS THIS ARTICLE in *Time* magazine on 'how the world eats'. It features what are supposed to be average families from five regions of the world, each family posing behind a stack of groceries. We are told that the authors travelled the world to learn what families in different countries eat in a week. Asia is represented by the Ukita family from Japan, composed of mother, father and two daughters. The caption reads: *Though wife Sayo usually prepares traditional dishes that favor fish and vegetables, her daughters often eat at fast-food restaurants.* The family's food expenditure for the week is $317.25. This includes grains and other starch; meat, fish and eggs; fruits, vegetables and nuts; condiments; snacks and desserts; prepared foods and beverages. Europe is represented by the Melander family of Germany, composed of the parents, a son and a daughter. Their weekly expenditure on the same categories of food as the Japanese family comes to $500.07. The caption tells us that the wife buys anything that's fresh and good for the family. Latin America is represented by the Casaleses of Mexico. The parents have three kids and their weekly food expenditure is $189.09 for the aforementioned categories of groceries. The caption tells us that: *A weakness for pricey soft drinks distorts their tight food budget.* The Revises proudly represent North America. They are an African American family of mother, father and two sons from the United States. Their weekly expenditure on the same categories of food is $341.98. The caption tells us: *The North Carolina family fights the effects of abundance with exercise.*

Indeed, one can see that these are average families in these countries. We are not told what their jobs are but they look like professional people.

Now, let's see who represents Africa. The Aboubakars live in Chad. The weekly expenditure on food for the woman and her five children is $1.23. But it is not really their expenditure, because all of their food is from charity. They pose with their tiny sisal bags of millet or sorghum and plastic container of cooking oil. The caption reads: *Sudanese widow D'jimia feeds her five children with the rations she receives at the Breidjing Refugee Camp.* Most of the food categories listed above, such as dairy and beverages, are not available to them. Even their water is provided by Oxfam. And this is your *average* African family?

Yes, there are such refugee families in Africa but they are not your *average* African family. What has been done here is the same as taking a family from Rome Township in southeast Ohio where there is so much hunger that some children go to bed without supper and the only meal for some of them is the school lunch, and presenting their plight as that of an average American family. Yes, in the United States of America there are such families and I work with some them every day in such hamlets as Kilvert. They depend on soup kitchens and food pantries; food donated by charities. Unlike the American family portrayed in this article, they don't have the abundance whose effects must be fought with exercise. Instead, many of them are obese because they have to depend on cheap foodstuffs that are replete with empty calories. Remember that a litre of Coca-Cola is much cheaper than a litre of milk. But these Appalachian families are not by any stretch of imagination representative of your average American family, in the same way that Sudanese refugees in Chad are not average African families. Refugees form the tiniest of minorities compared to the populations in the rest of Africa's countries.

If the editors of *Time* magazine had portrayed the diet of a cattle rancher in Botswana, a factory worker or taxi driver in South Africa, a mineworker in Lesotho, a school teacher in Ghana or a coffee farmer in Rwanda – to name but a few low- to middle-income occupations in Africa – it would have been clear to their readers that the average African family does have a diet of grains and other starchy foods; meat, fish and eggs; fruits, vegetables and nuts; prepared foods and beverages. And they buy these foods instead of getting them from charity. And they live in houses and not tattered tents like the depicted refugee family. But a fair portrayal of the real Africa would not have had any credibility. It would go against the expectations of readers of the magazine who have a set narrative in their minds of Africa as a continent of nothing but starvation, chaos and mayhem. It is a metonymic portrayal, a much prevaricated one, where the few flashpoints on the continent have come to stand in the West's collective imagination for the whole continent without exception. Western media's portrayal of Africa must therefore be consistent with that jelled narrative. It must not do anything that dishabituates established notions, but must reinforce the narrative that has congealed in the audience's mind. I am not suggesting that gatekeepers in the West are engaged in a conspiracy to discredit Africa. It is just force of habit. What sells to their readers and viewers is the Africa that they already 'know'.

I saw this some years back during the Winter Olympics in Sarajevo. In one event there was a competitor from Senegal. On the American television channel that was broadcasting the event, whenever an athlete was introduced the cameras took us to his or her home country and showed us some of its beautiful landmarks. When it came to the Senegalese athlete the cameras took us to some ramshackle grass hut that looked like an abandoned bird's nest. That was Senegal, and that was Africa. It did not matter that the athlete came from Dakar – a beautiful, modern, vibrant, clean city. He had never lived in any place like the one depicted on television. Senegal does have many beautiful landmarks too, but their portrayal would have gone against the viewers' expectations.

It is the same old story: whereas for other countries and continents the media portray what ranges from the average to the best case scenario, in Africa the representation must always be of the worst case scenario. It is the Africa we have come to know. Any other Africa would be discomfiting for us. My American students have been discomfited quite a few times by such South African movies as *Jerusalema*, *White Wedding* and *Swop!* that I occasionally screen in my textual analysis classes. Not only are they perplexed by the high production values that they associate with America rather than Africa, they are disappointed that this Africa of skyscrapers and luxury sedans and trains and gun-toting carjackers and prostitutes and high-walled mansions and gritty townships and golf courses and white weddings and fashion designers is not the 'real' Africa – the Africa they know. You see, they are experts on Africa, thanks to the congealed narrative.

I am reminded of the *Time* magazine article by the fact that I am challenging an expert on Africa whose expertise is solely based on the jelled narrative. His name is Dr Terry Harvey and he has been engaged by the court in Athens as the Guardian Ad Litem – a person appointed by the court to represent, in this case, the interests of the children in a divorce or custody action.

But before I get to his jelled narrative, let me tell you what happens after I come back from South Africa with the children. Forgive me for galloping through these events, but they could make a whole book on their own and I need to get to the conclusion of this woeful tale of a foolish outsider.

Before Adele's return to America we had a few confrontations in Johannesburg where I had gone for the launch of my new novel,

The Whale Caller, which was published by Penguin Books. I had left the kids with my brother Sonwabo at my Pomeroy Road apartment in Athens. At a reading to promote my new novel Adele invaded the venue accompanied by an attorney I didn't recognize and a policeman. The attorney served me with a document demanding that I return the children to Adele. They didn't reckon that I knew something about the law. For one thing, the attorney is not the sheriff of the court; he has no right to serve court process unless authorised to do so by a court. And this attorney guy didn't have any such authority. The document itself was irrelevant and meaningless in any event, and I told them so. I also admonished the policeman very strongly for allowing himself to be used by an unscrupulous lawyer in a civil matter when he should be chasing criminals all over Johannesburg.

'There is crime out there,' I yelled, as my audience, which included Gugu and Thandi, looked on aghast. 'Children are being raped as we speak, houses are being burglarised. And you are here to serve long-rescinded court process on a civil matter you know nothing about? Since when does the state get involved in divorce and custody matters?'

I didn't care about Adele and the lawyer. They were doing what they did best. I was focusing on the policeman whose salary I paid with my taxes. The three of them just stood there, at a loss as to what to do next. We left and drove away in Gugu's car.

On another occasion Adele attacked me physically in the presence of my son Neo, a truck driver and a few labourers when I returned the furniture that had been in storage to our common house. Even though she had kicked the tenant out of the house, she didn't want me to return the furniture. I didn't know why at the time, but learnt later that she had rented the house out to her own tenants so as to pocket the rent for herself. She threw stones at us and broke the windows of Neo's four-wheel-drive pickup truck. We laid a charge of assault and malicious damage to property against her.

On yet another occasion, she invaded Gugu's house and assaulted her. Gugu had to get a restraining order against her. But still she continued to skulk around the complex, at one time invading early in the morning accompanied by an armed policeman. Apparently she had made a complaint that I had assaulted her, hence the armed policeman. Of course, no charges were laid because such an assault was a figment of her imagination. In fact, it was a calculated ploy to stop me from returning to America to the children, hoping that they would be stranded without me and she would then regain custody. After two weeks of the book tour, with all those upheavals that amounted to an emotional tsunami, I went back to Athens, Ohio, to be with the children.

A few weeks later she also came back to Athens. I allowed her to see the children whenever she wanted to, as long as she did not take them away from my house. This was before the court finalised the custody arrangements. One night she arrived at my house and knocked violently on the door while yelling insults. I refused to open. Neighbours came out to watch the spectacle. When she persisted I called Buzz Ball, my lawyer, who advised me to call the police. I did.

'The police are on their way, Adele,' I shouted.

That was stupid of me. I shouldn't have warned her. When the patrol car arrived she was long gone. The next day I went to the police station to make a statement.

The court finally had a custody hearing. The magistrate, Karen Harvey – no relation to the Guardian Ad Litem, Terry Harvey, who I am going to tell you about – gave me the custody of the children pending the divorce hearing. She allowed Adele supervised visitations every other weekend. I opposed that because I wanted the kids to spend quality time with her unhampered by a supervisor. The magistrate then ruled that before she took the children from my house she had to deposit her passport with the court. The fear was that she would once again abduct them out of the jurisdiction of the court.

But she didn't give up. She was a fighter. She tried every trick in the book. She even went to My Sister's Place, a shelter for abused and battered women claiming that she was an abused woman. And, of course, My Sister's Place did not hesitate to get her a Petition for Domestic Violence Protection Order. As part of this order she demanded that I should immediately surrender possession of the Nissan Sentra. At the court hearing for this particular matter I was represented by Buzz Ball again and she was with two young female attorneys whose names I did not get. All the evidence pointed to the fact that she was the aggressor who had even invaded my house and I had had to call the police. The magistrate dismissed her petition for a protection order. She noted that I was the one who needed protection from her. After the magistrate ruled, it seemed to me that the people from My Sister's Place, who handle on a daily basis serious cases of women who are terribly abused by their husbands for real, were disappointed that in this case they had been had.

As for the car, there was no way she could have it back, the magistrate stated categorically. She had abandoned it when she abducted the kids. I donated it to the people of Kilvert who auctioned it to raise funds for their community centre which provides food for destitute people.

Now, let's come to the present: the Guardian Ad Litem. His job is to advise the court as to which of the parents should be the custodial parent. At this point I am the custodial parent, but that is a temporary arrangement until the divorce is finalised. Dr Terry Harvey occasionally visits my home at Euclid Drive; I have since moved from Pomeroy Road and am now renting a house so that the kids can have their own bedrooms. Adele now lives at the Carriage Hill Apartments which are owned by the university and are rented out to graduate students. Dr Harvey visits her there too to see how she lives and to assess whether the children will be better off with her or with me. He has lengthy interviews with her and with the children. He does the same with me too and with friends who occasionally help me look after the children, Spree McDonald and his wife, Tsibishi. Spree is a doctoral student and my graduate assistant. Dr Harvey also interviews the children. He compiles lengthy notes from which he writes his first report to the court.

I am absolutely miffed when I get a copy of the report. The good doctor has bought into Adele's story that our conflict emanates from my being the product of an African patriarchal system that turned against her because she was an educated African woman. She is a very smart woman who is using the established narrative in her favour. She's playing the gender card. Without testing Adele's story, without even attempting to find any evidence to corroborate it, and without examining my personal history and position on issues of gender and the oppression of women, the good doctor taps into the African narrative that has congealed in his mind from the time he watched *Tarzan* movies as a kid to all the horror stories of a dysfunctional continent he continues to consume in today's news and entertainment media and he concludes that indeed Adele's story is the whole truth and nothing but the truth.

Part of his 'Observation/Conclusions' reads:

> Adele has made a very convincing argument regarding her role as wife and mother in this family. I am not sure how the South African justice system compares to ours but assume it to be based on English Rule of Law since the country was once ruled by the English. Additionally, there are probably cultural differences that come into play in this case. Having been to S.A. myself, on more than one occasion, it is easy to recognize that women are often considered chattels in that country. There is a movement in that country for women to assume more modern roles as a partner in the marriage, involving themselves in politics and government as well. Adele apparently has broken that mold and has become assertive trying to educate herself and her children and involving herself in the family finances and other facets of the family. Adele says this attitude is described by Zakes as 'dictatorial'.

You can see the many glaring assumptions already in this piece that are based on the jelled narrative. Apparently it didn't occur to him to ascertain the accuracy of any of them because to him they are self-evident truths based on the Africa he 'knows'; the Africa that is reinforced by a documentary I saw recently titled *Babies*, which is touted as a 'visually stunning movie that captures the earliest stages of the journey of humanity'. It features babies from Namibia, Mongolia, Japan and the USA. Whereas the babies and their parents from the other cultures are clean and live in hygienic surroundings, the African babies have been selected from the 'exotic' Himba tribe which is on the verge of extinction; it now numbers about twenty thousand in all. They wallow in mud and dirt all day long. Flies feast on their mouths and eyes. Their mothers have their whole bodies, including the hair, caked in mud. To

528

ignorant Western viewers whose only point of reference is the established stereotype narrative, this Africa that has hardly emerged from the Stone Age is the 'real' Africa. They think that this is how we all grew up. Our mothers, wives, sisters and daughters are the 'chattels' of Dr Harvey's report.

That is why I must now quote my response to the above quote from Dr Harvey's report:

> I do not understand how Adele's argument of her role as wife and mother in this family is *convincing* to the Guardian Ad Litem since he knows nothing of our lives in the many years that I have been married to Adele and he sought no (tested) evidence from her to support her assertions most of which I have argued in this response are false. I do not understand what the Guardian Ad Litem is trying to imply about the South African legal system since he knows nothing about it. I think for matters like these he should seek expert advice, which is readily available in the African Studies Department at Ohio University. Our legal system in South Africa is Roman Dutch Law and not English Law. He claims that he was in South Africa. I would like to know when that was. When I spoke with him for the first time he told me that he went through a South African airport on a hunting trip to a neighbouring country many years ago – when apartheid was still in place. From that I understood that he has never been in South Africa. I doubt if he can tell me what city he went to in South Africa. The South Africa he describes here in his report is not the South Africa I know. In South Africa women are not considered chattels. That would be against the Constitution of the country, which is one of the only two Constitutions in the world (the other being Canada) that outlaw both gender discrimination and discrimination on the basis of sexual orientation. [*I have since learnt that there are two or three others, but my point still stands.*] The Guardian Ad Litem also mentions politics and government in South Africa, which again he knows nothing about. In South Africa the president is a man and the vice president is a woman. Of the 25 cabinet ministers, 12 are women. Of the 20 deputy ministers 10 are women. Of the 300 members of parliament 147 are women. I do not know if you can say the same

of the United States. But what I know is that South Africa is second only to Sweden in the number of women in government, particularly serving as ministers. This runs though all levels of government, and when we get to local government overall female participation is in fact in the majority! Are these women chattels? When I said Adele was 'dictatorial' throughout our marriage I was not afraid of her assertiveness but was afraid of her anger and violence. She never discussed things with me but always did things her way without consulting me. All I wanted was to be her equal partner not her subservient. It was part of her dictatorial attitude to take the children to South Africa without my knowledge. Can the Guardian Ad Litem point at one thing that I did that would support his conclusion. It is nonsense to say Adele broke the mold and became 'assertive trying to educate herself'. Good gracious! South Africa has millions of educated women. I am from a family of educated women myself. My grandmother was a school teacher, my mother a nurse. The Gugu that the Guardian Ad Litem has mentioned in this report has two master's degrees and is doing her PhD. [*Elsewhere in his report the Guardian Ad Litem implies that I left Adele for Gugu because Gugu is less educated and therefore less assertive.*] This is not extraordinary. The Guardian Ad Litem could have easily found information on the true situation in South Africa from the internet or from the African Studies Department at Ohio University instead of making such embarrassing statements. As a man who has written extensively on women's issues and whose books have been labelled feminist, I take offence at the Guardian Ad Litem's conclusions on this matter and I demand that they be tested in court through evidence since they bear great weight on whether I get the custody of the children or not.

I want to emphasise here that at the time this American man is accusing my country of treating women as chattels – and, please, I am not saying that women in South Africa have arrived where they should be; they still have a long way to go before we all live up to the values of our fine Constitution and banish our sexist and patriarchal attitudes – America ranks Number 31 in the World Economic Forum Global Gender Gap Report whereas South Africa ranks Number 6. The only countries that are ahead of South Africa are Iceland, Finland, Sweden, Norway and New Zealand. A small African country called Lesotho is ranked Number 10, twenty places above the United States. Now you tell me, who can preach to whom about gender equality?

Rather than have his assertions tested in court Dr Terry Harvey quickly draws a follow-up report where he sings a different tune altogether and recommends that I should get custody because I care for the extramural activities of the children and Adele does not. But this shows you how some decisions that may affect the life and death of other human beings are made at the whim of ignorant officials. If I had not demanded that these silly assertions of Dr Harvey's be tested in court I would have been metaphorically tarred and feathered as sexist on the basis of the jelled narrative.

All this happens in 2006. It is a year that is really taking its toll on me because so many things are happening, and all of them may serve to alter the course of my life for better or for worse. I have learnt to live with Adele's annoyances. She is using the kids as a tool to avenge herself for the decisions of the court that didn't go her way. The kids spend one week of every month with her, and during that time she does not take them for their extramural activities. She knows that's one thing that will rile me to madness. Zukile has karate and Zenzi has ice skating, karate and guitar lessons. Even when I offer to take them for their activities myself during what is supposed to be her parenting time, she refuses. I have to go to court many times to get court orders to compel her to do so. But her impunity prevails and Zenzi finally has to give up ice skating because she misses too many rehearsals and events and her instructors cannot tolerate that any more.

In June, I take the kids to South Africa to renew their visas. I had lodged their applications with the American Embassy in Lesotho when I was there the previous December to see my mother. They kept the applications and said that the kids needed to appear in person for their applications to be considered. In Johannesburg we book at Judith Lodge in Emmarentia. The kids have their own comfortable bedrooms and we turn this trip into a holiday. The last time they were in Johannesburg was the year before when they had been abducted by their mother, and for the most part we were on the run from one hotel to another. They never got to enjoy Johannesburg. I get Thandi from her home in Springs and she stays with us to help me look after the kids and take them for their daily swim at Virgin Active near Cresta Centre.

A few days later I borrow Gugu's car and we all drive to Lesotho. At the American Embassy in Maseru I am happy that I know the desk clerk who serves us. 'Mabereng used to be Willie Mafoso's girlfriend and they were so tight we all thought they would marry. Adele had already regarded her as a sister-in-law. Even after they broke up 'Mabereng and Adele continued to be buddies. The Embassy already has our applications and I have paid the necessary fees. She takes the children for an interview by the Consular Affairs staff and asks us to come next week to collect the passports with the visas stamped on them.

I take the kids to see Adele's relatives in Leribe and leave them there so that Adele's sister, 'Mapolao, can take them to the village to see Adele's parents. Gugu and I go to the Eastern Cape to see the Bee People. As usual we end up in Mafeteng to visit my mother. I find that she does not altogether remember me. Zwelakhe tells me that he plans to hold a very big party for her. I give him some money as my contribution towards the party.

On the 10th of July we get the visas and drive back to Johannesburg. Our holiday in Johannesburg is almost over since we only budgeted for two weeks. We have been here for twelve days already, so in two days' time we'll be flying back. The kids are looking forward to spending the rest of the summer at the Athens Community Swimming Pool with their friends.

The next day I get an email from Jed T Dornburg, the Vice-Consul at the US Embassy in Lesotho. It reads:

The U.S. Embassy is cancelling the H4 visas of Zukile Mda and Zukiswa Zenzile Moroesi Mda issued 10 July 2006. The visas were cancelled due to lack of custody on the part of the parent present at the interview. The Embassy requires either consent, in writing or in person, by both parents, or proof of permanent sole custody, without visitation rights, by the parent applying. Should the situation change the Embassy will be happy to consider the applicants for visas.

There is no way we can go back to America when the children's visas have been withdrawn. It turns out that 'Mabereng alerted Adele that I was applying for visas for the children and Adele sent an urgent fax to the Embassy, which was later given to me by the American Consulate in Johannesburg. *This letter informs you that I do not give permission to have my children's visas renewed*, she writes. She goes further to claim that I took the children out of South Africa despite the fact that she has custody of them. *Already we have learned that Zakes has actually taken leave from Ohio University for the Fall quarter, 2007 and there is no guarantee that the children will be brought back to Athens*, she adds. All this, of course, is patently false, she does not have custody, and I am not on leave but am returning with the kids to Athens to resume my job as a professor at the university there. She just wants to muddy the waters. But it is enough to have the visas withdrawn.

I do not understand why she does not want the kids to get visas and return to America when both of us, their parents, live in America. Buzz Ball consults with her lawyer and both lawyers try to persuade her to change her mind. Both lawyers fail.

While there is this flurry of correspondence between Buzz, Adele and even the Domestic Relations Court our time at Judith Lodge comes to an end. We have to move out. Thankfully, Gugu welcomes us at her townhouse. She looks after the kids while I fly to America to sort the matter out. Only the final decree of divorce will solve the problem, I tell my lawyer. A date is set for the divorce hearing, but Adele manages to have it postponed because she says she will be out of town. I have to return to Johannesburg empty-handed. The kids are beginning to get restless. Gugu and I take them to the skating rink at Northgate Mall and to the Gold Reef City amusement park to keep up the holiday spirit.

On one such trip we go to the Hector Peterson Museum in Soweto. We have parked the car just outside the museum. On the sidewalk vendors are selling all sorts of arts and crafts. We are just lazing around on the lawn eating *amagwinya* fat cakes and *atchaar* when suddenly we see Oprah Winfrey strolling towards us. She is with a girl in a green and yellow uniform. She is perhaps in her early to mid-teens and they are talking animatedly and laughing. Two gigantic African American guys are following them at a respectful distance. I reckon they are Ms Winfrey's bodyguards. There is also a cameraman who is walking backwards in front of them filming them. I think it is just for the archives rather than for her programme because she is in a very informal grey tracksuit and is not wearing any make-up. Gayle King, Ms Winfrey's friend, and another African American woman I do not recognise are standing next to us talking quite loudly and laughing.

Zenzi is jumping up and down with excitement at seeing these celebrities so close she could touch them. Zukile is nonchalant. Nothing ever seems to move him. Gugu and I have never given a hoot about celebrities, otherwise we would have struck up a conversation with Gayle King and her friend. We are just happy that we have made the kids' day bringing them to Soweto on this particular day when Ms Winfrey has decided to visit Soweto as well.

'I wish I was that kid who is with Oprah,' says Zenzi, looking at them longingly.

'That kid is with Oprah because she is poor,' I say. 'So, you wish you were poor.'

'Yes, just for today,' she says.

A young vendor thinks he will corner Ms Winfrey to buy something. He comes with a wooden carving of a giraffe but before he can get to her the bodyguards shoo him away. He returns to the rest of the vendors disappointed. They laugh at him.

One says, 'We told you, those big ugly Negroes will not let you talk to her.'

They still call African Americans Negroes in Soweto.

Fancy coming to Soweto and meeting Oprah Winfrey! We never meet her in America. But here in South Africa Gugu and I have this tendency of bumping into her at the oddest of places. I remember one year we went to Kokstad to visit my magistrate brother. Kokstad is out of the way, more than eight hours from Johannesburg. We drove through the KwaZulu-Natal Midlands crossing rivers and valleys at such villages as Ixopo, made famous by Alan Paton, and ascending and descending

534

some of the most hauntingly beautiful hills until we reached Kokstad in the evening. We didn't want to bother my brother for accommodation at that time so we thought we would just book in at one of the two hotels. It was fully booked. So was the second one. Oprah Winfrey was in town and all the rooms had been taken by her entourage. All the restaurants were full also, and we couldn't get any service.

We had to go and sleep at my brother's place.

Despite the holiday spirit that we have managed to create, the kids must go back to school in the United States. Judge Alan Goldsberry of the Athens County Common Pleas Court, Domestic Relations Division, in his final attempt to get the children back to Athens, issues a court order granting me permanent sole custody of the children, without visitation rights to Adele. I am hoping that with this order the visas will be granted. After all, Mr Dornburg's email to me states clearly that all he needs is proof of permanent sole custody without visitation rights. We drive to Lesotho again, our fourth trip to the American Embassy in Maseru. Once again the visa is denied. Mr Dornburg has moved the goalposts. Now he needs a decree of divorce. According to this apparatchik, a court order issued by a judge in his own country is not good enough for him. Once again, it turns out that Adele was warned by 'Maberang about my next visit to the Embassy and she sent an urgent fax to Mr Dornburg. She instructs him to ignore Judge Goldsberry's court order because it was made for visa purposes only. *I am aware that this court order is being brought to the Embassy this week and I still refuse that my children should be given visas without my consent,* she writes.

In the three months that the children are stranded in South Africa I go to America three times to address this problem without any success. It is mid-August and school has started. It seems their mother doesn't care whether they go to school or not. Zukile has responsibilities at the Athens Middle School where he is president of the students' council. He also wants to participate in track and football and cannot be picked if he is not there. He is brooding now because it seems to him and to his sister that they will never be able to return to Athens.

My friend Melanie Chait, who is a film-maker and also the founder and principal of a film-making school in Johannesburg, tries to find them a school in Johannesburg, even if it's on a temporary basis. She knows of an American school in one of the suburbs which may accommodate them. The kids are totally against the idea because it implies that we are giving up on ever returning to America.

Melanie has been trying to convince me not to return to America. In fact, she thinks I shouldn't have gone there in the first place. We were trying to establish our own television station when I left in 2002. I had promised her then that I was just going for one year and would come back as soon as Adele was admitted for her PhD and was settled with her own funding. When I stayed on she occasionally wrote and reminded me of my undertaking. There were many projects that we needed to be doing together. I can see that now she thinks this is her opportunity to convince me to stay and just enrol the kids at one of the schools in Johannesburg.

'Why go back to George Bush's America?' she asks.

In fact, many of my friends in South Africa feel sorry for me for living in America, especially at this time in history when South Africa is free and presents its black elite with boundless opportunities, and when America is, according to them, ruled by the war-mongering Bush. The Bush factor is very big with them. 'You're going back to Bush's America?' they ask incredulously. They don't understand that I don't live in Bush's America. I only see him on television as they do. I don't live in the America they see in the media either. I live in Athens, Ohio, a small college town with a very progressive mindset. My children ride bikes in the peaceful streets with kids from Ghana, Iran, Russia, China, Jamaica, Venezuela and every conceivable country in the world. There I can be alone while surrounded by the world. After every few months I can return to South Africa and enjoy great South African theatre at the Market Theatre and other world-class venues in Johannesburg, Pretoria and Cape Town; and feast on some of the best cuisine in the world at restaurants in those cities. I can drive to the Eastern Cape and harvest honey with the Bee People. I can breathe the air of my ancestors on the pink mountain. Then, after a few weeks, I can return to the succour of my family in Athens, Ohio, where I can once more be alone.

As for the boundless opportunities that they are talking about, you have seen already that they are not for me.

Buzz Ball finally manages to get a firm date for the divorce hearing. I fly back to the United States, once more leaving the children with Gugu in Johannesburg. On August 25, 2006, the case comes for a final hearing before Judge Alan Goldsberry. My brother Sonwabo has come down from Columbus to lend some moral support. My former student Spree McDonald is my character witness. The only other witness is Dr Terry Harvey, the Guardian Ad Litem. He tells the judge under oath that in his opinion I am the better parent. He has made a number of house visits to me unannounced and every time he has found the house very neat and clean. He observed that I personally cook for the children and don't feed them junk food. On some occasions he has come in the evening and found me helping them with the homework. Most importantly, I care very much about their extramural activities whereas their mother does not. Adele also presents her case through her attorney, Mr Walker. She wants custody of the children, all of the Weltevredenpark property (because, she insists, I have the Eastern Cape property) and half of all the royalties from my books.

The divorce is granted on the same day, and the judge decides I should be the primary custodial parent. Adele is given visitation rights every other weekend and one full week each month. She will not get any royalties and will only get half of the Weltevredenpark property. I think the fact that she abducted the kids last year and stubbornly refused to sign her permission for them to get visas this year counted against her. You will remember that I never wanted custody in the first place. All I wanted was reasonable access to my kids. Because of her actions, she has lost custody and I am not ever going to let her have it again. It is not in the interests of the children to deprive them of their father, just as it is not in their interests to rob them of their mother.

This time Adele signs the permission for visas because if she doesn't the judge will revive that order where he took away all her visitation rights. If she doesn't want her kids to return to the USA where she herself resides then she doesn't want visitation rights.

I fly back to Johannesburg with my freshly minted decree of divorce.

The first thing I do after my arrival is to go to Gugu's home to ask for her hand in marriage. Her parents, Josephine and Bra Phil, live in Piet Retief on the Swaziland border. The custom is that on such a mission I need to be accompanied by a male relative. I therefore ask Monwabisi to fly to Johannesburg so that we can drive to Piet Retief the next day. I will pay for his airfare. But he is not interested in being of assistance even though he tells me he is free that weekend, which doesn't surprise me because we have never been there for each other. And that cuts both ways. I adopt George Menoe, a film-maker who was my partner when I still owned a production company, as my relative for the day and we drive to Piet Retief. Gugu's parents welcome the idea. I had already met her mother Josephine and was delighted to meet her father who is quite garrulous and jocular.

On Monday, September 4, 2006, I marry Gugu at the Roodepoort Home Affairs office. My witness and best-lady is Nakedi Ribane. I can see that she is not impressed that I am getting married in my blue denim jeans and striped denim shirt. She was one of South Africa's top models and is still very particular about dressing well. Gugu is in a dress made of the *seshoeshoe* traditional cloth, courtesy of the young designers of Stoned Cherrie. She doesn't comment on my blue jeans. Her witness is her older sister, Pat Mphuthi. The only other people in the small wedding chapel are our kids – Gugu's three kids, Nonkululeko, Simphiwe and Gcinile; and my two, Zukile and Zenzile. But I am also with two of my older kids, Neo and Thandi. Nakedi came with her daughter Letsatsi. Dini is the only one who is not here. After the ceremony, which lasts less than thirty minutes, we go for lunch at the Hard Rock Café in the Town Square in Weltevredenpark.

Gugu is glowing. We are finally husband and wife. I don't know if I am glowing too because I can't see myself. But I know how I feel. Euphoric. It's been a long road. I have the satisfaction of a man who has finally reached a destination.

I remember that after my divorce from Mpho I immediately married Adele. I met an old friend, Khomo Mohapeloa, the mathematician and jazz musician I told you about earlier. He had heard of my divorce and congratulated me on it. He, too, was recently divorced, from a beautiful Swazi woman who was our local physician in Maseru.

'Now we can live in freedom as bachelors,' he said.

'Not me, mate,' I said. 'I just got married again.'

'Oh, man, you are a glutton for punishment,' he said.

He didn't know that he was being prophetic. He was merely expressing his disappointment in me. Well, I have let the side down again today, but I am confident that this time there is no room for self-fulfilling prophecies.

There is no honeymoon for us. We have work to do. As soon as we get back to her townhouse that very afternoon I phone the American Embassy in Maseru about the children's visas and they tell me that they have transferred our case to Johannesburg. This saves us a lot of travelling; Maseru is five hours away from Johannesburg. At the American Consulate they grant the children visas immediately; they don't even look at Adele's letter. They tell me that it was silly of the Embassy in Maseru to be swayed by Adele's faxes in the first place. The judge's orders were sufficient for them to grant the visas. *Now* they are telling me, after all the trouble I had, and the expense of flying to America on four occasions. They apologise for the inconvenience and give me all the letters that Adele wrote to the Embassy in Maseru in case I want to take action about the matter. But, of course, I am not going to waste my time on this matter any more. All I want is to take my kids back to their school in Athens, Ohio.

The kids and I fly back to the United States on the United Emirates airline. It doesn't bother us that we have to spend the whole day in Dubai. There is a lot to do and to see at that airport. There is a lot to eat too, all of it free if you are a passenger. But my thoughts are in Johannesburg where I have left my new wife. It will be another year before she joins me because her three kids are at a private school in Piet Retief where they live with their grandparents. It will take that long to make arrangements for them to transfer to a school in the United States, get visas for them, and buy a much bigger house for the family that has instantly more than doubled. Gugu also has a job which she can't just leave abruptly. All this doesn't really bother me because for the past few years I have been commuting to Johannesburg every two months or so to see her and my mother. I will continue to do so.

Zenzi and Zuki are late for school, but their teachers understand; they have been marooned in Johannesburg for three months.

I am only back in Athens for two weeks when a telephone call from my sister-in-law Johanna, summons me back to Lesotho. My mother is dead.

I ask Adele to stay with the children but she does not respond to my emails. That is how the court has advised us to communicate now, via emails so that there should be a record of our bickering. And indeed there are hundreds of emails covering the whole period of this ordeal. I don't expect her to respond because she has vowed that she will make my role as custodial parent very difficult. 'I'll make you wish you hadn't got custody,' she said. When I don't hear from her I know that she wants my trip to Lesotho to bury my mother to fail since I can't leave the children alone. The people who used to help me babysit are Spree McDonald and his wife Tsibishi, but they won't do it any more because, they tell me, Adele has threatened Tsibishi if she continued helping me with the kids. So she won't do it now because she says she fears for her life. But I have not run out of options. There is my brother in Columbus, and Sonwabo takes time off work and comes to Athens to look after my kids.

I am already in Johannesburg when I hear that Adele stormed into my house and demanded the kids from my brother. I'd suspected that would happen and I had told Sonwabo if it did he must just release the kids to her without any argument. I pick up Gugu and we proceed to Lesotho in her car.

At the funeral I meet Sonwabo's kids, Limpho, Mpumi, Thembi and Solomzi. When I tell them that I have left my kids with the father they have not seen in more than twenty years Solomzi says, 'You're a brave man. Are you not afraid that he will abandon your kids just as he abandoned us?'

What can I say to that? He is making his point and it is a valid one.

In Mafeteng my mother is lying in her coffin in Zwelakhe's living room, and people are sitting or standing around singing hymns softly. A few weeks ago I gave Zwelakhe some money because he was planning to organise a big party for her. Now she lies in a coffin and that money will go towards her funeral. I was sad that my mother was gone. But at the same time I was relieved. I couldn't bear seeing her the way she had been lately. She had lost her memory and couldn't remember me or anyone else. As she lies there I remember that before she lost it completely she would report to me that there was someone who kept on taking her perfume. I made a point of flying all the way from the USA every few months to see her. I actually saw her more often than my brother, the one who is a magistrate in Kokstad, even though I lived thousands of miles away. And she would have tears in her eyes as she told me about her perfume. I would have tears in my eyes too because I knew how much she valued that perfume. I bought it for her in Paris. Every time I went to Paris, which was twice or thrice a year, I bought my mother expensive perfume. I don't know who kept on relieving her of it. All sorts of people came to hang out in her bedroom even when she had lost her memory. One day as she was complaining about her missing perfume Nontuthuzelo, Zwelakhe's wife, heard her.

'*Hawu,* 'M'e Rose, what are you doing with perfume when you are so old?' she asked.

She was joking with her mother-in-law, of course. But that hurt me very much. I didn't say anything about it though. Unlike her husband, Nontuthuzelo is very nice to me. Her husband is gradually becoming nice to me too. I suspect his wife has a lot to do with it. It is my mother's daughters-in-law who have tried to bring our dysfunctional family together. For instance, Johanna, the wife that my brother Sonwabo abandoned, is a peacemaker and a voice of reason at family gatherings. She is the one to whom my mother used to confide her hurts.

As she lies in her coffin, her pastor from the Universal Church preaching the Gospel at her wake, the thought that she is resting at last fills me with sudden euphoria. She is not there, she's gone, she'll never suffer again. She was never herself again after her husband died in 1993. What pained her most were the tensions that existed among her children. It was worse that some of the battles were fought over her. There was a time, for instance, when my brother Monwabisi whisked her away to Kokstad against the wishes of Zwelakhe because Monwabisi felt that she was unhappy living with Zwelakhe. She lived with Monwabisi for a couple of months in that Eastern Cape town, but it turned out that my mother was extremely unhappy there. She felt like a stranger in Kokstad. She had lived in Lesotho for many years and all her friends were there. But most of all she missed her cat which had been left behind in Mafeteng. Monwabisi had to take her back to Zwelakhe's house. This exacerbated the hostilities. I myself stayed out of the spat, although I did go to see my mother in Kokstad and bought her a few things to make her comfortable in her new environment.

Now, tomorrow she is going to a different environment altogether, under the ground, and she won't feel a damn thing. Although by the time she died she had lost her memory completely, she was never diagnosed with either Alzheimer's or dementia. Her Soviet-trained doctor, a young man I was at Peka High School with, merely dismissed her condition as old age. 'There is nothing we can do about it,' he said. I didn't know there was a disease called old age. But why did my mother catch it at the young age of eighty-three when some of her friends who are much older don't suffer from it?

The next morning the funeral service is held in a marquee just outside Zwelakhe's yard. People from all corners of Mafeteng have gathered. There are some who have come from other parts of Lesotho and South Africa. My mother's relatives have come from Cape Town and the Eastern Cape. Her sister Nozipho has come from Tzaneen in Limpopo where she has lived for many years after marrying a man from there. The ANC is represented by Christopher Dumisani Nyangintsimbi, who is South Africa's ambassador in Lesotho. We grew up together in those mountains of Qoboshane, what today I call the Bee Place. His father was my teacher, and my father's teacher before me. Dumisani had joined the struggle and took up arms in the ANC guerrilla camps. When we got our liberation he was an officer in the new South African National Defence Force. He has always called my mother *umalumekazi*, which means aunt, so he is here not only as the representative of his government but as a member of our extended family. The PAC is represented by two young men from the Free State province. I never get their names. There are Lesotho politicians as well, mostly leaders of the opposition parties such as Kelibone Maope, an advocate and former cabinet minister with whom I was at Peka High. At the graveside I stand next to General Metsing Lekhanya who looks a shadow of the arrogant

542

military commander who overthrew Chief Leabua Jonathan and was himself overthrown by fellow officers who then ushered democracy back to Lesotho, making it possible for Ntsu Mokhehle to return and become the prime minister after winning the elections with his BCP. Lekhanya is now the president of the BNP – the very party he overthrew with his coup d'état – and therefore the leader of the opposition in parliament. He whispers his condolences and tells me how proud I should be to come from the loins of such a distinguished family. All I can think of is what an odious character he is.

Throughout the ceremony I wear a white Xhosa ceremonial blanket, which makes me feel rather silly. These are some of the traditional innovations that have been introduced by Cousin Nondyebo into our lives. We never used to practise any of these customs when my father was alive. We didn't even know about them. But, what the heck, it's only for a few hours. I might as well humour the neo-traditionalists in the family and wear the ridiculous blanket. It all has to do with the movement that is sweeping the country of black people trying to find their roots after having 'lost' their culture due to colonialism and apartheid. The problem with this movement is that it does not recognise the dynamism of culture but aims to resuscitate some of the most retrogressive and reactionary, and sometimes horrendous, elements of what used to be 'tribal' culture but have long fallen into disuse. There are many examples of this in, for instance, KwaZulu-Natal where a practice that demeans women known as 'virginity testing' is endorsed not only by the conservative King there, but by such conservative and yet influential ANC leaders as Jacob Zuma.

You know by now that I have this tendency to digress. Tough luck if you don't like it after coming with me this far. I was telling you about my mother's funeral. We laid her to rest. I read an isiXhosa poem in praise of her Cwerha Gxarha clan, descendants of the Khoikhoi people. I told the gathering of our association with Lesotho that dates back to 1880 when King Moorosi of the Baphuthi people gave refuge to my revered ancestor Mhlontlo. That is why today we have a lot of Mdas in the mountains of Mantsonyana who are breeders of sheep and goats.

Pat Pitso, a neighbour and the village comedian, cracks a few jokes about my mother and her expertise in giving patients an injection in their bums. There is laughter at this funeral, and I love it.

I am quite cheery when I drive back to Johannesburg. Before I return to America I have to sort out the issue of our Weltevredenpark property. Judge Goldsberry ordered that it be sold and that we divide the proceeds equally. Adele, as I have told you before, is renting it out and pocketing the money. I give my attorneys the decree of divorce and instruct them to facilitate the sale. I will get my half of the house but I have lost everything else that was in it, including some of my irreplaceable memorabilia, such as my literary awards and childhood photographs. I have lost the invaluable book that Father Frans Claerhout gave me after drawing a golden bird on the flyleaf and signing his name. I have also lost the LP records that represent the only thing that I inherited from my father, the original paintings by renowned artists Claerhout, Meshu and James Dorothy, and my stacks of *Asterix* comics. Up to this day, Adele will not say what she did with all these very personal effects.

I also take the opportunity to go to Piet Retief with Gugu because I want her to join me in America with her kids. There I meet her ex-husband William Shongwe at a restaurant and we talk about the kids. He says it is good that we should know each other; we cannot harbour hostilities towards each other because now the children are the glue that binds us together. I think he is a gentleman and quite civilised about it. I wish Adele could be just as civilised.

Another opportunity we take is to visit Mpho at her house in Springs. Gugu and I always enjoy our visits to Springs. Mpho is now a dignified matriarch with silver-grey hair. She still looks exactly like her twin sister, Mphonyane. Both of them find their happiness in their children and grandchildren, and in the Lord. They are devout Jehovah's Witnesses who go into the 'field' every week, preaching door to door to the unbelievers. But thankfully Mpho never preaches to us when we visit her.

It takes one whole year before Gugu and her children join me in Athens, Ohio. We have bought a comfortable house on the far eastside in suburban Athens where we live as a blended family of seven. There are three surnames under this roof; each one of us keeps the surname with which he or she was born.

Occasionally Gugu and I listen to Champion Jack Dupree and our eyes fill with tears of nostalgia. He is the bluesman of my youth. He is the bluesman of Gugu's youth too. Her father, Bra Phil, used to fill their house in Orlando West with the sounds of Champion Jack Dupree and the likes of Big Bill Broonzy. I have noticed that we avoid playing Mr Dupree most times. I guess we don't want to be crying all the time.

One of our greatest pleasures is the visits to Kilvert – the hamlet of the WIN people that I discovered with the help of a colleague by the name of Jill Cunningham. I have written a novel titled *Cion* set in Kilvert and in Virginia. But the main reason we go to Kilvert is to spend time with Irene Flowers and Barbara Parsons, the two formidable women who single-handedly run the Kilvert Community Center where they sew quilts to raise money to feed the poor and organise social functions for senior citizens and other residents of the area. We have adopted these women as our mothers because we find them very inspiring. We pitch in whenever we can with any assistance we are able to give. But most importantly for us, going to Kilvert is very much like our visits to my mother in Mafeteng. It is also very much like going back to my ancestral village where we sit in my uncle's restaurant, eRestu, and hold meetings with the Bee People, and listen to village gossip, and watch interesting characters come and go.

I am too happy to be a wanderer; I'd rather sit on my back porch and watch the birds and the deer and the rabbits and the turtles invade my lawn. So, I have cut my travels around the world to a minimum. But once in a while my publishers prevail on me to take a trip to a literary festival or some such event. Remember, they've got to sell books and therefore they have no sympathy for my disconnectedness. That is why I find myself sitting on the podium at the Constitution Center with Edward Rendell, the Governor of Pennsylvania, Michael Nutter, the Mayor of Philadelphia, and George Herbert Walker Bush, the former president of the United States and board member of the Constitution Center. They are here to honour Bono with the Liberty Medal and I am here to perform a poem that they commissioned. When my publishers told me about this commission I told them that this was not my kind of gig; I am not a praise singer. Especially where politicians are involved. But my publisher wants to sell books. 'Please, this is a great opportunity to give publicity to your new novel,' they tell me. These guys sent me on a nationwide tour of more than twenty-five cities. I cannot let them down now. So I agree and I write the poem. That is why I am sitting on this podium next to Bush the Father.

I told him when I was introduced to him as the featured poet that I can see why Nelson Mandela likes him; he is a nice guy for a Republican. It is true that Nelson Mandela does like him. I have heard him say nice things about him, whereas he has never had anything good to say about his son, Bush the Younger – especially after he invaded Iraq under false pretences. Bush the Father merely chuckles and grabs my hand very tightly.

After performing my poem titled 'Let them come with rain', I sit on this podium listening to the speeches and to Morris Goldberg playing the pennywhistle. Although he is a New Yorker he is associated with South African music a lot. I have heard his saxophone backing my ex-girlfriend, the Cape Town jazz singer and scatter, Sylvia Mdunyelwa.

Where did I go wrong? I cringe when I realise that I have become an establishment person. I am sitting with politicians in the glare of television cameras. Where did I go wrong?

THROUGH MY BEDROOM WINDOW I can see vapours of heat rising from the ground. One could easily drown from the humidity out there. I have to finish writing these memoirs of an outsider before the summer is over. I have moved my computer and my whole workstation upstairs to my bedroom so that I am not distracted by the kids. Gugu has gone to South Africa for her mother's funeral. Josephine left us a few weeks after suffering a stroke.

It is a killer summer, but I write relentlessly for hours on end. I must be done with these blinking memoirs because they have been holding up my other projects for the last three months. I have a novel set in old Mapungubwe to write. It is titled *The Sculptors of Mapungubwe* and it makes me restless like a hen that wants to lay an egg. I have a novel titled *Rickshaw* to write. It is set in contemporary Durban. I also have to follow Toloki into the American hinterland in my second American novel. And then write the story of Noria and how she meets her death in Lesotho in a joint sequel to *Ways of Dying* and *She Plays with the Darkness*. This one will be called *Ululants*. I must reclaim that title which initially belonged to *The Heart of Redness*. When all these are done I must follow, through the focalisation of a fictional family, the journey of my revered ancestor, Mhlontlo – he who slew the magistrate Hamilton Hope – from Qumbu to Quthing. These darn memoirs must get out of the way.

I must focus on nothing but them. I turn down everything that comes my way. I have just turned down an assignment to write an article for the *Wall Street Journal* and another one for the *Guardian* in London. In both cases these were going to be very short articles which I could have written in a day. But I can't afford to break my concentration.

Unfortunately, there are things that one cannot ignore. When my friend, Tony Award winning actor John Kani, sends me the script of his new play which he wants me to critique I can't say no. I read the script and write elaborate comments, pointing out both the strengths and the weaknesses of the play. Even these memoirs cannot stand in the way of my commitment to South African theatre.

My routine is a simple one: I wake up at five-thirty, take a forty-minute walk in the suburb, or on alternate days go to the neighbourhood gym for an hour, take a shower, have a light breakfast of oats or cream of wheat and an apple, then start writing, but only after checking my emails and dealing with those that are urgent. Out of the blue I receive an email from Brian Kuttner, a professor at Washington University. He tells me that his daughter has been assigned my novel *Ways of Dying* as part of her reading for a class on South Africa and he was reminded that he was once a client of my father's in Lesotho in 1976. *He was extremely efficient and quite severe with his clients*, he writes.

I chuckle to myself because it is exactly as I remember my father. I am curious, so I write back to the professor, asking him to share with me more of his impressions of my father. He responds:

> Your father advised me on two matters. The first was a ridiculous situation I got into with the *moruti* [a pastor] in the village where I was teaching secondary school. The preacher was denouncing me from the pulpit [calling him an Indian, a communist and a Christ killer – Kuttner is Jewish] and your father effectively got him to cease and desist. The second was a trust he set up and administered for the benefit of a student.
>
> I'm sure you remember the cinder block building his office was housed in on a footpath off the magistrates' courts. Inside, rather than having clients waiting – there was no waiting room – he saw 3 or 4 clients simultaneously – attorney client confidentiality notwithstanding. He was aided in this by a miraculously efficient secretary. He would switch from client to client, seated around his table, and the secretary would type on a manual typewriter as your father dictated, indenting when he gestured, so that a complete legal document was ready for the client's mark at the end of a one hour ordeal, which I will now describe. I gathered from my brief experience that many of the cases were for stock theft and the clients were often illiterate peasants. Your father would cajole the facts out of one client and then leave him to collect his thoughts while turning to the next one. I'll never forget he said to one old man, 'The trouble with you is this: you see this thing,' he brandished an ashtray at him. 'Instead of saying this thing is an ashtray. You say: "The first time I saw this thing it was in Johannesburg. I was visiting my son on the mines. He's a good boy and sends money to his mother every month".' Then he gave the old man strict instructions to formulate his thoughts and turned to the next client who was already cringing in anticipation. The secretary pulled multiple sheets of paper and carbon out of the typewriter and rolled in the next client's document. I have often thought the No. 1 Exile's Law Office would have made a much more entertaining and certainly less demeaning series.

This last reference alludes to Alexander McCall Smith's *The No. 1 Ladies Detective Agency*, which the professor obviously thinks is demeaning. I share his view.

What I find interesting about Brian Kuttner's description of my father and his methods is that it is exactly as I remember him, and the memory leaves me with a warm feeling. I get quite maudlin these days, especially about my father.

As I write these memoirs he haunts me in other ways too that may even be dangerous to my life. I am taken aback by this email that I receive from a South African woman called Naledi Mosaka:

> I am Paul Mosaka's last born. I was reading some of your articles on the internet in which my father's name was mentioned. I took offence to some of the adjectives used to describe my father. I would like you to explain to me if you may what you mean by my father having no personality. Given that my father has been dead for 45 years now, and that you are only 4 years my senior, it means you were a small boy when he died and even younger when he was in Fort Hare, so what could possibly give you the right to describe my father in such terms at such an early age and continue to perpetuate this judgment even in your adulthood. This shows total lack of disrespect for an African child, for ourselves as his children as well as his memory especially when he cannot respond to such comments for himself. The self-righteous living like you should refrain from castigating the dead simply because they have no voice. As far as I am concerned my father was a man of great integrity, a great mind whose life was cut short by diabetes, that he was short did not make him 'personalityless'. I bet you would like your family to read good things and bad things that are FACTUAL not based on opinion and personal perceptions when you are not around.

For the life of me, I have no idea what this lady is on about. I have never heard of any Paul Mosaka, let alone written all those disparaging things about him. And I tell this lady so. In all my writing, I explain to her, I have never referred to anybody as 'lacking personality'. When I criticise someone it is for the content of what they stand for (and what they do) rather than their personality. I hate *ad hominem* arguments. Most of my writing is in the realm of fiction, but even there I don't have a character called Paul Mosaka. I am hoping that my accuser will cease and desist, but she writes me an even more threatening letter. Instead of lying, I should be man enough to apologise publicly for disparaging her dead father, she says. I demand that she shows me the document she alleges I authored, but she claims she misplaced it or can't locate it again on the Internet. I am beginning to think that this is a scam. Only after I threaten legal action does she send me as an attachment a PDF document from some archive, an old interview that my father gave to some scholars. It turns out that Paul Mosaka was a politician in the early 1940s who was elected a member of the Native Representative Council, one of the government-created bodies through which the 'natives' were governed. Obviously my father would be at loggerheads with such a body and with the politicians who participated in it.

Here I was being crucified for the sins of my father.

I never get to see Naledi Mosaka's face but I hope that when she realises that she has been accusing the wrong Mda she is shamefaced. She never apologises, though.

The third haunting of the past that happens as I am winding down these memoirs does not involve my father directly, but his father, the Headman of Goodwell, Charles Gxumekelana Mda. I receive an email from a certain Dr Bernard Leeman. I learn that he used to be in the Lesotho Paramilitary Force, planted there by the PAC and its ally, the BCP, and he worked with the guerrilla wings of these parties for many years. He is now a scholar in Australia.

I am sorry if this may offend you, he writes, *but I wonder if you have ever heard any rumour that the true father of P.K. Leballo (1915–1986) was a member of the Mda clan, maybe your own grandfather?*

I told you about Potlako Leballo quite early on in my story. Just to remind you, he was the leader of the Pan Africanist Congress who once dispatched me to kidnap the children of the Boers in the Free State farms when I went AWOL from the Poqo guerrilla forces.

My blood relationship to him is news, of course, and I ask Dr Leeman about his sources for this kind of information. He says that Leballo told him this himself. Leballo claimed that he was not the son of his official father. There was some hanky-panky between his mother and my grandfather while his father was busy fighting against the Germans in the First World War. Leeman writes: *Leballo claimed Mda family history (the incident of the magistrate) as his own, housed with Owen Mda and was devoted to A.P.*

The 'incident of the magistrate' refers to the time when my people became refugees in Lesotho after Mhlontlo killed the magistrate in the Cape. Leballo was born in Lesotho.

I know that Uncle Owen liked Leballo a lot and Leballo regarded him as his younger brother. But it was news to me that Leballo was devoted to my father. When he swore me into membership of the PAC he actually denounced my father as a fence-sitter. My father, on the other hand, thought he was just a demagogue who had no content. He told me so himself. Scholars like Bob Edgar and Luyanda ka Msumza who have studied my father are sceptical of Leballo's or Leeman's story. But I guess we'll never know the truth. All the players are dead. But this confirms that there was a lot of drama in my family. A lot is yet untold.

Father haunts me like a song that persistently rings in my head. Like a jazz number that wiggles itself in and out of my consciousness. Like the deep and dark tone of Abbey Lincoln. I have just read in the paper that she is dead. An era is passing before my eyes. I remember her with Archie Shepp in 'Golden Lady'. But even more significantly I remember her with Coleman Hawkins in Max Roach's 'We Insist' – from the 'Freedom Now Suite'. It was music they created in honour of our freedom struggle in South Africa and the United States. It spoke of the atrocities of the Sharpeville massacre. Overwhelmed as a young revolutionary by Roach's drums, Michael Olatunji's congas, and the percussion of Raymond Mantilla and Tomas du Vall in 'Tears for Johannesburg' from the same Suite, I composed my poem 'A Sad Song' – *Who will bury us, we who died a painful death of the sounds of the drums of death? We whose screams were swallowed by the winds? It is not an untruth; our own shall be our own. In death and in life, We Insist!* This is the last stanza. I wailed the poem out like the wind at poetry performances in the exile of Lesotho.

Oh, how romantic it was to be a revolutionary those days! Our prophet was Frantz Fanon and jazz was the hymnal that nourished our souls. Yet there was death too. Real wars where sons and daughters of loving parents shed blood on the roadside. We were certain of victory. We were certain *matundu ya uhuru* – the fruits of liberation – would be enjoyed by all in a land of equal opportunity.

Equal opportunity?

Father haunts me in such a way that I cannot extricate myself from his ghost. I have become him for he lives in me. He shunned the limelight and was what he called a 'backroom boy' – a thinker behind the scenes. I am even worse in that regard; I am an ultimate outsider on a road to hermitage. Like him, I work with peasants in the villages, and despite myself I am satisfied with the little that I have, and give the rest away. We differ, though, because he was doing it for the people, as part of his commitment to the struggle. I am doing it for myself. For my own happiness.

Yet the void widens.

Acknowledgements

Here's to that beautiful Sculpture Climber of Des Moines, Melisa Klimaszewski, who read every chapter and gave me very useful feedback. I cannot thank you enough, dearest Melisa – Lover of the Figure 8. I also thank two of my former students, Dr Elly Williams and John Kachuba, who read the first two chapters and assured me I was on the right track. I greatly appreciate comments and encouragement by Maureen Isaacson (who flattered me by asking, 'Are you not a little young to write a memoir?'), Isobel Dixon and another former student, Dr Spree McDonald – all three read part of the work-in-progress.

The lines of poetry quoted on page 136 are from the book *The Dead Lecturer: Poems by LeRoi Jones* (New York: Grove Press Inc., 1964). (LeRoi Jones is now known as Amiri Baraka.)

Selected Index

A Note About the Author

Zakes Mda is a professor of creative writing at Ohio University. He has been a visiting professor at both Yale and the University of Vermont. Among his novels (all published by FSG and/or Picador), *The Heart of Redness* won the Hurston/Wright Legacy Award. He lives in Johannesburg and Athens, Ohio.